Croatia

timeout.com/croatia

Croatia

Time Out Croatia Guide 3

Published by Time Out Guides Ltd, a wholly owned subsidiary of Time Out Group Ltd.
Time Out and the Time Out logo are trademarks of Time Out Group Ltd.

© **Time Out Group Ltd 2006**

10 9 8 7 6 5 4 3 2 1

This edition first published in Great Britain in 2006 by Ebury Publishing
Ebury Publishing is a division of The Random House Group Ltd,
20 Vauxhall Bridge Road, London SW1V 2SA

Random House Australia Pty Limited 20 Alfred Street, Milsons Point, Sydney, New South Wales 2061, Australia
Random House New Zealand Limited 18 Poland Road, Glenfield, Auckland 10, New Zealand
Random House South Africa (Pty) Limited Isle of Houghton, Corner Boundary
Road & Carse O'Gowrie, Houghton 2198, South Africa

Random House UK Limited Reg. No. 954009

Distributed in USA by Publishers Group West
1700 Fourth Street, Berkeley, California 94710

Distributed in Canada by Penguin Canada Ltd
10 Alcorn Avenue, Toronto, Ontario, Canada M4V 3B2

For further distribution details, see www.timeout.com

ISBN 1-904978-70-3 (until January 2007)
ISBN 9781904978701 (after January 2007)

A CIP catalogue record for this book is available from the British Library

Colour reprographics by Wyndeham Icon, 3 & 4 Maverton Road, London E3 2JE

Printed and bound in Germany by Appl

Papers used by Ebury Publishing are natural, recyclable products made from wood grown in sustainable forests

Time Out Guides Limited
Universal House
251 Tottenham Court Road
London W1T 7AB
Tel + 44 (0)20 7813 3000
Fax + 44 (0)20 7813 6001
Email guides@timeout.com
www.timeout.com

Produced in association with Time Out Croatia
Directors David Plant, Vanda Vucicevic

Editorial

Editor Peterjon Cresswell
Sub Editors Ismay Atkins, Lily Dunn, Andrew Humphreys, Anna Norman
Proofreader Tamsin Shelton
Indexer Jonathan Cox

Editorial/Managing Director Peter Fiennes
Series Editor Ruth Jarvis
Deputy Series Editor Lesley McCave
Business Manager Gareth Garner
Guides Co-ordinator Holly Pick
Accountant Kemi Olufuwa

Design

Art Director Scott Moore
Art Editor Pinelope Kourmouzoglou
Senior Designer Josephine Spencer
Graphic Designer Henry Elphick
Digital Imaging Dan Conway
Ad Make-up Jenny Prichard

Picture Desk

Picture Editor Jael Marschner
Deputy Picture Editor Tracey Kerrigan
Picture Researcher Helen McFarland

Advertising

Sales Director Mark Phillips
International Sales Manager Ross Canadé
International Sales Executive Simon Davies
Advertising Sales (Croatia) Time Out Croatia: David Plant, Vanda Vucicevic, Maja Bosnic, Dino Zulumovic, Alison Radovanovic, Rajko Radovanovic, Jane Cody, John Nash
Advertising Assistant Kate Staddon

Marketing

Group Marketing Director John Luck
Marketing Manager Yvonne Poon
Marketing & Publicity Manager, US Rosella Albanese

Production

Group Production Director Mark Lamond
Production Manager Brendan McKeown
Production Coordinator Caroline Bradford

Time Out Group

Chairman Tony Elliott
Managing Director Mike Hardwick
Financial Director Richard Waterlow
TO Magazine Ltd MD David Pepper
Group General Manager/Director Nichola Coulthard
TO Communications Ltd MD David Pepper
Group Art Director John Oakey
Group IT Director Simon Chappell

Contributors

Introduction Peterjon Cresswell, Tom Popper. **History** Reuben Fowkes, Marcus Tanner. **Croatia Today** Marcus Tanner. **Food & Drink** Alison Radovanović, Reuben Fowkes, Boris Marelić. **Beaches** Peterjon Cresswell. **Outdoor Croatia** Shane Braddock, Jane Cody, Peterjon Cresswell. **Art & Architecture** Maja and Reuben Fowkes. **Nightlife** Peterjon Cresswell, Anja Mutić. **Zagreb** Anja Mutić, Peterjon Cresswell, Alex Dragaš, David Plant, Reuben Fowkes, Celia Hawkesworth. **Slavonia & Inland Croatia** Reuben Fowkes, Renato Pandža, Tom Popper, Marcus Tanner. **Istria** Alison Radovanović, Tom Popper, Peterjon Cresswell, Alex Dragaš. **Kvarner & Islands** Tom Popper, Renato Pandža, Peterjon Cresswell, John Kania, Alex Dragaš. **Zadar & Islands** Peterjon Cresswell, Renato Pandža, Maja and Reuben Fowkes, Anja Mutić, Mladen Masar. **Split & Islands** Peterjon Cresswell, Renato Pandža, Tom Popper, Alex Dragaš, Matthew Collin, Vanda Vucicevic. **Dubrovnik & Islands** Peterjon Cresswell, Vesna Marić, Vanda Vucicevic. **Directory** Brian Gallagher, Marcus Tanner.

Maps JS Graphics (john@jsgraphics.co.uk). Maps are based on material supplied by Netmaps.

Photography pages 5, 25, 37, 47, 71, 72, 91, 175, 205, 234, 253, 256, 282, 287 Carly Calhoun; pages 7, 10, 44 (bottom left), 45, 49, 67, 76, 81, 93, 209, 215, 223, 224/225, 232, 233, 254 Fumie Suzuki; pages 9, 301 Jenan Pekušić; pages 14, 34, 214 Jemma Masson; pages 19, 161 St. Valter/www.adriatica.net; pages 21, 22, 26, 41, 43, 44, 59, 61, 64, 83, 111, 113, 117, 118, 119, 120, 121, 122, 123, 124, 125, 126, 129, 130, 131, 132, 134, 135, 136, 137, 138, 140, 141, 142, 143, 145, 146, 151, 153, 155, 156, 159, 160, 167, 168, 169, 170, 172, 173 Rajko Radovanović; pages 28, 32 Corbis; pages 42, 77, 237, 241, 248, 251, 299 Vanda Vucicević; page 50 Damir Pacić; page 53 Sljeme Medvednica; pages 56, 57, 258 Sail Croatia; pages 63, 176, 203 Tanja Borović; page 79 Sljeme Medvednica; pages 82, 84, 85, 86 David Plant; pages 95, 99, 106, 178, 179, 193, 231, 277 Croatia National Tourist Office; page 101 Marijo Bandić; pages 103, 107, 197 Reuben Fowkes; page 104 Anikó Fenyvesi; page 109 (top) Marcus Tanner; page 164 Blue World; pages 181, 185, 190 Peterjon Cresswell; pages 183, 186, 191 Vlado Zrnić; pages 196, 200, 201 Anja Mutić; page 199 Azalea Hotel; page 227 Torcida; pages 244, 247 Bosnian Tourist Board; pages 275, 276, 285, 288, 289, 292, 295, 296 Rafael Estepania.

The following images were provided by the featured establishments/artist: pages 18, 19, 36, 60, 89, 90, 94, 105, 109 (bottom), 139, 171, 189, 228, 238, 267, 270, 279, 261, 280, 281, 283, 291.

Contents

Introduction

Croatia is the destination of the moment. Spain's coast has been ruined, Italy's is tacky, the French Med is exclusive. Croatia's coast is pure, nearly all 2,000 kilometres and 1,200 islands of it, and is open to all. Excepting a few pockets of package resorts and the odd port, the coast you're gawping at, and the reason for all the recent hype, is remarkably similar to how Roman Emperor Augustus, or the Venetians or Napoleon's troops would have seen it.

Only **Rijeka** and **Split** sully Croatia's sliver-thin littoral with industrial clutter – exactly because Rijeka and Split are the ports from which sleek, white Jadrolinija liners leave for idyllic islands several times a day in summer, for the foot-passenger price of a round of drinks in London or New York. And even then Rijeka has peeling Habsburg façades and Split has as its centrepiece a superb Roman palace whose nooks and crannies have been filled with oddball life of all kinds for 1700 years.

Few dawdle around either departure point, nonetheless. There's island hopping to be done.

Croatia by region

For the purposes of this guide we have divided Croatia into seven regions: **Zagreb**, the capital and its immediate surroundings of ski slopes and chocolate-box villages; **Slavonia & Inland Croatia**, the area known by locals as continental Croatia, of vineyards and medieval castles; **Istria**, Croatia's pocket Tuscany of hilltop villages and gastronomic delights; and **Kvarner & Islands**, the high-sided gulf populated by dolphins and accommodating Croatia's largest islands. **Dalmatia** has been split into three regions. Northern Dalmatia is called **Zadar & Islands**, central Dalmatia **Split & Islands** and southern Dalmatia **Dubrovnik & Islands**. The best known and most popular of the islands is the central section, where Hvar, Vis and Brač are easily accessible from Split. Dubrovnik tends to attract older tourists, happy to relax amid the pleasant greenery and historic sights of Mljet or Korčula. Zadar is little known, but its archipelago is every bit as beautiful and frequented, in the main, by locals.

Verdant islands, bare karst-rock islands, tiny dots of islands with nothing on them but a lighthouse recently converted to accommodate isolated holidaymakers (*see p19* **Lighthouse accommodation**), naturist islands, islands with just deer and naturists feeding them, islands with cocktail bars attracting the VIP set, islands for windsurfers, islands for sculptors, islands for Tito's political prisoners, islands for Tito's collection of safari animals, islands so remote they're nearer to Italy, islands called home by a family of 120 dolphins, islands of age-old fishing traditions, islands with a particular cave in which the sunlight turns a brilliant blue for an hour each day, islands known for their wine, cheese or anchovy pasties. More than 80 per cent of Croatia's islands have no people on them at all.

And all of them dot a crystal clear Adriatic, the smooth stones of its seabed visible through it at every one of the thousands and thousands of indents from Rijeka in the Kvarner Gulf down to Croatia's tapering tip past **Dubrovnik** at Montenegro. All kinds of water sports – sailing, especially, but also windsurfing and kayaking – are practised all summer long down the coast. The crystal clear sea, unusual wrecks from conflicts ancient and recent, and lack of sharks, mean that Croatia is one of Europe's best destinations for divers. Clubs, many happy to train beginners, dot the coastline.

Croatia is not just a pretty face, though. Croatia has history, Greek, Roman, Slav, Venetian, Napoleonic, Habsburg, Yugoslav, Nazi, Communist and now its own independent history. Much of this is still visible, most notably in Dubrovnik, a republic and a law unto itself for centuries, a history carved in beautiful white stone. There are churches glittering with Byzantine treasure, Orthodox churches, towering Gothic churches, simple stone churches from 800 AD.

Croatia can do modern, too. Dubrovnik is ringed by high-end, five-star hotels, whose fashionable spas and classy Mediterranean restaurants are embellished by the stunning Adriatic backdrop the designers were lucky enough to incorporate into their plans.

It must be said that Dubrovnik is hellishly busy for two months of the year, in part thanks to its heavyweight cultural festival of 50 years standing. But even in its compact Old Town in high season you can dive off the rocks and climb back up for a relaxed, moonlit beer at an intimate cluster of tables. And then there's

Unspoiled beaches stretch a short walk from **Dubrovnik**.

Istria. Away from the couple of resorts on the west coast, Istria, a small triangle of land linking Italy and continental Croatia, Istria is empty. Hardly any trains, few cars, even fewer buses, just a few medieval hilltop villages, rolling vineyards and the occasional stellar restaurant whose chef will sprinkle your steak or the house chocolate cake with truffles. The capital **Zagreb**, too, empties in summer, its Habsburg façades, traditional coffeehouses and meticulously planned green downtown spaces bereft of locals who flee for the coast. They reclaim their capital in September, when this manageable city of a million people reopens for business: new boutique hotels, chic restaurants, minimalist bars and one of the best live music scenes in Europe. Only recently has Zagreb realised that tourists also come in summer – especially now that there is a new UK budget connection with Wizz Air.

Away from the coast and Zagreb, forty per cent of Croatia is mountains, rising to nearly 2,000 metres (6.560feet). Twenty-five per cent of Croatia is forest. Eight national parks and ten nature parks contain waterfalls, lakes and, in the case of **Kornati**, a string of 140 islands (*see p14* **National Parks**). Running wild around them are bears, lynx, wolves, chamois, wild cats and wild boar. The little known **Velebit**

National Park alone has more than 2,500 species of plant life. Some 126 bird types have been found in **Plitvice** and the marshes of the **Kopački Rit Nature Park** contain rare black storks, white-tailed eagles and thousands of cormorants. **Brijuni** has elephants, zebras and authentic dinosaur footprints, remnants of the Tito era and prehistoric times. In the **Kvarner Gulf**, griffon vultures and dolphins both have conservation centres open to the public.

WAR AND PEACE

It would be easy to spend time at the resorts and not think about what went on here in 1941 and 1991. World War II was particularly brutal in what was Yugoslavia, of which Croatia was a reluctant junior member. Croatia played a major part in that shocking brutality. No getting away from it, Croatia has a nasty, Nazi past. For 35 years, a Socialist regime under Partisan war leader Tito held the whole shaky structure of Yugoslavia together, during which time Croatia developed a fully fledged package tourist industry – until Serbian nationalism tore up the rule book a decade after Tito's death. In 1991, Croatia became the victim: the towns of **Vukovar**, **Zadar** and Dubrovnik were bombarded and trapped in a state of siege as the significant Serb population of Croatia rose

The beautiful island of **Brač**. *See p228.*

up. The first fatality was the park ranger of Plitvice. The most gratuitous urban show of aggression was on Dubrovnik, its beautiful Old Town showered with shells, an act against a demilitarised World Heritage site that saw Europe sit up, notice and, perhaps hastily, grant Croatia its long sought independence. Meanwhile Vukovar got flattened. The Yugoslav War then flared up in Bosnia and Hercegovina. Croatia led a disastrous and often brutal intervention. All was ended, at least on paper, by the Dayton Agreement of 1995.

During this time, Croatia's main source of revenue, tourism, all but disappeared. For the local economy of a fledging state with little industry to speak of, the war was a double whammy on top of the familiar ills of a former Communist, centrally planned system having to cope with the free market. Croatia's closest and most natural trading partners, Serbia and Bosnia, had been enemies on the battlefield. Transport links to Serbia had been cut and relations with Slovenia were sullied by a border dispute. Important privatisation contracts were given to the cronies of the ruling Tudjman regime. Croatia's foreign debt ballooned.

Slowly, though, the tourists returned. The war most affected Croatia's inland region, and today you still see burned out villages if you

head in from the coast, particularly in northern Dalmatia. Dubrovnik was painstakingly and magnificently rebuilt. Zadar has all but recovered, **Šibenik** is still struggling. Zagreb was hardly touched, nor the whole of Istria.

The rest of the coast, islands especially, have been open for business since the mid 1990s. You could spend a whole summer – in fact, you won't find a better way of spending a summer – island hopping around the coast from Istria down to Montenegro, and not be aware of what was happening here 15 years ago. The graffiti is no worse than you will see in the Basque Country, and however many propaganda posters you might see in villages around Zadar declaring support for Major-General Ante Gotovina, the alleged Croatian war criminal is now behind bars awaiting trial in the Hague. His arrest in December 2005 is seen as the removal of the most major obstacle to Croatia joining the European Union. Accession talks began in earnest shortly after Gotovina's dramatic arrest in the Canary Islands.

You will see a lot of patches of red-and-white checkerboards, as used by the Croatian kings from the 10th century, then adopted by the pro-Nazi Croatian state during World War II, and now spread across the flags, football shirts and sun hats on sale at every stall all down the coast: the *šahovnica*. Croatia, Catholic and by tradition conservative, is a proud new nation. Great swaths of it were ruled from Venice, Vienna, Budapest and Belgrade for the best part of the last thousand years. Any nation might wave a flag or two.

MEETING THE LOCALS

Some words, then about, your hosts. First of all, there are four and a half million of them and all the men are huge – big, broad-shouldered Slavs, some descended from a rather ill-defined tribe known as Illyrians.

This being the Balkans, social interaction is very direct. Croats don't mumble and they don't beat about the bush. They are, as a general rule, delightfully hospitable, and not just because their economy depends on tourism. Nearly everyone in the service industry speaks basic English at worst, decent English in the main, the result of a classical education system and the fact that Western TV shows are subtitled, not dubbed. All grow up with popular culture and most Croats are music savvy. As well as the live music scene in the capital, the most prestigious clubs on the Dalmatian coast attract the world's top DJs every summer.

Sport is all-important, too, particularly in Split. Bidding to host the 2011 World Athletics Championships (just as Croatia is bidding to co-host football's European Championships the following year), Split is bonkers for sport. Home matches of local football club Hajduk are lively, colourful affairs, and the city turns out in force for its sporting heroes – as witnessed by the return of Goran Ivanišević after his Wimbledon triumph in 2001.

PLANNING YOUR TRIP

Croatia has been a package-tour destination since the 1960s. Today more than 100 tour operators (*see p309*) run trips to Croatia, offering holidays from archaeological walks around the old Roman towns of Dalmatia to naturist breaks in Istria.

With the recent introduction of budget air links between the UK and Croatia, there will be a surge of independent travellers coming into Croatia from the summer of 2006. Yet much of the local tourist industry is still in the package-tour mindset. For visitors to get the most out of Croatia, they may have to deal with a creaking infrastructure and unsatisfactory overland transport network.

Coming for a long weekend, there is little to worry about. Both Split and Dubrovnik have enough attractions and nearby islands to make any three- or four-day break a relatively easy and reasonably priced experience. From Split, **Hvar** and **Brač** have a daily catamaran service in high season, allowing for an overnight stay in town and quick jaunt across the Adriatic.

Although most hotels slap a 20 per cent surcharge on stays of less than three nights, at these destinations you should be able to find a simple room in a two- or three-star establishment without breaking the bank. Hvar is a party island, Brač is more family-oriented. To stay somewhere more upmarket on Hvar in July and August is going to cost a pretty penny. Another idea might be to base yourself in Dubrovnik and use the taxi boats to nearby **Lokrum** to spend the afternoons on the beach. The less crowded **Elafiti Islands** are also easily accessible in a day. Both towns have major cultural festivals in summer (*see p305*).

A week's break at either destination allows you to spend more time on the islands. From Split you could spend four or five nights on **Vis**, the least developed of the main islands. From Dubrovnik you could head for **Mljet** or **Korčula**. These islands offer unspoilt nature and, in the case of Korčula, a little history. There's not much by way of nightlife on either.

If you're looking to stay in Istria, the west coast, especially **Poreč** and **Rovinj**, can be very crowded in high summer. **Novigrad** can offer a relaxing few days away from the crowds without much by way of historic attractions. The beauty of Istria is that it's year-round. In fact, autumn is the best time to see it, when the rolling countryside is a golden colour and

The best Sailing getaways

Opat

South-east end of Kornat, Kornati National Park. Easy moorings.
Two rustic seafood restaurants are backdropped by stark wilderness in an otherwise deserted bay. An energetic walk up a signed path, to the top of the nearby hills, gives a spectacular panorama of the surrounding islands.

Vrboska

North coast of Hvar, an hour's walk from Jelsa. Easy moorings.
This unspoiled village offers several small stone bridges, intriguing back streets and a warm reception from the harbour master.

Uvala Vinogradišće

South coast of Sv Klement, Pakleni Islands near Hvar. Anchorage.
An idyllic bay with great restaurants. You can walk over the hill to the marina, on the north side of the island, for a boat taxi into Hvar

town. This avoids the hassle of negotiating the busy town harbour once you arrive.

Uvala Sv Fumija

South coast of Čiovo, joined to Trogir by a bridge. Anchorage.
Watch a fabulous sunset over an informal dinner in Konoba Duga, with just a dirt track to connect it to the distant main road. Good shingle beach and deserted anchorage.

Maslinica

West coast of Šolta. Anchorage.
One of the smallest inhabited islands has resisted embracing the burgeoning tourist industry. Maslinica is its prettiest settlement.

Polače

West end of the north coast of Mljet. Anchorage.
A spacious safe anchorage on one of the most unspoiled islands, with easy access to the saltwater lakes and the magnificent scenery of Mljet National Park.

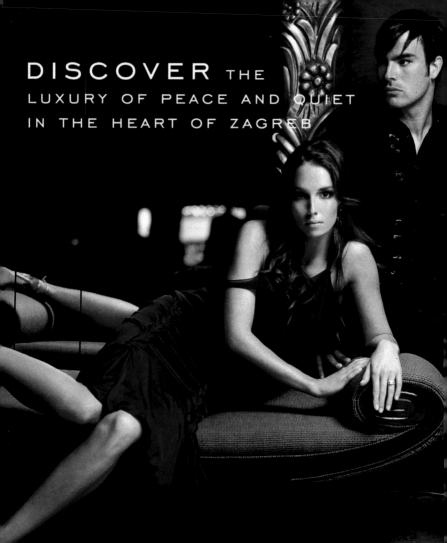

DISCOVER THE
LUXURY OF PEACE AND QUIET
IN THE HEART OF ZAGREB

LIVE THE LUXURY

THE
Regent

ESPLANADE ZAGREB

BY REZIDOR SAS

truffles feature on every restaurant menu.
Pula boasts an active off-season cultural life –
although the main event is the international
film festival (*see p117*) in early August at the
Roman amphitheatre, which also stages big-
name rock concerts from June. The little hilltop
village of **Motovun** is transformed every July
by an independent film festival (*see p128*
Motovun Film Festival) that turns into a
five-day party.

If you're staying for two weeks, you have
enough time to take the coastal ferry down from
Rijeka and call at a couple of the islands on the
way down to Dubrovnik. Using Rijeka as a
base, you are also easily placed to explore the
large islands of the Kvarner Gulf. **Krk** is the
most accessible, the site of Rijeka airport and
linked to the mainland by bridge; **Cres** is the
least developed.

The area of north Dalmatia is the least
known to UK visitors – mainly because it's the
most difficult to get to from the international
airports. Although not on any of the major ferry
routes, **Zadar** is a relatively easy overland hop
from Zagreb or Split, and well worth a three-
day visit. Its historic Roman centre contains
scores of churches, one with Byzantine
treasures, it's easy to get around and the local
nightlife scene has changed dramatically since
the opening of The Garden DJ terrace in 2004.
For those already familiar with the most
popular islands near Split and Dubrovnik, a
ferry journey to the **Zadar archipelago**
would be a rewarding one.

Wherever you go, the famous beaches are
just that, beaches. Stones and sea, sometimes
shingle and sea, all too rarely sand and sea.
No fun fairs, no amusement arcades, no theme
parks. If you're travelling with children and
they're happy with a paddle, a pedalo or a
snorkel, you're in luck. There's probably an
aquarium nearby, too – but that's your lot.
Croatia is still pretty cheap, its sea is calm and
generally safe, and locals love kids. If your
children need more thrills but aren't old or
motivated enough to try kite surfing or sea
kayaking, then boredom may be a factor.

GETTING AROUND

The major points of arrival into Croatia for
holidaymakers are the airports of Split and
Dubrovnik. In June 2006, easyJet introduced a
service to Rijeka. Visitors to Istria can also fly
to Trieste in Italy, a Ryanair destination.
Zagreb has recently been added to the Wizz Air
roster. A significant number also arrive by ferry
from Ancona or Pescara, usually to Split.

The best way to get around is by boat. The
state-run Jadrolinija ferry company is cheap
and pretty comfortable, though it's there to

By numbers

Geography

Area 56,542sq km (21,831sq miles)
Coastal sea area 31,067sq km (11,995sq miles)
Coastline (as the crow flies) 600km (373 miles)
Coastline (actual length with indents) 1,778km (1,105 miles)
Coastline (offshore islands) 4,012km (2,493 miles)
Coastline (total) 5,790km (3,598 miles)
Islands 1,185
Inhabited islands 66

Population

Croatia 4,495,904 (2005)
Zagreb 779,145 (2002)
Split 188,694 (2002)
Rijeka 144,043 (2002)
Osijek 114,616 (2002)
Ethnic groups Croat 87.8%; Serb 4.5%; other 5.9% (Bosniak, Hungarian, Slovene, Czech, Romany)
Religions Catholic 87.8%; Orthodox 4.4%; Slavic Muslim 1.28%; others 6.52%
Language Croatian (South Slavic using Roman script)
Health (2005 est.) Life expectancy male 71 years; female 78 years. Infant mortality 6.84 deaths/1,000 live births

Economy & finance

Currency Croatian kuna
Exchange rates (as of April 2006) One pound = 10.6kn. One euro = 7.3kn. One dollar = 6kn.
Real GDP growth (2004) 3.7%
Inflation rate (2004) 2.5%
Unemployment rate (2004) 13.8%

serve locals, not tourists. Many island services
leave very early in the morning, timed to come
back when the working day is done, not when
you might want to leave the beach. The upside
is that fares are kept low. A ten-minute journey
by Tube in London's Zone 1 costs more than a
two-hour glide to idyllic Hvar from Split.

In summer there's a catamaran service
on major short-hop routes too. Jadrolinija
(www.jadrolinija.hr) divides the coast into four
main regions, the main ports of departure being
Rijeka, Zadar, Split and Dubrovnik. Note that
once you arrive at your island of choice local
transport may not be so accommodating –
more of that soon.

Once daily in summer, a car ferry runs the length of the coast from Rijeka, a mainly overnight journey whose daylight course will be a wonderful holiday memory.

Car hire in Croatia is expensive, something around 500kn a day (50 pounds or 70 euros) for an average family car with unlimited mileage.

Most main companies have an office in Zagreb and at major airports. There is zero tolerance on alcohol. There are toll roads; the highway between Zagreb and Split was opened in 2005.

Croatia's strange boomerang shape and mountainous terrain doesn't lend itself to a quick, integrated transport system. Overland

National Parks

Since 1949, Croatia has created eight national parks and ten nature parks. The oldest is perhaps the most beautiful: **Plitvice** (*see p99*). Comprised of 16 lakes connected by waterfalls, this area is surrounded by dense forests of beech, fir and spruce. The two main entrances are easily accessible from Zagreb or main towns in Dalmatia, halfway down the country. Brown bear are among the animal types found here.

Mljet (*see p294*) is probably the best known of Croatia's protected areas. Nearly the whole of this island, a ferry ride from Dubrovnik or Split, has been left to nature, although only the western third is the officially designated National Park. Here you'll find the two natural salt lakes for which Mljet is famous. The area is perfect for cyclists and hire places abound.

Kornati (*see p192*) is the most dramatic of the parks, an archipelago of some 140 islands. Access is by boat only, with excursions departing from **Murter** (*see p194*). This is the region most known for the type of

tourism promoted as 'Robinson Crusoe', where visitors are offered the use of a simple, stone cottage and allowed to fend for themselves. **Šibenik** (*see p200*) is another departure point. Krka (*see p200* **Krka National Park**), an area of rugged limestone, plunging rapids and dramatic waterfalls, is also easily accessible from Šibenik.

The most unusual park is surely **Brijuni** (*see p118* **Tito's Xanadu**), a mostly inaccessible archipelago whose main island was used by the former Yugoslav leader Tito as his zoo and pleasure park. Sumptuous gardens complement the exotic wildlife, and there is evidence of habitation going as far back as the dinosaurs.

For serious hikers, mountaineers and potholers, the three key parks are **Risnjak** (*see p156*), **Northern Velebit** and **Paklenica** (*see p177*), all within easy reach of Kvarner, Istria, Zagreb and northern Dalmatia. Among the nature parks, **Kopački Rit** (*see 105*) and **Lonjsko Polje** (www.pp-lonjsko-polje.hr) are wetlands famous for their extensive bird life.

Zimmer frei

Your first contact with the locals in a Dalmatian town often comes as you disembark from the bus or boat that brought you. Little old ladies hold up a sign saying '*Zimmer frei*', enthusiastically grabbing your elbow saying '*sobe*', or rooms. Somehow, without any common words, you make out a price (usually around 200-300kn a room) and you understand that you should follow this woman for a short walk to a house nearby. She'll probably take you to a subdivided downtown flat or an upstairs bedroom in a holiday home, where the owners and their family are summering on the ground floor.

If you just go home with the first older woman you meet at the bus station, you might get a saggy bed, a weak shower or an untidy bathroom. To ensure a certain level of cleanliness and comfort, and to avoid

trekking around town, it helps to go to a travel agency. Agencies add about ten per cent to the final price of a room, but they're quick, and they screen accommodations for quality. Right where you got off the bus or boat, and all around a town's seaside, you'll find agencies that will confirm a vacancy by phone and then send you off to stay in someone's house. You are often asked to pay in advance at the agency, otherwise you're told the price that the owner is expecting from you. Travel agencies also book rooms in advance by phone and internet. The Croatian Tourist Board (www.croatia.hr) provides a free booklet, *Private & Confidential*, listing all the agencies in each region. If you reserve a couple months ahead, you can get cheap, comfortable accommodation right by the beach or in the heart of town.

travel is poor and longwinded. If they haven't got a car, Croatians travel by bus. All major towns are linked by a regular and cheap bus service. The main company is Autotrans (www.autotrans.hr) but there are several other operators. Most buses are quite old, the leg room minimal. If you are joining the bus somewhere along its journey – the smaller stops are just a concrete bunker with the town's name on it – you may have to stand. Sometimes there may not be room at all. Keep 7kn in change to pay for your luggage to be stored in the hold – there won't be room for much on the bus. The journey from Split to Dubrovnik, for example, takes four and a half hours and costs about 100kn. Note that a return fare is slightly discounted, but only if you travel back with the same company. Usually you buy your ticket in advance from the departure bus station and are given a seat number – although these are often ignored once you board. Timetables are posted up but there are few departure boards – usually there is a confusing gaggle of people around each platform. Look out for the little sign on the bottom left-hand side of the driver's window – and the name of the bus company.

Given the discomfort and hassle of long-distance bus travel, if you are touring the country it is worth considering internal flights. Croatia Airlines (www.croatiaairlines.com) keeps back a handful of cheap tickets until a couple of days before their departure on services between the main towns, so you could fly from Zagreb to Split for about 500kn return. This extra outlay of some 200kn means you're

not cramped up for a total return journey of 18 hours while the bus driver assaults your ears with loud folk tunes to keep himself awake. Note that some buses use a ferry for part of the journey – Dubrovnik-Korčula is one example.

Rail travel is extremely limited. Part of the reason is that the network was devised by the Habsburgs – in particular the Hungarians – with Budapest as its hub. Also the main routes used to link with Belgrade and Sarajevo. Today the only route worth mentioning is served by a new tilting train between Zagreb and Split. Even though it is only two or three carriages long, seats are generally plentiful and you can order one by a table. The single fare is about 140kn, coffee and a sandwich provided. Journey time is five and a half hours. Change halfway along at Knin for a slow regional train to Zadar. There is also a main line from Zagreb and Rijeka. There is no service up the coast and nothing at all to Dubrovnik.

ACCOMMODATION

First things first. Croatia doesn't do the kind of simple, cheap, two- or three-star, family-run pension that is such a great feature of France, Spain and Portugal. It was a Communist country that had no Western guests (apart from spies and diplomats), then it had package tourism, then it accommodated the business community with luxury hotels whose facilities ticked every box but the one marked 'character'.

Opatija was a five-star resort before there was ever Yugoslavia (those classy Habsburgs!). Dubrovnik was accommodating movie stars

while the first package tourists were arriving – and Zagreb has the great railway hotel, the Esplanade – but these are the exceptions. Until around 2003, most of Croatia's hotel stock was bland and functional.

Now that situation is changing – slowly. Starting with Dubrovnik (which has six five-star hotels and another opening in the summer of 2006), Croatia is beginning to realise that a hotel has to offer something special before it can charge Western prices. The tourist board slogan of 'The Mediterranean As It Once Was' still applies to many of the hotel rooms, with their dowdy furnishings and relatively basic facilities. Air-conditioning is not a given. For every Dubrovnik Palace or Pucić Palace (prime contenders for best hotel in Croatia) there are scores of others whose provision for tourists is merely adequate. The point about Croatia is that few here dare to be different, whether as hotel owner or restaurateur. Perhaps it's too much to risk, perhaps it's something in the national make-up.

Another trap for the independent traveller is the near universal rule of adding surcharges (about 20 per cent) on stays of less than three nights. Quite often the room prices given are for each guest – double it for the price for the pair of you. In this guide we have given the prices mainly in euros (unless requested to use kuna). Just because a hotel quotes its rates in euros does not mean it accepts them as payment – this is nearly always made in the local currency.

We give the rates for a double room, ranging from low to high season (whose dates vary, but generally the whole of July and August). Many hotels in the main tourist areas (particularly the Makarska Riviera) close between October and April – those in the larger towns tend to stay open. A nominal tourist tax applies throughout. Prices for higher-end establishments are quoted in euros, lower-end in kuna.

The real shortfall comes in the mid-range category. There isn't one to speak of. Honourable exceptions include the Hotel Cittar in Novigrad, the Villa Hrešć in Zadar and the Hotel Paula in Vis. In Split, Pula, Šibenik and Hvar town, the need for a couple of three- or four-stars with individuality is pressing.

The budget end is equally bereft – which is where the vast network of private rooms comes in (*see p15* **Zimmer frei**). In too many places the accommodation choice for individual travellers is between an overpriced four-star, a multi-storey package hotel or an old lady's front room. The modest handful of hostels (www.hfhs.com) do an adequate job. Campsites (*autokamp*) tend to be fairly basic but cheap, and pitching your tent in the stony soil can be a nightmare. For small groups, many homes are rented out as apartments (*apartmeni*) and out of high season this can be the ideal, reasonably priced solution.

The most obvious choice for a unique and memorable stay is a lighthouse (*see p19* **Lighthouse accommodation**). Some dozen

Maps

Place of interest and/or entertainment	
Railway station	
Park	
Hospital/university	
Military area	
Beach	
Neighbourhood	BEL AIR
Interstate highway	15
US highway	95
State or county highway	75
Ski resort	
Golf course	
Winery	

such remote settings have been converted into three-star accommodation units. Villa rental is nowhere near as extensive as it is in, say, Portugal. The exception here is Istria, whose Villas Forum (www.villasforum.com) sets the benchmark on how to renovate run-down regional properties in local architectural style, add a few touches such as a pool and a barbecue area, and earn repeat business. Istria also is leading the way on rural tourism, opening up farms for family stays and attracting visitors away from the coast.

Most tourist offices can provide a list of hotels in the vicinity and their phone numbers. Few will help with booking them. Local travel agencies (we list a couple for each main town) can do that job for you. In most tourist centres, one group controls the bulk of the hotel stock – Sunčani Hvar in Hvar town, for example.

A view from the **Dubrovnik Palace Hotel**.

ABOUT TIME OUT CITY GUIDES
Time Out Croatia is one of an expanding series of travel guides produced by the people behind London and New York's successful listings magazines. Our writers, a mix of expert locals and experienced travel writers aim to provide the most up-to-date information you'll need to explore the country, whether you're a local or first-time visitor.

THE LOWDOWN ON THE LISTINGS
Above all, we've tried to make this book as useful as possible. Throughout the guide, we've included telephone numbers, open or closed times and admission prices (where no price is given for a museum or other attraction, assume admission is free or nominal). For attractions, hotels, visitor centres and selected other businesses, we've added websites. In the chapter on Zagreb, listings incorporate travel directions unless the venue is an easy walk of the central square of Trg bana Josipa Jelačića.

As far as possible, we've given details of facilities, services and events, all checked and correct at the time we went to press. However, Croatia is a Balkan country. Opening hours are flexible. A place may stay open because it's full of guests or may close because the owner fancied the day at the beach. Before you go out of your way, call and check opening times, dates of events and other particulars. While every effort has been made to ensure the accuracy of the information contained in this guide, the publishers cannot accept responsibility for any errors it may contain.

PRICES AND PAYMENT
We have noted whether shops, restaurants and hotels accept the following credit cards: American Express (AmEx), Diners Club (DC), MasterCard (MC) and Visa (V).

The prices we've supplied should be treated as guidelines, not gospel. Fluctuating exchange rates and inflation can cause charges to change rapidly. If prices vary wildly from those we've quoted, ask whether there's a good reason. If not, go elsewhere, and then please let us know.

Advertisers

Lighthouse accommodation

Throughout the 19th century, the ruling
Austro-Hungarian monarchy built 48
lighthouses along the Croatian coast.
Families were born and raised there – the
lighthouse keeper had to be married.

They are longer used for the purpose of
navigation and today a dozen have been
converted to accommodate tourists. Some
are within easy reach of the mainland –
others, in particular **Palagruža** (*pictured*) are
so remote they are suitable only for the young
and hardy. Palagruža is also different in that
is nearly a mile long, allowing for a range of
flora and fauna to explore. Some, such as
Struga, have beaches suitable for children;
others, for example **Rt Zub** and **Pločica**
(*see p291* **Getting away from it all**) have
no lighthouse keeper and are perfect for
group visits.

Accommodation is usually quite basic but
three-star. Prices per person are reasonable,
although in some cases you pay a transfer
fee to reach the island from the nearest
mainland departure point. Tour company
adriatica (01 24 15 611, www.adriatica.net)
can arrange visits.

THE LIE OF THE LAND

Time Out Croatia is split into seven sections,
which have then been further subdivided to
cover the main town followed by the local
destinations easily accessible from it.

Each chapter begins with a map of the
region; more detailed maps of major towns and
attractions are included within the chapters. A
map of Croatia, showing how we've divided up
the country, is at the front of this guide. For a
full index of maps in the book, *see p17*.

PHONE NUMBERS AND ADDRESSES

All local landline numbers in this guide are
prefixed with their area code. From abroad, you
need to dial the access code 00, then the code for
Croatia, 385, followed by the area code minus
the first 0. So a number in Zagreb listed as 01 23
45 678 should be dialled 00 385 1 23 45 678 from
abroad. From elsewhere in Croatia, simply dial
the number given. If you're in the region itself,
you don't need the area code, just the six or
seven digits afterwards.

As not all venues have landlines, many locals
use mobile phones, prefixed by 091 or 098.
Where necessary, we have given these numbers
too. Calls to a Croatian mobile from a foreign
one can be expensive. For more *see p308*.

In Croatian a street is *ulica*, a square *trg*, an
embankment *obala*. *Cesta* is a road, route or
avenue. Quite often the street name will be
given as the person it has been named after, so
in Zagreb Ulica Nikole Tesle is referred to by
locals as Teslina. Many large roads or new ones
do not have numbered houses. In Croatian these
are given as '*bb*' or *bez broja* ('without a
number'). We have omitted 'bb' from our
addresses to lessen confusion. Note also that
waterfront promenades in Split and elsewhere
are often referred to as '*riva*'.

ESSENTIAL INFORMATION

For all the practical information you might need
for visiting Croatia – including customs and
visa information, disabled access, emergency
telephone numbers, a list of useful websites and
so on – turn to the Directory chapter at the back
of this guide. It starts on *p302*.

LET US KNOW WHAT YOU THINK

We hope you enjoy the Time Out Croatia guide,
and we'd like to know what you think of it. We
welcome tips for places that you consider we
should include in future editions and take notice
of your criticism of our choices. You can email
us at guides@timeout.com.

The New Tuscany

- ❀ Vineyards. olive groves, healthy food

- ❀ Good building standards

- ❀ Solid capital appreciation

- ❀ Close enough for long weekends (Ryan Air)

- ❀ English widely spoken

Apartments

Stone houses

In Context

Features

Pula amphitheatre.

History

A 1,000-year-old dream of nationhood fulfilled.

Scholars have yet to resolve the etymology and meaning of the word Croat, with clues as to its origins sought variously in the Greek words for 'people who have a lot of land', 'tree', 'a dance', and the inhabitants of the Island of Krk. The word has also been taken as evidence of distant Iranian roots, with an original meaning of 'friend' or 'protector'. Arriving at the shores of the Adriatic at the start of the seventh century, the Croats were among a wave of Slav invaders that reached their most western point of conquest in Istria at the gates of Italy. At the same time, the Slav tribes also pressed south, destroying Salona in AD 614, the magnificent capital of Roman Dalmatia.

In the face of the barbarian onslaught, the Romans, and other Romanised peoples of Illyria, moved to the islands, later returning to their cities on the mainland when it became clear that the Slavs were not interested at this stage in urban living. This resulted in an interesting situation, in which two quite different civilisations co-existed in close proximity during the seventh century. The Romans kept to the towns of Zadar, Trogir

and Split, while in the Dalmatian hinterland, tribes of Slavs maintained their own social systems, religion and language. There was a pragmatic exchange between the two societies, with the Romans ready to exchange craftwork and commercial services for the livestock and agricultural products of the Slavs. Over time, the two cultures intermixed. Rulers of the pagan Slavs came under the influence of the Christian civilisation of the cities, and the urban population became progressively less distinct from the more numerous ethnic Slavs living in the surrounding countryside.

In a pattern that was repeated over the centuries, the ups and downs of distant empires gradually changed the political constellation on the Adriatic coast. The struggle between the Franks and the Byzantines in the age of Charlemagne, crowned Emperor of the Holy Roman Empire in 800, had direct repercussions for Dalmatia. When Charlemagne and the Byzantine Emperor made peace in Aachen in 812, the Byzantines were allotted the Roman cities, while the Franks got the rural hinterland, founding a dukedom that was centred on Sisak.

DUX CROATORUM

The first historical document referring to Croatian state institutions dates from 852, when Trpimir (845-864) styled himself 'Dux Croatorum'. The small territory of this Croatian dukedom extended across the hinterlands of Zadar, Trogir and Split, but did not include the coastal cities themselves. Interestingly, there was also a fledgling Pannonian Croatian state, positioned along the River Drava, in an area that in the Middle Ages became known as Slavonia. Cautious progress by the Croat rulers was suggested by an agreement made between Byzantium and the Croatian state, according to which the cities on the Adriatic seaboard would pay a fee to the Croatians in exchange for the right to work their own fields. The Venetians, whose influence on Dalmatia was already on the rise, also paid the Croat leaders for the right of their ships to pass through unhindered.

The Croat ruler Tomislav (910-928) started out as a *dux*, but succeeded by 925 in becoming a full-blown *rex*. The Byzantine empire allowed him to rule the cities of the Adriatic as the Emperor's pro-consul. During his rule, there were two Church assemblies in Split in which vital questions facing the early medieval Church were discussed. Militarily, Tomislav kept the Hungarians in the north at bay and stopped Bulgarian Emperor Symeon's attempt to conquer the country. He was an administrative innovator, bringing the machinery of feudal government up to date, with the division of Croatia into 11 administrative districts.

Culture and religion in the kingdom were marked by the division between users of Latin and users of the Slavic alphabet, *Glagolica*. In the early years, inland Croatian priests knew no Latin, could marry, and wore their hair long like the Byzantine clergy, but by the 12th century, the papal authorities and the mostly Latin-speaking coastal nobility had brought the Croatian Church firmly within the established order of Roman Catholicism. Glagolitic survived as the secular alphabet for Croatian literature from the 14th to 16th centuries, and was to enjoy a partial revival in the 19th century, thanks to Romantic literary nationalists.

In one of those fateful accidents of royal marriage and inheritance that are hard for the modern mind to fathom, the Croatian crown passed in 1102 to King Kálmán of Hungary. He assumed the Croatian throne under a joint agreement that was to guarantee the separate but unequal existence of Croatia within the Hungarian kingdom until 1918. According to the *Pacta conventa* the Croatian nobility kept their Sabor (assembly) and local authority in the country. While Croatia continued to exist as a separate political entity, the process of state building was blocked for almost 900 years by the interests and competing sovereignties of the Ottomans, Venetians, Hungarians and the Habsburg empire.

DOMINATION AND HARDSHIP

The decline of the medieval Croatian kingdom was hastened by the rise of Venice, which in the 14th century consolidated its hold on Dalmatia. One low point was the sale of Dalmatia to the Venetians for 100,000 ducats, with the result that the Venetians ruled both the cities and islands of Dalmatia, with only the rump of Croatia in Slavonia left. After the fall of Bosnia in 1463, Croatian lands were more vunerable to Turkish attacks, and defeat at the Battle of Krbavsko Polje, in Lika, in 1493 ushered in a century of chaos and destruction. The situation was just as serious for the Habsburgs, who trembled as the Turks drew nearer and nearer to Vienna, crushing the Hungarians at the Battle of Mohács in 1526. With the King of Hungary killed at Mohács, the following year the Croatian nobility chose to put their faith in the Habsburg ruler King Ferdinand, in the hope that he would protect them from the Turks.

> **'After the fort at Bihać fell in 1592, the territory was referred to as the remnants of the remnants of the once great Croatian kingdom.'**

Croatian trust in the Habsburgs was not very generously rewarded. The Emperor Ferdinand I carved another slice off what was left of the Kingdom of Croatia with the establishment of a broad military zone, controlled from Vienna, along the border with the Ottoman empire. This was the 'Vojna Krajina', or Military Border. After the fort at Bihać fell in 1592, only small parts of Croatia remained unconquered. The remaining 16,800 square kilometres (6,486 square miles) were referred to as the 'remnants of the remnants of the once great Croatian kingdom'. The 16th century in Croatia was also the era of Matija Gubec's bloodily suppressed peasant uprising, and the Uskok pirate state in Senj, which had managed to harass the Venetians, Habsburgs and the Turks from its stronghold on the inhospitable coastline around Senj.

An exception in this story of hardship and imperial domination is provided by Dubrovnik. Known as Ragusa, and recognised as a sovereign republic, the city was the main Mediterranean centre for trade with the Ottoman empire by the 16th century, and maintained its independence until the Napoleonic Wars. Despite the difficult political situation, Dalmatia in the 15th and 16th centuries was something of a mecca for Renaissance culture. In this period, hundreds of Croat humanists studied at universities abroad, such as Padua. The strong cultural identity of the coastal cities of Dalmatia was as much connected to their sense of belonging to a cultural heritage going back to the Romans and Greeks, as to their Latin scholarship and the development of Croat vernacular literature. Italian humanists, along with painters, sculptors and architects, who came to work on the magnificent building projects of Renaissance Dalmatia, must have felt very much at home here.

The eventual reversal of Ottoman fortunes followed their defeat at the Battle of Sisak in 1593. But instead of relaxing Habsburg control of the country, Ferdinand II consolidated the imperial organisation of the Military Border, taking it completely out of the hands of the Croatian Parliament. Partly in response to such high-handed treatment, the noble Zrinski and Frankopan families plotted to eject the Habsburgs from Croatia, in an unlikely and desperate-sounding coalition with Louis XIV of France, the King of Poland, the Venetians and even the Turks. Unfortunately, word of the plot leaked out, and Peter Zrinski and his brother in law Franjo Frankopan were beheaded in Vienna Neustadt in 1671. The 17th and 18th centuries saw the power of the Croatian nobles in the Habsburg lands decline, with the Croatian Sabor in an increasingly weak position relative to the Vienna-appointed Governor, or Ban.

Following the Ottoman retreat after their second failed advance on Vienna in 1683, southern Slavonia was also brought into the Vojna Krajina. From the mid-16th century onwards, the Habsburgs had attracted border guards to the area with offers of free land without manorial obligations and by allowing freedom for Serbs to practise the Orthodox religion. Consequently, according to the first census of 1819 over half the population of the Military Border were Serbs, whose large presence in historic Croatia was to become a source of tension. The economy of the Military Border stagnated thanks to bureaucratic restrictions on the size and transfer of agricultural holdings, a complex customs regime and the fact that all men of military age had to spend much of the year on exercises. When the Hungarians tried under Ferenc Rákóczi to rid themselves of the Habsburgs, the Croatian nobility opted to collaborate with Vienna, signing the 'pragmatic sanction' that made possible Maria Teresa's ascension to the throne in 1740. This turned out to be a mistake, as during her 40-year rule she further

centralised power, shutting down the Croatian Sabor. Her son, the enlightened despot Joseph II, made some small improvements in the conditions of the peasantry, but was even more determined than his mother to carry out the Germanisation of the Habsburg empire.

ILLYRIANS OR SOUTH SLAVS?

After Venice fell to revolutionary France in 1797, her possessions in Dalmatia also fell under French control. French rule brought a number of advanced but short-lived administrative reforms, which included Napoleon's innovative establishment of an Illyrian kingdom, embracing Dalmatia and much of modern Slovenia. After Napoleon's defeat, Dalmatia passed into the control of the Habsburgs. At the same time, the growing strength of nationalism in Hungary was felt in Croatia, which many Hungarians treated as a province and attempted to 'magyarise'. It was against this background that a new direction in Croatian politics was defined, with the emergence of the Illyrian movement.

The fragmentation of the lands of the medieval Kingdom of Croatia had long been bemoaned, triggering calls for the 'Triune Kingdom of Croatia, Slavonia and Dalmatia' to be reunited under the House of Habsburg. However, the Slav activists of the early 19th century, fearing the term 'Croat' was too narrow, and following the example of the writer Ljudevit Gaj, instead described themselves as Illyrians, thereby hoping to bring under one umbrella the Habsburg empire's Croat, Slovene and Serb inhabitants.

Political Illyrianism ended after 1848. Although the Croatian Ban, Josip Jelačić, had helped the Habsburg monarchy suppress the Hungarian uprising, it earned him no favours from Vienna. Instead, during the authoritarian backlash against national independence movements between 1849 and 1860, the Sabor was not allowed to meet, and the Austrians ruled Croatia even more directly than before. Jelačić died a bitter man.

In the latter half of the 19th century, the Illyrian movement split. Ljudevit Gaj's heirs continued to champion a broad alliance with other Slavs, notably the Serbs. Now describing themselves as Jugoslavs (South Slavs) rather than Illyrians, their leader for many decades was the redoubtable scholar-Bishop of Djakovo, Josip Strossmayer. Their opponents, under Ante Starčević, rejecting the pan-Slav alliance with the Serbs as unworkable and as detrimental to Croat interest, gathered under the banner of the Party of Rights. A struggle between Strossmayer and Starčević for hearts and minds dominated Croat politics in the late 19th century.

Ban Josip Jelačić. *See p24.*

In 1867, after Austria's military defeat by Prussia, Vienna was forced to reach a historic compromise with restive Hungary. The division of the old Austrian empire into Austria-Hungary had enormous implications for the Croats, for while Dalmatia was left under the rule of Vienna, Slavonia fell squarely inside Hungary, albeit with a measure of autonomy. Cheated of all hopes of uniting Croat lands into one autonomous unit within the empire, Croat loyalty to the Habsburgs declined. One side-effect was the difficulty the government in Budapest experienced in managing the Sabor, which became increasingly ungovernable.

While the political situation resembled stalemate, the economic development of the country advanced apace. The ejection of the Ottomans from Bosnia in 1878 removed the the purpose of having a Military Border, and opened up new opportunities for both trade and mineral exploitation. The building of strategic railways made possible the industrial development of Slavonian cities such as Osijek and Slavonski Brod. The inland towns, which had stagnated for centuries, enjoyed an urban renaissance, with the transformation of Zagreb a case in point. A major earthquake provided an opportunity to remodel the city according to the civic ideals of the fin de siècle, creating a distinctive green horseshoe of squares and parks. The growth of Zagreb was partly the result of the policy of Ban Mažuranić, whose slogan 'from the inside and outside', reflected a practical strategy for modernisation that also gave the city the first European-style university in the Balkans.

THE FIRST YUGOSLAVIA

The coming of World War I tested the Croats' loyalty to the old order to its limits. At first most Croats fought loyally for the octogenarian Emperor Francis Joseph but, as the fighting dragged on and the prospect of defeat loomed, many Croats began pondering their future without the Habsburgs. The leaking of the terms of the secret London Treaty of 1915, by which the Entente Powers promised Italy most of Dalmatia if it were to come into the war on their side, shocked Croats into action. Alarmed by the possibility of partition between Italy in the west and Serbia in the east, opinion swung towards the establishment of a South Slav state embracing Serbia and Montenegro in order to guarantee the integrity of Croat lands. The first Croats to advance this programme were three Dalmatians, Supilo, Trumbić and the sculptor and architect Ivan Meštrović, who set up the Yugoslav Committee for this purpose in 1915.

The campaigners for Yugoslavia envisaged Croatian autonomy and equality within the new framework. But the state formed in 1918, after Austria-Hungary collapsed, disappointed them. It became clear that Yugoslavia's Serbian rulers saw Yugoslavia as an extension of Serbia and the imposition of a centralised constitution in 1921 discredited the Yugoslav cause in Croatia.

Well of Life by **Ivan Meštrović**.

Opinion now rallied to the separatist Stjepan Radić, leader of the Croat Republican Peasant Party, who had never supported the Yugoslav project. Having warned the Croats that 'they were rushing into union with Serbia like a band of drunken geese in a fog', he campaigned for an independent Croatian republic.

The young Yugoslav state was immediately faced with fierce opposition from Radić's party, which only became more radical and intransigent following his assassination in the Belgrade Parliament in 1928. His successor as leader was Vladko Maček, who maintained the Peasant Party's policy of non-violent struggle against Serb domination. Alongside this popular movement, which usually won the elections in Croatia, a more extremist opposition movement grew up on the far right under Ante Pavelić. His Ustashe movement traced its descent from Starčević's Party of Rights. But unlike the latter, it was prepared to engage in violence to achieve the goal of independence. An extreme solution on the left was offered by the Communist Party, destined to take control of the country later on, but in the 1920s and 30s a minority group.

'The assassination of Yugoslavia's authoritarian King Alexander in Marseille in 1934 put an end to the political stalemate.'

While in politics, the Kingdom of Yugoslavia drifted in the 1930s towards authoritarianism, in the cultural sphere there was a resurgence of opposition to parochialism and right-wing politics. The leading figure in Croatian literature in this period was Miroslav Krleža, who opposed the clerical right and the political dominance of the Peasant Party. He was aligned politically with the underground Communist Party, but in cultural matters he struggled against the confines of Socialist Realism.

The assassination of Yugoslavia's authoritarian King Alexander in Marseille in 1934 put an end to the political stalemate. Because the new King Peter was a minor, power passed to a regent, Prince Paul, an Anglophile liberal who was bent on solving Croat grievances without, however, conceding independence. Maček was brought in from the cold and after tortuous negotiations over borders and competencies, an autonomous Croat unit – the Banovina – was established within Yugoslavia in 1939. Dismissed as a façade by Pavelić's now-exiled Ustashe, the Banovina managed to alleviate Croat

frustration – a necessity for the whole of Yugoslavia now that Nazi Germany and Fascist Italy were threatening the balance of power within Europe.

The Banovina had no time to establish itself. After a pro-British faction in the Yugoslav army overthrew Prince Paul in 1941, Hitler invaded Yugoslavia and rapidly conquered the country. In Zagreb, Mussolini hurriedly installed Pavelić and his Ustashe cronies as lords of the new Independent State of Croatia (NDH), a name that belied its real status as an Italian dependency.

The NDH co-operated wholeheartedly with Nazi plans to exterminate the Jews and other minorities. Its agenda also included forcing Serbs to convert to Catholicism or be killed; many simply fled. As the Axis powers awarded the NDH the whole of Bosnia-Herzegovina, where Serbs made up the single largest ethnic group, the NDH was locked into civil war from the moment it was established in April 1941.

As World War II intensified, a frightful three-cornered conflict developed over Croatia between Communists, Serbian royalists, known as Četniks, and the Ustashe, who claimed the support of Nazi Germany and Fascist Italy. In reality, Italy was an ambivalent godparent of the NDH, making no secret of its eventual ambition to annex Dalmatia and realise Mussolini's goal of turning the Adriatic Sea into an Italian lake. Pavelić's poorly equipped army was no match for its opponents, and especially the well-organised Communist Partisans, led by Josip 'Tito' Broz (*see pp28-29* **Reinventing Tito**). The Partisans showed their strength by holding two congresses inside the NDH in 1942 and '43 at Bihać and Jajce, where they sketched out the foundations of a new Yugoslav state. This was to be a truly federal arrangement, with Serbs sharing power not only with Croats and Slovenes but with Macedonians, Montenegrins and Bosnians. It was to fall to the Communists to realise Strossmayer's programme.

COMMUNIST YUGOSLAVIA

With the defeat of the Nazis in 1945, Ustashe leader Ante Pavelić fled and it was the turn of the Communists to rule Croatia. Once more, Croatia was back inside Yugoslavia as one of six federal units. Its borders were smaller than those of the Banovina, owing to the Communists' decision to resurrect Bosnia as a federal unit. Those losses were partially offset by the inclusion in Croatia of the cities of Rijeka and Zadar and of most of Istria, which Italy had obtained from the Habsburg empire after 1918.

While there was little nostalgia for the bloodstained rule of Pavelić, now in exile in Argentina, the imposition of full-blown Soviet-

Reinventing Tito

Born in 1892 in the village of Kumrovec, Josip 'Tito' Broz, the ruler of Yugoslavia from 1945 until his death in 1980, remains a paradoxical figure in contemporary Croatian culture. On the one hand he is seen as a Communist dictator, who kept Croatia within Yugoslavia, crushing the Croatian Spring independence movement in 1971. Dependent for his power on terror and the secret police, he built the notorious Goli Otok island prison camp to punish his enemies. Seen from another perspective, he was a Croatian hero from the hilly region of Zagorje, the only World War II resistance leader to liberate his own country and tread a difficult third way between Stalin and the West during the Cold War, an ambassador of world peace, and the preserver of brotherhood and unity at home.

The paradox seems to have fuelled a wave of nostalgia for all things Tito, including a best-selling cookery book of his favourite recipes, the marketing of the Tito cult on Brijuni (*see p118* **Tito's Xanadu**), several films about his life, a photo exhibition of his travels, the planned restoration of his yacht *Galeb* as a tourist attraction by the city of Rijeka and a website www.titoville.com, full of his songs, speeches and pillow talk. In an intimate 4,000-word account of Tito's complex and colourful love life, the role of his widow, Jovanka Broz, is the most bizarre. Now living in squalid penury in a dilapidated, unheated house in Belgrade, Jovanka made the news in 2006 when details of her plight emerged. Suspecting her of plotting against him, Tito had her arrested in 1977, and she was dragged from her bed in her nightgown and interrogated. After his death, she was stripped of her possessions.

The fate of the former first lady is only a footnote in Tito's extraordinary life story. Raised on what is now the Slovene-Croatian border, Josip Broz left behind his peasant background to become an engineering worker, ending up at the Daimler-Benz works near Vienna. During World War I he was taken prisoner by the Russians but freed after the

style Communism grated on Croats, most of whom resented the persecution of the Catholic Church, symbolised by the trial and imprisonment of the Archbishop of Zagreb, Alojzije Stepinac, in 1946. A hate figure to Serbs for his initial colloboration with the NDH, Stepinac was correspondingly admired by Croats, especially in the countryside, and an official campaign against him merely fuelled a cult of Stepinac as a national martyr.

The tense atmosphere felt in Croatia lessened after Stepinac's death in 1960, which Tito cleverly exploited to bring about a rapprochement with the Church, allowing Stepinac a grand funeral in Zagreb to which foreign diplomats were invited. The Church took the proffered olive branch at face value and under Stepinac's successor, Cardinal Šeper, church-state relations lost their bitterness.

The development of mass tourism in the '60s also brought new life to the Croatian economy, especially in Dalmatia and Istria. It was helped by market reforms, accompanied by a considerable degree of local autonomy, allowing Croatia to become the second-most prosperous republic within Yugoslavia. Domestic production and Western imports led to an improved supply of both food and consumer goods. And Croatians took advantage of going to work abroad as 'guest workers', bringing back their hard-earned Deutschmarks to fuel a boom in Communist consumerism.

Bolshevik Revolution, staying on in Russia as a Red Guard during the civil war. On returning home, he worked in a flour mill, shipyard and foundry, and was made head of the Zagreb Communist Party in 1928. He was then arrested and spent six years in prison, using the time to study and debate Marxist theories with fellow prisoners. He later described the experience as 'my university'. After his release he went to Moscow and became a leading Communist functionary under the name Comrade Walter. He avoided becoming a victim of Stalinist purges and was appointed leader of the Yugoslav Communist Party in 1939. His nickname, Tito, came from his abrupt style of giving orders: '*Ti... to*' ('You... that!').

From 1941 he led the Yugoslav Partisan resistance against the Nazi invasion. Leading a braze guerrilla campaign up in the hills, he evaded Nazi capture and managed to persuade Churchill, through special envoy Fitzroy Maclean, to throw British support behind his Partisans. By October 1944 his men marched through Belgrade, and by May 1945 they were in Zagreb.

Head of a new, six-republic Yugoslavia from 1945, Tito was able to indulge his taste for palaces and conspicuous expenditure in general. He wore a gold-edged uniform with a belt buckle of pure gold, he wrote with a golden pen, he dyed his hair, and he often changed his clothes four times a day for various occasions. He had the archipelago of Brijuni transformed into an elite residence and playground, where he entertained world leaders and celebrities, such as Queen

Elizabeth II, Sophia Loren and Orson Welles. Priceless publicity shots of the time show Tito driving Princess Margaret round in a buggy and Richard Burton in a speedboat.

Tito was constantly on the move, on the state yacht *Galeb* (seagull) and in a specially kitted out 'Blue Train'. As the economy slowly began to grind to a halt, Tito strutted the world stage as a leading figure of the non-aligned movement.

When the news of Tito's death came on 4 May 1980 a key football match was abandoned and the players left the field in tears. Huge crowds packed the railway stations between Ljubljana where he died and Belgrade where he was buried, to watch the funeral train go past.

Today the towns that bore his name have been renamed, but public squares, such as Trg Maršala Tita in Zagreb, remain. All the wealth and property he amassed, in accordance with the principles of the Communist system, reverted to the state on his death. The presidents of independent Croatia have found themselves following in his footsteps and sleeping in his bedrooms, from the official Zagreb residency of Pantovčak to the villas of Brijuni.

Tito's old village Kumrovec (*see p97*) is now an ethnographic museum and a visitor attraction. The sleepy hamlet is not to everyone's taste, however. A recent bomb attack blew the head off Antun Augustinčić's famous statue of Tito. For months, there was a headless leader on a plinth, marching up and down at the darkest hour of the Partisan struggle.

Developments within the Communist Party further relaxed the political climate. The great event of the 1960s was the fall of Tito's deputy and presumed successor, Alexander Ranković. An ideological hardliner and a Serb, his presence beside Tito seemed a guarantee of ideological continuity. His abrupt removal in 1966 sent shockwaves through the country that Tito proved unable to contain. In several republics and provinces, including Macedonia and Kosovo, the post-war generation of leaders was challenged by relative youngsters offering a heady mix of liberalism and local nationalism.

In Croatia, these same elements were at work, bewildering the dogmatic older Communists with calls for more freedom and accountability.

The standard bearers for change in Croatia, Miko Tripalo and Savka Dabčević-Kučar, soon pushed aside Tito's colourless old henchman in Croatia, Vladimir Bakarić. Their supporters nicknamed the movement the Croatian Spring, or Maspok, short for *masovni pokret*, or mass movement. It was always a work in progress, however, and whether their ultimate aim was the reform of Communism or a multi-party democracy remained unclear.

THE CROATIAN SPRING

Maspok's immediate broad aims were economic and political reforms to secure Croatia a greater share of the wealth it generated and to increase Croatia's autonomy – and that of the other republics – within Yugoslavia. As such, the movement was seen, rightly, by many Serbs as a device to reduce their influence as an ethnic group in Yugoslavia, as well as to marginalise the role of the Communist Party.

The most pressing economic issues included the fact that although Croatia brought half the foreign capital into the country, it disposed of only 15 per cent of it. Centralisation of decision-making in Belgrade worked to the disadvantage of Croatia, and led to the widespread perception that Croatia was being economically exploited within the federation.

These economic grievances fed into other, more purely cultural worries about the loss of identity. Many intellectuals, including Tito's pet writer, Krleža – a member of the Croatian Communist Party's central committee, no less – were worried about the future of the Croatian language, which they claimed had been standardised along Serbian lines.

From Ranković's fall in 1966 to the autumn of 1969, the Croatian Spring swept all before it, with Tito's apparent support. Though worried by what he saw as its liberal excesses, at first Tito hoped Tripalo and Dabčević-Kučar could rein in the wilder elements. He also appreciated having Croat opinion on his side in 1968, when the Soviet invasion of Czechoslovakia made Yugoslavia jittery about its own security.

But by 1970 Tito was no longer afraid of Soviet intervention and was more worried by turbulence in Croatia, where demonstrations, strikes and student protests were shaking the Party's authority and alarming the mainly ethnic Serb officer corps of the Yugoslav army.

The crunch came in autumn in 1971, as the demands of the Croatian nationalists became increasingly radical, with calls for a separate Croatian currency and seat at the UN, as well as frontier changes with Bosnia. Croatia's 12 per cent Serb minority, concentrated in the old Military Border region, was increasingly agitated, as representatives accused Tripalo and Dabčević-Kučar of conniving for the return of the Ustashe.

In December 1971, urged on by the army and by Bakarić and the displaced old guard of the Croat Communist Party, Tito moved to crush the Croatian Spring. With tanks revving ominously at their army barracks, he summoned the leaders of the Croatian Party to his hunting lodge at Karadjordjevo, in Serbia, and ordered them to resign. They duly quit without demur, though their quiet exit did not save Croatia from a wide-ranging purge. The cultural organisation, Matica Hrvatska, was closed, hundreds of prison sentences were handed out and thousands of Party members were expelled. It was the end of an experiment

in a democratic form of Communism and its failure led to a great silence falling over Croatia, which gave rise to its new nickname in the late 1980s – 'the silent republic'.

The mute discontent of Tito's last years was alleviated by rising living standards based largely on foreign credits. But after Tito's death in 1980, the credits dried up and the economic situation worsened rapidly. As foreign debts spiralled and inflation spun out of control, the Communists rapidly lost prestige and the power to successfully suppress criticism. The old ideology of 'Brotherhood and Unity' became an object of general ridicule as the six republics fought openly over economic policy.

'A new Communist leader, Slobodan Milosevic, tore up the ground rules that had existed in Yugoslavia since 1945.'

However, it was not in Croatia that nationalism resurfaced in all its force but Serbia. There, a new Communist leader from 1987, Slobodan Milosevic, tore up the ground rules that had existed in Yugoslavia since 1945, openly promoting a violent and aggressive brand of Serb nationalism that paid no heed to the rights of Croats, Albanians, Bosnians or anyone else.

Milosevic's first target was Kosovo, the Albanian-dominated province in southern Yugoslavia that Serbs regarded as the cradle of their medieval state and whose autonomy Milosevic was determined to throttle. With the army behind him in 1989 he achieved his goal, albeit at the cost of the deaths of dozens of Albanian protesters, gunned down in the streets. He then turned his sights on Montenegro, which an internal coup delivered peacefully into his hands. While Serbs idolised 'Slobo' as a hero, the non-Serb majority in Yugoslavia was appalled and the League of Communists dissolved into its separate national components and lost control of events.

THE 1,000-YEAR-OLD DREAM

The rise of Milosevic forced other Communist leaders to look to their constituencies and concede democratic reforms. So it was that after 45 years of one-party rule, a plethora of parties appeared on the political scene, and with that, the prospect of multi-party elections. In Croatia the Communist Party leader since 1989, Ivica Račan, duly called a poll for 19 April 1990. Many thought Račan's skilful, temperate opposition to Milosevic's Serb chauvinism might bring him a democratic mandate. But Račan miscalculated the depth of Croat resentment to Communist rule and the prize went instead to the nationalist Croatian Democratic Union (HDZ) whose leader, a former general, Franjo Tudjman, had served several prison terms after the Croatian Spring.

Tudjman at first confined himself to arguing for a confederation and greater Croatian self-rule. But growing violence dictated its own course of events. No sooner was the 1990 election over than armed Serbs based in the hilly north Dalmatian town of Knin threw up roadblocks and proclaimed a separate Serb state within Croatia – the Republic of Serbian Krajina (RSK).

The RSK did not confine its remit to Serb-majority areas and, with Milosevic's energetic backing, rapidly annexed as much of the republic as possible. With Yugoslav army tanks as back-up, their task wasn't difficult. Facing a clamour from a panicked population, Tudjman edged towards proclaiming total independence – risking the threat of open war. The Croats also had to march in step with their Slovene neighbours, who were also busily proceeding towards independence anyway. The two republics agreed to jump ship together on 25 June 1991. But whereas Slovenia shrugged off Yugoslav control without effort, after a ten-day shoot-out with the Yugoslav army, Croatia faced determined opposition from Milosevic, the army and the 600,000 Croatian Serbs.

In the summer and autumn of '91, the RSK mopped up one district after another, at its highpoint controlling one-third of the republic, including most of northern Dalmatia, eastern Lika, Kordun and Banija, parts of western Slavonia and the regions of Baranja and Srijem in eastern Slavonia. The eastern border town of Vukovar (see p108 **Vukovar: Before and after**) came under especially prolonged joint RSK and army siege, reducing the graceful baroque streets to rubble. When the town fell on 17 November, the victorious Serbs committed one of the worst atrocities of the conflict, butchering more than 200 wounded soldiers lying in Vukovar hospital. With less success, hundreds of miles away, the army pounded away at the historic city of Dubrovnik. However, the blaze of international publicity intimidated them from repeating the tactics in Vukovar and the town stayed in Croat hands.

The horrific scenes from Croatia on television screens all over the world discredited Milosevic's claim to be fighting a defensive war to preserve a multinational Yugoslav state and fed a clamour to punish Belgrade through recognising its independence. France and Britain, Serbia's traditional allies, held out to the end but bowed to the inevitable after Germany – the destination of many Croat refugees – threatened to recognise Slovenia and Croatia unilaterally, if need be. Fearing an ugly open rupture in the European Union, its member states agreed jointly to recognise the two states at Christmas 1991, a decision that took effect in January 1992.

Tudjman perceived recognition as an historic victory and the fulfilment of what he called the '1,000-year-old dream' of a Croat state. Nevertheless, at first the victory seemed hollow. The war had cost thousands of lives and inflicted massive infrastructural damage. Towns, railways and factories lay in ruins, hundreds of thousands of people had been made homeless and the once lucrative tourist industry had collapsed. The RSK was also still in control of one-third of Croatia's territory, its gains seemingly cemented by a UN-brokered peace plan and by the deployment of peacekeepers along the frontline. Tudjman's problems only worsened in 1993-94, when he hurled the infant Croatian army on to the side of the ethnic Croats in Bosnia's own messy civil war – a fateful decision that didn't do the Bosnian Croats much good, and led to Croatia's virtual international isolation. Under strong pressure from the US in 1994, Tudjman executed a humiliating retreat from the Bosnian arena and endured considerable obloquy at home.

FROM WAR TO SUN WORSHIP

But Croatia's prospects brightened markedly soon after. By 1995 the US was desperately concerned to roll back the Serb juggernaut in Bosnia, end the war there and rescue the hard-pressed Muslim-led government in Sarajevo. Croatia was brought in from the cold as the US gave the green light for armament supplies, which made the Croatian army a significant regional force. Thus reinvigorated, Tudjman determined to reverse Serb gains in Croatia at the same time as doing US bidding in Bosnia. A *casus belli* presented itself in July when the Bosnian Serbs threatened to overrun the large but isolated Bosnian city of Bihać, near the Croatian border. As Bosnia appealed for foreign aid, Tudjman obligingly sent his army racing over the border, where, much to the outside world's surprise, they rapidly routed the supposedly invincible Serbs, relieving Bihać before doubling back south to sever the RSK's supply lines through Bosnia to Serbia. In Knin, the Serbs trembled, sensing rightly what was afoot. Convinced that Milosevic would not risk war with Croatia over the RSK, on 4 August 1995 Tudjman ordered an all-out attack on the RSK, codenamed Operation Storm. The RSK crumbled faster than anyone predicted and the next morning Croat soldiers were hosting their

The terrible siege of **Vukovar**, 1991. *See p31*.

red-and-white flag over the battlements of Knin whose inhabitants, along with about 150,000 other Serb inhabitants of the RSK, now fled eastwards to Serbia in a long column. Victory was complete. The remaining Serbian-controlled territories in eastern Slavonia, including Vukovar, were returned to Croatia in 1998 under UN supervision. Tudjman had only a short time to savour these triumphs, succumbing to cancer in December 1999.

Tens of thousands attended Tudjman's bitterly cold funeral in Zagreb, though few international leaders joined the throng. While most Croats mourned the man, they did not mourn the HDZ's increasingly corrupt and authoritarian style of government, turfing out Tudjman's henchmen at the next opportunity in the 2000 elections and putting back in the driving seat Ivica Račan, the old Communist leader recast as a Social Democrat. The Račan government acted fast to mend fences with Europe. The President's almost monarchical powers were massively trimmed, state interference with the media was curbed by law, the path was cleared for exiled Serbs to reclaim property and return, and Zagreb pledged never again to meddle in Bosnia.

The progress was not all plain sailing, as Europe made any serious rapprochement conditional on Croatia's absolute co-operation with The Hague war crimes tribunal. And the court's demand for the extradition of key military figures was deeply unpopular in a country still not recovered from the trauma of what was called the Homeland War.

Yet, with Tudjman now at rest under a vast marble tomb in Zagreb's Miragoj cemetery, and with Milosevic also gone, there was a distinct feeling that Croatia had turned a corner and passed key tests. The war had not delivered the political extremism so many foreign commentators had predicted, let alone the return from the grave of the Ustashe. The tourists were back in bigger numbers than ever and – much to the shock of locals – now buying up holiday homes. In December 2005 the arrest of alleged war criminal Ante Gotovina, after years on the run, won brownie points with the West (the hunt and subsequent arrest polarised the locals, however, with Gotovina hailed as a hero within some circles). With the hope of lasting stability, security and inclusion within the European fold, EU membership looks finally in sight.

Key events

AD 600s Croats settle Dalmatia and Pannonia.
820s Local warlords assume *dux* (duke) title.
c925 Tomislav crowned first Croatian King.
920s Grgur (Gregory) of Nin defends Slavic liturgy and alphabet, known as Glagolitic.
1089 King Zvonimir dies, without heir. Hungary's King Kálmán invades.
1102 *Pacta conventa* grants Croatia autonomy in Hungary. Croats keep their Ban (viceroy) and Sabor (assembly).
1125 Venetians destroy town of Biograd.
1202 Venetian crusaders sack Zadar.
1241 Tatars invade Hungary and Croatia; Bela IV flees to Trogir.
1242 Golden Bull of Bela IV awards Zagreb status of royal free city.
1493 Ottoman Turks crush Croats at Krbavsko Polje.
1526 Croats offer crown to Ferdinand of Habsburg who establishes Military Border, or Vojna Krajina.
1573 Matija Gubec leads peasant revolt against landlords.
1593 Battle of Sisak saves Zagreb from Ottoman Turks.
1601 Mavro Orbini's book *Kingdom of the Slavs* helps inspire Slavic renaissance.
1630 Ferdinand II confirms rights of Serb immigrants with *Statuta Valachorum* (statute of Vlachs).
1671 Zrinksi and Frankopan nobles executed for plotting against Habsburgs.
1686 Habsburg armies liberate Croatia from Turks.
1699 Treaty of Sremski Karlovski confirms Habsburgs' border with Ottoman empire.
1779 Empress Maria Teresa reduces Croatia's autonomy.
1805 Treaty of Pressburg awards Dalmatia to Napoleon.
1806 French troops enter Dubrovnik, ending city state's centuries-long independence.
1815 Congress of Vienna grants Dalmatia to Habsburg Austria.
1830s Ljudevit Gaj's Illyrian movement rallies Habsburg Slavs.
1848 Pro-Illyrian Ban Josip Jelačić demands union of Croatia and Dalmatia in the empire.
1848-9 Jelačić leads Croat army against Hungarian revolutionaries.
1866 Bishop Strossmayer founds Yugoslav Academy of Arts and Science in Zagreb.
1867 Austro-Hungarian compromise confirms division of Croatia and Dalmatia.

1874 Strossmayer founds University of Zagreb.
1880s Strossmayer's Yugoslavs compete with Starcevic's Party of Right Croat nationalists.
1905 Rijeka resolution again demands union of Dalmatia and Croatia. At Zadar, Croats and Serbs pledge to co-operate.
1915 Three Dalmatians, Trumbić, Supilo and Meštrović, set up Yugoslav Committee.
1917 Serbia consents to idea of Yugoslav state in Corfu Pact.
1918 Croatian Sabor votes for union with Serbia and Montenegro.
1921 Centralising constitution scraps Croatia's Ban and Sabor.
1928 Croat independence leader Stjepan Radić assassinated in Belgrade.
1929 Ante Pavelić founds extreme-right Ustashe movement.
1934 Ustashe assassinates Yugoslav King Alexander in Marseille.
1939 Regent Prince Paul grants Croatia autonomous 'Banovina'.
1941 Germany invades and establishes Fascist Independent State of Croatia (NDH). Rome Agreement forces NDH to cede much of Dalmatia to Italy.
1942-3 Partisan congresses at Bihać and Jajce set blueprint for new federal Yugoslavia.
1945 Pavelić flees as Partisans enter Zagreb.
1946 Archbishop Stepinac of Zagreb jailed.
1966 Fall of Ranković ushers in liberal 'Croatian Spring'.
1971 Tito fires Croatian Spring leaders at Karadjordjevo.
1980 Tito dies, economy plunges into recession.
1981 Apparition of Virgin Mary in Medjugorje, Bosnia, stirs ferment among Bosnian Croats.
1987 Slobodan Milosevic takes helm in Serbia, unleashing Serb nationalist ferment.
1989 Franjo Tudjman founds Croatian Democratic Union (HDZ) as anti-Communist alternative.
1990 HDZ wins election, ending 45 years of Communist rule. Tudjman made President.
1991 Croatia declares independence, Serbs revolt in Croatia and Yugoslav army besieges Dubrovnik and Vukovar.
1992 EU recognises Croatia's independence.
1995 Operation Storm overruns rebel Serb state in Krajina.
1999 Tudjman dies.
2000 Ivica Račan's centre-left wins elections.
2004 Croatia gains EU candidate status.

Croatia Today

You've never had it so good – at least on the Adriatic.

These are the images Croatia's tourist board would like the world to associate with the country: the sun sinking low over an azure Adriatic; yachts of the super-rich, Euro-royals among them, bobbing in sheltered coves, against a mountain backdrop; whitewashed baroque churches turning rose pink in the dusk; tanned tourists bathed in the amber glow of light reflected from honey-coloured stone walls. And these are the smells to accompany the images: a whiff of squid risotto from the kitchens of a Dalmatian taverna; the scent of oranges on the bulging fruit trees lining the boulevards of Dubrovnik; the salt tang of *paški sir*, the pungent cheese from the island of Pag; the heady aroma of lavender that covers Hvar like a purple blanket and that islanders turn into oil to sell on the quayside.

They are true images too. A thousand newspaper headlines in English, French, German and Italian proclaiming Dalmatia to be 'the new Tuscany' or 'the new Provence' (only cheaper) have done their work, luring a new wave of visitors prepared to pay for the privilege of seeing 'the Mediterranean as it once was', to echo the latest official motto. The poorer visitors from the old Yugoslavia and Eastern Europe who used to holiday on Croatia's long and heavily indented coastline are thin on the ground these days, intimidated by fast-rising hotel and restaurant prices, driven up by the spending power of visitors from Britain, Ireland, Italy and Germany, who are buying everything in sight, from stone barns to former Venetian palazzos. Every wealthy European seems now to hanker for a piece of Croatia's sunburned coast, with the achingly pretty islands of Hvar, Korčula, Brač and Vis as the prime targets. The locals may not like it (tales of foreigners 'buying up' Dalmatia regularly fill their newspapers) but the injection of money, and lots of it, has added a glossy sheen to what until the 1960s was a poor, half-forgotten corner of Europe.

Yet, venture 30 or 50 kilometres inland from the bustling coastline and you find a Croatia that the brochures don't mention – a scarred and depopulated landscape, littered with burned-out houses and lopped-off churches – the physical legacy of Croatia's war for independence from the Serb-dominated Yugoslav federation. Ethnic Serbs, once thick on the ground in this barren hilly interior, and a majority in many districts, fled en masse in the summer of 1995 after Serbia abandoned their breakaway state to its fate. Since then, nearly all have reclaimed their property, and some have returned to Croatia to live as a result of the Croatian government's warming relationship with Serbia.

But if the administrations in Zagreb and Belgrade are friends again, it hasn't filtered down to street-level. Serb returnees complain of overt discrimination at every turn, while Croats eye returnees with sullen resentment, having neither forgiven nor forgotten the tremendous destruction that the Serb forces inflicted on their country in the 1990s.

That the memory of the warfare of the '90s hangs over Croatia like a cloud is not simply down to local reluctance to 'move on'. The elephant in the living room of modern Croatia is the International Criminal Tribunal for the former Yugoslavia, based in the Hague, where popular ex-general Ante Gotovina is facing trial for the deaths of 150 Serbs in 1995.

'It's been a shock to discover that life without the Serbs as bosses hasn't delivered instant prosperity.'

If one aim of the tribunal was to foster a sense of closure and reconciliation, it has failed dismally as far as Croatia is concerned. The protracted hunt for Gotovina bitterly polarised people, ripping scabs off wounds that had barely started to heal and generally creating political mayhem. At one point some feared the ex-general's angry allies, who were shaking cities up and down Dalmatia, might overturn the elected government. In the event, sense prevailed and Croatia's infant democracy passed a major test. Bowing to huge pressure from Europe, which made it clear that the way

to the EU led through the Hague, Zagreb finally located and captured Gotovina in the Canary Islands, and handed him over to the tribunal's chief prosecutor Carla del Ponte in December 2005. But it hasn't defused tensions, as angry slogans scrawled on walls all over Croatia show only too clearly.

Lost in the shouting over whether Croatia should have 'given in' to Europe and its tribunal was the question of whether Gotovina was guilty or not. A debate on the darker side of the Homeland War, as the Croats term their independence struggle, is certainly needed. This is unlikely to happen as a result of the upcoming trial as Gotovina is enshrined in the mind of the public as a hero and a martyr. The trial's verdict is unlikely to alter anything.

Not everyone is so inflamed over the affair. Opinions are more nuanced by far in the rolling, vine-planted hills of Istria, on the border of Italy, an area that suffered little direct impact from the fighting in the 1990s and that, with its strong Italian imprint, is a land unto itself. The same goes for fertile, flat and just a little dull Slavonia, a region whose hardworking, somewhat Germanic inhabitants exercise a calming influence on the body politic.

PROS AND CONS OF EUROPE

The agile statesman attempting to straddle these sharp political and geographical divisions, and exorcise some of the demons from the past, is Ivo Sanader, can-do leader of the centre-right Croatian Democratic Union (Hrvatska Democratska Zajednica) and prime minister since December 2003. As the political heir to Franjo Tudjman, Croatia's cussed old warrior for independence, the smart money was on Sanader tilting firmly to the right once he ousted the Social Democrats and their leader, Ivica Račan, from power. Instead, Sanader disappointed many HDZ true believers, and the pro-Gotovina lobby, with his studiedly centrist approach, based on a foreign policy of close co-operation with the Hague tribunal and high-speed pursuit of membership of NATO and the EU. His reward was a thumbs-up from Ms Del Ponte in the autumn of 2005 over co-operation with the tribunal, which, in turn, removed the last obstacles preventing Croatia from gaining EU candidate status and opening accession talks with Brussels, with a view to joining alongside, or shortly after, Bulgaria and Romania in 2007.

Not bad for the leader of a party associated until recently with defiant isolationism from Europe's mainstream. But Sanader is a man of surprises; his other big volte-face has been to determinedly woo neighbouring Serbia, a land most nationalists regard as the eternal enemy. His government has passed laws granting visa-

SPECIJALNO IZDANJE

GL**O**US

8. 12. 2005.

Madrid

18:03

GOTOVINA

1613 DANA U BIJEGU

■ ŠPANJOLSKA VEZA Kako je general uhićen
■ GOTOVININ KRUG Obitelj, prijatelji i pomagači
■ VOJNA KARIJERA Hrvatska vojska i Legija stranaca
■ PARIŠKI DANI Slatki život bez uniforme
■ HAAŠKI SUD U pritvoru Carle Del Ponte

The arrest of **Ante Gotovina**.

free entry to Croatia for Serbian citizens and he has lobbied hard for Serbia's own eventual entry to the European family.

The price paid for pleasing Brussels is mounting criticism at home for what many consider a betrayal of national interests, of which Gotovina's handover is a prime example. Sanader can expect more trouble on that front in 2006, after Brussels upped pressure on Zagreb to join a free-trade zone in the western Balkans. The Brussels bureaucrats say it is the only way for the region to attract outside investors, who are currently deterred by the confusing difference in economic regulations between the various new states. Economists like the idea, too, saying it will cement Croatia's advantageous trade relations with its poorer neighbours, Bosnia and Serbia. But the right is livid, adamant that the free-trade zone is a stalking horse for the re-creation of some form of Yugoslavia, ensnaring the Croats once more.

IT'S THE ECONOMY, STUPID

Much of the paranoid talk of plots to deprive Croats of their new-found freedom is the predictable reaction of a country that hasn't known real self-determination since the 11th century. Much of the rest is down to money. Arguably, Croats would not feel so agitated about Gotovina, the Hague tribunal, Brussels bureaucrats and the plight of the Croats in neighbouring Bosnia, plus all the other pet causes of the right, if they weren't so badly off.

For decades Croats comforted themselves that the only reason they didn't live like the Austrians was because they were mismanaged and robbed by Belgrade and the Serbs in general. It has been a shock to discover that life without the Serbs as bosses has not delivered instant prosperity. Instead, the last decade has seen high unemployment of around 20 per cent, and price rises to roughly Western levels for most goods, including foodstuffs, with no equivalent rise in wages, which hover stubbornly around an average of $12,000 per year. Away from the tourist resorts where the surface glamour reflects the foreigners' spending, the results of this shortage of cash are apparent in one pinched-looking town after another, each with its peeling façades, one or two dreary cafés and, all too often, a run-down pizzeria as the only option for a night out.

Croats are now far better off – and better governed, for that matter – than their neighbours in Bosnia, Serbia and Montenegro. The problem is that voters don't accept Belgrade or Sarajevo as the benchmark and instead look further afield to the likes of Munich and Vienna. Factor in Croatia's worryingly high foreign debt and a yawning trade deficit with most trading partners, and the likelihood of that Western Europe-inspired dream being fulfilled in the near future recedes further than ever.

'All that's missing from the jigsaw is an element of the *dolce vita*.'

If this begins to sound like a recipe for bloody riots on the streets, that's far from the case. The Croats are emphatically not like the French, with their cult of barricades, revolutions and street action. We're talking Slavs here – champion grumblers and weavers of conspiracy theories, much given to melancholy and sighs of 'if only'. Moreover, there is no sign of the widespread frustration generated by the pains of economic transition translating into political extremism either of the left or right variety, as January 2005's presidential election of showed only too clearly. There, the crumpled figure of Stipe Mesić, a devout centrist, romped home easily, while the candidate of the extreme right won less than three per cent of the votes.

In its moderate, largely consensual politics, Croatia is already part of the European mainstream it longs to join. All that's missing from the jigsaw is an element of the *dolce vita*, which Croats see played out before their eyes each summer among the millions of foreign visitors – their benefactors and, at the same time, their tormentors.

Konoba Bako, Komiža. *See p253.*

Food & Drink

There's something fishy going on...

Croatia may be one of Europe's smaller nations but it packs a spectacular variety of culinary traditions into its cuisine. Take the landscape – the major dictator of what foods are produced where. In the space of only 56,500sq km (21,800sq miles), you've got alluvial plains formed from ancient sea beds, mountain ranges rising to over 1,980 metres (6,500 feet) above sea level and 2,000km (1,240 miles) of coastline (if you count the islands), as well as two of Europe's major rivers – the Danube and the Sava. Add to that, not just one but three distinct climatic regions – Continental, Alpine and Mediterranean – and top it all off with more cultural and political incursions than you can shake a stick at. No wonder Croatia's cuisine is so varied.

Istria is considered Croatia's culinary temple, its peasant traditions, fresh, seasonal ingredients and inventive chefs combining to make this small peninsula the destination of

choice for gastronomes. The celebrated use of truffles, to season steaks or added to chocolate cake, is only one example of the sophisticated dishes on offer (*see p124* **Istrian cuisine**). Dalmatia does the simple things right, relying on the high quality of the local olive oil, wine, garlic, tomatoes – and freshness of its seafood. Coastal or inland, Croatian **wine** (*see p44*), although rarely exported, can be excellent.

Croatian cuisine can be divided between the Central European tradition and that of the Central Mediterranean. For centuries the region was ruled by the Austro-Hungarian empire and the Venetian Republic and both cultures have left their culinary mark. This is not to dismiss the Slavic roots of Croatia's own tradition and the very real influence of the Ottoman empire. Each region of Croatia contributes its own specialities but it should be borne in mind that these are regarded as national dishes and can therefore be found all over the country. The only true demarcation derives from Croatia's love of fresh ingredients, which does tend to divide it up along the lines of meat-based and seafood cuisine.

SEA AND RIVERS

The Adriatic boasts more than 400 different species of fish, but with limited quantities of each kind. This is different from the North Sea, where some of the same species can be found in abundance, whereas others are not found at all, such as the renowned *zubatac* (dentex). The waters in Dalmatia are famously clean, producing wonderful fresh fish and seafood.

Dalmatia has a long culinary tradition, dating back to Greek, Roman and Byzantine times, of preparing fish and seafood. Oysters from Mali Ston, for instance, much prized today, were first farmed by the Romans after the Emperor Augustus conquered the Illyrian tribes. In the 16th century Renaissance poet Petar Hektorović wrote a famous account of a three-day fishing trip, detailing the fishermen's

tools, which fish they ate and the delicate way in which they prepared them. Recently, fish farms for striped sea bass (*lubin* or *brancin*) and gilthead sea bream (*orada*) have been set up in Ston and on Brač. As well as oysters, Dalmatian tuna (*tuna*) is highly prized by the Japanese who import as much of it as they can lay their hands on. Oddly, the popular and traditional *bakalar*, cod, is not a local fish, but was first imported into Dalmatia by merchants from Trieste and Venice in the 18th century. A few spoons of rice or potatoes, with a touch of salad, are the usual accompaniment. Look out also for *blitva*, local kale or Swiss chard.

Tourism came to Dalmatia well over a century ago, and mass tourism in the last 40 years. Fish and seafood dishes have always been essential to any restaurant menu, but some specialities have become increasingly rare. Sea dates (*prstaci*), which were once commonplace, are now a protected species in Croatia, but they can still be found – usually imported from the adjoining tiny coastline of

What's on the menu?

Useful phrases

Are these seats taken? *Da li je slobodno?*
Bon appetit! *Dobar tek!*
Do you have...? *Imate li...?*
I'm a vegetarian. *Ja sam vegetarijanac.*
I'm diabetic. *Ja sam dijabetičar.*
I'd like a table for two. *Molim stol za dvoje.*
The menu, please. *Molim vas jelovnik.*
I didn't order this. *Nisam ovo naručio.*
Thank you. *Hvala.*
The bill (please). *Račun (molim).*

Basics (*Osnovno*)

Ashtray *Pepeljara*
Bill *Račun*
Bread *Kruh*
Cup *Šalica*
Fork *Vilica*
Glass *Čaša*
Knife *Nož*
Milk *Mlijeko*
Napkin *Ubrus*
Oil *Ulje*
Pepper *Biber*
Plate *Tanjur*
Salt *Sol*
Spoon *Žlica*
Sugar *Šećer*
Teaspoon *Žličica*
Vinegar *Ocat*
Water *Voda*

Meat (*Meso*)

But leg
Govedina beef
Grah sa svinjskom koljenicom bean soup with pork knuckle
Guska goose
Gusta juha thick goulash soup
Janjetina lamb
Jetra liver
Kunić/zec rabbit
Odrezak escalope (generally veal or pork)
Patka duck
Piljetina chicken
Prsa breast
Purica/tuka turkey
Srnetina venison
Šunka ham
Svinjetina pork
Teletina veal

Fish/Seafood (*Riba/Plodovi mora*)

Grilled fish *Riba sa roštilja/na žaru*
Bakalar dried cod
Brancin sea bass
Brodet fish stew
Cipal golden grey mullet
Dagnje/mušule/školjke mussels
Hobotnica octopus
Jastog lobster
Kamenice/ostrige oysters
Kovač John Dory

Bosnia and Hercegovina. Cooked in white wine and garlic, sometimes with breadcrumbs, they are a delicacy beyond compare. *See p297* **Naughty finger food**.

Seafood is prepared in a few set, simple ways, the most common being *buzara*, gently poached in a tomato-based sauce. *Brodet* – fish stew – is also popular in Istria. Traditionally, in Dalmatia it should consist of three fish, ideally one of them *grdobina* or *rošpo* (monkfish, frogfish or angler fish). Seafood risottos are another feature, especially *crni rižot* with dark squid ink. If there is any made *od sipe*, from cuttlefish, these have stronger and tastier ink.

Fish is often just cooked on the grill, *na žaru*. Red mullet (*trilja*) is considered perfect for this. You can find it, cooked to perfection with a little olive oil, in small fishing villages, at a family-run *gostionica*, as distinct from a *restoran*, or fully fledged restaurant. By all means ask if the fish on offer is fresh, frozen or farmed. You will usually be shown the fresh fish on offer for you to choose. Fish is priced by the kilo, often in the 300kn range. About half a kilo should be enough for one person. You can ask how much it weighs, or have it weighed, and in many places you can watch it being cooked outside on the grill or you can look into the kitchen to see how it's done. Fish can also be baked (*pečnici*) or boiled (*lešo*). The cheaper fish, perhaps hake (*oslić*), will be fried (*prženi*) in breadcrumbs. Sole (*list*) is not highly regarded either.

Škrpina, scorpion fish, may be recommended, and its meat is deliciously tender, but it's the devil's own job for the uninitiated to pick through the bones. John Dory (*kovač*), golden grey mullet (*cipal*) and several members of the bream family (*pagar, arbun* and *pic*; common, sea and sheep's head) are also common finds – just ask what's fresh. Dentex is usually excellent.

You'll find grilled squid (*lignje na žaru*) on almost every menu. Octopus (*hobotnica*) is often used as a salad, normally just chopped portions mixed with onion and herbs. The most popular shellfish are scampi (*škampi*), served in their shells, and invariably *buzara*, in tomato sauce.

Lignje squid
List sole
Losos salmon
Lubin sea perch
Orada gilthead sea bream
Oslić hake
Pastrva trout
Šaran carp
Sipa cuttlefish
Škampi scampi
Trilja red mullet
Tuna tuna
Zubatac dentex

Accompaniments (*Prilozi*)
Kruh bread
Krumpir potatoes (*prženi krumpir* – chips)
Riža rice
Tjestenina pasta

Salads (*Salate*)
Cikla beetroot
Krastavac cucumber
Mješana salata mixed salad
Rajčica tomato
Rokula rocket
Zelena salata green (lettuce) salad

Vegetables (*Povrće*)
Cvjetača cauliflower
Gljive mushrooms

Grašak peas
Kuhani kukuruz sweetcorn
Leća lentils
Mahune green beans
Mrkva carrot
Paprika pepper
Šparoge asparagus
Špinat spinach

Fruit/Nuts (*Voće/Orasi*)
Dinja melon
Jabuka apple
Jagoda strawberry
Kruška pear
Malina raspberry
Marelica apricot
Naranča orange
Orah walnut
Šljiva plum
Trešnja cherry

Drinks (*Pića*)
Čaj tea
Kava coffee
Led ice
Mineralna voda mineral water
Penjušac sparkling wine
Pivo beer
Rakija brandy
Sok (*od naranče*) (orange) juice
Vino wine

DID YOU KNOW THAT THE NECKTIE ORIGINATED FROM THE CROATS

Young men and girls tied kerchiefs around their loved ones necks as a sign of fidelity. This spontaneous act of love spread around the world like wildfire, and these kerchiefs became known as cravats in the 17th century after the Croatian soldiers who wore them. At all contemporary weddings in the world a tie is a vital fashion accessory in all its variations (a cravat, a bow tie, a starched shirt front, a formal tie etc.) The kerchief,which the fiancée or wife tied around her

husband´s or fiancé´s neck was a sign of a lasting relationsh Today therefore, the clothes worn by a bride and groom a deeply related. In the tradition of that original tie, Croata recognized as the supreme expression of the fideli beauty and dignity of those entering into marriage, a as a symbol of the future before them. Croata ties, alwa so unique, personal and spontaneous, are tied arou an excellent shirt and framed by a top quality Croata su

Zagreb, Oktogon, Ilica5
Zagreb, Kaplol 13
Split, Mihovilova širina 7 (Voćni trg)

Rijeka, Trg Republike Hrvatske
Osijek, Županijska 2
Varaždin, Trg kralja Tomislava 2

Dubrovnik, Pred Dvorom 2
Dubrovnik, Hotel Excelsior
Cavtat, hotel Croatia

www.croata.hr

CROATA

Kantina, Pula. *See p121.*

If children are ordering this, warn them that it won't be neatly packaged in breadcrumbs. Use your fingers and expect it be pretty messy. Lobster (*jastog*) is invariably the dearest item on the menu, 500kn a kilo.

Continental Croatia is well known for its freshwater fish, including *šaran* (carp) and *štuka* (pike). *Fiš paprikaš*, freshwater fish stewed in a paprika broth, is another inland favourite. If you're inland but you don't want fish, then *čobanac*, a meaty, paprika goulash, is also a regular find.

HILLS, FIELDS AND FOREST

Croatians love their meat. Prime cuts such as *ombolo* (medallion of pork) and beefsteak are cooked quickly, often over an open fire, and served very simply. A favourite is a mixed grill, which might contain Turkish-style *ćevapčići* (minced meatballs) and kebabs together with typical Central European sausages and cutlets. *Pljeskavica* is like a Balkan hamburger. Dishes, such as *Zagrebački odrezak*, a schnitzel stuffed with cheese and ham, reflects a strong Austrian influence, while the hot, spicy *kulen* is a superb salami that's liberally permeated with paprika, showing the influence of Hungarian cuisine. Cured meats are a great tradition, with each region producing their own slightly different versions. *Pršut*, air-cured ham, is a delicacy in Istria and Dalmatia.

You frequently see roadside spits, roasting whole lambs or pigs, placed outside restaurants as an enticement to passers-by. This is typical of the mountainous Gorski Kotar region, which produces some of the finest lamb in Croatia. Your freshly carved meat is normally accompanied by raw spring onions and a basket of bread. Beef is also used in a slow-cooked stew, *pašticada*. The real deal you often must order a day in advance: *peka* or *od peke*, the cast-iron dome used to cover meat being slow-roasted with hot coals. Octopus can also be prepared in this way.

Cooked vegetables tend to be served as a main dish rather than as an accompaniment. Stuffed peppers, usually served with potatoes, are a frequent example. Pickled cabbage, or sauerkraut, is universally popular. The most common dishes are *sarma*, pickled cabbage leaves stuffed with spiced, minced pork and rice, and *lički lonac*, where pork meat is slow-braised, in shredded sauerkraut. Side vegetables tend to be raw – fresh salad or, especially in winter, a selection of pickled vegetables such as gherkins, green tomatoes or peppers.

More than 30 per cent of Croatia is covered in forest and hunting is a national pastime. The game widely available is mostly venison and wild boar. This meat is normally slow cooked either by braising on top of the stove or in rich,

Made in Croatia

A recent ruling gave Croatia a taste of EU bureaucracy and a warning of the difficulties it faces in trying to protect home-grown brands from foreign imports. 24 hours after being told that its 'Buy Croatian' campaign discriminated against imported products, the Croatian Chamber of Commerce dropped its popular slogan in exchange for a bland exhortation to 'Produce and Buy Quality Products'. Despite this, there is a strong feeling that locally made goods are of higher quality than foreign imports, with many resisting the lure of multinational brands and remaining loyal to all things Croatian.

Most shops stock the full range of local products, so you can see for yourself what all the fuss is about. Croatian natural springs are a source of some of the finest water in Europe. Jamnica's luxury bottled still water **Jana** always hits the spot on a scorching summer's day. You can't miss the endless rows of **Frank Coffee** packs in the shops. Its strong, Turkish flavour is so popular that the usual international coffee brands are almost impossible to find, even in supermarkets. This kind of coffee is traditionally made in a small, long-handled saucepan over the stove, and is hopeless in filter machines and percolators. In addition to cold water and strong coffee, ice-cream is another summer essential. There are **Ledo** stands on the beach and in cafés, selling tasty and not over-sweet ice-cream by the scoop in a range of classic flavours, while its ice lollies include low-key numbers such as **Snjeguljica** ('Snow White') and nutty **Njofra**.

Kraš is another highly visible Croatian brand, with sweet delicacies ranging from its excellent Bajadera range, to Napolitanka nougat wafers, and large bars of Dorina chocolate. Founded during the Yugoslav period, the company was named after Josip Kraš, an obscure Communist bakery worker who was killed by the Fascists in 1941.

With a heritage going back even earlier, **Gavrilović** was privatised in the early 1990s, and its new owners set out to bring about a return to traditional salami making. If you're faced with a deli counter of different brands, ask for Gavrilović. A classic picnic combination is a few slices of its *zimska* or winter salami (suitable for all-year consumption) and a pot of **Dukat** red-top *vrhnje*, sour cream.

Cedevita is a unique Croatian product and practically a national symbol. Generations have grown up on this strange drink that comes as an orange powder, mixed with water. Every student has a jar of it, even if there's nothing else to eat or drink in the flat, and typically quench their thirsts with pint-size glasses of the stuff. It is believed to have regenerative powers and to increase sporting ability, as well as to counteract the effects of a hangover. Another exotic powdery product is **Vegeta**, one of the best-known Croatian exports in the region. During the Communist period Yugoslav travellers used to carry large quantities of this highly flavoured stock to exchange with locals in neighbouring countries. Add a few teaspoons to a stew or soup and give the whole meal a distinctive and overwhelming Vegeta glow.

A fish platter fit for the whole family, typically garnished with potatoes and local greens.

meaty goulashes. They are frequently served with Italian-style gnocchi or polenta.

The saline climate of Pag and Cres produces exquisite lamb, raised on salty wild herbs, and *paški sir*, sharp sheep's cheese from Pag, dried, matured and prepared with olive oil.

An alternative dessert might be *palačinka*, a pancake filled with *marmalada* (jam), chocolate (*čokolada*) or *orah* (walnuts). In Dalmatia you'll find *rožata*, a kind of crème caramel. Ice-cream here is almost as good as in Italy.

Fast food tends to be Eastern in influence. *Burek*, a flaky pastry that's filled with either spiced mince or soft cheese, is popular, often accompanied by yoghurt. Look for the little jars of Ajvar, a paprika and aubergine relish, to garnish your *ćevapčići* meatballs. Croatia produces excellent, thin-crust pizzas, available by the slice if you're eating on the run.

MENUS AND HOW TO READ THEM

The *jelovnik*, menu, is divided rather differently from its British counterpart. First on the list will probably be *hladna jela* (cold food), the starter or antipasti. Typical dishes might be thin slices of *pršut*, *ovčiji sir* (sheep's cheese) or *kozji sir* (goat's cheese) or perhaps a carpaccio of meat or fish. Then there are the soups, *juhe*,

such as *riblja juha* (fish) or *govdja juha* (beef). *Mineštra/manistra* is a hearty soup of beans or other pulses and based on pork stock.

Gotova jela, finished food, are the dishes that are pre-prepared in quantity and therefore fast. *Gulaš*, goulash, would be a typical example, a rich stew usually served with pasta, gnocchi or polenta. Local *fuži*, pasta twists, are a popular form. *Divljač gulaš* is game, quite often *crna* (venison) or *svinja* (wild boar).

Jela sa roštilja is grilled meat (*meso*) or fish (*riba*), also rendered as *na žaru*. *Jela po narudžbi* are the house specialities, also known as *specijaliteti*. These are main courses and the ingredients will depend on which region of Croatia you are dining in. Istria will inevitably offer *tartufi* (truffles), while in Dalmatia it's likely to be a form of *buzara* sauce.

Prilozi i salate are side dishes and salads. This will include *krumpir* (potatoes), *blitva* (local kale), *mješana salata* (mixed salad), *rajčica* (tomato), *zelena* (green salad) and *rokula* (rocket). *Kruh* (bread) may also feature on the menu.

Kolači means cakes and this section covers puddings generally. As well as pancakes, there's *pita od jabuka*, apple strudel, and *kroštuli*, which are tiny, deep-fried doughnuts without the jam. *Sladoled* is ice-cream.

The better establishments offer a digestif, perhaps a herb grappa (*travarica*) or fruit brandy (*rakija*). Coffee (*kava*) is always strong.

WHAT TO DRINK

Croatia produces red and white wines, some 700 of them, in a tradition going back to the Romans. Until quite recently, coastal vineyards were encouraged to produce red wines, and continental ones whites – but this has changed with the rapid growth of new wine producers (*see p103* **Grapes on the 45th parallel**).

Of the coastal reds, the most renowned (and most expensive) is **Dingač**. Deep ruby red in colour, and a superb accompaniment to grilled fish (the tradition in Dalmatia), Dingač is produced in the restricted area of the same name on the steep south slopes of the Pelješac peninsula. The grape variety there is **Plavac Mali**, a cousin of Zinfandel. Native Croatian wine maker Miljenko Grgić, who gained his reputation in Napa Valley, California, came back to his homeland to produce quality wines

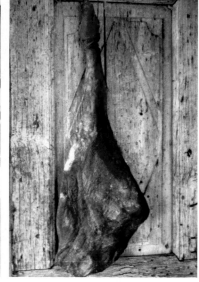

Market forces

The large open-air food market (*dolac*) in any main town is a great spot for an early-morning meander. The emphasis here is on 'early', as markets start around 7am and by noon are usually no more than a rather messy memory.

Expect to see masses of green stuff. During the summer months, there are salad vegetables by the ton. Unlike in Britain, stall-holders aren't afraid to repeat themselves. Stall A may well be selling exactly the same home-grown produce as stall B – at exactly the same price. It's all a question of being able to objectively judge the quality of the produce and then subjectively deciding which vendor you'd most like to hand your money over to. Don't expect them to make too much effort to attract your attention.

This is also where you can find home-made fruit grappas, local honey and olive oils. Seldom sold on their own, they are usually found nestling behind a pile of fresh rocket or whatever else the farmer pulled up from his garden that morning. The produce is truly fresh and these markets are some of the only places you'll find these things on sale. Out in the rural areas it's almost impossible to buy fresh salad greens. Because everybody grows their own what would be the point of local shopkeepers stocking them? If you're lucky, you might find a few wilted lettuces. Markets are a boon to self-catering tourists.

If you find it's getting too hot, you can escape into the cool interiors of the meat and fish areas. Especially with the fish, you'll see stall after stall of exactly the same offerings – whatever was taking the bait in the early hours. Service, however, can differ. Look out for the stall that's de-scaling its fish at no extra cost. In the larger markets you can also find specialist meat stalls – horse meat sausages are worth a try if you're up for it. In the north you'll find *kulen*, spicy salami. Creamy, home-made soft cheeses vary from region to region, and are brought in by little old ladies in headscarves. Bread also varies – Zagreb's *kukurzni kruh* is sold by the slice and won't be found anywhere else.

of the Plavac Mali variety. **Postup**, also from Pelješac, is equally reputed. **Babić** from Šibenik is a popular, well-priced alternative.

Because of the rocky, limestone soil, southern white wines are mostly dry, such as the golden yellow **Pošip**, strong in alcohol from the Čara vineyards on Korčula. **Grk**, its name ('Greek') echoing its ancient tradition, is another white from Korčula, from Lumbarda. Vis is known for **Vugava**, from the grape of the same name, Krk for **Vrbnička Žlahtina**. Inland, whites are dominated by the lightweight **Graševina**.

The primary wine of Istria is **Malvasia**. Possibly one of the oldest types in Europe, this white grape is grown in over two-thirds of Istria's vineyards. Malvasia is usually dry and it is best drunk young – normally within the first year of production. Fresh and flowery, Malvasia is often aged in oak barrels for a more complex taste. Because Istria has two distinctive soil types, Malvasia produced near the coast tends to be more robust; grapes from the hinterland provide a more delicate bouquet.

Istria's indigenous red wine is **Teran**, a rich ruby red tipple that has a strong, fruity flavour. Young Teran is often used to prepare Istrian *supa*, a traditional meal with warm, toasted bread and olive oil added to the wine and then served in a jug (*bukaleta*).

In addition to these native wines you can also find better-known varieties such as **Muscat**, notably produced around the town

Complaints, complaints

One of the bizarre hangovers from the old regime is the requirement for any food or drink establishment to stock a Complaints Book, *Knjiga Žalbe*. From top-notch five-star gourmet restaurants to grungy, bohemian dives, every place will have one. Look at any menu and on the back will be the advice, in at least three poorly translated versions, that customers can find the *Knjiga Žalbe* at the bar. Lo and behold, there tucked away on a shelf, will be a stern, A4-sized bound volume, awaiting comment.

It rarely, if ever, arrives. If you feel tempted to write something witty in it, don't.

Restaurant and bar owners are required to pay an annual fee to the state for the book, and it will be a government official who will come to chase up the case, said owner having had to send the complaint in triplicate to the right office within 24 or 48 hours of the irate scribble being entered.

In two years of running his successful, cool, minimalist DJ lounge terrace **The Garden** (*see p189*) in Zadar, the owner recalls one complaint, from a Belgian visitor moaning about the price of mineral water. Sure enough, an official explanation landed six months later on to a doormat in Ghent.

of Momjan, and the **Rosé Muscat** for which Poreč is known. The area of **Sovinjak** is famous for its champagne-style wines, with red champagne a particular speciality.

Many of Istria's best wines are being produced by a new generation of vintners, who formed **Vin Istra** (www.vinistra.hr), dedicated to improving the quality of local production and to the promotion of Istrian wines. The Istrian Tourist Board has established Wine Roads, making it easy for visitors to find the best cellars and taste these wines first-hand. A map showing the locations of all of Istria's leading vineyards can be picked up from any tourist information office.

Wine is either red (*crno*), white (*bijelo*) or rosé (*crveno*), dry (*suho*) or sweet (*slatko*). In

Dalmatia, the deep reds are mixed with water (as a *bevanda*), the whites in the north with mineral water (*gemišt*).

Croatian beers (**Ožujsko**, **Karlovačko**) are reasonable, although locals may prefer Slovenian **Laško** or **Union**. **Favorit** is from Istria. A glass of draught (*točeno*) beer is usually 30cl and costs about 10kn. Belgian varieties are widely available by the bottle.

Clear fruit brandy (*rakija*) is the common spirit. Grape brandy is *loza*. Regional varieties include mistletoe, *biska*, from Istria. There's also **Maraska**, a cherry liqueur from Zadar.

Coffee (*kava*) is strong and of high quality. It usually comes with milk on the side – otherwise ask for *kava sa mlijekom*. Tea, *čaj*, comes with lemon, as does fruit tea, *voćni čaj*.

Vis.

Beaches

It's what you've come for, so dive in.

The first thing the foreign visitor should know about beaches in Croatia is that very few of them are sandy. Fine shingle is the closest you're going to get – and, in most cases, the beach is one of smooth pebbles or rocks. Only in rare cases – such as the city beach of **Bačvice** in **Split** (see p211) – has someone come and dumped sand somewhere convenient because it's easier for people to play and lie on. What you see is what has been here for millennia, a long, rugged, indented coastline fringed by more than 1,000 islands, almost all of it unblemished by man, industry or motorboat.

Facilities around beaches are usually simple – at most a couple of cafés nearby. Don't expect showers or changing rooms, although beaches near hotels usually have a concrete platform to lay your towel on or dry off easily. Those in the main towns and major resorts will have the standard shops on hand, perhaps a restaurant with a panoramic view. In certain cases (see p176 **Balkan Ibiza** and p202 **Highway 65 revisited**) a beach will be the ideal location for a nightclub, but it would be wrong to suggest that Croatia's coastline is built up – yet. The

government sets strict guidelines on planning: no permission will be granted for a construction nearer than 100 metres from the Adriatic. Certain stretches of the coast were given over to package tourism in the 1970s – the **Makarska Riviera** (see p243) being the classic example. This is not likely to happen again. Croatia does not want to become another Spain, marred by ugly development. Croatia currently boasts 80 Blue Flag beaches (www.blueflag.org), meeting international standards of cleanliness and safety. Without much industry to speak of, the country depends on tourism, and here tourism depends on the quality of the country's beaches. Croatia's 1,780km (1,100 miles) of mainland littoral and 4,000km (2,480 miles) of island coastline are its riches.

HOBBIES AND HAZARDS

The key feature is the clarity of the sea. The Croatian Adriatic is crystal clear – you won't want to go near more familiar parts of the Med afterwards. This purity is helped by the currents, anti-clockwise up from Albania and Montenegro, so that by the time it heads up round Istria and down the Italian coast blighted

Urchins!

The sea is beautiful, the waves are calm, lunch was delicious, you've found your favourite spot back on the beach, what could possibly go wrong? Urchins, that's what. These small, black, spiky critters love the clear waters of the Adriatic – proof, at least, that the sea is clean.

On some islands, Lastovo, Korčula, Mljet (but not, oddly, Brač or Hvar), the sea urchin (*morksi jež*) is considered a delicacy and devoured, the red caviar-like eggs of the female in any case.

The most likely place you're going to find them is in between the rocks where the sea meets the shore. As in nearly all cases there isn't much of a wade out until the sea is deep enough to swim in, this means you should exercise care as you negotiate your way into the water. Croatians seem to do this instinctively, but then locals have been coming to the same spot for years. For foreigners, and especially for children, the

solution is simple, albeit a fashion disaster: plastic sandals. In fact, all children should have footwear if they go near the water, however barefoot the local kids might be.

If you do happen to step on one, or have one spike your finger as you're looking in rockpools (another area in which to exercise caution), the spike is annoying rather than dangerous, and you probably won't notice until you start stepping around again afterwards. Treatment tips are almost as numerous as species of *echinoidea*, sea urchins, themselves. (Urine, anybody?) Soaking your foot or hand in hot water is one. Hot vinegar is said to dissolve the spines. Tweezers can also be used but the danger is breaking the spine and leaving the other half still buried in your skin. After a few days, the splinter will work itself out anyway – but you'll be wasting valuable holiday time.

There's nothing for it but to invest a few kuna in plastic sandals.

by industrial clutter, it can be quite murky. Here it's as pure as you're going to get in Europe. And in most cases the seabed is shallow for a very short distance – you can dive in almost immediately. Close to the coast, the currents are quite mild, ideal for paddling, swimming and snorkelling. Tides are low and high waves are rare. The winds that do blow, the unpredictable *Bura*, the *Mistral* and the moderate *Jugo*, generally aid the water sports of **kitesurfing**, **windsurfing** and **sailing** (*see p56*). The coastal destinations best suited for windsurfers are **Viganj** (*see p300*) near Orebić on Pelješac, the famous **Zlatni Rat** (*see p229*) triangle of beach by Bol on Brač and **Premantura** (*see p120*), a short hop from Pula on the very southern tip of Istria.

Apart from the rare sighting of a shark (reported extensively in the local press), the only hazard is from the spiky, black sea urchin (*see p48* **Urchins!**). These are not venomous, only annoying, and children should wear sandals or flip-flops if they are going to wade on the rocks close to shore.

Topless bathing is commonly practised and naked bathing is not confined to hard-to-find pockets away from the crowds. Naturism here was introduced in **Rab** (*see p177*) in the early 20th century – famous exponents were King Edward VIII and Wallace Simpson before their marriage – and some 30 officially designated resorts (signposted as 'FKK') have been

popularised by Germans since the 1970s. There are hundreds of other unofficial ones, usually a stretch a short walk away from the main bathing site, where relaxing nude is the norm. The website www.cronatur.com has details.

ARE WE THERE YET?

Croatia isn't blighted by theme parks, funfairs or huge halls of amusement arcades. This means a holiday without bleeping noises, flashing lights and the constant demand for 5kn coins. On the down side, the kiddie used to a high-stimulation whirl of gos and rides is going to get bored pretty quickly.

A family going to Croatia has three main choices, depending on the age and boredom threshold of its younger members. The first is to go the whole hog on a package holiday – a number of UK tour operators (Thomson, Cosmos, Holiday Options) have the resorts of central Dalmatia's Makarska Riviera and Istria's west coast on its summer roster. Note that Croatia is very much geared to the high season. Even though the climate is quite mild during the half-term breaks of May and October, quite a few places either wouldn't have opened or would already have closed for the year. Locals like to earn their money for the year in a few short months and spend the winter repairing, renovating and recuperating.

This means that you can find some great bargains at the ones that are fully operational in the shoulder season. This might benefit those choosing option two, flying independently on a budget (Wizz Air, easyJet, Excel, flyglobespan) or national carrier (British Airways, Croatia Airlines) and finding their own accommodation. Hotels such as the **Kompas** (*see p282*) in **Dubrovnik**, the **Neptun** (*see p252*) in **Tučepi** on the Makarska Riviera, the **Say Adriatic** in **Murter** (*see p196*) or, in **Poreč** in Istria, the **Delfin**, the **Diamant** or (preferably) the **Hostin** (for all, *see p144*), all have family-friendly facilities, even entertainment programmes in the summer.

The third option, generally for older children, is one that might be easy in France or Spain but tricky in Croatia. Finding a reasonably priced, mid-range, family-run two- or three-star hotel or pension in a quiet village somewhere and using it as a base away from the crowds is a challenge, to say the least. For a start, few such places exist. Secondly, having a car would be essential – public transport simply isn't up to it. Driving to Croatia from the UK is too far and hiring a car is expensive (compared to the rest of the Med) and would cut into any savings you might make by finding that elusive little three-star in the first place.

Whichever you choose, the safest beaches for children include **Brela** (*see p243*) on the Makarska Riviera, whose white-pebble beaches have gentle slopes into the sea and, in the case of Punta Rata, have a lifeguard on duty; **Copacabana** (*see p269*) on the hotel-dotted **Babin Kuk** headland outside Dubrovnik, with sea-slides and all kinds of water sports; the **Vela Plaža** at **Baška** (*see p163*) on the southern shore of Krk, sheltered and well equipped; and **Rajska Plaža** at **Lopar**

Supetar, Brač

(*see p177*) on Rab, sandy (hooray!) and shallow. Unsurprisingly, all are swarmed at high season. Far less crowded, with sandy seafloors, the coves and beaches on the islands in the **Zadar archipelago** (*see p186*) may be an ideal solution if you're not looking for too much by way of facilities around them and are prepared to be flexible on transport.

The best Beaches

Gornja Vala, Gradac
Little known stretch of beautiful white pebbles at the southernmost end of the **Makarska Riviera**. See p243.

Pakleni Islands, Hvar
An easy hop by taxi boat, these unspoilt beauties include the naturist havens of **Stipanska** and **Jerolim**, and the famed botanical paradise of **Palmižana**. See p237.

Rajska Plaža, Lopar
Long, sandy, shaded and shallow, patrolled by lifeguards and with sports facilities nearby. On the **Lopar** peninsula, at the northern tip of Rab. See p177.

Telašćica Bay, Dugi Otok
On the Zadar archipelago, this nature park is within easy reach of **Sali**, linked to Zadar by catamaran. A warm, saltwater lake sits near numerous little coves. See p187.

Zelena Punta, Ugljan
The closest of the **Zadar archipelago** to the mainland, this is really a tourist village but has got plenty of equipment for hire – and a safe, sandy sea bed. See p187.

Zlatni Rat, Brač
Croatia's most famous beach, a shifting tongue of shingle near **Bol**. Ideal for windsurfers. See p229.

In Context

Outdoor Croatia

All kinds of Adriatic activities – and skiing too.

Sure, it's pretty, but Croatia's landscape of blue sea backdropped by limestone mountains is also a godsend for adventure sport devotees. Even for non-enthusiasts, the combination of gorgeous scenery and a balmy Mediterranean climate means that there's every temptation to expand holiday activities beyond just sun-bathing and nightclubbing.

For Croatians, many still with working ties to the land and sea through family farms and fishing boats, new sports are providing them with an appreciation for a difficult landscape that they have battled against for generations. They are also discovering there is more money to be made in businesses that rely on protecting rather than degrading their environment.

The Adriatic has been the facilitator of Croatian life, a conduit for invaders, merchants and crusaders. Now it's being reborn as a water enthusiast's paradise. The island-dotted sea lends itself to yacht cruising, sailing, swimming, kayaking, fishing and, above all, scuba diving. Forget the Caribbean or the Red Sea, the waters off the Croatian coast are enviably clear and,

thanks to the area's rich history, enlivened with centuries of explorable historical wrecks.

Back on dry land, the Dinaric Alps, the Croatian coastline's protective spine, are also increasingly a venue for adventure activities including hiking, climbing, biking, horse riding and paragliding. Outside Zagreb, an upgraded skiing centre at Sljeme, helped by the success of local Olympic champion Janica Kostelić, is now on the World Cup circuit and open to the public all winter (*see p53* **Ski Zagreb**).

Climbing

As the land masses that are Croatia and Italy slowly separated, the release in pressure caused the underlying limestone to push upwards and form the islands and mountains that now define the Croatian coastline. A happy by-product of this tectonic upheaval was the creation of a breathtaking environment for sport climbers.

The Dinaric Alps are a predominantly karst terrain, so the highly porous carbonate rock – like limestone – has been eroded by groundwater forming enlarged fissures and a subsurface drainage system. In other words, Croatia is also a dream for cave explorers.

For climbing, this rock is very firm but sometimes quite sharp. In Croatia there are numerous routes of all difficulties and lengths. The routes also vary in terms of how well they are equipped, ranging from no in-situ gear, to aided routes, to modern sport climbing routes. It's strongly recommended that climbers take along a set of nuts and friends, and a few slings.

Brač

A local climber, Ivo 'Šteka' Ljubetić, began developing climbing routes in the Nerežišća Canyon, on the north-western part of Brač, in 2000. Settled among pines, and with views of the nearby maritime town of Bobovišća and the idyllic village of Ložišće, the canyon is a superb place for climbing. There are around 60 routes, most in the 5a to 6c+ categories.

Named after a local cake, Kolač, situated near Nerežišća, is a great place to climb, a narrow natural arch with high-quality routes.

Hvar

There are two climbing areas on the island. The Suplja Stina wall is on the south side, located below the Sveti Nedjelja vineyards. The geomorphology of the Adriatic Islands is such that the southern sides tend to have dramatic limestone cliffs sliced by deep bays with pebble beaches. Long cliffs extend to the horizon around the town of Sveti Nedjelja. Most of these drop directly into the water, which precludes belaying – although it does allow for excellent deep-water soloing. However, at Suplja Stina, climbers can belay at the base of the wall, and still grab the opportunity for an après-climb swim. The site offers 43 long routes in a broad range of categories, from 5a to 7b.

The other climb site is on the north side of the island at the traditional fishing village of Velika Stiniva. Here, 20 newly developed routes are well shaded in the sides of a deep bay. Most of the routes are not particularly difficult (5a to 5+) and lend themselves to beginners, although there are also a number of very technical routes.

Marjan

Marjan is the wooded peninsula attached to the western end of Split. It's a protected nature reserve where locals come to relax, promenade and exercise. On the southern face of the peninsula, below towering cliffs, is a rock wall called Šantine Stine. It's riddled with hermits' caves, proof that the area has been

a place to get away from it all for hundreds of years. The wall also has a long history of use by trainee alpinists, and during the mid 1980s it began to attract sport climbers. One of the world's first sport climbing contests was held on Marjan in 1986. From the 70 established routes, most ranging in difficulty from 5a+ to 6c+, climbers have views over the Adriatic and islands. The routes are up to 30 metres (98ft) in length and, due to their outlook, can be climbed all year round.

Omiš

The Cetina river cuts a deep gorge as it snakes a 200-km (124-mile) course, breaching the cliffs at Omiš to join with the Adriatic. Pirates sheltered below these rock walls for centuries, building a town at their base and fortresses on their peaks. Sport climbers first set up routes here in the 1970s and they now number over 70, most in the 5a to 6c+ range. Some of the bolted multi-pitch routes are up to 300 metres (984ft) long.

Paklenica National Park

North-west of Zadar, this is the most popular and exciting climbing area in Croatia, with over 400 routes of all difficulties and lengths.

This area of extraordinary scenery and striking biodiversity contains 500 species of plants, 500 species of insects, including 80 types of butterflies, and 200 species of birds. To protect them, climbing is strictly controlled.

The park is centred on two gorges: Mala Paklenica and Velika Paklenica. The latter has two valleys, one cutting through the peaks of Debeli Kuk and Anića Kuk. This is the sole climbing area. The greatest number of sport climbing routes is in a section called Klanac.

There's an entrance fee to be paid for the park and you also need to purchase a climbing permit; a three-day permit costs 60kn, five days is 90kn and a one-year permit is 500kn.

The main climbing season is from spring to late autumn. At the end of April or beginning of May each year an international big-wall speed climbing competition is held in the park.

Useful information

Two guides to climbing in Croatia have been written by Boris Čujić, both published by Astroida DOO Zagreb: *The Croatian Climbing Guide* covers all climbing areas within Croatia, apart from the Paklenica National Park; *The Paklenica Climbing Guide* covers the park. The Croatian website **www.cro-climbing. com** lists all local climbing and alpinist clubs.

Diving

In addition to local plant and animal species, undoubtedly the most appealing diving sights in the Adriatic are the underwater cliff faces and caves, and the wrecks of old ships and World War II planes. The same limestone that makes up the Dinaric Alps drops away dramatically underwater, and is full of crevices, caves, sink holes and channels. Based on the number of caves so far discovered on land it is thought that there are 1,500 underwater caves and holes still undiscovered in the Adriatic.

Even more interesting are the underwater wrecks. The oldest of these are the remains of ships sunk in antiquity, while plying the routes from ancient Greece towards northern Italy. As trade increased, coastal towns Dubrovnik, Split and Zadar grew. Shipwrecks were a natural by-product of economic growth.

Naval battles of the 19th and 20th centuries also left monuments on the seabed. The steamship *Baron Gautsch* was launched in Trieste in 1908, and commandeered by the Austrian navy to transport men to Kotor, in present-day Montenegro. On 13 August 1914, returning from Kotor with a shipload of refugees, the *Gautsch* hit an Austrian mine, just north of the Brijuni Islands. Some 200 drowned, including many children. The ship sank to the sandy bottom, 40 metres (130ft) below the surface. The shipwreck was used by the Yugoslav navy for target practice but now, under the protection of the Ministry of Culture, it has become a home for large fish.

More recent historical events account for the US Air Force B17G bomber that lies 72 metres (236ft) under the surface, 100 metres (328ft) off the southern shore of Vis. It fell from the sky in 1943, although the crew was rescued by local fishermen. Divers can see the guns, engines and all instrumentation clearly.

Useful information

Annual growth in the number of dive tourists since the mid 1990s has led to an increase in the number of registered diving centres – to over 100; the best first points of reference are the **Croatian Diving Association** and the **Diving Tourism Group** (for both, *see below*).

To dive in Croatian waters you need an annual diving identity card, costing 100kn, and an 'individual permission for independent underwater activities', costing 2,400kn. If you are diving with a registered diving centre, the individual permission is not required. Diving in zones under special protection by the Ministry of Culture is allowed only in the company of a guide from an authorised diving centre.

In the event of a diving accident, contact the **Centre for Search and Rescue at Sea (SAR)** in Rijeka: telephone 9155, VHS channels 16 or 10.74. Hyperbaric chambers are located in Split (two chambers: one at the Institute for Maritime and Hyperbaric Medicine and a second at the Gošković Institute), in Pula (Polyclinic OXY Pula) and also in Zagreb (Polyclinic OXY Pula, Zagreb Branch, Dubrava Clinic Hospital).

Croatian Diving Association
Dalmatinska 12, Zagreb (01 484 8756).
The CDA is an association of amateur, non-profit-making diving clubs that promotes recreational diving and organises competitions. It also runs ecological-awareness campaigns.

Diving Petra
052 812 880/www.divingpetra.hr.
Based in Rovinj, Diving Petra organises dives on the *Baron Gautsch* (*see left*) and other recent wrecks.

Diving Tourism Group
Trumbićeva obala 4, Split (www.prodiving.hr/www.diving.hr).
The DTG (or Pro Diving Croatia) brings together local and foreign dive companies with the aim of promoting Croatian diving and improving the quality of equipment used and services rendered. Its website lists all registered dive centres.

Issa Diving Centre
Komiža, Vis (021 713 651/091 201 2731 mobile/www.scubadiving.hr).
The people to see to arrange a dive on the downed World War II US B17G bomber (*see left*) and other historical wrecks, or to complete a dive course with professional instructors on beautiful Vis.

Hiking

What Croatia's mountains lack in altitude (there's nothing higher than 2,000 metres or 6,560ft), they make up for in drama as they virtually explode from the sea. Belonging to the Dinaric Alps, the peaks are characterised by a sharpness of shape, the dominance of bare limestone, a lack of water, a poverty of vegetation and the harsh climate. It's a combination that means that hiking here can require as much effort as higher peaks elsewhere, particularly if attempted during the blazing summer. But it doesn't necessarily have to be difficult – there are a lot of relaxing hikes through rolling, forest-shaded hills dotted with hamlets, especially in Istria.

Markings along Croatian hiking trails are usually a red circle with a central white dot, or two parallel red lines with a white line between. Mountaineering clubs maintain the markings and most huts, shelters and lodges.

Ski Zagreb

Few would think of Croatia as a major skiing destination. Then again, Croatia didn't have any track record in the sport – until the arrival of Janica Kostelić. The greatest skier of the modern era, Zagreb-born Kostelić was raised in the sport by her father, Ante, who was also a former competitor. She learned to ski near her family home, on the slopes of Medvednica outside the Croatian capital, at the then modest centre of Sljeme.

Janica won her first World Cup race in 1999, at the age of 17. Injured shortly afterwards, she came back to win three gold medals at the Winter Games of 2002, the most successful single Olympic skiing performance in history. Her brother Janica is also a World Cup slalom champion, and silver medal winner at the 2006 Winter Games. She is Croatia's greatest sporting hero and the Kostelićes are the nation's greatest sporting family.

Riding on the popularity of the otherwise modest Janica (who refused having a Zagreb street named after her as it 'wouldn't have been appropriate for someone who's only 23'), ambitious Zagreb mayor Milan Bandić saw an opportunity to put his city on a world stage. With the country gripped by skiing fever, Bandić found the funds to upgrade the facilities at **Sljeme** to such an extent that the course could be considered suitable to stage top-class international competition. It worked. In 2005 Zagreb hosted its first World Cup event. The city has never known such sporting prestige.

For its citizens, apart from the chance to cheer on Kostelić at the so-called Snow Queen run every January, this means they now have a superb ski centre right on their doorstep. An easy cablecar ride from the outskirts of town (*see p78*), Sljeme offers all kinds of fun on the slopes. Open to all, Sljeme has blue, white and green runs for recreational skiers, and red ones for more advanced ones. The steep slope of Panjevina is ideal for snowboarding and ski training. Night skiing is staged twice a week. There's also sledging in nearby Činovnička meadow. Ski passes are reasonable, 50kn for half a day, 70kn for a day, with a number of seasonal discount tickets.

For those who would like to stay up in the hills, there are dozens of mountain huts (www.tzzz.hr/engleski/wintersports.htm), most within easy range of restaurants serving traditional turkey with *mlinci*, thin dried dough, and apple strudel. In keeping with Sljeme's new international profile, a four-star apartment hotel was opened in 2006. With a sauna and restaurant, the Snow Queen offers skiers and hikers comfortable lodgings within easy reach of the slopes. All details are available from the Sljeme office (01 48 25 470, www.sljeme.hr).

Istria

Istria's hiking trails incorporate medieval hilltop towns, patchwork valleys and historical monuments, from pre-Christian burial mounds to Secessionist villas for the Austrian nobility.

In the north-west, around **Buje**, **Grožnjan** and **Motovun**, hiking trails lead through woods, meadows, olive groves and vineyards. Country taverns provide somewere to stay, as well as menus of game and truffles, washed down with regional wines. From Buje, Gornja Bujština is a trail up to a lodge at Žbevnica. From here you get a fabulous view of the Dolomites and the Alps. The county town of **Pazin** is at the centre of the Zelengrad and Beram routes, and the region's oldest trail, the St Simeon. This 12-km (7.4-mile) trail begins in **Gračišće**, a small village 10km (six miles) east of Pazin, and can be quite rugged in parts.

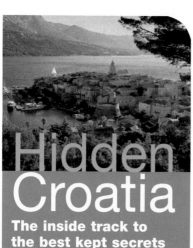

South-western trails lead from **Rovinj**, through **Vodnjan**, to the Roman city of **Pula**. Hikers on this trail can catch a ferry from Fažana to the **Brijuni National Park** (*see p118* **Tito's Xanadu**).

Above the resort of **Opatija** in Kvarner looms Mount Učka (1,300 metres/4,264ft). The peak's climbing lodge affords panoramic views over the Kvarner archipelago beyond. The trailhead to Istria's most popular walk is located nearby in **Poklon**; this 14-km (8.7-mile) path runs to the town of **Brgudac** and on to **Korita**, where there's a lodge for overnighting.

Velebit Nature Park

Velebit is simply massive. At 145km (90 miles) long, it stretches all the way from the Vratnik Saddle to the Zrmanje Valley. Its highest point is Vaganski Vrh at about 1,758 metres (5,766ft) above sea level. Because the coastal slope rises directly from sea level, the ascent to the top takes much longer from here than it does on the continental side (which starts at about 500 metres (1,640ft) above sea level.

Visually, there's a great deal of difference betweeen the two sides of the mountain. While the coastal face is almost completely bare, the interior slopes are forested in beech and populated by wolf, bear, deer, lynx and boar, not to mention some 92 species of flora. Velebit is best known for the majestic karst sculptures that rise above the forest. The largest and most impressive are situated around **Tulove Grede**. Following the route of the Krupa river, which has scored deep into the limestone creating numerous waterfalls, is another terrific hike.

Velebit is also rich in caves, many of which are little explored. **Cerovacke Pecine** is one of the biggest cave complexes in Croatia, with extraordinary formations and archaeological artefacts of Palaeolithic Man.

Be warned, the climate on Velebit is harsh. During winter the slopes get up to 130 days of snow cover, coupled with the gusty bura wind, which howls through the limited number of passes, and temperatures are very, very low. In contrast, during summer it's scorching.

There are hundreds of kilometres of hiking trails and 18 lodging sites – obligatory for anyone wanting to overnight as camping in the park is not permitted. The park is open all year and admission is free.

Useful information

Rudolf Abraham's book *Walking in Croatia* is essential reading for anyone serious about hiking around these parts.

Croatia Mountain Rescue Service
Kozarćeva 22, Zagreb (01 482 4142).
The Mountain Rescue Service (GSS) provides help beyond the regular ones. For emergencies call 985.

Croatian Mountaineering Association
Kozarćeva 22, Zagreb (01 482 3624/fax 01 48 24 142/http://hps.inet.hr).
The CMA is the best source for maps and contacts for huts and shelters, for mountaineers in Croatia.

Iglu Sport
Grahorova 4, Zagreb (01 370 0434/www.iglu sport.hr). **Open** 10am-7pm Mon-Fri; 9am-1pm Sat.
For camping equipment and hiking maps.
Branches: Varoški prilaz 4, Split (021 343 423); Franje Tudjmana 14, by Paklenica National Park, Stari Grad (023 369 889).

Paklenica National Park
www.paklenica.hr.

Velebit Nature Park
Kaniza, Gospic (053 560 450/www.pp-velebit.hr).

Kayaking

The Adriatic is excellent for kayakers of all levels. You are never further than a one-hour paddle from the next small fishing village and the protection afforded by the many islands means that it takes exceptionally strong winds to make conditions unmanageable.

Outfitters are found all along the coast; they can provide all the equipment and information required for anything from a few hours out on the water to a week-long expedition.

Dubrovnik

Approaching Dubrovnik's walls from the sea is something that anyone comfortable in a kayak must do; contact **Adriatic Kayak Tours** (*see p56*) for further details. If you have more time, it's also worth paddling out to nearby **Lokrum** (*see p269*). And if you're up for a seaborne expedition of a few days, then the **Elafiti Islands** (*see p270*) are a rewarding destination.

Hvar & Brač

For kayakers, the quiet south side of **Hvar**, shaped by cliffs and beaches, is perfect for relaxing days away from the crowds that throng the main town.

On **Brač** kayakers should paddle over to the beaches situated below the town of Murvica, and the Zmajeva Spilja (Dragon's Cave), or to the bay at the end of the trail to Pustinja Blaca, a 16th-century monastery.

Sea kayaking on the Adriatic's sheltered waters. *See p55.*

Kornati National Park

West of Šibenik and south of Zadar, 89 islands
are fringed by reefs and protected under the
umbrella of the **Kornati National Park** (*see
p192*). Kayakers get lost in this maze of bare
islands and bays, dining at shoreline seafood
restaurants and snorkelling the reefs.

Although the islands appear to be desolate,
they are home to hundreds of plant species and
an abundance of birdlife. Many of the islands
are criss-crossed by 17th-century stone walls.

The **national park office**, in Murter, is
where you get entrance tickets (50kn) and fishing
and diving permits, and arrange accommodation.
There are also two **Visitor Reception Centres**,
one in Zakan harbour on Ravni Žakan, the other
in Vroje on Kornat. Reception staff cruise around
on small boats to sell tickets as well.

Some islands are off-limits, no camping is
allowed at all and diving is limited to seven
zones. Visitors should bring food and water.

Useful information

Adriatic Kayak Tours

*020 312 770/091 722 0413 mobile/UK 0870 931
9672/www.adriatickayaktours.com.*
Tours around the walls of Dubrovnik.

Lifejacket Adventures

*021 315 888/098 931 6400 mobile/www.lifejacket
adventures.com.*
Kayaking tours in central Dalmatia.

Sailing

For a safe, gentle and relaxing introduction
to sailing, choose Croatia. Its Mediterranean
climate normally ensures calm, warm weather
and there are no major tides or currents to
worry about. You can take your pick of 1,185
islands and islets, basking in the crystal-clear
waters of the Adriatic. Spectacular scenery,
idyllic bays and warm hospitality await.

If the idea still sounds delicious yet daunting,
a qualified skipper from your charter company
will be able to show you the ropes, take you to
all the special places and ease you through your
learning curve. You might also want to learn to
sail properly at one of the schools on the coast
or, if you've got some experience and like to
travel in groups, join one of the flotilla holidays
available from the larger charter companies.

If you're looking for more challenging sailing,
visit outside of July and August, without the
heavy holiday traffic and when the winds are
freshening. The Pasman Canal, the islands
near Split and off the Pelješac peninsula are
favourites for keener sailors and windsurfers.
Many regattas are organised from Biograd and
Murter, near Zadar. See www.yc-biograd.com
and www.sailing-week.com for details.

CHARTER COMPANIES AND PRICES

Croatia can offer reputable international charter
companies and a number of good, smaller local
ones that can provide you with a tailor-made

experience, often at a more competitive price in the shoulder seasons. The best ones fill up fast in July and August. If you're a beginner or have young children, talk it through with the charter company and they'll find you the right skipper.

Charter companies can explain planning, pricing and the booking process. All offer skippered yachts to cater for beginners, as well as bare-boat charters for those with a qualified skipper in their group. Some also have motorboats. Most companies can help with travel to Croatia but it might be easier (and also cheaper) to book yourself. Get to the charter base early on the first day in order to have plenty of time for the briefing and to reach your first overnight destination in good time. It may mean spending the night before at a nearby hotel. The charter company may recommend a suitable place.

Prices are structured in several ways. Some companies do not supply prices on their websites but ask for basic information so they can provide a tailor-made quote. Others quote per person for four people sharing, including flights and transfers, some quote for the boat itself without flights. For a 39-foot boat with four people sharing, prices in high season for an international company and an established local one ranged from 9,243kn per person per week with flights and transfers to 5,088kn excluding flights and transfers. The rates in late September were 5,075kn and 2,871kn, respectively. A skipper will cost around 888kn per day for a yacht and 1,110kn for a motorboat. Companies normally ask for up to 50 per cent

of the charter price as a booking deposit, and the balance four weeks prior to your start date.

Charts and guides will be supplied, plus lifejackets, safety equipment and fresh linen and towels. Deals on fuel vary but the fuel and water tanks should normally be full when you depart and on return. A tender (small rubber boat) will be provided for safety and to get you from an anchorage to shore, but you may have to pay extra for an outboard engine if you don't fancy rowing. A night's mooring in a marina will cost around 244kn, with a ten per cent uplift at most in July and August. Town harbours will be slightly less and you will be charged a fee in some anchorages.

You're never far from a marina in Croatia. State-owned ACI runs 21 of the 45 around Croatia's coastline, and has its own charter fleets in Vodice and Trogir. Further details are available on www.aci-club.hr and in the brochure *Croatian Marinas*, available from the Tourist Board (www.croatia.hr). The newest marina in Kaštela (www.marina-kastela.hr) is not yet listed. Most coastal towns and villages in Croatia have their own harbours – some with electricity and water on tap, a few with showers and laundry services.

ANCHORS AWAY

Kremik (Primošten), Frapa (Rogoznica), Agana (Marina), Trogir, Kaštela and Split marinas are all less than an hour's drive from Split airport. Dubrovnik marina is an hour's drive from the airport on the other side of town. Zadar has far fewer international flights, so for the marinas in

Buoyant exploration of Europe's most beautiful coastline.

Borik, Zadar, Sukošan, Biograd, Murter, Tribunj, Vodice and Skradin you'll have to drive two hours from Split airport. EasyJet's new UK service to Rijeka makes bases in Istria and Kvarner more accessible.

Once you've arrived at your destination, met your skipper and purchased basic provisions, you're all ready to settle in to your temporary floating home. Your clothes should have been packed to fold away easily. You should also have brought sunglasses, sunscreen, a hat, deck shoes and protective long-sleeved shirts. The charter company will have recommended (with your input) the right sort of yacht for your budget and crew. A 40-footer provides generous space for a family of four, or even six, and you should be pleasantly surprised by the standard of fitting out. However, the layouts are all different so check the charter company websites for one that suits you. Once aboard, you will be fully briefed about the boat, the sailing area, routes, safety issues and special requirements. Your skipper will find out your preferences – marinas or anchorages, nightlife or tranquillity, short hops or longer distances, serious sailing or relaxed cruising – and recommend a route and the places for overnight stays and dining out.

Berthing in marinas, at many town harbours and at small bays where restaurants have laid pontoons, is made easy by 'lazy lines'. This is when marina staff, the harbour master or the restaurant owner will see you coming and run to the quay to pull a rope out of the water for you. A crew member picks it up with a boat hook and fastens it at the front of the boat if the boat is going backwards in. If the boat goes forwards in, the lazy line gets fastened at the back of the boat. Going backwards in is an easier option for novices and allows more privacy as cabins are generally at the front, away from passers-by.

Your choice of company might be influenced by location. Istria has some beautiful towns and adventurous cuisine but it doesn't have the variety and abundance of islands in Dalmatia. East of Istria, Kvarner contains the islands of **Krk**, **Cres**, **Lošinj** and **Rab**, all with their own marinas. Rab is great for sandy beaches, Krk is somewhat dominated by package resorts, and the long thin island of Cres has limited shelter for visiting boats. Lošinj is probably the most enticing, with the charming town of Mali Lošinj the most popular port of call.

A short sail from the busy marina of Zadar are the lesser developed islands of **Pašman**, **Ugljan** and **Dugi Otok**, all ideal for finding secluded bays. Nearby Biograd and the three marinas in Murter offer easy access to the stark natural wilderness of the **Kornati Islands**. Facilities are more limited and the sailing is a

bit tougher, with so many islands and islets about, but if you really want to commune with nature then this is the place for you. Also easily accessible are the small islands around Šibenik: Zlarin, Prvic, Kaprije and Žirje. Skradin, upstream from Šibenik, has spectacular waterfalls, well worth a detour.

As you head further south towards Split, Trogir has a marina full of charter companies, and a palm-tree lined promenade, a popular overnight mooring for luxury yachts. Near here is the newest marina of Kaštela, ten minutes' drive from Split airport, also with a good selection of charter companies.

The popular islands of Brač and Hvar are within easy cruising distance of Trogir, Kaštela and Split. Šolta and the Drvenik Islands are even nearer and still give the impression that time has stood still for 20 years. A little further south, easily accommodated on a two-week sailing holiday, are the islands of Korčula and Mljet, two of the greenest in Croatia.

From there, nearby Dubrovnik has a large marina with several charter companies.

Useful information

The **UK office of the Croatian Tourist Board** (0208 563 7979) has copies of the booklet Information for Boaters. **Team Sailing Croatia** (www.teamsailingcroatia.com), based at the Kaštela marina, offers RYA-approved courses. The **Adriatic Nautical Academy** (www.sailing-ana.hr) in Opatija has a range of courses, from beginners to advanced.

Baotic Yachting
www.baotic-yachting.com.
A good choice of motorboats as well as yachts. Based in Kornati, it also operates from Baška Voda, Dubrovnik, and Marina Frapa (Rogoznica). A new base on Dugi Otok is planned for 2006.

Bavadria
www.bavadria.com.
A fleet of yachts based at Kaštela marina.

Dalmatia Charter
www.dalmatiacharter.com.
A family-run business that operates from Trogir and Kremik marina, near Primošten. Yachts only.

Sail Croatia
www.sailcroatia.net.
Tailor-made holidays for any level of experience. At the Kaštela marina, Split, Pula and Dubrovnik, it also offers motorboats and crewed options.

Sunsail
www.sunsail.com.
Bases in Dubrovnik, Kornati (Biograd) and Kremik marina. It offers flotilla holidays. Yachts only.

Rajko Radovanović, Podrum Gallery.
See p61 **Basement revolutionaries.**

Art & Architecture

The broad brushstrokes of history colour local art,
but Croatia is there in the details.

For such a small country, the art scene in Croatia has always been surprisingly diverse and decentralised. Different towns and regions have taken a leading role at different times, with the artistic focus rotating between Dalmatia, Istria, Zagreb and the continental hinterland. Contrary to what many people in the capital choose to believe, many of the most active galleries are outside Zagreb, with the most independently minded projects originating in places such as Dubrovnik and Rijeka.

The history of Croatian art owes much to the spheres of artistic influence radiating from major cultural and political centres in Europe. This was Athens, then Rome; in early medieval times, the competing Christian centres of Orthodox Constantinople and Catholic Rome; in the later Middle Ages it was the Ottoman empire and the Habsburgs in Vienna. In more modern times, Soviet Socialist Realism and abstract stylings from the West were radically opposed poles of stylistic influence on Croatian artists in Tito's Yugoslavia.

PRE-MODERN

Archaeological evidence shows that there were Greek colonies on the islands of Vis, Hvar and Trogir. A fourth-century BC head of Artemis discovered on Vis (known to the Greeks as Issa) is an outstanding example of Hellenistic bronze work, and one of the few original Greek works to survive from this period anywhere in Europe. A chance find in Trogir unearthed a marble relief from the first century AD, depicting a naked running youth, a personification of Kairos, the god of the 'fleeting moment'.

Zagreb's **Museum of Contemporary Art**. *See p62.*

While the Greeks were a sea-based empire, the Romans conquered the whole of present-day Croatia. As was the case everywhere they went, they left deep traces in social and cultural life, founding cities, many adorned with large ceremonial buildings. The most spectacular of these include the Roman **amphitheatre** and temple of Augustus in **Pula** (*see p116*), the **Roman forum** in Zadar (*see p182*), and the **Diocletian Palace** in **Split** (*see p208*).

In the post-Roman world, Dalmatia found itself within the sphere of Byzantium, the influence of which is reflected in monuments such as the **Basilica of Bishop Euphrasius** in **Poreč** (*see p139*). The artistic culture that later emerged in the areas governed by the first Croatian state (from the seventh century onwards) is preserved in a scattering of small churches built on a circular plan; these are often decorated with the plaited relief sculptures that have come to be seen as typically Croatian.

In the later medieval period, a dynastic union with the Hungarian crown, as well as Venetian control of Dalmatia and Ottoman expansion inland, alternately pulled and squeezed the country from all sides. However, political turbulence seems to have spurred Croatians to new artistic heights, and this was the period when Dubrovnik built its majestic city walls, while a series of magnificent cathedrals were erected from Zagreb to Zadar. **Šibenik Cathedral** (*see p201*) is a masterwork of the early Renaissance, as is the recently restored

chapel of Trogir Cathedral. Italy was the main axis for artistic exchange, with Italians, such as Nicola Firentinac, working in Šibenik and Trogir, and Croatian artists working in Renaissance Italy, the most illustrious being the architect of Urbino, Lucian Laurana.

While in Dalmatia it was the towns that nurtured artistic life, in Istria the rural hinterland proved the most fertile ground. Istrian village churches, such as Beram and Oprtalj, preserve vivid cycles of Gothic frescoes executed in a folk style by local artists' workshops. In the 17th and 18th centuries Dalmatia waned while northern Croatia flourished. Monastic orders such as the Jesuits and Paulines propagated baroque with such success that it is easily the most visible style in the churches of continental Croatia. Fine examples include **St Catherine's** in **Zagreb** (*see p70*), Sv Maria in Belec and the Pauline Church in the Lepoglava monastery.

MODERN

When Vlaho Bukovac came to Zagreb in 1893, his arrival marked a turning point in Croatian art. As a child he had gone to America in a sailing boat with his uncle, ending up working in Peru and San Francisco, where he began painting. He was sent to Paris to the Ecole des Beaux-Arts to develop his talents. On returning to his homeland, he gathered a circle of young artists known as the 'colourful' Zagreb School and painted mystical masterpieces such as

Gundulić's Dream (which hangs in Zagreb's Modern Gallery, Hebrangova 1, 01 49 22 368). The first Zagreb Salon of 1898, which Bukovac initiated, caused a reactionary backlash against his work. He was denounced as a foreign agitator and destroyer of Croatian culture. Bukovac withdrew from Croatian artistic life and spent his last 20 years in Prague.

The sculptor Ivan Meštrović came to the fore exhibiting with the Secessionists in Vienna in the early 1900s. One of his best-known works is the extraordinary, Symbolist *Well of Life* (1905) outside the National Theatre in Zagreb, which he sculpted at the age of 22. Meštrović was a controversial figure, campaigning for Croatian liberation from the Austro-Hungarian empire, and for the unification of South Slav peoples. He left the country during the Nazi occupation and spent his last years in America. Along with many public monuments, there is a **gallery** of his work in **Split** (*see p210*) in his old villa.

The foundations that Bukovac laid for modern art in Croatia were built on by the painters of the Munich School, Vladimir Becić, Miroslav Kraljević and Josip Račić, although the promising careers of the latter two were cut short by their early deaths. A second wave of modernism is represented by the Group of Four, all graduates from the Prague Academy. The collectivist Zemlja Group brought together young Croatian artists who sympathised with the revolutionary movement. Their main ideologue was Krsto Hegedušić, who looked for inspiration in old Flemish paintings and in the traditional life of Croatian peasants, advocating politically engaged, content-based art. In the opposite corner was the Group of Three with its 'anti-movement' philosophy, which called for art without ideology and valorised the individual artistic act in contrast.

The immediate post-World War II period was marked by the increased politicisation of art. The career of Antun Augustinčić benefitted from his close association with Tito and his exposure to Soviet art. His approach was well suited to the creation of impressive public monuments, such as the Tito Monument in Kumrovec and the Monument to the Red Army in Batina Skela.

From the 1950s, after Tito split from Stalin, Zagreb started to host major exhibitions of

Basement revolutionaries

The Podrum Gallery in Zagreb was Croatia's first alternative space – a gallery outside the official system. Nearly all of today's contemporary artists came through it, most importantly the seminal Group of Six, plus Vladimir Dodig, Ivan Dorogi, Ladislav Galeta, Tomislav Gotovac, Vlado Gudac, Sanja Iveković, Zeljko Kipke, Antun Maračić, Dalibor Martinis, Marijan Molnar, Goran Petercol, Rajko Radovanović (*work pictured*), Josip Stočić and Goran Trbuljak.

These 20 artists felt the need for a joint activity different from that required by the traditional institutional presentation of art. In May 1978 they formed a Work Collective of Artists based in a small basement room called Podrum ('basement'). Each artist within a traditional medium opted for an analytical and critical approach to their medium and its social context. Characteristic of Yugoslav art at the time was an ironic representation of the signs and symbols of Socialist revolution.

The Group of Six – Željko Jerman, Mladen Stilinović, Sven Stilinović, Vlado Martek, Boris Demur and Fedor Vucemilović – opened up the Croatian arts scene. Before them, artists had to be academically trained and designated as Painters, Sculptors or Designers. None of the six had received formal arts education and they broke the institutional rules as to who could be an artist. Originally ineligible for admission to the Croatian Artists' Society and the official gallery scene, they took art to the streets and were responsible for introducing a post-'68 anti-establishment movement. As a direct result, at the beginning of the 1980s, the Croatian Artists' Society introduced a new, expanded media section.

international contemporary art, such as the series entitled 'New Tendencies'. By the fall of the Berlin Wall in 1989, the Yugoslav arts scene was already ahead of the game. This was also true of popular culture. Yugoslavs had been watching American TV shows and listening to Western rock music since the 1960s, and English was taught in schools. This helped set the scene apart from the rest of Eastern Europe.

CONTEMPORARY

The best of contemporary Croatian art is closely intertwined with the international scene. Leading figures such as Ivan Kožarić, Sanja Iveković, Braco Dimitrijević, Slaven Tolj and Andreja Kulunčić are all well known outside Croatia. There are also many highly regarded artists whose work is little known abroad but which successfully connects with local preoccupations. It's a small but decentralised scene, and one in which the dysfunctionality of established institutions acts as a catalyst for independent activity across the board.

Dubrovnik's Art Radionica Lazareti is run by Slaven Tolj, an artist who is known for powerful, often self-destructive performances that deal with everything from the siege of the city in 1992 to the end of a love affair. He was recently the curator for the Croatian Pavilion at the Venice Biennale, and pointedly chose six artists living and working outside Zagreb in order to represent a decentralised view of the country's art scene.

Rijeka and Split have art academies feeding a pool of local galleries and project spaces. **Split's Academia Ghetto Club** (see p214) is one of the more notable; its fashionable private views are frequented by the leading lights of the local cultural intelligentsia. In **Rijeka**, the **Museum of Modern and Contemporary Art** (see p155) hosts an international biennale. In continental Croatia, **Galerija Balen** in **Slavonski Brod** (see p108) has strong links with the art world of neighbouring Hungary and often features collaborative work. Further east, the Osijek scene revolves around the new Gallery of the Association of Fine Artists. Of the Osjiek artists, Ivan Faktor made his name from films dealing with the civilian experience of the war in the early 1990s, while the work of performance artist Boris Šincek also refers to the trauma of war, including a recent piece in which he takes a gunshot to the chest while wearing a bulletproof vest).

In Istria, the scene revolves around the artists' village of **Grožnjan** (see p128) and the region's major contemporary venue, the MMC Luka Gallery in Pula (Istarska 30, 052 214 408).

The new **Museum of Contemporary Art** (see p72) in **Zagreb** is either a strategic investment in the future of Croatian art or a massive white elephant. Due to open in 2008, the museum will have plenty of space to show Croatian art of the last 50 years. However, the forbidding glass and the concrete structure in the cultural desert of Novi Zagreb represents a very public test of its ability to pull in visitors. There are several interesting smaller galleries in Zagreb that do their part in shaping the scene. **Galerija Nova** (Teslina 7, 01 48 72 582) alternates between collaborations with international curators and solo shows by young Croatian artists; it's also a venue for one-off events, book launches and performances. The **MAMA Netclub** (Preradovićeva 18, 01 48 56 400, www.mi2.hr) hosts alternative art happenings, often with an element of social and political critique, and always involving computers and new media. The **Croatian Artists' Centre** (see p77) has its base in a beautiful, mosque-like building designed by Ivan Meštrović. The institution suffers most of the time from internal politics but its white-domed Gallery of Extended Media has a diverse and worthwhile exhibition programme.

Galerija Zona (Berislavićeva 20, 01 48 37 590), run by the son of Edo Murtić, a standard bearer of the Croatian jet set, is the place to view – and perhaps purchase – work by the most high-profile local artists. That would certainly include Tomislav Buntak, a young painter who daubs mythical scenes on large canvases, walls and even ceilings. Matko Vekić is another youthful talent whose favourite subjects are cars and diggers, painted on very large canvases, with references to astrology, ideally revolving on a flashy advertising panel.

International players include Igor Grubić, Kristina Leko and also Andreja Kulunčić. Grubić seeks to draw attention to perceived social injustices through guerrilla acts; he painted the floor of the ancient Peristil in Split black as a protest against nationalism (referencing the time it was painted red by anti-Communist artists in the 1960s). Leko orchestrated the milkmaids of Zagreb market in a work intended as a rebuke to EU regulations that threatened local dairy produce. Kulunčić's work has explored ethical issues in genetic engineering and appropriated the medium of advertising to draw attention to unemployment and the exploitative treatment of immigrants in the EU.

Croatian art may still be taking its cues from larger, more powerful neighbours, but that should never be mistaken for slavish imitation. Biting the hand that feeds it is one of the most enduring, even endearing, of local artistic traits.

Hacienda.

Nightlife

Lively party scene on the coast despite the rise of turbofolk.

Is Croatia the new Ibiza? No, but the local DJ scene has come on leaps and bounds since the early 1990s when Kiki, Felver and Frajman played Zagreb's first techno bashes and ravers were finding old mosques, abandoned mansions in the Sljeme ski slopes and the Grič Tunnel bomb shelter to party in.

As the war died down, the Zagreb scene quickly switched to the coast from June through September. Now there is a clear seasonal divide and, come June, Zagreb ups sticks for the Adriatic. Even the long-established landmark venue in the capital, **Aquarius** (*see p88*), sets up a branch at Croatia's big beach party at Zrće on Pag (*see p176* **Balkan Ibiza**).

Inevitably, everything has become less underground and more commercialised – albeit on a different scale to the UK or even Ibiza. Still, the key clubs on Croatia's coast these days are large, slick operations, with enough clout and reputation to attract decent international names. There are no superclubs as such but the two most important venues, **Aurora** (*see p199*) near Primošten and **Hacienda** (*see p204*) at Vodice near Šibenik, can regularly pull in two or three thousand and have Carl Cox, David Morales or John Digweed manning their decks. Pleased with the audience reaction and the Adriatic setting, most make regular returns.

THE COAST WITH THE MOST

Set up in the early 1990s, these two clubs switched focus to the coast road, the Magistrala, halfway between Zadar and Split (*see p202* **Highway 65 revisited**). With the Zagreb-Split highway in place, party-goers can head down from the capital or up from Croatia's second city and go wild for the weekend. Other clubs have not been slow in setting up in the same hub, such as **Exit** (*see p204*) in Vodice.

The best Clubs

Aquarius, Zagreb
The oldest and the best. *See p88*.

Aurora, Primošten
Name DJs, prime Adriatic site. *See p199*.

Hacienda, Vodice
Best rated venue in Croatia. *See p204*.

Zrće beach, Novalja
Three all-night beach clubs in one.
See p176 **Balkan Ibiza**.

When two British guys opened outdoor DJ terrace lounge **The Garden** (*see p189* **Cool clubs**) in northern Dalmatia's capital of Zadar in the summer of 2005, it was a happy coincidence – the two owners had holidayed there in 2004 – but it does reinforce the regional focus. Having made a great success of the Garden (and also introduced the DJ bar **Space Lab** right in central Zadar, too; *see p188*), the management spent the winter of 2005/06 setting up the Garden's first festival for the first weekend of June, **The Garden Get Together**, on the headland of Petrčane outside town. As well as the seafront, the crew are making use of the classic Socialist Realist annexe to the Tito-era Hotel Pinija nearby. While domestic club owners do their best to make venues as chic and Western as possible, UK movers and shakers seem to like authentic historic atmosphere. The Garden is set in Zadar's original Venetian fortifications. Neil Lewis' swish **Vertigo** (*see p241*) club, opened on the party island of Hvar in 2005, is in an old-fashioned building in the small, sleepy harbour town of Jelsa.

Hvar attracts high-end party-goers by the bucketload, the yachting fraternity dropping anchor at landmark cocktail bar **Carpe Diem** (*see p234* **Cool clubs**) on Hvar town harbour. The island's fame stems from its golden era just before the Yugoslav war. It's got this cachet back, but has had to go upmarket to get it. While locals hang out at the basic **Hula Hula Beach Bar** (*see p239*), Roman Abramovich is ordering class-A vodka from his spot on Carpe Diem's legendary VIP terrace.

Brač has its own little scene, centred on the **Faces Club** (*see p232*), the kind of big, brash venue typical of Split (**Master's**, **Metropolis**, **Tribu**; for all, *see p221*) and Dubrovnik (Lazareti and **East-West**; *see p279*).

NORTHERN LIGHTS

Up in Kvarner and Istria, the scene is more diverse. Cases in point are **Fun Academy** (*see p158*) and **Club Točka** (*see p158*) near Rijeka, a town that has its fair share of DJ action at city-centre bars at weekends. Pula's nightlife venues are mainstream – although you might chance on something unusual at **Club Uljanik** (*see p123*). In Istria, focus falls on the all-in-one entertainment centre of **Monvi** in Rovinj (*see p149*). Less well known are adjacent **Girandella** and **Golbujera** beaches within easy reach of Rabac on Istria's east coast, with DJ festivals (www.soundform.org) in summer. **Pudarica** beach on Rab, between Rab town and Barbat, is home to the hot place of 2005, **Santos** (*see p178*). Typical of the genre – lounge bar by day, post-beach bar in the evening, cocktail and DJ venue by night, go-go dancers, pool, multi-level dancefloor, the works – Santos offers unsophisticated fun.

And what of Zagreb? Opened since the early '90s, **Aquarius** still sets the pace. This lakeside landmark has seen the rise of glitzier, more commercial venues on its doorstep, **Best** and **Gallery** (for both, *see p88*), both capable of bringing big international names to their decks, but Aquarius always seems to do everything with such professional panache, it holds on to its loyal crowd.

Aquarius - Zagreb's lively lakeside landmark.

The key to Zagreb is its penchant for live music (*see p84* **Zagreb music city**). Indie, surf-punk, country, chances are it's been here. Most places double up and host live acts and DJs. The mecca of grunge, **Močvara** (*see p92*) has DJ nights; Aquarius stages concerts once a week (usually Tuesdays). At somewhere like **KSET** (*see p92*) or **Boogaloo** (*see p90*), Jeff Mills might be programmed in the same week as a Nirvana tribute band – which is exactly what happened in March 2006.

Aquarius plays mainstream hip hop at weekends, but will throw something left-field into the mix. Its long-running **Kontrapunkt** nights were set up by **Eddy&Dus**, inventive broken beats whose popularity was the springboard for the most interesting domestic DJ around, Eddy Ramich.

EDDY, IVAN AND PERO

Born in Holland into a Slovak-Croatian family, **Eddy Ramich** had a global upbringing, much of it spent with his violin. He began DJing – hip hop, acid jazz – in the student clubs of Zagreb in the early 1990s. He got his first residency at the Aquarius, and his own show on Radio 101. He teamed up with Dus, gaining cult status for Sun Ra and Morricone remixes, before signing to French label Penso Positivo. The LP *High Life* earned good reviews in the UK.

Keeping Kontrapunkt going with guest DJs such as Gilles Peterson and Carl Craig, Eddy then played with Jana Valdevit, aka **Yannah**, a jazz pianist with whom Eddy&Dus had collaborated in 2000. The result was Eddy Meets Yannah – and a deal with respected German label Compost Records. Bringing in Domu (Dominic Stanton) for off-the-wall remixes, the *Shamed* EP released at the end of 2005 earned plaudits across the board. It also established a Mediterranean sound, rhythmic, soulful, slightly melancholy, sprinkled with touches of nu jazz.

The other local name to look out for is **Ivan Komlinović**, a DJ and producer, recently linked to Carl Cox's label Intec. Mainly working in the techno/tech-house field, Komlinović played long, polished sets throughout the '90s, his experience and talent now shining through in the studio. The other prime mover on the scene is **Pero Fullhouse**, one of the prolific names from the early days. Split-based Pero, a promoter and now resident DJ at Aurora, has played almost every big dance festival in Croatia since the mid 1990s. Another to work mainly in the techno/tech-house arena (trance cuts no mustard on this side of the Adriatic), Pero set up his own label, OmegaRitam, in 2002. Most of the domestic DJs Pero cites as worth catching, either Split- (**Iva** from the **Crobot**

Turbofolk

Croatia is awash with turbofolk. Simple, pumping dance music with vague folk roots and mindless lyrics, you can't escape it. A newspaper survey showed that 43 per cent of 17 year olds listened to turbofolk. In the spring of 2006, Zagreb clubs Pasha, Blue Night and the notorious Ludnica ('the Asylum', set near one such institution) came under city council scrutiny after a series of shootings in town. All are now threatened with midnight closing times.

So, how did turbofolk get here? You can blame the Serbs. Belgrade's Pink TV's popularised it in the '90s. Defiantly Balkan, turbofolk sang of risqué love, glamorous crime and easy wealth – perhaps not unlike dancehall or gangsta rap. It was best delivered by leggy, busty bimbos in scant clothing. The most successful exponent was Ceca. Pink TV's defining moment came in 1995 when Ceca married paramilitary commander Arkan on air, the pairing of Balkan pop and aggressive, macho values.

Almost perversely, soldiers and widows from all sides of the conflict tuned into turbofolk. Pink TV became the biggest success story in the Balkans.

It still is. Singers such as Seka Aleksić, Mile Kitić and the unstoppable Ceca (who lost her husband in a hail of bullets in Belgrade in 2000) are the pop stars of the day. Loved by teenagers in both Belgrade and Zagreb, turbofolk is an easy and lucrative option for club owners in each city. It all proves that however close EU membership might be, much of Croatia is in a Balkan mindset.

crew, **Lushi**, **Yelle**) or Zagreb-based (**Petar Dundov**, **Zero**), work in techno or house. He, much as others in the business, fears the rise of bland, basic, Balkan disco music (*see above* **Turbofolk**) sweeping Croatia.

Still rocking the house, though, are Kiki, Felver and Frajman, proving that there is enough work for everyone in Croatia – and perhaps not enough young, new names coming through. Three websites provide information of DJ parties and festivals across Croatia: www.pegla.com; www.radiodeejay.hr and www.klubskascena.com. Dates and names should be relatively easy to pick out. The site www.brija.com covers Istria and for Dubrovnik click on www.clubpages.net.

Zagreb

Features

Maps

Zagreb

Habsburg by tradition, the Croatian capital is being fashionably reinvented.

'A room with a sea view, please!' The marketing manager of Zagreb's most prestigious hotel, the **Regent Esplanade**, laughs at the number of visitors who arrive at the Croatian capital expecting it to be on the Adriatic. Nearer to Vienna than Dubrovnik, the pocket-sized metropolis is also closer in character to Central Europe. Expanded under the Habsburgs, with pretty parks and elegant façades, Zagreb had been an ecclesiastical and political hub from medieval times – what it lacked was a country to rule. With capital-city status only gained after independence in the 1990s, Zagreb is now surprised to find tourists turning up on its doorstep. They in turn are surprised to find a slightly shabby Central European city rapidly trying to gentrify itself – and no sea.

Set by Mount Medvednica, where the last foothills of the Alps meet the Pannonian Plain, Zagreb grew up on the north bank of the Sava. It comprised two rival hilltop settlements, **Gradec** and **Kaptol**, the site of today's **Sabor**, or Croatian Parliament, and the **Cathedral**. After Hungarian King Ladislas founded a diocese here in 1094, it remained under the archbishopric of Hungary until 1852. Kaptol and Gradec fought for most of that millennium. A testament to their animosity can be found in the naming of **Krvavi most**, Bloody Bridge, the alley at the western end of Skalinska and scene of battles between them.

By the 17th century, with the Governor (Ban) of Croatia and the Sabor based here, Zagreb's importance overshadowed the local rivalry. By the 19th, its development reflected a growing search for a Croatian identity. Prestigious buildings such as the **Academy of Arts and Sciences** and the **National Theatre** centrepieced a neat spread of grid-patterned streets and squares between the **Upper Town** (Gornji Grad) of Kaptol and Gradec, and the new railway station. Habsburgian in appearance, it gained the name of **Lower Town** (Donji Grad). A main square, Harmica, was laid out where the Upper and Lower Towns met.

Power still rested in the twin Habsburg capitals of Vienna and Budapest. With the clamour for reform, in 1848, the Croatian Ban, **Josip Jelačić**, led an army into Hungary. His bid failed and Jelačić died a broken man. He was honoured with a statue on Harmica, on his horse, his sword pointed in defiance. Tito had it taken down and the square named Trg republike. With the fall of Communist rule in 1990, the statue was reassembled and the square renamed **Trg bana Josipa Jelačića**.

Across the Sava, Tito built the Socialist-style housing estate of **Novi Zagreb**. Zagreb, as the second city of Yugoslavia, acquired an industrial edge. Many Socialist-era shopfronts can still be seen around the Lower Town. At the same time, an underground rock and art scene flourished and a Zagreb spirit emerged, distinct from the bourgeois atmosphere between the two world wars. It was savvy, independent, liberal, certainly not supportive of rule from Belgrade, but neither comfortable with the nationalist undercurrents of Tudjman and his cronies. Apart from an audacious rocket attack in 1991 on the Ban's Palace and one on citizens in 1995, Zagreb was spared the worst of the war. Its population swelled by refugees from Bosnia and the countryside, Zagreb and its outskirts did see a significant political shift to the right. This has been dissipated with the need for post-war recovery. Zagreb, in the mid-point between Mitteleuropa and the Mediterreanean, knows its future lies with Europe. The arrest of alleged war criminal Ante Gotovina in December 2005 saw nationalist protests in north Dalmatia. That same night, the bohemian bars of the capital played the prison songs of Johnny Cash (*gotovina* is the Croatian word for 'cash'), understanding that a major hurdle to union with Europe had been overcome.

The war and the economic struggle after independence froze the city in its two seminal points in time, 19th-century Habsburg and 20th-century Socialist. The visitor to Zagreb in 1996 would have seen little change to the city from, say, 1976, when the Rolling Stones played here. Only recently, since the turn of the new century, have trendy businesses sprung up: a cool bar quarter on **Preradovićeva** near Jelačić, designer stores along Ilica off Jelačić and a business quarter along **Savska**, south-west of Donji Grad. 2005 was the first summer

The phone code for **Zagreb** is 01. Here we give the full number for each listing – drop the '0' if dialling from abroad. In Zagreb itself you don't need to dial the 01.

Things to do

See the **Bloody Bridge** (*see p69*) where Zagreb's medieval history was fought out. Spend the morning at the **Dolac** (see p91), Zagreb's daily outdoor and indoor produce market. Take the **funicular** (*see p70*) from Ilica to the Upper Town. Browse at **Victor** (*see p89* **Zagreb by design**), Croatia's first concept store. Wander around the **Botanical Gardens** (*see p77*) or **Maksimir Park & Zoo** (*see p78*). Go for a cycle around **Lake Jarun** (*see p72*) or ski down **Sljeme** (*see p78*).

Places to stay

The **Regent Esplanade** (*see p93* **Hot hotels**) shows its Charleston-era class. For contemporary fittings, try Zagreb's first designer hotel, the **Arcotel Allegra** (*see p92*) or the swish comfort of the **Sheraton Zagreb Hotel** (*see p93*). Best centrally located cheapie? No question, the **Hotel Laguna** (*see p92*).

Places to eat

Baltazar (*see p79*) offers authentic regional meaty delicacies in rustic surroundings. **Gostionica Tip-Top** (*see p79*) is steeped in literary history. Ambitious, pricy **Marcellino** (*see p77* **Top tables**) is worth every kuna. **Okrugljak** (*see p80*) is the grande dame of Zagreb eateries. You can dine in opulent surroundings at **Paviljon** (*see p81*).

Nightlife

Kolaž (*see p87*) and **Krivi Put** (*see p87*) are the new bars in town. **Maraschino** (*see p87*) and **Sedmica** (*see p86* **Best bars**) are cool but crowded – **Škola** (*see p82* **Best bars**) is still the place to be. **Gallery** (*see p88*) is now challenging **Aquarius** (*see p88*) for Zagreb's most happening club.

Culture

Observe some neat handiwork by Ivan Meštrović in the **Cathedral** (*see p73*), **St Mark's Church** (*see p73*) and his own **Atelijer** (*see p73*). Catch a temporary exhibition at the **Museum of Contemporary Art** (*see p73*) or the **Galerija Klovićevi Dvori** (*see p73*). Wander around the Manets and Rembrandts at the **Mimara Museum** (*see p76*) or the Breughels and El Grecos at **Strossmayer's Gallery of Old Masters** (*see p76*).

that restaurateurs became aware of significant numbers of tourists – before, nearly all used to close their doors and head for the coast.

Tourists are hardly encouraged by a lack of mid-range hotels and no clear signs as to what they should go out and see. There are few explanatory plaques at historical spots around town and no real must-see attraction apart from a cathedral wrapped in scaffolding. The local authorities seem to have set their sights on earning money hosting conferences and conventions. The introduction of a budget air link with London will change weekend visitor figures here – and maybe local attitudes.

IN THE CITY

Zagreb still lacks the urban gravitas of a Vienna or a Budapest but this is part of its charm. You can walk to most appointments. If not, many of its 16 tram routes pass through Jelačić, where you might start your day pondering a map over a slow coffee. Two walking tours of the city, one north to Gradec and Kaptol, the other south around the Lower Town, become apparent. Each takes about 90 minutes. You might finish one in time for *gablec*, the local version of elevenses (look out for café signs saying *gableci*), before completing the next one by lunchtime.

Next to Jelačić on the map but a short, steep climb away are the well-stocked and always busy daily market, **Dolac**, and the cathedral. Further over on Gradac, the other side of Bloody Bridge, is a cluster of sights around the main one of St Mark's Church.

This group of churches and galleries is best accessed from a funicular (Tomićeva, every 10mins, 6.30am-9pm daily, 3kn) by Ilica, a gentrifying commercial street running west from Jelačić. The short ride takes you to the **Lotrščak Tower** (Strossmayerovo šetalište 9, 01 48 51 768, open 11am-8pm Tue-Sun, 10kn), a lookout tower built in the 13th century, reached by climbing a winding wooden staircase. It has since housed a sweet shop and, on the first floor, Zagreb's first pool hall. Every day since 1877, a couple of loud cannon blasts from here signal noon sharp.

Leafy Strossmayerovo šetalište runs by the tower giving a lovely view of the rooftops. Near the tower stands **St Catherine's Church** (Katarinski trg, 01 48 51 950, open 10am-1pm daily), built by the Jesuits in the 17th century, with a beautiful baroque interior of pink-and-white stucco. Three main galleries are clustered around it: the **Croatian Museum of Naive Art**, **Klovićevi Dvori** and the **Museum of Contemporary Art**. Just north of Klovićevi Dvori stands the Stone Gate (Kamenita Vrata), the only remaining medieval entrance to the

Rattle and hum – Zagreb's blue trams are a regular feature of city life.

Upper Town. It's more of a short, bendy tunnel than a gate, and is a shrine to mark a fire that consumed everything here but a painting of the Virgin Mary in 1731. Prayers are whispered, flowers laid and candles lit.

Passing through it, you wander around the cobbled streets of Gradec, looking into little squares, perhaps popping into the **Croatian History Museum** (Matoševa 9, 01 48 51 900, www.hismus.hr, open 10am-5pm Mon-Fri, 10am-1pm Sat, Sun, 10kn), a lovely baroque mansion with a collection of photographs, furniture, paintings and weapons thematically relating to Croatia's development.

At the heart of Gradec stands **St Mark's Church** on Markov trg, a modest square considering it houses the Croatian Parliament and the Ban's Palace. North, edging towards the verdant slopes of Mount Medvednica, are the **Meštrović Atelijer**, a natural history museum (Demetrova 1, 01 48 51 700, www.hpm.hr, 10am-5pm Tue-Fri, 10am-1pm Sat, Sun) and the **Zagreb City Museum**.

Walking back through the Stone Gate, you come into Radićeva and, crossing back over Bloody Bridge, to one of the most atmospheric and lively streets in Zagreb, **Tkalčićeva**. Pastel-shaded low-rise old houses accommodate galleries, bars and boutiques. The parallel street

of Opatovina, once home of the legendary Kvazar bar, has long lost its verve and is now lined with display cases of cheap clothes.

Crossing the indoor and outdoor markets, your eyes are drawn towards the spires of the cathedral, surrounded on three sides by the ivy walls of the Archbishop's Palace. Around it runs Vlaška, which brings you up to the park of Ribnjak, pleasant by day, filled with amorous teenagers after dark at weekends.

The Lower Town begins at Jelačić. A criss-cross of streets begins with a pedestrianised zone around Preradovićeva flower market, by the new bar quarter of **Gajeva**, Preradovićeva and **Margaretska**. Stern, grey Habsburg façades run down to the station, some with shopfronts unchanged since 1965. Parallel to them are two neatly planned rectangles of green public space stretching north-south as far as the train station, bookended by the **Botanical Gardens**. This is the so-called Horseshoe, an attempt by 19th-century urban designer Milan Lenuci to create a city in the Austrian mode. Each park is parcelled up into three parts, centrepieced by grandiose landmark buildings of prominent institutions: the Academy of Arts and Sciences; the National Theatre, and the **Mimara Museum** alongside. **Zrinjevac**, the northernmost section, features tree-lined paths, a gazebo and a fountain designed by Herman Bollé, responsible for many of Zagreb's major architectural works, including the cathedral. Linked to Jelačić by Masarykova, the former café-lined hub of the underground music scene, Trg Maršala Tita is notable not only for the neo-baroque **Croatian National Theatre** but also for the fact that the square has kept its name, Tito. In front of the theatre stands one of the most famous works by sculptor Ivan Meštrović, *The Well of Life*.

The Lower Town ends at the railtracks and another fin-de-siècle façade, the neo-classical train station, Glavni kolodvor. A major stop on the Orient Express, it echoes another era, when arrival by train was the norm. Next to it was built one of Europe's great railway hotels, the Esplanade, now surrounded by a pedestrianised square of fountains and an underground shopping mall. The main rail lines still run to Vienna and Budapest – only in 2005 was a fast service introduced to Split.

South and west run a right-angle of broad avenues: Savska, with its burgeoning business quarter; and Vukovarska, where Orson Welles shot part of his film version of Kafka's *The Trial* in 1962.

AWAY FROM THE NUMBERS

Across the Sava river spread the suburbs of Novi Zagreb, Socialist-era housing blocks with the usual urban ills. Novi Zagreb is the site for the **Museum of Contemporary Art** (www.mdc.hr/msu), due to open in 2007/08, at the corner of Avenija Dubrovnik and Avenija Većeslava Holjevca. The first museum to be built in Zagreb for 125 years, and the largest ever built in Croatia, it will be big enough to display the 9,000 items currently held, many of which are in storage. The museum's current site at Katarinin trg (*see p73*) holds only temporary exhibitions. There will also be a multiplex cinema this side of the Sava. With downtown gridlocked almost through the day, more businesses are looking to set up in Novi Zagreb.

Further afield, three main attractions are accessible on public transport from the city centre. **Jarun** is a recreational lake by the Sava, on tram route No.17 south-west of Jelačić. Built for the World Student Games in 1987, it's a haven for cyclists and rowers. It also houses Zagreb's landmark nightclub, **Aquarius**. Another easy tram hop is to **Maksimir**, the city's main park, with public gardens, the zoo and, across the main road, the national football

Zagreb's central square – **Trg bana Josipa Jelačića**. *See p69.*

stadium, home of Dinamo Zagreb. North-east of the city, the beautiful tree-lined cemetery of **Mirogoj** (open dawn-sunset daily), designed by Herman Bollé, is filled with ivy-strewn cupolas and pavilions. The motley gravestones include five-pointed stars, Cyrillic inscriptions, Stars of David and Islamic half-moons, pointing at Croatia's ethnic tapestry. Works by renowned Croatian sculptors line the neo-Renaissance arcades. From the cathedral, take bus No.106.

For more adventurous trips out, including the cablecar to the new skiing centre at **Sljeme** (*see p78* and *p53* **Ski Zagreb**).

The more prestigious museums charge 20kn entrance, 10kn for students, children and pensioners. If you're doing any serious gallery gawping, invest in a three-day **Zagreb Card** (www.zagrebcard.fivestars.hr, 90kn) from the tourist office (*see p94*) on Jelačić.

The majority of these sights are within walking distance of Jelačić. Transport details are given for those further afield.

Cathedral
Kaptol 31 (01 48 14 727). **Open** 10am-5pm Mon-Sat; 1-5pm Sun.
Zagreb Cathedral, or Cathedral of the Assumption of the Holy Virgin Mary (Katedrala uznesenja blažene djevice Marije) to give it its proper name, has been built and rebuilt so many times it's no wonder it's been clad in scaffolding for most of the last decade. It doesn't stop busloads of tourists parking outside – this is Zagreb's number one attraction. Its neo-Gothic twin towers, visible across the city, are as close as Zagreb gets to a visual identity. The original church was destroyed by the Tatars in 1242 and later reconstructions were damaged by fire. A more serious job was needed after an earthquake struck in 1880 and the city hired Viennese architect Hermann Bollé. Looking to the cathedral's medieval past, Bollé added a monumental pair of 105m-high (345-foot) belltowers, fitting for a developing metropolis. As there was little money left once the spires were built, the interior is quite austere. It features a clutch of medieval frescoes, a baroque marble pulpit, a Renaissance triptych altar attributed to Albrecht Dürer and an Ivan Meštrović relief that marks the resting place of controversial Croatian Archbishop Alojzije Stepinac.

St Mark's Church
Trg sv Marka 5 (01 48 51 611). **Open** 9am-noon, 5-5.45pm daily.
Two coats of arms grace the distinct red-white-and-blue chequered roof of this emblematic church – Zagreb's and Croatia's, the latter symbolising the former kingdoms of Croatia, Dalmatia and Slavonia. Since the 13th century when the Romanesque original was built, the church has gone through many architectural styles, such as an elaborate Gothic south portal and a baroque, copper-covered belltower. Inside are hand-painted walls by Jozo Kljaković and a crucifix by Meštrović. The rectangular square outside, housing the Ban's Palace and the Sabor (the Croatian Parliament), has been the hub of political activity since the 1500s.

Museum of Contemporary Art
Katarinin trg 2 (01 48 51 808/www.mdc.hr/msu). **Open** 11am-7pm Tue-Sat; 10am-1pm Sun. **Admission** 15kn. **No credit cards**.
Currently only large enough to display temporary exhibitions – and with its office at Habdelićeva – the Museum of Contemporary Art will be relocating in 2007/08 to a new building in Novi Zagreb. *See p62*.

Croatian Museum of Naive Art
Ćirilometodska ulica 3 (01 48 51 911/ www.hmnu.org). **Open** 10am-6pm Tue-Fri; 10am-1pm Sat, Sun. **Admission** 10kn. **Credit** AmEx, V.
This collection of 50 or so paintings is a decent introduction to Croatia's naive art movement. Housed on the second floor of the 18th-century Raffay Palace, the Hrvatski muzej naivne umjetnosti has a small permanent exhibit of colourful peasant life representations executed in the traditional way by village painters. Particular accent is placed on the Hlebine School, including works by the internationally famous Ivan Generalić and Ivan Lacković Croata. Also represented are lesser known Croatian naive painters, plus a couple of international modern primitives. The presentation could be better – a further 1,600 works are still in storage. Guided tours are available if arranged in advance.

I. Meštrović Atelijer
Mletačka 8 (01 48 51 123/www.mdc.hr/mestrovic). **Open** 10am-6pm Tue-Fri; 10am-2pm Sat, Sun. **Admission** 20kn. **Credit** *50kn min* AmEx, DC, MC, V.
Croatia's most internationally renowned sculptor, Ivan Meštrović, lived in this restored trio of adjoining 17th-century mansions in Gornji Grad between 1923 and 1942. The collection is spectacular, representing major works from the artist's prolific first four decades. Marble, stone, wood and bronze sculptures, as well as reliefs, drawings and graphics grace two floors of the house, the front atrium and his atelier just off the ivy-covered courtyard. The dimly lit interiors are lined with beautiful wood panelling and exude an intimate ambience.

Galerija Klovićevi Dvori
Jezuitski trg 4 (01 48 51 926/www.galerijaklovic.hr). **Open** 11am-7pm Tue-Sun. **Admission** 20kn. **No credit cards**.
This high-profile gallery, set in the stunning space of a former Jesuit monastery in Gornji Grad, is known for curating first-rate temporary exhibits of big-name local and international artists. Recent shows have focused on the Hlebine School of naive art, China, Picasso and the Russian avant-garde movement.

Ethnographic Museum
Trg Ivana Mažuranića 14 (01 48 26 220/ www.etnografski-muzej.hr). **Open** 10am-6pm Tue-Thur; 10am-1pm Fri-Sun. **Admission** 15kn; free Thur.

Dolac. See p91.

Eclectic two-floor collection of folk artefacts set inside a Secessionist palace. Downstairs is a permanent collection of traditional costumes from different regions of Croatia, as well as a hodgepodge of overseas items brought home by Croatian explorers, including ritual masks from the Congo, Indian textiles, tree-bark paintings from Australia and Chinese ceremonial dresses. Often the more interesting displays are temporary ones on the second floor, organised around local and global themes.

Zagreb City Museum

Opatička ulica 20 (01 48 51 361/www.mdc.hr/mgz).
Open 10am-6pm Tue-Fri; 10am-1pm Sat, Sun.
Admission 20kn. **No credit cards.**
Occupying the 17th-century Convent of the Clares in Gradec, the City Museum is a worthwhile one to visit. Its permanent collection presents 4,500 objects tracing Zagreb's history from prehistoric times. Themed sections include recent Iron Age finds, walk-through reconstructions of 19th-century Ilica shops and study rooms of famous Croatian artists. Other captivating nuggets include old packaging, watches and automatic music machines. You'll even find Chagall's *Lady with a Bird*, once owned by a German actress who made Zagreb her home in World War II. Propaganda posters of 20th-century political and religious figures act as a finale. Many exhibits are interactive and it's all well documented in English. An intimate attic hosts temporary shows. The sundial in the courtyard is the city's oldest, still showing the right time.

Mimara Museum

Rooseveltov trg 5 (01 48 28 100). **Open** 10am-5pm Tue, Wed, Fri, Sat; 10am-7pm Thur; 10am-2pm Sun.
Admission 20kn. **No credit cards.**
Zagreb's most impressive art collection was donated to the city by Dalmatia-born Ante Topić Mimara. Inside a neo-Renaissance former school from 1895, 42 exhibition rooms contain 1,700 objects. These range from paintings to statues and archeological tidbits, organised chronologically and thematically but with nothing by way of English explanation. Attractions include a collection of carpets, medieval icons, Chinese porcelain, and paintings by Raphael, Velázquez, Rubens, Rembrandt and Manet. The collection is vast – only a third is on display – and controversial, as nobody knows how Mimara acquired his wealth or collected all these objects.

Museum of Arts & Crafts

Trg maršala Tita 3 (01 48 82 111/www.muo.hr).
Open 10am-7pm Tue-Sat; 10am-2pm Sun.
Admission 20kn. **No credit cards.**
Inside this grand Hermann Bollé-designed palace opposite the National Theatre is an assortment of 160,000 items, 3,000 of them on permanent display. Having celebrated its 125th anniversary in 2005, the museum could do with English-language explanations at this point. As it is, you have to take everything at face value. Exhibits are presented in a series

of halls around an imposing galleried atrium. Items span the period between the 14th and 20th centuries – from Gothic to art deco – ranging from furniture, pottery, glass and ivory to musical instruments, clothes, textiles and photo equipment.

Strossmayer's Gallery of Old Masters

Trg NŠ Zrinskog 11 (01 48 95 117/www.mdc.hr/ strossmayer). **Open** 10am-1pm, 5-7pm Tue; 10am-1pm Wed-Sun. **Admission** 10kn. **No credit cards**.
Built in 1884 to accommodate Bishop Josip Juraj Strossmayer's anthology of European masterpieces, this neo-Renaissance palace showcases a delightful selection of well-chosen works spanning the 14th to 19th centuries. Of the 4,000 items in the permanent collection, only 256 are on display at any given time, in ten intimate rooms on the building's second floor. Italians, including Tintoretto and Beato Angelico, lead the pack in the first six, followed by Flemish (Brueghel), Dutch and German (Dürer) painters in the next three. French and Spanish (El Greco, Delacroix, Ingres) complete the collection.

Croatian Artists' Centre

Trg žrtava fašizma (01 46 11 818/www.hdlu.hr).
Open 11am-7pm Tue-Fri; 10am-2pm Sat, Sun.
Admission 15kn. **No credit cards**.
This Ivan Meštrović-designed 1930s masterpiece is among Zagreb's most unusual architectural sights. Classical columns support a white circular structure made entirely of stone from Brač. In 1941, to attract more Muslims to Croatia's Fascist regime, the building was turned into a mosque. Locals still call it *Džamija*, despite the fact that the three minarets were demolished in 1949. Since 2003 it has housed the Croatian Association of Artists, serving as its main exhibition space. Contemporary local artists, with an occasional international name, are showcased in the three chic galleries.

Technical Museum

Savska 18 (01 48 44 050/www.mdc.hr/tehnicki).
Tram 12 to Tehnički muzej. **Open** 9am-5pm Tue-Fri; 9am-1pm Sat, Sun. **Admission** 10kn for permanent collection; 10kn for planetarium; tram rides free.
No credit cards.
The city's quirkiest museum contains an offbeat collection including 19th-century fire engines, 1930s locomotives, a collection of classic cars, a Dubrovnik tram from 1912, a 1930s diving suit, old Yugoslav planes and a World War II Italian submarine that you can climb into. Available by guided tour only (3-4.30pm Tue-Fri, 10.30am-noon Sat, Sun; must request an English-speaking guide in advance) are three special exhibits: Nikola Tesla's demonstration cabinet, with re-creations of the inventor's machines and devices; a replica mineshaft; and a planetarium. On Sundays at 9.30am, hop on the museum's 1924 tram that does a city tour to Maksimir and back.

Botanical Gardens

Marulićev trg 9a (01 48 44 002). **Open** *Apr-Nov* 9am-2.30pm Mon, Tue; 9am-dusk Wed-Sun.

Top tables # Marcellino

A five-minute drive from the centre, arrival at **Marcellino** (*see p80*), as with so many places in Zagreb, is confusing. Am I in the right place? Where do I go? Walk on through the glass doors to find a 45-seater modern restaurant dominated by a glass wall overlooking a mature wood. Get a window seat if you can; when warm the glass doors open and you're sitting in a king's tree house. At night, lights illuminate the trees – stunning and almost magical. For interesting, ambitious international food, at a price, go no further.

The owner and head chef Mario personally oversees each ordered, symmetrical and delicate plate, training a surrounding army of sous chefs as he goes. Food as art comes at a price; a meal for two with wine will cost you around 1,000 kunas, a price even by London and New York standards. Having said this, if you want fillet of beef with rocket, parmesan and truffles, or venison with blueberries, chestnuts, pears and wine, or prawns with orange juice and olive oil, in a memorable setting, you won't be disappointed. This is a place to impress, to share your meal with embassy staff and local celebrities. Serious without being dull; formal without being stuffy. Zagreb's version of Gordon Ramsay at Claridge's may be pushing it but it's not a million miles away.

These lovely gardens, founded in 1889, contain giant trees, lily-pad-covered ponds, an English-style arboretum, symmetrical French-inspired flower beds and ten glasshouses, the latter closed to the public. About 10,000 plant species come mainly from Croatia, some from as far as Asia. It's a nice, shaded spot in summer, with plenty of benches.

Maksimir Park & Zoo

Maksimirski perivoj (01 23 02 198/www.zoo.hr). *Trams 11, 12 to Bukovačka.* **Open** *Park 8am-sunset* daily. *Zoo summer 9am-7pm daily; spring & autumn* 9am-6pm daily; winter 9am-3pm daily. *Ticket office closes 1hr before closing time.* **Admission** *Park free.* *Zoo 20kn; 10kn under-7s & Mon.* **No credit cards.**

A ten-minute tram ride east of the centre, 18 hectares (45 acres) of green expanse were opened to the public in 1794, with what was termed English-style landscaping. You can happily spend a day around its dense forests, long meadows, tree-lined alleys and man-made lakes. There are follies, too: the 1840 Echo Pavilion, the recently restored Swiss House and the three-floor Vidikovac Tower or Belvedere. At the far eastern end is the City Zoo with a modest collection of creatures and daily feeding times of seals, sea lions, otters and piranhas. Across the main road is Croatia's main football stadium and home of Dinamo Zagreb, also called the Maksimir. Its renovation in the summer of 2006 may be put on hold in order to host a Euro 2008 qualifying match with England in October. Thereafter it will be key to Croatia's bid to co-host Euro 2012 with Hungary.

Excursions

The forested slopes of **Mount Medvednica** beckon nature lovers for a hike, or a cablecar ride above the trees to the highest peak of **Sljeme**. More than half of Medvednica, Bear Mountain, is wooded, featuring forests of beech, oak, fir and maple, with extensive flora that includes 14 endemic and 93 endangered plant species. In spring and autumn, the area is at its most beautiful, with colourful flowers – from saffron to dog-tooth violets – and clear crisp horizons.

Sljeme (www.sljeme.hr) offers stellar vistas of Zagreb and the Zagorje countryside. This is where four-time Olympic champion Janica Kostelic learned to ski. It is now a major ski centre, recently introduced on to the prestigious World Cup programme, the course open for amateurs through the winter. There is night skiing, sledging and snowboarding too.

See p53 **Ski Zagreb**.

It can be reached by one of the many well-marked paths leading up from the foothills of Medvednica or by the 20-minute cablecar ride from the village of Gračanski Bliznec. A popular two-hour hike on central Medvednica leads from Tomislavov Dom hotel and restaurant to Medvedgrad, a recently renovated feudal fort erected in the 13th century, worth a wander for the views. The park's newest attraction is the renovated **Zrinski Mine** (10am-4pm Sat, Sun, 15kn/10kn) near the popular Grafičar mountain hut on central Medvednica, with life-size statues of miners, sounds of dripping water, pick blows in the rock and the creaking of wooden wheelbarrows.

The most popular day trip from Zagreb is one to **Samobor**, 23km (14 miles) west of the city, on the eastern slopes of the Samobor Hills. With medieval origins and baroque architecture, this charming village centres on Trg kralja Tomislava, a lovingly restored square lined with pastel-coloured 19th-century townhouses, traditional cafés and a clutch of churches. On the western side of the square stands the modest town museum (Livadičeva 7, 01 33 61 014, open 9am-3pm Tue-Fri, 9am-1pm Sat, Sun), with its small assortment of archaeological and ethnological items including furniture, pottery and a section on Croatian mountaineering. Just off the square is Little Venice, where wooden bridges criss-cross the Gradna brook. Try and see the collection at the **Marton Museum** (Jurjevska 7, 01 33 26 426, www.muzej-marton.hr, open 10am-1pm Sat, Sun, 15kn) showcasing 1,000 exhibits from Biedermeier furniture to 19th-century silverware and Russian porcelain. That aside, the reason why so many locals come here is for the famous Samobor *kremšnite*, the trademark cream pie available at central cafés such as **U prolazu** and **Livadić**.

For the region's best hiking and biking, head to **Žumberak-Samobor Mountains Nature Park**, which starts just 5km (3 miles) west of Samobor and extends a further 30km (19 miles). The area is difficult to reach by public transport, but if you do find your way here, you'll encounter a fantastic wilderness dotted with hilltop hamlets, extensive vineyards, karst canyons with waterfalls and old-fashioned watermills. Two information and eco centers are located at **Slani Dol** 6km (3.5 miles) west of Samobor and in the village of **Budinjak** 35km (22 miles) from town, with an archaeological site from the late Bronze Age.

Resources

For information on hiking trails and park attractions visit www.pp-medvednica.hr or www.sljeme.hr. To reach the cablecar, take tram No.14 to Mihaljevac then tram No.15 to the terminal at Dolje. You then have a ten-minute walk through a pedestrian tunnel for the cable-car station at Gračanski Bliznec.

For information about Žumberak-Samobor Mountains Nature Park, check www.ppzsg.org. For local buses, see the Samoborček (www.samoborcek.hr) schedule to Slani Dol and Budinjak. The Zagreb County Tourist Board (Preradovićeva 42, www.tzzz.hr) offers information and a set of excellent maps of the region's biking routes (www.pedala.hr). Samobor is a 45-minute ride by frequent buses from Zagreb's main bus station or from the Črnomerec bus terminal.

Where to eat

Zagreb is gentrifying fast, but you can still count on the fingers of one hand the genuinely quality global restaurants. As far as domestic ones go, you can taste traditional specialities from just about any region of Croatia – from Dalmatia to Zagorje – and in any price range. *Purgeri*, people from Zagreb, are meat lovers, so the capital is a carnivores' delight, particularly where pork and veal are concerned. The other local favourite is *štrukli*, little dough ravioli filled with cottage cheese, sometimes covered in breadcrumbs. Domestic restaurants abound in the city centre. If you're looking for a pricy blow-out, head for **Marcellino** or **Ogruljak**.

Transport details are given below where the venue is not within walking distance of Jelačić.

Asia
Šenoina 1 (01 48 41 218). **Open** noon-midnight daily. **Credit** AmEx, DC, MC, V.
While you can't expect a cheap feed at this upscale venue, you can expect the best Chinese in town. The kitsch is understated, the mix of Asian and Croatian staff courteous and swift, the clientele mainly businessmen, dignitaries and politicos. Offerings include the usual rice and noodle dishes with vegetables, meat or pricier seafood, plus specialities such as Asian duck with pancakes and Szechuan treats.

Baltazar
Nova Ves 4 (01 46 66 808). **Open** noon-midnight Mon-Sat. **Credit** AmEx, DC, MC, V.
In a little Kaptol courtyard, this rustic-style restaurant attracts an upmarket clientele with its superb traditional grills and regional meats from Zagorje and Slavonia. Duck and turkey are also featured. Service and presentation are impeccable, allowing the bill to creep up to 300kn a head with wine, but carnivores won't begrudge it in the slightest. In summer a pretty terrace of similarly rustic character comes into its own.

Boban
Gajeva 9 (01 48 11 549). **Open** 10am-midnight daily. **Credit** AmEx, DC, MC, V.
Named after its owner, Croatian World Cup star Zvonimir Boban, this popular two-storey operation is handily located just off Jelačić. Upstairs is a café, downstairs a faux-rustic, mainly Italian restaurant. Carlo Conforti's kitchen turns out a vast range of pastas (tagliolini with truffles, spaghetti with calamari and black olives) at giveaway prices of around

The snowy paths of **Medvednica**. *See p78.*

50kn a dish – and the portions are staggering. You probably won't need a starter, unless a group of you is sharing a Hunter's Plate (49kn) of venison salami and various cold meats. There are meaty mains, too, including veal chop (57kn) and grilled horsemeat (54kn). Dalmatian crème caramel, *rožata*, is among the desserts, and there are plenty of domestic wines.

Gostionica Tip-Top
Gundulićeva 18 (01 48 30 349). **Open** 7am-10pm Mon-Sat. **Credit** AmEx, DC, MC, V.
Locals know this age-old eatery as Blato as it's run by restaurateurs from Korčula. Little has changed here since Tin Ujević (*see p81* **The cat in the hat**) and his literary gang were regulars in the 1940s – except that their pictures have been mounted and an outline of Tin's iconic hat etched on to the windows. The front bar is authentically retro, the back dining room intimate. There are specials every day, Thursday's a quite outstanding octopus goulash (45kn) but you can also opt for red mullet, sole or sea bass at 300kn a kilo. Plenty of Pošip and other Korčula varieties on the wine list.

Ivica i Marica

Tkalčićeva 70 (01 48 28 999). **Open** noon-11pm
Tue-Sun. *Bakery* 9am-11pm daily. **Credit** AmEx,
DC, MC, V.
Named after Hansel and Gretel, this newly opened
venue next door to the bakery of the same name,
done out like in the fairy story, is Zagreb's leading
health-food restaurant. Its mission, as the board outside on atmospheric Tkalčićeva explains, is to serve
national staples with no preservatives, artificial
colouring or GMO ingredients. Expect seitan or tofu
instead of meat; wholewheat flour and brown sugar
replace the white varieties, even in the ice-cream.
The fish, though, is genuine, and delicious, the cod,
grouper and tuna available on Fridays. All bread,
noodles and pastries are made on the premises
(try *šufnudle*, boiled dumplings). Organic salads are
also available. The monthly five-course menu is
excellent value at 90kn.

Kerempuh

Kaptol 3 (01 48 19 000/www.kerempuh.hr). **Open**
9am-3pm, 7-11pm Mon-Sat. **Credit** AmEx, DC, MC, V.
So geared to the popular Kerempuh to the market
place it overlooks that it was only towards the end
of 2005 that it opened its doors in the evening. Then
as now, Anna Ugarković, who gained experience as
a cook in London's restaurants, rushes round the
market first thing in the morning to find fresh ingredients for the daily changing menu. Once decided
on, this is immediately posted up on the restaurant's
website so that the membership of laid-back young
professionals can choose their dish before they
arrive. There are always a couple of attractive vegetarian options among the reasonably priced meaty
ones. Relaxing atmosphere.

Korčula

Teslina 17 (01 48 72 159). **Open** *Mid Aug-mid July*
9am-10pm Mon-Sat; 9am-4pm Sun. **Closed** mid July-
mid Aug. **Credit** AmEx, DC, MC. V.
As traditional as it gets, this fish restaurant on the
corner of Teslina and Preradovićeva was here long
before the trendy bars set up around it. The huge
portions, the old-school staff, the dining booths, it
could be 1976. The kitchen turns out high-quality
versions of seafood standards, tuna fillets or grilled
squid with *blitva*, as well as a few specialities worth
trying, in particular a succulent baked octopus with
potatoes (92kn). There are scallops, breaded frog's
legs, and grouper or John Dory at 350kn a kilo.
Meats include Dalmatian *pašticada* (75kn), stewed
beef in wine sauce. Decent bottles of Dingač and
Pošip highlight a good wine selection of similarly
Dalmatian provenance.

Mano

Medvedgradska 2 (01 46 69 432). **Open** noon-11pm
Mon-Sat. **Credit** AmEx, DC, MC, V.
One of the newcomers on the Zagreb dining scene,
this is a classic case of style over substance, fashion over function. Up by the Kaptol Centar, Mano
presents itself as a fancy version of a traditional

steakhouse. In an airy interior of bare stone walls
and steel pillars, black-clad waiters deliver mainly
meaty mains with steep price tags. Specialities
include beef-steak Mano with peppers and rosemary, Lomo steak prepared on your own little table
grill, breaded venison with chestnuts, and wild-
boar polenta with gorgonzola. Stray from these
carnivorous choices and you find yourself and the
waitstaff struggling. Fish comes in small, poorly
presented portions, the cheese selection includes an
inexplicable brie from Dalmatia, a mystery to you
and your waiter. For an average price of 150kn a
main course, you might expect something better
around the edges.

Marcellino

Jurjevska 71 (01 46 77 111). **Open** *Sept-July* noon-
11pm Mon-Sat. **Closed** Aug. **Credit** AmEx, MC, V.
For interesting, ambitious international food, at a
price, go no further. *See p77* **Top tables.**

Maskin i lata

Andrije Hebranga 11a (01 48 18 273/
www.masklinilata.hr). **Open** noon-11pm Mon-Sat.
Credit AmEx, DC, MC, V.
Named after traditional Dalmatian wine-making
tools, this wine-cellar restaurant beneath the Old
Pharmacy pub, Maskini lata offers a taste of the
sea in the heart of the city. Only opened in 1999, it's
got the small, traditional, relaxed family feel just
about right. Most of the offerings have a fish or
seafood base – lobster, cod, monkfish, squid,
prawns, octopus – all combined with home-made
pasta, gnocchi, risotto, wild asparagus, Istrian truffles or turned into great stews. Try the *brodet* or
gregada or a big plate of mixed fish (priced by the
kilo) with *blitva* (a local green somewhere between
spinach and kale), the traditional accompaniment.
The meat, cheese and desserts are all good, too, but
it's the fish and the 45 different southern Croatian
wines that are the real stars here. Round off a few
lazy hours with a medica (sweet, warming honey
rakija) digestif. The old ship lamps lining the walls
and the friendly staff ensure Maskin i lata is calm
and confident without being showy or elitist.
Thoroughly recommended.

Okrugljak

Mlinovi 28 (01 46 74 112/www.okrugljak.hr). Tram
14 to Mihaljevac then a 300m walk. **Open** 10am-1am
daily. **Credit** AmEx, DC, MC, V.
The grande dame of Zagreb restaurants is a worthy
destination despite the hike to reach it. Its cachet
attracts old money and new jet set, munching and
mingling in the two high-ceilinged wooden-clad dining halls in a suburb below Sljeme. Top-rated traditional dishes from the Continent and the coast are
prepared with special care – from juicy barbecue meats
and uplifting blood sausages to super-fresh tuna fillets
and delectable lobster carpaccios. The pasta is made
on the premises, while the wine list boasts up to 100
domestic and overseas varieties. Reserve at weekends.
Average main course in the 150kn range.

The cat in the hat

Augustin 'Tin' Ujević (1891-1955) is widely considered the most important Croatian poet of the first half of the 20th century. A man of brilliant mind and wide education, with mastery of six languages, a deep knowledge of European culture and the world's religions, Tin was also a colourful character, with a reputation for bohemian living.

Something of his unconventional life is reflected in the fact that all kinds of Zagreb landmarks bear his name or image: the city's most famous second-hand bookshop on Zrinjevac; any number of bars and restaurants with his photograph or outline of his trademark hat (in particular his old haunt, the **Gostionica Tip-Top**, *pictured*; *see p79*); and, bizarrely but proudly, the duty-free bar at International Departures at Zagreb's Pleso airport. Your last drink will be in honour of Tin. Several schools in Croatia bear his name, and one of Jadrolinija's gleaming ferries.

Born in Dalmatia, Tin attended secondary school in Split and university in Zagreb. He was a rebellious student, actively opposing Austro-Hungarian rule and promoting the Serb-Croat-Slovene alliance that was to come into being in 1918. Arrested once in 1912 and twice in 1913 for his political ideas, he was drawn, like so many writers at the turn of the 20th century, to Paris, where he lived through World War I, spending many a noisy, sleepless night among the artists he met there. During the 1920s he lived mainly in the capital of the new Yugoslav state, Belgrade, and had the dubious honour of being expelled from the city on a number of occasions – in 1925, for instance, charged with 'vagrancy, indolence and bohemian disorderliness'. From 1930 to 1937, he lived in Sarajevo, then in Split, before settling finally in Zagreb

in 1940. There his name is associated particularly with the Kažalisna kavana (the Theatre Café), where he held court among a large group of admiring followers, although his sharp tongue often led to heated exchanges. Profoundly contemptuous of all convention and regulated urban life, he nonetheless loved Zagreb, where a bench in one of the local parks would often offer him a late night's rest.

A prolific poet, essayist and translator, Ujević struck a chord with many of his contemporaries through his highly original talent. His poetry is a serious endeavour to express the bewilderment of modern man in the face of general disillusion, isolation and lack of faith. Something, surely, we can all raise a glass to.

Opium Oriental Bar & Restaurant

Level -1, Branimir Centar, Branimirova 29 (01 46 15 679/www.opium.hr). **Open** 11am-midnight Thur-Sun; 11am-1am Fri, Sat. **Credit** AmEx, DC, MC, V.
This dark basement eatery by the Arcotel Allegra Hotel, in the bland surroundings of a shopping mall, serves pan-Asian food of a reasonable local standard, concentrating on Thai and Malay mainstays. Generous portions of curries and noodles, with teriyaki options, are served in an intimate purple and red, leather and wood interior with about a dozen tables. The glass cage kitchen displays oriental chefs busying themselves around woks, so preparation seems reasonably authentic,

although the place wouldn't last five minutes in London. An adjoining bar pulls in a lively crowd for its cheap cocktails.

Paviljon

Trg kralja Tomislava 22 (01 48 13 066). **Open** noon-midnight Mon-Sat. **Credit** AmEx, DC, MC, V.
Located at the Art Pavilion, opened in 1898, the Paviljon treats customers in a manner fitting to the ornate surroundings. A complimentary taster of a croissant with prosciutto arrives before your meal, and an equally complimentary herb brandy from Hvar completes it. In between, you can choose from a long list of Stanko Erceg's intelligently conceived

Best bars

Škola

This is the most fashionable bar in town – and you wouldn't know it was here. Among the façades of pedestrianised Bogovićeva, a plaque reads 'Škola' in four languages. The corridor gives nothing away, only a choice of cheap books. Another little sign suggests you mount the staircase. After passing lime-green sofa cut-outs, you enter an apartment door on the second floor and – wow! Everything is done in sci-fi film-set white, pink-shirted staff flitting between low sofas. It's no surprise that the main owner Boris Gregorić was a film producer. The 1.5 million euro overhaul of this former school (get it?) in 2002 set decorative standards for bar design in Croatia – and the trend for lounge bars in Zagreb. If a roof terrace is added in the summer of 2006, **Škola** (*see p87*) will be another first. Despite the cool minimalism, most cocktails are the same price as elsewhere, Caipiroskas, Appletinis and Daiquiris in the 40kn bracket. The 'Special & Unique' range (60kn) is mixed with several types of spirits, the long, mainly domestic wine list is well chosen, and snacks include tofu burgers and tortilla wraps – standard for London, revolutionary for Zagreb. There's a full-blown restaurant up a spiral staircase. DJs spin at weekends but there's a buzz all week, people knowing they're in the right place at the right time.

dishes featuring saffron, sage, basil and other herbs, laden with healthy vegetables. Appetisers (80kn-120kn) include swordfish carpaccio, shrimp and fennel salad and goose liver in Cumberland sauce, salads (70kn-80kn) including spinach with bacon and prawn or lentil, mint and grilled cheese. For the mains (about 100kn), the crispy roast duck comes with red cabbage and figs, the grilled swordfish with fennel seeds and the pork medallions in truffle sauce with polenta and parsley. A side dish of steamed vegetables (25kn) is a fine accompaniment. Wines run from a Zlatna Otok (65kn) to a Grgić Plavac Mali (195kn), with several fine examples from Slovenia.

Pod Gričkim Topom

Zakmardijeve stube 5 (01 48 33 607). **Open** *July, Aug* 7-11pm Mon-Sat. *Sept-June* 11am-11pm Mon-Sat; 11am-5pm Sun. **Credit** AmEx, DC, MC, V.

This leafy enclave is right underneath the Grič cannon. The terrace, lined with colourful flowerpots and paintings of Zagreb, is a summer evening favourite. On offer are dishes from different regions of Croatia: Dalmatian *pašticada* and monkfish carpaccio, Zagreb steak (filled with ham and cheese) and *zagorski štrukli* for dessert. The portions are well sized, service is excellent and the clientele cosmopolitan. It's a hive of activity when the weather's nice, so do make dinner reservations.

TakeNoko

Kaptol Centar, Nova Ves 17 (01 48 60 530/ www.takenoko.hr). **Open** noon-1am Mon-Sat; noon-6pm Sun. **Credit** AmEx, DC, MC, V.

The only Japanese restaurant in town, an upmarket restaurant on the ground floor of the Kaptol Centar at the top of Tkalčićeva, provides a welcome break from the usual heavy stomach-filling options elsewhere in town. The three-part menu and the wine list get rave reviews by local critics and foodies, and the menu features fusion dishes like grilled goose liver with mooli and shiitake mushrooms along with the usual sushi and tempura ones. Not cheap, mains at 150kn-200kn a go, but worth every lipa.

Vinodol

Teslina 10 (01 48 11 427/www.vinodol-zg.hr). **Open** 10am-midnight daily. **Credit** AmEx, DC, MC, V.

Well-prepared Central European fare at moderate prices, and a mixed bag of local and overseas patrons. You can dine on the covered patio terrace accessed through an ivy-clad passageway off Teslina; the cold weather alternative is the massive dining hall with vaulted stone ceilings. The service is swift and the cuisine heavy on meat. Highlights include the succulent lamb; veal and potatoes under *peka* (traditionally baked in a coal oven); and more unusual options like pork fillets with dried plum sauce. Of the lighter alternatives, go for trout with almonds or grilled *bukovače* (local wild mushrooms). A popular lunchtime spot, so be prepared to wait.

Immaculate pedigree and lovely lakeside location – nightspot **Aquarius**. *See p88.*

Where to drink

A new bar scene has hit town, flagshipped by the self-styled coolest spot in town, **Škola**. The handful of trendy new joints around it – **Apartman**, Golf Caffè, Pif, **Maraschino** – now create a right-angle of chic drinking by the flower market on Preradovićev trg, two minutes from Jelačić. On the other side of the square, by the market, run the parallel pair of streets that comprised the bar quarter through the 1980s and '90s: **Opatinova** and **Tkalčićeva**. The latter has lost its verve, but Tkalčićeva is still a great night out. Bohemian **Melin** is a shabby wonder, and the simple **Funk Club** comes alive at night. A bar crawl here is ramshackle and random, a world away from the cosmopolitan sheen of Preradovićeva.

Mention must be made of Zagreb's penchant for music bars and clubs – fine establishments such as **Spunk** and **Limb** are too small to stage live acts, but they are laudably fussy about the sounds they play. *See p84* **Zagreb music city**.

Transport details are given below if the venue is a trek from Jelačić. Note that few bars accept credit cards; details are given of those that do.

Apartman

Preradovićeva 7 (01 48 72 168). **Open** 9am-midnight Mon-Wed, Sun; 9am-1am Thur-Sat.

One of the new collective of bars near the flower market, Apartman is a funky first-floor spot on the corner with Teslina. Incongruously, it was the HQ of the local scouts' association, signified by a plaque and an outdoor scene covering one wall. A young clientele intertwine on big bright cushions by day; by night, DJs occasionally take over.

Booksa

Martićeva 14d (01 46 16 124/www.booksa.hr). *Trams 1 & 17 to Trg burze.* **Open** 9am-11pm Tue-Sun.

Zagreb's first and so far only literary club doubles as a café, a collective run by three enthusiastic women. The books are Croatian only, but the music is good, the atmosphere laid-back and regular events include exhibits, concerts and readings, some by visiting English speakers. Worth the quick tram ride or 15-minute walk from the centre.

Cica Bar

Tkalčićeva 18 (no phone). **Open** 9am-11pm daily.

This tiny storefront 'graperia, cafeteria and galleria' is the most underground place you'll find on the tatty Tkalčićeva strip. A funky interior contains works by local artists, flea market finds and frequently changing, controversial art installations in the side window. Grab a seat here or at an outside table to try the home-made *rakija* fruit brandy for which Cica is famous: blueberry, honey, nut, fig, anis, mixed herbs. Staff also sprinkle the coffee with cinnamon, a nice touch. Cica hosts grills and DJ sessions, but hedonism and random sounds seem to be the main attraction here.

Zagreb music city

The Zagreb live music scene is rediscovering itself after a decade of isolation. The domestic and international acts performing here every month are of a quality and variety way above what should be expected of a young capital of only a million people. The punk scene of the Kulušic and the Lapidarij clubs, captured by Igor Mirkovic in his 2003 film *Sretno Dijete* ('Lucky Child'), has long gone. Gone, too, are the 1990s that followed, when artists feared to visit. Zagreb is open again, its audiences cool, lively and astute.

Zagreb boasts a handful of small and mid-range venues, plus large halls for the big names. You can find everything from underground to post-rock, avant-jazz to hip hop, by unknowns or cultish artists such as Lambchop and Thievery Corporation. DJ clubs such as **Aquarius** (*see p88*) host live bands and notable live music spots host DJs.

Watch out for posters along Ilica or flyers in bars such as **Sedmica** (*see p86*) and **Dobar Zvuk** (*see p86*). Check also the websites of the key venues, given in the listings section, plus the portal www.muzika.hr.

For an intimate, adventurously programmed venue, head straight for **KSET** (*see p88*). A club for 400 people, it's part of the University of Electrotechnical Science and for the last 25 years has actively promoted new bands,

domestic and international. Since 1999, thanks to an agile promoter, KSET has become an oasis for underground, post-rock, americana, avant-jazz, punk and lots of other stylistically diverse artists. At least one night a week, generally at the weekend, the speakers are given over to electronic music, often drum 'n' bass. It's a very friendly atmosphere, with an easygoing crowd enjoying cheap drinks.

In a similar vein but more underground, the **Močvara** (*see p88*) on the banks of the Sava holds 700 people in an abandoned factory imaginatively muralled by Igor Hofbauer. Shows here are completely random: punk, metal, world music, whatever, plus DJ nights at least monthly. Art-rock, anarcho-punk types haunt the bar.

The new venue in town, **Boogaloo** (*see p88*), has a long pedigree. It occupies the OTV Dom building on Vukovarska, scene of seminal shows by Laibach and Einstürzende Neubauten in the early 1980s. Holding 1,000 people, it mixes live music (Bill Wyman's Rhythm Kings) and DJs (Sven Väth). The best mid-sized venue is **Tvornica** (*see p90*), run by the man responsible for the legendary Kulušic. With a capacity of 1,500, its gig list since opening in 1999 includes the Asian Dub Foundation, the Residents, Henry Rollins,

David Byrne and the MC5. World music is big on the agenda as well as club nights such as Stereo Studio. Good bar too.

Pauk (Jarunska 2, tram 17 to Horvati) is set in student halls of residence; **Purgeraj** (Ribnjak 1, www.purgeraj.hr) has live blues and rockabilly, plus plenty of local brands of *rakija*. The age-old **Jabuka** (Jabukovac 28, 01 48 34 397, bus 101 from Britanski trg) was an important live venue in its day but now plays the punk hits of yesteryear.

The **BP Club** (*see p88*) in the centre of town is a temple of jazz. Run by Croatia's most important jazz musician, vibraphonist Boško Petrović, this intimate basement is lined with pictures of the famous exponents (Art Farmer, Joe Pass, Ronnie Scott) who have played on its tiny stage in the corner. Superb choice of wines, beers and spirits too. It stages two festivals: Springtime Jazz Fever in late March and Hrvatski Jazz Sabor in early October. At the other side of Jelačić, Sax! (Palmotićeva 22, 01 48 72 836, www.sax-zg.hr) is owned by the Croatian Musicians' Union and holds impromptu sessions and album promotions from Tuesday to Saturday.

Zagreb is also a master of the music bar. These are hangouts where there is no admission, perhaps a DJ, but where the management is fussy about the music being played. The music bar *par excellence* is **Spunk** (*see p87*). With comic-book decor by the same designer, Igor Hofbauer, as the nearby Močvara, it's a place for garage punk c1966 and underground rock 'n' roll c1985. If that's your bag, come here on a Friday night and treat your ears till 3am. Near KSET, **Limb** (*see p87*) is another must. A cult bar for ten years, it's run by Selma, with a Tarantino sense of musical drama: Tex-Mex, French chansons, the Strokes. At weekends you'll find her by the stereo and playing weird CDs by herself. The former Limb barman Željko now runs downtown **Dobar Zvuk** (*see p86*), a rock music hangout for pretty young punks.

Sedmica (*see p86*) plays ambient, lounge and trip hop with occasional dollops of indie. For honest to goodness, classic hard-drinking rock and blues, **Route 66** (*see p87*), with photos of Bill Wyman and Cliff Williams from AC/DC from their respective visits, is a low-ceiling, cheap-drink, dirty roadhouse bar and musicians' hangout. Many come for the Velebit, the best Croatian beer, others for the country cover bands on Thursdays or demo debuts.The current nightcap venue is **Papillon** (*see p87*), a riverboat, playing reggae and world music till the early hours. You might even catch stand-up on Fridays. Sign the petition against its 11am closure.

Best bars Sedmica

Sedmica (*see right*) does not seek publicity or wish to attract the casual passers-by. It's one of those cult bars that prefer not to be listed in guidebooks, and do little to advertise their presence on the street. It's easily missed, even if you know where you're going, the only clue being a small protruding Guinness sign above a residential doorway. Around a decade ago, a group of students from the nearby Academy of Fine Arts discovered Sedmica and decided to adopt it. Today it's the favourite meeting place of current and former students from all fields of creative arts, who gather here from the mid-morning until late at night to talk and drink. It's an obvious rendezvous before a private view at a trendy gallery or for an impromptu cast party.

You enter through a corridor lined with concert and exhibition posters and invitation cards pinned to the wall. Inside, a small room contains a crowded bar counter upon which stand taps of Fischer's and Erdinger. Long, thin marble tables provide a place to prop, otherwise you can join the boho crew on the wrought-iron mezzanine behind. The most regular of the regulars include the informal Zagreb artists' group made up of the sculptor Denis Krašković, painter Danko Friščić, video artist Davor Mezak and performance artist Marijan Crtalič. They are famous for their provocative group shows that usually include giant installations constructed from discarded TVs and other urban detritus, and for artistic reconstructions of sci-fi horror movies. They're part of the furniture, proud of their own interventions in the space over the years, including the wall designs behind the bar and countless live performances between friends.

Dobar Zvuk

Gajeva 18 (01 48 72 222). **Open** noon-11pm Mon-Sat.
Suitably set in an old hi-fi store, this superior music bar is a lively and popular rendezvous for younger, spiky-haired locals and older rockers. *See p84* **Zagreb music city**.

Fanatik

Ribnjak 26 (no phone). **Open** 8pm-4am Tue-Sat.
On the Ribnjak slope, this red-lit, zebra-striped room attracts a gay/straight mix. A busy bar in the mid 1990s, the Fanatik closed for a while, reopening as

a mature late-night club-bar, the perfect antidote to the teenage fumblings in the park across the road.

Funk Club

Tkalčićeva 52 (no phone). **Open** 9am-1am daily.
A standard café-bar by day, by night the Funk Club becomes a lively scene indeed. Spontaneous interaction sparks around a horseshoe bar, while thumping beats come up from the cellar. Down a spiral staircase, in a small plain basement with stone vaulted ceilings, DJs spin catchy tunes (house, jazz and broken beats) to a dance-happy crowd. Unqualified fun.

Hemingway Lounge Bar

Trg Maršala Tita (www.hemingway.hr). **Open** 7am-3am daily. **Credit** AmEx, DC, MC, V.

Hemingway is a chain of upmarket cocktail bars with three branches in Zagreb. This one is the most popular, mainly because of its location opposite the National Theatre. The classy one is at Tuškanac (No.1, no phone, open 9am-2am Mon-Thur, 9am-5am Fri, Sat) in leafy Gradec, with a pay-in club (25kn) at weekends. Look out for Marin Nekić's original mixes, such as My Way Or The Highway or a Royal Red Virus, shaken with aplomb at mixology contests around the world. Here, three small, stylish rooms have TVs, crystal chandeliers and photos of Papa. In summer pavement tables pack with the pretty set posing over cocochinos and finger food by day, Mai Tais and Long Island Ice Teas at night.

Indy Bar

Vranicanijeva 6 (no phone). **Open** 9am-1am daily.

An eclectic cocktail bar set in a cobbled Upper Town courtyard, the Indy presents a contemporary, jazzy musical backdrop (with occasional jazz concerts) to complement a decorative one of an old radiogram, a ceiling constructed of surfboards and a back bar display of magnifying glasses. The drinks list is extensive and cheap, the service friendly. Not as bohemian as it makes out to be, but a welcome pit stop after a sightseeing wander.

Kolaž

Amruševa 11 (no phone). **Open** 7am-11pm Mon-Sat.

Owned by a one-time staff member at Limb (*see below*), this small red-brick basement bar attracted much attention when it opened at the end of 2005. Draught beers are Starobrno and (unusually) dark Gösser, with a few Belgian varieties (Kriek, Chimay of all colours) by the bottle. It's a rare Lower Town spot for breakfast, offering coffee for 18kn, orange juice and toast, and by the evening a well-chosen music backdrop (Velvets, indie) kicks in.

Krivi Put

Runjaninova (no phone). **Open** 6pm-1am Mon-Sat.

Already rich in kudos – this bare courtyard building was the first site of the Močvara (*see p90*) club – Wrong Way comes to you from the people behind the Melin (*see right*) in Tkalčićeva. The naked lightbulbs in primary colours are a decorative statement, the sparse art and Stefan Lupino photographs being illuminated by strip lighting. One end features a sturdy bar counter, the other a small stage. Expect this to be a prime hangout by the autumn of 2006.

Limb

Plitvička 16 (01 61 71 683). Tram 13 to Miramarska. **Open** 9am-1am Mon-Sat.

Back in the day, Limb was *the* spot for music fans. Underground, understated, right by the KSET club, it was everyone's hangout. It's since lost its edge, although older boho types still occupy the three tiny colourful rooms and the glass-enclosed terrace with a tree in the middle. Chatty Francophile bar owner

Selma is still responsible for the music (*see p84* **Zagreb music city**), providing Beaujolais in the autumn and chansons on the stereo all year round.

Maraschino

Margaretska 1 (01 48 12 612). **Open** 8am-1am Mon-Sat; 9am-1am Sun.

Named after the sweet cherry liqueur from Zadar, Maraska, this two-floor spot in trendy bar central is packed to the rafters in the evenings, but a low-key place to try a few local tipples by day. Its brown interior decked out in old Maraska promotional posters, it offers Maraska-infused coffee or hot chocolate, long drinks, and Malvazija and Babić wines. Expect DJ sessions at weekends.

Melin

Tkalčićeva 47 (01 48 28 966). **Open** 9am-1am daily.

The spirit of old Zagreb, Melin is a cult spot off Tkalčićeva, scruffy but with bags of character. The colourful interior is grungy, the air thick with smoke and the music deafening. At weekends drunken teenagers and older alternative types spill out on to the side terrace, the playground on the grounds in front or the Portal alongside. The recent move of management to the Krivi Put (*see left*) may see a more bland musical soundtrack at weekends.

Papillon

Veslačka (www.papillon-zg.hr). Trams 14 & 17 to Veslačka. **Open** 8pm-late daily.

The trendiest of the riverboat bars, currently organising a petition to stay open later than a threatened 11pm closure. *See p84* **Zagreb music city**.

Route 66

Paromlinska 47 (01 61 18 737). Tram 13 to Lisinski. **Open** 9am-1am daily.

Zagreb's rock bar par excellence, Route 66 features live music, pool tables and highly sought-after Velebitsko beer. *See p84* **Zagreb music city**.

Sedmica

Kačićeva 7a (01 48 46 689). Trams 1, 6, 11 to Britanski trg. **Open** 8am-11pm daily.

Cult bar under a Guinness sign. *See p86* **Best bars**.

Škola

Bogovićeva 7 (01 48 28 197/www.skolalounge bar.com). **Open** 9am-1am Mon-Wed; 9am-4am Thur-Sat. **Credit** MC, V.

The place to be. *See p82* **Best bars**.

Spunk

Hrvatske bratske zajednice (01 61 51 528). Tram 13 to Lisinski. **Open** 7am-midnight Mon-Wed; 7am-3am Thur-Sat; 6pm-midnight Sun.

Top of the music bars and hangout places in Zagreb. By the National and University Libraries, Spunk is a coffee-break bar for students during the day, assuming an identity of garage rock bar serving discerning bohos by night. Perhaps it's the comic-book murals of Igor Hofbauer, artist at the Močvara club (*see p92*) nearby. *See p84* **Zagreb music city**.

Nightlife

The thriving club scene of the mid 1990s has gone. **Aquarius**, the number one club for electronic music since 1992, still rules but its status is being challenged by the fancier, more exclusive and internationally prestigious **Gallery**. The music scene itself is being taken over by the infamous **turbofolk** (*see p65*). Vulgar, banal and defiantly Balkan, its mix of mindless electropop and folk is taking hold, helped by the influential Pink TV beamed in from Belgrade. At weekends, a blanket policy of house and techno seems to dampen out any taste for R&B and hip hop during the week. In summer, the scene ups sticks and moves to the coast.

Most venues cannot run by just DJs or live bands alone. Key live venues, such as **KSET**, **Močvara** and **Tvornica** will have at least one night a month set aside for electronic music.

Mention must be made of the recently opened **Boogaloo**, the former OTV Dom, offering more of a DJ scene than live action. Zagreb's pedigree as far as the latter is concerned is second to none. *See p84* **Zagreb music city**.

Transport details are given if the venue is a trek from Jelačić. Few places accept credit cards; details are given of those that do. Admission prices are generally 30kn-60kn. Gallery, especially, demands smart wear.

Aquarius

Aleja Matije Ljubeka (01 36 40 231/www.aquarius.hr). Tram 17 to Horvati. **Open** *Café* 9am-9pm daily. *Club* 10pm-6am daily.

This highly professional Jarun lakeside club pioneered many of the firsts in Zagreb, including the one for electronic music. Opened in 1992, this 1,300-capacity two-floor venue lead the scene through the '90s and still is ahead of the field. This is partly due to the fresh sounds of Kontrapunkt DJs (in particular Eddy Ramich) who offer future jazz and broken beat treats, and partly because of the adaptability of the venue itself. Aquarius can turn itself into a mid-sized concert hall, hosting Mercury Rev in late 2005, for example. Fridays are sacrosanct, Blackout Lounge seeing the dancefloor and huge covered terrace jammed with young things getting down to commercial hip hop and R&B. In summer, Aquarius opens its beach branch at Zrče at Novalja on Pag. *See p176* **Balkan Ibiza**.

Best

Jarunska cesta 5 (01 30 11 943/www.thebest.hr). Trams 14 & 17 to Savski Most. **Open** 10pm-7am Fri, Sat.

This is the closest Zagreb gets to having a mega-club, with a schedule of mainstream events and lots of glitz. Body & Soul weekend parties are all the rage; the once-monthly Astralis trance fest also pulls in a crowd. The music, house, techno and disco, is invariably commercial, though you might catch a new local DJ talent on the decks.

Boogaloo

OTV Dom, Vukovarska 68 (01 63 13 021/www. boogaloo.hr). Tram 13 to Miramarksa. **Open** Call for details.

A 15-minute walk from Jelačić, Boogaloo is a DJ club and live venue, recently opened in the OTV Dom building. *See p84* **Zagreb music city**.

BP Club

Teslina 7 (01 48 14 444/www.bpclub.hr). **Open** 10am-2am Mon-Sat; 5pm-2am Sun.

BP is Zagreb's most prestigious jazz club, managed by vibraphonist Boško Petrović. *See p84* **Zagreb music city**.

Gallery

Matije Ljubeka (091 113 32 21 mobile). Tram 17 to Horvati. **Open** 10am-1am Mon-Wed, Sun; 10am-4am Thur-Sat. **Credit** DC, MC, V.

Damir and the crew from the hugely successful Hacienda in Vodice on the coast opened this exclusive club in the former premises of the Baobab by Lake Jarun. DJs who have starred at the Hacienda, such as Ian Pooley, David Guetta, Martin Solveig, as well as Hector Romero and David Morales, all performed here in 2005/6. An aura of exclusivity is maintained by the club keeping a tight control on ticket numbers, its doormen huge and dress code pretty strict. No trainers here, please. Once you've passed the face test, you get to rub shoulders with the Croatian variety of bling, with a random hipster thrown in. Inside is pretty funky, certainly not swanky, and the wooden terrace is a boon, with intimate tent-like booths. If you're in, it's good fun.

Global

Pavla Hatza 14 (01 48 14 878/www.globalclubzg.hr). **Open** *Cafe & shop* 8pm-2am Mon, Tue, Sun. *Club* 8pm-4am Wed-Sat.

The first and so far only dedicated gay club in Zagreb attracts a mixed crowd. A café and sex shop by day, it's a hopping spot after dark, with three bars, a VIP lounge, a dancefloor and a darkroom. A programme of strippers and queer movie nights is part of the build-up to the big event of the week, Saturday Night Fever.

KSET

Unska 3 (01 61 29 999/www.kset.org). Tram 13 to Miramarska. **Open** 8pm-midnight Mon-Fri; 9pm-3am Sat.

Excellent, adventurous music venue for live music during the week and DJs at weekends, and well worth the hassle of finding it. *See p84* **Zagreb music city**.

Močvara

Trnjanski nasip (01 60 55 599/www.mochvara.hr). Tram 13 to Lisinski. **Open** 8pm-1am Mon-Thur, Sun; 8pm-4am Fri, Sat.

Zagreb by design

Three shops illustrate Zagreb's burgeoning fashion scene. The most recent to open is also the most revolutionary: Victor. Spread over three floors, **Victor** (*pictured right; see p92*) brings the concept of a concept store to Croatia. Best illustrated by trend-setting Colette in Paris (the inspiration for Victor), the concept store gathers exclusive, quirky and sought-after products under one smartly designed roof, in a three-dimensional one-stop lifestyle shop window. Victor is thus a first for the region. The womenswear (ground floor) and menswear (first floor) sections feature the best Croatian names, including **I-GLE** (*see below*), and global ones such as JP Gaultier, Patrick Cox, Yohji Yamamoto and Comme des Garçons. Alongside are exclusive perfumes, cookbooks, candles and other accessories. A delicatessen in the basement contains authentic Croatian products (Dalmatian jams, olive oils, bottles of *rakija*), all tastefully packaged, and a stylish flower shop. The top-floor café is worth a visit alone, white floors and walls, clear perspex chairs with an orchid flower on each and a beautiful art deco white sofa in the middle. It's all as intentionally random as the birch logs in the menswear area, setting an intriguing tone.

The staff are well trained, offering friendly advice but leaving you be to enjoy the space.

I-GLE (*see p91*) is the flagship store of local designers Martina Vrdoljak Ranilović and Nataša Mihaljčišin. The name a play on words ('sewing needle' and 'look!'), I-GLE offers striking designs for womens- and menswear, some in manifold layers, others with bizarre colour combinations. Their label enjoys cult status in Zagreb, where they have made clothes for several theatre productions.

More mainstream and hugely successful, the refined feminine glamour of the **Gharani Štrok** line was created in 1995 by Nargess Gharani and Vanja Štrok, graduates from the Surrey Institute of Art & Design near London. Vanja's mother Renata is a renowned interior designer, her father Goran owns the Adriatic Luxury Hotels group. Gharani Štrok's first outlet was at Dubrovnik's Hotel Excelsior, their second (*pictured left; see p92*) opened in Zagreb in May 2005, a store they designed themselves. In between, the global renown of their pret-à-porter label spread: five catwalk shows at London Fashion Week, and the GS line stocked at Debenham's stores over the UK. With ten factories running, GS are branching into interiors, shoes and jewellery.

Musical differences Hladno Pivo

Punk is still alive and kicking in Zagreb. The evidence? **Hladno Pivo** ('Cold Beer'), currently the most popular rock band in the country. With five studio albums in 12 years, Hladno Pivo are listened to by teenagers and thirtysomethings alike. Their simple, fast, loud and energetic tunes sing of Croatian society from the early 1990s to date, their lyrics pouring irony, humour and cynicism on to politicans, the police and band members themselves. It's streetwise. They didn't have to look too far. When Hladno Pivo received their first national music award, the Porin, in 1994, two band members were selling newspapers on the streets of their native Gajnice, a working-class suburb on the western outskirts of Zagreb. Broke, living at home with unemployed parents, the punk life. These days, they sell out Zagreb's 10,000-capacity Dom Sportova (as a landmark show in 2005 proved). Hladno Pivo sell out? They'd drink warm beer first.

The Swamp is where young alternatives gather for underground fun. *See p84* **Zagreb music city**.

Tvornica

Šubićeva 2 (01 46 5 5 007/www.tvornica-kulture.hr).
Trams 1 & 17 to Šubićeva. **Open** *Café* 8am-10pm daily. *Club* 10pm-4am daily.
Concert venue with an excellent local pedigree. *See p84* **Zagreb music city**.

Where to shop

Nothing reflects Zagreb's rapid gentrification more than its shopping scene. Three businesses stand out in particular: **I-GLE**, flagship of local designers Martina Vrdoljak Ranilović and Nataša Mihaljčišin who stock their menswear at **Victor**, the region's first concept store; and **Gharani Štrok**, an established global brand at the forefront of the pret-à-porter market (*see p89* **Zagreb by design**). All are Croatian, all have key stores in Zagreb's city centre.

The other main name in the world of local fashion design is **Sinha-Stanić**. The big hit at London Fashion Week in 2005, British-born Fiona Sinha and Aleksandar Stanić from Zagreb met at St Martin's College, joined forces in 2004 and such was the reception for their first collection at Fashion Fringe that prestigious Italian luxury goods company AEFFE signed them up. On sale at

London's Selfridges and Harvey Nichols, they're tipped to be the next big thing.

Kathy Balogh (Radićeva 22, 01 48 13 290, open 8am-noon, 4-7pm Mon-Fri, 9am-2pm Sat) is avant-garde of the old school, but reliably challenging, and always likely to surprise you. **Leonarda L.** (Gajeva 9, 01 48 75 045, open 9am-8pm Mon-Fri, 9am-3pm Sat) is unusual in that it's run by the wife of star footballer Zvonimir Boban, but whose designs are tasteful, more bohemian than bling.

Croata is the renowned brand of handmade silk ties, their heritage dating back to the very origins of the word 'cravat'. Neckties *à la croate* became chic in 17th-century France after being worn by Croatian soldiers. The Croata company has nine branches across the country, including two in Zagreb.

Ilica is the traditional hub of Zagreb's shopping scene. Today the little shopfronts of its two-storey houses contain Mango, Lush and local fashion stores **Image Haddad** (No.6, 01 48 31 035) and **Heruc Galerija** (No.26, 01 48 33 569) beside shops unchanged since 1978.

Off Ilica, **Frankopanska** is Zagreb's exclusive shopping street. Here you find upmarket outlets such as Lacoste and Diesel as well as Gaultier, Galliano and Moschino. Shoe shops include many UK and European high-street brands.

The recently opened **Centar Kaptol** (www.centarkaptol.hr), past the cathedral on Nova Ves, is as posh as any shopping mall gets in Zagreb. This is where you'll find the likes of Marks & Spencer, Paul & Shark Yachting and Hugo Boss.

Britanski trg off Ilica is good for antiques on Sundays though prices can look steep – it's up to you to bargain. For a **flea market**, **Hreljić** in the far south-eastern corner of Novi Zagreb runs on Sundays. Leave yourself half a day to get there by bus and rummage through the mountains of junk. Back in town, both the **flower market** on Preradovićev trg and the main **Dolac** produce market off Jelačić are excellent. If you're looking for Croatian products as presents, look no further than **Bornstein** (Kaptol 19, 01 48 12 361, open 9am-8pm Mon-Sat), a delightful wine cellar in Kaptol stocking global as well as the best quality domestic wines, olive oils and other local gourmet items.

For books and magazines, particularly English-language ones, **Algoritam** (Gajeva 1, 01 48 18 672, open 8am-9pm Mon-Fri, 8am-3pm Sat) is well stocked and right on Jelačić. Good selection of travel guides too.

Croata

Prolaz Oktogon, Ilica 5 (01 48 12 726/ www.croata.hr). **Open** 8am-8pm Mon-Fri; 8am-3pm Sat. **Credit** AmEx, DC, MC, V.

One of the most fashionable stores in town when it opened in 1995, the Croata flagship salon in the capital offers scarves, shawls, shirts and vests, along with its trademark ties with traditional Croatian designs. Shops in Split, Dubrovnik and elsewhere. **Branch**: Kaptol 13 (01 48 14 600).

Dolac

Dolac. **Open** 6am-2pm Mon-Fri; 6am-3pm Sat; 6am-2pm Sun.

The daily market on a raised square a set of stairs up from Jelačić has been the city's major trading place since 1930. Farmers from surrounding villages come to sell their homemade foodstuffs and some of the freshest fruit and veg you'll ever taste. In the covered market downstairs are butchers, fishmongers and old ladies selling *sir i vrhnje* (cottage cheese and cream). Fresh flowers and lace are also sold.

I-GLE

Radićeva 25 (01 48 12 952/www.i-gle.com). **Open** 9am-8pm Mon-Fri; 9am-3pm Sat. **Credit** AmEx, DC, MC, V.

Striking threads. *See p89* **Zagreb by design.**

Trg bana Josipa Jelačića. See p69.

Gharani Štrok

*Dežmanov prolaz 5 (01 48 46 152/www.gharani
strok.co.uk).* **Open** 9am-1pm, 5-8pm Mon-Fri; 9am-
1pm Sat. **Credit** AmEx, DC, MC, V.
This flagship store for the pret-à-porter label was
opened in May 2005. *See p89* **Zagreb by design**.

Victor

Kralja Držislava 10 (01 45 72 921/www.victor.hr).
Open 10am-8pm Mon-Fri; 9am-3pm Sat. **Credit**
AmEx, DC, MC, V.
Croatia's very first concept store. *See p89* **Zagreb
by design**.

Where to stay

The lack of affordable accommodation is one
of the reasons why Zagreb still hasn't come
up from its up-and-coming status. While you'll
find plenty of luxury lodging options in the city
centre, mid-range alternatives are thin on the
ground. Most are a tram ride away and only
about 100kn less expensive than their city-
centre counterparts. A couple of hostels cater
for the budget traveller looking for a no-frills
overnight – but the central Omladinski
(Petrinjska 77, 01 48 41 267, 600kn) is in need of
renovation. Most hotels hike their prices by 20
per cent for trade fairs in April and September.

If you're staying at least three days, you
may want to consider short-term rental through
Nemoj Stati (www.nest.hr), an agency with
apartments – from studios to two bedrooms –
in the city centre. Prices range between 400kn
and 640kn per night; all include bedding and
towels, plus cleaning and laundry once a week.
Discounts apply for stays longer than 14 nights.

Arcotel Allegra

*Branimirova 29 (01 46 96 000/fax 01 46 96 096/
www.arcotel.at).* **Rates** €152-€162 double; €14
breakfast. **Credit** AmEx, DC, MC, V.
Zagreb's first designer hotel, owned by an Austrian
chain. It's a self-consciously chic spot with a Med
theme and young staff. The marble-clad lobby, with
an aquarium and colourful fish, gives access to the
easily passable Radicchio restaurant. The 151
uncluttered rooms come with good soundproofing,
pine furniture, funky fabrics with portraits of
celebrities (Kahlo, Picasso and Kafka) and DVD
players. Look out for the world map, with a red dot
marking Zagreb, on the blue carpets in hallways
and rooms, and star constellations on elevator ceilings. The top floor has a sauna and gym, and nice
rooftop views. The on-site Joe's Bar hosts weekly
Latino nights with dance shows. Ask about attractive weekend rates.

Best Western Hotel Astoria

*Petrinjska 71 (01 48 08 900/910/fax 01 48 17 053/
www.bestwestern.com).* **Rates** €114-€147 double.
Credit AmEx, DC, MC, V.

Best Western bought this 1932 hotel between the
train station and Jelačić, and, after a floor-to-ceiling
makeover, unveiled it in 2005 as one of its 45 pre-
mier properties. A lobby of wood panelling, plush
red armchairs and marble floors leads to red-
carpeted hallways lined by replicas of Croatian masterpieces. Rooms range from smallish twins and
queens to more spacious executives and suites with
window-paned sliding doors. Decor features a
palette of beiges, yellows and creams and contemporary paintings. High-speed internet too.

Hotel Central

*Branimirova 3 (01 48 41 122/40 555/fax 01 48 41
304/www.hotel-central.hr).* **Rates** €99-€107 double.
Credit AmEx, DC, MC, V.
If you're arriving by train, this is the cheapest decent
place to stay, right opposite the train station. The
nondescript four-storey building features a pokey
lobby and 79 smallish but clean rooms with en-suite
bathrooms (some with showers, some with tubs),
wall-to-wall green carpeting and an abundance of
unnecessary furniture. Request one of the larger
courtyard-facing rooms on the top floors – these are
quiet, with leafy views.

Hotel Dubrovnik

*Gajeva 1 (01 48 63 500/501/fax 01 48 63 506/
www.hotel-dubrovnik.hr).* **Rates** €142-€163 double.
Credit AmEx, DC, MC, V.
Watch Zagreb's daily action unroll from your window at this four-star right off the main square. The
complex comprises two six-storey buildings. The
older, from 1929, has a beautifully spruced-up
façade; the younger is a 1980s glass extravaganza.
Inside the pair, 258 en-suite rooms come in different
shapes and sizes, but all boast unfussy decor with
Old World flair, dark wood furniture and modern
trimmings such as modem connections. Rooms in
the new part come with smaller windows, so book a
Jelačić-facing room in the old building – preferably
a corner room with lots of windows.

Hotel Laguna

*Kranjčevićeva 29 (01 30 47 000/fax 01 30 47 077/
www.hotel-laguna.hr).* Tram 12 to Tehnički muzej.
Rates €70 single; €86 double. **Credit** AmEx, DC,
MC, V.
For all its design modesty c1975, this three-star is a
handy little option three stops on the No.9 tram from
the main station. Note that rates for a double room
compare favourably with those in hostels at the nearby Student Centre or station – and the Laguna has a
sauna and gym and internet access. 160 rooms.

Hotel Palace

*Trg JJ Strossmayera 10 (01 48 14 611/fax 01
48 11 357/www.palace.hr).* **Rates** €130-€160 double.
Credit AmEx, DC, MC, V.
This grand Secessionist mansion, the Schlessinger
Palace, houses Zagreb's first hotel, opened in 1907.
Almost a century later, it's still one of the city's most
elegant properties, catering to the moneyed and
the famous. All 123 rooms, three suites and two

semi-suites are a mix of art nouveau decor and contemporary amenities: sturdy dark wood furniture, huge windows, a yellow-and-blue colour theme, original paintings and spacious bathrooms with tubs. For minimum noise and the best views of Sljeme in the distance, book a courtyard-facing room. Look for the fantastic fresco in the back of the ground-floor café with its Austro-Hungarian finesse.

Pansion Jägerhorn

Ilica 14 (01 48 33 877/30 161/fax 01 48 33 573/ www.hotel-pansion-jaegerhorn.hr). **Rates** €101 double. **Credit** AmEx, DC, MC, V.

For some peace, quiet and a family atmosphere, stay at this intimate little spot in a commercial passageway at the Jelačić end of Ilica. Eight smallish and clean doubles fill the top floor of a heritage building

right below the leafy Upper Town. Rooms have capacious bathrooms, sloping walls and standard trimmings. There are also two suites with a separate living room and a kitchenette.

Regent Esplanade

Mihanovićeva 1 (01 45 66 021/fax 01 45 66 050/ www.regenthotels.com). **Rates** *Mon-Thur* €200-€215 double; *Fri-Sun* €149 double; €20 breakfast. **Credit** AmEx, DC, MC, V.

Art nouveau gem. *See p93* **Hot hotels.**

Sheraton Zagreb Hotel

Kneza Borne 2 (01 45 53 535/fax 01 45 53 035/ www.sheraton.com). **Rates** €130-€190 double. **Credit** AmEx, DC, MC, V.

International comfort available at this unsurprisingly classy business and conference hotel in the

Hot hotels The Regent Esplanade

Fabulous luxury and top-notch service are the name of the game at this art nouveau gem beside the train station. Since it opened in 1925 to cater to travellers on the *Orient Express*, the **Regent Esplanade** (*see above*) has accommodated Elizabeth Taylor, Queen Elizabeth II, the King of Spain and Louis Armstrong. Less famously, it also served as the Gestapo headquarters during World War II. It closed for most of the 1990s. After a complete refurbishment, it reopened in 2004 as the Regent Hotels chain's first in Europe. The lobby is a veneered wonder, clocks over

the door showing the time in six world cities. Stylish guestrooms range in size and configuration, but all come with perks such as heated floors, goose-down bedding, mist-free mirrors and fancy toiletries in the marble bathrooms. The chef at Zinfandel's restaurant conjures up modern Med cuisine with a California-meets-Asia twist, while Le Bistro does the best *štrukli* in town. There's a terrace for coffee sipping, a casino and a fitness club. Look out for the year-round weekend rates, valid except for the trade fair in mid September.

Musical differences
Pips Chips & Videoclips

In the early 1990s Zagreb's Pips Chips & Videoclips achieved instant notoriety with the song 'Dinamo ja volim', dedicated to the fans of local football club Dinamo. At the time Croatian president Tudjman had taken the unpopular step of ordering Dinamo to change its name to Croatia Zagreb. Based on the football anthem 'You'll Never Walk Alone', the song bridged the gap between football and rock. An illegal cassette pressing sold 5,000 copies – it could have sold tens of thousands of CDs. It was a local cult classic.

From that time on, the band changed. After flirting with Britpop on the albums *Fred Astaire* and *Bog*, their last offering *Drvece i rijeke*, mixed by Dave Fridmann of Mercury Rev and Flaming Lips fame, received global acclaim. P C & V are a rare Croatian band to have successfully combined Anglo-American indie-pop and native alternative sounds.

Lower Town: marble bathrooms in all 306 rooms and suites, heated indoor pool, massage treatments. The Four Points branch in the business quarter is the shiny blue-glass tower you see for miles around. **Branch**: Four Points Panorama Hotel by Sheraton, Trg sportova 9 (01 36 58 333/fax 01 30 92 657).

Getting there & around

Zagreb's Pleso **airport** is 17km (10.5 miles) south-east of the city centre. Buses (30mins journey time, 25kn) run to Zagreb bus station every half-hour 7am-8pm daily, then after each flight. From the bus station, buses run every half-hour, 4.30am-9am Mon-Fri (from 4am Sat, Sun), then 10am, 11am, then every half-hour until 8pm. A taxi should cost about 200kn.

Tram line Nos.2 and 6 run three stops from the bus station to the train station, Glavni kolodvor. No.6 passes through Jelačić, the city's main crossing point. There are 16 tram routes altogether, including No.15 between Mihaljevac and the cablecar terminus at Dolje. A tram ticket costs 6.50kn from a newsstand (stamp on board), 8kn from the driver. It is valid for 90 minutes if travelling in one direction. A day ticket is 18kn. There is also a four-line network of night trams. Tariffs and network maps are available at www.zet.hr.

Buses serve outlying areas, many setting off from the ranks on the suburban side of the train station. Ticket tariffs are the same.

Taxis are picked up from ranks around town, including the station and just off Jelačić. The standard rate is 25kn plus 7kn per kilometre, hiked up 20 per cent 10pm-5am, Sundays and holidays. Luggage is charged at 5kn per piece. Call 01 66 00 671 or 970.

Resources

Internet
Sublink Internet Centar *Teslina 12 (01 48 11 329/www.sublink.hr)*. **Open** 9am-10pm Mon-Sat; 3-10pm Sun.
Cheap and conveniently located internet office.

Pharmacy
Ilica 43 (01 48 48 450). **Open** 24hrs daily.

Police
92.

Post office
Branimirova 4 (01 48 40 340). **Open** 24hrs Mon-Sat; 1pm-midnight Sun.
Open almost all hours and right by the station.

Tourist information
Zagreb tourist office *Trg bana Jelačića 11 (01 48 14 051/www.zagreb-touristinfo.hr)*. **Open** *Mid June-Aug* 8.30am-10pm Mon-Fri, 9am-5pm Sat; 10am-2pm Sun. *Sept-mid June* 8.30am-8pm Mon-Fri; 9am-5pm Sat; 10am-2pm Sun.
Free brochures, maps and the three-day Zagreb Card (www.zagrebcard.fivestars.hr) at 90kn.

Slavonia & Inland Croatia

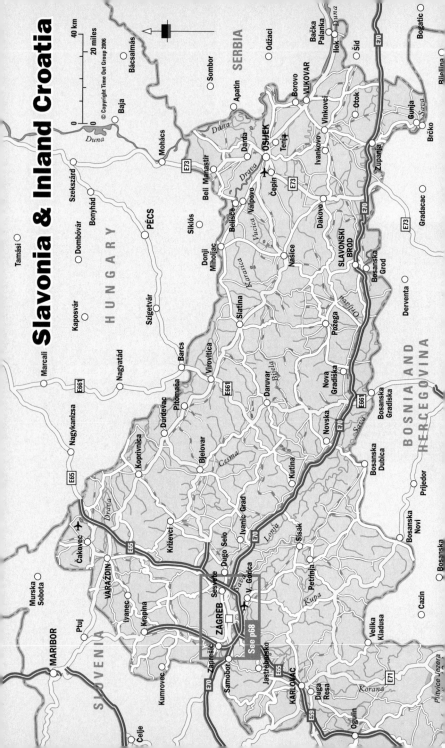

Slavonia & Inland Croatia

Slavonia & Inland Croatia

Medieval castles, cascading waterfalls, rolling vineyards – and tragic stories from the Yugoslav war.

Continental Croatia, as locals refer to it, is the north of the country that isn't Istria. Zagreb may be considered separate due to its capital status. It comprises the bucolic area of Hrvatsko Zagorje, dotted with medieval castles and centrepieced by the pretty, baroque former capital of **Varaždin**; the stunning **Plitvice Lakes**, Croatia's oldest and most attractive national park; and the rolling cornfields of Slavonia, whose main towns include **Osijek**, **Slavonski Brod**, **Vinkovci** and **Vukovar**.

It is an area best explored by car, although there are train (and more likely) bus services from Zagreb. It is also an area that was most affected by the Yugoslav war, particularly eastern Slavonia. Whereas much of life is slowly returning to normal, you are bound to see burned-out villages and, off the beaten track, signs warning of uncleared minefields. In the borderlands with Serbia and Bosnia, keep to the main towns and villages, and roads in between.

Hrvatsko Zagorje

The closest trip from Zagreb is to Hrvatsko Zagorje, squeezed up between the capital and Slovenia. Amid the picturesque villages and vineyards, its main attractions are the castles of **Trakošćan** and **Veliki Tabor**, Tito's home village of **Kumrovec** and Varaždin.

If heading for Trakošćan don't miss the lovely town of **Krapina** (www.krapina.com), with one of the world's richest Neanderthal sites boasting fossil remnants of Homo sapiens.

Up by the Slovenian border is the fairy-tale castle of Trakošćan (www.trakoscan.hr, open May-Sept 9am-6pm daily, Oct-Apr 9am-4pm daily, 20kn), some 80km (50 miles) north of Zagreb. Perched on a small hill fronted by a picture-perfect lake, Trakošćan is a 19th-century neo-Gothic version of the medieval original, complete with turrets, a drawbridge and a landscaped park. The living quarters of the castle's last owners, Count Drašković and his family, are open as a museum, with furniture from different periods (baroque,

rococo and Biedermeier), a series of family portraits and antique weapons dating back to the 15th century.

More impressive and less crowded is the UNESCO-protected hilltop castle of Veliki Tabor, 40km (25 miles) north-west of Zagreb (www.veliki-tabor.hr, open Apr-Sept 10am-5pm daily, Oct-Mar 9am-3pm daily, 20kn). This golden, pentagonal fortification dates back to the 12th century, with four semicircular towers added in the 15th. The three-level maze of galleries around the central courtyard contains knight armours, antique rifles and curios such as an 1883 chandelier from a transatlantic steamboat and the skull of Veronika Desinić, a peasant girl who, according to legend, was drowned and bricked up in the castle wall for falling in love with the castle owner's son. The castle hosts events from medieval battles to falcon hunting tournaments. Nearby, every July the Tuhelj thermal baths stage a film festival with DJ parties (www.taborfilmfestival.com). With the best view of the castle from the opposite hilltop, and traditional Zagorje specialities made with cottage cheese, Grešna Gorica (049 343 001, www.gresna-gorica.com) is a rustic restaurant also steeped in the Desinić legend. Its name means the Hill of Sin.

Another highlight is the open-air museum of Kumrovec, a village best known as the birthplace of Josip 'Tito' Broz. The Old Village Museum (www.mdc.hr/kumrovec, open Apr-Sept 9am-7pm daily, Oct-Mar 9am-4pm daily, 20kn) shows the core of a reconstructed village, with peasant houses, farmsteads and the house where Tito was born.

> ▶ The phone code for each area of continental Croatia varies. In this chapter we provide the full phone number for each venue – drop the first '0' if dialling from abroad, followed by the number. If you're dialling within the area, you don't need the first three numbers. Numbers beginning 091 or 098 are mobiles and are expensive to call from most foreign phones.

Slavonia & Inland Croatia

Things to do

Visit the house where Tito was born in **Kumrovec** (*see p97*). Gawp at the cascading waterfalls of the **Plitvice Lakes** (*see p99*) – better yet, take one of the ferry boats, included in the admission price. Take your binoculars to the **Kopački rit Nature Park**, home to 260 species of birds. Spend the day at a Slavonian village festival, or **kirvaj** (*see p100*). Take a tour of the **Zdjelarević vineyards** (*see p103*) at Brodski Stupnik.

Places to stay

Lagus (*see p98*) outside Varaždin offers beautiful views of the baroque town. Relax in the steam room after a day at the Plitvice Lakes National Park at the **Hotel Jezero** (*see p102*). Admire art deco trimmings at the century-old **Hotel Waldinger** (*see p106*) in Osijek. Stay in smart, four-star comfort at the **Hotel Lav** (*see p110*) in Vukovar.

Places to eat

Grešna Gorica (*see p97*) in Hrvatsko Zagorje offers top-notch regional delicacies with a hilltop view of Veliki Tabor castle. **Zlatna Guska** (*see below*) is in a 350-year-old palace in historic Varaždin. Try the trout in picturesque surroundings at **Lička kuća** (*see p102*) in Plitvice – or the traditional Slavonian venison stew at the **Slavonska kuća** (*see p106*) in Osijek. Dine on delicious freshwater fish at **Vrške** (*see p110*), a survivor of the 1991 siege of Vukovar.

Nightlife

Papa Joe (*see p106*) is the new place to be in Osijek. Slavonski Brod has Slavonia's best bar crawl, down the **Drunk Street** of **Starčevićeva** (*see p107*) – although **Snoopy** (*see p107*) is the best bar. The **Danielle Bar** (*see p110*) offers house and ambient music in Vukovar.

Culture

Observe reconstructed peasant life at the **Old Village Museum** (*see p97*) in Kumrovec. Take a look at the life's work of renowned sculptor **Antun Augustinčić** (*see below*) in Klanjec. See what's going on at the **Galerija Balen** (*see p108*), known for its bold art programme, in Slavonski Brod.

Klanjec, a pretty little town close to the Slovenian border, contains the Antun Augustinčić Gallery (www.mdc.hr/augustincic, open Apr-Sept 9am-5pm daily, Oct-Mar 9am-3pm Tue-Sun, 20kn); three exhibition rooms offer a chronological look at the career of this prolific sculptor. Look out for a replica of his most celebrated work, *Peace*; the original stands outside the UN building in New York.

Varaždin

Varaždin is the cultural, economic and administrative centre of Hrvatsko Zagorje. It's a pretty, baroque city, its skyline punctured by church towers, its centre lined with parks and gardens. Historically, Varaždin was a fortress town, a stronghold against Turkish raids. It passed through the hands of several owners, including the aristocratic Erdödy family, until 1925. For a brief time in the 18th century, it was the capital of Croatia, hosting the Parliament ('Sabor') and the Royal Croatian Council.

The city's pedestrianised baroque centre has a noble feel about it. The 14th-century **Castle** (042 210 339, www.mdc.hr/varazdin, open summer 10am-5pm Tue-Sun, winter 10am-3pm Tue-Sun, 20kn) houses the **City Museum**, with displays of arms, local crafts and furniture. **Varaždin Cathedral** (Pavlinska 5), built in 1647, is distinguished by its baroque entrance and 18th-century altar. In between castle and cathedral, the **Town Hall**, built in 1523, hosts the changing of the guard every Saturday.

To dine in historic surroundings, head for the **Zlatna Guska** (Jurja Habdelića 4, 042 213 393), in the basement of the 350-year-old Zakmardy Palace. Both decor and dishes have historic themes. It's set in parkland by the Croatian National Theatre. In less ornate surroundings, **Cimplet** (Braće Radić 102, 042 206 101) serves veal steaks and freshwater fish, the chef using modern takes on traditional dishes. **Mea Culpa** (Ivana Padovca 1, 042 300 868) is a standard, swish lounge bar. By the Town Hall, **Galliano** (Trg kralja Tomislava 4, 091 570 5883 mobile) is a stylish café by day and, upstairs at weekends, a cocktail bar by night. The main hotel in town is the three-star **Turist** (Aleja kralja Zvonimira 1, 042 395 395, www.hotel-turist.hr, 450kn), with 100 comfortable rooms behind a Socialist façade. If you're with the car, the **Lagus** (Varaždinbreg, Turčin, 042 652 940, www.hotel-lagus.hr, 400kn), 6km (3.5 miles) from town, offers beautiful views of Varaždin and a recommended restaurant.

Varaždin Tourist Office

Ivana Padovca 3 (042 210 987/www.tourism-varazdin.hr). **Open** *Apr-Oct* 8am-6pm Mon-Fri; 9am-1pm Sat. *Nov-Mar* 8am-4pm Mon-Fri.

Getting there & around

Due to the sporadic and unreliable public transport to and around Zagorje, a day trip from Zagreb to the castles and villages is only viable with a car or as part of a tour. Consult **Event Tours** (www.event.hr) or **Mystik Tours** (www.mystik-tours.hr) for details. For more information on Croatian castles and museums, visit www.mdc.hr. Buses between Zagreb and Varaždin (1hr 45mins) leave almost hourly; equally regular trains take 2hrs 15mins.

Plitvice

Plitvice National Park is one of Croatia's natural wonders. Cascades of water tumble from steep mountains into the aquamarine Plitvice Lakes, raising a mist that sprays the jungle-like vegetation shading the lakeshore. The scene is repeated over and over around the 16 lakes, where more than a dozen large cataracts and many smaller waterfalls create a magical preserve of almost unnatural beauty.

The flow from the rivers Crna and Bijela (Black and White) drops a kilometre in altitude by the time it travels through a 5km-long (3-mile) chain of lakes linked by waterfalls. Along the way, it rushes past pockmarked cliffs that have been eroded into surreal, fairy-tale shapes. The striking landscape is in a constant state of change, due to a natural process that has been continuing for thousands of years.

Only a couple of hours' drive from the coast, Plitvice National Park's rushing water and shady mountain forests offer a pleasantly cool contrast to the sun-baked shore. The lake area of 2sq km (0.8sq miles), and natural reserve of 295sq km (114sq miles) around it, can keep you happily diverted for several days. Hotels in the park and a campsite make it easy to dawdle. By car it's a relatively easy day trip, as the park's two main entrances are on the old main road between Zagreb and Dalmatia, parallel to the new motorway. Buses usually stop at each entrance. Leaving Plitvice may be trickier at busy times of year, as services between the main cities are often full and you may have to wait for a couple to pass.

You can hike among the lakes via an 18km (11-mile) trail, crossing wooden walkways that let you stroll over streams and boggy stretches. This trail is well served by open-air sightseeing buses, ferry boats, small snack bars and public toilets, but you can still hit long stretches where you feel at one with the wilderness.

Veliki Tabor. *See p97.*

Kirvaj: The village fete Slavonian style

Kirvaj is the traditional village feast in Slavonia that takes place on the saint's day of the local church. This celebration is taken very seriously by villagers, and is preceded by a month of ritual preparation, including whitewashing the house and doing the garden, as well as buying a new set of clothes for everyone in the family. Relatives and friends are invited to lunch and the hosts are careful not to miss out anyone from neighbouring villages that they visit on their feast day. It's a whole-day affair, often starting with a mass in the local church, and transforms seemingly deserted villages into hives of activity.

While in Dalmatia village feasts tend to take place on the streets and squares, Slavonian feasts are more insular, taking place mainly in people's homes. The survival of the custom of *kirvaj* into the 21st century is a sign of a strong sense of belonging and cultural identity, and part of what makes Slavonia such an atmospheric and friendly region to visit.

Lunch is the main event and is served according to the standard Slavonian menu for special occasions. First up is clear soup with threads of pasta. The main ingredient probably had a good life pecking around the yard, because, according to a village saying, 'the older the hen, the better the soup'. Connoisseurs of the *kirvaj* menu look for a good strong, fatty soup, with the thinnest possible threads of home-made egg pasta. Next to come is cold boiled meat with red sauce. The cold chicken and beef were used to make the soup, and are livened up with tomato sauce, which is made in season and kept in jars till the big day. This is followed by *sarma*, which are moist bundles of paprika or cabbage stuffed with spicy rice and minced pork. Although you may already be feeling quite full, the best is still to come.

The pièce de résistance of the Slavonian feast menu is *pečenka*, or cold roast pork. Like the hen, the pig also probably lived in the yard, and was fatted up on cobs of corn grown expressly for the purpose. The animal would have been slaughtered by the menfolk, with help from friends and family, before being baked in a traditional outdoor bread oven. A fire is made inside the brick stove

and then the hot embers are removed. The heat in the bricks is enough to cook a whole pig to perfection in three to four hours. The skin should be 'golden as if it was cooked by the sun', as someone is bound to remark, and deliciously crispy, while the most highly prized chunks are the fatty underbelly and the ribs. *Pečenka* is served on long trays with bread cut from huge home-made loaves, with an optional bowl of cabbage salad, the only concession to vegetarians in the menu.

Miraculously, plates of 20 to 30 types of cake begin to appear, many with bizarre names such as Seventh Heaven, Parachutist, Londoner, Hungarian Girl, Greta Garbo, Japanese Wind and Cat's Eyes. These cakes are delicately served in small cubes or slices, to maximise everyone's chance of trying as many as possible, and are rich in organic eggs and walnuts from the host family's own personal walnut tree. *Rakija* or plum brandy (of course from the hosts' own plums and made in their own still) is the traditional aperitif, followed by white wine and mineral water to wash it all down. When one complete sitting on the long wooden table is finished, it's all change, and the hosts begin the whole service again for the next round of honoured guests that seem to keep on coming throughout the day.

The *kirvaj* is an opportunity for lots of talking and catching up on news from friends and extended family, and depending on the hosts, can get quite lively, with singing and joking. Entertainment is provided by groups of *tamboraši* musicians playing traditional Croatian instruments and going house to house – alternatively there is bound to be a concert of its contemporary inheritor, the grim turbofolk (*see p45* **Turbofolk**), for the younger ones in the village hall.

Children associate the feast with the lines of stalls that are set up along the road, selling all kinds of disposable objects made in distant lands. Every child goes to spend their pocket money on balloons, plastic guns, plastic glasses, false hair, water pistols, dollies or action men.

If you want to see a real Slavonian *kirvaj*, you could time a visit to **Slavonski Brod** for 13 June, and head for the nearby village of **Podvinje** to celebrate St Anthony's Day.

If you only have an afternoon to visit the park, you can start at Entrance 2, the southernmost access to the lake area, for a few hours' stroll around **Lake Gradinsko**, which has the most intense concentration of waterfalls. Go south from the entrance to the trails that wind around Lake Gradinsko and end with a ferry ride that carries you across **Lake Kozjak**, the largest, back to where you started. Another possible half-day itinerary could take you to the **Great Falls** (Velike kaskade) near Entrance 1. Or you can use the sightseeing buses to reach key spots quickly. Clear, detailed maps are available at each entrance.

With more time, you can hike the park's mountain forests, for a chance to see an impressive variety of flora and fauna that exists in such huge biodiversity. Plitvice hosts more than 50 species of mammal, from the tiny dormouse to wolves and the brown bear, both rare finds in Europe. Both are shy of humans. Hiking the hinterlands of the park, you have more chance of spotting second-hand signs of their presence. Another rare mammal in the park is the lynx, which was wiped out in Croatia and has since been reintroduced with some success. There are known to be 60 pairs of lynx in the country, and many live in Plitvice park. Otters thrive in the streams and rivers of the park. You can also see wild boar, deer, foxes, hares and martens.

These animals live in a forest of mainly beech, with tall, straight silvery trunks. Firs grow in the higher areas. Forests, meadows and

The waterfalls of **Plitvice National Park**. *See p99.*

lakeside habitats attract some 140 species of birds, including many types of owl. There are also many species of butterflies, occasionally gathering in large, colourful flocks. Listen out for the tiny treefrogs, hard to spot but easy to hear when they start to chirp. They are most visible during the summer spawning season.

Where to stay

There are three hotels inside the park, located next to each other at Entrance 2, right by the lakes. There is also a motel nearby, a campsite and rooms for rent. The hotels close from mid October to mid April. To find private rooms in the villages near the park, call the national park office, and expect to pay about €20-€35 a head. The campsite has bungalows for those who left their tent at home. Campers may be tempted to find a secluded spot in the park to sleep for free, but it's not allowed and patrols are regular, so you are likely to get caught.

Campsite Korana

Catrnja (053 751 888). **Rates** *Camping* €7 per person. *Bungalows* €17-€20 single; €24-€34 double. **Credit** AmEx, DC, MC, V.
Buses from Zagreb and Zadar stop at this busy site, in a tiny village on the main road, about 6km (3.7 miles) from Entrance 1. There are 42 'bungalows' containing two beds with fresh linen, so you don't have to bring camping gear for cheap accommodation. The site has a restaurant and grocery store.

Hotel Bellevue

Entrance 2, Velika poljana (053 751 015). **Rates** €39-€54 single; €52-€72 double. **Credit** AmEx, DC, MC, V.
A two-star with 70 en-suite rooms has the cheapest accommodation next to the lakes. Even if the rooms are drab, the beds are comfortable and you're not likely to spend a lot of time indoors when you come to Plitvice. Breakfasts are served at the hotel, but there is no restaurant for lunch or dinner.

Hotel Jezero

Entrance 2, Velika poljana (053 751 015). **Rates** €60-€82 single; €84-€116 double. **Credit** AmEx, DC, MC, V.
This 229-room modern three-star is the fanciest hotel in the park. The simple rooms are nicely decorated and comfortable, and there are suites available. You can unwind from a day's hike around the park in the whirlpool or one of the steam rooms. There is a restaurant and a bar/nightclub on the premises.

Hotel Plitvice

Entrance 2, Velika poljana (053 751 015). **Rates** €45-€71 single; €64-€100 double. **Credit** AmEx, DC, MC, V.
The mid-range option among the park's hotels, the Plitvice was renovated in 1997 and is still in good shape. Out of the 51 rooms, almost half are higher

rated, with better views, but if you're not spending too much time indoors, the smaller, economy rooms should be fine.

Motel Grabovac

Grabovac Dreznicki (053 751 999). **Rates** €39-€51 single; €52-€68 double. **Credit** AmEx, DC, MC, V.
A simple, recently renovated motel, on the edge of the nature preserve and about 12km (7.5 miles) north of the lakes. Buses from Zagreb stop here on the way to the heart of the park, but you'll probably want a car to get back and forth between your bed and the lakes. The en-suite rooms are ordinary-looking but in good shape. There is a restaurant, a self-service cafeteria and a small bar on the premises.

Where to eat

There are a few restaurants around Plitvice, adequate for the purpose. They invariably offer grilled meats such as *pljeskavica* or *ćevapčići*, hams and sausages. Some also serve locally caught trout, usually excellent in these parts.

Lička kuća

Entrance 1 (053 751 024). **Open** *Apr-Oct* 10am-10pm daily. **Credit** AmEx, DC, MC, V.
The better restaurant in the park is a sprawling place with a big terrace designed to feed hordes of tourists. A big outdoor grill produces all kinds of meats. The trout is excellent, and the restaurant recommends its speciality, *Lička juha*, a heavy, sausage-based stew.

Resources

Plitvice Lakes National Park

053 751 015/www.np-plitvicka-jezera.hr. **Open** 8am-7pm daily. **Admission** 50kn-95kn; 25kn-55kn 7-18s; free under-7s. **Credit** AmEx, DC, MC, V.
Official information offices are prominently located at both entrances to the lake area inside the park. These, and the branch office in Zagreb, pretty much run a monopoly on booking accommodation in and around the park, or offering other tourist services. **Branch**: Trg kralja Tomislava 19, Zagreb (01 46 13 586).

Getting there & around

The lake area has two entrances, with parking, a few kilometres apart on the old main road between Zagreb and Dalmatia, the E59/E71. The new A1 motorway parallel to it has turn-offs at Otočac and Gorna Ploča. The more northern Entrance 1 is next to the biggest restaurant. Entrance 2 has the hotels and easy access to the heart of the park.
Buses from Zagreb or Zadar should get you there in about three hours and cost about 60kn. All buses going between Zagreb and Zadar stop in Plitvice, but they do not pick up passengers if

Grapes on the 45th parallel

Višnja and Davor **Zdjelarević** run Croatia's first wine hotel, following a family tradition dating back to 1866. Neglected under communism, the vineyard in Brodksi Stupnik, 20km (12.5 miles) from Slavonski Brod, was restored, the ancestral home repaired and vines replanted at a time when others were fleeing the war-torn region. More than a decade on, they now have a small hotel and restaurant, underneath which are prize-winning wine cellars.

Slavonian wine-growing traditions and drinking habits are oriented towards white wine, often drunk with a dash of soda water. Graševina is the typical Slavonian indigenous variety and the backbone of the vineyard. It has been supplemented with international varieties, such as Chardonnay, Riesling and Pinot Noir. There is no reason why red wine should not prosper here too, except there was a decision made during the communist era that in order to simplify mass production vineyards on the coast had to specialise in reds, while continental wine-growers would confine themselves to whites. The Zdjelarevićs have planted nine hectares of red wine grape varieties, from Cabernet Sauvignon to Shiraz.

The couple are proud to point out that Brodski Stupnik, at 45'10 degrees, is on the same latitude as the best French wine-growing regions. It benefits from an excellent microclimate – the area has on average more sunny days than anywhere else in continental Croatia – as well as the excellent soil.

The restaurant broadmindedly stocks wine from the best producers across Slavonia, so you could do some advance tasting as research for your next stop on the vineyard trail. The menu is a modern take on the possibilities offered by local produce and cooking traditions, with a seasonal approach, so the waiter will encourage you to try game stew in autumn and organic lamb in the spring. You don't need to be staying at the hotel to visit the restaurant or wine cellars, although there are 15 reasonably priced guestrooms. if you have your own transport, the hotel is a good base for exploring the surrounding region, visiting some of the other local wine producers.

There is a lot of scope for walking and there are also mountain bikes at the disposal of guests. Other activities include horseriding at a local stable. The Zdjelaravić hotel, restaurant and vineyards are a pioneer of sustainable rural tourism in Slavonia and a great way to get a taste for authentic Slavonian food and wine.

To reach Brodski Stupnik, take a bus from Slavonski Brod station. It's then a 2.5km (1.5-mile) signposted walk uphill to the vineyards.

Zdjelarević Vineyard
Vinogradska 102, Brodski Stupnik, Slavonski Brod (035 427 775/www.zdjelarevic.hr). **Rates** 395kn single, 580kn double. **Credit** AmEx, DC, MC, V.

they are full. This means it can be risky to try to leave the park on the last bus of the night during high season.

No cars or buses are allowed inside the protected area around the lakes. Open-sided sightseeing trains quickly get you to points of interest and let you admire the scenery as you go past. There are also a couple of ferry boats that make strategic connections across Kozjak, the largest lake. The buses and ferries are free of charge once you pay admission to the park.

Slavonia

The fertile plains of Slavonia lie between the rivers Sava to the south, Drava to the north and Danube to the east. They are home to around a million Slavonians, famous in the rest of Croatia for their warm hospitality, love of hearty but wholesome food, and strong sense of local identity. The mesmerising sight of endless flat fields of wheat and corn is broken in places by forested hills that hide lush valleys and tiny villages, strategically located off the beaten track in the hope of being overlooked by the marauding bandits and foreign conscripts that have traversed Slavonia over the centuries. The region has a continental climate of freezing winters and scorching summers, and shares the Pannonian love for roast pork, stuffed peppers and young wine.

There are 25 municipalities, most small market towns serving the surrounding villages with a slow charm. The capital is **Osijek**, five hours by train from Zagreb, Slavonia's only university town. It has a vibrant urban scene with many galleries, theatres and a lively nightlife. **Slavonski Brod** is the second city of

The killing fields

Plitvice Lakes is in the region of Krajina, originally the 'Vojna Krajina', the Military Border so named by the Habsburgs. To make sure the Ottomans stayed on the other side of it, they granted the land to Morlachs, a peripatetic group of Vlach shepherds who were allowed freedom from serfdom in exchange for keeping the Turks at bay. The local Morlachs were mostly Serbian Orthodox practitioners, and until 1995, the region contained a majority Serbian population.

As Croatia was preparing to declare independence in 1991, ethnic Serbs from Krajina, preferring to keep ties with Belgrade, seized the park. Josip Jović, a Croatian police officer at the park headquarters, was killed and is remembered as the first victim of the war. There is a monument to him near Entrance 2.

The Krajina Serbs received support from the Belgrade-backed Yugoslav army, gaining control of the region before a 1992 ceasefire froze the borders in a position that reduced Croatia's size by almost 30 per cent. Local Serbs created the Republic of Serbian Krajina and ethnically cleansed their minority Croatian neighbours through evictions and murder, forcing about 43,000 Croats to flee.

The Croatian army retook the area in a successful 1995 offensive that reclaimed the country's traditional borderlands. Serb forces were expelled within a matter of days, and then Krajina's majority Serbs became the victims of ethnic cleansing in a campaign that lasted for months and was notoriously brutal. Depending on who you ask, an estimated 150,000-300,000 Serbs were forced to flee the region. About 14,000 were killed before they could leave. It was the largest exodus of Serbs from Croatia caused by the war.

Along the road from the coast to Plitvice, you will pass villages where every fifth or sixth house has been burned to its foundations, indicating enforced eviction. Other houses have gaping holes from shelling. The old Serbian Orthodox churches in this area are burned to bare stone. Its all a vivid reminder of the turbulent period of history from which Croatia has only so very recently emerged.

Hotel Osijek. *See p106.*

the region and, along with its historical fortress and attractive riverfront, makes a good base for exploring the hills, forests and vineyards of central Slavonia. Within easy reach of both, **Djakovo** (www.djakovo.net) makes an interesting detour purely because of its neo-Gothic St Peter's Cathedral, home of historic figure Bishop Strossmayer. A town of 25,000 people, it has successfully preserved the scale and feel of its 19th-century heyday. **Vinkovci** also preserves its folk traditions, observed throughout the region on annual village feast days (*see p100* **Kirvaj: The village fete Slavonian style**).

In the Yugoslav war, some of the heaviest fighting took place in eastern Slavonia, and the fate of **Vukovar** is a symbol of Croatian self-defence and sacrifice. *See p108* **Vukovar: Before and after**.

Osijek

Osijek is in Croatia's far north-eastern corner, near the Hungarian and Serbian borders. The main town of the Slavonia and Baranja region, Osijek is set on the right bank of the Drava, near its mouth into the Danube.

The town centre is divided into three parts: **Gornji grad** (Upper Town), **Donji grad** (Lower Town) with the historic fortified centre of **Tvrdja** in the middle. Recent municipal plans call for extending the Drava embankment walkway from the Upper Town to the Lower.

It's a slow-paced sort of place, with scatterings of Secessionist architecture and a long history. A thriving village in the Middle Ages, it was destroyed by the Ottoman Turks, who built several mosques and an 8km-long (5-mile) wooden bridge, said to be one of the

architectural wonders in the reign of the Ottoman sultan Suleyman the Magnificent (1495-1566).

After liberation from the Turks in 1687, Osijek was again destroyed. The new Austrian authorities built a fortress, Tvrdja, a residential and military complex in the heart of town. Army buildings are set alongside baroque family houses. Here you will find the baroque façade of the former Jesuit church of St Michael and **Museum of Slavonia**.

Three parts of the town were united in 1786, when Osijek became the administrative centre of Slavonia. In 1779 a new wooden bridge was built across the Drava, connecting Osijek with Hungary and the rest of Central Europe.

Osijek suffered a nine-month bombardment during the Yugoslav war, the scars still to be seen as the city continues its recovery.

Focal Trg Ante Starčević, in the Upper Town, is the site of the St Peter and St Paul Cathedral. Built with a 90-metre-high (295-foot) spire in neo-Gothic style at the end of the 19th century, it's the town's only major attraction outside of the fortress. The main local cultural institutions line Europska avenija.

Osijek otherwise offers simple pleasures. On the other side of the Drava from Tvrdja, just over the footbridge, are the main city park and Copacabana Recreation Centre ('Kopika'), with pools and riverside sports.

The **Nature Park of Kopački rit**, a few kilometres north-east of Osijek, is also slowly recovering after the Yugoslav war. Its wetlands are home to 260 species of birds, although many of the animals have disappeared. Not all of the territory has been cleared of mines – stick to the main roads and look out for signs. The Osijek tourist office (*see p106*) has full details.

As if to compensate for the relative lack of museums and galleries, the town has plenty of restaurant and nightlife options. The most renowned venue for freshwater fish – and Dalmatian seafood, too – is **Laguna Croatica** (Dubrovačka 13, 031 369 203), which combines southern decor with a Slavonian ambience. To dine on lamb and veal specialities with the locals, head for **Bijelo-plavi** (Martina Divalta 8, 031 571 000), by the football stadium and decked out in the namesake colours of blue and white. In Tvrdja, **Slavonska kuća** (Kamila Firingera 26, 031 208 277, closed Sun) is a traditional venue with rustic decor, offering the local venison stew, *čobanac*, and a mixed freshwater-fish salad. If you're just in Osijek for one day, dine here.

By day, **San Francisco** (Radićeva 12, 031 860 8022) and **Cappuccino** (Šetalište kardinala Franje Šepera 8, 031 203 090) are the best places for a coffee. The town's new destination is **Papa Joe** (Kuhačeva 25, 031 252 020), which operates as a café in the morning and lounge bar by night, running until 3am at weekends.

The town has two four-star hotels. The landmark **Waldinger** (Županijska 8, 031 250 450, www.waldinger.hr, 750kn single, 950kn double), set in the beautiful century-old art-deco Baumgartner House, is beautifully furnished in the architectural style of its heritage. It has a capacity of 15 rooms with seven three-star ones available in a back courtyard. Centrally located, this is a classy place to stay. The other, in the same price range, is the **Osijek** (Šamaška 4, 031 230 333, www.hotelosijek.hr, 965kn). Completely renovated in 2004, this is one of the best equipped hotels in Slavonia, with a fitness centre, dry and steam saunas, and internet access in each of the 140 rooms.

A handy mid-range option is the **Hotel Central** (Trg Ante Starčićeva 6, 031 283 399, www.hotel-central-os.hr, 515kn), built in 1899 and recently renovated to three-star status. It's on the main square, opposite the cathedral. The 39 rooms are comfortable with standard fittings. Prices include breakfast, with good half-board options.

Museum of Slavonia

Trg Sv Trojstva 6 (031 208 501). **Open** 10am-1pm Tue-Fri, Sun; 6-9pm Sat. **Admission** 12kn.
Bronze Age and Roman remains from across the region. There is usually an interesting temporary exhibition on too.

Osijek Tourist Board

Šupanijska 2, 31000 Osijek (031 203 755/ www.tzosijek.hr). **Open** *Summer* 7am-8pm Mon-Fri; 8am-noon Sat, Sun. *Winter* 7am-4pm Mon-Fri; 8am-noon Sat.

Slavonski Brod

Situated at the ancient crossroads between the Pannonian plain and Bosnia, halfway on the motorway between Zagreb and Belgrade, the fate of Slavonski Brod has owed a lot to shifting borders. Following the liberation of the region from Turkish rule in 1691, this ancient river crossing point (*brod*) was chosen as the location for an Austrian military garrison and an important Franciscan monastery. With the incorporation of Bosnia into the Austrian empire and the building of a strategic railway bridge, the fortunes of the city took a turn for the better. The late 1800s was marked by the building of grand merchants' houses on one of the largest public squares in the country. The 20th century has not been so kind. The town was transformed according to Socialist urban planning after its destruction by Allied bombing, and it became a centre of heavy industry. From 1991 the city has again sat on an international border, that between Croatia and Bosnia, weathering the rapid decline of its heavy industry through an influx of thousands of business-minded refugees from Bosnia.

The main site of historical interest in town is the **Fortress**, which until the mid 1990s was in the hands of the military. It has since been

Osijek Cathedral. *See p105.*

Snoopy, Slavonski Brod

Snoopy (*see below*) is the home of the alternative crowd in Slavonski Brod, where the music does not falter from the path of ex-Yu cult rock and Anglo-Saxon indie bands. The decor recalls a desert island, with a bamboo-clad bar and baggy grey sacks hanging from the ceiling. Many of the guests clearly wish they could close their eyes and wake up on a desert island, free of the drudgery of the mainstream. Regulars include members of environmental activist group PUŽ, a Croatian acronym for 'Layer of Urban Living', high-school dropouts, ex- and eternal students and a very tall basketball player. While there are people who've never heard of Snoopy, there are those who'd never drink anywhere else.

Snoopy is a quiet bar when it's calm and a nightlife hotspot when it's swinging. There's no dancefloor as such, but full use is made of the space above and below the tables when the atmosphere gets hedonistic. There's also a backroom with a dartboard, but most of the action takes place around the bar, where Dado dispenses doses of tequila, beer and other party poisons.

If you do find your way to this genuine outpost of underground music and culture, don't be put off by the policeman walking up and down outside. He's guarding the police station, which, apart from Snoopy, is the only establishment of any importance in the street of Mažuranićeva.

restored and integrated into the city, now housing two schools, the Town Hall and the uninspiring Ružić art gallery. Despite the renovation, it feels quite bare, giving locals little temptation to cross the moat. The **Franciscan monastery**, also dating back to the early 18th century, has an impressive baroque church and atmospheric cloisters. Sunday morning services are an important civic ritual, followed up with a visit to one of the city's many cafés. The nearby café-lined Sava embankment is the ideal spot.

For dining, try the regional specialities in the **Slavonski Podrum** (A Štampara 1, 035 444 856), a wood-panelled cellar, especially the grilled fish from the Sava. **Pizzeria Uno** (Nikole Zrinskog 7, 035 442 107) offers reliable pizzas from a wood-fired oven and Slavonian specialities from Grah.

The nightlife scene revolves around the riverside promenade, Šetalište braće Radić (try **Green Park** or the **Iguana**, whose live iguana died from smoke inhalation); and what locals refer to as Drunk Street, **Starčevićeva**. Here **Alfa** (No.19, 035 233 800) is a good place to start the night and **TNT** (No.1, no phone) a fine place to finish it. Mention must be made of the dive bar **Rupa** (Trg Ivane Brlić-Mažuranić 5, 035 410 010) and the lounge bar on the same square, **Navigator** (No.8, 098 341 541 mobile). Don't miss **Snoopy** (Mažuranićeva 10; *see above*), the hangout for the alternative crowd.

The main hotel in town is the **Park** (Trg Pobjede 1, 035 410 228, 336kn), ideally located on the main square, but it is in urgent need of renovation. **Lotos** (Trg Ivane Brlić-Mažuranić 10, 035 405 555, 380kn) is a modest guesthouse,

Vukovar: Before and after

The very word still has the power to make Croats wince and some shed tears. Vukovar. Or, as it became known in 1991, VukoWAR. Some even called it Croatia's Stalingrad.

The town symbolised Croatia's David and Goliath struggle against a stronger Serbian enemy in 1991. The comparison with Stalingrad, though, was exaggerated. Vukovar was no strategic city but a town lying off the beaten track, and one housing large Serbian, Slovak, Ruthene and Ukrainian minorities.

Vukovar's rise to a fame it never sought began in the spring and summer of 1991, after Croatia declared independence and Serbia, under Slobodan Milosevic, began deploying the Yugoslav army at full throttle in support of Croatia's home-grown Serb rebels.

As the easternmost town in Croatia, it was an obvious target and by late summer the various Serb formations had it surrounded.

But instead of the expected walkover, the embattled garrison under Mile Dedaković held out for months, delaying the advance of the Yugoslav army and electrifying Croatia, for whom the sleepy Danube town suddenly became the loaded symbol of their independence war.

Nightly, the country tuned into broadcasts by sole remaining reporter, Siniša Glavišević, who recorded the street-by-street battles of the retreating Croat fighters, the demolition of the infrastructure by the tanks and artillery of the Serbs and the heroic work of Dr Vesna Bosanac in Vukovar's ruined hospital.

By November it was over, the Serbs having razed much of the place to its foundations. On 17 November the last fighters surrendered and the bedraggled civilian remnants came up from their freezing underground cellars – their exit from the town on foot through mud and rubble becoming one of the lasting images of the war.

The conquest of Vukovar did not end the town's agony, for the Yugoslav army then executed more than 200 wounded men lying in the hospital in the worst single war crime of the entire conflict, dumping the bodies in pits in a nearby farm at Ovčara. Glavišević perished also and only an international outcry saved Dr Bosanac. Meanwhile, in Croatia the fall of 'our Stalingrad' triggered accusations against President Franjo Tudjman, with some claiming he let the town die a lingering death to attract international attention. It was true that recognition did follow within weeks, but Tudjman furiously denied he sacrificed Vukovar to get it.

For the next six years, Vukovar remained under Serb rule, filling up with Serbs expelled from other parts of Croatia. With no jobs and no money, it remained largely ruined, and after the fall of the Croatian Serb army in Knin in 1995, Belgrade relinquished it without fuss to the Croats under an internationally brokered plan in 1995, called the Erdut Agreement. Zagreb resumed full control on 15 January 1998.

Today the ruins have been swept away and a splendid new hotel, the four-star Lav (*pictured, below right*), has risen to join the old Hotel Dunav, where journalists were housed during the conflict. As thousands of Croats have come home, and most of the Serbs remained, the streets are again full. But there has been no reconciliation. The two communities attend their own schools, churches, cafés and clubs and ignore one another. The Serbs are unrepentant – most, in any case, are refugees from other towns. The Croat returnees are bitter about their long exile. Outside town stands a monument to the victims, a stark reminder of the horror of the fratricidal struggle that soaked this corner of Slavonia in blood.

---

and pizzeria near the Sava. The best riverside option is the **Rezidencija Uno** (Šetalište braće Radić 6, 035 415 000, www.uno-brod.hr, 600kn), a delightfully renovated townhouse, while the cheapest choice is the **Magnus Rooms** (JJ Strošmajera 46, 035 436 536, 180kn), clean private rooms near the market.

With time and transport, try and arrange to stay at Croatia's first wine hotel, **Zdjelarević**, 20km (12.5 miles) from Slavonski Brod in Brodski Stupnik. *See p103* **Grapes on the 45th parallel**.

Regional Museum of Brodsko Posavlje

Starčevićeva 40 (035 447 415). **Open** 9am-7pm daily. **Admission** free.

While the original building of the museum is being restored, temporary exhibitions take place in a newly built wing. Expect to see anything from exquisite Slavonian folk handicrafts to hunting paraphernalia and bizarre local archaeological finds. Down in the courtyard there's an independent art gallery, Galerija Balen, known for its sociable openings and bold exhibition programme.

Slavonski Brod Tourist Office

Trg Pobjede 30 (035 445 765/www.tzgsb.hr).
Open *Summer* 7am-9pm Mon-Sat. *Winter* 7am-7.30pm Mon-Sat.

Vinkovci

Vinkovci is a small, typical Slavonian town on the banks of the river Bosut. It's elongated and devoid of elevation but enlivened by a baroque town centre, including the main square, park and parish church built in 1777.

The town's heritage is not only architectural. As Cibalae, it was populated by the Romans and was the birthplace of two emperors, Valens and Valentinian I. In the 11th century the Slavs renamed the place Sv Ilija. After the Turks, the Austrians ruled. After industrialisation, Vinkovci became a major railway junction.

The composer of the Croatian national anthem, Josip Runjanin, was born here. Today the most important event in the calendar is **Vinkovačke jeseni** ('Vinkovci Autumn'), a traditional folk fete held each September.

The best-known restaurant in town is **Lamut** (Ulica kralja Zvonimira 23, 032 332 588), offering local specialities such as pork shank in sauerkraut. **Prkos** (Ulica Stjepana Radića 27, 098 1663 3918) is at pains to provide authentic food from a century ago: game in mushroom sauce, a variety of sausages (*kulin*, *švargle* and *kravavice*) and stews (particularly venison and fish). It also makes its own bread on the premises. **Marabú** (Glagoljaška 8, 098 901 3753 mobile) and **Mystique** (Ulica kralja Zvonimira 32, no phone) are two ethnically themed cafés that stand out from the norm.

The town has three main hotels. The **Cibalia** (Ulica Ante Starčićeva 51, 032 339 222, www.hotel-cibalia.com, 600kn) is the newest in town, opened in 2000, a standard three-star near the bus and train stations. The oldest (and biggest) is the **Slavonija** (Duga ulica 1, 032 342 555, www.son-ugo-cor.com, 375kn), renovated in 2000, but still with boxy rooms. The **Gem** (Ulica kralja Zvonimira 120, 032 367 911, www.hotelgem.hr, 440kn) is unusual in that it has two indoor tennis courts, as well as a sauna and billiard room.

Vinkovci Tourist Board
Trg Bana Josipa Šokčevića 3 (032 334 653/www.tz-vinkovci.hr). **Open** 8am-3pm Mon-Fri; 8am-1pm Sat.

Vukovar

Of all the towns in continental Croatia, the one that has the most resonance is Vukovar. Almost completely destroyed in 1991, Vukovar's ruins were ruled by the Serbs until 1995. Handed over to the Croats in 1998, Vukovar has led a strange double existence, the two communities living two separate lives. Rebuilding has been a slow and painful process but the town now boasts a new four-star hotel and a few businesses have gradually started to open. *See p108* **Vukovar: Before and after**.

Vukovar was always a mixed city and, in former times, a beautiful one. After the Turks retreated in the 1600s, Germans, Jews, Serbs, Ukrainians and Hungarians flooded in. A German entrepreneurial family by the name of **Eltz** developed it as a craft and trading centre. Their palace, damaged but still in operation, now houses the town's museum. By the 1900s its baroque façades were home to a thriving bourgeois community, with significant Ruthene and Slovak citizens too. When the Yugoslav war started, Vukovar was still a major centre for manufacturing, mainly tyres.

The town holds a particular place in the Croatian psyche. Its bravery under siege means that its name is chanted at football matches; the anniversary of its surrender on 18 November is commemorated with sombre programmes on the radio. A visit here can be a shocking experience but one not without reward.

The main restaurant in town is **Vrške** (Parobrodksa 3, 032 441 788), one of the very few buildings to have survived 1991 completely unscathed. A simple place with a terrace on the Danube, it offers a diverse range of freshwater fish. The most popular dish is pike-perch prepared in croquettes with a pinch of beer inside. Meat dishes are prepared on a wood-fired grill. Other specialities include *Vučedolski uštipak*, a fritter of ground meat with bacon and cheese, and grilled hamburger with goat's cheese. Vukovar's new four-star hotel, **Lav** (*see below*), on the opposite bank houses an equally swish restaurant, with local delicacies such as smoked pork sausage (*kulin*), fried frog's legs, venison stew (*čobanac*), plus local cheese (*Vukovarski podlivani sir*) for dessert. Some 100 Slavonian wines are available.

The **Danielle Bar** (Ulica Marija Jurić Zagorke 6, 032 410 387), in the half-destroyed, half-renovated neighbourhood of Mitnica, is an unexpected delight, with friendly faces and a music programme of house and ambient. The first bar to open after the war was **Ferrari** (Ulica dr Franje Tudjmana 5, 032 442 500), now with weekend parties. The only disco is **Quo Vadis** (Ulica bana Josipa Jelačića 98, 098 311 204 mobile), a multi-floored venue, one half café, one half nightclub with DJ decks.

The **Hotel Lav** ('lion') opened in 2005 – or rather reopened in 2005, as the first hotel to open in town was the Lav in 1840. In the 1960s it was a Socialist-style building, and this was the one destroyed in 1991. This current model (Ulica Josipa Jurja Strossmayera 18, 032 445 100, www.hotel-lav.hr, 900kn) is a smart business hotel. It has a restaurant (*see above*), conference facilities and 39 well-equipped rooms. The two-star **Dunav** (Trg republike Hrvatske 1, 032 441 285, 420kn), which housed journalists during the 1991 siege, is still in operation. It has 56 simple rooms, all ensuite, half with televisions.

Vukovar Tourist Board
Ulica Josipa Jurja Strossmayera 15 (032 442 889). **Open** 8am-3pm Mon-Fri; 8am-1pm Sat.

Getting there & around

There is a train service every two hours from **Zagreb** to **Osijek** (5hrs) and **Slavonski Brod** (2hrs 30mins). Buses are more frequent, but with equivalent journey times. Buses run every hour between **Vinkovci** and **Vukovar** (50mins). Hourly buses from Osijek run to Slavonski Brod (2hrs) and Vukovar (45mins).

Istria

Features

Maps

Istria

Istria

Terra Magica to the Romans, is truffle-rich Istria the new Tuscany?

Traditional Istria – hilltop villages, vineyards and accordion players.

Christened 'Terra Magica' by the Romans, this small, triangular peninsula is Croatia's most westerly region. What makes Istria so extraordinary and enchanting is its scale – a dramatic, monumental landscape shrunk down to human size. You can drive north to south in just over an hour and you are never more than 30 minutes from the coast – yet the range and diversity of locations are amazing. It feels like a continent in miniature.

Istria feels separate from the rest of Croatia. From the early 1800s to World War II, Italian was its official language. Older locals speak Italian, place names have an Italian equivalent and street signs are often dual language. Istria has its own, celebrated gastronomy (*see p124* **Istrian cuisine**), its own wines and olive oils, even its own beer, Favorit. Most of all, Istria is more Westernised than the rest of the country, and appeals to the visitor looking for something more satisfying than standard tourist menus and pebbly beaches. Dalmatia doesn't have to try too hard. Istria is swiftly developing rural tourism (*see p140* **Down on the farm**) and a network of authentic villas for hire.

Bordered by mountains to the north and the Adriatic on either side, Istria has existed as a regional entity since the times of the ancient Greeks – when it was known by exactly the same name as today. Self-contained and self-sustaining, it has survived many occupations – most of Europe's major historical powers have laid claim to the region at some time or another. The Romans ruled here from 177 BC, creating a capital in **Pula** at Istria's southern tip. Still the main administrative centre, Pula's superb Roman remains include a well-preserved amphitheatre. Slav tribes settled here from the seventh century, although many locals spoke a Latin tongue for centuries afterwards. Istria

> ▶ The phone code for **Istria** is 052. In this chapter we provide the full phone number for each venue – drop the first '0' if dialling from abroad, followed by the number. If you're dialling within the area, you don't need the 052. Numbers beginning 091 or 098 are mobiles and are expensive to call from most foreign phones.

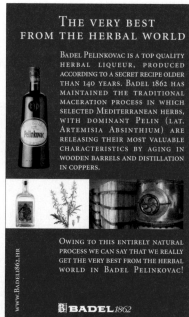

came under Venetian, then Habsburg control, until 1918 when the Italians took over. After Mussolini came to power in 1922, many aspects of Croatian life were frowned upon or banned.

Throughout its history, no matter who was in power, Istria had always been geographically defined as stretching from Trieste to Rijeka. Today, although neither of these two towns are in Istria, they are the main point of entry here by low-cost flights from the UK. Much as Istria was promised to the Italians by the West in World War I, Tito saw the peninsula and key ports of Pula and Trieste as spoils of war. Trieste was controlled by the Americans as Zone A; Zone B inland was under Yugoslav authority. Locals lobbied to keep their region intact. You can still see graffiti from this period, saying 'Trieste is ours'. In 1954 the London Memorandum assigned Zone A to Italy and Zone B to Yugoslavia. A mass exodus to Italy ensued. Tito attracted other Yugoslavs to the region by developing a tourist industry here in the 1960s. Istria was too far removed from the Yugoslav war to be affected by it, apart from the economic effect of dwindling tourism for a couple of years.

The west coast, with its medieval harbour towns, is best known to visitors. The major resorts of **Rovinj** and **Poreč** are picturesque and resonant with historical undertones. **Novigrad** is an underrated gem. Nearer Pula, the islands of **Brijuni** (*see p118* **Brijuni: Tito's Xanadu**) are a major draw, for their natural beauty and bizarre historical and zoological attractions. Until recently, tourists only kept to these coastal destinations.

Today they are discovering inland Istria, and small, historical towns such as **Grožnjan** and **Hum**. Central Istria is famous for the medieval hilltop towns that dot this spectacular area. **Motovun**, in the glorious Mirna Valley, is probably the best-known location, partly thanks to its film festival (*see p128* **Motovun Film Festival**) in July. This is the heart of truffle country and home to some of the finest wines and olive oils in this part of the Mediterranean.

The mountains of Ćićarija and Učka form the region's northern boundary, a haven for hikers, climbers, cavers and paragliders, and a popular destination for extreme sports fans. The east coast remains rugged with forests reaching right down to the rocky coastline giving views out to the islands of the Kvarner Bay.

The joy of Istria is that nothing is ever very far away and inland Istria is every bit as beautiful as the coast. The road network is good although, unfortunately, away from the urban centres, public transport is exceedingly limited. If you have the time and the inclination to hire a car, however, the investment will not be wasted.

The best Istria

Things to do

Take a boat to Tito's bizarre menagerie amid the authentic dinosaur footprints of **Brijuni** (*see p118* **Brijuni: Tito's Xanadu**). Visit hilltop **Grožnjan** (*see p128*), a town inhabited only by artists. Walk around the world's smallest town, **Hum** (*see p130*). See the gorge that inspired Jules Verne in **Pazin** (*p145* **Jules Verne's Pazin**).

Places to stay

Valsabbion (*see p127*) in Pula has a panoramic pool and beauty treatments. The new five-star **Hotel Nautica** (*see p136*) in Novigrad shows the changing face of the marina. The **Hotel Fortuna** (*see p144*) has the run of an island off Poreč. Rovinj's historic **Hotel Villa Angelo d'Oro** (*see p150*) is one of the best in Croatia. **Karoca** (*see p140* **Down on the farm**) near Buzet offers a taste of authentic Istria.

Places to eat

Where to start? **Marino** (*see p131* **Top tables**), perhaps, or **Vrh** (*see p146* **Top tables**) in Buzet, both superb examples of gastronomic excellence in inland Istria. In Pula, don't miss the renowned **Valsabbion** (*see p122*), while **Damir i Ornella** (*see p134*) in Novigrad mixes Croatian and Japanese techniques. **La Puntulina** (*see p148*) in Rovinj offers fabulous views and authentic Italian flavours.

Nightlife

Monvi (*see p149*) in Rovinj is one of the biggest nightlife spots in Croatia. **Colonia Iulia Parentium** (*see p143*) is Poreč's place to be. For live music, Pula's **Club Uljanik** (*see p123*) can't be beat. **Fakin** (*see p133*) is where all the action is in Motovun. Get sassy cocktails and sea views at **Vitriol** (*see p136*) in Novigrad.

Culture

Pula's **amphitheatre** (*see p116*) is a Roman masterpiece – visit in summer and you can catch the **Pula Film Festival** (*see p117*) too. For independent cinema, head for the **Motovun Film Festival** (*see p128*) in July. The village of **Grožnjan** (*see p128*) contains nothing but galleries and artists' studios. The **Euphrasian Basilica** (*see p139*) in Poreč contains stunning Byzantine art.

Istria

Pula

Pula should have everything going for it. The economic powerhouse and only town of any size in the region is a well-located port set by the bottom tip of the Istrian peninsula – seemingly the gateway to the string of idyllic Adriatic islands stretching way down to the south.

Croatia's most interesting national park, the Brijuni Islands, is on its doorstep. So important to the Romans they built the sixth-largest amphitheatre in the Roman world there, Pula contains a well-preserved arch, floor mosaic and Forum from the same era, all in the city centre. It has a strong Italian heritage, a couple of outstanding restaurants, one very good hotel

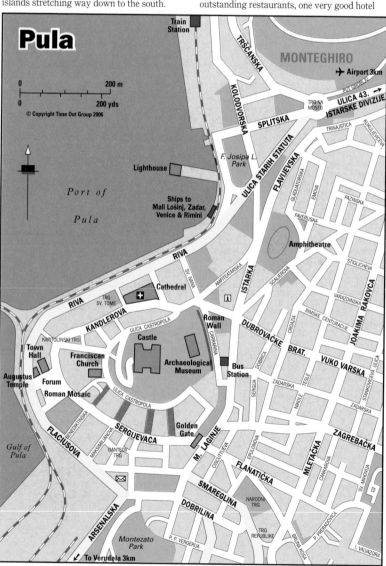

Pula

0 ——— 200 m
0 ——— 200 yds
© Copyright Time Out Group 2006

Istria

Train Station
TRŠĆANSKA
MONTEGHIRO
✈ Airport 3km
KOLODVORSKA
PUT GRGURA...
TRG NA MOSTU
ULICA 43.
SPLITSKA
ISTARSKE DIVIZIJE
TRINAJSTICA
KUKULJEVIĆA
F. Josipa L. Park
ULICA STARIH STATUTA
FLAVIJEVSKA
GLADIATORSKA
EMVIA
PAZINSKA
Lighthouse
FAVERUSKA
Port of Pula
Ships to Mali Lošinj, Zadar, Venice & Rimini
Amphitheatre
STIGLICHEVA
RIVA
AMFITEATARSKA
ISTARKA
SCALIEROVA
VARAZDINSKA
JOAKIMA RAKOVCA
SV. IVANA
Cathedral
RIVA
TRG SV. TOME
KANDLEROVA
RIMSKE CENTURACIJE
CROAZIA
Roman Wall
DUBROVAČKE
VUKO VARSKA
KARTOLINSKI TRG
ULICA CASTROPOLA
Castle
CARRARINA
BRAT.
DOBRIĆA
Town Hall
Franciscan Church
Archaeological Museum
Bus Station
SERGIJA
ZADARSKA
TESLE
NIKOLE
STANKOVIĆEVA
ULICA
Augustus Temple
Forum
Roman Mosaic
ULICA CASTROPOLA
ZADARSKA
Gulf of Pula
FLACIUSOVA
BENEDIKTINSKA
SERGIJEVACA
Golden Gate
ZAGREBAČKA
MAKSIMILIANOVA
DANTEOV TRG
M. LAGINJE
EPULONOVA
CISCUTTIJEVA
FLANATIČKA
MLETAČKA
CANKAROVA
SV. MIHOVILA
✉
SMAREGLINA
NARODNI TRG
DOBRILINA
P. P. VERGERIJA
TRG REPUBLIKE
BRUNA KOSA
P. PRERADOVIĆA
Montezato Park
I. VALVAZORA
ARSENALSKA
↙ To Verudela 3km

The **Roman Amphitheatre** in **Pula** – scene of the annual **Film Festival**.

and a reputation for staging cultural events based on a film festival of 50 years' vintage and an adventurous music festival of the mid 1990s. Oh, and the only airport in Istria, with a budget UK connection all summer.

Alas. When describing Pula, travel writers use phrases like 'a mixed bag' and 'an enigma'. The tourists who fill the town in summer wander somewhat haphazardly after seeing the small clutch of admittedly historic sights. Visitors are mainly housed in the suburbs – downtown has remarkably few hotels. The decent hotels and restaurants here are at **Verudela**, a fair trek from town. The dock area is industrial and serves only seasonal traffic to Mali Lošinj, Zadar, Venice and Rimini. Unlike nearly every seaboard destination in Croatia, Pula has no pretty harbourfront. It is poorly connected by sea, in fact – for Brijuni you must get a bus to Fažana, and then a boat. Its Italian heritage doesn't extend to its clothes shops, and although the city authorities saw fit to put up green-and-yellow street signs in two languages, they're in lettering so small it's impossible to read from across the road. As for UK budget flights, flyglobespan runs once a week from Edinburgh and Glasgow only – easyJet decided on Rijeka for its London-Adriatic link. No buses run between town and Pula airport.

Most of all, there is a sense of doom where culture is concerned. The summer of 2005 was marked by a dispute between local concert promoters and the Church over whether Pula should stage a Marilyn Manson concert or not. (It did.) Meanwhile, the **Pula Film Festival**, glamorous 40 years ago when Tito was inviting Sophia Loren and other stars here, is a mainly domestic affair (www.pulafilmfestival.hr) overshadowed by the joyous cinematic get-

together at Motovun (*see p128*) down the road a month later. The alternative music and arts festival has long gone. The main live music venue, the **Rock Club Uljanik**, is a shadow of itself due to a draconian local law forbidding downtown drinking after midnight.

Things are perhaps not as bad as when James Joyce wintered here immediately after eloping with Nora Barnacle in 1904, writing desperate letters home comparing the place to Siberia. The house where he taught is now a café, the **Uliks** (Ulysses).

Pula was then Pola, the naval base for the Austro-Hungarian empire. This was its second great era in history, some two millennia after its first. The Romans arrived in 177 BC. It became a Roman colony a century later, producing wine and olive oil, and by the time of Augustus from 63 BC Pietas Iulia was a thriving urban centre with a forum, temples and city walls.

Between Augustus and the Habsburgs, Pula diminished to a minor port of a few hundred citizens. Industrialised under the Austrians, who built an arsenal here in 1856, it passed into Italian hands in 1918 and was heavily bombed by the Allies in World War II. Industrialised again under Tito, it saw a rise in package tourism in purpose-built hotels outside town. Pula is certainly worth a weekend visit – and is one of the rare coastal towns where life goes on in winter.

ROMANS AND HABSBURGS

The must-see attraction is, of course, Pula's **amphitheatre** (Flavijevska, 052 219 028, open summer 8am-7pm daily, winter 9am-5pm daily, 20kn). Set a short walk north of the city centre, its outer walls are remarkably preserved, and a wonderful backdrop for the film festival and big-name concerts that take place here every

Istria

Brijuni: Tito's Xanadu

The Brijuni archipelago lies off Istria's west coast, a 15-minute boat journey from Fažana, just north of Pula. Most of the 14 islands are off-limits to the public. This is Croatia's equivalent of Camp David — you have to be a member of the world's elite to get an invite here. Luckily, there is so much to see on the other two you're unlikely to feel hard done by. An open-air time machine, Brijuni records 5,000 years of human history and 150 million years of prehistory when dinosaurs patrolled the islands – you can even follow in their petrified footsteps (*pictured right*).

Veliki Brijuni is by far the largest of the islands and contains the vast majority of its treasures. Beautiful and vaguely surreal – English country estate meets Jurassic Park – it consists of hectares of well-maintained, green parkland surrounded by the dazzling Adriatic and planted up with avenues of prehistoric-looking pines. This is where you will find a golf course, a bird sanctuary, botanical gardens, the zoo and safari park, three museums and the main archaeological sites. A clear map of the islands is posted at its harbour — including details of where to find the dinosaur footprints that dot the island's shoreline.

The oldest remains of human habitation date from 3,000 BC. Built in the bay of Javorika, this Neolithic settlement is only one small part of over 40 hectares (100 acres) of archaeological sites contained on the islands.

After 177 BC the Romans built many villas along with facilities for processing olive oil and the manufacture of amphorae. The last of their olive trees, dating from AD 400, still flourish on the main island. The largest Roman complex is sited in the bay of Verige. This impressive development includes a summerhouse built over three terraces, a series of temples, thermal baths and even a freshwater fish pond. It also included a working harbour that remained in use well into the sixth century.

After the Romans, the Goths left behind little but a few brooches, on display at Brijuni's **main museum**. Byzantium added fortified walls to the main Roman complexes, breached in 788 by Frankish King Carlo the Great, who built his palace on the south-eastern corner of Verige, using the existing Roman sanitation and central heating.

In 1312 plague wiped out the population, so when the Venetians claimed the islands in 1331 there was no one to resist. Brijuni was used for its quarries, the stone transported to Venice. During this time, the area became marshy and a haven for mosquitoes. When Napoleon arrived, he ordered a full survey with a view to their draining and developing the area. After he fell, and Austria took charge, Brijuni had to wait until 1893 before it was rescued from its malaria-infested stupor. The Austrian steel magnate, Paul Kupelwieser bought Brijuni as real estate for

75,000 gold florins. His dream was to create an English-style country park and he devoted the rest of his life to doing so. Today's Brijuni is Kupelwieser's legacy.

How do you create paradise for the rich and famous in the middle of a malaria-ridden swamp? Renowned microbiologist Robert Koch was Kupelwieser's saviour. In 1900 Koch was about to begin experiments into the eradication of malaria in Tuscany. The Austrian read about this in the newspapers and immediately contacted Koch, suggesting he carry out his preliminary research on Brijuni. It was a stroke of genius – and an unqualified success. In 1905 Koch was awarded the Nobel Prize for medicine. He had also succeeded in isolating the cholera and tuberculosis bacteria. A carved monument erected in his honour stands by the harbour in Veliki Brijuni.

Kupelwieser set to work. He excavated the archaeological treasures. He built villas for himself and his friends. He planted trees. He landscaped gardens. He built continental Europe's first 18-hole golf course. He established a zoo. In time, Kupelwieser created his own Xanadu, but he didn't live long enough to see it. After he died in 1918, the Great Depression hit and bankruptcy caused his son to commit suicide. In 1933 Brijuni passed into the hands of another state: Mussolini's Italy.

After the war, the Brijuni archipelago, along with the rest of Istria, became part of Tito's Yugoslavia (*see p28* **Reinventing Tito**). The leader used Brijuni as his base, conducting diplomacy away from spying eyes, setting up the Non-Aligned Movement with India and Egypt here in 1956 and inviting the world's rich and famous to his idyllic playground. As you step onto Veliki Brijuni's quayside you are following in the footsteps of Haile Selassie, Queen Elizabeth II, her sister Margaret, JFK, Richard Burton, Elizabeth Taylor, Sophia Loren – anyone who was anyone in the 1960s. You can see them documented in the 'Josip Broz Tito on Brijuni' exhibition housed in the main museum. Another, 'From the Memory of an Old Austrian', celebrates the vision and achievements of Kupelwieser.

As the Non-Aligned founder, Tito was regularly presented with exotic animals by its various political leaders. As a result, the zoo on Veliki Brijuni continued to expand. You can

still see many of the animals, including Indira Gandhi's elephants Sony and Lanka. Those who died were stuffed and placed in Brijuni's Natural History Museum, part of a three-museum complex near the harbour. Visitors are reassured that all animals died from natural causes, although the Tito exhibition next door contains many photographs of him with his trusty hunting rifle. An ethnographic museum has been closed since 1991.

The Brijuni National Park offices are on the quayside at Fažana. You can book excursions plus yachting, golf and diving expeditions. The organised tour (160kn) passes Veliki Brijuni's main sights on a little train with an accompanying guide. It takes about four hours including the sea crossing from Fažana. Independent travellers can hire a bike or a little electric buggy.

There's more than enough to see on Veliki Brijuni to stay a couple of nights in one of the three hotels near the harbour, each with a restaurant, or three luxury seaside villas, where you get your own maid and private beach. There are three standard villas too. You book rooms at the office in Fažana or from 052 521 367, www.brijuni.hr.

summer. Inside is a bit of a mess, of green plastic seating and clumps of stone, the view at the top of the sloping interior a disappointing one of the grass verge running to the harbour and crane after crane beyond. But you do get a sense of the gladiatorial contests held here until AD 400, particularly when you go down to the corridors on the sea-facing side where the lions were kept. Through a long tunnel lined with Roman masonry, you'll now find a few displays about olive oil production and a rather detailed map of Via Flavia, which connected Pula with Trieste. Outside is a modest souvenir shop with the same opening hours as the arena.

The second of the Roman attractions stands at the south-east entrance to the town centre. The **Arch of the Sergians**, or **Golden Gate**, was built in 30 BC. Its most notable aspects are the reliefs of grapes and winged victories on the inner façade. Passing through the arch and past the statue of James Joyce, marking where the author taught in 1904-05, you walk down the Roman-era high street, the **Sergijevaca**. It leads to the heart of Pula, the Roman **mosaic** and **Forum**, and **Temple of Augustus**. The mosaic dates to the second century AD and has geometric motifs representing the twins Amphion and Zethos. Alongside is the Forum, still the main square, today lined with cafés (including the landmark **Cvajner**), the Town Hall, tourist office and, lining the far side, the six classical Corinthian columns of the Temple of Augustus. Inside is a modest collection of Roman finds (052 218 689, open summer only, 9am-3pm daily, 10kn).

Pula's main two religious buildings, the Gothic-style Franciscan church and the cathedral, a Renaissance façade built on a Roman temple, are set near the Forum, below the centrepiece **Fortress** (Kaštel). Neither contain much of great interest. The Fortress, originally the Roman Capitol, was built by the Venetians in the 17th century; it houses the disappointing **Istrian Historical Museum** (Gradinski uspon 6, 052 211 566, open summer 8am-8pm daily, winter 9am-5pm daily, 10kn). Towards the old Roman wall is the worthwhile **Archaeological Museum of Istria**.

Anything else of interest lies south of the city centre, on or off the main Veruda road leading to the hotel hub and best beaches of Verudela. Halfway to the two nearest beaches, at Stoja and Valsaline, is the ornate, verdant **Naval Cemetery**, built by the Habsburgs, the perfect spot for a stroll on a hot summer's afternoon.

Archaelogical Museum of Istria

Carrarina 3 (052 218 603/www.mdc.hr/pula).
Open *Summer* 9am-8pm Mon-Sat; 10am-3pm Sun. *Winter* 9am-2pm Mon-Fri. **Admission** 10kn. **No credit cards**.

Rovinj. *See p147.*

Many of the best local Illyrian and Roman finds have been put on display here, a three-storey traditional museum with good English-language documentation. You'll find jewellery, coins and weapons from Roman and medieval times, ceramics and fossils from pre-history, plus mosaics and sarcophagi.

Beaches

Central Pula has no beaches. The nearest ones at Stoja and along Lungomare between Veruda and Valsaline are adequate, but if you're having to take a city bus (Nos.1 and 4 respectively) to get there, you may as well take the Nos.2a and 3a to Verudela, its nicer shingle beaches and best-in-town lunches. If you've come for a beach holiday, leave Pula for **Medulin** and the windsurfing centre of **Premantura** (*see below*), both a regular bus journey from Pula.

Excursions

For holiday-makers, the most obvious hike from Pula is to **Medulin** and/or **Premantura**, at the southernmost tip of Istria. Pulapromet buses run almost hourly to Medulin (No.25) and Premantura (No.26), journey time about 30 minutes. Both are good centres for windsurfing, (www.windsurfing.hr), Medulin particularly for beginners. Each has long stretches of beach and shallow water. Medulin's Bajeca has water slides for kids and there are taxi boats to nearby little islands. For details of the well-equipped tourist hotels and camping sites,

contact TZO Medulin (Centar 223, Medulin,
052 577 145, www.tzom.hr). The main diving
club, KL Sub, has its office in Medulin (Ližnan
186a, 052 545 116, www.divingindie.com) but
dives near the Indie campsite at Banjole, which
is nearer Pula. Behind Premantura is the nature
park of **Kamenjak**, some 10km (6 miles) of
coves, inlets and tiny islands, some preferred
by naturists.

The major excursion from Pula is to the
Brijuni Islands (*see p118* **Brijuni: Tito's
Xanadu**). Boats only go from Fažana, 7km (4.5
miles) north-west of Pula by hourly bus No.21.

Vodnjan, 11km (7 miles) north of Pula (bus
No.22, 20mins), houses the biggest church in
Istria, St Blaise (052 511 420, open summer 9am-
7pm Mon-Sat, 2-7pm Sun, winter by reservation
only). Its main attraction lies in an area
curtained off behind the altar: mummified
bodies of three saints brought here from Venice.
There is a 35kn charge to see them. There are
also hundreds of saintly relics in the sacristy
(30kn). The rustic Vodnjanka (Istarska, 052 511
435, open summer 10am-1pm, 5pm-midnight
daily, winter 10am-1pm, 5pm-midnight Mon-
Sat) serves superb Istrian specialities.

Where to eat

As the main town in Istria, Pula cannot fail to
have decent restaurants. Three would make
the nationwide top ten list of many a local
gourmet critic: the **Valsabbion**, the **Milan**
and the **Vela Nera**. All three are out of town,
in Verudela and Stoja. In town, the **Kantina**
and **Scaletta** are recommended. The Forum
and side streets are lined with terrace venues,
but none are particularly notable.

Borghese

Monte Paradiso 21 (052 392 111). **Open** 11am-
midnight daily. **Credit** AmEx, DC, MC, V.
Reputable fish and seafood restaurant in Verudela
with prices to match. Starched white tablecloths and
napkins await the diner in an interior embellished
with natural light. The fish is fresh and finely prepared, but don't miss out on the recommended
starter of mixed salad with fruits de mer and speciality main dish of scampi ravioli.

Kantina

Flanatička 16 (052 214 054). **Open** 8am-midnight
daily. **Credit** AmEx, DC, MC, V.
Hidden behind the main market, this lovely terrace
restaurant serves Istrian delicacies in a converted
Habsburg villa. The decor is contemporary, as is the
careful presentation of the food. Truffles feature
heavily, either with steak (95kn) or, more traditionally, with *fuži*, Istrian pasta twists. There are plenty of greens, rocket particularly, some 40 types of
wine and the cake selection is outstanding.

Milan

Stoja 4 (052 300 200/www.milan1967.hr). **Open**
Summer 11am-midnight daily. *Winter* 11am-
midnight Mon-Sat. **Credit** AmEx, DC, MC, V.
One of the top three restaurants in town is set in a
modern three-star hotel by the Naval Cemetery –
both are friendly and family-run but the ground-
floor restaurant is the biggest attraction. A display

Cabahia bar, Pula. *See right.*

case heaves with riches fresh from the sea, duly listed on a long main menu. Most types are 300kn a kilo, reasonable considering the quality on offer. Shellfish come in all types, although risotto portions are (in Croatian terms) quite small. Frog's legs with polenta is a speciality. For wine, you're literally spoilt for choice, as the cellar here has 700 examples, running up to 1,000kn a bottle. Let the waiter advise.

Scaletta

Flavijevska 26 (052 541 599). **Open** *Summer* 10.30am-11pm daily. *Winter* 10.30am-11pm Mon-Sat. **Credit** AmEx, DC, MC, V.
Scaletta is two venues in one, a pavilion on one side of the main road up from the amphitheatre, and a dinky little dining room on the other, where you'll find its charming hotel (*see p127*), round the corner up a slight incline. Scaletta is a splendid option for its location – and its kitchen. A risotto Scaletta with fruits de mer is delicately seasoned with saffron and sprinkled with raisins. Steak comes with white truffles, lobster with Istrian noodles, *rezanci*. Malvazija and other Istrian tipples are the customary accompaniments, although you can order up an Erdinger wheat beer – Scaletta is German-owned.

Valsabbion

Pješčana uvala IX/26 (052 218 033/www.valsabbion. net). **Open** *Feb-Dec* 10am-midnight daily. **Closed** Jan. **Credit** AmEx, DC, MC, V.
The best table in town and certainly one of the top five in Croatia. Attached to the high-quality hotel of the same name (*see p127*), Valsabbion comprises two dozen tables, half on a bay-view terrace under a bright white canopy, half in a tasteful, art deco interior of refined pastel colours. The food more than equals this establishment's international reputation,

inventive and satisfying. If money is not an issue (how often do you dine at Valsabbion?), try the tasting menu (495kn) of ten gourmet creations, perhaps truffle carpaccio or wild asparagus, all wonderfully presented. À la carte, locally sourced Kvarner Bay shrimps or Premantura crabs are teased with touches of greenery. The wine list is some 200 strong.

Vela Nera

Pješčana uvala (052 219 209/www.velanera.hr). **Open** 8am-midnight daily. **Credit** AmEx, DC, MC, V.
Incongruously set next to a supermarket, but with a terrace overlooking the pretty Marina Veruda, this is Pula's second-most notable restaurant. Its modern, spacious interior is a refreshing change from the starched-white formal approach common elsewhere in town. Informal, too, are some of the combinations adventurously thrown together. The salmon and whisky carpaccio as a cold starter, for example, or the peaches and champagne mingled with scampi in the house risotto. Dining partners can dip into the house fish platter (280kn) or meat version (140kn). More than 100 wines to choose from too.

Where to drink

Pula has decent little bars but few in prominent locations. Local law forbids a city-centre bar opening after midnight, particularly open-air venues. Places like **P14**, **Epidemija** and **Scandal Express** are classic downtown bars the first-time visitor would never find. Towards Verudela, where Buducinova and Tomasinijeva meet, is a hub of spacious terrace venues. The best are **Podroom** and **Cabahia**.

Cabahia

Širolina 4 (no phone). **Open** 10am-midnight Mon-Sat; noon-midnight Sun.

Great spot for a summer evening, this, in the bar hub halfway between town and Verudela. A light Latin American theme runs through the leafy front garden and jumble-sale back room bar – Café do Brasil sacks, a Che Guevara flag and cocktail – although the beer is Slovenian Laško.

Caffè Uliks

Trg Portarata 1 (052 219 158). **Open** 6.30am-10pm daily.

The statue outside gives it away. A century ago James Joyce taught at a school in this building by the Roman arch. He and his eloper are also honoured with a Joyce cocktail (Jameson's, Martini Bianco and Krašokova pear) and a Nora of Bailey's, Bacardi and cream. Other Irish drinks include bottled Guinness and Kilkenny (and tasty Irish coffee) in this otherwise standard bar in a pedestrianised square.

Cvajner

Forum 2 (052 216 502). **Open** 8am-11pm daily.

Or to give it its official title, the Kunstkafe-Cvajner. Either way, it's an absolutely splendid bar for the main square of a tourist-swamped historic Roman town centre. Part gallery, part junkshop, the Cvajner is bohemian in appearance but not gratuitously so. Unmatching furniture, sculptures and an old carriage are placed around a spacious, high-ceilinged interior where parts of an old wall are dated AD 1928. Bottles of Chimay and dark Laško complement the standard 40kn cocktails, best partaken on the Forum terrace.

Epidemija

Kandlerova 12 (no phone). **Open** 6am-midnight Mon-Fri; 8am-midnight Sat, Sun.

The Union Pivo sign outside says 'Coco'. Ignore it. The beer is Laško, the place is Epidemija and local media types have been meeting here in a fug of cigarette smoke since it opened in 2004. By the cathedral, beneath the Fortress, it's a strange find but a popular one for those in the know.

Podroom

Buducinova 16 (no phone). **Open** 9am-1am daily.

Candidate for best bar in Pula, the Podroom makes good use of its leafy garden with a stone waterfall, plonking a bar in the middle of it and seats all around. Inside is a bit of a mess – a picture of a woman with a fried egg, a sign saying 'Harley Davidson Motorcycle Club' – but a friendly, clubby vibe wins the day. Plenty of 40kn cocktails too.

P14

Preradovićeva 14 (052 382 987). **Open** 5pm-midnight daily.

Jozo Ćurković's wonderful little alternative haunt at the far end of Flanatička attracts an arty clientele for impromptu stand-up performances and one-off events. Centrepieced by a snake-shaped bar table, decorated with mushrooms and a lit-up globe, P14

is an address like no other downtown bar. Dark Laško on draught and plenty of Istrian spirits from the bar propped up by friendly regulars.

Scandal Express

Ciscuttijeva 15 (052 212 106). **Open** 7am-midnight Mon-Fri; 7am-2pm, 6pm-midnight Sat; 8am-2pm, 6pm-midnight Sun.

A tiny, smoky dive where local bohemians meet, you'll find this place near the theatre at the Giardini end of Flanatička. There's no room around the bar at all, so regulars hug the corners by the entrance or, more usually, spill out on to the narrow street.

Nightlife

With downtown closing early, nightlife is limited to certain bars in Veruda (*see above*) and a couple of mainstream clubs north-east of the centre. The best is **Aruba** (Šijanska cesta 1), with a bar outdoors and packed two-room disco inside. **Club Uljanik** (Dobrilina 2, 098 285 969 mobile, www.clubuljanik.hr) by the harbour has an agenda of alternative bands and DJ nights. The Napleonic **Fort Bourguignon** near Valsaline Bay hosts regular summer DJ events. Outside Pula, name DJs make it to **Joy** in **Premantura** and the **Disco Imperial** (Fucane 72, 098 193 8984 mobile, www.disco-imperial.com) in **Medulin**.

Regular James Joyce at the **Caffè Uliks**.

Istrian cuisine

Istria is a world away from Dalmatia, where tourist-friendly restaurants serve similar types of seafood in uniform sauces (*see p37* **Food & Drink**). Istria has its own gastronomic identity. Pasta, gnocchi, *rižot* (risotto) and polenta feature strongly on all domestic menus but the prime ingredients will differ. The reason for this is that the basis of Istrian cuisine lies in the freshness and ready availability of its ingredients. If you are on the coast then it's fish and if you're inland it's not. Although Istria is a small peninsula – you're never more than 32km (20 miles) from the sea – it's as if there's an invisible 'food wall' dividing the cuisine in two.

This is a peasant cuisine, of the finest tradition, which still bows to the seasonal cycle of gastronomic delights. Spring brings the wild asparagus. Summer is awash with fresh fruits and vegetables. Autumn is dominated by mushrooms and Christmas marks the pig-killing season with its home-made sausages and the hanging of *pršut*. The whole is punctuated by seafood or game depending on your location. With modern-day food preservation techniques, many of these seasonal foods are available all year round for the burgeoning restaurant market. However, you will regularly – and somewhat apologetically – be informed if the truffles on your pasta have been frozen. In the best restaurants the time of year will still dictate what you find on your plate. So, remember,

if you happen to be enjoying strawberries in November then you've seriously strayed into foreign territory.

The coast provides a wealth of fresh fish and crustaceans. To give you an idea of the sheer range available there are seven different types of mussel alone. Scampi is a particular favourite. Fresh and huge, they are invariably served in their shells – use of fingers is mandatory – and be prepared to eat the heads if you want to look like a local. Squid (*lignje*) is also ubiquitous, fried, stuffed, grilled or sautéed in 'black' risottos. Lovers of Dover sole should make a point of trying the Istrian version, locally known as *list*. This is exactly the same fish but, having made its migration to Istria, it's leaner, sweeter and altogether tastier than when it left UK waters. Forget subtle filleting or heavy, complicated sauces, when you order fish that's exactly what you get.

Inland, the menus are based on beef, pork and game. If you're ordering veal, remember that in Croatia this simply means young beef and not the questionably produced white meat that we know in Britain. *Divlje* (game) will be a toss up between wild boar and venison, depending on what the local hunters have managed to shoot. Interestingly, game birds rarely feature although some form of chicken dish is usually available. Rabbit is another favourite but you normally have to order this at least a day in advance.

Options for vegetarian are typically limited to a handful of specialities such as wild asparagus, which is usually served with scrambled eggs, or truffles with pasta. A traditional Istrian salad is another good bet; based on bitter leaves such as radicchio or endive, it also contains beans and hard-boiled eggs for added sustenance.

The pearls of Istrian produce, however, are available throughout the region. *Pršut* – air-cured ham – is an integral part of the Istrian identity. Winter's bitingly cold north-easterly wind – the *bura* – together with the air's exceptional purity, is credited for the fine taste of this regional speciality. Traditionally reserved for feast days and celebrations, a platter of *pršut* and local cheese is now commonplace as a first course in most restaurants. This goes hand in hand with the traditional bean soup, *maneštra*, which is based on stock made from these bones. In leaner times these *pršut* bones would have been passed from house to house to ensure that the whole village shared in the dish.

Olive oil is another staple and, in Roman times, it was considered the empire's finest to such an extent that only oil from the 'golden triangle' between Vodnjan, Barbariga and Fažana was considered fit to grace the tables of the Caesars. Today, oil production has been revived and Istria is once again credited with producing some of the highest quality oil in the world. The 'Olive Oil Roads of Istria' have now been established to enable enthusiasts to tour local producers and sample their wares first hand.

Far more recent but no less important are the high quality black and white truffles of central Istria. Mainly located in the vast Motovun Forest, these valuable funghi were accidentally discovered by Mussolini's cohorts in 1936. No doubt they had been happily growing away for years but, unlike the Italians, the locals were oblivious to their existence. Now, however, Istrian truffles are big business. Much of the local population now regularly scour the forest with their trusty truffle dogs.

Underpinning everything, however, are Istria's omnipresent vineyards. Wine isn't simply something you drink: it's a way of life here. The Istrian wine-making tradition dates back to the times of ancient Greece. On the east coast lies an area known as Kalavojna.

The name is derived from *kalos oinos*, Greek for 'good wine'. In fact, Greece was the origin of Istria's main grape variety, Malvasia. White Malvasia, red Teran and refreshing Muscat account for the vast majority of Istria's vineyards. In the mid 20th century Istrians were depressingly regarded as excellent grape growers but poor wine makers. This has changed beyond recognition over the past 15 years. A new generation of young vintners is ensuring Istria's growing reputation for fine wines. You can discover these wines for yourself by touring the 'Wine Roads of Istria'. As with the Olive Oil roads you can pick up this information from any tourist office.

And then there's the grappa. If it grows then some Istrian, somewhere, will have popped it into grappa. Fruits, berries, nuts, herbs, bushes, trees, even truffles. The range is staggering. The main types, commercially available, are Medovača (honey), Biska (mistletoe leaves, a speciality of Hum and Roč), Erba Luiga (herbal grappa, great for hangovers), Orahovac (walnuts) and any number of fruit brandies, which you'll often find being sold from small, roadside stalls. In most restaurants you will be offered a complimentary grappa on settling your bill, so why not experiment a little?

Where to stay

Downtown Pula has a grand total of four modest hotels. The classy options are all 5km (3 miles) south of town in Verudela, which is accessible by bus Nos.2a and 3a, or with a 60kn taxi ride. The best there is the boutique **Valsabbion**; the four-star **Histria** offers a more traditional high-standard stay. The nearby **Palma** is in the same group – for details of the seasonally opening others, check website www.arenaturist.hr.

Hotel Histria

Verudela (052 590 000/fax 052 214 175/ www.arenaturist.hr). **Rates** €84-€156 double. **Credit** AmEx, DC, MC, V.

Top tables Konoba Morgan, Buje

Morgan is one of Istria's most exciting restaurants. Self-effacing to the point of suicidal – it's not even signposted – it's full throughout the year, often with Italians who travel to eat here on a regular basis.

Marko Morgan, the young restaurateur, has a simple mission. He aims to excite his guests by producing excellent but simple dishes based on authentic Istrian recipes.

The top-quality ingredients are all sourced locally and attention to detail predominates. The veal must be female – higher fat means tastier meat. The process involves the whole family, Morgan senior hunting the wide selection of game, mother and sister working in the kitchen.

Specialities include home-made polenta with game (rabbit, pheasant, wild boar, venison or quail); pasta stuffed with chestnut purée; and *krestine*, red pasta filled with white, cockerel meat. Morgan also places great emphasis on blending wine with food. The restaurant has an excellent selection of the region's finest vintages including some almost-forgotten varieties such as Plavina and Hrvatica.

Morgan is pleasingly fresh and unpretentious. The instruments lying around testify to Marko's training as a musician. After hours, he might play piano for his guests, perhaps on the large, covered terrace. The view is relaxing although the surroundings are somewhat ramshackle. Note the dilapidated farm building with its Communist red star still precariously perched on the roof.

And the name? Bizarrely, it's a common name in this part of Istria. Legend has it that the infamous pirate Captain Henry Morgan hid from his pursuers in the Limski Kanal and was happy to fraternise with the womenfolk.

For Morgan, take the main road from Buje to Brtonigla, then the track on the left-hand side about 1km (half a mile) before Brtonigla. *Bracanija 1, Buje (052 774 520)*. **Closed** Mid Sept-mid Oct. **Open** *Mid Oct-mid Sept* 11am-10pm daily. **Credit** AmEx, DC, V.

A landmark four-star, this, commanding a view of Verudela Bay from the bank facing the Valsabbion (*see below*). All 240 simply furnished rooms have sea-facing balconies. Facilities include a circular outdoor pool, a heated indoor one, both with seawater, a sauna, gym and disco. Some 20 tennis courts and other sports pitches are nearby. It also has a casino and conference centre. Although pricy considering the prosaic nature of the rooms, the hotel's half-board rates are a snip at €5 over the price of a room.

Hotel Milan

Stoja 4 (052 210 200/fax 052 210 500/ www.milan1967.hr). **Rates** 490kn-590kn single; 620kn-850kn double. **Credit** AmEx, DC, MC, V.
By the Naval Cemetery before you get to the Stoja headland, the Milan is best known for its quality restaurant (*see p121*). Its dozen three-star rooms are clean and comfortable, and within easy reach of the modest beach at Valkane Bay.

Hotel Omir

Sergija Dobriča 6 (052 210 614/fax 052 213 944). **Rates** 450kn single; 600kn double. **Credit** AmEx, DC, MC, V.
Handy cheapie in the centre of town, a Socialist-style guesthouse with old furnishings and light fittings, and a wonderfully weird breakfast room decked out with art and an aquarium. Nineteen quiet rooms and a pizzeria downstairs. Round the corner is the ten-room three-star Galija (Epulonova 3, 052 383 802, fax 052 383 804, www.hotel-galija-pula.com, 550kn) with its own restaurant.

Hotel Palma

Verudela (052 590 000/fax 052 214 175/ www.arenaturist.hr). **Rates** €58-€112 double. **Credit** AmEx, DC, MC, V.
The three-star Palma shares some of the facilities of the nearby Histria, particularly the 20 tennis courts. Guests have the use of three outdoor pools, one with a water slide, and a bowling alley. Rooms have balconies, although the hotel faces inwards away from the sea. Attractive half-board rates only add €3 to the price of a double. The Palma is open year round.

Hotel Riviera

Splitska 1 (052 211 166/fax 052 219 117/ www.arenaturist.hr). **Rates** 465kn-615kn double. **Credit** AmEx, DC, MC, V.
Classic old Habsburg hotel whose grand façade and marble lobby belie the fact that its 65 rooms need renovation. It's in the Arena Turist hotel group, so, hopefully, this won't be too long in coming. In the meantime, it's a handy base if you're just in by train – the station is five minutes away – and want to see the amphitheatre and a few sights around town.

Hotel Scaletta

Flavijevska 26 (052 541 599/fax 052 540 285/ www.hotel-scaletta.com). **Rates** €55-€68 single; €71-€99 double. **Credit** AmEx, DC, MC, V.
Conveniently located, German-run hotel and restaurant (*see p122*) a short walk towards the station from

the amphitheatre. The dozen rooms (ten doubles, two singles) are all simple and comfortable, and a decent breakfast is included in the price.

Valsabbion

Pješčana uvala IX/26 (052 218 033/fax 052 222 991/www.valsabbion.net). **Rates** €69-€113 double. **Credit** AmEx, DC, MC, V.
Ten immaculately conceived rooms comprise the hotel accommodation at the high-class restaurant Valsabbion. Half have sea-view balconies, all are equipped with fine taste. Six are doubles in two categories, two are two categories of suite. An outstanding buffet breakfast is €11.50, but included in the half-board rates in certain weeks, of just over twice the room rate but also covering a four-course dinner in one of Istria's finest restaurants. There's also a panoramic pool, fitness facilities and various beauty treatments.

Resources

Hospital

Zagrebačka 30 (052 214 433/376 500).

Internet

Cyber@Café *Flanatička 14 (052 215 345/098 943 4240 mobile).* **Open** 8am-10pm daily.

Pharmacy

Giardini 15 (052 222 551). **Open** 24hrs daily. Ring the bell for night service.

Police

Trg republike 2 (052 532 111).

Post office

Danteov trg 4 (052 215 955). **Open** 7am-8pm Mon-Fri; 7am-2pm Sat.

Tourist information

Arena Turist *Hotel Riviera, Splitska 1 (052 529 400/www.arenaturist.hr).* **Open** 9am-6pm Mon-Sat.
Main booking desk for the local chain of hotels, in the branch nearest to the train station. Can also help with private rooms.
Atlas *Starih Statuta 1 (052 393 040/www.atlas-croatia.com).* **Open** 9am-6pm Mon-Sat.
Books accommodation and finds private rooms.
Pula Tourist Office *Forum 3 (052 219 197/ www.pulainfo.hr).* **Open** 8am-8pm Mon-Sat; 9am-8pm Sun.
Helpful office occupying an old Roman building.

Getting there & around

Pula **airport** (052 530 105/www.airport-pula.com) is 6km (3.5 miles) north-east of the centre. Flyglobespan (www.flyglobespan.com) runs a weekly service from late May to the end of October with Edinburgh (Sun) and Glasgow (Tue). Croatia Airlines runs a service with Zagreb at least once a day. There is no public transport into town. A taxi costs about 200kn.

In summer there is a twice-weekly fast-boat service with **Rimini** and **Venice**. You can find details at www.find-croatia.com/ferries-croatia. The only service within Croatia is a **car ferry** between **Zadar**, **Mali Lošinj** and Pula, from mid June to early September. It leaves Zadar five times a week at 6.30am, returning from Pula mid afternoon. The journey time is eight hours, foot passenger fare for Zadar–Pula about €15. For details see www.losinjska-plovidba.hr/Ljetni.htm.

The **train** station is north on Kolodvorska, a ten-minute walk from the centre. A service from Zagreb runs four times a day, journey time about seven hours, with a bus between Rijeka and Lupoglav. There is also a daily service with Ljubljana (4hrs).

Pula has two **bus stations**, one in the city centre at Istarska, the other north-east of the amphitheatre at Trg Istarske Brigade (052 502 997). There are daily international services from Trieste and Venice and a summer one on Fridays from Milan. There are buses every hour from Zagreb and regular ones from the main towns in Istria. Details of all can be found at www.pulainfo.hr/en/autobus.asp. The local bus company **Pulapromet** (www.pulapromet.hr) runs services to nearby Vodnjan, Premantura and Medulin as well as ones within town. Buses for Stoja (No.1) and Verudela (Nos.2a and 3a) leave every 20 minutes (15mins). Nearly all stop at both stations in town. Tickets are 6kn from a newsstand, 10kn on board. There is a **taxi** office by the Roman wall at Carrarina (052 223 228/098 715 230 mobile).

Grožnjan

Now known as the 'Town of Artists', Grožnjan is a place with an instinct for survival. Twice now it has nearly been wiped of the map but remarkably has managed to survive.

Grožnjan is one of Istria's prettiest medieval hilltop towns, 228 metres (750 feet) above sea level, just north of the main road between Buje and Vižinada. Its position provides spectacular views, the Adriatic coast to the west and the dramatic landscape of the glorious Mirna Valley to the east. The northern region of Istria is rich with these ancient, Italianate settlements. What sets Grožnjan apart is that this town feels loved, alive and cared for. Amazing when you consider that, just 40 years ago, it lay derelict and deserted – and not for the first time.

In 1630 bubonic plague swept across Istria wreaking death and catastrophe. Nowhere was worse hit than Grožnjan. Almost overnight this thriving centre became a ghost town. The Venetian republic couldn't afford to let such a formerly prosperous area stand idle so it set about revitalising the municipality. It brought in Italian families from the provinces of Veneto, Carnia and Furlania. Tradesmen and artisans settled in the town itself. For the surrounding villages, the republic brought in peasants to work the land: Dalmatians, Montenegrins and Albanians, the Illyrian provinces were never short of strong backs. As an inducement, these new settlers were exempt from taxes for 20 years on condition that the land was cultivated and productive within five.

Motovun Film Festival

Motovun's annual film festival is central Istria's cultural highlight of the year. For five days in late July this tiny medieval town is transformed into a party-mad hub, occasionally patronised by some of the most famous names in the business, a cross between Sundance and Glastonbury. Expect enchanting open-air screenings in the historic main square on balmy summer evenings.

Established in 1999 with the stated aim of promoting independent films and films originating in countries with modest movie industries, this small festival has burgeoned beyond all expectations. It's almost become too big. With a resident population of only a couple of hundred, Motovun's annual inundation of 50,000-plus souls has the little hilltop village bursting at the seams. But then again, that's all part of the fun.

The festival presents 80 documentaries, features and shorts. The top prize is the Propeller of Motovun. In 2004 it went to Ken Loach for *Ae Fond Kiss* and there are usually a handful of offerings from UK independents. Other awards include From A to A, for the best regional film from Albania to Austria. You can also access some 30 shorts from the festival's website.

Screenings are scheduled around Motovun over the five days from 10am to midnight, followed by live music until 3am or 4am. The festival becomes a 24-hour party and you don't have to be a film buff to enjoy it. People arrive from all over Europe; accommodation is at a premium. A campsite is set up in Pod Motovun at the bottom of the hill but many just sleep in their cars. For more details, contact www.motovunfilmfestival.com.

Hilltop **Grožnjan** – former ghost town repopulated entirely by artists.

Grožnjan grew and prospered. In 1902 Austrians built the Paranzana Railway (*see p132* **Train in vain**), opening up new markets in Koper and Trieste. In 1910 the local census recorded 1,658 residents in town and 4,028 in the municipality. The depression of the 1920s saw the beginnings of slow economic migration to centres of employment like Trieste, although the new Italian rulers brought electrification and waterworks.

After World War II, this part of Istria was assigned to Tito's Yugoslavia. By 1956 some two-thirds of north-west Istria had emigrated to Italy. In Grožnjan only 20 souls remained. It was 1630 all over again. Neighbouring towns such as Završje never recovered. Not Grožnjan.

Artists also have an instinct for survival and they know a prime location when they see one. At the beginning of the 1960s a group of artists stumbled across the decaying and deserted town of Grožnjan. Stunning views and masses of studio space going begging became the perfect place for an artists' colony. They started moving in and by 1965 they had managed to make it official. Grožnjan was formally declared a 'Town of Artists' and the keys were handed over. Little by little, artists from Croatia and Slovenia began to transform the abandoned houses into homes, workshops, studios and galleries. Premises were allocated for the **International Cultural Centre for Young Musicians** (MKC HGM Grožnjan, Umberta Gorjana 2, 052 776 106).

Today a disproportionate number of residents are cultural professionals of one sort or another. As a consequence Grožnjan's street signs are hand-painted ceramics, rather than state-manufactured enamel; the colours of the shutters are subtle but just right; there are ancient-looking stone seats perfectly sited for enjoying the view; and everywhere you look, there's a gallery. There's a perfect little town square and outside the town loggia on balmy, summer evenings are recitals by operatic tenors or noodling jazzers, all performing as part of the **Grožnjan Musical Summer** (www.hgm.hr).

In a way the town has come full circle. Today's artists and crafts-people are the tradesmen and artisans of the 17th century. The spirit of Grožnjan continues – beautiful, creative and very much alive.

Where to eat & drink

Art'A

Trg corner 3 (no phone). **Open** 8am-midnight Tue-Sun. **No credit cards**.
Suitably arty café with a panoramic terrace, one of the few places in town open all year round. Not much by way of food, though.

Bastia

1 Svibanja 1 (052 776 370). **Open** *Mid June-Aug* 8am-2am daily. *Mar-mid June, Sept-mid Jan* 9am-10pm. **Closed** Mid Jan-Feb. **No credit cards**.

Istria

Hum.

Under the church tower, this large traditional restaurant is the main one in town. Fabulous local dishes include home-made sausage, rumpsteak with truffles and twisted pasta ties (*fuži*) with wild game. There's a little bar with a piano in the back.

Where to stay

Apart from the **Pintur**, a couple of familes are happy to take in paying guests – just ask at the **Bastia**. During the music festival, most are happy to sleep where they fall, in the main square. If you happen to be performing and need some proper shut-eye, the nearby **Radanić Hotel** (052 776 353, 091 783 3772 mobile), run by an old local of the same name, is a friendly, cheap, traditional guesthouse.

Pintur
M Gorjana 9 (052 731 055). **Closed** Jan-Mar. **Rates** *Apr-Dec* 300kn double. **No credit cards.**
Modest little guesthouse and eatery (closed Mon) opposite the Bastia, with four three-star rooms.

Galleries

Fronticus Gallery
Trg Lože 3 (052 776 357/eugen.v.b.@inet.hr). **Open** varies.
The main public gallery in town.

Multimedia Cultural Centre
Palača Spinotti Morteani (052 776 349/ ziri-podzupanica@pu.tel.hr).

Tourist information

Grožnjan Tourist Office
Umberta Gorjana 3 (052 776 131/www.groznjan-grisignana.hr).

Getting there & around

There is no public transport to Grožnjan. Your only option is to take the Buzet-Buje bus and ask the driver to drop you off at Bijele Zemlje, and walk the 3km (2 miles) uphill from there.

Hum

Wrapped around by thick, medieval walls, Hum is billed as the smallest town in the world. To qualify as a town, a settlement must contain a school, a church, a post office, a town hall and a pub. Squeeze in a dozen houses and that's Hum. Traditionally it's been home to just two families, with the priest also the publican.

But things are changing. As you wander round the town's single, circular street, be careful not to trip over any building rubble. People have cottoned on to Hum's charm and slowly the town is coming to life.

As you pass through the town's massive, metal doors you enter a cave-like antechamber hewn straight out of the rock. Above is the Town Hall. On the walls are stone tablets inscribed in ancient Glagolitic, a Slavic script for which Hum is famous (*see p143* **The alley of Glagolites**). Ahead is the main square; to the left is the ludicrously large **Church of the Exalted and Blessed Virgin Mary** with its magnificent crenellated belltower. The consecration chapel of **Sv Jeronima** in the graveyard houses 12th-century frescoes covered with Glagolitic graffiti.

Left is a Lilliputian house with a picturesque loggia. This is the main street – the only street. A small gallery signed 'Imela' is the source of Hum's second claim to fame: **Biska**, grappa flavoured with mistletoe – made from the leaves rather than the poisonous berries. It's either bright green or golden brown in colour, depending on whether fresh or dried leaves have been used.

Further up the street is the **Hum Museum** (052 662 596, open summer 11am-5pm daily), really a souvenir shop but with a small collection of old Istrian furniture and artefacts. You can also buy Glagolitic alphabet charts.

Finish the circuit of the town and step out of the main gate and into Hum's single restaurant, only open at weekends: the **Konoba Hum** (052 660 005, open 11am-11pm Sat-Sun) has a covered terrace with a beautiful view down into the valley – this is the perfect setting to share a

Istria

bukaleta (drinking jug) of traditional Istrian *supa*. Clearly invented by a peasant with no food in the house, this speciality consists of red wine topped off with warm, toasted bread liberally sprinkled with olive oil.

Hum lies near **Roč**, famous for its musical associations (*see p136* **Roč Accordion Festival**), and is 5km (3 miles) from the main Buzet-Lupoglav road. There is no public transport but coach tours can be booked throughout the summer from most tourist offices in Istria.

Motovun

Motovun – Montona to the Romans – is one of the most beautiful and best preserved of Istria's medieval hilltop settlements. These days it's best known for its film festival (*see p128* **Motovun Film Festival**), which transforms this otherwise sleepy town into a cultural and party hub for one week every summer.

Motovun is sited on the summit of a 277-metre (910-foot) hill in the middle of the Mirna Valley, surrounded by truffle-rich forest. When the original prehistoric settlement was founded, it would have been surrounded by water. In those days the estuary stretched right up to the 'Gates of Buzet' at the head of the valley. It was down this ancient inlet that Jason and his Argonauts are supposed to have fled after having captured the Golden Fleece.

In its day, Motovun was the communications hub for all of inland Istria. From its strategic position, it controlled the merchant routes that wound across the valley floor on the way to the coast. In 1278 Motovun came under the rule of Venice, a major outpost on its border with the Austrian empire. Although depopulated as a result of the Italian exodus after World War II, a new wave of inhabitants – many of them artists and writers – has set up home here in recent times. The result is the Motovun Film Festival, set up in 1999.

Top tables Marino, Momjan

The small, superbly conceived menu at **Marino** is seasonal, taking full advantage of the area's fresh produce. Spring sees wild asparagus teamed with cured pork and pasta or with eggs and tender pork medallions. Fresh black truffles make their appearance from June onwards. These relatively mild types are often employed with other, indigenous wild mushrooms such as *vrganji* and *lisičice* in interesting and innovative combinations. Autumn brings game and the pungent white truffles for which Istria is now famous – they even garnish the signature hot, chocolate cake at the close of the meal. If you happen to find yourself here out of truffle season, don't despair. Marino's head chef, Marko Rastović, produces excellent dishes using the preserved variety.

Owner Marino Markezić also runs the family winery, Kabola, founded in 1891 and now recognised as one of Istria's leading wine producers, ensuring an excellent choice to accompany your meal. A short distance away, the cellars contain a museum of wine-making artefacts. It is here that Marino, aficionado of the Slow Food movement, hosts gourmet meals. You can book through the main restaurant.

Marino is situated on the main road between Buje and Momjan. Full directions are available on the website.

Kremenje 96b, Momjan (052 779 047/ www.konoba-marino-kremenje.hr). **Closed** Jan. **Open** *Feb-Dec* noon-10pm Mon, Wed-Sun. **No credit cards**.

Train in vain

Named after Parenzo, the Italian name for Poreč, **Parenzana** was a narrow-gauge railway and a major feat of engineering that brought wealth and prosperity to inland Istria.

When the Habsburgs took over Istria, transport became a priority. This land-locked regime was keen to exploit its newly acquired access to the sea. A rail line was built to link Vienna to Trieste and in 1876 it was extended to Pula, with a branch line from Kanfanar to Rovinj. Investment was driven by Pula's booming shipbuilding industry and Austria's military interests. The next step was to tie in the west-coast port of Poreč and traverse through the most populous and agriculturally productive part of the region. This was to be a tall order.

Climbing over the spectacular hills of north-west Istria was a major challenge and Austrian engineers got to work in the 1880s. By 1902 the Parenzarner Bahn was opened. Follow the route on the map and you see why it took so long. From Poreč, the line went through Visnjan, Baldaši, Visinada, Racatole, Karojba, Motovun, Livade, Opatalj, Završje, Kastanja, Grožnjan and so to Buje. After that it continued downhill, through today's Slovenia, until the terminus at Trieste. This means that from a sea-level start at Poreč,

the railway had to climb 273 metres (896 feet) at Baldaši and then down again to Livade, 13 metres (443 feet) above sea level, and all the way up to 293 metres (961 feet) at Grožnjan. They wiggled the route through natural passes where possible. In Motovun, they simply tunnelled straight underneath.

Just like the Wild West, the railroad brought economic development. Livade, a tiny village in the flat Mirna Valley, became a major depot almost overnight. Farmers along the line could transport wine and olive oil to the ports. Inland Istria boomed.

It wasn't to last. Partly because of road transport but mostly because of Mussolini, Paranzana ceased to exist in 1935. Il Duce was set on empire building and Abyssinia, today's Ethiopia, was his goal. Benito decided to rip up the railway and ship it out to Africa. Not one of his better ideas: the cargo ship sank off the Egyptian coast and the bulk of the Paranzana railway lies rusting at the bottom of the sea.

You can still appreciate the engineering genius and sheer graft that gave birth to Parenzana. Tourist offices provide hiking and cycling routes that run alongside. What you can't do, even to this day, is take a train across Istria.

Non-residents are banned from driving the town's narrow cobbled streets (there's a car park at the bottom of the hill).

Motovun's two sets of fortified walls divide the town into three sections – the higher you climb, the older it gets. As you wend your way upwards, past rather dilapidated, 16th- and 17th-century Venetian-style houses, you pass several small shops, offering wine, truffles and local grappa.

As the road levels it passes through the main city gate dating from the 15th century. Its walls are hung with Roman tombstones taken from the cemetery of Karojba, a village 5km (3 miles) away on the road to Pazin. Within the gate is a museum of antique weaponry. The entrance is on the far side of the gate. Also here is the town's art gallery. Next door is a small café whose terrace is sited on the other side of the street, against the first set of fortified walls. Sitting here you have a clear view to the Adriatic. Just in case, a telescope has been thoughtfully provided. There's a cashpoint opposite, the only one in the area.

A few steps further, facing the town loggia, is the 13th-century gate into the original heart of Motovun. This walkway is particularly steep and slippery – use the handrail. This entrance houses a small restaurant, **Pod Voltum**. From the archway you walk on to the main square. Dominated by a magnificent 13th-century belltower, the piazza is sited over a huge *cisterna*, or water collection pit, which used to supply the town. You can still see the 14th-century well. Next to the tower is the baroque Church of St Stephen and, opposite, a Renaissance palace citadel, housing the local cinema. The piazza also houses Motovun's only hotel, the **Kaštel**.

It's at this point that all the climbing pays off. Stroll along the original 13th-century walls and a stunning 360-degree panoramic view reveals the whole of inland Istria laid out before you.

Motovun only has two main roads. If you turn left and follow the second route down, you come out close to the car park. Known as Pod Motovun (Under Motovun), the locality has a couple of café bars (including the **Fakin**) and shops but, most importantly, a petrol station.

Where to eat

Pod Voltum

Šetalište V Nazora (052 681 923). **Open** *Summer* noon-11pm daily. *Winter* noon-11pm Mon-Tue, Thur-Sun. **No credit cards.**
Under the Arch by the old city gate serves a selection of honest, regional fare, including truffles, and can always be relied upon to have a fire blazing in winter. A rare non-smoking establishment.

Where to drink

Fakin

Zadrugarska 8 (052 681 978). **Open** 8am-11pm Mon-Sat. **Closed** 2wks Jan.
Wild at festival time, the funky Fakin attracts the friendly local biker fraternity thanks to owner Damir, whose pictures adorn the walls. In winter you might only hear the click of chess pieces, the clack of pool balls and the cluck of local chatter about the price of truffles.

Where to stay

Kaštel

Trg Andrea Antico 7 (052 681 607/fax 052 681 652/www.hotel-kastel-motovun.hr). **Rates** €39-€48.50 single; €66-€111 double. **Credit** AmEx, DC, MC, V.
Behind the bright red façade of Motovun's only hotel are 28 spacious three-star rooms set around little patios. Some have balconies. Attractive half-board rates are available at the renowned in-house restaurant (8am-10pm daily), offering game, truffles and other Istrian specialities in a chestnut-shaded garden or recently renovated dining room.

Tourist information

Motovun Tourist Office

Trg Andrea Antico 1 (052 681 758).

Getting there & around

The bus from the transport hub of Pazin takes 45 minutes. There are five a day in summer, two in winter. The twice-daily Pula-Buzet line also drops off at Motovun.

Novigrad

The pleasantly sleepy nature of the former Venetian town of Novigrad may soon change. Round the harbour from the town centre, a marina complex is being built, with a five-star hotel, an artificial island and moorings for 100 boats. All should be in place by 2007.

The heart of Novigrad, its medieval structure intact, occupies the peninsula opposite. Called Cittanova under the Venetians, it contains a couple of modest sights and a surprising number of decent bars, hotels and restaurants for a community of fewer than 3,000 people. The more modern part of town stretches less than a kilometre east, as far as the bus station and a small hotel complex.

Between town and facilities, you can walk along the main road of Murve or the pleasant seaside promenade of Rivarella. Even in high season, tourists are light compared to nearby Poreč, the hub for buses from Zagreb or Pula.

Konoba Mura. *See right*.

The Venetian-style campanile beside **St Pelagius**, a baroque 18th-century church built on the foundations of a basilica from the Middle Ages, rises over the narrow network of streets. Here in the main square, Veliki trg and the main street of Velika ulica, stands a Venetian loggia, containing the Town Hall. North of town at Karpinjan, near the new marina, is the **Rigo Palace**, built in 1760. It contains a display of ancient tombstones and Byzantine fragments.

Otherwise, time in Novigrad is best spent dining well and wandering along the seafront. For a romantic getaway, you won't find better in Istria. Until the new marina opens, that is.

Where to eat

Novigrad boasts three restaurants worth writing home about: **Damir i Ornella**, **Mandrać** and the **Konoba Čok**. There are a handful of others on Rivarella with a sea-view terrace and a good kitchen. Menus are often in Croatian, Italian and Germany only.

Damir i Ornella

Zidine 5 (052 758 134). **Open** noon-3pm, 6.30-11.30pm Tue-Sun. **Credit** AmEx, DC, V.
Commonly acknowledged to be the best place in town, this 28-seat diner is worth booking at least a day in advance. Signposted on Velika ulica, it's set in a narrow side street near the seafront. Inside, a simple, tasteful bare-brick interior is a comfortable setting for raw fish and shrimp specialities. The grilled lobster is excellent too. Desserts include a popular kiwi flan. Expect to pay about 400kn a head.

Konoba Čok

Sv Antona 2 (052 757 643). **Open** noon-3pm, 6-11pm daily. **Credit** AmEx, DC, V.
On an enclosed front terrace by a roundabout on the edge of the Old Town, a board reads: 'Welcome from Family Jugovac'. While his son Viljan runs the kitchen, Sergio takes care of guests and the wide range of Istrian wines on offer. This simple, well-run seafood eaterie is indeed a welcome treat, with fresh sea bream, sea perch and sole , lobster, and all kinds of shellfish including oysters. Truffles decorate the steak and pasta starters, and meals are generally bookended by a complimentary fruit brandy.

Mandrać

Mandrać 6 (052 757 369). **Open** noon-3pm, 6-11pm daily. **Credit** AmEx, DC, V.
The walls of Mandrać's backroom are covered in gastronomic awards and even though there are seats for 200 diners, it's best to reserve in summer. Fresh fish and grilled meats are well presented on warmed plates, garnished according to the friendly advice offered by the waiter. Despite the high standard of service and preparation, prices are a reasonable 250kn-300kn per kilo of sole, sea bass or sea bream. House wine is an equally reasonable 60kn a litre, although there are plenty of vintages on view in a cabinet in the back. If it's full, try the traditional Sidro (052 757 601) next door.

Taverna Tabasco

Bolnička 8 (052 757 004). **Open** 9am-10pm daily. **No credit cards**.
Opened in the summer of 2005, this friendly little konoba is the perfect for *merenda*, elevenses. The two tables in the alleyway catch the mid-morning sun and for 20kn you can order a plate of little fish or meat snacks to keep you going until lunchtime. If you're here for a full meal, you shouldn't be disappointed either: standard fish and meat dishes at reasonable prices in a sturdy interior of white stone walls and fishermen's knick-knacks.

Tri Palme

Karpinjan 14 (052 757 081). **Open** *Apr-Oct* noon-midnight daily. **Closed** Nov-Mar. **No credit cards**.
Friendly terrace grill near the new marina run by local musician Željko Kmet. While shrimps, steaks and *ćevapčići* sizzle on the grill, Favorit beers and

Istria

local wines flow, and a guitar might be produced if the mood takes. Regular starters (sheep's cheese, *prosciutto*) are also available and everything is priced at reasonable local rates.

Where to drink

Half-a-dozen decent bars dot the town centre, including the superb **Vitriol** and characterful **Konoba Mura**. You could make a little barhop from the Vitriol, to **Aquarius**, **K Ribaru**, **Lite**, and ending up opposite the Hotel Cittar at the chaotic late-night **Delfin** or grungy **Ara**. Any discos are to be found in high season around the hotel complex on the eastern outskirts of town.

Kavana Ogledala

Gradska vrata 24 (no phone). **Open** 8am-midnight daily.
Also known as Caffè degli Specchi, this is nothing like the grand coffeehouse of the same name in Trieste. It's a simple café serving frothy coffee and gooey cakes whose character and colour change

on a Sunday afternoon. Then it transforms into the local branch of the AC Milan fan club; its modest interior is decked out in red and black and buoyant with an unthreatening sense of celebration.

Konoba Mura

Zidine 10 (052 757 902). **Open** 7am-midnight daily.
Opposite the trendy Damir i Ornella, regulars play cards around the bar counter, the same men depicted in the proud stripes of RK Novigrad's 1965 team framed and mounted. Gilberto, the cook with the handlebar moustache and chef's hat with a five-pointed red star in honour of Heineken beer, serves standard meat dishes to diners in the side room and back terrace. The Mura is ideal for TV football – Torino paraphernalia graces the fireplace.

Little Caffè

Gradska vrata 15 (098 939 7573 mobile). **Open** 8am-midnight Mon-Thur; 8am-1am Fri, Sat.
A young, professional crowd hangs out in this swish café in the heart of Novigrad. A little art on the walls, a decent choice of whiskies and Istrian bitters,

Yesterday, Poreč

Yesterday was, fittingly enough, in 1965. That was when McCartney wrote the song and Jackie Carnihan made what would be a fateful journey to Poreč from Oldham. Until then, Jackie's only claim to fame was that she had sneaked in backstage at the Oldham Odeon to give Paul a loveheart necklace. Fan and young star got their picture taken by the *Oldham Chronicle*. Two years later, on holiday, Jackie gave her heart to a hotel receptionist in

the burgeoning resort of Poreč. They went on to have two children, one of whom, son Nicolas opened this nostalgia-fest of a bar (*see p143*) in 2005. Covered with Beatles memorabilia, including the picture taken of Mum with Macca four decades ago, Yesterday plays music from the era, while untried and unplugged locals appear on Friday nights. Jackie, meanwhile still lives in the area, in a small village called Kufci.

Guinness and Kilkenny by the bottle, it's a cut above most bars in the Old Town. Could do with a touch of music, a shortcoming in these parts.

Vitriol

Ribarnička 6 (052 758 270). **Open** 8am-midnight daily.

Best bar in Novigrad. Its terrace lapped by the sea, overlooking the setting sun, the Vitriol is trendy enough to appeal to weekending Italians without losing its young, lively, local character. Concoctions have a distinct Italian flavour (Negroni, Garibaldi) but include a zingy Novigrad Beach of gin, Campari and orange juice (35kn). Local wines are chalked up on a board outside, beers include Kriek and Kilkenny and there are enough hot drinks to fill an entire menu. Ideal for a summer's eve or winter's afternoon. Sharp staff too.

Where to stay

The new five-star **Hotel Nautica** (052 600 400, www.hotel-nautica.com), when open in the summer of 2006, will take accommodation in Novigrad on to a different level. Until then the Old Town contains a number of mid-range

Roč Accordion Festival

Picture a small, medieval hilltop town, surrounded by thick stone walls. Erect an open-air stage in the largest space available, cram the place with the widest mix of people imaginable and add music. That's the Roč Accordion Festival.

Held on the second Sunday of May, the festival is something really special. A thumping good day out and a beacon of cultural heritage, it's an experience not to be missed. Nearly all the participants are amateurs and their primary reason for playing is to share a collective love of music and have a cracking good time. Performances can range from the sublime to the not so and the musicians from fresh-faced young shavers to grizzled old men with shovels for hands. With some 70 performers, festivities last all day and well into the evening.

There's a serious side too, which is the celebration of the diatonic accordion or *trieština*, a unique five-tone instrument quite unlike the better-known octave-based accordion of Bavarian bierkellers. *Trieština* players were a dying breed when the Roč festival was begun in 1989. That May, just 16 players gathered in the town square. The following year they were joined by a handful of amateurs, and so on, until the big bash of today. More young musicians are taking up the instrument and, thanks to the festival, its future now looks assured.

Sip a Novigrad Beach over a stunning Novigrad sunset at the **Vitriol**. *See left.*

options, the most notable of which is the
Cittar. For a resort holiday, head for the
seasonal **Maestral** or **Laguna** (www.laguna-
novigrad.hr) near the bus station.

Hotel Cittar

Prolaz Venecija 1 (052 757 737/fax 052 757 340).
Rates 560kn-736kn double. **Credit** AmEx, DC,
MC, V.
Its exterior built into a section of Venetian wall in
the city centre, the Cittar is one of the best mid-range
hotels in Istria. Run by a small, friendly team under
Sergio Cittar, it contains 14 rooms with smooth, var-
nished floors, comfortable, big beds and capacious
baths. A breakfast of warm croissants, meats and
cheeses is taken in the sunny conservatory at the
front. Half-board of an extra 75kn per person is
offered in summer, when it's best to reserve at least
a week in advance.

Hotel Laguna

*Terre (052 757 050/fax 052 757 026/www.laguna-
novigrad.hr).* **Closed** Mid Oct-Mar. **Rates** *Apr-mid
Oct* €36-€70 single; €54-€120 double. **Credit** AmEx,
DC, MC, V.
One of two resort hotels in this holiday complex east
of town, the Laguna is set in a simple, white building with two pools outside. There's a large, three-
cornered one for adults and a smaller one with a slide
for kids. Discounts for families are generous: children up to 7 sharing with their parents are free, those
from 7 to 14 get a 50% discount. The prices quoted
are for half-board accommodation – drop the rates
by €5 if you prefer bed and breakfast only.

Hotel Maestral

*Terre (052 757 557/fax 052 757 462/www.laguna-
novigrad.hr).* **Closed** Mid Oct-Mar. **Rates** *Apr-mid
Oct* €44-€88 single; €64-€134 double. **Credit** AmEx,
DC, MC, V.

The larger and more expensive of the two hotels in
the Laguna organisation, the Maestral also contains
more amenities, including a heated indoor pool with
seawater, a modest gym and a sauna. All is furnished in authentic retro brown – the casino is a
major local attraction.

Hotel Rotonda

*Rotonda 1 (052 757 110/fax 052 726 177/
www.hotel-rotonda.hr).* **Closed** Nov-Apr. **Rates**
May-Oct €52-€106 double. **Credit** AmEx, DC, MC, V.
Well-located three-star on the seafront. The 35
rooms are pretty standard, although some have sea
views, and the terrace bar-restaurant is a nice spot
on a summer's evening. It has its own stretch of pretty plain beach, but the half-board deals are good,
especially in the shoulder months.

Torci 18

*Torci 34 (052 757 799/fax 052 757 174/
www.torci18.hr).* **Closed** Oct-Apr. **Rates** *May-Sept*
€50-€60 double. **No credit cards.**
Sturdy three-star pension and restaurant in the centre of town with 12 plain rooms, some overlooking
a courtyard. The restaurant is standard but stretches to lobster and grouper fish.

Resources

Internet

Internet Centar *Mandrać 20 (052 726 280).*
Open *Summer* 8am-midnight daily. *Winter* 9am-
noon, 5-8pm Mon-Sat.
Handy place by the marina that also sells souvenirs.

Tourist information

Novigrad tourist office *Porporella 1 (052 757
075/ www.istra.com/novigrad).* **Open** *Summer* 8am-
8pm daily. *Winter* 8am-3pm Mon-Fri; 8am-1pm Sat.
Friendly little office full of brochures on the seafront.

Istria

Getting there & around

Novigrad is poorly served by public transport. There are only four buses a day from Zagreb and Pula. It might be quicker to get to **Poreč** and change for a more regular service between the two towns 18km (11 miles) apart. The bus station is a ten-minute walk outside town. For a taxi, call 052 757 224, 098 806 349 mobile.

Poreč

The ancient settlement of Poreč, with its treasured sixth-century basilica and sublime seaside views, is overrun by tourists and the businesses that cater to them. Buses and boats deliver holidaying families who check into the c1970 concrete resort hotels for their all-inclusive packages combining beach-side accommodation with activities and meals. Restaurant staff in the pedestrianised **Old Town**, politely attempt to ensnare passers-by. Small shops selling expensive designer clothing, costume jewellery, traditional lace or T-shirts printed with bawdy jokes cram **Decumanus**, a 2,000-year-old thoroughfare. English, Italian and German are more commonly heard than Croatian.

The tackiness can be off-putting but the town's mix of Roman, Byzantine and Venetian architecture remains charming, the beaches are stunning and the clamour of bars, restaurants and casinos offers ample diversion.

For a romantic getaway or a feel for Croatia and its people, avoid Poreč. Families who want something for all ages, and want it organised for them, will find the resort suits them fine.

Even those who don't like package tours can spend a rewarding day here, visiting the **Basilica** and **Bishop's Palace** and enjoying beach time. It's an easy day trip from Rovinj or other points in Istria. It's also the starting point for ferries to Venice.

OLD TOWN AND NEW RESORTS

The Old Town is on a small, mostly car-free peninsula, packed with restaurants, expensive shops and many reminders of Poreč's rich history. The stone-paved main artery, Decumanus, the ivy-covered, shaded square at its seaward end, **Trg Marafor**, and the ruins of the **temples of Neptune and Mars**, west of the square, were built by Romans, who took over the region in 200 BC and made the peninsula of Poreč the local administrative centre. The town's jewel, the **Basilica of Bishop Euphrasius**, was built in the sixth century by a Byzantine civilisation, who held the town until the eighth century and were followed by Frankish rulers.

Hospitable **Hotel Cittar**, Novigrad. *See p137.*

The **harbour** contains ornate buildings with tall arched windows, reminders of Venetian dominance from 1267 until the 18th century, when Poreč was ruled by Napoleon and then the Habsburgs. The Venetians also built a town wall in the 15th century, which stretched from the harbourside **Round Tower**, now occupied by a bar (**Torre Rotonda**), to the inland **Pentagonal Tower**, now occupied by a restaurant (**Peterokutna kula**). Italy ruled Poreč from 1918 to 1943, at which point it was taken over by German forces and subsequently attracted heavy Allied bombing in 1944. It then became part of Yugoslavia.

The tourists invaded as long ago as 1844, when Poreč was a stop for luxury liners sailing out of Trieste. The town became a playground for the rich, and tourism was soon the main industry. The town is so good at this industry it wins awards every year for its efforts to attract and satisfy its visitors. The staff of hotels, restaurants and other establishments take pride in delivering top service, so those who do check into the big resorts are sure to feel looked after.

Most of the resort hotels are located outside town, on a green strip where pine forests run right up to the beach. The hotspots are **Plava Laguna** (Blue Lagoon), 4km (2.5 miles) south, and **Zelena Laguna** (Green Lagoon), 6km (3.5

Istria

miles) south. They contain resort complexes, with sports centres, discos, mini golf courses, bike or boat rentals – and beaches. The paved trail leading out to the resorts is a fine seaside walk or bike ride. There's also an open-air tourist train, more of a long, skinny bus, that runs along the path, hitting all the resorts.

Euphrasian Basilica & Bishop's Palace

Sv Eleuterija (052 431 635). **Open** 10am-5pm daily. **Admission** *Church* free. *Belfry* 10kn. *Museum* 10kn. The basilica, built in the sixth century by Bishop Euphrasius, is an important surviving example of Byzantine art. The surrounding complex offers impressive sights, too – you can absorb the best in 20 minutes or linger for a couple of hours. The main attractions are the wonderfully preserved gold-gilt and mother-of-pearl mosaics, which shine with a brightness that belies their age. The largest and most striking is in the apse, above and behind the altar, depicting a procession of saints and angels around the Virgin Mary holding the baby Jesus. On the left of Mary is Bishop Euphrasius, conveniently labelled for those who don't know what he looks like, carrying a model of his church. Behind the bishop, also labelled in mosaic tile, is his brother Claudius, and between them, Claudius's young son. Below this mosaic is another, depicting biblical scenes and saints. Inside the archway of the apse is a mosaic showing individual pictures of the 12 apostles with the lamb, symbolising Christ, in the apex of the arch. Euphrasius built his three-nave basilica on the foundation of a fifth-century church. Mosaics from earlier churches are still visible in the floor of the northern nave. The three naves are separated by columns supporting curved archways, topped with Byzantine-style capitals; above them are medallions bearing the bishop's initials.

In the front is an atrium with tall columns topped by Byzantine capitals. Beside it is an eight-sided baptistery, and beyond a belfry, which you can climb for a view of the seaside and the surroundings.

Next to the church is the former Bishop's Palace, also from the sixth century, housing a museum that contains mosaics gathered from earlier churches. Outside, the seaside stretch is free of tourist shops, and a nice spot for an evening stroll when the rocks along the water fill up with nocturnal crabs.

Beaches

South or north of town there are pleasant walkways that follow the coast, going past bustling rocky or pebbly beaches. Some stretches of shore are reserved for residents of a nearby resort, but most of the beaches are open – and packed with people from a nearby resort. The stroll south, toward Plava Laguna and Zelena Laguna, can be the most rewarding. Just outside of town, you'll pass a long stretch of pine forest before you hit the resort area. The beaches here are rocky, but may be less crowded. You can also take the tourist train from Trg Slobode and get driven down the 6km (3.5-mile) walkway to Zelena Laguna, to join the masses on the pebbly beaches. If you continue south of the **Hotel Delfin** (*see p144*), the beaches are rocky but more private.

Musical differences Gustafi

Gustafi are the most popular band from Istria. They combine local pentatonical folk-music flavours with Tex-Mex roots, and sing in local dialect. Their concerts last from three to six hours, whether it's a pub, the public square, a meadow or the backyard. They have played them all, 150 shows a year in 15 years, usually nine members on stage, sometimes even more. Are they the best live band in Croatia? Almost certainly. When he was in Zagreb promoting his photography exhibition, David Byrne couldn't resist getting up to join them. They could keep the saloons of Austin, Texas happy for a year but they don't even bother playing Italy round the corner. To celebrate the patron saint of wine-makers on St Martin's Day in Zagreb's Tvornica in 2005, Gustafi played their usual three-hour set and 1,300 people drank 1,200 bottles before half of it was over.

Down on the farm

For first-hand experience of Istria's lifestyle and culture, rural tourism is the way to go. Small-scale, personal and inexpensive, this type of accommodation provides a genuine opportunity to see how the other half live.

Current tourist facilities can be clearly divided either side of 1991. The traditional tourist industry was decimated by the Yugoslav war. The upside was that Istria was forced to sit back and reassess its strategy. With the effects of mass tourism in Spain and the erosion of traditional, rural communities in Tuscany, there was plenty to ponder while sitting out the lean times.

Over the last decade, rural tourism has been the vanguard of Istria's masterplan for a high quality, low-density visitor experience. 'Agritourism' has expanded to include stays in renovated cottages, a form of farm-based accommodation that is now spreading down the Dalmatian coast and into the inland regions of Gorski Kotar, Zagorje and Slavonia. Helping stem the depopulation of rural areas, it places a strong emphasis on the protection of the environment, traditional architecture and cultural heritage.

The standards are high – the local tourist board vets these places thoroughly – and tariffs are low, generally around €15-€25 per night. Accommodation is usually self-catering, either apartments in converted farm buildings or renovated houses. The original architecture has been adhered to, so places are often full of charm and character. Don't expect luxury

but, by way of compensation, you tend to get vine covered terraces and beamed ceilings.

To qualify as Agritourism, owners must sell exclusively home-grown food and wines. Therefore many also run a restaurant. One good example is **Karoca** (052 663 039, www.karoca.com, open 12.30-10pm Tue-Sun, no credit cards; *pictured*), in the pretty village of Sovinjak, between Buzet and Istarska Toplica. Everything on the menu, including the bread, is made on the premises. Also available are wild boar, venison, home-made sausages and plenty of truffles. The house wine comes from the owner's vineyards, as does the grappa. The garden surveys rolling hills, dotted with vineyards and tiny villages.

Agritourism venues are sited away from the coastal resorts so you won't have to contend with swarms of holidaymakers. There's lots of space for children to run around and plenty to keep them occupied. Being working farms there is usually livestock plus the ubiquitous olive groves and vineyards. Many places also offer horse riding, mushroom and fruit picking. You are welcome to be as involved as you like – especially during the grape harvest. Privacy is respected, it's up to you.

To get the most out of your stay, car hire is generally essential. The advantage of staying with locals is that they can offer tips you wouldn't find anywhere else. Not all speak English so check before. The Istrian tourist board (www.istra.hr) lists the languages spoken at each venue.

For a little more privacy, take the boat over to Sv Nikola (*see below*) from the harbour. Here you'll find pine-shaded paved and pebble beaches, the most notable being the circular one of Oliva near the **Hotel Fortuna** (*see p144*).

Excursions

A taxi boat (every 30mins, 7am-11pm daily, 12kn) takes five minutes to reach the island of **Sv Nikola**, a popular resort since the late 1800s. These days it's dominated by the Hotel Fortuna (*see p144*), which means the beaches are reasonably crowded all summer – but the hotel's sporting facilities are open to other residents in the local Riviera hotel chain.

There are regular trips to the limestone caves near Nova Vas at **Baredine** (052 421 333, www.baredine.com, open July, Aug 9.30am-6pm daily, May, June, Sept 10am-5pm daily, Apr, 1st 2wks Oct 10am-4pm daily). The guided tour lasts 40 minutes and is included in the price of the excursion. See **Atlas** (*p147*) for details.

Where to eat

Restaurants are found by the harbour, along Decumanus and in the two squares at either end of it, Trg Slobode and Trg Marafor. There are also some stand-out spots in Plava Laguna and Zelena Laguna. A bad place wouldn't last long in this competitive atmosphere, so most choices are likely to please, with outdoor seating and decent seafood options. Look out for Istrian *prosciutto*, baked fish, pasta with lobster, truffles and, in spring and early summer, fresh asparagus. The proximity of Italy and need to please Italian tourists mean that pizzas and pastas are going to be good. Service is of a high standard and friendly staff earn their tips.

Dvi Murve

Grožnjanska 17 (052 434 115/www.dvimurve.hr). **Open** Feb-Dec noon-11pm daily. **Closed** Jan. **Credit** AmEx, DC, MC, V.
Outside the more touristy part of town is a popular konoba with a large, pleasantly shaded terrace with a busy grill in one corner. They cook up fine seafood, including the standards and local specialities such as sea bass baked in salt and lobster in spaghetti. This is also a good place to stray away from the standards and opt for traditional Istrian dishes such as stew with dried lamb, goulash and noodles, wild game or a plate of grilled meats.

Istra

Bože Milanovića 30 (052 434 636). **Open** noon-midnight daily. **Credit** AmEx, DC.
In an unexciting location near the bus station, with terrace seating where the main view is passing tourists, sits one of the more popular restaurants in

Euphrasian Basilica, Poreč. *See p139.*

town. Regulars swear by the seafood, standards and specialities such as baked fish and lobster with pasta. The mixed seafood starter is a pleasant way to enjoy a gastronomic tour of Istria. Friendly service and the homey atmosphere add to the pleasure.

Korta

Zelena Laguna, near Hotel Plavi (052 410 535). **Open** 10am-midnight daily. **Credit** AmEx, DC, MC, V.
Counting the indoor section and outdoors, there is seating for 500 in a stretch of the Zelena Laguna resort with few other restaurants nearby. Though it does handle big crowds, the nicely landscaped garden-like terrace with shady trees offers some intimacy, and the excellent service and fine seafood do the rest. The menu has the typical family-pleasing combination of fish, pizza, pasta and steaks.

Nono

Zagrebačka 4 (052 453 088/427 300). **Open** noon-midnight daily. **Credit** AmEx, DC, MC, V.
It may not have a sea view, but this down-to-earth pizzeria in the Old Town draws diners away from the harbour for huge, brick-oven baked pizza with a soft crust. Locals pack the place, sometimes making

it hard to find a table at lunch, but if you want the best pizza in town, it's worth the wait. There are some decent salads, too, and fresh seafood.

Peterokutna kula
Decumanus 1 (052 451 378). **Open** noon-midnight daily. **Credit** AmEx, DC, MC, V.
In a pentagonal tower built in 1447, near the entryway to the Old Town, this restaurant offers indoor and outdoor seating in nicely restored spaces. As a 170-seater, it's clearly touristy, and in high season the atmosphere can seem a bit hectic, but the tables are roomy and comfortable. The cuisine is designed to show off the best of Istria, with truffles appearing in several dishes, such as the satisfying steak with truffles.

Rialto
Ljudevita Gaja 3 (091 250 8331 mobile). **Open** *May-Sept* 10am-midnight daily. **Closed** Oct-Apr. **Credit** MC, V.
This friendly family-run place with a festive atmosphere is the only eaterie on the quiet stretch of seaside behind the bishop's palace. The awning-shaded terrace is removed from the crowds but still has a sea view. Although it does fine seafood and grilled meats, it is a pizzeria, with simple, delicious varieties as if from nearby Italy. Look out for the tempting and lively selection of home-made grappas.

Tri Ribara
Zelena Laguna, near Hotel Zorna (052 410 508). **Open** 11am-midnight daily. **Credit** AmEx, DC, MC, V.
A decent choice in Zelena Laguna specialises in fish and has some fancier seafood offerings, like lobster and sole. Pizzas and pastas are also handled well.

The terrace and the grounds are pleasantly surrounded by greenery and right next to the sea. Quick and courteous service and a good list of local wines.

Ulixes
Decumanus 2 (052 451 132). **Open** noon-midnight daily. **Credit** AmEx, DC, MC, V.
Step off crowded Decumanus, down a few steps, and into a cool, cavernous old stone room, charmingly cluttered with antiques and old shipping paraphernalia. The garden behind, in a secluded courtyard, is equally attractive. The speciality is the Istrian version of 'surf and turf': seafood and truffles. Surf includes calamari, octopus salad and fresh fish, and less common varieties like ray and sole. Truffles can be had in pasta or as part of various starters such as sheep's cheese or carpaccio. There are usually some interesting daily specials.

Where to drink

The focus on family tourism means that cafés cater to a tamer crowd after ice-cream or a post-dinner cocktail. Trg Marafor has several terrace bars, including **Mango Mambo**, a cocktail bar with a slightly hipper vibe. Although the world does not need another Beatles theme bar, at least **Yesterday** (*see p135* **Best bars**) has a McCartneyesque storyline to it.

Caffè Bar C&D
Obala maršala Tita 12. **Open** 8am-2am daily.
In one of the busiest sections of the harbour, this slick-looking bar offers good drinks and conversation with fellow travellers.

Poreč.

The alley of Glagolites

Rekonst glagoljsi Polače.

A major feature of the Buzet region is the remnants of Croatia's ancient Glagolitic script. The focus of this historical heritage is the Alley of Glagolites: a narrow, winding road between **Roč** and **Hum**, a 7km (4.5 miles) route with 11 stone monuments. Beginning with the Pillar of the Chakavian Parliament and ending with the refurbished medieval gates of Hum itself (*see p130*), the sculptures lie scattered along the roadside. They were erected between 1977 and 1983 to celebrate of the rebirth of Croatian literacy and culture in Istria.

A forerunner of Cyrillic, the Glagolitic script was created in the ninth century to aid Slavs convert to Christianity. Two brothers from Thessaloniki, Cyril and Methodius, came up with the alphabet to represent the Slavic tongue. Widespread on the coast, it was used for the translation of religious texts, some of which still survive. The *Roč Missal*, the first Croatian book, from c1483, is one example. It was produced by Žakn Jurij, whose bust stands at Roč parish church.

Today the Glagolitic tradition is kept alive in large part through the efforts of the Mala Glagoljaška Akademija, a script workshop staged in Roč every July. Children come from all over Croatia to learn about their literary heritage. Something between Celtic and Cyrillic lettering, the beautiful script also turns up on local road signs, Hum being a classic example.

Epoca

Obala maršala Tita 24. **Open** 8am-2am daily.
Good music, friendly staff and a sociable buzz sets this place apart from the other harbourside bars. Near the tip of the peninsula that holds the Old Town, at the beginning of the busy strip of cafés and restaurants, Epoca offers a spacious indoor bar and sea views. Dancing has been known to break out in the evening, though the crowd you'll be schmoozing with will be mostly fellow travellers. Good cocktails.

Kavana Dalí

Rade Končara 1. **Open** 8am-1am daily.
Funky modern café between the Hotel Poreč and the marina, away from the package-tourist scene. A relaxing place for a long daytime coffee and a lively one at night. It's set in a spacious conservatory facing the harbour – there's a definite sense of being somewhere special. Hopefully, closure for refurbishment in early 2006 won't last until the summer.

Lapidarij

Sveta Maura 10 (052 431 595). **Open** noon-midnight daily.
Within the City Museum's garden is a pleasant courtyard bar that provides sanctuary from the crowds in the Old Town. It hosts concerts, particularly Wednesday's jazz residency, bringing the best practitioners of all its various forms – from swing to acid jazz – into Poreč for jam sessions.

Torre Rotonda

Narodni trg 3A (098 255 731 mobile). **Open** *Apr-Oct* 10am-1am daily. **Closed** Nov-Mar.
As with every other space on the waterfront, this bulky round tower built in 1473 has been taken over by tourists. Go up the winding staircase to the first-floor bar, a sociable space amid the ancient stone walls. If you continue on up, you'll get to the flat roof of the tower, with an umbrella-shaded terrace and a commanding view of the harbour and the sea.

Yesterday

Park Olge Ban 2 (098 190 662 mobile). **Open** *Summer* 7am-1am daily. *Winter* 7am-11pm daily.
This Beatles-themed bar has come to Poreč by way of Oldham. *See p135* **Best bars**.

Nightlife

In the resorts, the discos can feel part of a package tour. You'll be mingling with fellow tourists and some nights you may not find a crowd unless you bring your own. The best spot is therefore the Colonia Iulia Parentium, both a bar and a danceclub.

Colonia Iulia Parentium

Gradkso Kupalište, Šetalište A Štifanića, south of the Old Town before Brulo (no phone). **Open** *Apr-Sept* 8pm-4am daily. **Closed** Oct-Mar.

The seaside terrace Colonia, the best place in town for dancing, is equally entertaining as a local bar. A nightly programme of live acts and DJs offers an eclectic range of music, from house to acid jazz to rock. The crowd is a fun mix of foreign and Croatian tourists plus the odd local.

International Club

Zelena Laguna, near Hotel Delfin. **Open** *Apr-Sept* 10pm-4am daily. **Closed** Oct-Mar.

This spacious indoor and outdoor disco by the resorts of Zelena Laguna draws big crowds subjected to mediocre selections of commercial summer hits. Expect go-go dancers on raised platforms. A bacchanalian, party mood nonetheless.

Plava

Plava Laguna, near Hotel Laguna Galijot. **Open** *Apr-Sept* 10pm-4am Wed-Sat. **Closed** Oct-Mar.

A small round structure in resort land with an adjacent terrace contains a club attracting a youthful crowd. DJs and bands are shipped in from around Croatia and Central Europe. With reasonable prices and a selection of cocktails, it's a good alternative to the International. If the dancefloor isn't happening, there's not much else to the place.

Where to stay

The 30 hotels and hundreds of rooms for rent in and around Poreč provide thousands of beds. Most hotels are owned by the chains Riviera (052 408 200/www.riviera.hr) and Plava Laguna (052 410 295/www.plavalaguna.hr). Of their resort venues, the **Hotel Diamant** is the better option in Brulo, the **Hotel Laguna Galijot** in Plava Laguna and the **Hotel Delfin** in Zelena Laguna. Check their websites for others. Private rooms range from a bedroom to agritourism on someone's working farm.

Several hotels offer central accommodation without the add-ons. Some allow you to use the extensive **Hotel Fortuna** facilities on Sv Nikola Island, a few minutes away by boat.

Hotel Delfin

Zelena Laguna (052 414 000/fax 052 451 658/ www.plavalaguna.hr). **Closed** Nov-Mar. **Rates** *Apr-Oct* €23-€41 single; €42-€78 double. **Credit** AmEx, DC, MC, V.

This low-frills resort offers a decent budget option for families. The huge complex, built in 1971 and looking a little worse for wear, has 793 rooms on a hilltop in a pretty pine-forested peninsula. The rooms are small, basic and plain, but reasonably cool in the pine-shaded building despite the lack of air-conditioning. Pebble and less crowded rocky beaches nearby are separate enough from the rest of Zelena Laguna to be used mostly by hotel guests. Large grounds provide spots for sunbathing. There's a sports centre right next to the hotel, plus an outdoor pool with saltwater. Dinner at the decent buffet restaurant is included in the price of the room.

Hotel Diamant

Naselje Brulo 1 (052 400 000/fax 052 451 440/ www.riviera.hr). **Rates** €49-€90 single; €78-€158 double. **Credit** AmEx, DC, MC, V.

This bland 11-storey building houses the most luxurious and most expensive of Poreč's family-style resorts. The sports facilities, spa centre, children's play area and entertainment programmes are designed to keep the whole family content to hang around the hotel and the nearby beach. Other attractions include tennis courts and an adjacent 'adrenalin park', with bungee jumping, skateboard ramps and plenty of other potentially insurance-worrying other distractions. Also contains an indoor pool with a bar. Comfortable, air-conditioned rooms have helped earn the Diamant its four-star status. Self-catering apartments, separated from the main building, allow for more privacy and independence from the communal activities. Guests at nearby cheaper Kristal (052 400 500) can pay a fee to make use of the amenities at the Diamant.

Hotel Fortuna

Sv Nikola (052 406 000/fax 052 451 440/ www.riviera.hr). **Closed** Nov-Mar. **Rates** *Apr-Oct* €35-€77 single; €58-€132 double. **Credit** AmEx, DC, MC, V.

The Fortuna offers a resort atmosphere and the relative isolation of a small island a five-minute boat ride from the centre of town. Sv Nikola Island has nice beaches, a small pine forest and a couple of restaurants. It is pretty much dominated by the hotel, a cluster of detached apartments and a sports facility open to guests from other hotels in the Riviera chain. The eye-pleasing, modern, white building has an attractive outdoor swimming pool and a big pool-side patio. There is a children's playground and children's entertainment programmes, and a sports centre including tennis court. Room prices generally include dinner; if you'd rather eat elsewhere, you'll get a €6 reduction. The only air-conditioned space is the restaurant.

Hotel Hostin

Rade Končara 4 (052 408 800/fax 052 408 857/ www.hostin.hr). **Rates** €39-€85 single; €52-€122 double. **Credit** AmEx, DC, MC, V.

The Hostin chain only has one hotel in Poreč, and it offers competitive luxury at decent prices. The modern but attractive resort complex, surrounded by pines, is next to the marina by a strip of seaside greenery that holds all the resorts. It's easy to hit the town from here, though management strives to make this a self-contained holiday. Amenities include a pool, sauna, whirlpool, steam room, gym and nearby pebble beach. Diving, boat and bike rentals are nearby. It offers a half-board deal, where you can have dinner at the decent hotel restaurant for an extra €6, but it might be more rewarding to explore the scores of options in the nearby harbour. The hotel was completed only recently, and the tastefully designed, well-appointed rooms are in good shape.

Hotel Jadran

*Obala maršala Tita 21 (052 431 236/465 100/
fax 052 451 440/www.riviera.hr).* **Closed** Nov-Mar.
Rates *Apr-Oct* €22-€52 single; €34-€82 double.
Credit AmEx, DC, MC, V.

This pretty old harbourside building with beautiful
arches provides low-frills lodging near a busy section of the waterfront. There are only 22 basic rooms,
with no air-conditioning or TV, but they're clean and
well kept up. There's a good bar and terrace downstairs. Sea-view rooms cost extra and can suffer
overspill noise from the bustle of the harbour. It

would suit anyone who won't be lounging around
the hotel all day long and is just looking for a cheap
central place to sleep.

Hotel Laguna Galijot

*Plava Laguna (052 415 800/fax 052 415 818/
www.plavalaguna.hr).* **Closed** Nov-Mar. **Rates** *Apr-
Oct* €53-€126 single; €72-€170 double. **Credit**
AmEx, DC, MC V.

It's still a package-tour resort, but the four-star Hotel
Laguna Galijot is one of the more pleasant venues
of its kind around Poreč. An attractive two-storey

Jules Verne's Pazin

The county town of **Pazin** is positively large
by Istrian standards, with all the amenities
you could wish for. It has a bus station. It
even has a train station. You can get to
Rijeka or Zagreb. It has a cinema, a theatre,
a seminary, a department store, a street
market and a hospital. It houses Istria's
favourite jump-off point for suicides. But
more than anything, Pazin is at pains to pay
homage to Jules Verne.

Pazin loves Jules Verne so much that it
names streets after him. The local Jules
Verne Society (Stari trg 8, 052 622 460,
www.ice.hr/davors/ejvclub.htm) meets
here regularly.

Which is all very strange when you consider
that the French author never set foot here.
However, he did use Pazin Castle as a major
location in his 1885 novel, *Mathias Sandorf*.

Over 1,000 years old, Pazin Castle was the
prison where Sandorf and his colleagues were
held before making their desperate escape
through the underground river that flows
beneath the castle walls. And it's all still
here: the forbidding stone stronghold, the
magnificent 130-metre deep (427-foot) gorge
below (the local suicide venue of choice) and
the mysterious river at the bottom, which
really does disappear underground. All is
exactly as described in the book.

Verne kept a correspondence with the then
mayor, Giuseppe Cech. He gained further
material from French travel writer Charles
Yriarte, who really had been to Pazin. Apart
from that, there is no proof that Verne ever
came near Istria – although local experts are
convinced they have proof that he sailed
close to the shore.

Istria

building is hidden behind a fenced-in pine grove on its own tiny peninsula, offering relative seclusion. The hotel has a private beach, which is rocky, so you'll want to bathe with sandals. The grounds have tall, shady trees, nice gardens and lush lawns with comfortable spots for sunbathing. Most rooms have sea views and a balcony. The adjacent one-storey 'village' has several smaller, separate structures that add another 52 rooms, and another cluster of smaller structures holds 86 self-catering apartments. There isn't the array of activities other resorts offer but it does have its own marina and diving school – there is a sports centre and the Plava Disco nearby. Prices include champagne breakfast and a decent dinner. Outdoor pool with heated saltwater.

Hotel Mediteran

Plava Laguna (052 415 900/fax 052 415 901/ www.plavalaguna.hr). **Closed** Nov-Mar. **Rates** *Apr-Oct* €29-€62 single; €50-€116 double. **Credit** AmEx, DC, MC, V.

This affordable family resort has 332 rooms without air-conditioning inside an ugly concrete building surrounded by pine forest above a rocky beach. Extensive activities available include a sports cen-

tre with four tennis courts, a children's playground, beach volleyball, a rifle range, table tennis, bike rentals and mini golf. Sailboats and rowboats are available for rent nearby.

Hotel Parentino

Obala maršala Tita 17 (052 431 925/052 465 100/ fax 052 451 440/www.riviera.hr). **Closed** Nov-Mar. **Rates** *Apr-Oct* €24-€38 single; €36-€82 double. **Credit** AmEx, DC, MC, V.

This small, 14-room, two-star hotel is set in a pretty 19th-century building on the busy harbour. The old-style rooms have high ceilings and simple, functional decor. Although it's not a resort, you can use the sports facilities and swimming pools of the Fortuna (*see p144*). Convenient to the action but too central for those who want to go to sleep early.

Hotel Poreč

Rade Končara 1 (tel/fax 052 451 811/www.hotel porec.com). **Rates** €36-€64 single; €52-€98 double. **Credit** AmEx, DC, MC V.

This blocky concrete building with 54 rooms is close to the bus station and a small park by the marina. Of all the hotels in town, this is furthest from the

Vrh, Buzet

When it comes to classic Istrian cuisine, the consistently high quality here marks out Vrh as one of the best in its field.

The menu includes standards such as *fuži* (Istrian pasta twists), gnocchi with game goulash or truffles, steak with truffles, and

home-made sausages. Meat is prepared under *peka,* the Croatian speciality of slow-cooking under a dome of cast iron, covered by hot ashes. There are also some pleasant surprises, such as the selection of *fuži* fillings, which includes forest mushrooms and wild asparagus. The nettle pâté is particularly good too.

Host Nevio Petohlep produces the house wine. Of particular note is his Malvasija Frizante, which comes with a local legend. A soldier from Napoleon's invading army was wounded and left for dead at the roadside. An Istrian girl took him in and nursed him back to health. As a token of his appreciation, the Frenchman, a native of Reims, divulged his wine-making secrets to his benefactress's family. Istrian *frizante* or 'champagne' has been a local tradition ever since. Red champagne is a particular favourite.

Vrh also produces some of the region's finest grappa, sold directly to cellars in Zagreb. There's even a truffle variety.

You'll find Vrh on the main road between Ponte Porton and Buzet. Take the turn after Motovun, signposted Butoniga. The left-hand turn to Vrh is signposted 2km (1.25 miles) down the road.

Vrh 2, Buzet (052 667 123). **Open** 1-10pm Tue-Sat; 12.30-10pm Sun. **No credit cards**.

holidaymaker bustle. All the comfortable rooms have balconies, although the views are a little mundane – and there's no air-conditioning.

Tourist information

Adria Tourist Service
Hvarska 5 (052 423 303/www.ats.hr). **Open** *Apr-Oct* 8am-9pm daily.
Trips to Venice, accommodation, rentals and other local excursions.

Atlas Travel
Eufrazijeva 63 (052 434 933/www.atlas-croatia.com). **Open** *Apr-Oct* 8am-9pm daily.
Hotel and private room booking, currency exchange, ferry tickets and rentals.

Poreč Tourist Office
Zagrebačka 9 (052 451 293/www.istra.com/porec). **Open** 8am-10pm daily.
Free maps and brochure *Tourist Info.*

Getting there & around

The nearest airports are in **Pula** and **Trieste**, Italy (00 39 0481 773 224). Half a dozen services a day run to Poreč bus station (Rade Končara 1, 052 432 153) from each main town in Istria, and Zagreb. A tourist train runs from Trg Slobode, the main square by the bus station, to Zelena Laguna, stopping at Plava Laguna and various resorts on the way. There is also a boat that makes the trip out to Zelena Laguna, and an hourly pink bus from the bus station in high season. There is a taxi stand at the bus station. You can also call 052 432 465 or 052 438 347, 098 209 675 mobile.

Adria (*see above*) organises ferry boats and day trips to **Venice**. From late June to mid September, Tirrenia (www.tirrenia.it) runs a fast boat from **Trieste** (8am Wed, Thur, Fri, journey time 3hrs, €16 single, €32 return). It continues to Rovinj and Brijuni, returning to Poreč between 5-6pm.

Rovinj

Seen from a distance, the weathered stone houses of Rovinj's Old Town, with their backs jammed up against the sea in a tight cluster, appear to have grown organically from the rocky peninsula. Up close, the narrow cobbled streets that wind between these houses also look more natural than man-made.

The mix of seaside scenery, old architecture and shaded rocky beaches in this idyllic fishing town has been bringing in groups of tourists since 1845, when a steamship line from Trieste stopped here. Since then, the town has been a star destination on Istria's tourist-crowded coast. And yet tourism has not overwhelmed Rovinj or closed the local fishing trade, which brings fresh catches to its excellent restaurants. Rather than overdevelop, Rovinj has sought to retain its old charm – a charm for which tourists pay a premium. This is one of Croatia's nicer, and pricier, resort towns.

Rovinj has been settled since at least the seventh century, when it was an island centred around a low, cone-shaped hill sticking out of the sea. The populace overflowed to the mainland, and in 1763 Habsburg engineers attached Rovinj Island to the rest of Croatia, turning it into a peninsula. The hill still defines the shape of the mostly car-free Old Town, and an easy stroll up the spiralling road to the top affords views of surreal beauty.

Some of the best panoramic views are from the **Cathedral of St Euphemia** (10am-2pm, 3-6pm daily), which caps the hilltop. This baroque structure was built in 1736 to house the remains of Euphemia, a virgin martyr, who was fed to the lions by Emperor Diocletian around 304. Legend says her massive stone coffin disappeared from Constantinople and miraculously floated ashore in Rovinj, providing a fishing town with a catch from heaven and a patron saint. St Euphemia's tomb and relics can be seen inside the cathedral.

Other sights worth spotting in town are the **open-air market** and the **City Museum** (Trg maršala Tita 11, 052 816 720, www.muzej-rovinj.com, open summer 9am-noon, 7-10pm Tue-Sun, winter 9am-1pm Tue-Sat, 15kn) next to the Balbi Arch, the original town gate. The museum has some historical exhibits as well as some good contemporary art. Rovinj has a reputation as a home for artists – and galleries. **Grisia**, a stone-paved thoroughfare leading up to the cathedral, is packed with dozens of galleries and ateliers, selling crafts, kitsch and amateur seascapes. In summer, most galleries on Grisia spill out on to the pavement. Every August, in a festival of outdoor shows, anyone selling art can set up shop on Grisia.

Beaches

In town there is a small busy beach area in front of the **Hotel Rovinj** (*see p150*). For the pine-forested beaches at the edge of town, you'll need sandals to wade on the jagged shore, but the lack of sand means the sea is incredibly clear, great for snorkelling or diving. Head south of town, past the marina and the **Hotel Park**, to the area of **Monte Mullini** and the wooded peninsula of **Zlatni Rt** (Golden Cape). The walk along the water is a little more than a kilometre from town. There is a cluster of resorts around here, but it's uphill, so the beaches are mostly undisturbed nature. If you keep going south, there are some quiet stretches where you can find your own private boulder to sun on. About 3km (2 miles) south of town are two nudist beaches, **Polari Bay** and the adjacent **Cape Eve**. The 13 small islands here have thick forests surrounded by rocky beach.

Excursions

The most popular excursions are to nearby **St Katarina Island** and dazzling **Crveni otok** (Red Island), both a short hop by taxi boat from the main harbour. Each has a hotel but offers enough secluded cover to warrant the 10kn-20kn return journey.

Another is offered by most travel agencies in town. The **Limski Kanal**, 13km (8 miles) north-east of Rovinj, is a stunning fjord, turquoise in colour and with dramatic, steep sides. It's best explored in a car, allowing you to dine at the panoramic **Viking** restaurant (052 448 223, open 11am-3.30pm, 6.30-11pm daily), with mussels, oysters farmed at the fjord and fresh fish. The restaurant is named after the 1963 film *The Long Ships*, starring Richard Widmark, some of which was filmed here. The film's caterer decided to open this restaurant afterwards. In high season, excursion boats take one-hour tours of the waters.

Where to eat

Amorfa

Obala Alda Rismondo 23 (052 816 663). **Open** 11am-midnight daily. **Credit** AmEx, DC, MC, V.
The Amorfa, right on the harbourside, is one of the pricier places in town. The slick service and the decor, which includes an indoor goldfish pond and a nicely appointed terrace decked in white tablecloths, help make your meal more of an event. The dishes include hearty portions of excellently prepared seafood standards, along with a few special items, like salted sea bass. There is an impressive list of top local and foreign wines. It's undeniably a good restaurant in a great location, but you can probably find the same quality food for less than the average 120kn a main dish elsewhere in town.

Calisona

Trg na mostu 4 (052 815 313). **Open** 8am-midnight daily. **Credit** AmEx, MC, V.
Just beyond the Balbi Arch is a small square where a large awning covers a relaxing terrace serving sophisticated seafood. Along with Istrian standards like fetuccine with truffle, lobster with tagliatelle and succulent fresh grilled fish, there are creative offerings such as squid stuffed with scampi, Dalmatian-style octopus salad, and sole in Chardonnay. Meat includes steak, a grilled platter for two and *ražnjici*, a spiced Balkan-style pork kebab.

Casa Mia

Driovier 24 (052 830 069). **Open** 10am-11pm daily. **Credit** AmEx, DC, MC, V.
Near the big outdoor market, on the bustling seaside square of Valdibora, this terrace offers a place to relax and watch the waves roll by while enjoying fine food at reasonable prices. With seafood like sea bass, dentex, grouper, lobster and several types of shellfish, coming fresh from the next-door market, it's not hard to make a good meal, and the kitchen is up to the task. It also serves pizzas in 17 varieties, steaks and pork dishes.

Giannino

Augusto Ferri 38 (052 813 402). **Open** 11am-3pm, 6-11pm daily. **Credit** AmEx, DC.
Popular restaurant by the Old Town draws repeat customers with its Italian cuisine. The menu is dominated by fresh catches from Rovinj's fishermen, but the sauces, and the pastas, have an Italian influence. Seafood and pasta meet in great dishes like noodles *mare monti* or rigatoni with lobster, a very Istrian recipe. Local ingredients get shown off in tempting offerings like sole with truffles.

Neptun

Joakima Rakovca 10 (052 816 086). **Open** *Summer* 8am-1am daily. *Winter* 11am-11pm daily. **No credit cards**.
In a narrow thoroughfare, a street away from the harbour, this friendly restaurant has a comfortable, rustic interior and a few pavement tables. The photo-illustrated menu is a bit touristy, but the food tastes better than the pictures look. As well as the usual fish offerings, there is stand-out pasta with truffles, meaty *ćevapčići* and *vjesaličia*, puffy-crusted pizza from a brick oven. Neptun also offers *peka* meats, the closed pan covered with coals and cooked for 90 minutes. If you fancy lamb or veal this way, make sure you order in advance.

La Puntulina

Sv Križa 38 (052 813 186). **Open** noon-3pm, 6pm-midnight daily. *Cocktail bar* 6pm-2am daily. **No credit cards**.
Perched on a straight drop above the sea, this new family-run establishment puts a gourmet Italian touch into local cuisine. La Puntulina starts with the same fresh ingredients sold around town, but here dishes stand out through creative sauces and a careful mix of flavours. The fish fillet Puntulina, with a delicately spiced tomato sauce, the scallops in brandy, the local squid in polenta and the fish carpaccio all provide exciting ways to enjoy fresh seafood. The local mushroom is treated well in truffled fish fillet, ravioli with truffles and beef fillet in truffle sauce. Italian-style desserts include *panna cotta* and *crema Catalana*. The wine bar serves local, French and Italian wines by the glass or bottle and staff will recommend the right vintage for your meal. Get the table nearest the window for a sea view and afterwards go downstairs to the cocktail bar, with a stunning secluded terrace on the sea.

Toni
Driovier 3 (052 815 303). **Open** noon-3pm, 6-11pm Mon-Tue, Thur-Sun. **Credit** AmEx, MC.
Simple, well-respected eaterie in a compact dining room filled with green-and-white checked table-cloths. With mid-range prices, the standard fish and pasta dishes are well prepared and equally well presented. Plenty of Istrian wines too.

Veli Jože
Sv Križa 1 (052 816 337). **Open** 10am-1pm daily. **Credit** AmEx, DC, MC, V.
Istrian-style dishes flavour the menu of this quaint spot near the harbour with a high-ceilinged interior crammed with antiques and seagoing kitsch. There is seating for 50 on a pavement terrace. Specialities include shellfish lasagne, crab with truffles, cod in white wine and baked lamb with potatoes.

Where to drink

The cafés at the north-west end of Rovinj harbour, such as the cocktail bar in **La Puntulina**, **Valentino** or the **Zanzibar**, are great places for sundowners. After dark, the best bar crawl is in the tiny streets at the bend of **Obala Alda Rismondo** and in **Joakima Rakovca**, a little street near the harbour; don't miss **Buzz** (No.5), **Hannibal** (No.36) or the **Rock Café Roxy** (No.15).

Rio Bar
Obala Alda Rismondo 13 (052 813 564). **Open** 11am-1am daily.
On the harbour, the Rio's comfortable terrace offers a scenic spot to start the evening. Outgoing staff and patrons give the place a lively atmosphere and set you up for a night of barhopping.

Valentino
Sv Križa 28 (052 830 683). **Open** 11am-1am daily.
Pricy cocktail bar at the end of the harbour has fab outdoor seating on a terrace a few feet over the sea. Step off the street, lose the crowds and commune with nature, your cocktail and your companion.

Zanzibar
Obala Pina Budičina (052 813 206). **Open** 11am-1am daily.
Big, loungey wicker chairs with bright red cushions surround low drinking tables on the terrace of this popular cocktail bar near a busy section of the harbour. At happy hour, tables fill with people here to gawp at people or the gorgeous sunsets over the sea. Inside, the DJs encourage you to hang around for the rest of the night, a pricy proposition with cocktails running at 60kn plus.

Nightlife

The two main choices are the huge **Monvi** complex and the centrally located **Labyrinth** (*see below* **Gay & lesbian**).

Monvi Entertainment Centre
Luja Adamoviča, Monvi, south of the marina at the resort area (052 545 117/www.monvicenter.com). **Open** *Summer* 11am-4am daily. *Winter* see agenda.
One of the most profitable nightspots in Croatia, this large complex has several bars, a pizzeria, a Mexican restaurant, an amphitheatre for live music, and a huge, air-conditioned dancefloor packed with young tourists and locals all year. This has become a major stop for bands or DJs touring the country, and on summer nights the club can get some serious talent – on the decks and on the dancefloor. The collection of bars can make the place feel a bit shopping mall-ish, but as the evening wears on, there's a sense of security in knowing there are about a half-dozen places to slip away for a drink and a chat. The club is south of town, near the big resort hotels but far enough away for everything to go all night.

Gay & lesbian

There are nude beaches on Polari Bay and Cape Eve ideal for casual socialising.

Labyrinth
Sv Križa 59, by the terrace of Hotel Rovinj (www.labyrinth.hr). **Open** *Summer* 10pm-4am Fri, Sat and party nights.
A gay and mixed crowd enjoys great dance music in this club hidden away in the heart of the Old Town. It's inside a catacomb-like space under an old stone embattlement constructed around the cathedral. The moderate-sized, round dancefloor is surrounded by a mural with scenes from Rovinj and beefcake interpretations of Michelangelo's work. DJs from all over Europe drop in to play moving commercial, house and progressive music. It's not as crowded as the Monvi, but everyone seems just as ready to party.

Lobby Bar
Zdenac 16 (www.labyrinth.hr). **Open** 11am-1am daily.
Gay and gay-friendly bar in the heart of the Old Town serves fancy cocktails allowing for down-to-earth conversation amid classy decor. Run by the folks who do the Labyrinth Club nearby, it's the logical place to begin a quest for the gay side of Rovinj.

Where to shop

Open-air market
Trg Valdibora. **Open** 7am-4pm daily.
Valdibora hosts a hectic open-air market selling the day's catch and local produce. The array of fresh seafood is almost reason enough to go self-catering. Browsing is great fun and there are plenty of items you can take with you: home-made grappa, wine and lavender oil. By 1pm, many fresh-food vendors go, leaving souvenir shops hawking knick-knacks made from shells, Croatian-flag beach towels, paintings, postcards and other non-essentials.

Where to stay

Much of the accommodation around Rovinj is in package hotels, the majority run by **Maistra** (www.maistra.hr). These include the **Hotel Eden** (Luja Adamovića, 052 800 400, €88-€198) with tennis courts and bowling alley, the **Hotel Park** (Ivana Maletić Ronigova, 052 811 077, €62-€148) with scuba diving, boat rentals and children's clubs and the self-catering **Amarin Apartments** (Monsena, 052 802 000, €36-€75 for two). The latter is a great option as it shares a pool and restaurants so that you're not tied to making your own food and entertainment.

Private rooms can be arranged with local travel agencies. With the beach less than 2km (1.25 miles) away, taking a simple room in the Old Town for 200kn-250kn can be a great way to enjoy Rovinj. Book ahead in high season if you want to be near town or the beach.

Hotel Adriatic

Obala Pina Budičina 2 (052 815 088/fax 052 813 573/www.maistra.hr). **Closed** mid Oct-Mar. **Rates** *Apr-mid Oct* €41-€66 single; €61-€112 double. **Credit** AmEx, DC, MC, V.

Simple three-star on the harbour lets 27 rooms in a central location for mid-range rates. Although it's the oldest hotel in town, built a century ago, the large, basic rooms are in good shape. The hotel's pleasant terrace café is one of many along the busy harbour. The noise from the harbour can be a bit of a problem in sea-view rooms, but this is a great place for couples and anyone looking for fun in town.

Hotel Katrina

St Katarina Island (052 804 100/fax 052 804 111/ www.hotelinsel-katarina.com). **Closed** mid Oct-mid Apr. **Rates** *mid Apr-mid Oct* €122-€178 double. **Credit** AmEx, DC, MC, V.

St Katarina, a pine-covered island in the harbour about the same size as Rovinj's Old Town, is dominated by a modern, 120-room resort hotel built around a former mansion by a luxury chain also responsible for high-standard hotels in Alpine resorts and the Miramar outside Opatija. The island and its rocky beaches are pretty much taken over by hotel guests, who have the run of a beach bar, tennis courts, two swimming pools, garden spaces and beautiful stretches of pine forest. A free boat leaves every half-hour for the five-minute journey between the Old Town and the car-free island. Meals are included in the room price.

Hotel Rovinj

Sv Križa 59 (052 811 288/fax 052 840 757/ hotel-rovinj@pu.t-com.hr). **Closed** mid Oct-late Mar. **Rates** *Late Mar-mid Oct* €33-€50 single; €56-€84 double. **Credit** AmEx, MC, V.

This affordable hotel has a great downtown location: on a hill, with its back to the base of the cathedral and its front facing St Katarina Island and the sea. Although it's in the heart of town, it's far enough away from the harbour to avoid the noise. The 70 rooms are basic and without air-conditioning, but the location and reasonable prices make up for the lack of frills. Service is courteous and efficient.

Hotel Villa Angelo d'Oro

Via Švalba 38-42 (052 840 502/fax 052 840 111/ www.rovinj.at). **Closed** Sept-mid Mar. **Rates** *Mid Mar-Aug* €78-€124 single; €128-€220 double. **Credit** AmEx, DC, MC, V.

Rovinj's only five-star is in a beautifully restored old building on the site of a 17th-century bishop's palace. The location, along a narrow, winding stone-paved street halfway up the hill that defines Rovinj's Old Town, is both quiet and central. The lobby, the museum-quality stairway and the individually styled rooms all ooze antique opulence. The garden café, hidden from the street by ancient stone walls, and the sheltered rooftop loggia, with its beautiful sea views, provide stunning sanctuary. The 'wellness area' includes a sauna, jacuzzi and solarium. It has a superb seafood restaurant worth visiting even if you're not staying and a wine cellar where you can arrange tastings. Quick, courteous service and attention to detail add to the luxurious feel of the place. Only 24 rooms, so book early.

Resources

Internet

A-Mar *Karera 26 (052 841 211).* **Open** *Summer* 9am-11pm daily.

Tourist information

Delfin *Obala Vladimira Nazora (052 812 266).* **Open** *Summer* 10am-9pm daily.
Excursions and boats to the islands around Rovinj, accommodation booking and moped rental.
Globtour *Obala Alda Rismondo 2 (052 814 130/ www.globtour-turizam.hr).* **Open** *Summer* 10am-8pm daily.
Right in the harbour, accommodation booking and and excursions to Venice and elsewhere.
Planet *Svetog Križa 1 (052 840 494/www. planetrovinj.com).* **Open** *Summer* 10am-9pm daily.
Internet café, excursions (including ferries to Venice) and all types of accommodation.
Rovinj Tourist Office *Obala P Budičina 12 (052 811 566).* **Open** *mid June-mid Sept* 8am-9pm daily; *mid Sept-mid June* 8am-3pm Mon Sat.
Free maps and English-language brochures.

Getting there & around

There are regular bus services from Zagreb and Pula, site of the nearest airport. The bus station is at **Trg na Lokri**, a short walk east of the Old Town. For a **taxi**, call 052 811 100.

From late June to mid September, Tirrenia (www.tirrenia.it) runs a fast boat from **Trieste** every day but Monday at 8am (3-4hrs, €20 single, €40 return). Three times a week it continues to Brijuni.

Istria

Kvarner
& Islands

Features

Maps

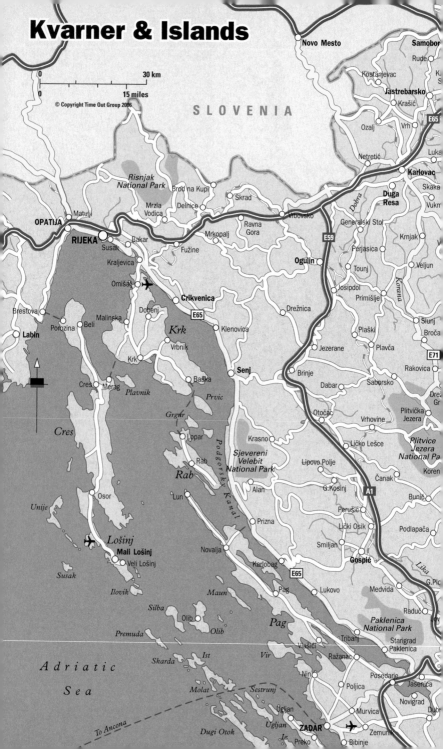

Kvarner & Islands

Bay of dolphins, carnivals and griffon vultures.

Trsat Castle overlooking the Kvarner Bay from the heights of Rijeka. *See p156.*

The deep Kvarner Gulf, bounded on three sides by steep mountains, contains Croatia's largest Adriatic islands. Some, such as **Krk, Lošinj** and **Rab**, have long been developed for tourism. Others, in particular **Cres**, are relatively untouched. Natural beauty abounds. Rare colonies of griffon vultures and dolphins (*see p164* **The day of the dolphins**) are two of the region's big attractions; the two main national parks of **Risnjak** and **Paklenice** offer superb scope for hiking and climbing.

Of the other destinations, **Pag** offers both isolation and the summer-long DJ scene of **Zrće** (*see p176* **Balkan Ibiza**). Although Pag doesn't officially belong to Kvarner – this long, arid island is administratively divided between the mainland and Zadar – it is included in this section as it is so closely connected with the other islands in the gulf. Easy transport links are one of the area's boons – both Krk and Pag have bridges to continental Croatia and most ferry hops are short and frequent.

The two main towns are chalk and cheese. For much of its recent past, the gritty port of **Rijeka** didn't belong to Croatia at all, but Italy

and Hungary. It's now its third largest town after Zagreb and Split, and a vital transport hub. A major regeneration scheme should wake Rijeka from its post-industrial slumber. A major departure point for the coast, Rijeka is best known for its carnival (*see p161* **Rio in Rijeka**), which takes place every February.

Next door, **Opatija** had its glory days in the late 19th century. Here the Habsburgs built ornate villas and grand spa hotels, many of which can still be checked in to – at a price.

Whatever travel plans you have – Kvarner connects Istria to the rest of Croatia – may be affected by the *Bura* wind, which blasts down through the mountain passes above the gulf. When it roars, the Krk bridge (linking to the region's only airport, now a budget air destination from the UK) is forced to close and no boats can go out.

▶ The phone code for **Kvarner & Islands** is 051, in **Pag** 023. You don't need to dial the code within the region itself.

Kvarner & Islands

Things to do

Take a boat from Veli Lošinj to see the dolphin colony (*see p164* **The day of the dolphins**). Catch Croatia's craziest **carnival** at Mardi Gras in Rijeka (*see p161* **Rio in Rijeka**). Go hiking around the **Risnjak National Park** (*see p156*) or climbing among the karst slopes of the **Paklenica National Park** (*see p177*). Enjoy an expert massage at one of the classic spa hotels of **Opatija** (*see p167*).

Places to stay

Take an Adriatic dip at the recently renovated **Jadran** (*see p160*) in Rijeka. The **Zlatni Lav** (*see p163*) at Martinšćica on Cres is a new three-star with a sea view, as is the **Kanajt** (*see p165*) at Punat on Krk. Take your pick of Habsburg elegance in Opatija – the **Hotel Kvarner** (*see p172*) is affordable.

Places to eat

Sveti Jakov (*see p167* **Top tables**) and **Le Mandrać** (*see p168* **Top tables**) are the key places in Opatija and nearby Volosko. Rijeka's top table is the downtown **Municipium** (*see p157*). Tuck into famous Cres lamb at **Bukaleta** (*see p162*) and typical Krk pasta,

šurlice, at the **Corsaro** (*see p165*). **Artatore** (*see p166*) near Mali Lošinj is a classic, traditional village eaterie.

Nightlife

Zrće near Novalja on Pag (*see p176* **Balkan Ibiza**) is Croatia's leading party spot all summer. For late DJ bars, Rijeka can offer the **Karolina** (*see p157*) and the **Opium Buddha Bar** (*see p156* **Best bars**). **Jungle** (*see p165*) in Krk town is where the beat goes on there. Lounge bars line **Vladimira Gortana** (*see p166*) in Mali Lošinj. Tired of gooey cakes and frothy coffees? Head for **Monokini** (*see p172*), Opatija's rare nod to the 21st century.

Culture

Rijeka's **Modern and Contemporary Art Museum** (*see p155*) exhibits the best young Croatian artists. Discover local history at the **Petrić Palace** (*see p162*) on Cres, and look out for the medieval treasures of the Frankopans on display at the **Church of St Quirinus** (*see p163*) in Krk town. Modern Croatian and classic Italian works are exhibited at the **Art Collections** (*see p166*) in Mali Lošinj.

Rijeka

Excited visitors sit atop Rijeka's **Kavana Ri**, resting their cold beer on its terrace overlooking their sleek Jadrolinija liner soon bound for idyllic Adriatic islands. They must wonder what they're leaving behind, a town whose main building is called Big Skyscraper, where Socialist blocks are stuck to Austro-Hungarian confectionery, a kind of Bratislava with boats.

There's a weird wind that blows through Rijeka. And it's not just the *Bura* rattling the cranes and ugly industrial clutter of the waterfront – turbulence becomes it.

Rijeka is also called 'river' by the Italians and the Hungarians, except that their version is Fiume and their ways of nabbing Croatia's biggest port for various lengths of time in recent history were somewhat twisted.

Founded by the Romans, and Habsburg from the 1400s, Rijeka fell under Hungary in the late 1700s. The landlocked Magyars built a new harbour, baroque landmarks and sundry industries (including the world's first torpedo), though the nearest Hungarian town was 350km (217 miles) away. When their legitimacy was

challenged in 1868, the Hungarians switched papers on Emperor Franz Josef at the signing ceremony, and a majority Slav population endured 50 more years of rule from Budapest.

As a result of the indignation expressed in the influential local newspaper *Riječki Novi List*, displaced Dalmatian intellectuals stirred up a groundswell of opinion resulting in the Declaration of Fiume 1905, a call for a united land of South Slavs. It failed.

After the Habsburgs collapsed in 1918, the Hungarian Governor fled his magnificent palace, and in marched Italian patriot, pilot and poet Gabriele D'Annunzio with 200 soldiers and proclaimed Fiume to be Italian and his own state. Rome disowned him. His totalitarian rule lasted over a year, providing Mussolini with the inspiration for his March on Rome in 1922.

Mussolini's men took Rijeka a year later, the Germans in 1943. Rijeka industrialised under Tito, rusted in the 1990s, but recent developments in transport infrastructure – the motorway from Zagreb, the road bridge from the nearest airport at Krk island where easyJet flies in to from June 2006 – may see a change in fortunes. Two newly renovated four-star hotels

opened in 2006, the **Bonavia** and the **Jadran**.
Moreover, the **Gateway Project**, signed with
the World Bank in 2003 for an estimated
€300 million, will see the Rijeka waterfront
transformed in ten years. A new passenger
terminal, a nautical centre and marina, and a
link road with the Rijeka roundabout – and
Zagreb and Budapest – will all be in place.

The tourist board has a dinky new office in
Rijeka's pedestrianised high street, the **Korzo**.
One of its tasks is to turn February's carnival,
Croatia's biggest, into a major visitor attraction.
For the rest of the year, tourists must make do
with the baroque remnants of Magyar rule and
the rather splendid castle of **Trsat**.

GOVERNORS AND GLAGOLITES

The Korzo runs parallel to the embankment
Riva. A few baroque façades (including the
remake of the original medieval **City Tower**)
fade behind modern shops and cafés. A short
walk west is the main bus station, backdropped
by the bizarre, two-level **Capuchin Church**.
West another ten minutes is the train station,
still with two services a day to Budapest.
Beyond is **Opatija**, almost a suburb these days.
East, the Korzo ends at the local bus station
(for services to Opatija) and the so-called **Dead
Canal**, actually pretty and pedestrianised. Its
nearby continuation, the Rječina, is the division
between Rijeka and the former separate areas of
Sušak and Trsat. Between the wars, this stream
was the border of Italy and Yugoslavia.

From here you can trek up the 538 steps of
Stube Petra Kružića to Trsat – or take the No.1
bus for a lovely hilltop stroll and take the steps
back. If you've an afternoon to kill before your
boat, spend it around Trsat Castle. If you've
only a couple of hours, turn left from the canal
at Titov trg into Žrtava fašima (Rijeka still
swears by Socialist street names) and four
mildly diverting attractions.

First up is **St Vitus' Church** (Grivica 11,
051 330 897, 9am-noon, 5-7pm daily), topped by
a baroque rotunda, a Venetian-inspired creation
from the 1600s. You're now at the edge of the
Old Town. Just above it stands the suitably
stately Governor's Palace, commanding a view
of the sea; D'Annunzio would have seen the
battleship sent from Rome in 1920. Exhibits
belonging to the **History and Maritime
Museum** here (Muzejski trg 1, 051 213 578,
9am-8pm Tue-Fri, 9am-1pm Sat, 10kn) are
overshadowed by Alajos Hauszmann's
sumptuous state rooms. Next door, the **City
Museum** (Muzejski trg 1/1, 051 336 711, open
10am-1pm, 5-8pm Mon-Fri, 10am-1pm Sat,
20kn) contains modest, temporary exhibitions
in a modern, two-floor space. Overlooking these
two buildings is the **Natural History**

Museum (Lorenzov prolaz 1, 051 553 669, 9am-
7pm Mon-Sat, 9am-3pm Sun, 10kn), with an
aquarium, geological displays and recently
opened botanical garden outside.

Spinal Frana Supila leads from the
neighbourhood of the museums towards
three main squares: Jadranski trg and the Big
Skyscraper (the office block also named Rijeka
Skyscraper); Trg Riječki rezolucije (after the
1905 Resolution); and Trg republike Hrvatske,
with the University Library, which houses the
Modern and Contemporary Art Museum
(Dolac 1/II, 051 334 280, www.mmsu.hr, open
10am-1pm, 6-9pm Tue-Sun). Only big enough
for temporary exhibitions, the second-floor
MCAM aspires to compete with the Museum
of Contemporary Art in Zagreb with its regular
agenda of young Croatian artists. On the
ground floor are a few installations relating to
the old Glagolitic alphabet (*see p143* **The alley
of Glagolites**). The pedestrianised square
extends down as far as the Riva.

Radio Rijeka on the **Korzo**.

Trsat Castle

Petra Zrinskoga (no phone). **Closed** Jan. **Open** *Apr-Nov* 9am-midnight daily. *Dec, Feb, Mar* 9am-3pm daily.

Visit this fort for the panoramic view alone, best enjoyed from the Gradina terrace café beneath the Nugent mausoleum. Irish-born Austro-Hungarian naval commander Laval Nugent-Westmeath fought Napoleon and bought this medieval Frankopan fortress to house his family and his art collection, the latter no longer open. The mausoleum is worth a look in, if only for the bad press it gives Nugent's daughter, the 'evil and eccentric' Countess Ana. Down back towards the No.1 bus terminal, you pass the Sabrage café (*see p158*), Our Lady of Trsat Church and the small Franciscan monastery.

Beaches & excursions

There is not much by way of a beach at Rijeka, although if you stay at the **Jadran** (*see p160*) you get easy access to the sea. Better beaches are a short hop from **Opatija** (*see p167*).

Some 40km (25 miles) north-east of Rijeka stretches the thick, steep forest of the **Risnjak National Park**, centred by the 1,528-metre-high (5,013-foot) mountain of the same name. Here reside bears, wolves, lynx and chamois. Without a car, the park is tricky to reach. There are several buses to Delnice (1hr 15mins), but the shuttle bus to the park's office and entry point of Crni Lug (Bijela Vodica 48, Crni Lug,

---

Best bars Opium Buddha Bar, Rijeka

One of Rijeka's unusual venues (*see p158*) is set out with a live six-foot iguana in an 18-foot terrarium in one corner and, in the other, a seven-foot, seated, gold-painted statue of a svelte Buddha. In between it's a half-block-long stretch of intimate darkness with comfy chairs circled around low coffee tables and dim, sexy red lights. There is also a very big bar, behind which a TV constantly shows the Fashion Channel with the sound turned off. A fun, young crowd does a good job of filling the big space with loud conversation and quiet smooching. There are DJs and dancing at weekends, and the rest of the music selected is eclectic and usually good. The fantastic terrace out front is a wide, awning-covered stretch of pavement on the Riva, across the street from the harbour, with more comfy chairs and tables. Staff are young and hip, but not too cool to give service with a smile.

Kvarner & Islands

051 836 133, www.risnjak.hr, open 7am-10pm daily, 30kn) leaves late afternoon. Agencies in Rijeka (*see p161*) offer excursions.

Where to eat

For fine dining, head to **Opatija** (*see p167*). Rijeka has working-men's konobas around the harbour and market, busy at late-morning *marenda*, a few reasonable places by the Korzo and the panoramic **Trsatika** up in Trsat.

Belgian Beer Café Brasserie
Trg republike Hrvatske 2 (051 212 148).
Open 6am-1am Mon-Thur, Sun; 6am-2am Fri, Sat. **Credit** MC, V.
Genuine brasserie atmosphere to this place, set so close to the harbour you can see ships passing from the handful of tables outside. Inside is wooden, with Flemish inscriptions on the walls and almost authentic pissoirs. Most of all, the cuisine is tasty and hearty: Brabant roast chicken in Leffe with celery mash (45kn); Belgian sausages with red cabbage (40kn); even beer sausages (120kn). There are four menus of the day (48kn-58kn), one vegetarian, and four other meat-free choices. Disappointingly slender selection of Belgian beers but the kitchen runs late and staff are swift.

Feral
Matije Gupca 5B (051 212 274). **Open** 9am-11pm Mon-Sat. **Credit** MC, V.
Handy little downtown eaterie specialising in seafood, with a few meaty options too. Cooked frog with potatoes and kale is one of the more unusual of these, otherwise the menu features the standard white sea fish and scampi. Mozzarella salad makes a nice change from seafood, Löwenbräu beer something different than the stock Istrian wines. Front terrace open in summer.

Municipium
Trg Riječke rezolucije 5 (051 213 000). **Open** 10am-11pm Mon-Sat. **Credit** AmEx, DC, MC, V.
One of the classiest names around town – if not *the* classiest – Municipium is set in a grand Habsburg-era building, tucked away in a quiet courtyard right in the centre of town. Door staff greet you at the entrance – decorum is all. The menu is vast and fish-oriented, most of it priced in the 300kn/kg range, very reasonable considering the quality of service, presentation and the fare itself. Zucchini, wild asparagus and other greens get a look-in and the wine list runs to 150 (mainly Croatian) varieties. If you're going to splash out, do it here.

Trsatika
Šetalište J Rakovca 33 (051 217 455). **Open** 11am-11pm Mon, Tue, Thur-Sun. **Credit** MC, V.
Fabulously located up in Trsat, this part pizzeria, part grill offers high-grade versions of renowned standards, with a terrace view to boot. Specialities include roast suckling pig, grilled, roasted or boiled lamb, *šurlice* pasta and goulash from Krk, and roast veal knuckle. A rustic oven in the corner turns out large, cheap pizzas in two sizes, the house Trsatika with ham, mussels, scampi and cheese coming in at under 40kn. If you have a day in Rijeka, set aside a couple of hours here.

Zlatna Školjka
Kružna 12a (051 213 782). **Open** 11am-11pm Mon-Sat. **Credit** AmEx, DC, MC, V.
With a good location and a reputation as one of the best places in town, this busy cellar restaurant can charge higher prices than most. Along with usual seafood offerings, appetisers include fish carpaccio with capers, and marinated salmon. The day's fish is displayed on ice, with a wide selection of molluscs. The hefty salads can work as a small meal, followed by a number of cheeses. Snappy service adds to a pleasant atmosphere.

Where to drink

Trendy cafés now line the Riva. The most notable is the **Opium Buddha Bar** (*see p156* **Best bars**), but nearby are also **Capitano** and **Karolina**. The Korzo and its continuation of Ante Starčevića contain many venues: the naff but renowned El Rio; Hemingway; and the superior **Mali Café**, **Cinema Kvarner** and **Dva Lva**, the latter better after dark.

Capitano
Adamićeva 3 (051 213 399). **Open** 7am-4am daily.
Beautiful old-style bar in a sumptuously large indoor-outdoor space right on the harbour attracts a young, fashionable crowd. The dark wood and marble interior, with a huge old-fashioned mirror behind the bar, has expensive-looking decor and pleasant gallery seating. The indoor back terrace is inside a shopping centre, where DJs spin for dancers at weekends. The real terrace, out front facing the harbour, is one of the nicer ones in Rijeka. Relax in wicker while you watch crowds and boats go past.

Cinema Kvarner
Ante Starčevića 4 (no phone). **Open** 7am-midnight daily.
On the ground floor of a former movie house, this smallish bar on the end of the Korzo has pleasant, expensive-looking decor that includes photos from theatre performances in town. The staff could be a little more helpful and enthusiastic, but there is still a good atmosphere. A fine list of cocktails and a friendly, chatting crowd keep the place going until closing hour. When it shuts, there are plenty of options nearby.

Karolina
Gat Karoline Riječke (051 330 909). **Open** 6am-midnight Sun-Thur; 6am-2am Fri; 6am-4am Sat.
A slick, modern glass-enclosed structure, sitting all by itself on a pier in the main harbour, houses an upmarket bar that draws a mix of yuppies, tourists,

hipsters and hard-drinking barflies. The bar's terrace is right on the sea, and it makes a fantastic place for a daytime drink outdoors. Inside is a carefully designed, dimly lit space, with high tables and tall stools in the middle of the bar area, and lower chairs with zebra-striped cushions at the two ends. The darkness releases inhibitions, and the techno and trance music inspires a good time. DJs and dancing at weekends.

Kavana Ri

Brodokomerc Forum, Riva (051 311 019). **Open** 8am-11pm daily.

If you're sitting on the upper harbourfront terrace of the Ri, chances are you've got a ship to catch. There she is, right in front of you, gleaming white and blue, while your waitress (slowly) brings out a dirt-cheap cold beer for you to raise a glass to adventures ahead. The place is a Socialist timewarp, the decor, the furniture, the service, but hey, rather this than any Western chain café at twice the price. Accessed via a concrete staircase round the back of the building opposite Gat Karoline Riječke.

Mali Café

Korzo 18 (051 335 606). **Open** 7am-midnight daily.

The young, chatty crowd helps make this friendly spot one of the better places to drink along the Korzo, small ('mali') but comfortable. The strange mural of a naval battle on the wall seems a bit incongruous, but the rest of the modern, mostly black-and-white interior is tasteful and well thought out. Music tending toward trance and jazz styles, big cocktails and extremely nice staff make this a great place to start a bar crawl or spend most of the evening.

Opium Buddha Bar

Riva 12a (051 336 397). **Open** 7am-3am Mon-Wed; 7am-5am Thur-Sun.

Landmark rendezvous on the Rijeka waterfront. *See p156* **Best bars**.

River Pub

Frana Supila 12 (051 213 406). **Open** 7am-2am Mon-Wed; 10am-4am Thur-Sat; 6pm-2am Sun.

Behind a big, wooden, unsignposted door opposite the Optani opticians, halfway down from the museums, this is a rare case of a truly pub-like pub in continental Europe. Beautifully upholstered furniture sits on an old tiled floor, while a sturdy bar counter holds up taps of Bass, Caffrey's, Guinness and Kilkenny. The framed photographs from around Istria are a nice touch, old regional maps too, with a few busts of Irish writers rather than the silly usual Oirish toot you see elsewhere.

Sabrage

Petra Zrinskog 2 (091 793 1536 mobile). **Open** 7am-midnight daily.

Up in Trsat between the church and castle, this is a lovely spot to while away a few hours. Manager Ante Žezelj felt the need to post up his diploma from the American Bartending School, but he needn't have bothered – this place is well stocked, well run

and well staffed. Along with classic cocktails and long drinks (25kn-40kn) there's a long wine list, a Tinto Reserva hiding among the bottles of Zlatni Plavac and Dingač. There are whiskies, 14-year-old Oban and ten-year-old Talisker, to be sipped in an elegantly carved wooden interior decorated with portraits of famous locals. Nice hot chocolates too.

Nightlife

The two main bar strips of the Korzo and the Riva are as lively at night-time as they are during the day, and venues such as **Capitano** and **Karolina** (*see p157*) operate as seminightclubs. Some of the boats on the waterfront also double up as late-night places of entertainment – **Nina** is a recent example. Nearby places that are used after dark are commercial dance bars are the **Dva Lava**, **Teuta** and the **Phanas Pub**. Look out for DJ nights at the **Fun Academy** (www.funacademy.hr) at the windsurfing haven of Preluk towards Opatija, and **Točka** (Luki 19, 098 920 2135 mobile, 091 156 9426 mobile) outside town. The grunge scene centres on the **Palach Club**, but if the **Spirit Club** (www.spirit-ri.hr) finds another venue to replace the one recently closed by the train station, you can expect a string of alternative acts from Croatia, Italy and beyond.

Dva Lava

Ante Starčićeva 8 (051 332 390). **Open** 8am-11pm Mon-Wed; 8am-3am Thur-Sat.

The Two Lions comprises two cramped storeys of edgy flirting in a sci-fi film set. The music is commendable, usually veering from the mainstream, cocktails are dangerously cheap, and local youth eye their potential catches from the lounge bar/viewing platform upstairs. No entrance fee unless a name act is programmed, standard bar prices.

Palach Club

Kružna 6 (051 215 063). **Open** 9am-11pm Mon-Fri; 5pm-1am Sat; 5-11pm Sun.

Turn off the Korzo and you're on a gritty, graffiti-adorned side street, where teenagers with perfect punk haircuts and new Doc Marten's loiter by the entrance to Rijeka's main alternative club. Inside, the recently expanded Palach spreads out across a ground-floor complex with several rooms dedicated to either dancing, art display or tables for drinking and chatting. Decor varies from shiny industrial to an all-black dance hall. The café is open all day. By early evening the place begins to fill up with students, slackers and other party animals, chatting by the main bar, dancing to DJs or watching concerts by bands from Croatia and around Europe. Named after Jan Palach, the Czech student who set himself on fire during the Prague Spring of 1968, the place can take itself too seriously, but the staff are down-to-earth, and the people who come to party are mostly out for fun.

The **Hotel Continental** (*top*) and the **Dead Canal**. See *p160* and *p155*.

Palach Club. *See p158.*

Phanas Pub

Ivana Zajca 9 (051 312 377). **Open** 7am-1am Mon-Wed; 7am-3am Thur-Sat.

Down at the harbour, this place can only be experienced late at night – that is, if you can get in. An otherwise innocent two-floor wooden pub with maritime knick-knacks is thick with hormones, pinging around to a commercial dance and rock soundtrack. Guinness, Kilkenny and Stella, some quality wines and cheap cocktails offer alternatives to the standard Ožujsko, but the drinks are almost secondary to the action around the long bar counter.

Teuta

Užarska 1 (051 335 712). **Open** 7am-1am Mon-Wed; 7am-3am Thur; 7am-4am Fri, Sat; 4pm-1am Sun.

Another Jekyll and Hyde job, this is a laid-back café by day and a DJ haunt by night, particularly at weekends. It could be more consistent, but in a town full of bars packed with local youth on the pull, this is a handy find if you're serious about your music.

Where to stay

Despite the recent reopening of two keynote venues in town, the **Bonavia** and the **Jadran**, both four-star, the hotel stock in Croatia's third-biggest town is pretty sad. The Jadran is run by the Hoteli Jadran group (www.hoteli-jadran.hr), which also runs the somewhat tatty **Continental** and museum-piece **Neboder**.

Continental

Šetalište Andrije Kačića-Miošiča 1 (051 372 008/fax 051 372 009/www.jadran-hoteli.hr). **Rates** €53 single; €62 double. **Credit** AmEx, DC, MC, V.

It looks grander than it is, but at these prices in the centre of town, overlooking the canal and with a pretty terrace internet café on its doorstep, you can't really complain. Last renovated in 1989, a century after it opened, the Continental offers convenience rather than comfort in its 38 rooms. Brown was all the rage in 1989, apparently.

Grand Hotel Bonavia

Dolac 4 (051 357 100/fax 051 335 969/www.bonavia.hr). **Rates** €93-€145 single; €116-€175 double. **Credit** AmEx, DC, MC, V.

Rijeka's class option, in the seriously high-end Adriatic Luxury Hotels group. Don't expect heated pools and hot cocktail bars, this is a recently renovated business hotel, but a spa and gym are promised. The 120 rooms are tastefully done, the in-house Bonavia Classic restaurant is one of the best in town, and the terrace café overlooks the city.

Jadran

Šetalište XIII Divizije 46 (051 216 600/fax 051 216 458/www.jadran-hoteli.hr). **Rates** €77-€90 single; €90-€107 double. **Credit** AmEx, DC, MC, V.

Completely renovated in 2005, the seafront Jadran has also upgraded its prices considerably. The 66 rooms are nicely fitted, but you're paying for the location. Set by Rijeka's first stretch of swimmable sea, with its own stop on the No.2 bus route east of town in Pećine, the Jadran ('Adriatic') has been a spot for bathing and relaxation since it opened in 1914. There's a price supplement for sea-facing rooms. Half- and full-board deals also available.

Neboder

Strossmayerova 1 (051 373 538/fax 051 373 551/www.jadran-hoteli.hr). **Rates** €67 single; €68 double. **Credit** AmEx, DC, MC, V.

Yes, it's that bloody big (14-floor) skyscraper on the flyover behind the Continental. If you're looking for a (relative) cheapie in town and the Continental is full, you'll have to come here. The renovated rooms are adequate, the unrenovated ones rather tatty at best. The unreconstituted Socialist Realist lobby gives it away, really – this is 1975 all over again. Actually, the name doesn't help – Skyscraper.

Youth Hostel Rijeka

Šetalište XIII Divizije 23 (051 406 420/www.hfhs.hr). **Rates** 110kn-125kn dorm bed; 270kn-300kn double. **No credit cards.**

Opened by the mayor in February 2006, the former Villa Kozulič has been transformed into a modern, 60-bed youth hostel, the first one in town. Well sited in Pećine, east of town by the sea on the No.2 bus route from the train and bus stations, in addition to dorm beds it offers three comfortably equipped double rooms in the attic, a snip for the price and location. The hostel is open all year and has a TV room, internet and a kitchen.

Resources

Hospital
Krešimirova 42 (051 658 111).
General hospital near the train station.

Internet
Inter Club Cont *Šetalište Andrije Kačića-Miošiča 1 (051 371 630/www.interclub-cont.com).* **Open** 7am-11pm daily.
Easily the best internet centre in town, conveniently located by the Hotel Continental – plenty of terminals, gooey cakes and coffee. Grab a canal-side table under the chestnut trees when you finish your session. At 3kn for the first 15 minutes, you won't find cheaper.

Pharmacy
Korzo 22 (051 211 036). **Open** 24hrs daily.

Police
92.

Post office
Korzo 13 (051 525 515). **Open** 7am-9pm Mon-Fri; 7am-2pm Sat.

Tourist information
Generalturist *Trg 128.brigade Hrvatske vojske 8 (051 214 590/www.generalturist.com).*
Excursions and other services for tourists.
Rijeka Tourist Office *Korzo 33 (051 335 882/ www.tz-rijeka.hr).* **Open** Mid June-mid Sept 8am-8pm Mon-Sat; 9am-2pm Sun. Mid Sept-mid June 8am-8pm Mon-Sat; 9am-2pm Sun.
New office on the main drag with a touchscreen outside is manned by friendly, able, English-speaking staff happy to dish out maps and advice.

Getting there & around
Rijeka airport (051 842 040/www.rijeka-airport.hr) is on the northern tip of the island of Krk, near Omišalj, 25km (15.5 miles) south of town. An Autorolej bus meets the weekly Croatia Airlines arrival (45mins, 30kn). Services should be increased for new easyJet services from London Luton and Bristol from June 2006. Its terminus is the suburban bus station near the canal in the city centre. **Taxis** are supposed to have a set fee of 160kn, but many can charge at least 300kn.

Rio in Rijeka

Croatia's biggest carnival takes place in Rijeka, a colourful procession of thousands on the Sunday before Shrove Tuesday.
The Mardi Gras tradition here dates back centuries, when it was a pagan festival to welcome the coming of spring and scare off any lurking Turks. Then as now, masks were elaborate and ugly, and evil spirits were sent packing by local menfolk dressed in animal skins and huge, clanging cowbells: the *zvončari.* Always up for a spot of costumed

fun, the Habsburgs revived the concept in the late 1800s, before Rijeka got tangled up in too much political torment to entertain street parties. In 1982 three masked groups walked down a Korzo of bemused onlookers. Participants grew every year, so that by 2001 4,000 took part in the parades.
Rijeka Carnival (www.ri-karneval.com.hr) runs over four days in January and February. Depending on when Shrove Tuesday falls, the Queen's Pageant usually takes place on the third Friday in January, followed by the Zvončari Parade the next day. By tradition, these bell-ringers clang their instruments and move in steps according to their village of origin. Thirteen days before Shrove Tuesday, on the Saturday lunchtime, the Children's Parade runs through the streets of town. The big event is the International Carnival Parade, which begins at noon on the following Sunday. It usually takes the whole afternoon for floats to pass down the main streets before celebrations into the night at stalls and tents set up around the canal.
Rijeka's modest hotel stock is usually booked way in advance before carnival day. Tour companies such as adriatica put together all-in packages for visitors – check www.adriatica.net for details.

Rijeka is Croatia's biggest transport hub and biggest port. Jadrolinija catamarans serve Cres and Mali Lošinj, and Rab and Novalja. The main coastal ferry runs once a day in summer, twice a week in winter, between Rijeka and Stari Grad (Hvar), Korčula and Dubrovnik. The main office of **Jadrolinija** (051 211 444, www.jadrolinija.hr, open 7am-6pm Mon-Fri, 8am-2.30pm Sat, noon-3pm Sun) is by the harbour at Riva 16 . The **harbour** is right in town, a short hop from both the **suburban bus station** by the canal, and the **national bus station** just west of the Korzo, on Trg Žabica. There are hourly buses from Zagreb (3hrs 30mins) and regular ones from Split (8hrs 30mins) and Zadar (4hrs 30mins).

The **train station** is a short walk west from the national bus station. There are four trains a day from Zagreb (around 4hrs), and daily services from Ljubljana, Vienna, Munich and Budapest. For Pula, a bus runs as far as Lupoglav and is then met by a train.

You should only need to use the **city bus** network if you're going to Trsat (No.1) or Pećine (No.2) – the centre is compact. Tickets are 10kn for these zone 1 destinations. The **No.32 bus** for Opatija (25mins, 14kn) leaves every 20 minutes from the suburban bus station by the canal, passing the train station.

For a **taxi** call 051 332 893.

Cres

Cres is one of the largest and least developed of Croatia's islands. It is connected with **Lošinj** (*see p166*) by a mobile bridge, its southern neighbour much the opposite in terms of hotel and restaurant provision. Cres is long enough to have two distinct landscapes, verdant in the north, known as Tramuntana, barren to the south. The north contains the two settlements of **Beli** and **Cres town**, the south the former regional capital of **Osor**. In between are the ancient villages of **Lubenice** and **Valun**, and a rich natural life, characterised by the presence of at least 140 griffon vultures, which have been protected on Cres since 1986. In the middle of the island, freshwater Lake Vrana, its waters above sea level, its depths below the sea bottom, supplies both Cres and Lošinj. **Porozina** at the northern tip is the main point of entry from the little port of Brestova, on the Istria–Kvarner border.

The tiny hilltop village of Beli is the base for ornithological research. Here the Caput Insulae (051 840 525, www.caput-insulae.com) ecology centre monitors and cares for the griffon vulture population. You'll find an exhibition and details of a hiking route leading from here through woods and abandoned villages. Near Beli is a

complete Roman bridge, evidence of man's long-term presence here – both Cres and Lošinj were settled in prehistoric times.

You can see a collection of local finds in Cres town's museum housed in the **Petrić Palace**, named after the local 16th-century philosopher. This town is marked with a small, medieval harbour, Gothic and Renaissance churches, and remains of the Venetian city walls.

Also on the island's western side, Lubenice offers an insight into island life as it once was. This spectacular 4,000-year-old settlement is home to about 20 ageing souls and a crumbling collection of stone buildings, including a 15th-century parish church and a Romanesque chapel used as storage space by a local family. Below this wind-slammed place spreads the jagged coast and a series of secluded pebble coves accessible by a steep footpath leading through the underbrush. Rijeka-based Ekopark Pernat (www.ekoparkpernat.org) has set about the restoration of the old parish building and introduced photo exhibitions, art and craft workshops and the annual **Lubenice Music Nights**, open-air classical concerts held every Friday in summer. Nearby Valun is a charming fishing village whose parish church contains the **Valun Tablet**. Its inscription from the 11th century is an early example of the ancient local tongue of Glagolitic (*see p143* **The alley of Glagolites**).

The Liburni tribe who lived in modern-day Osor were probably the ones who dug the channel that now separates Cres and Lošinj. An important trading town, as Apsorus, Osor was the largest Roman town on the Croatian Adriatic after Pula. Since then, it has been in permanent decline, although its Archaelogical Museum (open 10am-noon, 7-9pm daily, 10kn) shows that medieval Osor was still sizeable.

The most convenient spots to eat and drink are to be found on the waterfront of Cres town: **Marina** (Jadranska obala, 051 571 072) is a newly opened restaurant at the marina, where the extensive meat selection includes the Cres Plate of steak in green pepper sauce. **Šumica** (Lungomare sv Mikule 17, 051 571 891) on Cres town beach serves the renowned local lamb and octopus *ispod peke*, slow cooked in the traditional way. If you have a car, drive the ten minutes from Cres to the hilltop hamlet of Loznati, and the family-run **Bukaleta** (051 571 606) restaurant. The attraction here is the famous Cres lamb, baked, boiled, fried or barbecued. The family has its own olive groves and produces fine olive oil too.

In Valun, **Toš Juna** (051 525 084, open Apr-Oct noon-4pm, 6-11pm daily) serves freshly grilled lamb in an old olive mill. **Mali raj** (Vidovići 11, 098 715 856 mobile, open June-Sept

7-11pm daily) is a family-run konoba in the small village of Vidovići, 2km (1.25 miles) from Martinščica, with a panoramic terrace. Everything served is home-grown or reared, from lamb cutlets to the wine and brandies. On Lubenice's main square, **Lubenička loža** (051 840 427) confines its dishes to sheep's cheese (*skuta*) and prosciutto sandwiches, but compensates with spectacular views from its terrace across to St Ivan Bay.

Štala (Turion 3, 098 491 975 mobile) is the island's sole nightclub, in Cres town.

Cres only has two hotels: **Kimen** (Melin I 16, Cres town, 051 571 322, www.hotel-kimen.com, open Easter-mid Oct), a two-star in a garden setting near the beach; and **Zlatni Lav** (Martin, 18d, 051 574 020, www.hotel-zlatni-lav.com, open Apr-Oct), a new three-star with a beautiful sea view in Martinščica, on the main road. **Kovačine** (Melin I 20, Cres town, 051 573 150, www.camp-kovacine.com, open Easter-mid Oct) is a popular campsite that also offers 13 rooms with a bathroom, TV and balconies with sea view.

For more information, contact the **Cres Tourist Office** (Cons 10, Cres town, 051 571 535, www.tzg-cres.hr).

Two ferries hop to Cres: from **Brestova** on the Istrian mainland to **Porozina**; and from **Valbiska** on **Krk** to **Merag**. Both run every hour or so and take 30 minutes. In summer a daily catamaran links with **Rijeka** (1hr 20mins) and **Mali Lošinj**, all going into Cres town, some to **Martinščica**. At least five buses a day run between Cres town and Mali Lošinj, two linking with **Zagreb**. Summer weekdays, some six buses a day run between **Cres town** and **Osor**, significantly fewer at weekends and in winter. Transport to north Cres is scarce. There is a **taxi** rank at **Cres town bus station** (Zazid 4, 051 571 664, 098 947 5592 mobile).

Krk

Krk isn't your typical Croatian island. First, it has been attached to the mainland by a road bridge since 1981. Secondly, it has an airport, the one serving Rijeka, in fact. Thirdly, it has a developed road network, so that the main tourist centres in western Krk – **Malinska**, **Njivice** and **Omišalj** – are easily accessible. The beach at **Baška** is as popular as almost any in the Adriatic. Finally, Krk has a few of its own gastronomic delicacies, namely long, thin tubes of pasta, *šurlice*, to be eaten with goulash or lamb stew, and local white wine Vrbnička. Krk is the largest of Croatia's islands.

As the base for the powerful medieval dukes the **Frankopans**, Krk has played a significant role in Croatian history. It was populated by

Illyrians, Greeks and Romans, before the Croats and, from the 12th century, the Frankopans who at one point held half of modern-day Croatia. After Venice took over here in 1480, the Frankopans still ruled significant portions of the mainland for another 200 years. Much of Krk's recent history centres on tourism.

Krk town is the island's administrative and cultural centre. Although it has long spilled over the surrounding hills, its centre sits on 3,000 years of history and is contained within its intact city walls dating from various eras. All summer tourists flood the focal squares of Bana Jelačića Vela placa, and main street of Strossmayera. The chief historical sight is the **Cathedral of the Assumption** (Trg sv Kvirina, open 9.30am-1pm, 5-7pm daily), built in the late 12th century, a Romanesque structure with Roman columns from its previous incarnation as a baths. Attached to it are the Romanesque **Church of St Quirinus**, with its Frankopan silver altarpiece from 1477; and the **Bishop's Palace** with works by Paolo Veneziano and other Italian masters.

Near Krk town, the former agricultural village of **Punat** is set in a beautiful bay with islet **Košljun** in the middle. Upon it stands a 15th-century Franciscan monastery with a significant religious treasury. Punat has one of the biggest harbours in the region; boats take tourists across to Košljun and back for 20kn.

Krk's other main draw is Baška, whose famous Blue Flag sandy **beach** is, at nearly 2km (1.25 miles), one of the largest on the coast. Tourists first started coming here in 1908, when Baška was the largest town on Krk. Just before Baška as you approach from Krk town is the village of **Jurandvor**, containing a copy of the most significant historical find in the vicinity, the Baška tablet, the original once housed in the **Church of St Lucy**. This is the oldest dated (11th-century) written example of the original Croatian language of Glagolitic. A couple of more minor churches stand over the tangle of medieval streets in Baška.

Foodies and wine buffs should head to the east coast and **Vrbnik**, a medieval town set on a high cliff. Well-preserved narrow streets contain old churches, some housing Glagolitic scripts, but mostly any number of little restaurants whose wine cellars are stocked with bottles of the famous local Vrbnička. **Nada** (Glavaca 22, 051 857 065, open Mar-Oct 11am-2am daily, Nov-Feb 11am-midnight Sat, Sun) has a restaurant upstairs, while downstairs is a traditional konoba complete with barrels, hanging smoked hams and massive wooden tables. **Gospoja** (Frankopanska 1, 051 857 142) and **Katunar vinarija** (Sv Nedija, 051 857 393, open June-Sept 11am-midnight daily, closed

The day of the dolphins

The clean waters of the northern Adriatic are home to the bottlenose dolphin, in particular the area around Cres and Lošinj, where a population of 120 resides. This figure is pretty accurate, as this is also home to **Blue World**, a marine research and conservation organisation. Based at Veli Lošinj, Blue World (Kaštel 24, 051 604 666, www.blue-world.org) runs the Adriatic Dolphin Project, a long-term study of the local dolphin population. The creatures are tracked photographed and taperecorded in an effort to better understand their social behaviour and feeding patterns.

Blue World doesn't lay on boat trips for tourists, only for school groups, workshop students and volunteers (*see below*), but does work together with the handful of local excursion companies who take tourists out to look for dolphins. Note that high season happens to be the time when you're least likely to find them. Firms based at Veli Lošinj harbour include **Fran** (098 627 012 mobile) and **Happy Boat** (091 792 1035 mobile). Blue World is at pains to point out that under no circumstances should visitors attempt to swim with dolphins – not only is it illegal but such contact could ruin years of research into the creatures in their natural habitat.

For a better understanding of how dolphins behave, Blue World runs the Lošinj Marine Education Centre (July, Aug 9am-1pm, 6-9pm daily, June, Sept 9am-2pm, 6-8pm Mon-Fri, 9am-2pm Sat, May, Oct 9am-4pm Mon-Fri, 9am-2pm Sat, Nov-Apr 10am-2pm Mon-Fri, 10kn, 7kn 6-10s, free under-6s), with interactive displays and exhibitions on the ground floor, a library and specialised workshops upstairs. Payment is extra for the regular series of lectures given in four languages. The centre also organises longer workshops, some of which include boat trips. In the summer, 12-day volunteer courses are set up, with residency in Rovenska Bay near Veli Lošinj. Check the Blue World site for more information.

Kvarner & Islands

Oct-May) are known for their wine, the latter combining a wine cellar, shop and à la carte restaurant serving shark steak in Vrbnička.

Back in Krk town, full-blown dining options include **Konoba Šime** (Antona Malmića 1, 051 220 042, closed Dec-Feb), a typical Adriatic restaurant with an atypical setting in the city wall. Space is tight but there's a huge terrace. Neighbouring **Corsaro** (Obala Hrvatske mornarice 2) also has a fine terrace. The food here is more innovative: this is the place to try the famed *šurlice* pasta tubes with goulash, or steak with truffles. **Galija** (Frankopanska 38, 051 221 250) is part konoba, part pizzeria.

The historic building that houses Krk's **Casa di Padrone** (Šetalište sv Bernandina, 091 229 4602 mobile, open 8am-midnight daily) has been a fishmonger's, a pharmacy and now houses a lounge bar with a beautiful boat terrace. **Volsonis** (Vela placa 8, 091 511 9554 mobile, open 8am-1am daily) is a café-bar in a basement where renovations uncovered Roman archaeological remains, some finds displayed here. The venue hosts temporary exhibitions and cultural events.

Beachfront dining in Baška is best enjoyed at **Cicibela** (Emila Geistlicha, 051 856 013, open Mar-Oct 10am-midnight daily, closed Nov-Feb), run by the Bogdešić family and renowned for its creative cooking. You can choose your lobster or opt for one of the pasta-seafood combos including black pasta with cuttlefish or scampi spaghetti. **Pirun** (Palada 92, 051 864 061) is a konoba-style eatery with a fire for winter dining and an open terrace for summer. With a location dockside, the fish is as fresh as it gets, although the place is also known for horsemeat (served as a 350g cutlet) and, in particular, colt. A few steps from the harbour, **Konoba TU-TU** (Palada 36, 051 856 674, open May-mid Sept 10am-midnight daily, mid Sept-Apr 7pm-midnight daily) is rated for its choice of wines from all over Croatia.

Punat's **Marina** (Puntica 9, 051 854 132, open Mar-mid Jan 11am-11pm Mon-Thur, 8am-11pm Fri-Sun, closed mid Jan-Feb) boasts the services of celebrated chef Krešimir Crvenković, ensuring regular appearances in national Best Restaurants lists. Expect superior seafood and views across Punat Bay.

The owners of **Bracera** (Kvarnerska 1, 051 858 700, open Feb-Dec 10am-11pm Tue-Sun, closed Jan) in Malinska have their own fishing boat, the *Angelina*, supplying the kitchens. The restaurant is done out konoba style, with old family photos, antiquey furniture, barrels, nets and old tools. **Rivica** (Ribarska obala 13, 051 846 101, open Feb-Dec noon-midnight, closed Jan) in Njivice has been running a kitchen since 1934. It's a classy place that takes cooking

seriously and offers a seasonal menu heavy on lamb in spring, asparagus in summer, squid and calamari in autumn, and white fish in winter. The family runs a konoba next door.

The main nightlife option is the **Jungle** club in Krk town (S Radića), near Vela placa, fun but mainstream, open from 10pm every night in summer, weekends in winter.

The **Hoteli Krk group** (Ružmarinska 6, 051 655 755, fax 051 221 022, www.hotelikrk.hr) runs most of the lodging options in town. The **Marina** (Obala Hrvatske mornarice, 051 221 128, open May-Sept, €46-€94, closed Oct-Apr) is ideally located by the port, although noisy on weekend nights. The group has a complex of tourist hotels with pools and sports facilities around the **Hotel Dražica** – see the website for details. The **Bor** (Šetalište Dražica 5, 051 220 200, www.hotelbor.hr, open mid Apr-Oct, €38-€128, closed Nov-mid Apr) sits in pinewoods near the sea, five minutes' walk from the city centre; **Koralj** (Vlade Tomašića, 052 408 200, www.valamar.com, open Apr-Oct, €42-€140, closed Nov-Mar) is bigger, with nearly 200 rooms and suites, internet, a gym and beauty salon, sauna and solarium, with the same access to pine woods and the sea.

The Baška Hotels group (051 656 111, www.hotelibaska.hr) runs a complex of tourist hotels. The **Corinthia** (Emila Geistlicha 34, open Apr-Oct, 480kn-1,080kn, closed Nov-Mar) is three hotels in one, of varying ages but with masses of facilities including four indoor and three outdoor swimming pools, and a spa centre (www.wellness-baska.info). The **Zvonimir** (same address, open Apr-Oct, 702kn-1,230kn, closed Nov-Mar) is more upmarket than its neighbour but uses its services and facilities.

In Punat, **Kanajt** (Kanajt 5, 051 654 340, www.kanajt.com, €60-€130) is a recently renovated three-star in a former bishop's villa built in 1528. It's by the marina with nice views across the bay. It's worth the little extra for a balcony. The **Omorika** (Frankopanska, 051 654 500, www.omorika-punat.com, open Apr-Oct, €50-€106, closed Nov-Mar) is a sizeable but relaxed three-star close to the beach, where half-board rates are a snip. The polished **Falkensteiner Hotel Park Punat** (Obala 100, 051 854 024, www.falkensteiner.com, open late Mar-Oct, €54-€120, closed Nov-late Mar) is set in parkland in the centre of Punat, just across the promenade from the sea. Part of the Falkensteiner group, it's great for kids, with indoor and outdoor playgrounds and summer entertainment. The management also runs a naturist campsite, available to hotel guests.

One of the better hotels in the pretty resort of Malinska, the **Malin** (Kralja Tomislava 23, 051 850 234, www.hotelmalin.com, 460kn-760kn), right on the promenade, is a medium-sized place with facilities including a sauna, gym, diving centre, marina and its own beach. Minimum stay is three nights. A short distance away in the fishing village of Porat, the **Pinia** (Porat 31, 051 866 333, www.hotel-pinia.hr, open mid Mar-Oct, rates vary, closed Nov-mid Mar) is a four-star opened in 2003 with 26 well-equipped rooms with views across Kvarner Bay. The hotel has a private beach.

For more details, contact the **Krk Island Tourist Office** (Trg sv Kvirina 1, 051 221 359, www.krk.hr) and **Krk town Tourist Office** (Vela placa 1/1, 051 221 414, www.tz-krk.hr).

The **airport** by **Omišalj** on the northern tip of Krk serves **Rijeka** on the mainland. At present there is no public transport to Krk town, 20km (12 miles) away, although that might change with the new easyJet connection from June 2006. A taxi should cost about 250kn-300kn. Regular **buses** run from **Rijeka** (1hr 40mins) to **Krk town**, via **Malinska** and then down to **Baška**. A couple a day come from **Zagreb** (5hrs 30mins). **Ferries** hop between **Valbiska** and **Merag** on **Cres** (30mins), and **Baška** and **Lopar** on **Rab** (50mins). In high season only, there is a regular service between **Crikvenica** on the mainland and **Šilo** on Krk's north-eastern tip (30mins).

Lošinj

Life in Lošinj centres on the two tourist-friendly settlements of **Mali** and **Veli Lošinj**, at the other end of the narrow divide with Osor on Cres. The island, separated from Cres by the Liburni tribe before the Romans came, developed rapidly with the shipbuilding industry in the 18th and 19th centuries, before tourism took over. Today Mali Lošinj is the biggest town on all the Croatian islands and the island lives from tourism. Part of its charm is the presence of a colony of dolphins, protected by non-profit-making Blue World based in Veli Lošinj (*see p164* **The day of the dolphins**).

Mali Lošinj ('Small Lošinj', in fact bigger than Veli Lošinj, 'Great Lošinj') is located in the most protected part of the bay. Its houses are placed above the harbour, which features a new and well-equipped marina. Tourism is centred on **Čikat Bay**, frequented by the health-seeking Austrian aristocracy in the 19th century and now known for its windsurfing.

Sights include a couple of minor churches – note the bust of Josip Kašman, the baritone who sang at the opening of the New York Met in 1883, outside the **Chapel of St Anthony**. Mali Lošinj also contains the **Art Collections** (Vladimira Gortana 35, 051 231 173, open 10am-noon, 7-9pm daily), modern Croatian and 17th-

and 18th-century Italian works, once in the hands of two locals. Of note are urban scenes by fin-de-siècle painter Emanuel Vidović.

Quieter Veli Lošinj shares a similar history to its neighbour – it's a pleasant 45-minute walk between them. It also has a Church of St Anthony, whose pink façade dominates the port, and which contains seven baroque altars and works by Vivarini and other Italian masters. Exhibitions are also staged at the Venetian Tower, built in 1455, but most come to see the famous bronze statue of Apoxymenos, either Greek from the fourth century BC or Roman. It was found off Lošinj in 1999.

In the heart of Mali Lošinj, **Baracuda** (Priko 31, 051 233 309, open Apr-Oct) offers fresh seafood served up in nautical surroundings. **Cigale** (051 238 583) offers similar in Čikat Bay. Some 10km (6 miles) outside town at the village of the same name, **Artatore** (051 232 932, open Mar-Nov, 10am-midnight daily) is a great little find. In the same family for three decades, it offers lobster done Artatore style in *buzara* sauce, and oven-baked lamb. Leave room for the peach pie, and try and get a table on the terrace overlooking the bay. **Marina** (051 236 178) in Veli Lošinj harbour facing St Anthony is the best choice there.

For fun, terrace bars line Vladimira Gortana, including **Nautica** (No.77, open Mar-Oct). **Godimento** (Riva lošinjskih kapetana 10, 051 231 419, open Apr-Oct) is the latest trendy lounge bar; **Priko** (Priko 2, 051 231 185, open July-Aug until 3am daily, Sept-June until 11pm daily) a mainstream disco popular with the crowd from Zagreb. **Mini Marina** (Del Conte Giovanni 1, 051 231 888), known as Katakomba, is a small club with a tiny stage filled nightly by local musicians. More live music is on offer at the **Positivo Bar** (Dražica 1, 051 233 187, open Apr-Oct until 3am daily), on the road to Dražica Bay next to a supermarket. Owner Krešo is a drummer from Zagreb. The **Downtown Pub** (Braće Vidulića 60, 051 233 951, open 7am-3am Mon-Sat, 3pm-midnight Sun) is another out-of-town venue with DJ parties, with a busy local winter trade. Look out for flyers and posters in Mali Lošinj. **Disco Energy** (open July-Sept 11pm-5pm daily) is a club space in an abandoned warehouse in the industrial zone at Dražica.

Two companies take care of much of the accommodation on Lošinj: **Asl** (051 236 256, www.island-losinj.com) and **Jadranka** (051 661 101, www.jadranka.hr). The latter runs the three-star **Bellevue** near the sea in Čikat Bay (051 231 222, open mid Feb-mid Nov, €49-€104, closed mid Nov-mid Feb) and the **Dependansa Hortensia** in the same complex, containing an indoor swimming pool with heated seawater and sundry sports facilities. Open all year, the **Villa Favorita** (Sunčana uvala, 051 520 640, www.villafavorita.hr, €98-€144) is a four-star set in a Habsburg villa by the sea, offering eight luxury rooms. Rates are half-board and the hotel has a sauna and outdoor seawater pool. Minimum stay three nights. Other old villa lodging includes the **Margarita** (Bošac 64, 051 233 837, www.vud.hr, open Apr-Oct, €60-€90). Jadranka also runs the huge hotel complex **Punta** at Veli Lošinj (Šestavina, 051 662 000, rates vary), with a mix of 300 package-style rooms and apartments, and sports facilities.

For more details, contact the **Mali Lošinj Tourist Office** (Riva lošinjskih kapetana 29, 051 231 884, www.tz-malilosinj.hr).

From mid June to early September a **car ferry** runs almost daily to Mali Lošinj from Zadar and Pula (www.losinjska-plovidba.hr/ Ljetni.htm).

Buses run almost every hour between Cres town and Mali Lošinj (1hr), four a day coming from Rijeka (3hrs 30mins).

Opatija

The grand villas surrounded by palm groves and regal century-old hotels lining the steep wooded shoreline speak of Opatija's pedigree as a resort destination. In the late 19th century, when the Austro-Hungarian empire reached its apex, the Habsburgs made this town of dazzling vistas and rocky beaches one of the hottest

Top tables Sveti Jakov, Opatija

The restaurant (*see p170*) of the five-star Hotel Milenij serves some of Opatija's best meals in the exquisite surroundings of a historic 1886 villa. This former home of Dr Julius Glax lived and worked in the late 19th century. Glax was a specialist in respiratory diseases and helped put Opatija on the map as a health destination. His house has a noble-looking arched portico covering half of the restaurant's terrace in the park. Inside, the decor beams with baroque opulence, gold-coloured wallpaper and a striking oil painting on the ceiling.

Sveti Jakov's capable kitchen does wonderful things with fresh seafood, like octopus served in wine sauce or catch of the day, an assortment of fresh fish brought out on a plate for detailed discussion and selection. It also ventures well beyond fish, with special menus containing meatier, Central European dishes that are meant to recreate the typical meals of the Habsburg empire. Boost your protein levels with lamb in white wine sauce, beef fillet with black truffles, turkey breast stuffed with olives or veal with *fuži*, Istrian pasta twists.

Kvarner & Islands

Le Mandrać, Volosko

In the little fishing village of Volosko, a pleasant 15-minute walk up the promenade from downtown Opatija, one of the more unusual restaurants on the coast uses local ingredients to create nouvelle-style cuisine and fusion recipes with an Asian influence.

Le Mandrać (*see p170*) has a fancier, more sophisticated feel than other restaurants, but it doesn't overdo it or stray too far from its Croatian roots. Even the decor, a sleek, modern glassed-in terrace, manages to stand out among the neighbouring canvas awnings and still blend well with the antiquity of the village square.

The food succeeds because, although the kitchen is experimental, flavour is clearly more important than eclecticism. Dentex in tempura, sashimi, fishcakes in the house barbecue sauce or cold orange-and-carrot soup served with home-smoked Kvarner octopus, are all delicious. You can sample a broad range of the offerings with special tastings menus. The ingredients change depending on what's in season. Attentive, friendly staff are happy to expalain and recommend good dishes, as well as wines, from the long list of Croatian, Italian, French and Slovenian vintages.

Kvarner & Islands

spots in Europe. Opatija was the place where royalty took their holidays and Isadora Duncan took her lovers.

Wealthy socialites built Secessionist and neo-classical mansions on the rocks above the sea, or stayed in hotels of imperial elegance. Unlike most Croatian resorts, where tourism infrastructure was added on to an existing settlement, Opatija's Old Town was purpose-built for tourists – rich ones. This legacy lingers in the stunning architecture, Viennese-style coffeehouses and Central European atmosphere, kept alive by the large number of Austrian tourists. Opatija still has slightly higher prices than other places on Croatia's coast, and it tends to draw wealthy, conservative visitors, who prefer seaside strolls to raucous nightlife.

You needn't be loaded to soak up Habsburg splendour, however – Ms Duncan's favourite, the **Kvarner**, is now a three-star that any holiday-maker could afford.

Opatija is arranged on a steep hill facing the sea, which means all over town you can get gorgeous views over the Bay of Kvarner and the hilly islands of Krk and Cres. Further vistas and several beaches can be found along a 12km (7.5 mile) shaded promenade, carved into the side of the hill, just above the rocky coast. Called the Lungomare, it was conceived so that visitors could take healthy lungfulls of sea air during rigorous walks.

Perambulating the Lungomare was advised by 19th-century respiratory specialists, who were proclaiming the health benefits of Opatija while Mahler, Puccini and Chekhov were adding to its social cachet.

Before 1844, Opatija was nothing but a fishing village with 35 houses and a church. Higinio von Scarpa then built opulent **Villa Angolina**, named after his wife, and surrounded it with a menagerie, an exotic garden and influential guests. The villa, with its neo-classical interior featuring trompe l'oeil frescoes, now hosts jazz and classical concerts, as well as exhibitions.

A stroll around the villa's Angolina Park will take you to the Lido and an entertaining stretch of Lungomare promenade, where you'll find commanding views from the terrace of the Hotel Kvarner, wonderful seaside restaurants like **Bevanda** and **Miramar**, and the landmark **Hemingway** cocktail bar. Continue north-east along the pine-sheltered promenade to reach sporadic stretches of rocky beach fronted by towering fin-de-siècle villas. Many mansions are restored, but some still sit abandoned, surrounded by groves of bamboo that was once raised in an exotic garden and now grows wild. Such scenes make it easy to imagine the glory days of this former playground for royalty.

You can continue down the Lungomare for quieter, pebbly shores of **Ičići** and **Lovran**, and then on to **Medveja**, whose lovely shingle beach might be more crowded in high season.

Where to eat

Competition keeps every kitchen on its toes. Seafood served in almost any restaurant here is likely to be fresh and cooked well. In a town with so much luxury accommodation, some of the finer meals can be had in hotel restaurants.

Bevanda
Zert 8 (051 712 772/www.bevanda.hr). **Open** 12.30-11.30pm daily. **Credit** AmEx, DC, MC, V.
Sumptuous seafood is served under a regal-looking glass atrium that covers a seaside terrace on the promenade in Opatija's Lido, near Villa Angolina. A good variety of fresh fish is prepared simply but expertly, making this one of the better places in a town full of top-quality seafood. The restaurant also

Opatija.

Monokini. *See p172.*

has a large, well-decorated interior, but the glass-roofed terrace is a magical place to sit, so it's a good idea to book an outdoor table ahead of time. The food, the location and the pampering service make this one of the best dinner choices in town.

Hotel Miramar Restaurant
Ive Kaline 11 (051 280 000/www.hotel-miramar. info). **Open** 12.30-11.30pm daily. **Credit** AmEx, DC, MC, V.
At a serene turning point in the promenade, near the edge of town, this resort hotel's restaurant serves fine seafood on a terrace with an exquisite view of the Adriatic. The kitchen uses good local ingredients, like truffles, available with fillet of beef or with *fuži*, pasta twists. The house grilled fish, mixed fish, sea bass and calamari are all well prepared. You can also order an à la carte menu, and receive the meal that hotel guests get for the price of their room. You'll probably do better to select from the main menu, but either way you're in for a satisfying meal. A winning combination of location and good food.

Le Mandrać
Obala Frana Supila 10, Volosko (051 701 357/ www.lemandrac.com). **Open** 11am-midnight daily. **Credit** AmEx, DC, MC, V.

Classy and inventive establishment in the gastronomic enclave of Volosko, 2km (1.25 miles) from Opatija. See *p168* **Top tables**.

Pomo D'oro
Obala maršala Tita 136 (051 711 195). **Open** noon-midnight Mon-Thur, Sun; noon-2am Fri, Sat. **No credit cards.**
Good, affordable pizzas, sold by the slice, make this a great place for a simple lunch or a midnight snack. The pizza is Sicilian-style, rectangular shaped with a thick soft crust, and one or two slices can feel like a meal. The late opening hours make this place a lifesaver when you need some post-bar nosh.

Sveti Jakov
Hotel Milenij, Sv Jakov Park, Obala maršala Tita 109 (051 202 000/www.ugohoteli.hr). **Open** noon-midnight daily. **Credit** AmEx, DC, MC, V.
Villa setting, five-star staff. See *p167* **Top tables**.

Vongola
Šetalište maršala Tita 113 (051 711 854). **Open** 11am-midnight daily. **Credit** AmEx, DC, MC, V.
The Vongola pairs a good kitchen with a fantastic location. Downstairs from the promenade, on the concrete beach in the heart of town, is a swath of

umbrella-covered terrace offering good renditions of Croatian standards. Order from a moderate selection of fresh, well-prepared fish and molluscs. The sole in white wine sauce is a standout, and you can't go wrong with the seafood platter for two. Non-fish dishes include the usual pastas, risottos and pizza. There are also steaks and schnitzel, but the real carnivore's treat is the *ćevapčići* and *pljeskavica*, two Balkan specialities made of mixed ground meats.

Where to drink

Hotel terraces on the promenade can be a great spot for a daylight refresher, but as the evening wears on, the choice of venues narrows, with **Hemingway**, adjacent **Galeb** and **Monokini** the best bets post-midnight.

Café Wagner

Obala maršala Tita 109 (051 202 071). **Open** 7am-midnight daily.
A Viennese-style café invoking Opatija's Habsburg heritage with its creamy cakes gets mobbed for 4pm coffee time. Superior Central European desserts are prepared with seasonal local ingredients. The quality of the espressos, cappuccinos and other brews stands up to the cakes.

Galija

Zert 3 (051 272 242). **Open** 7am-2am Mon-Thur, Sun; 7am-3am Fri, Sat.
A pleasant spot across from Hemingway (*see below*) and next to a marina that has a good terrace that draws overflow from its neighbour and adds to the buzz on this section of the promenade. Despite the old neon adverts on the wall, there are no cocktails here – it's more for beers and local grappa. The service is fast and friendly and there is usually an upbeat atmosphere, especially when there's good partying next door. There are DJs at weekends, but the music is pretty reliable most of the time.

Hemingway

Zert 2 (051 711 205/www.hemingway.hr). **Open** 7am-2am Mon-Thur, Sun; 7am-5am Fri, Sat.
In tame Opatija, this slick seaside space boasting several bars and two small dancefloors is the main spot in town to drink and party. Hemingway has a buzz mid-afternoon, and past sundown it can get heaving, with fun-seeking holidaymakers looking to mingle over Opatija's best cocktails. The book-sized drinks menu lists most major spirits. Plush, low chairs can make it hard to leave the covered terrace, with its view of the marina on one side and the open sea on the other. The dancefloors, often staffed by separate DJs and gratuitous go-go dancers, are generally full, but the conversation and cavorting are the big action here. You'll find the service to be smart, fast and professional, and it all adds to the general upmarket atmosphere.

Kavana Coretto

Obala maršala Tita 119 (no phone). **Open** 7am-11pm Mon-Thur, Sun; 7am-midnight Fri, Sat.
This cocktail bar is on a terrace raised above the downtown beach, in a busy section of the promenade. Lounge in a swinging chair or sink into a low, cushiony couch, listen to clubby music and take in passers-by and the sea vistas. It's easy to start a

Musical Differences Let 3

For the better part of the last 20 years **Let 3**, from Rijeka, have played the part of an art-rock band, almost rock-theatre band. In the early days, they could be happily compared to the Butthole Surfers. Today they are more provocative. Also, Let 3 are far more popular than the majority of art-rock or alt-rock bands in other countries. Musically, Let 3 are alternative, with a big sound, excellent production and often a range of collaborative musicians, such as large choirs or big brass bands from small coastal towns. Their new album *Bombardiranje Srbije i Čačka* (*Bombing Serbia and Čačak*) mixes the Stooges and Nirvana and melodies from Croatian operas based on folk music. Their recent hit song is 'Kurcem u čelo' ('Dick to the Forehead'). Live, few bands can touch them. They play half or completely naked, in fantastic costumes, sometimes in underground clubs, sometimes at fashion revues, sometimes at rock festivals. People even wanted to buy their CD of complete silence. Their statements and their stance are almost as important as their music itself.

night in the Coretto, where happy hour buzzes on for several, but by the time midnight comes, you'll have to head to the later bars.

Monokini

Obala maršala Tita 96 (051 703 888). **Open** 7am-2am daily.

The main alternative bar in town has a younger, more bohemian crowd than the slightly yuppie types you're likely to find round at Hemingway. Friendly staff give enthusiastic service, even though things can get a bit hectic, especially later on. The bar, which is on the main commercial road through the heart of town, is decorated with alternative, arty decor that includes revolving exhibitions by Croatian artists. CDs range from techno to rock, all of it generally lively. The internet café at the back can be a convenient extra.

Where to stay

Opatija's long history as a resort town means it's full of elegant hotels, built at the turn of the last century. Visiting one of these old gems, some of which have been renovated to various states of luxury, can be pricy fun. Affordable private rooms can usually be found at one of the travel agencies (*see p174*), but the town's supply of inexpensive accommodation is limited, so it's a good idea to book ahead during high season. Nearly all places open year-round. If you're looking to spend time in the region, **Beller** rents out tourist apartments in a four-star villa near town.

Beller

Poljanska cesta 12, Ičići (051 704 101/091 791 6842 mobile/fax 051 704 296/www.beller.hr). **Rates** €64-€108/apartment. **Credit** AmEx, DC, MC, V.

Seven comfortable apartments set in a four-star villa a short way down the Lungomare from Opatija near the ACI marina at Ičići. Properties can be hired out by the night or, except in summer, by the month (€600-€700). All come with a private terrace, internet facilities and air-conditioning, and private parking is a boon for traffic-swamped Opatija. Units accommodate two people comfortably, four easily, and are a short walk from the sea and a sports centre with tennis courts.

Hotel Bristol Opatija

Obala maršala Tita 108 (051 706 300/fax 051 271 317/www.hotel-bristol.hr). **Rates** €70-€100 single; €100-€145 double. **Credit** AmEx, DC, MC, V.

The Bristol, a lovely Habsburg-era hotel from 1906, was renovated and reopened 99 years later as a pleasant four-star in the middle of town. The rooms may be small, but they are tastefully decorated in an antique style that evokes baroque elegance, and they are kept in immaculate condition. All 78 feature air-conditioning, Wi-Fi internet access, a minibar, a trouser press and room service. There is a good restaurant and a Viennese-style café, which serves cakes and cocktails. The young staff are courteous and caring, all of which helps to make the Bristol a very attractive luxury option.

Hotel Kvarner

P Tomašića 1-4 (051 271 202/fax 051 271 202/ www.liburnia.hr). **Rates** €60-€80 single; €100-€150 double. **Credit** AmEx, DC, MC, V.

Croatia's first luxury hotel on the Adriatic, the Kvarner, right on the promenade, is still an imposing imperial presence in the heart of Opatija. Some of the sheen has come off since its glory days, which is why this revered institution is now one of the better bargains in town. Fans of grandeur will love the majestic size of the Crystal Ballroom, the ornate hotel lobby and the splendid seaside terrace beyond it. The rooms themselves are large, furnished in antique style but do not have modern conveniences like air-conditioning. Prices are a little higher for the sea-view rooms, but worth it, as these are usually larger. With a restaurant, a bar and the terrace café, there are plenty of good places to lounge, plus there's massage treatments, a sauna and an indoor pool. The grounds include an outdoor pool surrounded by a patio and steps leading down to the hotel beach.

Hotel Milenij

Obala maršala Tita 109 (051 202 000/fax 051 201 020/www.ugohoteli.hr/milenij). **Rates** €93-€109 single; €179-€207 double. **Credit** AmEx, DC, MC, V.
A newly renovated villa from the late 1800s and an adjacent modern building, both located in a pretty park in the middle of town, offer some of Opatija's fanciest and certainly most expensive accommodation– though the Milenij can sometimes seem to be struggling to deserve its five-star status. The rooms are tastefully decorated and kept in impeccable shape, but they're small. Staff are plentiful and enthusiastic, but perhaps a bit inexperienced. Still, there are no few luxuries, like a pool with a retractable glass roof, 24-hour room service and a spa centre with sauna, steamroom, jacuzzi, beauty treatments and massages. The rooms are all air-conditioned, with internet connections and fluffy bathrobes. The hotel's nearby Sveti Jakov restaurant (*see p167* **Top tables**) is one of the best – even possibly *the* best – in the area, but those who have dinner included in the price of the room may only be offered buffet-style service, which is unlikely to be as good as the restaurant's regular fare. Hence, it might be best to pay for your own dinners.

Hotel Miramar

Ive Kaline 11 (051 280 000/fax 051 280 028/www.hotel-miramar.info). **Rates** €83-€125 single; €116-€400 double. **Credit** AmEx, DC, MC, V.
The 1876 Villa Neptune has been beautifully renovated – and expanded with the addition of three guest villas – to create a full-service resort hotel with its own rocky beach. All rooms are stylish, comfortable and air-conditioned, with a bathroom and a separate toilet, with their own balcony or terrace. The four-star Miramar offers live music in the evenings and a separate spa centre, with a heated pool, a whirlpool, saunas, a steam room and beauty treatments. It has tasteful exteriors and they've done a nice job of blending the traditional main building with the newer additions. The indoor-outdoor pool, surrounded by a patio and sculpted garden, is downright attractive. The Miramar is right along the promenade, ten minutes' walk from downtown, and you take a footbridge over the promenade to get to the hotel's private fenced-in beach. The terrace restaurant (*see p170*), raised just above the promenade, has fantastic views and excellent food, handy as breakfasts and dinners are included in the price. The service is excellent.

Café Wagner. *See p171.*

Kvarner & Islands

Hotel Opatija

Gortanov trg 2/1 (051 271 388/fax 051 271 317/ www.hotel-opatija.hr). **Rates** €42-€63 single; €46-€96 double. **Credit** AmEx, DC, MC, V.

A grand old building originally built for the swells who flocked to Opatija in the town's earlier glory days is now a no-frills, reasonably priced way to stay where royalty once vacationed. The hotel building is located by a beautifully manicured baroque-style park. The large, attractive terrace café has a stunning view of the park, and the sea beyond. The rooms are basic, but they all have a bathroom and WC, and air-conditioning is thrown in for an additional fee of €10. If you don't mind attic rooms without a view, you can get a double in high season for as little as €68.

Hotel Palace-Bellevue

Obala maršala Tita 144-146 (051 271 811/fax 051 271 964/www.liburnia.hr). **Rates** €45-€64 single; €70-€108 double. **Credit** AmEx, DC, MC, V.

Two century-old hotels, both across the street from the sea in the middle of town, have been joined to create one large, three-star complex with a feeling of past glory at mid-level prices. Renovation work in 2000 and 2002 have helped spruce up the antique interiors, and the 212 rooms are in excellent condition, though they lack air-conditioning and other modern amenities. The two buildings with different entrances share many facilities, including bars, a restaurant, an internet café, a sauna and an indoor pool. The first-floor terrace restaurant offers gorgeous sea views. Downstairs, there are a couple of shops in the hotel buildings, as well as all the conveniences of downtown Opatija.

Tourist information

Atlas

Obala maršala Tita 116 (051 271 032/ www.atlas-croatia.com). **Open** 8am-10pm daily.
Arranges hotel rooms, private accommodation, excursions and tickets.

Da Riva

Obala maršala Tita 170 (051 272 990/ www.da-riva.hr/). **Open** 8am-10pm daily.
Accommodation, excursions and other services.

Opatija Tourist Office

Obala maršala Tita 101 (051 271 310/www.opatija-tourism.hr). **Open** *June-Sept* 8am-9pm Mon-Sat; 6-9pm Sun. *Sept-June* 8am-3pm Mon-Fri; 8am-2pm Sat.

Getting there

Bus No.32 runs every 20 minutes from **Rijeka** suburban bus station, by the canal, to Opatija (25min, 14kn). It also stops at Rijeka train station on the way. From Opatija, it leaves for Rijeka from the slight incline by the bus information office in the middle of town.

Pag

Approaching Pag by a regular 20-minute ferry hop from the mainland, you may be forgiven for thinking that you've landed on the moon. The east coast is a bleak, forbidding landscape of stark white and barren limestone karst against the blue expanse of sea and sky, blown bare by the bura wind. When it's hot, it's baking.

Pag is thin and 64km (40 miles) long, made up of two parallel mountain ranges. Settlements are mainly sleepy fishing villages, with two main towns, **Novalja** and **Pag town**. The island is pleasingly unspoilt by mass tourism and retains much of its tradition. It has been populated since prehistory, was fortified by the Romans and became an important salt-producing centre under Venice from 1403.

The south-west is a little greener, covered mainly in sage brush and maquis with sheltered valleys that grow vines and olives. There are also more beaches, which are mainly pebbles, in sheltered coves, some reached from precipitous tracks. The 24km (15-mile) peninsula leading to the island's western tip at **Lun** is worth the trip out. **Jakišnica** is a picturesque fishing village on this peninsula, off the beaten track but with excellent fish restaurants and good, cheap accommodation.

Novalja is a traditional seaside tourist resort situated to the south of the central plain of Pag. The town has Roman origins, even a famous underground aqueduct, and an arts centre, but that's not why anyone comes here. Novalja – or rather its **Zrće** beach – is where people come to party (*see p176* **Balkan Ibiza**). Surrounding the club scene are new resort developments and, filling them, throngs of family holidaymakers. The town opens out to extensive (mainly pebble) beaches backing up into pine forest. Nearly all the island's campsites are here along with diving clubs and other activity sports.

In contrast, the 15th-century administrative and commercial capital of Pag town exudes cultural heritage. In old Pag, with its narrow, fortified medieval streets beneath a 15th-century Gothic cathedral, the pace of daily life proceeds at a crawl. The sun beats hard off the white stone pavement, as seemingly equally ancient ladies painstakingly stitch together local lacework in doorways and alleys. From the bars and restaurants of the old harbour, the sea gives way through a series of dykes into saltpans, in use for 600 years.

Across the bay, near Pag town's beaches, clusters of modern apartment buildings and crumbling Tito-era hotels sit incongruously. Even historic Pag town has succumbed to tack, for here the Club Vanga offers pole-dancing and 'dirt wrestling'.

The landscape of **Pag**, famous for sheep, old lacemakers and cheese.

Balkan Ibiza

The brash, tacky disco scene on **Zrće** ('*Zirr-Ché*') beach near Novalja brings flocks of party-goers from all over Croatia to descend on its three key clubs of **Kalypso**, **Papaya** and **Aquarius**. As none charges entry, people dip in and out from one to the other, looking for better music or company. Most days in high season each place stays open 24 hours, or as near as dammit. Summer starts either at the last weekend in May or first weekend in June, with each club trying to outdo each other with the biggest entertainment programme and domestic DJs.

All three are open-air, stretched out on the long, white pebble beach of Zrće. Of the three, Kalypso (www.novalja.com/kalypso) has been here the longest, of nearly 20 years standing. A classic beach club with straw sunshades, Kalypso puts a volleyball court in front of the venue for sports activities during the day – there's darts and badminton as well. By night, DJs take over till the early hours. The music seems to appeal to a broader generational range.

Aquarius is the Zrće branch of the renowned Zagreb club (*see p88*), although the music played here tends to be more commercial than its counterpart in the capital. The venue is superbly equipped, with aerobics and massages during the day, as well as a water bar and a full restaurant/pizzeria. Breakfast is served at 5am and Aquarius even organise weddings here. Live bands as well as DJs.

Papaya (*pictured*) is also a Zagreb venue with a branch here. Its two pools with water slides and jacuzzis attract the best after-beach parties, with drinks promotions through the summer. All cools down about sunrise.

Clubbers can get a little shuttle bus running up to Zrće from downtown Novalja.

At Pag's south-eastern tip a spectacular road bridge leads to the **Paklenica National Park** (023 369 202, www.paklenica.hr), near the town of Starigrad. It contains 150km (93 miles) of hiking trails amid dramatic karst rock formations, also ideal for climbers and ornithologists (*see p51*).

The flavours on the Pag dinner table are influenced by the arid, saline environment. Inhabited by more sheep than humans, Pag lamb is deeply flavoured with the aromatic herbs sheep consume, as is the trademark Pag cheese (*paški sir*). Pag fish has a particular flavour, due to the lower oxygen levels in the highly saline waters. Accompanied by a bottle of local Žutica dry white wine and a digestif of Travarica herb brandy, the Pag culinary experience is complete.

The poshest restaurant in Pag town is **Na Tale** (S Radića 2, 023 611 194), overlooking the bay. Octopus lasagne and Pag lamb are among the specialities. In Novalja, try the **Starac i More** (Braće Radić, 023 662 423) on the embankment, with tidy seafood dishes.

The swankiest accommodation in Pag town is the **Hotel Plaža** (Marka Marulića 14, 023 600 855, www.plaza-croatia.com, open late May-late Sept, €82-€132, closed late Sept-late May), a relatively modern four-star with views across the bay to the Old Town. The 20 spacious rooms in the **Hotel Tony** (Dubrovačka 39, 023 611 370, www.hotel-tony.com, open Apr-Sept, 300kn-450kn, closed Oct-Mar) are soon taken, so book early. Just north-east of Pag Old Town, it has its own restaurant. **Villa Olea** (023 697 439, www.villaolea.hr, apartments from €60/person) is a good example of the family-run apartment accommodation springing up on Pag. It's in the quiet fishing village of **Šimuni**, 10km (6 miles) from Pag town and offers full board in six air-conditioned two- or three-bedroom apartments. There are pension rooms available from €30 per night.

Novalja is bursting with apartment rentals (www.novatours.com). If you prefer to overnight at a comfortable hotel, check in at four-star **Hotel Boškinac** (Novalja Polje, 053 663 500, www.boskinac.com, doubles from €100). Its 25 rooms are air-conditioned and boast views of the surrounding pine forest. The hotel also has its own vineyards and winery, a fine restaurant, and organises trekking and fishing excursions. Check www.turno.hr for cheaper downtown hotels; the two-star **Loža** (Trg Loža, 023 661 315, 405kn-913kn) is one.

For further information on places to stay, contact the **Pag town Tourist Office** (Od Špitale 2, 023 611 286, www.pag-tourism.hr). There is a **Novalja** office too (023 661 404, www.tz-novalja.hr).

The easiest hop to Pag is the hourly ferry from **Prizna** on the mainland to **Žigljen** (20mins) on Pag's north-eastern tip, 5km (3 miles) north of Novalja. Twice daily buses between **Rijeka** and **Zadar** call at both Novalja and Pag town, the only public transport link (30mins) between the two settlements. Pag town is an hour from Zadar, three hours from Rijeka and five hours from Zagreb – there are five buses a day from the capital.

In summer a daily Jadrolinija **catamaran** runs in the morning from Novalja to Pag town (45mins) and **Rijeka** (2hrs 30mins), turning round at Rijeka in the late afternoon. Two days a week it leaves from **Mali Lošinj** to reach Novalja two hours later, and then on to Rijeka.

Rab

The southernmost of the Kvarner islands, verdant Rab is also the busiest. Its namesake **capital**, a pretty, well-preserved medieval town protected from the bura wind by the nearby Kamenjak Hill, is dotted with architectural treasures, including Romanesque churches. The island was colonised by Greeks, Romans, then the Venetians, when two waves of plague hit in the 15th century. Venice allowed refugees to come in and run local businesses, and the island was developed for tourism from the late 19th century. Rab was one of Europe's first naturist resorts; before his abdication, King Edward VIII and Wallis Simpson swam naked here. These days holidaymakers flock to **Lopar** at the north tip of the island, famous for its sandy beaches.

Rab town is on a small peninsula, bounded within city walls, distinguished by its four church towers and precise network of streets. Three main streets – Upper, Middle and Lower – are interlinked with tiny lanes. The town is also divided into the oldest quarter, **Kaldanac**, at the far south-eastern end, and **Varoš**, dating from the time after the plague, with elegant Gothic and Renaissance buildings. The historic core is accessed by focal Trg sv Kristofera, with the pretty city parks of **Komrčar** nearby. The **Church of St Mary the Great** (open 10am-1pm, 7.30-10pm daily) has the biggest of Rab's four towers. The church itself, consecrated in 1176, is quite plain with Renaissance touches. You can climb the campanile (5kn) for superb views. The oldest belltower is **St Andrew's**, the church a mix of Renaissance and baroque styles. The **Church of St Justine** contains a modest collection of sacred art. Of the secular buildings, the **City Lodge**, built in Renaissance style in 1509, shows occasional exhibitions.

The best beaches nearest to Rab town are at **Kampor**, 6km (3.5 miles) north-west, and **Pudarica**, 10km (6 miles) south-east towards

Rab – naturist haven kept as nature intended.

Barbat. This is the scene of Rab's first beach club, the **Santos**, with a programme of domestic DJs and live pop acts. By day it offers a lounge bar and volleyball. Some 14km (8.5 miles) north of Rab town, Lopar is known for its 2km (1.25 miles) of sandy beach and shallow waters, ideal for children. Although crowded in summer, it lives up to its name of **Rajski plaža** (Paradise beach) in the off-season. A 15-minute walk away are the more remote beaches of Stolac and Sahara, which are used by naturists.

Rab town boasts two landmark restaurants: the **Labirint** (Srednja 9, 051 771 145, open Mar-Oct 11am-3pm, 6pm-midnight daily, closed Nov-Feb), run by the Pičuljan family, known for its seafood; and the upmarket **Santa Maria** (Dinka Dokule/Srednja, 051 724 196, open 10am-2pm, 5-11pm daily), set in an 18th-century palace with a stupendous view, known for its scampi and seafood. The main bar in town is the **Forum** (Donja 9A, open summer 7pm-2am daily), playing all styles of music over the course of an evening.

Imperial (051 724 184, www.imperial.hr) is the local group that runs the standard **hotel** (Palit, 051 724 522, 450kn-600kn) of the same name near Rab bus station in Komrčar. The **Istra** (Šetalište Markantuna Dominisa, 051 724 134, 350kn-500kn) is more convenient. **Ros Maris** (Obala kralja P Krešimira 4, 051 778 899, www.rosmaris.com, €94-€220), facing the marina, is the best and most conveniently sited hotel in town, with a heated outdoor pool, spa and, from the summer of 2006, a crèche.

For all information, contact the **Rab Tourist Office** (Trg Municipium Arba 8, 051 771 111, www.tzg-rab.hr).

The quickest ferry hop to Rab is the frequent one from **Jablanac** (30mins) on the mainland to **Mišnjak** on the island's southern tip. A regular bus service runs from Mišnjak via Rab town to Lopar. **Lopar** then links with **Baška** on Krk (50mins). In summer there's also a daily **catamaran** from **Rijeka** (2hrs), going on to **Novalja** on Pag (50mins). Three buses a day run from Rijeka to Rab town (3hrs 30mins), two daily in high season from Zagreb (6hrs).

Zadar & Islands

Features

Maps

Crikvenica
Drežnica
Josipdol
Klenovica
E65
Plaški
Slunj
Bročanac
Dvc
Vrbnik
Kk
Olezerane
Plavča
Rakovica
Senj
Brinje
Dabar
Saborsko
Drežnik Grad
Cazin
Baška
Prvic
Otočac
Vrhovine
Plitvička Jezera
Bosanska Krupa
Grgur
Lopar
Krasno
Ličko Lešce
Plitvice Jezera National Park
Bihać
BOSNIA AND
E59
HERCEGOVINA
Rab
Rab
Sjeverni Velebit National Park
Lipovo Polje
E71
Korenica
Lun
Alan
G.Kosinj
A1
Čanak
Nebljusi
Prizna
Perušić
Bunić
Pecani
Novalja
E65
Lički Osik
Podlapača
E71
D.Lapac
Doljani
Karlobag
Smiljan
Udbina
Mazin
Maun
Gospić
Lukovo
Medvida
G.Ploča
Srb
Silba
Pag
Lika
Otrić
Olib
Pag
Radučc
Lovinac
Zrmanja Vrelo
Olib
Tribanj
Paklenica National Park
Gračac
E59
Skarda
Ist
Vr
Vlašići
Ražanac
Starigrad Paklenica
Molat
Sestrunj
Nin
Posedarje
Jasenica
Obrovac
Zrmanja
Ervenik
Poljica
Novigrad
Padjene
 Ugljan
Murvica
ZADAR
Smilčić
Dubraja
Medvida
Kovač
Ugljan
Zemunik
Dubraja
Knin
Preko
Bibinje
Benkovac
Vrbnik
Iz
E65
Polača
Kistanje
Krka
Dugi Otok
Pašman
Biograd na Moru
Vrana
Devrske
Krka National Park
Drniš
Siverić
Sali
Pakoštane
Vransko jezero
Stankovci
Žažvic
A1
Zut
Pirovac
Skradin
Litnic
Komat
Muter
Tisno
Proklansja jezero
Piskera
Kornat National Park
Vodice
Perkovic
Neves
Kurba Vela
Žirjanski Kanal
ŠIBENIK
Kaprije
Primošten
Prgomet
Žirje
Blizna
Trogir
Adriatic
Rogožnica
Marina
E65
D.Seget
Sea
Drvenik
Grohote
Šolta

0   30 km
0   15 miles
© Copyright Time Out Group 2006

Zadar & Islands

Zadar & Islands

Byzantine treasures and seafront clubbing in Northern Dalmatia.

What made Zadar famous – the local cherry liqueur **Maraska**. *See p182.*

Northern Dalmatia is the lesser known stretch of Croatia's Adriatic coast. Centrepieced by the port of **Zadar**, it has as much Roman, Byzantine and Venetian history as the more familiar hubs of Split and Dubrovnik further south. This part of the coast also suffered most from the Yugoslav war – Zadar was shelled and nearly occupied. The lack of an international air connection means that much of what has gone on since – in particular a thriving nightlife scene (*see p202* **Highway 65 revisited**) – is only known to those in Croatia. This is gradually changing, in part thanks to the success of Brit-run bar and DJ terrace **The Garden**, in Zadar.

The **Zadar archipelago** and the 140 islands that make up the **Kornati National Park** are reason alone to visit this region. Of the other destinations, **Šibenik** is a quiet, cathedral city with easy access to the other great natural attraction of the area, the **Krka National Park**; although connected by bridge to the mainland, the island of **Murter** still has a traditional way of life; and **Primošten** is a fine little seaside town relatively free of tourists.

Zadar

The chief city of northern Dalmatia is stuck out on a peninsula halfway between Split and Rijeka and, as a consequence, has been isolated from the mainland for much of recent history. Italian (Zara) between the wars, after severe Allied bombing Zadar became part of Tito's Yugoslavia until 1991. In more recent times, under serious threat by Serbian forces for four years, Zadar was cut off from Zagreb completely for 14 months. Recovery has been slow, and parts of the compact old Roman city centre are still, as we write, clad in scaffolding. Recently, a handful of key spots, notably the DJ bar **Space Lab**, the multi-purpose arts venue the **Arsenal** and the marvellous **Sea Organ** installation, have brought a welcome burst of new energy to the city.

▶ The code for **Zadar** is 023, and 022 for some of the surrounding area. For calls in the same area, you don't need the code.

Things to do

Sign up for a boat tour of the unique **Kornati National Park** (*see p192*) – or hire a yacht and do it yourself. Visit the child-friendly, hands-on **Bunari Museum** (*see p201*) in Šibenik. Get the rowing boat (*see p186* **The boatman of Zadar**) over the water in Zadar to the north quay – then take in the red sunset amously admired by Alfred Hitchcock (*see p185* **Sunset boulevard**) over the south quay afterwards. Splash about at the bottom of the Skradinski buk waterfall at Krka (*see p200* **Krka National Park**).

Places to stay

The luxury **Villa Hrešć** (*see p190* **Hot hotels**) occupies a lovely spot overlooking Maestral Bay, near Zadar city centre. For something a little more isolated, the stone houses (*see p194*) stuck amid the 140 islands in the **Kornati National Parks** offer what's being marketed as 'Robinson Crusoe' tourism. **Say Adriatic** (*see p196*) has recently opened as an upmarket, kiddie-friendly hotel in Jezera marina on Murter island. The **Hotel Maestral** (*see p202*) is a hidden gem, tucked away on the island of Prvić off Šibenik.

Places to eat

The **Kornat** (*see p187*) in Zadar is convenient and classy. The **Konoba Idro** (*see p194*) in Kornati fills with singing fishermen. **Konoba Papec** (*see p198*) in Primošten serves bite-sized delicacies from the surrounding villages. The **Zlatna Ribica** (*see p203*) near Šibenik has gourmet cachet.

Nightlife

Space Lab (*see p188*) and **The Garden** (*see p189* **Cool clubs**) have brought UK cool to Zadar, while downtown **Stomorica** (*see p188*) is the place to bar hop. The coast road between Primošten and Pirovac boasts four key clubs (*see p202* **Highway 65 revisited**). Try and catch a DJ night at **Čigradja** (*see p196*) on Murter island.

Culture

The **Treasury** in **St Mary's Church** (*see p185*) in Zadar is filled with shining Byzantine craftsmanship. Nikola Bašić's **Sea Organ** (*see p196*) in Zadar is just truly bizarre. **Nin**, near Zadar, contains the oldest church in Croatia (*see p187*). The **Cathedral of St Jacob** (*see p201*) in Šibenik is a Gothic and Renaissance masterpiece.

Zadar's isolation has allowed for bizarre historical quirks. The city clock has no hour hand. Zadar has its own drink, the cherry liqueur Maraska – you'll see the sign all over town, including at the railway station where the sign for Zadar should be. Alfred Hitchcock loved the place (*see p185* **Sunset boulevard**). Hitch was drawn by the same blood-red sunsets as encouraged a UK crew to set up seminal club **The Garden** (*see p189* **Cool clubs**) in the walls of the old Venetian fortress. Although there are ample historic sights, tourists seem thin on the ground – most are accommodated in the resort hotels situated at Puntamika, ten minutes away by bus. The most central point of entry is by boat, with three ferry points dotted on the north embankment below the Venetian fortifications. The bus and adjacent train stations are a kilometre east of the centre.

Everything takes place in a criss-cross of streets on a tongue of land some 600 metres (1,968 feet) long and 300 metres (985 feet) wide, encircled by the fortifications, with scenic embankments below and the sea beyond. Cars are only allowed as far as these quays, so what you'll see in town are locals scurrying about

their business in the narrow streets. To reach the mainland, pedestrians either have to walk as far as the narrow section of channel at Foša, halfway to the bus station; cross the busy footbridge enclosing the border of the marina of Jazine; or, as people have been doing for centuries, pay a ferryman to take them across the water (*see p186* **The boatman of Zadar**).

The Romans may have used this same method as they built Iadera on the peninsula, with a regulated street pattern, four gates and a forum – much of which you still see today.

JEWEL IN THE CROWN

Part of the old Roman Forum forms focal Zeleni trg; the rest, with sundry sections of pillar, peters out towards the south quay of Obala kralja Petra Krešimira IV. On and adjacent to Zeleni trg are Zadar's five main sights: **St Donat's Church**; the **Cathedral**; the **Archaelogical Museum**; and **St Mary's Church & Treasury**. The Byzantine treats of the Treasury are the don't miss.

Alongside the Forum runs the spinal street of Široka, linking the new cultural hub of Three Wells (Trg tri bunara) to historic Five Wells

(Trg pet bunara) at each extremity of the city centre. Around the edge, the south embankment is somewhat forlorn these days. This was once the chic side of town, with a pier for fast passenger ships and four-storey buildings in the classic, Habsburg mould. Much was built with Maraksa money, the local manufacturers grown rich from liqueur sales. Here the Hotel Bristol and its namesake coffeehouse were landmarks, even when the Italians moved in and renamed them Excelsior. The quay was almost completely destroyed by Allied bombing. All that remained was the hotel, renamed the Zagreb and today the subject of a long-running saga to rebuild it.

Focus has shifted to the north shore. As if by way of announcing it, as you turn the south-west corner of the quay to head north, bizarre noises greet you, sounding not unlike the Clangers sighing for want of soup. Thirty-five organ pipes emit unworldly tones through holes bored into the smooth, new paving stones, their size and velocity played by the waves of the sea. The eccentric Sea Organ, inaugurated in 2005, was designed by Nikola Bašić and built in nearby Murter.

Further round you find the three ferry terminals including a new cruiser pier; one of Croatia's biggest and best morning markets; and the Port Gate, one of two Renaissance-era stone entrances to town that carry the carved Lion of Venice.

The eastern end of the Old Town is centred on Narodni trg, surrounded by the Guard House and City loggia, both original Renaissance structures built by the Venetians. The former is now rediscovering its role as the Ethnographic Museum, the exhibits slowly returning after wartime storage; the latter is an art gallery. Nearby is St Simeon's Church (Trg Šime Budinića, 023 211 705, open 8am-noon, 4-7pm daily), named after Zadar's patron saint. It houses the ornate Silver Casket of St Simeon, commissioned by Elizabeth of Hungary in 1377.

Here around Five Wells is the Venetian Land Gate, the narrow channel of Foša and the little warrens of the old Varoš quarter, including curving, bar-lined Stomorica.

St Donat's Church

Zeleni trg. **Open** 9am-10pm daily. **Admission** 6kn.
No longer in service but the rounded cylinder shapes of this Byzantine church are the symbol of Zadar itself. Built at the beginning of the ninth century, in the pre-Romanesque period, its interior is a simple, high-ceilinged space with perfect acoustics for recitals, for which the church is used today.

Cathedral

Trg Sv Stošije. **Open** 8am-1pm, 5-8pm daily.
Campanile 10am-1pm, 5.30-8pm Mon-Sat.
Admission *Campanile* 10kn.
The Cathedral of St Anastasia (Katedrala Sv Stošije) beside St Donat's was built in late Romanesque style in the 12th century. Decorative friezes and delicate stonework depict birds, animals and religious fig-

Space Lab, Zadar. *See p188.*

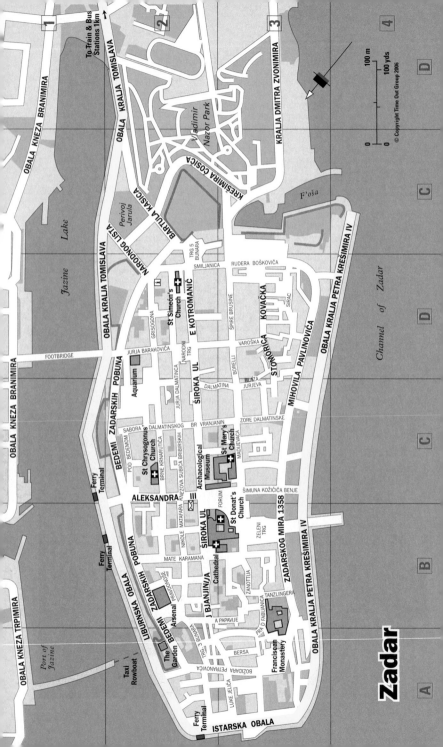

Zadar

To Train & Bus Stations 1km

OBALA KNEZA BRANIMIRA

OBALA KRALJA TOMISLAVA

BARTULA KAŠICA

KREŠIMIRA COSICA

KRALJA DMITRA ZVONIMIRA

Vladimir Nazor Park

Lake

Jazine

OBALA KNEZA BRANIMIRA

FOOTBRIDGE

Perivoj Jarula

F'oša

NARODNOG LISTA

OBALA KRALJA TOMISLAVA

TRG 5 BUNARA

SMILJANICA

RUĐERA BOŠKOVIĆA

St Simeon's Church

E KOTROMANIĆ

ŠPIRE BRUSINE

SIRAC

Channel of Zadar

BEDEMI ZADARSKIH POBUNA

Aquarium

JURJA BARAKOVIĆA

GRISOGONA

NARODNI TRG

ŠIROKA UL

VAROŠKA

BORELLI

KOVAČKA

STOMORICA

OBALA KRALJA PETRA KREŠIMIRA IV

DALMATINA

JURJA DALMATINCA

BLAŽA JURJEVA

MIHOVILA PAVLINOVIĆA

SABORA

POD BEDEMOM

DALMATINSKOG

BR VRANJANIN

ZORE DALMATINSKE

St Chrysogonus' Church

BRNE KRNARUTIĆA

KNEZOVA ŠUBIĆA BRIBIRSKIH

Archaeological Museum

St Mary's Church

MADIJEVACA

ALEKSANDRA

III

NIKOLE MATAFARA

FORUM

St Donat's Church

ŠIMUNA KOŽIČIĆA BENJE

ŠIROKA UL

ZELENI TRG

ZADARSKOG MIRA 1358

LIBURNSKA OBALA

Ferry Terminal

Ferry Terminal

BEDEMI ZADARSKIH POBUNA

MATE KARAMANA

Cathedral

J BJANJINJA

ZANOTTIJA

TANZLINGERA

OBALA KRALJA PETRA KREŠIMIRA IV

The Garden

BEDEMI ZADARSKI

Arsenal

PRADVONOSE

TRG 3 BUNARA

A PAPAVIJE

TRG D FABIJANICA

Taxi Rowboat

Port of Jazine

OBALA KNEZA TRPIMIRA

BOŽIDARA PETRANOVIĆA

LUKE JELIĆA

BERSA

Franciscan Monastery

Ferry Terminal

ISTARSKA OBALA

OBALA KRALJA PETRA KREŠIMIRA IV

100 m
100 yds

© Copyright Time Out Group 2006

ures, although most enter to climb the belltower for the fabulous view of Zadar, and mountains and sea either side. The campanile was completed by English architect TG Jackson in the late 1800s.

Archaeological Museum

Trg Opatice Čike (023 250 516). **Open** *Summer* 9am-1pm, 6-8.30pm Mon-Sat. *Winter* 9am-1pm, 5-7pm Mon-Fri; 10am-1pm Sat. **Admission** 10kn. Founded in 1832 but since rehoused in a modern building, 100,000 artefacts are arranged on three floors: begin above with a prehistoric section of ceramics and weaponry; down to a Roman and Liburnian floor (including a model of how the Forum would have looked); end in the Middle Ages on the ground floor, with bizarre local gravestones.

St Mary's Church & Treasury

Trg Opatice Čike (023 250 496). **Open** *Church* 8am-noon, 5-8pm daily. *Treasury Summer* 10am-1pm, 6-8pm Mon-Sat; 10am-1pm Sun. *Winter* 10am-12.30pm, 6-7.30pm Mon-Sat; 10am-12.30pm Sun. **Admission** 20kn.

The jewel in Zadar's crown. St Mary's is the church of this Benedictine convent, a 16th-century remake of an early Romanesque one dating back to 1066. The belltower, restored after Allied damage, also dates to this early period. The nuns were responsible for curating the stunning treasures next door, a collection known as the Gold and Silver of Zadar (Zlato i Srebro Zadra). Set over two floors, the Treasury houses Zadar's finest ecclesiastical arte-

Sunset boulevard

As you take an evening stroll along the south quay of Zadar, Obala kralja Petra Krešimira IV, to one side will be a wide grass embankment covering what was a long façade of elegant fin-de-siècle buildings, lost in World War II; to the other, a red, red sunset, the result of Zadar's setting among a string of islands and the Velebit mountain range. You lose yourself in cinematic reverie until – good gravy! Alfred Hitchcock! What's he doing here in my movie?

The reason is the very sunset you're gawping at. Hitchcock came here at the recommendation of actor Cliff Robertson, who was familiar with Dalmatia and thought Zadar and its sunset might make a good shooting location. Hitch and Alma, his wife and production assistant, were in Yugoslavia and drove into Zadar in their Lincoln on Friday, 15 May 1964. Photos exist of their arrival. The director deliberately booked room No.204 at the Hotel Zagreb as it reputedly had the best view and offered the best chances to capture the famous sunset. Try as they might, angles or technical aspects looked tricky.

The Zagreb being the only hotel in town, word spread fast. That morning, a crowd had gathered around the hotel and its then elegant coffeehouse (today the dull Zadar restaurant). Then working on a local weekly, now famous photographer Ante Brkan joined the throng, as Hitch wandered down the quay, signing autographs and taking pictures with his camera and tripod. At one point he stopped and gave a speech: 'Zadar has the most beautiful sunset in the world, more beautiful than the one in Key West, Florida, applauded at every evening'. Brkan snapped his portrait, a famous image that would win

a prize that year in Paris, early international recognition that would lead to a brilliant artistic career.

With applause from proud locals ringing in their ears, Hitch and Alma were off by noon. They never returned and never shot that film.

Brkan's image still stands on Zadar's south quay. Both bellboys at the hotel, liftboys and receptionist are dead. The manager is still alive, but not talking. Little other trace remains of Alfred's day in the sun.

The boatman of Zadar

Of all the various forms of public transport you may have used – the communal lifts of Lisbon, the *vaporetti* of Venice, the elevators of Monaco – surely the most romantic is to cross town by rowing boat. The rowing boat service in Zadar has been running since before the Venetians and connects two city landmarks: the Maraska factory and The Garden DJ lounge terrace. Yes, clubbers get to The Garden by rowing boat.

Between the tip of the long breakwater on the mainland and the north-west lip of the Zadar peninsula, the section of the original Venetian fortification housing The Garden is a short distance, 80 metres (262 feet) to be precise. But to drive it, you would have to go around the little marina, then the length of the Jazine harbour and negotiate the busy traffic jammed at the one entrance to the only stretch within the Old Town open to traffic. To walk it, even using the main footbridge, would

be unnecessarily long-winded. So do as residents of Zadar have done for centuries and let the *barjakoli* take the strain.

The boatmen, *barjakoli,* of Zadar were mentioned in historical archives in 1200. Certainly, the little café on the breakwater is called Barka, 'The Boat'. If you ask your boatman how long his service has been going, he replies: 'Two thousand years.' The silver you cross his palm with, 3kn, gets chucked on to a pile on a stretch of sack-cloth at his feet. Next to it, a few swigs of Karlovačko slowly rock in a permanently half-full bottle. With muscles like Popeye, the *barjakol* takes his cargo smoothly over the water. The job, in the safe hands of the same three families for generations ('my son will be the next one'), has been municipal since medieval times. The day is a long one, in summer from 6am to midnight, in winter until 5pm, and taken in shifts.

facts, finely carved, ornate examples of Byzantine craft and religious Venetian art from the 16th century. Saints' limbs are enclosed in sumptuous gold and silver reliquaries, icons, crucifixes, and everything is beautifully presented and illuminated. The collection spans 1,000 years, until the 18th century.

Beaches & excursions

There are family-friendly beaches lining the seafront complex of **Borik**, ten minutes from town on bus No.5, catering for package tourists.

For real beach relaxation, take a catamaran or boat from Zadar to the relatively unspoilt archipelago nearby. An island hop might require an overnight stay but the reward is sandy seafloors and dramatic scenery. Most routes are run by Jadrolinija and take about 90 minutes. The exception is the hydrofoil service to **Sali** on **Dugi otok** run by Mia Tours (www.miatours.hr), which leaves early most mornings from Zadar, takes 40 minutes and costs 18kn. With 200 islands and islets, the possibilities are complex and none of the

Zadar

islands has much by way of transport once you arrive. The largest is **Dugi otok**, Long Island, 50km (31 miles) long in fact. Its intricate, indented coastline hides any number of coves and beaches. Many are only accessible by boat. The lovely nature park of **Telašćica Bay** is within relatively easy reach of Sali, and is characterised by its verdant cliffs and saltwater lake. This northern tip of the island intertwines with the northern end of **Kornati** (*see p192*), with whom it compares for natural beauty. The northern tip of Dugi otok is best accessed via catamaran from Zadar to **Božava**. There is also a bus from the main ferry port halfway down the island, **Brbinj**, to Božava. (There is nothing between Brbinj and Sali.) The attraction here is the white sandy beach of **Saharun**, just south of the village of Veli Rat, and the sandy beach of **Pantera Bay**.

The most accessible island from Zadar is **Ugljan**, with hourly boats to the largest village of **Preko** (20mins), so close it feels like part of the city. Pick a quiet weekday to swim around here. **Silba**, linked to Zadar by catamaran, has lovely pebble beaches within fairly easy reach of the harbour.

A trip to **Nin**, 45 minutes from Zadar by bus, gives you the option of the morning poking around old churches and the afternoon at the sandy beach 15 minutes' walk north of town. Nin is a historic, fortified town set on a small island in a lagoon. An old Roman settlement, it was the residence of the first Croatian kings, as a look around its excellent **Archaeological Museum** (023 264 160, open summer 9am-10pm Mon-Sat, winter 9am-noon Mon-Sat, 10kn) will illustrate. The tiny Church of the Holy Cross is the oldest in Croatia.

Where to eat

Zadar doesn't have a stand-out restaurant as such, but half-a-dozen good ones. If you're only here for one night, the **Kornat** is the best in town, or the **Lungo Mare** if you don't mind a little trek. Look out for cherry-cake desserts using Maraska liqueur native to Zadar.

Dva Ribara

Blaža Jurjeva 1 (023 213 445). **Open** 11am-11pm daily. **Credit** AmEx, DC, MC, V.
The heavy leather menu informs you, in four languages, that this is a local restaurant of the old school, not unlike its sister operation Foša (*see below*) a short walk away. This one is firmly downtown, adjacent to the bar quarter of Stomorica, its terrace set in a quiet street nearby. Despite the name, the Two Fishermen, meat is the order of the day here, the signature dishes being hulking carnivorous platters for two. There's a pizza oven in the corner, too, and standard seafood offerings.

Foša

Kralja Dmitra Zvonimira 2 (023 314 421). **Open** 11am-11pm daily. **Credit** AmEx, DC, MC, V.
This well-known, old-school fish restaurant stands in and is named after the narrow channel by the city walls. Its stone square of terrace sits atop the waters with a fine view of the Zadar archipelago – it's as if you were dining on a public square. All the standard white fish and shellfish are served, either with traditional *blitva* kale and potatoes, or as part of a seafood risotto or pasta dish. Nice prices too.

Konoba Skoblar

Trg Petra Zoranića (023 213 236). **Open** 7am-midnight daily. **No credit cards.**
Skoblar is a traditional tavern located between St Simeon's Church and Five Wells. Football fans may recognise the name – Josip Skoblar was a star player in France in the 1970s. This used to be his bar and was recently taken over by a cousin. It still fills with people from the local media, especially for *marenda* time at elevenish, snacking on salted anchovies or octopus salad while mulling over the fate of the popular local basketball team. Skoblar does full lunches and dinners too, and in summer the meat offerings are reduced to leave kitchen space for plenty of fish and shellfish dishes – there are at least three kinds of shells in the black risotto. Sweet desserts are the house speciality here, either *kalelarga* cheesecake or Sv Stošija, a cherry cake made with Maraska, the local fruit liqueur.

Kornat

Liburnska obala 6 (023 254 501). **Open** 11am-11pm daily. **Credit** AmEx, DC, MC, V.
Reasonable candidate for best restaurant in town. By the ferry port adjacent to the Maya bar, the Kornat is classy enough to have a cloakroom and refined enough to have a superb selection of Croatian wines but relaxed enough to avoid giving a stuffy dining experience. The bottles are on display around a bright, modern interior, its 20 tables ably manned by equally bright, fluent-English staff. Although prices are much as elsewhere in town, the ingredients are not: truffles are used in sauces to garnish the stand-out monkfish, dry porcini mushrooms to help flavour the steak. Your appetite is first tempted by the complimentary pâté nibbles, teased by a cold starter of beef carpaccio with rocket, and satisfied by sea bass in scampi sauce. Istrian delicacies include *fuži* pasta twists or ravioli with truffles.

Lungo Mare

Obala kneza Trpimira 23 (023 331 533/091 1692 335 mobile). **Open** 10.30am-midnight daily. **Credit** AmEx, DC, MC, V.
This loveliest restaurant terrace in Zadar overlooks the sunset on Draženica Bay, a 15-minute walk from town. Inside is beautifully tiled, with a little art, the decor more modern than the traditional, neat waitstaff would suggest. Lungo Mare is equally appreciated for its fresh seafood and meat dishes, such as the house fish plate or pork fillet, stuffed with

scampi, cheese or *pršut* and mushrooms. The wine list, possibly teh best in town, runs into three figures and includes a few French and Italian names among the classic Croatian ones. Do try the famous house dessert, cheesecake.

Niko

Obala kneza Domagoja 9 (023 337 888). **Open** 11.30am-midnight daily. **Credit** AmEx, DC, MC, V.

One of the first restaurants to be privatised in former Yugoslavia, Niko looks pretty grim from the outside, but inside is one of the most popular kitchens in Zadar. Set near the Marina Borik on Puntamika's southernmost headland, Niko contains both a modest hotel (double rooms at €120-€135) and proud restaurant. Fresh fish arrives daily and is then prepared with carefully selected olive oil over a wood-fire grill. Regulars tend to go for the green tagliatelle with scampi. A spacious terrace overlooks the sea and enjoys its pleasant breeze.

Šime

Matije Gupca 15 (023 334 848). **Open** noon-midnight daily. **No credit cards**.

Commonly considered the best pizzeria in town, up near the hotel complex in Borik. Its terrace is huge, and invariably packed in high season, but the quality of the pizzas makes it worth the wait. Inside is trendy enough to attract Zadar's in crowd, particularly as there's an underground parking. Kids are well taken care of, the house pancakes or ice-cream a vote winner every time.

Where to drink

Downtown Zadar is full of strange little bars in the warren of side streets and alleyways leading off the main squares and thoroughfares. Café drinking is best enjoyed on the Forum, although the elegant coffeehouses of yesteryear along the south quay were lost to Allied bombs. A short stretch of **Stomorica**, just behind the once opulent Zadar restaurant on the south quay, is lined with tiny bars and fills with revellers on sunny nights. At the other end of the Old Town, by Five Wells, the passageway Poljana Pavla Pavlovića off Rudjera Boškovića housing the cool **Space Lab**, contains the smart **Coffee Lounge** (No.6, 023 318 870), pointing to the burgeoning of a bar hub in the student quarter.

Djina

Varoška 2 (no phone). **Open** 8am-11pm daily.

Great little gallery bar off the main square, done out with bizarre egg-shaped heads designed by Silvijana Dražković. A trendy crowd gathers by day to drink any number of fruit teas, the electronic musical backdrop increasing as the night wears on. There's a couple of chairs on the busy street outside.

Kantun

Stomorica 5 (no phone). **Open** 7am-midnight Mon-Fri; 8am-2pm, 6pm-midnight Sat.

Best venue in bar-lined Stomorica, although you could make a case for Lotus, with its Stones pin-up c1965. Others may prefer the in place of 2005, Kult, with its front garden and swings, great if you're 19 and on the pull but little by way of character. Character, Kantun has in spades. Centre of the alternative music scene, Kantun is all animated chat and awesome glugging, observed by a large portrait of the poet Tin (*see p81* **The cat in the hat**). A solitary tap of Laško, a little Gene Vincent coming over the speakers and Bob's your uncle.

Maya Pub

Liburnska obala 6 (023 251 716). **Open** 7am-2am daily.

'Meet different styles' runs the banner over the entrance to this ethno-themed hangout by the ferry terminal. And styles there are, most of them eastern, Buddhist, Hindu or Balinese, in this barn of a place big enough to accommodate local live acts on a stage set up to one side. Most of the time it's DJ sounds, nothing too fierce, and it's not a bad place for a quiet pint of Guinness or Kilkenny of an afternoon.

Rio

Putvac 5 (no phone). **Open** noon-1am daily.

Wonderfully wacky little Stomorica bar, just off the main drag, behind the Hotel Zagreb. It's tiny, just big enough for two rooms, four plasma TV screens, a picture of McDowell in *Clockwork Orange* mode and a sign saying '[shoe-be-do]'. The music and characters who come in to shout above it seem to have been selected by random play. Recommended.

Space Lab

Poljana Pavla Pavlovića, Rudjera Boškovića 6 (023 301 310). **Open** *Summer* 8am-1am daily. *Winter* 8am-midnight Mon-Sat.

The bods behind The Garden (*see p189* **Cool clubs**) opened this bar in 2005, a chilled-out minimalist white space hidden in a modern passageway in the student quarter. It's a breakfast-through-to-bedtime operation, the day beginning with one of SL's speciality 'mind and body' teas, a Geisha or a Harmony. This is best taken on one of the white-cushioned chairs outside. Life moves to the narrow space indoors, ludo boards are brought out and a slow musical build-up ensues. By the early evening, cocktails are on the go, someone has manned the DJ decks and the regulars arrive: people in the local music business, boutique owners, DJs.

Viaz

Široka (no phone). **Open** 7am-midnight daily.

Pumping techno booms around the two floors of this recently opened café on Zadar's main downtown street. It's a weird design, some stones under glass by the main entrance, boxy furniture all in orange and green, but it seems to draw in some of the city's most attractive young people. Although it has no street number, you'll find it opposite a busy courtyard bar, named the Kale Larga after the name everyone calls Široka.

Cool clubs | The Garden, Zadar

The story goes that James Brown, drummer of UB40, and his mate, music producer Nick Colgan, were holidaying in Zadar and fell in love with the place. Seeing an opportunity, a year later they came back to open their own bar: The Garden.

High up in the city's fortifications, with a vast terrace bathed each evening in a red sunset, The Garden has the most wonderful location. Croatians are used to their clubs having flashing lights over a showy dancefloor but The Garden has minimalist white furniture. It also has 'beds'. When locals first visited, with the paint still drying on the watering can logos, they walked around the beds, not knowing what to do. But they soon chilled and by the end of 2005, national newspaper *Večernji List* was placing The Garden third on its chart of most important things to have happened in Croatia (the opening of the Zagreb–Split motorway came first).

By then, Nick and his team had opened a chill-out café in town, the **Space Lab** (*see p188*). In June 2006, they stage The Garden Get Together DJ festival, on the **Petrčane** headland north of town.

And The Garden? By day, it's relaxed: people play board games, read the papers, watch passing ships. By night, late May through to mid September, there's a full DJ programme, 2006 climaxing with Gilles Peterson. Drinks are racy and reasonable: cocktails 30kn, a bottle of Dingač for 200kn, Belgian and Croatian beers from 11kn. A Garden compilation CD mixed by Steve Cobby of Fila Brazillia is on local and UK release.

More than anything, The Garden has put Zadar on the map. Soon to publish its own left-field guide to the city, *Zadar Confidential*, The Garden may yet be involved in any number of spin-off projects, all of which would have been inconceivable three years ago.

Hot hotels
Villa Hrešć

Overlooking the Maestral Bay a ten-minute walk from town, the **Villa Hrešć** (*see p192*) is by far the best option for comfort and convenience in Zadar. Mediterranean luxury comes at mid-range prices; the three-storey Hrešć contains two rooms and six suites (€100-€200). These are suitable for two to four guests, six at a push for an extra €15 each. These roomy suites are more like condominiums, with a living room and kitchenette, dining room, bedroom and modern bathroom with marble washbasin, all capacious, all immaculately furnished – and all overlooking the sea. The larger ones have a terrace, the largest one has a terrace the size of half a football pitch. And the view is stunning: Zadar, the sea around it and archipelago beyond, the same line of vision as you swim in the outdoor pool with its fierce water jet in the corner. Patris runs a friendly ship (check the visitors' book) with a pretty restaurant on the ground floor where the inclusive buffet breakfast is served. Guests can also dine in the terrace garden restaurant, where local specialities are served twice a day. Opened in 2003, the Hrešć is now firmly established as the lodging of choice for UK clubbers flying in for a weekend at The Garden. And it sure beats having to trek out to Puntamika.

Nightlife

The new nexus of nightlife centres on a small area around Three Wells, at the western tip of the peninsula. Here in the Venetian walls is **The Garden** (*see p189* **Cool clubs**), whose success after two summers has put Zadar on the map; and the **Arsenal**, a music stage, gallery, bar and restaurant in a historic building almost next door. Of the venues established before them, **City Club Forum** (Marka Marulića, 023 214 556, open summer from 11pm daily, winter 11pm Thur-Sat) is a small, popular place near the eastern edge of Jazine playing house and hip hop; and **Gotham** (Marka Oreškovića 1, 023 200 289, same hours) is a large entertainment complex done out in a Batman theme for twentysomethings, located north of the city centre by the Nova Banka tower.

Locals also head over to the nearby name clubs of **Aurora** in Primošten, **Hacienda** and **Exit** in and near **Vodice**, Šibenik and the party scene at **Zrće**, Novalja on Pag. *See p176* **Balkan Ibiza** and *p202* **Highway 65 revisited**.

Arsenal
Trg Tri bunara 1 (www.arsenalzadar.com).
Set in a renovated 18th-century warehouse, Arsenal is, for want of a better term, an arts centre. It has boutiques, too, and a local information office, but the gallery, cocktail bar, restaurant and music stage are the most prominent attractions. Every town should have one – no other Croatian town does. The stage is spacious, the sound superb, and between the band and a smart, island bar, drinkers lounge and diners dine. Martinis (25kn-30kn), coffees (including the Zadar with chocolate crumbs, 16kn), Babić and other wines are served by swift staff. Superior snacks and a full menu of mains too.

The Garden
Liburnska obala 6 (023 364 739/www.thegarden zadar.com). **Open** *Late May-mid Sept* 10am-1am daily.
Wonderfully located UK-owned lounge bar and club staging name DJs all summer. *See p189* **Cool clubs**.

Where to stay

Given the dearth of hotels in downtown Zadar, the attraction of four-star apartment hotel the **Villa Hrešć** (*see left* **Hot hotels**) becomes more apparent. Apart from a Socialist-style three-star and a basic cheapie for barhoppers, that's it for central Zadar. Nearly all hotels are out of town, at **Puntamika**, in a tourist complex called **Borik**. Some 4km (2.5 miles) north-west of town, a quick ride on the No.5 bus, Borik's somewhat dated 1980s feel has been transformed by the Tyrol-based group

The Venetian lion proudly atop Zadar's **Land Gate**. *See p183.*

Falkensteiner, which owns a trio of seaside venues: the **Hotel Adriana Select**, the **Funimation** and the standard **Hotel Donat** (Majstora Radovana 7, 023 206 637, fax 023 332 065, www.falkensteiner.com).

Hotel Adriana Select

Majstora Radovana 7 (023 206 636/fax 023 332 065/www.falkensteiner.com). **Closed** Nov-Mar. **Rates** *Apr-Oct* €118-€272 double. **Credit** AmEx, DC, MC, V.
A newly built four-star in the Falkensteiner group, appealing to quieter couples with a little money to spend. All 48 rooms are junior suites and are offered on a half-board basis – hence the steep rates in high season. Full board is an extra €10 a day. Although it has its own pool area, Adriana guests can use the Acquapura spa at the Funimation (*see below*) nearby. Easy access to the sea.

Hotel Funimation

Majstora Radovana 7 (023 206 100/fax 023 332 065/www.falkensteiner.com). **Rates** €62-€161 single; €84-€212 double. **Credit** AmEx, DC, MC, V.
The big attraction of this four-star family hotel – apart from its year-round availability – is its Acquapura spa complex ('the largest spa sphere in Croatia'). This comprises four areas: a spa with thalasso seawater treatments; a steam and dry sauna; indoor and heated outdoor pools, and one for kids; and a fitness centre. The thalasso area contains 16 treatment rooms alone. Throughout the summer, the Funimation (Fun + Animation, get it?) puts on numerous events for kids, the so-called Falky-Land.

A whole bunch of sports, windsurfing, tennis and volleyball – plus three daily buffet meals – are included in the price, and you pay extra for courses in diving and sailing.

Hotel Kolovare

Bože Peričića 14 (023 203 200/fax 023 203 300/ www.hotel-kolovare-zadar.htnet.hr). **Rates** €92-€102 single; €130-€140 double. **Credit** AmEx, DC, MC, V.
Recently upgraded classic old Socialist hotel, on the edge of the city centre towards the bus station. It's surprisingly large, 230 rooms, a third of them singles for the passing domestic business crowd. Giving out on to the beach, it also has an outdoor pool and a gym, but the rooms are pretty bland.

Hotel President

Vladana Desnice 16 (023 333 696/www.hotel-president.hr). **Rates** €124-€166 single; €151-€194 double. **Credit** AmEx, DC, MC, V.
Self-styled classy four-star in the Borik area, where much is made of the decorative aesthetic, the porcelain dishes and cherrywood furniture. Whether it's all in good taste is another matter – the Vivaldi restaurant has glass table dividers etched with the score from the *Four Seasons*. Still, there's 24hr room service and all rooms have balconies.

Hotel Venera

Šime Ljubića 4a (023 214 098). **Rates** 350kn single; 450kn double. **No credit cards.**
A modest cheapie in a narrow side street of the bar quarter of Stomorica. A dozen rooms over a travel agents have been renovated (although the budget

didn't run to door numbers – you'll have to count as you go along the corridor) to incorporate a little shower and twin beds for simple, clean comfort. Rates vary slightly between summer and winter. It's also referred to as the Jović Guesthouse.

Villa Hrešć
Obala kneza Trpimira 28 (023 337 570/fax 023 334 336/www.villa-hresc.hr). **Rates** €60-€86 single; €86-€107 double. **Credit** AmEx, DC, MC, V.
Fabulous mid-range option overlooking the sea a short walk from town. *See p190* **Hot hotels**.

Resources

Hospital
Bože Peričića 5 (023 315 677).
By the Hotel Kolovare, towards the bus station.

Internet
Multinet *Stomorica 8 (023 302 270)*. **Open** 8am-9pm daily.
Relaxing first-floor space in the bar quarter.

Pharmacy
Ljekarna Centar *Jurja Barakovića 2 (023 302 931)*. **Open** 7am-8.30pm Mon-Fri; 8am-1.30pm Sat.

Police station
Zore Dalmatinska 1 (023 345 141).

Post Office
Central Post Office *Kralja S Držislava 1 (023 316 552)*. **Open** 7am-9pm Mon-Sat.

Tourist Information
Zadar Tourist Office *Ilije Smiljanića 5 (023 212 222/www.zadar.hr)*. **Open** *Summer* 8am-10pm daily. *Winter* 8am-3pm Sat, Sun.
Small office just by the Forum.

Getting there & around

Croatia Airlines buses (25kn, 15mins) meet domestic arrivals to Zadar **airport**, 8km (5 miles) south-east of town at Zemunik Donji and run to the bus station before terminating at the ferry terminal. Buses are scheduled to set off from the same points 60-80 minutes before each departure. Sky Europe passengers should check for the nearest Croatia Airlines flight to theirs, or take a taxi (expect to pay about 150kn-200kn).

Ferries serving Rijeka and Dubrovnik, and the islands in the Zadar archipelago, dock at the northern quay right by the Old Town.

There are buses almost hourly from Zagreb (5hrs), Rijeka (4.5hrs) and Split (3.5hrs) to Zadar. A modest train service links with Knin (2.5hrs) and the InterCity line between Zagreb and Split. Zadar **bus** and **train** stations are next to each other 1.5km (a mile) east of the Old Town centre, a 15-minute walk.

Buses Nos.2 and 4 run to the ferry terminals, bus No.5 goes to Puntamika and Borik via the modern centre of town. Tickets are 6kn, pay on board. For a **taxi**, call 023 251 400.

Kornati

The Kornati archipelago has qualities that make it unique. It is made up of 140 islands and islets in an area only 35km (22 miles) long and 14km (8.5 miles) wide. Between the long, thin island of **Kornat**, which faces the coast, and the chain of islands on the other side, there is a stretch of water naturally protected from the open sea, with dozens of safe bays to drop anchor. Once you pass through one of the two narrow gates to the north and south, you leave the worst of the waves behind, and enter a strange, other-worldly environment, with barren-looking, treeless hills all around.

The islands on the inside of the national park seem deserted. You might sight the occasional sheep, or a small votive chapel, built by a grateful sailor saved from a storm by the natural barrier of the islands, otherwise there's little sign of human habitation. It's a very meditative and minimal landscape, unlike any other island chain in the Adriatic. When you enter Kornati, you've arrived somewhere completely different.

Whether you have your own yacht, or come on one of the many tour boats offering day trips around the national park, you will also get to experience the outer side of the archipelago. The contrast between the calm inner space of Kornati and the wild world of the open sea is unmistakable, not least in the geomorphology of the exposed rocks. Sheer cliffs offer spectacular scenes and dramatic sounds, from crashing waves to the echo of the human voice. The seaward side of the island of **Mana** is the most impressive; boats can come right up close to the 100-metre (328-foot) cliffs that stretch for 1.5 km (1 mile). If the sea is not too rough, the outer edge of Kornati is a superlative place to swim and snorkel, with a happening marine life just below the surface of the rocky shoreline.

National Park status, set in 1980, should allow the natural world of Kornati, above and below the sea, to recover from over exploitation. A few centuries back the islands were reputedly covered with oaks – now even most of the soil has gone, leaving a thorny, stony environment, where the largest surviving wild animals are frogs, lizards, snakes and birds. The wildest part of the park is in the far south, where a 500-metre (1,640-foot) exclusion zone has been declared around the islet of **Purara**, to allow the development of natural life. One hopeful sign is a colony of dolphins that lives between

Zadar

Kornati and the mainland and manages to co-exist with the fishermen, thrilling lucky visitors who get a leaping dolphin escort across the straits.

Kornati comes to life on the first Sunday in July for the **Feast of Kornati**, when an armada of boats and yachts from all over Dalmatia converges on the church of **Our Lady of Tarac** on Kornat for a celebration led by the bishop. The tiny bay by the church crams with boats and worshippers jump from deck to deck to reach the shore.

Visiting Kornati

Although signposts at the motorway exit for Murter suggest it's an easy journey from there to Kornati, visiting the national park is more complicated in practice. There is no ferry or public transport, and no way to get around the islands without a boat. There are also very few accommodation options in Kornati; most overnight visitors stay on their own yachts. If you have an international captain's licence,

then you can rent your own sea-borne transport – otherwise the only way to reach the park is on a tour. The best are the ones offered by the fishermen of Murter (*see p195* **The old salts of St Nikola**). Tourist boats also leave from Vodice, Pirovac and **Šibenik** (*see p200*).

Visitors pay a day fee, 40kn for excursion tourists, 80kn for yachtsmen and guests. Recreational fishing permits are 150kn per day.

BY YACHT

With your own boat the ideal place to enter Kornati is through the straits of **Opat**, between the south side of Kornat and **Smokvica**. You will be accosted by park rangers on speedboats, who sell you an entrance ticket. There are reception centres on the islands of **Ravni Žakan** and in the village of **Vruje**. Overnight mooring is possible in a dozen bays in the park, mostly at floating moorings marked by red buoys. Among the best bays for overnighting are Lavsa, Levrnaka and Ravni Žakan. There is also a marina on the island of **Piškera**, which is only open in the summer months.

The **Kornati archipelago** makes up Croatia's most unique national park.

ON AN ORGANISED EXCURSION

The nearest departure points for an excursion to Kornati are on the island of **Murter** (*see below*). If you take a stroll along the harbours of Jezera or Murter town, you'll see several boats offering day trips to Kornati – there'll probably be someone standing with a clipboard trying to sell tickets. All these trips offer a similar sort of deal, including entry to the national park, a journey around the most impressive natural sights, the chance to swim, and a fish barbecue washed down with a couple of glasses of the local red. Most of the vessels are converted fishing boats, and many of them convert back during the winter months, when the surly tourist guides return – perhaps gratefully – to their true profession.

Where to eat

There are around 20 restaurants in Kornati, most of which offer excellent fresh fish, as well as the islands' traditional aromatic lamb. Most guests find a spot on the jetty, or anchor in the bay, and the restaurants cater to the upmarket sailing crowd rather than day-trippers.

Konoba Idro

Lavsa Bay. **Closed** 15 Sept-20 June. **Open** *21 June-14 Sept* 9am-11.30pm daily. **No credit cards**.
Set in one of the safest bays in the national park, there always seems to be a party going on at the Idro, with singing going on into the night. Plenty of buoys, a long jetty and very good scampi make this a popular choice.

Restoran Piccolo

Smokvica Bay. **Closed** Oct-Apr. **Open** *May-Sept* 7am-midnight daily. **No credit cards**.
Turn left as you enter Kornati through the strait of Opata for this fabulous restaurant, with the full range of Dalmatian specialities: scampi, calamari, lobster and first-class fish on the grill. The Piccolo runs on solar energy, so there's no distracting hum from a diesel electricity generator.

Restoran Piškera

Piškera island. **Closed** 15 Oct-15 Mar. **Open** *16 Mar-14 Oct* 8am-midnight daily. **No credit cards**.
Its place opposite the only marina in the national park is the reason why this restaurant has a longer season in Kornati. The chef prepares the freshest, locally caught fish for the many returning guests.

Where to stay

Apart from staying on a private yacht, the only other options in the national park are the small, semi-legal campsite on the island of **Levrnaka**, or renting one of the few inhabitable stone houses on the islands. You can arrange this through one of the agencies in **Murter town**

(*see below*). As there is no public transport to the islands, your hosts will take you to the cottage by boat, and leave you there for an agreed period of time – take ample food and drink. This popular kind of tourism is touted locally as 'Robinson Crusoe'.

Resources

Kornati National Park (www.kornati.hr) has two reception centres: Ravni Žakan and Vruje. The main office is in Murter town (Butina 2, 022 435 740). Nearby are a couple of agencies (*see p197*) that organise tours and accommodation.

Murter

The island of Murter is connected by road bridge from the mainland. You won't find many gems of Dalmatian medieval architecture but there are breathtaking views of Kornati, pretty villages with an existence beyond the tourist trade, and tempting paths leading to secluded bays and beaches. It's also a main centre for sailing, diving and big-game fishing. Finally, Murter is ideally placed for exploring the **Kornati National Park** (*see p192*).

Jezera is the fishing village, **Betina** is the home of shipbuilding, and slightly aristocratic owners of the uninhabited Kornati Islands live in **Murter town**. All spots are linked by one road, accessible by frequent bus services, interrupted for half-an-hour at 9am and 5pm when Tisno Bridge is raised to allow sailing boats to pass.

EXPLORING THE ISLAND

The town of Murter is the biggest settlement on the island, famous for its sandy beach Slanica and its social life. A short walk up hill from the crowded centre takes you to the **Ghetto**, with its maze of steep side streets and traditional architecture.

Betina is a picturesque stone town set on a hill, with circular streets that offer enjoyable walks up to the village church. If you're lucky, the local priest will let you scramble up the steps to the top of the church tower for a view of the island. Local craftsmen still practise the ancient art of boat- building, making the distinctive *Gajeta* fishing boats with their lucky painted eyes. The centre of town is a café-lined square, which is the place to watch teams play water polo at the old port, while the town's older residents concentrate on their games of bowls.

Jezera is the island's best-kept secret. This is where the island's fishermen reside, as its bay provides the nearest safe harbour to the

Zadar

The old salts of St Nikola

The bay of **Sv Nikola** has always been an important location for boats returning from fishing trips around Kornati, as it is one of the few safe harbours on the seaward side of **Murter**. A tiny hamlet grew up around the now disused *soliona* (salting house), where sardines and anchovies were brought for preservation in brine before the era of refrigeration. There's a small chapel with resident donkey and one house. It used to be the home of the man in charge of the salting house and now belongs to his son, local fishing legend Tade.

The community of Sv Nikola has always lived from fishing, supplemented by olive trees, a fruit orchard, vineyard and vegetable garden, as well as a herd of goats. They still use the full range of traditional fishing methods, although declining stocks threaten their age-old way of life. These include the *migavica* net, which is stretched across the mouth of the bay and dragged towards the shore. They also take their *koča* boat out,

dragging a net behind that reaches to the sea floor and scoops up scampi. One of the most viable methods today is the *parangal*, which is a line of baited hooks that are dropped from a small boat around rocky islets. The fisherman returns a few hours later, hauling in the long line, and hoping for a good catch of sea eels that were hiding in the rocks, but tempted out by a morsel of whitebait.

Womenfolk also fish, a local tradition dating back to the days when they had to fill the places of fishermen who left to work on the mainland or emigrated. Today you still see a fisherwoman harpooning a stray octopus from the shore or pulling up a basket trap full of fruits de mer from a rowing boat. The fishing family who live in the house on Sv Nikola Bay have arguably the best sea view on the island. Visitors to this idyllic and sheltered spot might ask for fresh fish, wine or even olive oil. They are often happy to rent out their two sea-view apartments (022 438 325) – ask for Sanja.

---

open sea. Around the harbour at sunset, as fishermen return home, a crowd jostles by the boats to buy extremely fresh fish. There are excellent restaurants too.

Beaches

You don't need more than a mountain bike to reach any number of secluded beaches and bays around the island. A favourite is **Koromašna Bay**, signposted from Jezera, which has a small half-island with an unbeatable sea view. **Slanica** is a fair walk from Murter town, but it's one of the best beaches on the island, and much better than the downtown alternative. It has an amazingly turquoise sea, its shallowness ideal for games of frisbee and general fooling about in the water. It can get very crowded in mid-summer, the cafés and pizzerias noisy, so get there early, or walk through the campsite to the next bay, which has similar qualities but is virtually undiscovered.

At **Jezera** the municipal beach is a simple concrete and pebble affair, but there's a little beach bar and a fabulous view of the islands. Continue walking along the beach to find your own peaceful spot under the shade of an olive tree and watch the fishing boats and yachts come in and out of Jezera harbour. There is also a waterslide and rentable paddle boats.

Where to eat & drink

Bubizzeria Zameo ih vjetar

Hrvatskih Vladara 5, Murter town (022 435 304). **Closed** Dec-Mar. **Open** *Apr-Nov* noon-2pm, 5pm-midnight daily. **Credit** AmEx, DC, MC. V.
At this elegantly designed modern restaurant, it's hard to resist the *bubizza* or 'sister of the pizza,' topped with roasted vegetables such as courgette and artichoke. This is also a good place to try a range of unusual starters and main courses, from baked octopus to chickpea salad. The restaurant belongs to the family of the architect Bašić, famous for creating the Sea Organ of Zadar, so open your eyes for interesting details.

Gallileo

Obala Sv Ivana 31, Jezera. **Open** *Summer* 10am-2am daily. **No credit cards.**
Usually the noisiest bar on the harbour, this blue neon bar is a favourite with local young fishermen and the summer party crowd. On a lively night, locals go in for cheap brandy chasers or just don't bother with beer at all. The trail from here leads up to the Zenit nightclub (*see p196*) at the car wash, and from there on it can only be downhill.

Konoba Leut

Ribarska 7, Jezera (022 438 346). **Open** noon-midnight daily. **No credit cards.**
Just behind the harbour, in an authentic fisherman's street, the Leut is better value than the restaurants

Zadar

on the bay. Its signature dish is a fish platter for two, or the simple *oslić* fillet with *blitva*: hake with kale and potatoes. Service is friendly but slow, the fish is fresh and locally caught.

Čakula

Obala sv Ivana 30, Jezera (022 439 042). **Closed** Oct-Mar. **Open** *Apr-Sept* 7am-2am daily. **No credit cards**.

This Caribbean-themed café is run by the local wall painter, a crazy Hajduk Split fan who is also responsible for the decoration of the bar. Regulars gather round the little telly for games, waving scarves and winding up wailing nautical sirens. There's even a donkey decorated in club colours who sometimes travels for home games. Čakula is easily the most spontaneous and fun bar in Jezera, its location catching sunset over the harbour.

Tic Tac

Hrokešina 5, Murter town (098 278 494). **Closed** Oct-Mar. **Open** *Apr-Sept* noon-2pm, 3pm-midnight daily. **Credit** AmEx, DC, MC, V.

As this is one of the most famous restaurants on the Adriatic, it can be hard to find a table in high season. Tic Tac is tucked down an alleyway that leads straight to the sea, with tables all the way along. The restaurant became famous for offering sushi dishes as an alternative to traditional Dalmatian fare. Highly recommended is its *brodetto* with monkfish and imaginative starters, although not every dish seems to work.

Tony's

Obala Sv Ivana, Jezera. **Closed** Oct-Mar. **Open** *Apr-Sept* 8am-1am daily. **No credit cards**.

If you happen to be here when the sport fishermen come back, you may see a large tuna strung up. If you're interested in seeing how it's done, ask at the bar as Tony runs most of the boats moored at the jetty. Otherwise, just turn up for fresh drinks at the closest café to the beach.

Nightlife

The options after the bars close are limited: there's the **Zenit** by the car wash, on the island road outside Tisno; **Čigradja** in Murter town; or head for three venues a short drive away on the mainland, the Hacienda and Exit at Vodice or the Porat Club at Pirovac. *See p202* **Highway 65 revisited**.

Čigradja

Put Škole 1, Čigradja Bay (no phone). **Open** *Summer, days and times depend on programme*.

This café on Murter town beach is known for occasional parties and club nights, always well advertised on billboards around the island. It mainly caters for more mature musical tastes, jazz and blues, but guest DJ nights also make the most of a great seaside setting. This is the logical late night option if you're based in Murter town.

Zenit

Autopraonica, Jezera. **Open** *Summer most nights* 10pm-4am.

Watch the noticeboards of villages across the island for posters advertising trashy nights such as Miss Tanga or Foam Party, periodically torn down by appalled older locals. On the plus side, Zenit is the only place open in the small hours and has a disco and outdoor bar in a courtyard behind the car wash.

Where to stay

Murter has three hotels and several campsites in great seaside locations. Private rooms are available, too – *see p197* **Resources**.

Camp Slanica

Slanica Bay (022 445 255). **Closed** 16 Nov-14 May. **Rates** *15 May-15 Nov* €3.6/person; €3/tent; €2.4/car. **No credit cards**.

In the middle of a pine-tree forest, Slanica's also just a stone's throw from Slanica beach, less crowded Lučica beach and the half island of Školjić. Two restaurants, a supermarket and tennis courts.

Hotel Borovnik

Trg dr Sime Vlasica 3, Tisno (022 439 265). **Rates** €40-€60 double. **No credit cards**.

This hotel overlooks the bridge to the island in Tisno. Recently renovated, it has a restaurant and small outdoor pool, appealing to larger groups.

Hotel Colentum

Butina 2, Murter town (022 431 111). **Rates** €30-€70 double. **No credit cards**.

The 200-bed hotel in Slanica Bay has an excellent location, if your priority is to be first on the beach in the morning. For Murter town it's a bit of a trek.

Jezera Lovišća

Jezera Lovišća (022 439 600). **Rates** €7/person; €11/tent. **No credit cards**.

This is the biggest campsite and apartment village on the island, a short walk from Tisno and Jezera. Set in its own bay, it has tennis courts, a diving centre, restaurant and shop. It's at the start of a pleasant bike-friendly walk on the old road to Betina.

Kosirina

Kosirina Bay (022 435 218). **Rates** €3/person; €3/tent. **No credit cards**.

Probably the most beautiful campsite here, in a spot where no one passes without stopping for stunning views of the Kornati archipelago, clearest when the *bura* blows. There are unspoilt inlets and rocky outcrops easily reached on foot. Basic facilities.

Say Adriatic

ACI Marina, Jezera (022 439 300). **Rates** *apartment* €55-€105. **No credit cards**.

Say Adriatic is a newly built, upmarket hotel 50 metres (165 feet) from the Jezera Marina, family-friendly as can be, with a kids' playground, pool and a large car park.

Murter. *See p194.*

Tourist information

Coronata
Zrtava ratova 17, Murter town (022 435 089/ coronata@si.t-com.hr). **Open** *Summer* 8am-8pm daily.
Accommodation and Kornati excursions.

Jezeratours
Domagojeva 7, Jezera (022 438064/jezeratours @strojevina.hr). **Open** *Summer* 9am-7pm daily.
Accommodation, excursions and rentals.

Kornatturist
Hrvatskih vladara 2, Murter town (022 435 855/ www.kornatturist.hr). **Open** *Summer* 8am-8pm daily.
Private rooms in Murter and 'Robinson Crusoe' holidays on Žut and Kornat.

Murter Tourist Office
Trg Rudina (022 434 995/www.tzo-murter.hr). **Open** *July, Aug* 8am-10pm daily. *Sept-June* 8am-noon Mon-Fri.
Small office able to advise on trips around Kornati.

Vivatours
Ribarska 20, Jezera (022 438 330/vivatours@si.t-com.hr). **Open** *Summer* 9am-7pm daily.
Private rooms and trips to Kornati.

Getting there & around

Buses go to Murter town from **Šibenik** (1hr) and **Vodice** (30mins) about every 2hrs. There are two daily buses from **Zadar** (2hrs). The bus serving the main road along the island is pretty frequent and fares are pretty nominal.

Primošten

Primošten, 28km (17 miles) south-east of Šibenik, is a languid little seaside town. Despite its lack of tourist attractions – or tourists, come to that – this half-island is a decent spot for a couple of days' unwinding. Fragrant pines back its pretty beaches, hilltop restaurants offer fresh seafood and stunning views, and seafront cafés fill with locals. Visitors don't come for any of this: they come to Primošten for the **Aurora**, one of the best (and certainly the best located) club in Croatia (*see p202* **Highway 65 revisited**).

Primošten's car-free core is set on a small picturesque island linked to the mainland by a short causeway. Winding alleys lined with green-shuttered stone houses lead uphill to the **Church of St George**. From the small church cemetery of this 1485 edifice, stellar sunset views stretch to the open sea and the seven islets that front the coastline. A promenade around the Old Town features a mix of nicely restored stone mansions and their modern concrete counterparts.

North of here, the **Raduća peninsula** contains pine forests, pebbly beaches and Primošten's only hotel, the **Zora**. Raduća and the Old Town are linked by the Mala Raduća cove. Beyond, a scenic hinterland contains rolling vineyards and 30-odd hamlets. The most famous and most visited of them is the village of **Primošten Burnji**, where locals make red Babić wine.

Primošten.

Where to eat & drink

Identikit eateries lining the seafront of the Old Town and the Mala Raduća cove churn out forgettable pizza, spaghetti and seafood. On the hilltop of the Old Town a clutch of restaurants serve fresh seafood, with prices to match the panoramic views. The daily catch of fish and shellfish is customarily washed down by the locally produced red Babić wine.

Konoba Papec

Splitska 9 (no phone). **Open** *Summer* 7pm-midnight daily. **No credit cards**.
Don't miss the pre-dinner samples of local specialties at this rustic tavern in one of Primošten's oldest and most photographed townhouses. A small, dark interior with thick stone walls is decorated with traditional costumes and wine-making equipment. Outside, wooden benches and wine-barrel tables provide lovely seafront seating. The friendly owner, born in the house, brings out reasonably priced bite-size portions of goat's cheese soaked in olive oil, prosciutto and olives, paired with a glass of Babić wine or a shot of *rakija*, all own-made in the local villages.

Restaurant Kamenar

Trg biskupa J Arnerića 5 (022 570 889). **Open** *Easter-Dec* 9am-1am daily. **Credit** AmEx, MC, V.
Mulberry and acacia trees shade the terrace of this pair of renovated stone houses facing the Old Town gates. The pricy menu runs the full gamut of seafood mainstays. Just name your fish – sea bass, grouper, John Dory, bream – and it will come to you fresh and delicious. House specialities include steak in scampi sauce and anglerfish in lemon. Of the two dining rooms, pick the one in the back with family bric-a-brac: black-and-white snapshots, an old radio and aerial photos of Primošten from the 1960s.

Restoran Panorama

Ribarska 26 (022 570 011). **Open** *Summer* noon-2pm, 6pm-midnight daily. **No credit cards**.
Gorgeous sea vistas complement a well-executed repertoire of Adriatic seafood at this recent addition to Primošten's terrace dining scene. Right below the church, it's often less crowded than its hilltop neighbours, and better for a romantic sunset meal. Forget the tiny, non-descript interior and grab a white wooden bench outside, by a small swimming pool. The monkfish fillet is nicely prepared and the mixed fish platter for two great value. Recommended.

from the suggestions below. You can reserve a private room through **Daltours** (Dalmatinska 7A, 022 571 572, www.daltours.com) or **Nik** (Trg S Radića, 022 571 200, www.nik.hr).

Hotel Zora
Raduća (022 570 048/fax 022 571 120/www.azalea-hotels.com). **Closed** Nov-Mar. **Rates** *Apr-Oct* €91-€203 double. **Credit** AmEx, DC, MC, V.
After a recent makeover by Austrian chain Azalea, this complex of nine low-rise buildings, set in pine forest, has modern decorative touches. Marble floors, armchairs and shiny columns dress the lobby. The café-bar offers a lovely sea-facing terrace, while freshly painted rooms, although small, come with balconies, pine floors and colourful wall prints. Strangely, air-conditioning is only switched on from 5pm to 1am in high season. On the positive side, a new glass-domed seaside swimming pool has a series of underground treatment rooms. There's a full entertainment programme for kids too. All-inclusive stays are required in high season; half-board rates are available in the shoulder months.

Kamenar
Trg Biskupa J Arnerića 5 (022 570 451/fax 022 571 888/www.crodirect.com/kamenar/index.htm). **Closed** Dec-Feb. **Rates** *Mar-Nov* €40-€50 double. **No credit cards**.
This is the most old-world charm you can get for your money in Primošten, in a 150-year-old stone building at the entrance to the Old Town. Above the restaurant of the same name (*see p198*) is a family-run collection of six small but pleasant rooms with pine-wood floors. The small communal balcony has lovely views of the surrounding rooftops, all very intimate and informal. Prices include a modest breakfast at the restaurant.

Villa Koša
Bana Jelačića 4 (022 570 365/fax 022 571 365/ www.villa-kosa.htnet.hr). **Rates** €27-€35 double; €35-€50 suite. **No credit cards**.
A ten-minute walk east of the Old Town, this duo of garish pink-yellow buildings has a string of modern suites inside and a pebble beach just in front. Units vary in size and layout – some have kitchens and separate living room areas – but all come with natural light, a balcony or loggia and a nod to 1970s decor principles: kitschy furniture and a vague attempt at colour-matching bedspreads and curtains. Great views of the old town. Air-conditioning is charged extra at €6. Breakfast is up to you.

Villa Silvija
Rupe 24 (022 570 533/fax 022 571 720/ www.hotelsilvija.com). **Rates** €48-€70 double. **Credit** AmEx, DC, MC, V.
For unobstructed sea and Old Town views, book one of the 11 well-equipped suites inside this white modern structure, which is just a ten-minute walk uphill from the busy main road. Don't expect villa-like luxury, but you can count on balconies, kitchenettes, separate bedrooms and air-conditioning in most of

Nightlife
Primošten is the home of the **Aurora**, a local landmark since the early 1990s. Three major venues further north, the **Hacienda**, **Exit** and the **Porat Club** (*see p202* **Highway 65 revisited**), are within easy reach by car.

Back in town beforehand, young party-goers hit the dozen café-bars lining the Mala Raduća seafront. Crowds spill out on to the street and venues merge, but popular spots include **Popaj**, at the town entrance, and **Nautica**, a few steps down the seafront towards the Old Town.

Aurora
Magistrala (098 668 502/www.auroraclub.hr). **Open** *June-Sept* 8pm-4am daily.
Set 2km (1.25 miles) from town, Aurora usually gets going about 1am. *See p202.*

Where to stay
With only one package-style hotel in town, most visitors opt for private accommodation. The best option is to book a villa apartment

Krka National Park

Krka is a spectacular spread of nature a short boat or bus ride from **Šibenik**. This forested area comes complete with seven waterfalls, islets, lakes and rapids, water mills and a couple of ancient monasteries including a Byzantine-style Orthodox church dating back to 1402. The most visited sight is **Skradinski buk**, the park's tallest waterfall, with 17 cascades running the length of 800 metres (2,625 feet); daytrippers take refreshing dips in the small emerald pool at the bottom.

Buses run from Šibenik – see the tourist office for details (*see p204*). Various agencies in Šibenik offer day trips by boat, prices ranging between €30 and €40, with transport, a guide and entrance fees.
Krka National Park Office *Trg Ivana Pavla II 5, Šibenik (22 217 720/www.npkrka.hr).* **Admission** *July, Aug* €8; €6 7-14s; free under-7s. *Apr-June, Sept, Oct* €7 €5 7-14s; free under-7s. *Nov-Mar* €3 €1.5 7-14s; free under-7s.

the units. The floor plans do differ – some bathrooms are on the small side – but the decor is standard 1970s chintz. The owners, who run a café in town, plan to open a swimming pool to make up for the lack of nearby beach.

Tourist information

Primošten Tourist Office

Trg biskupa J Arnerića 2 (022 571 111/ www.summernet.hr/primosten). **Open** *July, Aug* 8am-10pm daily. *June, Sept, Oct* 8am-9pm daily. *Nov-May* 8am-2pm Mon-Fri.
Located just as you enter the Old Town.

Getting there & around

Primošten is an easy hop from near northern neighbour **Šibenik** (*see below*). Buses leave every couple of hours and take 25 minutes. Once in Primošten, walking is the only option.

Šibenik

One of the most overlooked destinations on the northern Dalmatian coast, Šibenik is a hillside maze of cobblestone alleyways and tightly packed squares topped by the Venetian **St Anne's Fortress**. On the estuary of the Krka River, this lesser visited workaday town makes for a good if brief stop-off point on the way down south. The town has yet to recover from the economic hardship of the war and its hotel stock is poor. It contains one unmissable historical site, the **Cathedral of St Jacob**, and a rare child-friendly modern one, the **Bunari Museum**. It's handy for the **Krka National Park** and the little-known islands of **Zlarin** and **Prvić**. Many also come for Croatia's best club, the **Hacienda**, or for **Exit** in Vodice itself and, for those in the know, the **Porat** near Pirovac.

First mentioned in 1066 by King Petar Krešimir IV, Šibenik is one of few Adriatic towns with a Croatian rather than Greco-Roman heritage. Despite Byzantine, Austro-Hungarian and French occupation, it was Venetian rule (1412-1797) and the Ottoman presence that left the deepest imprint. Most buildings in the historic centre, including the star attraction the **Cathedral of St Jacob**, date from this era.

Down an alley beside the church is the **City Museum** (Gradska vrata 3, 022 213 880, open 10am-1pm, 7-10pm daily), occupying what under the Venetians was the Duke's Palace, residence and office of the prince. A large permanent collection remains in storage but temporary exhibitions (local art, archaeological finds, folkloric costumes) can be worth a look. Enter by the cannons from the waterfront.

South of the cathedral and main square, the 15th-century Gothic St Barbara's church hosts the **Museum of Sacred Art** (Kralja Tomislava 19, open 9.30am-noon, 4-7pm Mon-Fri, 9.30am-noon Sat, 7kn, closed Oct-May). It's a modest collection spanning the 14th to 17th centuries, with religious paintings, polyptychs, ancient manuscripts, wood engravings and silver and gold objects.

After three more churches on Zagrebačka, the road slopes steeply to emerge at St Anne's Fortress (open dawn-sunset, 10kn). Built during Venetian rule as protection from the Turks, this now decrepit structure rises on the site of an earlier stronghold. Nothing impresses so much as the rooftop and sea views.

Beyond this small smattering of attractions in the historic quarter (plus the recently opened **Bunari Museum** down on the riverfront), there's little else to detain the visitor. The town is still recovering from the 1990s – perhaps the huge Dalmare shopping complex sitting among the suburbs of rusting factories is what the future might look like.

Bunari Museum

Palih omladinaca 2 (098 341 175 mobile/ www.experia.hr). **Open** 8am-midnight daily. **Admission** 30kn; 20kn 7-16s; free under-7s.
British design firm JANVS created the multimedia exhibits that fill this 15th-century vaulted water storage, transformed into a delightful interactive museum. Instead of the 20,800 barrels of water once held down here, there are now seven themed areas that lead visitors on a chronological tour of Šibenik's past. It's loads of fun for children, who can build an ancient fort in 25 seconds or play a shipwreck-themed flipper game. Adult-oriented exhibits include informative text boards, video displays and glass-encased ancient amphorae. Entrance in winter is through the attached café, which doubles as a showcase for local artists.

Cathedral of St Jacob

Trg republike Hrvatske (022 214 899). **Open** *July-Aug* 8.30am-9pm daily. *Sept-June* 9am-noon, 4-8pm daily. **Admission** free.
Gothic and Renaissance fuse beautifully in this monumental three-aisled basilica. Hampered by plague and fire, it took over 100 years to build, with the work overseen by a series of architects, most notably the Zadar-born Juraj Dalmatinac and his successor

The historic quarter of **Šibenik**.

Nikola Fiorentinac. The cathedral was eventually consecrated in 1555. An Ivan Meštrović statue of Dalmatinac stands outside the main entrance. Inside, the features of note include the octagonal cupola; the stunningly ornamented baptistery with a vaulted ceiling boasting angels and cherubs; and an external wall frieze that manages to span all three apses with 74 sculpted stone faces of prominent Šibenik citizens.

Excursions

A short ferry hop from Šibenik are the lovely islands of **Zlarin** and **Prvić**. A landscape of olive groves and vineyards is dotted with typical Dalmatian fishing villages and fringed with quiet pebble and rock beaches. A couple of restaurants, hotels – including a stunner, the **Maestral** – and an occasional apartment rental reveal recent signs of tourist development.

Zlarin is half-an-hour by ferry, its sleepy bay village featuring a 15th-century church, a single hotel-restaurant, the **Koralj** (Zlarinska obala 17, 022 553 621, www.4lionszlarin.com, €66), and shops selling coral, the ancient local trade all but fading out. A further 15-minute boat ride takes you to **Prvić Luka**, the main village on the island of Prvić. Here you'll find one of the most stylish hotels on any Adriatic island,

the **Hotel Maestral** (Rodina 1, 022 448 300, www.hotelmaestral.com, €50-€90), a 19th-century schoolhouse on the main village square, where 12 air-conditioned, mostly sea-facing rooms combine sleek contemporary decor with typical local elements such as exposed stone walls and green wooden shutters. The house restaurant, **Val**, serves excellent Med fare on a waterfront terrace. From here, a scenic path leads north-west to the picture-perfect village, Šepurine. Were it not for the classy **Ribarski Dvor** restaurant, it would feel frozen in time.

In high season, five ferries connect Šibenik to the islands from Monday to Saturday, and two on Sundays. Off-season, boats are less frequent. Allow 25 minutes for Zlarin and 40 for Prvić.

Where to eat

Šibenik offers a selection of reasonable restaurants serving up Dalmatian meat staples and the usual run of fresh but pricy seafood. The best can be sampled out of town at the legendary **Zlatna Ribica** in Brodarica.

No.4/Četvorka

Trg Dinka Zavorovića 1 (022 217 517). **Open** *June-Aug* 2pm-1am daily. *Sept-May* 2-11pm daily. **No credit cards**.

Highway 65 revisited

Much as Spain had its Ruta del Bacalao, a 400km (250-mile) stretch of highway between Madrid and Valencia once packed with weekend clubbers, Croatia has its coast road 65. There may be a shining new motorway with pricy toll gates all the way up it from Split to Zagreb, but locals prefer the old coast road: the Magistrala. Winding up from Dubrovnik, through Split, then Zadar and Rijeka, the Magistrala swells out to take in the blips of Primošten, Vodice and Pirovac. This relatively short section is familar territory to Croatian clubbers, for it links four key nightspots upon which a whole summer's entertainment depends.

Aurora (*pictured*; *see p199*) is 2km (1.25 miles) before Primošten up the Magistrala from Split. Opened just as war was breaking out in May 1991, it has spanned many trends in dance music and hosted almost every known domestic DJ, plus international names. The first floor, containing a cocktail bar, steakhouse, pizzeria and pool tables, is open during the day, and after 11pm the

second level swings into action: three dancefloors, an open-air palm-fringed area, six bars, a swimming pool and a chill-out lounge zone, all open till 4am. Resident DJ Pero is well connected and attracts good names here: Carl Cox, Laurent Garnier, Roger Sanchez, David Morales and John Digweed. National pop stars are also a regular feature. Expect foam parties, retro nights, R&B and hip hop, and a crowd of anything up to 3,500.

From Primošten, the Magistrala leads up towards Vodice, and the **Hacienda** (*see p204*). Commonly acknowledged to be the best summer club in Croatia, this huge open-air venue 15km (9.5 miles) north of Šibenik is the closest Croatia gets to a superclub. A powerful laser beams out for 50km (31 miles), pointing to the spot where 2,000 clubbers come together from Split to Zadar on several dancefloors. Recent DJs here include David Guetta, Martin Solveig and Ian Pooley and it regularly hosts star DJs, and the club management also has another elite venue, the **Gallery** (*see p88*), in Zagreb.

Meat is the name of the game at this steakhouse on a small square right off Zagrebačka, where a young bunch munches on pepper, cheese or truffle steaks, or one of the gnocchi or lasagne dishes. In the mornings, it's a café; at night, a cocktail bar. The terrace is a pleasant and shady place, while the traditional stone house has an intimate wooden-roofed balcony on the second floor, with four red-checkered tables, and nice views of a Gothic-Renaissance church.

Peškarija

Obala palih omladinaca (022 217 797). **Open** 11am-midnight daily. **Credit** AmEx, DC, MC, V.
Walk through an atmospheric stone passageway and you reach a terrace under the hillside of the Old Town, with a couple of tables and benches set in greenery. To look at the water instead of the pink decor inside, sit in the glass-enclosed loggia in the back. Quality fish and meat options include standards and offbeat dishes such as fried shark, Dalmatian frog's legs and Mexican paella with chicken, veal and vegetables. Save space for the baked ice-cream in breadcrumbs.

Tinel

Trg pučkih kapetana 1 (022 331 815). **Open** noon-3pm, 6.30-11pm daily. **Credit** AmEx, DC, MC, V.
Sample well-prepared regional mainstays served with creativity at this stylish little spot on a small square across from St Chrysogonus's church, the town's oldest. In summer, reserve a table on the tree-shaded stone terrace. The narrow townhouse offers two-floor seating inside elegant but crammed interiors with seashell-themed paintings and lots of ambience. Specialities include *pašticada* (beef, bacon and gnocchi in a wine and vinegar sauce) and ray fish fillet with rocket, courgettes and tomato sauce. Dried figs in wine are the best dessert choice.

Uzorita

Bana Jelačića 58 (022 213 660/www.uzorita.com). **Open** 11am-1am daily. **Credit** AmEx, DC, MC, V.
A local favourite in Šubićevac, a 20-minute walk from the Old Town, has been dishing out some of the area's best Dalmatian food since 1898. The cool patio terrace features a lovely open hearth and vine-covered seating. The glass-enclosed interior has exposed stone walls and an old-fashioned fireplace. Try the seafood kebabs or the mussels raised in the restaurant's own farm.

Zlatna Ribica

Krapanjskih Spužvara 46, Brodarica (022 350 695/www.zlatna-ribica.hr). **Open** 11am-11pm daily. **Credit** AmEx, DC, MC, V.
It may have lost some of its cachet but this gourmet institution still provides consistent excellence in the seafood arena. Since 1961 it's been drawing locals with its fabulously fresh daily catch. Now tourists have discovered it, too; there's a private dock for

If you head back on to the Magistrala into Vodice, at the marina you'll find one of the most promoted clubs on the coast: the **Exit** (see p204). Quite small, with a modest admission fee and two-floor interior, it's quite commercial but fun on its night. An expansive terrace overlooks the bobbing boats, the music is pretty standard domestic fare and there's a pizza kitchen if you get hungry. It hasn't got a website, but you can't miss the posters all the way up from Šibenik.

The least commercial club is also the most talked about: the **Porat** (*see p204*). To find it, drive 2km (1.25 miles) out of Pirovac on the Magistrala towards Zadar, then take a track on your left and look for glowing olive trees. Set in a forgotten olive grove, this open-air club by the sea is something of an enigma. Every tree is illuminated in a different colour, and there are two dance-floors, catering to a chilled crowd of clued-up party-goers. How did the best of the Croatian alternative dance scene end up here, miles from town, in a field off a forgotten stretch of the old coast road?

yachters. The yellow-painted covered terrace has a scenic view to the island of Krapanj, while the interior comes with kitschy floral decor. The meal starts with a customary bread basket and homemade fish pâté, followed by your pick of fish from the big platter at the entrance. If in doubt, order the excellent gilthead sea bream or sea bass (350kn/kg) with *blitva* or the fish platter for two. Meat dishes and veggies from the salad bar are easily passable. Worth the 8km (5-mile) taxi ride.

Nightlife

The biggest name summer club in Croatia, the **Hacienda**, stands outside Šibenik on the way to Vodice. Its success has spawned a couple of others, **Exit** in **Vodice** and **Porat** near **Pirovac** (*see p202* **Highway 65 revisited**). Also look out for posters for events inside **St Nicholas's Fortress**, located on a small island in St Anthony's Channel, which range from classical to techno. **Cromovens** (*see below*) has schedules and tickets, which include boat transport to the island. In town, bar tables line seafront **Obala prvoboraca**, with pre-clubbers until all head off.

Exit

Obala Jurčića Cota, Vodice Marina (no phone). **Open** *Summer* 11pm until dawn daily.
The most brashly promoted of the area's big three nightclubs, on Vodice marina. *See p202.*

Hacienda

Magistrala, Vodice (www.hacienda.hr). **Open** *Summer* 11pm-dawn daily.
Possibly Croatia's best club, just outside Vodice on the road for Šibenik. *See p202.*

Porat Club

Piroška, near Pirovac. **Open** *Summer according to programme* 11pm until dawn.
The most underground of the clubs in the region, just outside of Pirovac. *See p202.*

Where to stay

With only one poor hotel in town and few private rooms in the old quarter, Šibenik offers few reasons to stay overnight. Most people opt for private accommodation (for agencies, *see below*) in the nearby resorts of Brodarica and Vodice. A large hotel complex 6km (3.5 miles) south of town, the **Solaris** (Hotelsko naselje, 022 361 007, www.solaris.hr, €52-€116, closed Nov-Mar), set in pine forest, is an option.

Hotel Jadran

Obala dr Franje Tudjmana 52 (022 212 644/ fax 022 212 480/www.rivijera.hr). **Rates** €77-€93 double. **Credit** AmEx, DC, MC, V.
Aching for renovation and pricy with it, Šibenik's sole hotel occupies an unseemly four-floor building

on the waterfront. After negotiating the tiny lobby, small rooms have equally miniature tubs in the en-suite bathrooms but no air-conditioning or balconies. Request a sea-facing room, the same price as the others. Nice views from the terrace café too.

Hotel Panorama

Šibenski most (022 213 398/fax 022 213 111/ www.hotel-panorama.hr). **Rates** €44-€73 double. **Credit** AmEx, DC, MC, V.
Fab views of the Krka estuary are the main draw of this 1970s concrete-and-glass cube by the Šibenik Bridge, 4km (2.5 miles) west of town. This former motel has a marble-floored lobby with a vaguely nautical theme extending to its series of blue-carpeted rooms. These en-suite units are on the dark side but all come with air-conditioning, balconies and cherry-wood furniture. For best panoramas, pick one of the eight south-facing rooms. The terrace café-restaurant serves up better vistas than the food. There are plans to open a fitness centre and tennis courts – already there's bungee jumping from the bridge. Regular buses ply this route; a taxi charges about 75kn.

Tourist information

Atlas Šibenik

Trg republike Hrvatske 2 (022 330 232). **Open** 8am-5pm Mon-Fri.
Can organise private rooms in Šibenik and trips to Krka National Park.

Cromovens

Trg republike Hrvatske 4 (022 212 515/ www.cromovens.hr). **Open** 8am-5pm Mon-Fri.
As Atlas Šibenik *above.*

Nik

Ante Šupuka 5 (022 338 550/www.nik.hr). **Open** 8am-5pm Mon-Fri.
As Atlas Šibenik *above.*

Šibenik Tourist Office

Fausta Vrančića 18 (022 212 075/fax 022 214 266/ www.summernet.hr/sibenik). **Open** 9am-3pm Mon-Fri.
There's a separate tourist office on the waterfront for the nearby islands, Obala dr Franje Tudjmana 5 (022 214 411, open May-Oct 8am-8pm daily, Nov-Apr 8am-2pm Mon-Fri).

Getting there & around

Šibenik is two hours from **Split** and one and a half hours from **Zadar** by hourly bus. **Knin** is one hour 20 minutes, linking with the InterCity train line between Zagreb and Split. **Šibenik bus station** is near the ferry terminal at Obala Hrvatske mornarice, just south of the town centre. There are currently no mainline ferry services into Šibenik, only services to the nearby islands (*see p202*).

Split & Islands

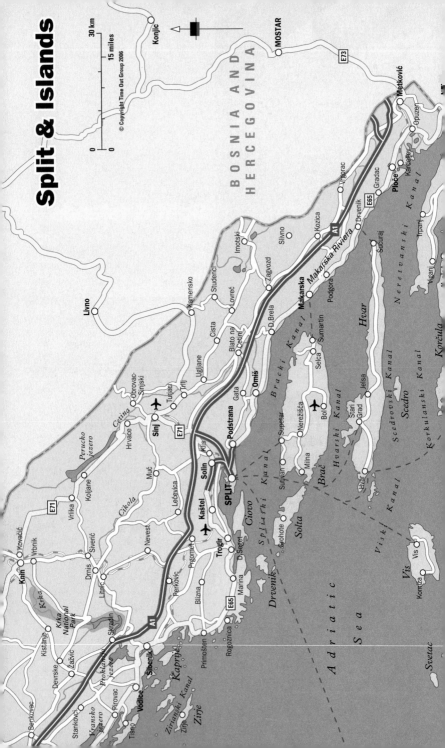

Split & Islands

Split & Islands

Get in with the in crowd.

Central Dalmatia is where the action is. Croatia's three sexiest island destinations of **Brač**, **Hvar** and **Vis** are all here, a quick, easy and cheap ferry hop from the transport hub of **Split**. With the 2005 opening of a motorway and inter-city train service with Zagreb, Croatia's second city is no longer isolated from the north of the country. As of May 2006, a low-cost air link between Split and the UK will also be in place, another first. All roads lead to Split and business on the islands is booming.

Tourists are also beginning to regard the de facto capital of Dalmatia as a destination in itself. Centrepieced by a ruined Roman palace, a maze of dark alleyways filled with all kinds of activity not least a vibrant bar culture (*see p216* **Croatia's best bar crawl**), Split is a sport-mad port, fiery, down-to-earth and forever thumbing its nose at the capital, Zagreb. Unlike Dalmatia's other regional centres of Dubrovnik and Zadar, Split didn't suffer bombardment in the Yugoslav war, but industry rusted and tourism dwindled. Flooded with refugees from nearby Bosnia, Split spent much of the 1990s in recession and is only just emerging. Every year the highbrow **Split Summer Festival** (www.splitsko-ljeto.hr) gets more prestigious and underground culture more organised – the city is the cradle of satirical magazine *Feral Tribune* (*see p222* **Tribute to the Tribune**). No more edgy than, say, Rotterdam or Hamburg (and certainly safer than Naples), it gives the visitor a jolt of in-yer-face urbanism, a lively city break but unsuitable for chilled relaxation.

For this, you must head to the islands. From Split harbour, right by the centre of town, 30 kuna will get you to Brač, Hvar or Vis. Blessed with Croatia's iconic beach, Zlatni Rat, Brač is the most family-friendly of the three, having long ago resigned itself to being a holiday destination, pure and simple. One of the few islands with its own airport, it is flooded with visitors all summer, the twin hubs of Bol and Supetar almost unbearably crowded. Culture comes in the form of stone, a particularly bright and supple variety composing the landscape, material for generations of famous sculptors.

Away from mass tourism, the former army base of Vis, remote and rocky, is much sought after. Celebrities are drawn to the traditional way of life still part of the daily fabric here –

that, and a number of key restaurants in Komiža and the Kut district by Vis town.

For 20 years now, Hvar has been the place to be. Always distinct from the mainland – 500 years ago it was a hub of Croatian culture – this most Venetian of islands was where discerning Croats went in the 1980s. Now that Westerners have picked up on it, the main harbour of Hvar town is awash with posh yachts, with key British ventures opening in the other towns of Jelsa and Stari Grad. If any island is going to be the next Ibiza, it will be Hvar.

South of Split towards Dubrovnik, the coast offers a disappointing preponderance of tourist-built hotels, a stretch named after the main town of Makarska. Although some of the beaches are pleasant, dramatically offset by the high rocky edifices of the Biokovo Nature Park, the **Makarska Riviera** is best suited to package tourists and families with children.

Split

'*Mais, c'est propre!*' comments a passing Frenchman on the cleanliness of the passageways riddling the gutted Roman palace forming the heart of Split. Descended on by hordes of his compatriots in the summer of 2005, the de facto capital and transport hub of Dalmatia is starting to attract tourists in its own right.

In rapidly increasing numbers (18 per cent more annual tourists in 2005 and twice as many from France), foreigners are filling the palace and the adjoining hub of the Riva, the palm-fringed Adriatic promenade. Five minutes away is the harbour for boats to Brač, Hvar, Vis and Italy, by the station for buses to Dubrovnik, Zadar and Bosnia and new trains to Zagreb.

It will take another ten years for Split to reverse the past decade of industrial and economic decay. In the meantime, it has a dearth of decent, centrally located hotels,

▶ The phone code for Split & Islands is 021. In this chapter we provide the full phone number for each venue – drop the first '0' if dialling from abroad, followed by the six-digit number. If you're dialling within the area, you don't need the 021. Numbers beginning 091 or 098 are mobiles and are expensive to call from most foreign phones.

At the hop

Split is the handiest hub for island hopping along the whole Adriatic coast. The key islands of **Brač**, **Hvar** and **Vis** are all easily accessible within a couple of hours at a nominal fee for foot passengers.

For Brač, several car ferries a day run to Supetar and one catamaran to Bol. Bol and Jelsa on Hvar are connected by the same catamaran. *See p233.*

For Hvar, car ferries shuttle between Split and Stari Grad and one hydrofoil a day between Split and Hvar town. Foot passengers can take advantage of the one daily ferry from Split to Hvar town, but not car drivers. *See p242.*

Two ferries a day and two hydrofoils run between Split and Vis town. *See p260.*

Split is also the starting point for ferries to Vela Luka on **Korčula** (*see p302*).

chaotic traffic and curt staff running its tourist office. What it also has is the sense to appreciate the riches that lie under its feet, namely one of the world's most perfectly preserved Roman palaces – and to keep it tidy enough for French visitors to praise.

Some 1,700 years on, the Emperor Diocletian would still recognise his palace – or the shell of it, at least. This vast, rectangular complex fell into disuse in the sixth century, 300 years after its construction as a grand retirement home by the locally born leader of the Imperial Guard. In AD 614 refugees flooded in from nearby Salona (today's Solin) and locals have been eking out a living in its manifold alcoves and alleyways ever since. Today its two-metre-thick (seven-foot) walls hide any number of shops, bars and businesses. Kids play football under groaning washing lines, cats scamper into dark recesses and palpitating Dalmatian pop music blares from decrepit windowsills. Local bar culture thrives (*see p216* **Croatia's best bar crawl**).

PALACE LIFE

Wandering aimlessly around the palace is one of Split's essential experiences. There is no ticket office or protocol – you just stroll in. Four gates guard its main entrances: Golden, Silver, Iron and Bronze. The latter gives access, through the basement of Diocletian's old Central Hall, now filled with souvenir and craft stalls, to the Riva. Much is under reconstruction and clad in scaffolding. You're bound to get lost but this is half the fun.

Amid the chaos, added to over the centuries, two landmarks stand out: the courtyard of **Peristil**, a major crossing point, and, beside it, the **Katedral Sveti Duje**. Once the site of Diocletian's mausoleum, and still guarded by a granite sphinx from ancient Egypt, this octagonal building was converted into a church by the refugees from Salona. Through the Middle Ages, it was given finely carved doors, an equally beautiful pulpit and eventually a belltower offering a panoramic view of the palace. The climb (5kn) can be quite dizzying, so only try it if you have a head for heights.

The urban layout below was meticulously studied by Scottish architect Robert Adam 250 years ago, who correctly felt its Roman symmetry would be of benefit to contemporary European design. His resultant publication influenced the Georgian designs in Bath, Bristol and London.

Adam was in Split when it was a thriving part of the Venetian empire. The population had long since spread outside the palace walls and Split's role as the main access point for trade in fast boats between Venice and the East – thus avoiding the pirate-infested waters further north – helped the local economy prosper. A short period of French rule saw rapid urban development, such as the landscaping of the waterfront embankment below the arches that once enclosed Diocletian's living quarters.

The **Riva**, now officially known as the – big breath – Obala hrvatskog narodnog preporoda, is where the city socialises, dedicating a lifetime's worth of afternoons to chit-chatting over coffee after coffee after coffee. Alongside, the calm blue of the Adriatic is softly broken by the regular glide of passing liners.

The palace is fringed by two prominent statues by Dalmatian sculptor Ivan Meštrović: one of literary scholar Marko Marulić in Trg braće Radić in the south-west corner, the other of medieval bishop Grgur Ninski by the Golden Gate. To the east, the Silver Gate was only discovered accidentally after Italian bombs in 1941 shattered a later outer wall. Nearby, the city's main produce market runs daily. The equally busy **fish market** is found on the west side of the palace, in a little square alongside Kraj Sv Marije. Adjacent runs Marmontova, another Napoleonic introduction, a smart(ish) pedestrianised avenue, Split's main shopping street and location of the French Institute. At the top stands the stern edifice of the Croatian National Theatre. A short walk north-west takes you to Stari plac, the old ground of local football club Hajduk Split (*see p226* **Maracana in miniature**). Although the pitch is now used for rugby, the bars here fill with football fans whenever Hajduk or national team Croatia are

Dosud, Split. *See p214.*

playing at the main Poljud stadium another ten minutes further up Zrinsko-Frankopanska.

Away from the palace, much of Split is an ugly spread of high-rise blocks thrown up when Tito industrialised the city after 1945. A handful of cultural attractions is set within reasonably easy reach. The most rewarding is **Ivan Meštrović**'s own **Gallery** (Setalište Ivana Meštrovića 46, 021 340 800, open summer 9am-9pm Tue-Sat, noon-9pm Sun, winter 9am-4pm Tue-Sat, 10am-3pm Sun, 20kn), a neo-classical villa built by the sculptor himself in 1931. Although he only lived here for two years before fleeing the Italian invasion, Meštrović was able to use it both as a workshop and exhibition space. Today its two floors and garden contain some 100 of his works, some of a patriotic nature, some sensual. Nearby, the **Kaštelet** at No.39 (same admission ticket) accommodates his religious carvings.

The city's other leading attraction, the **Archaeological Museum** (Zrinsko-Frankopanska 25, 021 318 720, open summer 9am-1pm Tue-Fri, 5-8pm, 9am-1pm Sat, Sun, winter 9am-2pm Tue-Fri, 9am-1pm Sat, Sun, 20kn), stands 15 minutes' walk from the palace, the other side of the National Theatre from pedestrianised Marmontova. Key historical finds from the nearby Roman capital of Salona are the main draw here, mosaics, sarcophagi and such like. The **Split City Museum** in the north-east corner of the palace (Papalić Palace, Papalićeva 1, 021 360 171) is worth visiting for the 15th-century Gothic building itself rather than the handful of paintings and medieval weaponry.

A 72-hour discount **Split Card** for museum admissions (60kn) is available from the tourist information bureaux (*see p225*) – although most visitors are happy to see a couple of sights, spend a long lunch at a café-restaurant on the Riva and hit the nearby city beach of Bačvice for the afternoon. Further east, the waterfront developments at Firula and Zenta contain a number of key restaurants and mainstream nightspots.

(see p225)

The best # Split & Islands

Split & Islands

Things to do

Take a boat to the natural wonder of the **Blue Cave** at **Biševo** off Komiža, Vis (*see p258* **The big blue**), or a water taxi from Hvar to the mainly uninhabited, nudist-friendly **Pakleni Islands** (*see p235*). On Brač you can spend the day on the shifting sands of Croatia's distinctive beach, **Zlatni Rat** (*see p229*), or climb to the highest point on the Adriatic islands, **Vidova Gora** (*see p229*). For an urban experience, climb the campanile of **Split Cathedral** (*see p208*) and see the original Roman layout that inspired the Georgian design of London, Bath and Bristol.

Places to stay

Le Meridien (*see p221*) in Split will be the city's finest when open in the autumn of 2006. Near Bol on Brač, the **Villa Giardino** (*see p233*) is much sought after, as is the charming, individually designed **Hotel Paula** (*see p260*) in Vis. **Hotel Podstine** (*see p242*) is a lovely, non-chain option in Hvar town. When ready in July 2006, the **stonehouse** (*see p238* **Hot hotels**) near Jelsa on Hvar will be the most high-end choice on the Adriatic isles. The modest **Riva** (*see p252*) in Brist provides seclusion along a stretch of coast characterised by package tourism. **Neptun** (*see p252*) in Tučepi is best for kids.

Places to eat

Šumica (*see p213*) in Split offers top-notch Dalmatian delicacies with a sea view. **Jastog** (*see p230*) in Supetar, Brač, is impeccable; in Bol, choose the **Ribarska kućica** (*see p230*). Under a starlit roof, stylish **Luna** (*see p236*) in Hvar town dishes out variations of seafood favourites, while across the island in Jelsa, **Nono** (*see p237*) is solid and welcoming. **Jeny** (*see p245*) overlooking Tučepi on the Makarska Riviera will give you a memorable meal with a dramatic vista. On Vis island you and visiting Hollywood stars are spoiled for choice: the **Konoba Bako** (*see p253* **Top tables**), the **Konoba Jastožera** (*see p257*), or the **Vila Kaliopa** (*see p259*).

Nightlife

The ruined Roman palace in the heart of Split is barfly heaven (*see p216* **Croatia's best bar crawl**). Bol's **Faces Club** (*see p232*) is the most happening thing on Brač. Everyone comes to cocktail bar **Carpe Diem** (*see p234* **Cool clubs**) in Hvar town harbour, but away from the posh yachts, **Zimmer Frei** (*see p239*) is perfect for a pre-club snifter. In Jelsa, hit **Tarentela** (*see p239*) before heading for chic Brit-run **Vertigo** (*see p241*). On Vis, late-night slackers love the **Caffè Bar Bejbi** (*see p259*) in Komiža harbour.

Beaches

Recently awarded a blue flag, **Bačvice** beach is where locals head after work. Set by a modern leisure complex of the same name and a couple of lively bars, Bačvice is a short walk from the main harbour, bus and train stations – simply cross the walkway over the train tracks and the beach is ahead of you. Showers stand at either end and a changing room in the main building. A post-swim drink at the panoramic **Tropic Club Equador** (*see p220*) is recommended.

Where to eat

Central Split contains a number of places offering standard Adriatic dishes and pizzas – the **Adriana** on the Riva, the **Sarajevo** in the palace and **Konoba Kod Jože** just outside will all serve you a reasonable meal. For something a little special, the **Šperun** is the best downtown option; otherwise head to the ones recommended in Bačvice and beyond.

Culture

See the works of Croatia's most famous sculptor in his own villa at the **Ivan Meštrović Gallery** (*see p210*) in Split. The city's open-plan **Roman palace** (*see p208*) itself has history aplenty, including an Egyptian sphinx which has survived since antiquity. Brač stone built much of the Adriatic – see it put to fine use at **Supetar cemetery** (*see p229*). Bol's **Dominican monastery** (*see p229*) houses Greek artefacts and an unexpected Tintoretto. The summer retreat of 16th-century poet Petar Hektorović, the **Tvrdalj** in Stari Grad, Hvar (*see p235*), is an icon of Croatian culture. Locally found Greek and Roman pottery and sculpture are displayed at the **Archaeological Museum** (*see p255*) in Vis.

Sport & activities

Brits can watch **rugby** or **football** in **Split** (*see p208* and *p226* **Maracana in miniature**) and, bizarrely, **cricket** on **Vis** (*see p255*). **Brač** is a leading **windsurfing** and **kite-surfing** centre (*see p229*). **Sailing** is all the rage on **Hvar** (*see p236*). The hilly **Biokovo Nature Park** (*see p243*) is ideal for hikers. Old shipwrecks and underwater caves surround **Vis** (*see p257*), explored every summer by **divers** of all levels.

Adriana

Obala hrvatskog narodnog preporoda 8 (021 340 000). **Open** 8am-11pm daily. **Credit** MC, V.
Nothing wrong with this waterfront pizzeria, except that locals tend to avoid it due to the preponderance of tourists filling the bustling terrace all summer. The food is absolutely fine, whether it's the huge pizzas (40kn-50kn), vast platters of meat (160kn) and fish (220kn) for two or fresh squid (280kn/kg). Octopus salad (60kn) is a decent starter, by which time you should have become acquainted with the local Pošip wine (80kn). Waistcoated service can be a little slow on busy nights but if you grab a study table in the old-style wooden interior, you'll catch someone's eye soon enough.

Bekan

Zenta (021 389 400). **Open** 11am-midnight daily. **Credit** AmEx, DC, MC, V.
A taxi journey or a 2.5km (1.5 mile) walk from the centre, the Bekan is highly regarded by locals. Traditional in decor and kitchen, it is set in the modern Zenta centre overlooking the waterfront just east of Firule. Superior versions of Dalmatian seafood specialities are served here, fish soup particularly, best enjoyed on the expansive terrace. Cheesecake desserts make a change from the usual gooey variety; equally, Malvazija wine from Istria is a welcome diversion from the familiar Dalmatian types.

Boban

Hektorovićeva 49 (021 543 300/098 205 575 mobile). **Open** 11am-midnight daily. **Credit** AmEx, DC, MC, V.
Showered with praise in all the leading local gastronomic guides, the Boban is hardly set in a picturesque location. Tucked among residential buildings a steep walk up from the Firula tennis courts – from town just give the taxi driver the name, he'll find it – Boban is at least a pleasant downhill stroll to the sea and along to Bačvice. The modern decor is pleasant enough, if a little sterile, but there is little to quibble about when the food arrives. An experienced hand will have taken care of the sauces embellishing your fat, fresh mussels or scampi of equal quality. Ask what's on that day, but a pricier catch such as *grdobina* (best translated as frogfish) will push the bill to at least €40 per head.

Bota Šare

Bačvice (021 488 648). **Open** 11am-midnight daily. **Credit** AmEx, DC, MC, V.
One of two key restaurants in the Bačvice beach leisure complex, this one is traditional Dalmatian and nautically themed. Prices are more than fair – a Dalmatian platter for two (smoked ham, octopus, shellfish) is 100kn, handy as a starter or main. The Bota seafood platter is 130kn, 190kn if lobster is included, and there are all kinds of sea truffles, crabs and mussels as main courses. Occasional musical folksy entertainment, but don't let that put you off.

Enoteka Terra

Prilaž braće Kaliterna 6 (021 314 800). **Open** 9am-3pm, 4pm-midnight daily. **Credit** AmEx, MC, DC, V.
The closest Split gets to slow food is this erudite enoteca run by experienced wine traders Marijana and Edi Gantar. This is both a boutique, offering shelves and shelves of Dalmatian and Istrian vintages (as well as olive oil) and an atmospheric candlelit cellar eaterie. You'll have to seek it out, as it's in the rustic basement of a century-old building behind Bačvice beach, but once inside the heavy wooden interior you'll be here for a while – that is if your credit card can tough it out. Once you choose your large glass of wine after elaborate explanation in good English, you will be presented with a plate of small tasters: hams, cheeses, smoked fish. If your appetite is more substantial, you can order a carefully prepared fish of the day in truffle and wine sauce or fillet of smoked sea bass. It's food to savour, with a 300kn per head price tag.

Konoba Kod Jože

Sredmanuška 4 (021 347 397). **Open** 10am-11pm daily. **Credit** MC, V.
Jože's Tavern is central but slightly off the beaten track – head out of the palace via the Golden Gate, over the park with the fountains and Sredmanuška is over the main road up a slight incline. A tidy terrace and rustic downstairs interior await – as well as splendid local food at very reasonable prices. After a tasty starter of Dalmatian ham or one of eight soups, you're ready for whichever fish you

chose (grouper, maybe, or dentex) from the tray of the day's catch – each is 330kn a kilo, and each will be prepared simply but satisfyingly. Adjacent street life provides the entertainment, friendly service ensures repeat business.

Noštromo

Kraj Sv Marije 10 (091 405 6666 mobile). **Open** 11am-11pm daily. **Credit** MC, V.
Two eateries by Split's open-air little fish market make a living from its products. This one is a proper sit-down restaurant; neighbouring Zlatna Ribica (open 6am-9pm Mon-Fri, 6am-2pm Sat, Sun) is a bar offering 30kn squid and 10kn beer. As for Noštromo, it's smart inside, smart enough to charge 150kn for a bottle of local Pošip wine and 320kn for the fish platter for two – fresh and well presented. Similar judgement can be passed on the shellfish, too, but you'll be lucky to leave with a bill under 500kn for the two of you.

Noštromo-Bellevue

Bana Josipa Jelačića 2 (021 347 499). **Open** noon-11pm daily. **Credit** MC, V.
Although quite prominent, running half the length of a loggia-arcade lining Trg republike, this hotel restaurant tends to get overlooked. Yet the kitchen delivers perfectly acceptable versions of Dalmatian (mainly) seafood standards, often much quicker than the time you may have to wait on a busy summer evening round the corner on the Riva. Perched on the terrace, within earshot of the waterfront, you

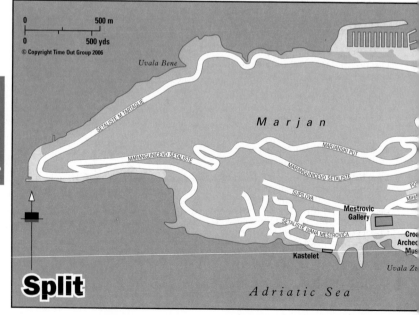

wouldn't really know it was part of a rather dowdy hotel until you walk through the traditional interior to the toilets. By then you probably would have happily dined on 130kn's worth of delicious fresh squid and a 30kn half-litre of reasonable house white.

Sarajevo
Domaldova 6 (021 347 454). **Open** noon-11pm daily. **Credit** AmEx, DC, MC, V.
Fifteen years ago, this would have been an upmarket venue. Now it's a somewhat quaint, old-school establishment – but that in itself can be an experience. A large, sturdy wooden interior lined with dining booths is waited on by timeless staff who nod sagely as you offer your choice from the menu of reliably time-honoured standards. Everything is two-thirds of the price of more contemporary places near the Riva, and everything, the squid ink risottos, the grilled meats, the pastas, is equally as good.

Šperun
Šperun 3 (021 346 999). **Open** 11am-11pm daily. **Credit** MC, V.
Lovely little Dalmatian buffet just behind Sv Frane church a minute's walk from the Riva. A neat rustic interior is fronted by a little coffeebar and, through a doorway, a table groaning with Adriatic goodies – little fish, fresh vegetables, olive oils and so on. Prices here are completely reasonable, and you would pay the same for bog standard fare within a ten-minute radius. Here, for 60kn-70kn, you can get a blue fish mixed grill (*miješana plava riba na žaru*),

grilled tuna fish with capers (*tunjevina na žaru sa kaparima*) or oven-roasted sea bream with olives (*lubin pečeni u škrovadi sa maslinama*). Marinated cheese and octopus macropus salad feature among the many starters. Veal, lamb and sirloin steak, too, plus an impressive array of local wines.

Stellon
Bačvice (021 489 200/www.stellon-split.com). **Open** 8am-midnight Mon-Thur, Sun; 8am-1am Fri, Sat. **Credit** MC, V.
Named after a founder of local football club Hajduk, this café-restaurant is owned by former player Goran Vučević. It's a fine place for a drink or dine out, beautifully located overlooking the sea by Bačvice beach. The terrace is divided equally between bar and restaurant, modestly described as a pizzeria – although it offers much more than that. Pizzas there are, either big (38kn-42kn) or small (29kn-32kn), but there's plenty of grilled fish, sea bream, angler and the like. Inside the decor is modern and funky, and you'll have to book at the weekend by passing by during the day.

Šumica
Put Firula 6 (021 389 897). **Open** 11am-midnight daily. **Credit** AmEx, DC, MC, V.
Vying to be the best place in town, the seafront Šumica is hidden behind pine trees halfway between Bačvice and Firula a little further east. Superb seafood can be enjoyed on the expansive terrace, and although you'll be paying about 250kn a head,

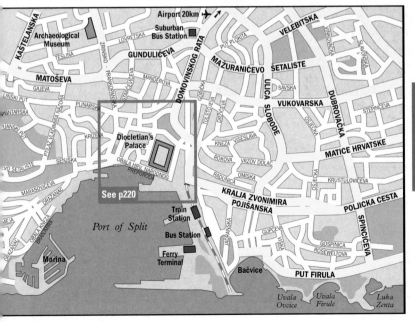

Katedral Sveti Duje. *See p208.*

you're practically guaranteed a very pleasurable dining experience. A favourite for wedding receptions, so do phone ahead.

Where to drink

By day, everyone hangs out at a terrace café on the Riva – anywhere that's not full of tourists. After dark, Split moves into the maze of alleyways of the Roman palace (*see p216* **Croatia's best bar crawl**). Bars abound – some with entrances in two streets, others in streets with no name at all, and at least one you'll love but know you'll never find again. Short of taking a ball of string, you're going to have to find one hub and use it as a landmark. The best might be the tangle of bars (Porta, Teak, Kala) in **Majstora Jurja** by the northern

wall or **Dosud** (**Puls**, Fluid, **Academia Ghetto Club**) near Trg braće Radić, just in from the Riva. Venues close at 1am.

Thereafter you have two choices: an easy walk to Bačvice or a taxi to a club such as **Tribu** or **Master's** (*see p221* **Nightlife**).

Academia Ghetto Club
Dosud 10 (021 346 879/091 566 7000 mobile). **Open** 10am-1am daily.
Calling itself a Free International University, the AGC is a bohemian hangout for arty nighthawks. Comprising a front courtyard, a small bar leading to a muralled main room with a vaguely erotic theme ('Welcome to the House of Love'), and an upstairs gallery, it's everybody's favourite bar. If there's an exhibition opening or film happening, then the separate bar upstairs may stay open a little longer. Great tunes too. It forms one end of the narrow, stepped Dosud bar run, passing by Fluid opposite and finishing at Puls – or vice versa.

Ave
Rodrigina (no phone). **Open** noon-midnight daily.
Excellent funky little bar, this – if you can find it. Rodrigina is the narrow street in the north-west corner of the palace. Either cut through the faux-Roman Divus bar on busy Bosanska, whose back door leads to Rodrigina, or turn left at the end of Majstora Jurja. Boutique and arty, with unusual pictures of fish on the walls, it attracts a varied but interesting crowd and offers a different take on the get-trashed-quick approach of most bars in the vicinity. You can spy on courtyard bar action in the Majstora Jurja bar hub from the dinky back room.

Bifora
Bernardov prilaz/Poljana stare Gimnazije (no phone). **Open** 6pm-midnight daily.
Another of the palace bars you wish you could find again, this DJ den is set on an unmapped square just behind Iza Luže and the cocktail tomfoolery of the younger crowd at Gaga. Look out for the sign saying Remixed Records, which should give you a clue. As well as some of the best sounds downtown, Bifora boasts a giggly, bohemian clientele unfazed by the mural of red-spotted mushrooms and grinning pixies. Has its own terrace in a deserted square.

Dioklecijan
Dosud 9/Alješina (021 346 683). **Open** 9am-midnight daily.
Locals would class this as a restaurant, and it serves food, to be sure. They would also call it the Tre Volte, after the arches overlooking the sea, the reason for coming here in the first place. To find it, mount the steps by the sphinx at Peristil, cut through the vestibule with the hole in the roof. Past the chairs outside the Hotel Vestibule Palace on your right will be a yellow arrow saying 'Grill'. Follow it. You will find the only bar overlooking the waterfront from above, an enclosed terrace of tables ideally located for a sundown beer. Inside is

a traditional *konoba*, cheap meats and such like, and saggy old locals getting into serious drinking by the bar counter. If you're hungry, call up a doorstep sandwich of cheese and ham carved from the huge hock behind the bar.

Gaga
Iza Loža 5 (no phone). **Open** 9am-midnight daily.
Just behind Narodni trg, Gaga is a permanently busy cocktail bar filling a tiny old square (check out the authentically retro barber's signs) with a young, party atmosphere. Cocktails, the only drink served from the counter set up outside, are dangerously cheap: 30kn for a Cuba Libre or Tequila Sunrise. Inside a standard interior, loud mainstream music keeps beer drinkers from too much conversation.

Luxor
Kraj sv Ivana 11 (no phone). **Open** 9am-midnight daily.
An upmarket café on Peristil, not particularly popular considering its prime location, Luxor offers relaxation from the brutal afternoon sun. Its vague Egyptian theme somehow means that the floor of the main bar is covered in shiny gold paper, although more money has been spent at IKEA on those springy, low-slung, high-backed chairs. Through the back is a gallery and a grand staircase leading to the toilets. Nothing wrong with it, but more adventurous management might ignore its proximity to the sphinx and surprise a few people.

Planet Jazz
Poljana Grgura Ninskoga 3 (no phone). **Open** noon-midnight daily.

Now a palace landmark – note the upmarket and inferior XVII Stoljeća since installed opposite – Planet Jazz is a tiny wooden cubbyhole of a bar. Seemingly, it has little to recommend it above the others, until you find a table on the terrace, enjoy the jazzy, clubby sounds emerging from within and realise there's probably no place you'd rather be right now. There's not much of a view – people's washing, in fact – but it's captivating nonetheless.

Po Bota
Subićeva 2 (no phone). **Open** 6pm-1am Mon-Sat.
The address is a little misleading – the tiny Po Bota is tucked away at the end of a cul-de-sac along the northern fringe of Trg braće Radić, to the left of the Milesi Palace if you have your back to the sea. What you'll find is a small, arty space with just enough room for a couple of tables and a tiny corner of bar counter. Oh, and a beer tap of Stare Brno. Bare brick, fish motifs and a little colourful art make up the rest. An in-the-know alternative to the Academia Ghetto Club (*see p214*), Po Bota accommodates off-their-face louche regulars who like to hold court and smoke like beagles.

Puls
Buvinina 1 (no phone). **Open** 10am-1am daily.
Just follow the noise round the corner from the green awnings of the Shook Café by the statue on Trg braće Radić. Puls is a well-established two-storey party bar, its young custom spilling out on to the alleyway that bookends the mini bar run of this Dosud intersection. Always packed, its downstairs bar is a smoky hangout for drinkers, while upstairs offers a little dancing and eye-contact games.

Daily life in the **Diocletian's Palace**. *See p208.*

Croatia's best bar crawl

1 F Café
2 Twins
3 Romana
4 France Style
5 Adriana
6 Dujam
7 Veneranda
8 Buža
9 Gradska Kavana
10 Shook Café
11 Puls
12 Fluid
13 Academia Ghetto Club
14 Dioklecijan
15 Luxor
16 Duje
17 Duje No.1
18 Duje No.2
19 Planet Jazz
20 XVIII Stoljeća
21 Red Room
22 Get
23 Teak
24 Kala
25 Porta
26 Dante
27 Whisky Bar
28 U Kantinu
29 Ave
30 Divus
31 Gaga
32 La Linea
33 Bifora
34 Po Bota
35 Caffè Galerija Plava

Nothing beats a bar crawl of the gutted Roman palace at the heart of Split. From 300 AD when the Emperor Diocletian conceived his palatial retirement home to the mid 1700s when Scottish architect Robert Adam traced its neat, logical lines to assist Georgian town planning back home, every nook and cranny of the palace filled with locals and their businesses. All daily life was here. It still is.

History, anthropology and architecture all come into play as you scoot around the Diocletian's dark, unmapped passages, discovering wonderfully random bars as you do. DJ bars, gallery bars, Goth bars, cocktail bars, bars with pseudo Ancient Egyptian themes, bars with pseudo Roman themes, bars in deserted open squares, bars with the only bird's eye view of the palm-fringed promenade. It would make a great board game, the squares and secret corridors designed two millennia ago. The object? No hotel on Mayfair or murderer unmasked, but inspired inebriation and stimulating ensozzlement. Privacy in the heart of a town of half-a-million people, communality in

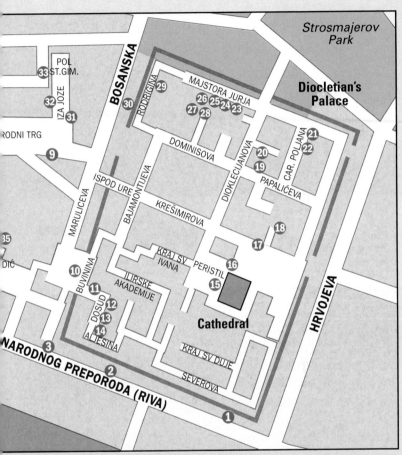

crowded, lively cafés rife with party spirit. For now, you're the counter, let the dice and the good times roll.

For a relaxing, panoramic start to the evening, pick any terrace café along the Riva. Venues change in popularity according to the day's passage to sunset, the bars at the eastern, port end (**F Café**, for example) nearest the market slowly emptying as those running west (**Twins**, **Romana**, **France Style**, **Adriana**, **Dujam**, **Veneranda**) fill from lunchtime on. Don dark shades to merge with the locals. You can dip your toe in the water

by a quick visit to the tiny **Buža** (Petra Priroda 7), in an intimate courtyard halfway between Zadarska and Kraj Sv Marije. A swift half, a blast of the Beach Boys and a smile from the regulars and you're away.

Kraj Sv Marije leads to focal square Narodni trg, where the landmark **Gradska Kavana** in the corner provides an ample terrace for observation; from Zadarska you can turn right into Dobrić and the equally busy, expansive square Trg braće Radić leads to the green awning of the **Shook Café** (Mihovilova širina 4) behind the statue of Marko Marulić by Ivan

Croatia's best bar crawl (continued)

Meštrović. Both main squares are ideal springboards from which to storm the palace; both adjoin obscure bar hubs better for a visit later on. From Narodni, you can turn immediately right from the Gradska Kavana down the commercial street of Marulićeva and arrive at the same Shook Café at the bottom.

Alongside the Shook Café runs a short, narrow alley with **Puls** (see p215) at the end. This may be your last port of call, but see it in daylight to get your bearings. Adjacent is the Hotel Slavija and a gently sloping, stepped alleyway with **Fluid** at the top. Turn left into Dosud; on your right is the doorway for the **Academia Ghetto Club** (see p214), its garden ideal in the early evening, its arty interior the perfect setting for late drinks.

Moving on, a right turn takes you to Aljesina, parallel to the promenade wall and the enclosed courtyard terrace of the **Dioklecijan** (see p214). Named the Tre Volte after the arches in the wall, its terrace tables allow a perfect view of sunset over the Riva and sea beyond. With your back to the arches, turn right, then left and you're by the open-roofed vestibule that leads to the main crossing point of the palace, Peristil. Along one side of the main square is the reasonably swish, Egyptian-themed **Luxor** (see p215), worth a look in; in one corner of the side section by the tourist information office is the terrace of the **Duje**. Two other Duje bars (**Nos.1** and **2**) occupy corners of the dog-leg alleyway running alongside. These are smoky hidey-holes for chainsmoking Goth- and punk-styled teenagers.

Back in Peristil, walking towards the Golden Gate along the northern edge along Dioklecijanova brings you to Papalićeva. Near the Split City Museum is signposted one of the best palace bars, **Planet Jazz** (see p215), with good DJ sounds. Its low terrace tables occupy the mini square of Poljana Grgura Ninskoga, the rather swish **XVIII Stoljeća** (No.7) occupying at the other end.

Between Papalićeva and the northern palace rim is a ruined square, with one wall covered in football graffiti: Carrarina poljana. At the far end is a new, chic DJ bar, **Red Room** (see p220); on an adjoining wall is **Get**, a small football bar, almost always empty. Kids and cats run around the square outside, an old couple might be dining on their own postage-stamp square of courtyard.

Back on Papalićeva, a left turn leads back on to a Dioklecijanova and, a short walk towards the Golden Gate, a little covered corner passageway with an icon above it. Turn here and you're in Majstora Jurja.

This is the main hub of bars furthest from the Riva, all attractively decked out. On the far wall is **Teak** and **Kala**, by a little square the always busy **Porta** and **Dante**, and in the square itself the **Whisky Bar** and **U Kantinu**. The square buzzes all summer long.

Turning left at the end of Majstora Jurja brings you into Rodrigina. On the left-hand side is a great little arty bar, the **Ave** (see p214). Further along, on the right-hand side, is the **Divus** (Bosanska 2). Walk through the faux-Roman and maritime knick-knacks of its interior and its other, main entrance leads out of the palace and onto the busy, commercial street of Bosanska.

If you need it, there are a couple of takeaway food spots further up the street. Otherwise, walking a short way to the left, down Bosanska, brings you back to Narodni trg. Beside the loggia façade of the Communal Palace is a narrow alley and a small square, Iza Lože. On summer evenings it is filled with a young gaggle of cocktail drinkers at **Gaga** (see p215) while, at the back, older locals ignore the bustle and cluster at **La Linea**. Two alleys run either side of La Linea. Bernadinova to the left leads to the fabulous DJ bar **Bifora** (see p214) in its own little square.

By now you should be three sheets to the wind and ready for anything. Follow your tracks back to Narodni trg, the Gradska Kavana and left down Marulićeva to Trg braće Radić. Beside the baroque Milesi Palace is a cul-de-sac, bookended by the brilliant, arty **Po Bota** (see p215) – and adjoining it the **Caffè Galerija Plava**, a gallery with a central courtyard.

If you're up for more action, pop back to the square, turn left behind the statue and, walking beside the Shook Café, the Buvinina alleyway is full of action: there's dancing on the top floor of Puls, glugging outside Fluid and bohemian interaction inside the sassy Academia Ghetto Club.

All has to close at 1am. It's no distance from here to the Riva and a ten-minute walk left past the bus station and over the railway tracks to the all-night action at Bačvice.

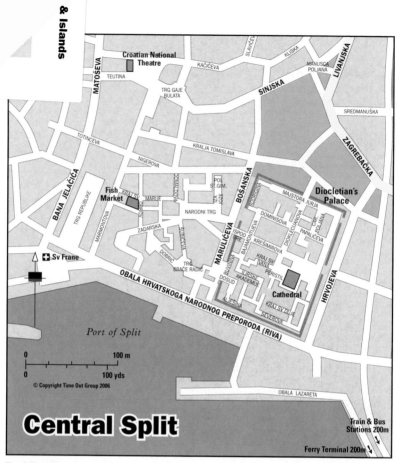

Central Split

Red Room

Carrarina poljana 4 (no phone). **Open** 9am-midnight Mon-Thur; 9am-1am Fri, Sat.

The latest DJ bar in the palace, this one opposite a wall of football graffiti in a crumbling square in the north-east corner, the Red Room comprises two spaces. By the entrance is a leopard-spotted bar counter and adjacent, filled with cushions in exotic colours, is a chill-out zone quickly filled with eagerly coupling couples. Could be the place to be in the summer of 2006.

Tropic Club Equador

Bačvice (no phone). **Open** 10am-2am daily.

Occupying a sweeping first-floor terrace that juts out over the Adriatic, the Equador is a refreshingly unglitzy café lounge/nightspot. By day it's the ideal place to take a post-bathe beer and watch the sun go down over Bačvice. By night it becomes a disco bar, with crowds milling around each bar counter and finding floor space to dance near the half-moon of starlit patio. When it closes, everyone drifts to the adjoining open-air Bačvice bar, which keeps serving way after you should have long gone home.

Vanilla

Baženi Poljud, Poljudsko šetalište (021 381 283). **Open** 9am-3am Mon-Thur; 9am-4am Fri, Sat.

Attached to the Tribu club in the beachside sports complex by the Poljud football stadium, Vanilla overlooks the swimming pool. It's the kind of place that Croatians call 'fancy' – which means it sells cocktails to a well-dressed young crowd. As a pre-club 'disco bar' it does a job, although really it's just some wicker furniture, a little music and drinks with umbrellas in them.

Žbirac

Bačvice (no phone). **Open** 7am-midnight Mon-Fri; 7am-1am Fri, Sat.

The best of the Bačvice bars, this one is a small detached terrace right on the beach whose popularity is due to a slightly older and more clued-up clientele than the young locals on the pull in the main complex. The little touches make it, too – the framed old colour photographs of the same Bačvice view you're gawping at, the comical picture of fat blokes playing football on the menu cover. A nice buzz.

Nightlife

To get an idea of what's going on, get a copy of the free monthly listings brochures *Splitski Navigator* or *Scena* from the tourist bureau at Riva 12 (*see p226*). They're not that detailed, but if a certain DJ or band is in town, it'll be mentioned. Flyers can be found in **Ave**, **Planet Jazz** and **Žbirac**, all reviewed above.

Since its change of management from cheesy disco to haven of electronica, the club to head to is **Master's**. Undergoing a complete refit in the winter of 2005/06, with a new sound system, it's located on Osječka (021 536 983) and runs most nights of the week, certainly from Wednesday. Name DJs, some of them international, mean an entry fee of 60kn; otherwise at weekends expect to pay 40kn. Its rival is the more commercial **Metropolis** (Matice hrvatske 11), a throwback to the 1980s. Both shut in high season, when the action moves to the beach. In the sports area at the Poljud, **Tribu** (Osmih Mediteranskih igara 3-5, 021 321 477, 098 982 9267 mobile) is a big name, with mainstream music and trendies sipping cocktails. Samba is popular, but rumour has it that Tribu is turning to turbofolk.

If there is anything you must avoid like the plague in Croatia, the sea urchin of local entertainment, it is turbofolk. Poppy boom-boom music with a Balkan beat and a pseudo-glamorous following, the most notorious elements drawn from the underworld, turbofolk isn't even funny. When you climb half-cut into a taxi and say, 'Take me to a club', you must then say, 'No turbofolk – under any circumstances.' If you can remember your pin code, you can remember this. Make sure the baffled taxi driver understands. *See p65* **Turbofolk**.

Away from discotheques, two venues have recently emerged. Towards the shipyards along Dubrovačka, a late-night DJ coffee-bar called **4 i Po Sobe** ('Four-and-a-half Rooms') is making ripples in the local scene. Another is **Admiral**, a former disco beneath the Hotel Marjan (*see p223*) with regular live music, including the big names on the local alternative circuit.

Finally, if (ever) the legendary **Discovery** re-opens in Bačvice, you should be in for a treat.

Where to stay

Split's poor hotel stock is gradually improving. The end of 2006 sees the appearance of the first major chain hotel. The 382-room Meridien (www.lemeridien.com), in Podstrana, 6km (3.5 miles) outside town towards Omiš, will contain a spa, gym and conference facilities.

For the moment, the best hotels here are the **Park**, the **Vestibul** and the **Globo**. If you are arriving on spec at the bus station, you will be bombarded by offers of private rooms.

Diocletian's Palace. *See p208.*

Tribute to the *Tribune*

A glance at one of *Feral Tribune*'s most notorious covers – an image of the wartime Croatian president Franjo Tudjman locked in a homoerotic embrace with the former Yugoslav strongman Slobodan Milosevic – illustrates why the provocative Split-based news magazine made more than a few enemies during the 1990s. It was one of the few media outlets to challenge the official orthodoxies of the Croatian 'patriotic war' for independence, digging up evidence of war crimes by Croatian troops and risking accusations of treachery. It braved an onslaught of punitive court cases and managed, although somewhat bloodied, to survive the Tudjman era and establish itself as one of the critical, independent voices of the post-war period.

Its roots are in the late Communist era of the mid 1980s, when it started as a satirical political leaflet, but it began to establish itself as a vital force when Yugoslavia started to self-destruct. The highly charged combination of nationalist ideology, homeland propaganda and wartime profiteering provided endless material for muck-raking investigations and bitter humour. The authorities responded with a series of law suits intended to cripple the magazine, while its staff were subjected to

intimidation and death threats. In one of the best-known cases, *Feral*'s editor-in-chief was prosecuted for comparing Tudjman to General Franco and the World War II-era Croat Fascist leader, Ante Pavelić. Neither did it endear itself to the Nationalists when, just before Operation Storm, the military operation that took back Serb-held areas for the Croats in 1995, it put the words 'Stop the War in Croatia' on its cover – in the Cyrillic lettering preferred by more traditional Serbs.

Feral says it still sells around 20,000 copies an issue, but it has struggled to survive in the harsher, free market of contemporary Croatia, and has reverted from colour to black and white. It still attracts a few writs, and its impudent cover caricatures remain deliciously savage. As the country moves unsteadily towards the European Union while struggling to face up to its recent past, there is still no shortage of scandals and cover-ups to investigate. But, as its deputy editor-in-chief Drago Hedl admits, the death of President Tudjman in 1999 deprived the magazine of the nemesis that so inspired it. 'We must be honest – Franjo Tudjman was unrepeatable and unique,' says Hedl. 'We miss him so much.

Adriana
Riva 8 (021 340 000/fax 021 340 008/www.hotel-adriana.hr). **Rates** 650kn-850kn double. **Credit** V.
The handful of well-priced three-star rooms above this waterfront pizzeria are much sought after, offering a simple, comfortable stay within an easy walk of the harbour. Terrace breakfast included in the price.

Hotel Art
Ulica Slobode 41 (021 302 302/fax 021 302 300/arthotel@net.hr). **Rates** 1,300kn single; 1,200kn double. **Credit** AmEx, DC, MC, V.
Split's first self-named boutique hotel is having trouble finding its feet. Although opened in May 2005,

by March 2006 it still didn't have a website and time will see whether the promised spa facilities will be in place for the summer of 2006. In its favour, it's set in a nicely renovated factory building, a short taxi journey north of the palace where the main roads of Slobode and Domovinskog rata meet. Rooms are spacious, beds are huge and the lounge bar near the lobby is a suitable place for an upmarket chit-chat. Parking is available at 50kn.

Hotel Bellevue
Bana Josipa Jelačića 2 (021 347 499/fax 021 362 383/www.hotel-bellevue-split.hr). **Rates** 670kn-960kn double. **Credit** MC, V.

This superbly located 19th-century edifice at the far end of the Riva forms one flank of the Venetian-style Trg republike. Once inside, you'll find that the Bellevue's 50 rooms are in serious need of tarting up. They're not uncomfortable, just dreary, not justifying the price tag. For a room near the harbour, try the Adriana (*see p222*) or the Slavija (*see p224*).

Hotel Consul
Tršćanska 34 (021 340 130/fax 021 340 133/ www.hotel-consul.net). **Rates** 590kn single; 820kn double. **Credit** MC, V.
A handy little hotel this, a 15-minute walk north of the palace, with 15 well-facilitated rooms and four suites. Nice big terrace, too, and half- and full-board rates are available at reasonable supplements. Quickly booked out, so phone well in advance.

Hotel Globo
Lovretksa 18 (021 481 111/fax 021 481 118/ www.hotelglobo.com). **Rates** €94-€117 single; €115-€151 double. **Credit** AmEx, DC, MC, V.
Opened in 2001, this smart, modern four-star is located north of the palace, a 15-minute walk from the Riva. The 26 bedrooms include 20 doubles, geared towards the business community – hence the fully equipped congress room. From 2006 a sauna and gym will be operational.

Hotel Jupiter
Grabovčeva širina 1 (tel/fax 021 344 801/ www.hotel-jupiter.info). **Closed** Mid Nov-mid Mar. **Rates** *Mid Mar-mid Nov* 200kn per person. **No credit cards**.

Hotel Jupiter offers the cheapest rooms in the Roman palace. Opened in 2004, this basic hostel-type pension offers 13 clean rooms with showers in the corridors. Rooms are spacious enough for two people but couples will have to push the single beds together. No breakfast, no frills, but located right in the palace – look out for the black-and-yellow Jupiter pizzeria sign behind Buvinina. The hotel is opposite, across a quiet inner courtyard square.

Hotel Marjan
Obala Kneza Branimira 8 (021 302 211/fax 021 399 210/www.hotel-marjan.com). **Rates** 590kn single; 875kn double. **Credit** AmEx, DC, MC, V.
Long surpassed as the best hotel in town, this is still a reasonable choice a ten-minute walk from the Riva in the opposite direction to the main harbour. The sea view is welcome, and the 100 or so rooms are of an acceptable standard.

Hotel Park
Hatzoev perivoj 3 (021 406 400/fax 021 406 401/www.hotelpark-split.hr). **Rates** €103-€127 single; €130-€154 double. **Credit** AmEx, DC, MC, V.
For the moment, this well-appointed four-star set in quiet grounds behind Bačvice beach gets our vote for the best hotel in town. An elegant pre-war villa given a fairly modern makeover, the Park offers 54 rooms and three suites with all the usual facilities (internet, TV, minibar, safe, air-conditioning) – plus a panoramic terrace fringed by palm trees, a health club and lavish buffet breakfast.

Split fish market. *See p208.*

Heaven up here – Adriatic islands beckon from **Split harbour**. *See p227.*

Hotel Peristil

Poljana kraljice Jelene 5 (021 329 070/fax 021 329 088/www.hotelperistil.com). **Rates** €88-€115 single; €108-€135 double. **Credit** AmEx, MC, V.

Another new hotel in the palace, this one with a terrace restaurant overlooking the Peristil. This three-star contains nine simple, but comfortable doubles and three suites, all reasonable for the price and location.

Hotel Slavija

Buvinina 2 (021 323 840/fax 021 323 868/ www.hotelslavija.com). **Rates** 500kn single; 650kn double. **Credit** MC, V.

For years this was the only budget accommodation option – in fact, the only accommodation option – in the palace. Back then, in the mid 1990s this operated as a Socialist style hostel. Modernisation has seen all 25 rooms fitted with showers and a TV, but they're still pretty basic despite what the smart reception area might promise. If you want to go budget and you're not too fussed about having your own private facilities, then a single in the Jupiter (*see p223*) round the corner is just over half the price. Note also that rooms overlooking the bar-lined alleyway outside will have nightlife noise drifting up until 1am at least.

Hotel Vestibul Palace

Iza Vestibula 4 (021 329 329/fax 021 329 333/ www.vestibulpalace.com). **Rates** €110-€155 single; €190-€220 double. **Credit** AmEx, DC, MC, V.

Recently opened in a little building adjoining the open-roofed vestibule in the palace, this seven-room boutique hotel is pretty swish inside, but unless your company is paying, you may find it hard to justify the €200 outlay. Rooms have an internet connection and nice touches, such as natural brick. The Vestibul Palace may have a superb location, but the building simply isn't big enough to allow for any additional facilities. Lovely, all the same.

Kaštel

Mihovilova širina 5 (098 973 8601 mobile/www. kastelsplit.com). **Rates** €38-€100 double. **No credit cards**.

Little-known three-star in the palace, at the end of a narrow alleyway near the Shook Café. Of the seven quite spartan but en-suite rooms, three have a sea view. Extra beds are charged at a nominal €5-€10. In short, Kaštel is ideal for a small group of palace-bound party-goers.

Simoni

Zlodrina poljana (021 488 479/098 974 7439 mobile/www.sobesimoni.com). **Rates** 150kn-250kn single; 200kn-300kn double. **No credit cards**.

You're arriving late into the harbour or bus station, you need a simple room and can't be bothered paying over the odds on the Riva. Phone the Simoni. Seven simple rooms with showers are for hire, in a renovated modern house just the other side of the train tracks as you walk through the station – you'll see the blue-and-yellow sign.

Resources

Internet

Dencall, Obala Kneza Domagoja (021 345 014/ www.dencall.com). **Open** 8am-11pm daily.

Friendly internet café by the post office opposite the harbour. There's a separate one next door and a branch in the old town (Zadarska 4, 021 332 810, open 9am-11pm Mon-Sat, 10am-11pm Sun). Dencall also issues cheap international telephone cards.

Police station

Trg hrvatske bratske zajednice 9 (021 307 022).

Post office

Obala Kneza Domagoja 3. **Open** 7am-9pm Mon-Sat. Facing the harbour, convenient for making cheap international phone calls.

Tourist information

Split Tourist Office *Peristil (021 345 606, www.visitsplit.com)*. **Open** *Summer* 9am-8pm Mon-Sat; 9am-1pm Sun. *Winter* 9am-5pm Mon-Fri. Recalcitrant staff provide basic information from a little office in the heart of the old town.

Hotel Split

Put Trstenika 19 (021 303 111/www.hotelsplit.hr). **Rates** €78-€98 single; €108-€140 double. **Credit** AmEx, DC, MC, V.

Surprisingly only categorised as a three-star, the Split is a well-equipped resort hotel right on the Adriatic 4km (2.5 miles) east of the city centre past Firula. All 200 rooms have a balcony, with the somewhat dearer ones overlooking the sea, and guests can take advantage of the hotel's large, octagonal outdoor pool and private stretch of beach. A couple of well-run restaurants and a large terrace are part of the modern complex.

Maracana in miniature

For the flagship football club of Dalmatia, and one representing the sport-mad city of Split, **Hajduk** are in a sorry state. A familiar name from European tournaments (invariably mispronounced by English football supporters as 'Had-zhook' rather than 'Hay-dook'), Hajduk's demise is mourned by one of the most passionate and colourful fan cultures in Europe. A big night at the stadium, the Poljud, will live as long in the visitor's memory as any major game in Madrid, Rome or Rio.

The Brazilian comparison is pertinent, for Rio was the role model used by Hajduk fans to introduce South American football culture, including torch flames, colourful banners and co-ordinated chants, to European terraces in 1950. Fiery celebrations were copied from grainy cinema newsreel footage of the Brazil World Cup of that year. Christening themselves the Torcida after their Brazilian counterparts, Hajduk fans created a storm for a game against visitors Red Star Belgrade, earning the wrath of Tito for the fanatical scenes in the stadium and around the city that day. The Riva had seen nothing like it.

A tradition had been established, by a Dalmatian diaspora who follow the Hajduk flag. Back in 1950, it was only a few thousand Dalmatian residents of Zagreb who braved the half-day's journey to Split — and back again. By the 1980s, supporters were flying in from Australia, North America or whichever shore-leave port their ship happened to have docked at.

The tradition continues to this day. Match build-up at its best involves a tribal gathering of Dalmatians. The Riva reverberates all afternoon with fireworks and parades, another tradition. And the patriotic, populist Torcida, banned in 1950, is happy to challenge the football club in authority. These days it's Zagreb – Dinamo Zagreb.

By the time the Torcida could support more demonstrably, after Tito's death in 1980, Hajduk had a new stadium. Opened by Tito himself to host the Mediterranean Games the year before, the Poljud is north of the city centre, superbly backdropped by the Adriatic.

The old one is where fans still gather. A short walk from the National Theatre, Stari Plac is now used for rugby internationals, but the sports bars here fill with football fans on match days. Between the Bili AS ('The Whites') and the Pivnica Rugby, a tatty, light-blue door could be easily missed. But inside, one floor up, is an authentic fans' bar, recently renovated, its walls illustrating in careful detail the history of Hajduk. Framed is a portrait of the four Split students meeting in 1911 at the U Fleku pub in Prague to discuss the foundation of a club in their home town. Trophy-clutching players are carried on the shoulders of crowds, trilby hats are thrown in unison from terraces, glorious European runs are celebrated on newspaper back pages. The bar at No.17 Zrinsko-Frankopanska, opens daily from 11am.

Neither the Torcida, players or management have covered themselves in glory of late. Although Hajduk won both domestic trophies in 2004 and 2005, it is in a weak Croatian championship dominated by two rival clubs, the other being Dinamo Zagreb. When the two clubs met at the Poljud in February 2006, the Torcida unfurled a banner saying: 'Maksimir Zoo, Cago, Eto and Da Silva', a reference to Zagreb's black players and the caged animals on display near Dinamo's stadium. Hajduk, mired in mid-table, were forced to play the next home game behind closed doors. Recently in Europe, Hajduk have gone out to Irish minnows Shelbourne and, even worse, to Hungarian team Debrecen 8-0, including a 5-0 embarrassment at the Poljud.

Turist Buro *Riva 12 (021 347 100).* **Open** 7.30am-9pm Mon-Fri; 8am-8pm Sat.
Handy travel agency who run a booking service for private rooms. Pay the fee at the desk and staff will show you where to go and give you a key.

Getting there & around

Split airport is 20km (12.5 miles) north-west of town between Kaštela and Trogir. Getting into town is easy – a **Croatia Airlines bus** is usually waiting (30kn, 30min journey time).

If you're flying back on Croatia Airlines, its buses depart 90 minutes before each flight from the stop by the Jadrolinija kiosks at the harbour end of the Riva. If you're not flying Croatia Airlines, the journey to the airport can be a nightmare. You have to check Croatia Airlines flight times at its office on the Riva – they're not posted up at the bus stop. Simply take the most convenient bus. If none coincide, then you must take the rundown city bus No.37 from bay No.3 or No.4 from the suburban station at the corner of Domovinskog rata and Gundulićeva –

Deep in financial difficulty – a consortium of former players have even had to bail them out – the club still bungles, hiring controversial coach Čiro Blažević (doh!) and selling key winger Darijo Srna (doh!) to Shaktar Donetsk. Pin-up boy Niko Kranjčar, a controversial steal from Dinamo, is rumoured to be leaving for the West, too.

For the innocent foreigner, a trip to watch Hajduk at the Poljud provides loud and colourful entertainment, and only edgy when Dinamo Zagreb are in town. As the stadium is also used for occasional home matches of the Croatian national team, there can be also a sense of national solidarity in the air, rather than brute regional pride. Improvements to the stadium can be expected if Croatia win an ambitious bid to co-host the 2012 European Championships with Hungary.

Tickets are available at office hours a few days before each game from the desk by the main entrance. *Tribina zapad* and *istok* are nice seats along the touchline (60kn-80kn), *tribina sjever* (30kn) is behind the goal with the home boys. Bus No.17 (direction Špinut) runs to the Poljud from the National Theatre, or it's a 15-minute walk uphill – via the bar at Stari Plac, of course.

a steep 15-minute trek up the main road opposite the statue of Grgur Ninski at the north-east corner of the palace. You must buy a 19kn ticket from the station kiosk or café and stamp it on board. The bus (every 20-30mins from 4am-11.30pm) goes to Trogir – the stop by the airport is not named as such, so keep a look out. A **taxi** either way costs 250kn-300kn.

Walking is the only practical way to get around the town centre. To reach the hilly peninsula of Marjan, take a city bus (7kn) from either end of the Riva at Trg republike or Zagrebačka by the market. Taxis such as Radio Taxi (970) or Taxi Riva (021 347 777) are parked at either end of the Riva.

Hops to the islands of Hvar, Brač and Vis require a couple of hours and a nominal foot passenger fare of around 30kn. The ferry terminal is a short walk from the Riva, a large building you can't miss diagonally opposite the bus station. Catamarans and hydrofoils leave from the Riva, behind a building surrounded by cafés on the main waterfront. Tickets and information are available at the harbour

Musical differences TBF

TBF ('The Beat Fleet') use their local slang to describe real-life stories from the craziest town in Croatia, their native Split. Combining lazily spoken rap rhymes or full-speed assault with a rock-funk-jazz band behind them, the three TBF rappers are an unstoppable machine when giving deserving victims a tongue-lashing, and soft lyricists when describing the Dalmatian way of life or unforgettable summers. TBF started their rise to popularity with the song *Trilogija jada* ('Trilogy of Misery'), offering the same crime story told through the eyes of the perpitrator, the policeman and the judge. Their most tongue-in-cheek work is *Herojix*, a polemical song about war veterans. Only a native would get the cultural references, but to place TBF somewhere between De La Soul, Public Enemy and Rage Against the Machine would not be horribly wrong. The band's third CD, *Maxon Universal*, was acclaimed as the best domestic pop album of 2004. Only their very laid-back Dalmatian nature will stop them becoming the biggest band in Croatia.

terminal or the Jadrolinija and SEM Marina kiosks at the Riva end of the harbourfront.

The main bus and train stations are next to each other, opposite the harbour. If you're making the four-and-a-half-hour journey by bus to **Dubrovnik** (*see p263*), keep your passport to hand, as part of the journey crosses Bosnia. Split has a comfortable, new inter-city train link with **Zagreb** (*see p69*), with two services a day. The journey takes about five hours and reservations are compulsory.

Brač

Dalmatia's largest island is easily accessible from the mainland – almost too accessible. Every summer thousands pour in by ferry or catamaran from Split, by plane from Zagreb or boat from the Makarska Riviera, to flock to its two family-friendly resorts of **Supetar** on the north coast and **Bol** on the south.

Bol is blessed with the most famous beach in all Croatia, the iconic **Zlatni Rat**, or Golden Cape, whose 500-metre-long (1,640-foot) finger of fine shingle sticks out into the sea like a natural pier. It is constantly in motion, its shape shifting with the tides. High waves and gentle winds make for superb swimming and windsurfing. This means that Bol is unbearably crowded in high season – but just about perfect in the shoulder months.

Supetar, the main port, is an attractive resort in its own right, with sand and pebble beaches as well as decent bars and restaurants. Large hotels were thrown up in the 1970s.

The rest of Brač – 40km (25 miles) long, 15km (9.5 miles) wide – is karst rock, but not just any old karst rock. This supple white stone, used over the centuries by Croatia's finest sculptors, built Split and Dubrovnik (although not the White House, as is commonly claimed). You can see local examples in the cemetery near Supetar, filled with tombs of Byzantine and art nouveau fancy created by local fin-de-siècle sculptor Ivan Rendić. It was one of his contemporaries, Toma Rosandić, who designed the beautiful **Petrinović Mausoleum**, the most impressive monument here. Another easy excursion from Supetar is to the ancient hilltop settlement of Skrip, where the **Museum of Brač** (021 630 033, generally 10am-6pm daily) in the **Radojković Tower** contains a Roman relief and various artefacts depicting the agricultural livelihood on the island – once verdant with vineyards and olive groves. It's a nice longish downhill stroll back to the sea at Splitska down the coast from Supetar.

Supetar is the setting-off point for the handful of buses a day to other spots on the island: the old fishing village of **Milna** and the quieter beaches around it, and Bol, with Zlatni Rat beach and other attractions nearby. The most noteworthy of these is the dramatic clifftop **Blaca Hermitage**, some three hours' walk (021 630 033; ask about excursions in Bol), with a wonderfully obscure collection of astronomical instruments, clocks and an atlas from 1623. On the way you pass **Murvica**, set below the Dragon's Cave, covered with old pagan paintings of wild beasts carved in the 15th century – ask at the Bol tourist office for the arbitrary opening times. East of Bol, at Glavica, stand the **Dominican church and monastery** (021 778 000, open May-June, Sept 10am-noon, 5-7pm daily, July, Aug 10am-noon, 5-9pm daily, 10kn), whose museum contains prehistoric finds, Greek coins and Tintoretto's *Madonna with Child*.

The most obvious option for a day out from Bol is the mountain standing right behind it: **Vidova Gora**. At 778 metres (2,552 feet), this is the highest point in the islands and offers the most stupendous view of Brač spread out before it. Allow two hours for the walk from the baroque **Church of Our Lady of Carmel** in the centre of Bol – and there's the Vladimir Nazor tavern (021 549 061, 098 225 999 mobile) at the top.

Beaches

Zlatni Rat is the reason why many visit Brač – and certainly why they visit Bol. The Golden Cape is the money shot in every tourist brochure. Walk west from the harbour where buses and ferries drop you off, until you reach Put Zlatnog Rata, the promenade, a shaded walkway through a pine forest that follows a rise above the beach. The resort hotels are uphill

from the promenade, among the pines, and the coast is below. The first big swimming area you come to is **Potočine beach**, about a kilometre (half a mile) outside town. This pretty cove with small, roundish pebbles draws windsurfers and sunbathers and is packed in high season. Further on is the Zlatni Rat, altogether some 30 minutes from Bol, sticking out into the sea. This peninsula has a bigger, more entertaining surf than many other beaches in Croatia, especially on the westward side, where the waves come from the open Adriatic. Zlatni Rat will be covered with bathers all summer and the atmosphere is jovial. The water is shallow and the seabed relatively smooth – ideal for kids. If you want more privacy, continue west. The first area you pass is the nudist beach of **Paklina**. Beyond this, the coast gets rockier and you'll need to swim with sandals. Further is a secluded location with few other bathers. There is also a small cove with a beach of sand and small pebbles a short walk east of the harbour, right before the Dominican monastery. This is close to town and can fill with bathers at times.

If you're staying in Supetar, just west of the harbour, still in the middle of town, is a sizeable child-friendly fine-pebble beach that draws scores of bathers from the nearby resorts. If you follow the beachside path west, past the park on a small peninsula, you find more smooth pebbly beaches. If you don't mind a rocky coast, put on a pair of swimming sandals and continue west for another couple of kilometres, along a tall stone fence. Here you'll find isolated spots where you can sunbathe on flat rocks and swim, right next to an aromatic pine forest.

The nearest sandy beach – the only one on Brač – is at **Lovrecina**, 10km (six miles) east of Supetar. Again, don't expect privacy in high season. To escape the crowds, the rocky beaches at **Sutivan** on the north coast and near Milna on the west are generally quiet. **Milna** has a smooth pebbly beach near town too.

Excursions

If you get off the beaten tourist path on Brač, using a rented boat or motor scooter, you'll find paths along the sea leading to isolated rocky beaches that you can call your own for an afternoon. All the towns on the island are accessible by bus from Supetar. Travel agencies arrange a variety of day trips.

Thanks to its location, Brač is a major windsurfing and kite-surfing centre. Between the end of May and the beginning of August, through the afternoon, a strong Maestral wind comes in from the west to create ideal conditions for the sport. Clubs line up along Bol beach, including **Big Blue Sport** near Hotel Borak

(Podan Glavice 2, 021 635 614, 098 497 080 mobile, www.big-blue-sport.hr), dealing in windsurfing and sea kayaking, and the main kite-surfing centre, **Yellow Cat** (098 288 581 mobile, www.zutimacak.hr/kite) near Zlatni Rat. Both have lessons for beginners.

Diving is another speciality. Big Blue Sport (*see above*) offers diving at all levels, including scuba for beginners. **Orca Sport** (021 740 625, www.orca-sport.com) on Potočine beach, is another windsurfing and diving centre. The best area is between Bol and Milna on the south-east corner of the island.

For a week in mid July, **Sutivan** on the north coast attracts a young crowd for its **Extreme Sports Festival** (www.vankaregule.com).

Where to eat

It almost never rains in summer on Brač – al fresco is the way to dine. Seafood is ubiquitous but almost everywhere serves pork, steaks and Balkan favourites *pljeskavica* and *ćevapčići*. Bol and Supetar both have great places in the harbour – walk a little way east in Bol and you can also find a romantic spot near an old monastery with scenic gardens.

Borak

Put Zlatnog Rata, Bol (021 306 223). **Open** *Summer* 11am-2am daily. **No credit cards**.
The Borak Hotel's beachside terrace is one of the nicer places on the promenade, under shade on a small, busy cove beach. The seafood is great – with scallops and mussels not found everywhere here – and the prices only a little higher than in the harbour. Follow the signs for a stairway from the promenade to Plaža Borak, a swimming spot where Potočine Beach begins, across from the Hotel Riu Borak.

Jastog

Bana Josipa Jelačića 7, Supetar (021 631 486). **Open** *Summer* noon-1am daily. **No credit cards**.
One of the more elegant and expensive places in Supetar, just up the hill from the harbour. If money's no object, Jastog is probably the best choice for a sumptuous langouste lobster dinner or well-prepared shellfish. 'The Lobster' is also known for its lamb and veal *ispod peke*, country-style with hot coals, its homemade ice creams, cakes and traditional herb liqueurs. Fine local wines and impeccable service.

Konoba Mlin

Ante Starčevića 11, Bol (021 635 376). **Open** *Summer* 5pm-midnight daily. **No credit cards**.
This romantic old mill, east of the main harbour, has a secluded, tree-shaded terrace above the sea. Fabulous sea fish sizzle on an outdoor grill while the menu offers interesting Dalmatian specialities such as 'octopus under glass'. Good meat dishes, too, and appetisers include thinly sliced Dalmatian ham. Decent selection of Croatian wines.

Punta

Punta 1, Supetar (021 631 507). **Open** *Summer* 8am-2am daily. **No credit cards**.
This big house, more secluded than the terraces on the busy harbour, has plentiful scenic, outdoor seating right on the beach. You can watch windsurfers cavort while choosing from a classic *konoba*-style menu with a wider-than-average range of fresh fish, including John Dory and grouper. Meat lovers can try the good assortment of Balkan-style ground lamb dishes and steaks, like the châteaubriand for two at 150kn. All prices are reasonable, in fact. Vegetarian options among the pizzas.

Ribarska kućica

Ante Starčevića, Bol (021 635 033/098 423 003 mobile). **Open** *Summer* 9am-1am daily. **No credit cards**.
Slightly more expensive this, but worth every lipa. A beautiful old structure on a rocky seaside walkway just out of the town's centre offers views of Bol's hilltop monastery, a secluded cove beach and the Adriatic. Each floor of the multi-layered terrace has tables and the interior is luxuriously appointed. The seafood here is fresh, including more unusual offerings such as tuna, and if you're only going to have one langouste lobster on Brač, it should be here. There is also a surprisingly adventurous selection of sauces and side dishes and a comprehensive list of quality local wines. Book ahead. Recommended.

Vinotoka

Jobova 6, Supetar (021 630 969/098 207 447 mobile). **Open** *Summer* 11am-1am daily. *Winter* 11am-11 pm daily. **No credit cards**.
Listed among the top 40 Adriatic restaurants by local nautical magazine *More*, this tranquil old house in a steep street offers excellent authentic Dalmatian food, primarily from the sea. The family has a fishing boat and produces its own olive oil. Specialities include scallop with gorgonzola. Locals swear by it, although the traditional Dalmatian choir (*klapa*) may put some people off.

Where to drink

In Supetar, **Put Vele Luke**, the small street that starts near the town's beach, is the main drag for drinking and nightlife. Bar staff on Brač don't like to interrupt a good party so places often open past the stated closing time. Most close in winter or open for much shorter hours. In Bol, the action is down by the harbour.

Caffè Bar Loža

Porat bolskih Pomoraca, Bol (021 635 877). **Open** *Summer* 7am-1am Mon-Thur, Sun; 7am-2am Fri, Sat.
Sit under the old stone arches of this friendly café, built into the back wall of the harbour, or find a seat beneath a big umbrella. It's the perfect spot to hide from the sun and watch the downtown crowds. There's also ice cream, and home-made doughnuts make a fine breakfast with the excellent coffee.

Zlatni Rat – the Golden Cape, Croatia's most famous beach. *See p229.*

Caffè Bar Marina

Porat, Supetar (021 630 557). **Open** *Summer* 7am-
1am daily. *Winter* 8am-10pm daily.
The Marina has a small terrace on the harbour and
a large, elegant-looking bar indoors. After dining, a
lively crowd of fun seekers comes here for a quality
cocktail or a shot of local grappa. Decent jazz and
pop tunes on the speakers, lively staff and warm
locals give the place a homely feel. In winter, menfolk gather round the bleeping gambling machines
and moan on about football, women and politics.

Caffè Bar Monaco

Put Vele Luke, Supetar (021 630 082). **Open**
Summer 10am-2am Mon-Thur, Sun; 10am-3am Fri-
Sat. *Winter* 10am-11pm daily.
The happy young crowd helps this bar along, its
subdued reddish lighting and touches of neon
pulling you in on the busy strip. Fast-paced techno
and hip hop keep people dancing on the semi-
enclosed terrace. Cocktails are generous and the
young staff are charming, if sometimes lost. You'll
find it near the corner of 1. Svibnja.

Cocktail Bar Bolero

Put Zlatnog Rata, Bol (no phone). **Open** *Summer*
9am-1am daily.
At a scenic high point on the promenade, plush
cushioned wicker chairs and sofas tempt you to
take a seat in this pine-shaded terrace cocktail bar
and admire the view of windsurfers in the cove and
Hvar beyond. The bar gets a good crowd by late
afternoon, and stays lively into the evening. It is
the perfect spot for that post-dip Tequila Sunrise
at sunset.

Pivnica Moby Dick

Loža 13, Bol (021 635 281). **Open** *Summer* 9am-
2am daily.
A relaxing terrace with a sea view over the harbour
affords the chance to gawp at waterside crowds and
Hvar island to the south. Many of the regulars here
are locals – it could well be the DJ sounds later on –
so foreigners coming here don't feel deep in tourist
central. Moby Dick is always a good bet for late
nights – it's generally one of the last places to stay
open near the harbour.

Brač.

Nightlife

The main club is **Faces**, owned by football star Igor Štimac, at the northern end of Bol. The bar strip **Put Vele Luke** in Supetar can go late on and offer dancing in various spots.

Faces Club Kaltemberg

Bračke ceste, Bol (021 635 410). **Open** *Summer* 9pm-late daily.
The only club to draw top international names – its posters are all over Split. Take the main road out of town and climb the steep hill till a clearing with a great view over the sea. Arches prop up a sophisticated array of moving lights over an open-air dancefloor in a 2,000-capacity mainstream club. A young crowd goes until the sunrise over Hvar down below.

XXL

Put Vele Luke, Supetar (021 630 699/091 729 6594 mobile). **Open** 10am-2am Mon-Thur, Sun; 10am-5am Fri-Sat.
Go downstairs to enter this large dark bar with a dancefloor. Foreign and talented local DJs attract a young, energetic set who come here to seriously shake it. It's hard to get away from the beat for a quiet chat, but if you don't mind shouting, the bar is friendly enough. The same management runs Space Fun, a cocktail fiesta joint on the beach.

Where to stay

Aside from the large, upscale resort complex by Supetar beach, there are affordable pensions, low-frills hotels and ample private rooms, offered by locals meeting the ferry from Split.

For Bol, the wooded area on the promenade to Zlatni Rat (www.zlatni-rat.hr) is the best spot in town, dominated by larger resort complexes. They have a whole range of activities: archery, children's play clubs, saunas, gyms, a tennis centre and any number of equipment rentals; holiday packages are available. The fanciest is the Riu Borak (021 306 202, €85-€120 single, €130-€200 double). The Elaphusa (021 306 200, €75-€110 single, €55-€200 double) does not have air-conditioning in every room, though Bol's breezes do keep evenings cool. The Riu Bonaca (021 306 269, €60-€100 single with meals, €120-€200 double with meals) is more child-oriented.

More affordable and less uniform accommodation is available a short walk away. With the number of rooms and apartments to let, you can almost certainly drop into Bol on spec, even in high season, and find somewhere.

For Milna, the Illyrian Resort complex (021 636 533, www.illyrian-resort.hr) and two-star Hotel M (021 636 116, www.hotelm.com) suffice.

Hotel Kaštil

Frane Radića 1, Bol (021 635 995/fax 021 635 997/ www.kastil.hr). **Rates** €44-€96 single; €64-€140 double. **Credit** AmEx, DC, MC, V.
Thirty-two renovated rooms (including four triple) are set inside a pretty old stone building with its back right on the harbour, in the heart of town. It also contains the pizzeria Vusio and Varadero cocktail bar. Once you're out, you can go straight from your last drinks on the waterside to your bed. Many rooms have a sea view but are above the terrace restaurant and busy harbour so noise might be an issue.

Pansion Palute

Put Pašika 16, Supetar (021 631 541). **Rates** €22-€25 single; €38-€44 double. **No credit cards**.
A comfortable, affordable, family-run pension with a loyal following. Breakfast on the veranda is extra but reasonable – there are half-board packages, too, in the recommended restaurant – and all the rooms have their own shower. Open all year.

Villa Giardino

Novi put 2, Bol (021 635 286). **Rates** €75 single; €87 double. **No credit cards**.
This must just be the best hotel deal on Brač. It's a family-run establishment, located in a beautiful old villa with 14 rooms, and it's usually booked in high season – but if you manage to snag one and you'll feel like you're a guest in someone's mansion. Though the building is old, the interior is comfortable and nicely renovated, with antiques furnishing many of the rooms. Breakfast is served on the front terrace and dinner can be enjoyed in a beautiful garden at the back – although this is not a full-time restaurant. A friendly, efficient and unobtrusive service draws rave reviews in the visitors' book.

Waterman Resort

Put Vele Luke 4, Supetar (021 640 155/www.water manresorts.com). **Rates** €23-€90 single; €46-€138 double. **Credit** AmEx, DC, MC, V.
This package-tourist complex composed of several hotels under the same management takes up a chunk of space near the main beaches right in the heart of town. The shared facilities at Waterman Resort include a spa and sports centre. There are three restaurants, too. It has easy access to the town beaches and offers equipment rental.

Resources

Internet

M@3X *Rudina 6, Bol (no phone).* **Open** *Summer* 8am-8pm daily.
Ideally situated by the harbour.

Midea Rental Services *Put Vele Luke 15, Supetar (098 175 2249 mobile).* **Open** *Summer* 8am-8pm daily.
Internet, plus scooter, bike and boat rental.

Tourist information

Adria-Tours Bol *Vladimira Nazora 28, Bol (021 635 966/www.adria-bol.hr).* **Open** *Summer* 8am-9pm daily.
Accommodation booked from hotels to private rooms, diving, scooter and boat rental. Currency exchange too.

Atlas Supetar *Porat 10, Supetar (021 631 105/www.atlas-croatia.com).* **Open** *Summer* 8am-10pm daily.
Accommodation, excursions plus equipment rental and currency exchange.

Bol Tourist Office *Porat bolskih Pomoraca (021 635 638/www.bol.hr).* **Open** *June-Aug* 8.30am-10pm daily. *Sept-May* 8.30am-3pm Mon-Fri.
In an old building by the port, this has details of excursions to the nearby attractions of the Dragon's Cave and Blaca Hermitage.

Supetar Tourist Office *Porat 1 (021 630 551/www.supetar.hr).* **Open** *June-Sept* 8am-10pm daily. *May, Oct* 8am-4pm Mon-Sat. *Nov-Apr* 8am-4pm Mon-Fri.
Right by the ferry port, this office is laden with brochures and excursion information.

Getting there & around

Brač is one of the few Adriatic islands to have its own **airport** (021 631 370, 021 648 615, www.airport-brac.hr), 15km (9.5 miles) north-east of Bol. Nearly all traffic comes from charter flights or from Zagreb – in summer you can find a Croatia Airlines (www.croatiaairlines.hr) flight for as little as €55. A minibus meets arrivals and takes passengers (25kn) to Bol. For Supetar, a taxi (098 264 741 mobile, 098 781 377 mobile) costs 150kn-200kn.

Supetar is the gateway to Brač. Jadrolinija (021 631 357, www.jadrolinija.hr) sends a dozen ferries a day from Split (25kn, 1hr). A car costs about 200kn. From Supetar buses (021 631 122) run to most other destinations on Brač – in summer there are five a day to Bol or Milna. The bus station is located just east of the ferry port.

In summer Jadrolinija runs a catamaran (85kn, 50mins) from Split to Bol once a day. It links Bol with Jelsa on Hvar (20mins). SEM Marina (021 325 533, www.sem-marina.hr)

runs a catamaran from Split to Milna, and then on to Bol – price about 85kn. Two ferries a day (about 25kn, 30mins) shuttle between Makarska on the mainland and Sumartin on the far east cape of Brač. Two buses a day run from Sumartin to Supetar – but not connecting with the afternoon ferry.

Hvar

Hvar is the closest Croatia comes to Cannes – at least as far as its namesake capital is concerned. In fact, a cut-price Cannes wouldn't be a bad analogy, although Hvar won't be cut-price for much longer. Luxembourg-based

property group Orco is developing all the hotels in the Sunčani Hvar monopoly in town – cheap(ish) two-star stays will be at a premium by 2007.

By then a prominent UK businessman will have his high-end lifestyle hotel up and running, complementing his already landmark Vertigo club, and Brighton's renowned boutique hotel Blanch House will have opened its first branch – all right here on Hvar.

Everyone wants a piece of the action in the sunniest and most happening of the Adriatic islands. Its hub is **Hvar town** harbour. In high season Roman Abramovich parks his yacht, film stars get the best tables on the VIP

Cool clubs Carpe Diem, Hvar

Where the yachts docks at Hvar town harbour, **Carpe Diem** (see p239) is a landmark. Behind a loggia façade, it's surprisingly – and pleasingly – ordinary inside, with just higher-than-ordinary prices and standard music for the genre. Its reputation stems from its VIP scene in high season, upon which Hvar hype is fuelled. Its reservation-only policy in August (put your name on the list as you pass by during the day) means that the terrace (and separate bar) operate as a celebrity zone. In 2005 Roman Abramovich ordered bottles of

the finest vodka, Gérard Depardieu demanded the cheapest house plonk. Opened in 1999, Carpe Diem carries its signature sun motif on its comprehensive cocktail menu. Ignore the bad philosophy – the bar staff wear bandanas, too – and dive into a Swimming Pool (55kn, pitcher 170kn) of vodka and coconut or fiery house Voodoo (68kn, pitcher 220kn). September is the best time here, no stars, just egalitarian shimmying à deux on the makeshift dance floor inside. The lease runs out in 2007 – expect changes thereafter.

terrace at waterside nightspot **Carpe Diem** (*see left*), and this pretty, petite Venetian capital of 3,000 locals overflows with 30,000 visitors every day. They swarm the attractive waterfront and adjoining main square, known as Pjaca, doing coffee, the nearby market and the modest selection of sights by morning, the beach by day and the bars by night.

The bright lights of Hvar town on the south-west tip overshadow the rest of the lavender-covered island, extending east in a thin strip for 60km (37 miles) as far as the isolated port of Sucuraj – but this, too, will change. British entrepreneur Neil Lewis, based near **Jelsa**, is putting the north coast on the map. Like the Austrian tourists who first holidayed on Hvar 150 years ago, Lewis loved the island and kept coming back. After successfully opening quality nightclub Vertigo in 2005, Lewis's next step is a bold one: stonehouse (*see p238*), a secluded mountain farm converted into a lifestyle hotel with appropriate leisure amenities, overlooking – but hidden from – Jelsa's pretty harbour. July 2006 is the launch date. Down below, a cocktail bar will be set up at the edge of an idyllic uninhabited island opposite – behind, a private plane can shuttle passengers to Split and thence London in two hours. Along the same north coast at Hvar's other hub of Stari Grad, Brighton-based boutique hotel and restaurant team Blanch House will open six chic rooms and a top-notch cocktail bar in 2007.

Between Hvar town and Jelsa, **Stari Grad** is the point of entry for car ferries from Split. It was here that Greeks from Paros settled in 385 BC and named it Pharos. The Croatian tribe who later congregated here bastardised the name as 'Hvar'. Invading Venetians then shifted the centre of power (and the name) to the west coast port of today's Hvar town. While the Venetians were building their capital, the island became the hub of a Croatian cultural renaissance.

Today the most prominent sight in Stari Grad is the summer retreat of 16th-century poet Petar Hektorović, the **Tvrdalj** (021 765 068, open summer 10am-1pm, 6-8pm daily, 10kn), known for its inscribed walls, gardens and fishpond. Nearby, a 15th-century **Dominican monastery** houses a museum (10am-noon, 6-8pm Mon-Fri, 10kn) containing other Hektorović artefacts, Greek gravestones and a Tintoretto, *The Mourning of Christ*, claimed to feature Hektorović himself. More Greek, Roman and maritime items are on display at the **Bianchini Palace** (021 765 910, summer 10am-noon, 7-9pm daily, 10kn) by the Tvrdalj.

Hektorović never saw his Tvrdalj finished. As a preliminary to the crucial naval Battle of Lepanto near Corfu in 1571, the Turks attacked Stari Grad, Jelsa and Hvar town. The capital you see today is the one rebuilt by the Venetians in the early 1600s. It is centrepieced by **Pjaca**, or Trg sv Stjepana, the rectangular main square lined with shops and restaurants, bookended by the harbour and **Arsenal** at one end, the market and **St Stephen's Cathedral** at the other. Constructed in late Renaissance style with an intricate Venetian belltower and baroque altars from the 17th century (plus one donated by the Hektorović family from 1220), the church also features a treasury (open summer 9am-noon, 5-7pm daily, winter 10am-noon daily, 10kn) containing a scattering of religious objects and two late Renaissance paintings. The most striking edifice left by the Venetians is the Arsenal. The beautiful arched doorways at street level accommodated ships in for repair; upstairs was one of Europe's first public theatres, opened in 1612. Today it is a tourist sight (021 741 009, open summer 9.30am-1pm, 5-9pm daily, 10kn) and also used as a contemporary art gallery.

Off the square run narrow, pedestrianised alleyways (traffic stops at the main car park by the market) providing shade by day, and café and restaurant activity by night. Above it stands the **Venetian Citadel** (Španjola, 021 742 620, open summer 8am-midnight daily, 10kn), with a display of Greek and Roman finds, and a stupendous view from the ramparts.

Below, beyond the harbour, are dotted the 11 nearby pine-covered **Pakleni Islands** (*see p237* **Palmižana: Back to nature**), uninhabited except for the regular cheap taxi boats from Hvar town all summer.

Beaches

Each of the main settlements has its own modest beach: Hvar town has one just down from the harbour near the Dalmacija hotel; Stari Grad has beaches lining each side of the bay, the southern one towards **Borić** less crowded; and Jelsa has child-friendly **Mina**. Other bathing areas nearby include **Grebišće**, approximately 1.5km (a mile) away, with the bar-restaurant Corni Petar to hand. Taxi boats run to the **Glavica** peninsula and the nudist beach on nearby **Zečevo** island.

Much of Hvar is indented with little coves – although you'll need transport to reach them. On the undeveloped south coast, **Zavala**, **Dubovica** and **Sveti Nedelja** are secluded spots and a relatively cheap taxi journey from any of the main three towns.

Most prefer to take the boat taxi (about 15kn, 30 mins) to the beaches of the Pakleni Islands, in particular the sandy one at Palmižana (*see p237* **Palmižana: Back to nature**), base of the Meneghello family. Such is the reverence in which the Meneghellos' idyll is held – culture centre, self-catering apartments and restaurant all in one – that Palmižana is considered a separate island. It's on the north-east coast of the main island (Veliki Otok) or Sv Klement. Naturists gather at the nearest island to Hvar town, **Jerolim**, and **Stipanska** on neighbouring Marinkovac.

Excursions

To explore this lovely, lavender-scented island dotted with secluded coves, you'll have to hire a car, bike or scooter. In Hvar town, contact **Navigare** on the main square (021 718 721, 098 727 070 mobile) or **Luka Rent** at the harbour (021 742 946, 091 591 7111 mobile).

Sailing is big news on Hvar. In Hvar town **Zvir** (Krizna Luka, 021 741 415, www.jkzvir.hr) is a renowned sailing club. Marinas include the **Adriatic Croatia International Vrboska** (021 774 018, m.vrboska@aci-club.hr) and the **ACI Marina** in Palmižana (021 744 995, m.palmizana@aci-club.hr).

Diving is best organised at the **Diving Center Jurgovan** (021 742 490, 098 321 229 mobile, www.divecenter-hvar.com) by the Hotel Amfora, a short walk around the harbour away from the action. Between Jurgovan and the harbour is the Hotel Adriatic, base for the **Diving Center** (098 440 353 mobile, www. diving-hvar.com), which organises diving courses and all-in packages taking place at Soline beach in Vrboska.

The north coast between Jelsa, Vrboska and Stari Grad is ideally suited to cycling.

Where to eat

In Hvar town terrace restaurants line the waterfront, the main square and immediately above it Petra Hektorovića, an alleyway usually referred to as **Groda** after the locality. Here everyone raves about **Macondo**, but **Luna** might be a more enjoyable experience. Stari Grad and Jelsa also contain a couple of key places listed below. If you have transport, head out for **Humac**, a memorable experience.

Dominko

Jelsa (021 761 933). **Open** *Summer* 6pm-midnight daily. **No credit cards**.
Located in the back of the old town up a leafy (and nameless) incline – but signposted from the harbour and announced by its name in white paint on an overhead plank – this friendly local *konoba* features a fabulous terrace for summer dining. Host Martin prides himself on *peka* specialities, producing succulent meats and lobster from under the traditional coal-covered bell-shaped metal lid. Try and warn him of group visits in advance.

Eremitaž

Priko, Stari Grad (021 765 056/091 542 8395 mobile). **Open** *Mid Apr-mid Oct* noon-3pm, 7pm-midnight daily. **Credit** AmEx, DC, MC, V.
This 15th-century sea-view stone house between the harbour and the tourist hotels offers well-made, reasonably priced Dalmatian standards on a pretty, shaded front terrace. The building used to house sick sailors in quarantine.

Humac

091 523 9463 mobile. **Open** *Summer* noon-10pm daily. **No credit cards**.
In an abandoned village of the same name surrounded by lavender fields some 8km (5 miles) east of Jelsa signposted on the bumpy main road to Sućuraj, this traditional *konoba* serves all the classic Dalmatian specialities by candlelight on an open flame. This is no gimmick – as well as no inhabitants, Humac has no electricity. A memorable treat.

Jurin Podrum

Donja kola, Stari Grad (021 765 804). **Open** *Summer* noon-2.30pm, 7pm-midnight daily. **Credit** AmEx, DC, MC, V.
Set in the tangle of streets in the old town – some sources give the address as Srinja kola – this is a fine local eaterie to suit all budgets. Brighton foody owners of Blanch House, due to set up next door in 2007, were so taken with the cuisine here they decided not to bother with their own. All the usual shellfish in sauces with handy diversions such as octopus and courgette spaghetti.

Luna

Petra Hektorovića, Groda, Hvar town (021 741 400/ 098 748 695 mobile). **Open** *Apr-Dec* noon-3pm, 6pm-midnight daily. **Credit** AmEx, DC, V.
Possibly the best dining experience in Hvar town, partly thanks to the starlit roof terrace (accessed via the 'stairway to heaven') and partly thanks to an adventurous and well-priced menu. Starters include marinated aubergine (25kn) and shrimp gazpacho (30kn); mains sea bass in caper sauce (90kn), lobster in tomato, white wine and brandy sauce (460kn/kg) and afters livanjski cheese (30kn) alongside the usual paški variety. Tomas and the buzzy staff in neat blue uniforms provide patter and a tasty gratis pâté starter with warm toast. Recommended.

Macondo

Petra Hektorovića, Groda, Hvar town (021 742 850). **Open** *Apr-Oct* noon-2pm, 6.30pm-midnight Mon-Sat; 6.30pm-midnight Sun. **Credit** AmEx, DC, MC, V.
The starched white tablecloths of the most renowned table in town fill the harbour end of this Groda alleyway. You'll be lucky to snag a terrace spot in high season unless you reserve but the interior is homely enough – a fireplace and modern art on display. Seafood is the big draw here, either standards such as scampi *buzara* or curiosities like lobster risotto. The grilled fish, though pricy, is generally excellent. Regulars swear by it, but first-time visitors have not always had a good experience.

Palmižana: Back to nature

When locals in Hvar town say they are going to the beach, they don't mean the modest spots by the harbour. They take a quick taxi boat to the Pakleni Islands, to relax, naked if they feel like it, amid the smell of fragrant pines, uninhibited in uninhabited nature. Facilities are equally bare, with one stellar exception: **Palmižana**.

Set in a natural harbour on the north-east coast of the main island of Veliki Otok (also known as Sv Klement), Palmižana flourished thanks to botanist Eugen Meneghello, who created a unique garden of rare, exotic species here. His son Giorgio-Toto, and his wife Dagmar, then built a holiday complex

around it, now run by their three children: the Pansion Meneghello. Offering culture, gastronomy and idyllic relaxation rolled into one, the **Pansion Meneghello** (021 717 270, 091 478 3110 mobile, fax 021 717 268, www.palmizana.hr) hires out its dozen comfortable stone bungalows by the week from Saturday to Saturday, April to October. Prices are set at about 250kn per night per person, with Dagmar Meneghello's superb cuisine 150kn per meal. Art workshops, courses in diving, fishing, sailing, as well as sandy beaches and classical concerts, it's all here. And the nightlife of Hvar town is only a taxi boat away. Book well in advance.

Nono
Banski dolac, Jelsa (021 761 901). **Open** *Mid Apr-mid Oct* 6pm-midnight daily. **No credit cards.**
Behind the church from the main square, this family-owned terrace restaurant is a great find. Evo greets everyone with enthusiasm, recommends the freshest fish and tries to get Nono's superb steaks to the table as quickly as possible – even when Italians swamp the place in summer. Best selection of wines in town.

Paradise Garden
Petra Hektorovića, Groda, Hvar town (021 741 310). **Open** *Summer* noon-2.30pm, 6.30pm-midnight Mon-Sat. **Credit** AmEx, DC, MC, V.
Lovely, secluded location this, at the church end of Groda, a pretty contained terrace garden serviced by lively, friendly staff. Few surprises on the menu – langoustines, pastas with fruits de mer – but it's no less enjoyable for all that. Book in high season.

Zlatna Školjka
Petra Hektorovića, Groda, Hvar town (098 168 8797 mobile). **Open** *Summer* noon-3pm, 7pm-midnight daily. **No credit cards.**

Billing itself as a slow food restaurant, the Golden Shell, on the corner of Hektorovića and the first street to the right of the main square from the church, does a number of welcome inventive dishes along with Dalmatian standards. Varieties of lamb stew are a house speciality as well as cheeses in olive oils, partaken on a simple shaded terrace with unpretentious checked tablecloths. Not cheap, all the same.

Where to drink

The landmark **Carpe Diem** in Hvar town harbour, although open during the day, is considered more club than bar (*see p234*). Other Hvar bar life is set around the harbour and main square – don't miss **Zimmer Frei** or the **Kiva Bar**.

In Stari Grad, you probably won't do better than Antika (021 765 479), a little multi-storeyed bar-restaurant set in a nameless side street in the old town. Staff look like they know what to do with a cocktail. Nice snacks too.

Jelsa is coming up, partly thanks to the 2005 success of newly opened club **Vertigo** (*see p241*). **Tarentela**, **Dgigibaoo** and **Libido** have come into their own as key pre-club venues – and early-opening café Hit on Jelsa harbour is essential for that post-session breakfast.

Batuda
Burak 66, Hvar town (no phone). **Open** *Summer* 10am-midnight daily. **No credit cards.**
Tucked away immediately above the Riva, this is an odd little place frequented by young, off-scene locals – but somehow it's nice to plonk yourself on one of the bright cushions in this steep cobblestone street and not feel you have to be in the centre of things. Standard drinks at cheap(ish) prices.

Caffè Bar Atelier
Trg sv Stjepana 4, Hvar town (no phone). **Open** *Summer* 8am-11pm daily.
One of several bars lining the main square – the Loco isn't bad either – the Atelier can mix a reasonable, strong Tequila Sunrise for 50kn, plus the usual range of Caipirinha, Caipiroska and Caipirissima. Twenty kuna sambucca shots make excellent preparation for a night on the hoy at the Carpe Diem.

Dgigibaoo
Jelsa waterfront (no phone/www.dgigibaoo.com). **Open** *Summer* noon-3am daily.
Located by Libido (*see right*), where the beach meets the eastern edge of the harbour, this is a cool terrace for cocktails by day and a vibrant music bar by night. Once the action moves from idyllic sunset to

Hot hotels
stonehouse, Hvar

The stonehouse is ambitious in the extreme. The brainchild of UK entrepreneur Neil Lewis, owner of the Vertigo club, the stonehouse (*see p242*) is a converted 200-year-old mountain farm, tucked away from the Bura wind on verdant headland high above Jelsa, secluded and self-contained. Planned and constructed over two years – including a transatlantic search for far-flung branches of the family who owned it – the stonehouse is due to open in July 2006.

Of the ten buildings, eight are stone-house bedrooms with Philippe Starck bathrooms and rain showers. The spacious communal area, backdropped by a pinch-yourself sea vista, comprises three terraces, an infinity pool, a

cocktail bar with guest shakers flown in from London, a sauna, jacuzzi, games room and a chapel for weddings. It has its own section of beach. After top-notch cocktails at sundown, a water taxi whisks guests to a Brazilian beach bar on a deserted island opposite.

Operating as a boutique hotel with courses in art and cookery for six months of the year, and a luxury retreat in July and August – when groups of 20 or so pay €30,000 for a week's exclusive use of the property with a chef and chauffeurs – the stonehouse will be the last word in lifestyle. Oh yes, it adjoins an airstrip, in case you might want a private plane shuttle to Split airport at €150 for three people. Luxury to London in three hours.

pitch black painted room, DJs rock the place with deep and funky house. Occasional live music, too, sometimes jazz. That bear-like guy is owner Nico, as friendly as can be.

Kavana Pjaca

Trg sv Stjepana, Hvar town (no phone). **Open** Summer 8am-11pm daily.

An expanse of wicker chairs occupies a right angle of flagstone at the harbour end of the main square, the perfect spot for a morning coffee and sweetcorn croissant, afternoon vanilla scoop with maraschino cherries, or post-beach Campari. There are local wines, too, and a selection of proper whiskies – including ten-year-old Talisker and the like. Part of the recently purchased Sunčani Hvar hotel group, so expect some renovation for 2006/07.

Kiva Bar

Fabrika, Hvar town (no phone). **Open** Summer 6pm-1am daily.

Viva la Kiva! When all around is wicker chairs and dainty cocktails – that means you, Nautika next door – the Kiva is an honest-to-goodness bar. It says so on the wall ('It's A Bar!') and is as good as its word, playing old hip hop faves and sundry dance and indie tunes in a loud, intimate, stone room. True, it also displays the lyrics to *Imagine*, a cheap toy guitar and peace signs, but with music this good and drinking this serious, they must be having us on. Set on the far quay near the Hotel Palace (*see p241*).

Libido

Jelsa waterfront (no phone). **Open** Summer noon-3am daily.

Another landmark bar where the beach meets the harbour, Libido is a first-floor terrace bar with jaw-dropping views, set above Gringo's pizzeria – Ivan ('Gringo') owns both. It's pretty trendy, but not so trendy that you can't dance to the clubby music or tune out over the seriously strong cocktails and gawp at all that ocean. Big screen for TV sports.

Tabu

Jelsa waterfront (no phone). **Open** Summer noon-3am daily.

At the harbour's far edge, away from Dgigbaao and Libido, this lounge bar is as chilled as it gets. A terrace of loungers and white linen seats extends right up to the yachts gently swaying with the sea and owner Davor's practised DJ rhythms. Late crowd.

Tarentela

Pjaca, Jelsa (no phone). **Open** Summer noon-3am daily.

On the main square, Jelsa's best bar comprises a modest interior and wide terrace where the action happens. Named after the funny snub-nosed lizard native to Hvar, Tarentela has generated a great gang of regulars over the last five years, a fine collection of CDs and buzzy staff – crazy Mario and the crew – overseen by progressive bar owner Dominic. Chilled by day, cool for cocktails at sundown and absolutely ideal pre-club.

Zimmer Frei

Groda, Hvar town (098 559 6182 mobile). **Open** 9pm-3am daily.

If Carpe Diem is the best club, then Zimmer Frei is the best bar in Hvar town, hands down. Look out for the white cushions spread on a narrow side street to the right of the main square from the church, a stark colour scheme adhered to within. It's all so wonderfully simple: the greaseproof paper lampshades over the bar, the clubby music, the up-for-it clientele. Jugo, who cut his teeth bartending in Germany, runs a tidy ship. The cocktails (40kn) are decent, the signature Zimmer Frei (50kn) of Bacardi, Malibu, grenadine and coconut juice a knockout. It has nice touches, too – the bar chairs come from Aloha, the first proper bar in Hvar town. Open all year round.

Nightlife

Hvar is party island. It attracted switched-on locals from the late 1980s onwards, but took off around 1999 when landmark venues such as **Carpe Diem** (*see p234*) and **Tarentela** (*see left*) started to happen. Even in those days, you might have come here, sunk a couple of cocktails at either and wondered what the fuss was all about. Today Hvar still has 3am closing times (5am for clubs), and the two stalwart nightclubs, **Veneranda** in Hvar town and Villa Verde in Jelsa, are pretty standard. Most post-bar partying still takes place on private yachts.

The bar scene, though, has changed. Venues such as **Libido**, **Tabu** and **Zimmer Frei** (*for all, see above*) have upped the ante. Carpe Diem now enjoys something close to Côte d'Azur status – although in actual fact it's really just a fun DJ and cocktail bar with a VIP reputation. And a new venue has brought real clubbing to Hvar. Opened in 2005, Brit-owned **Vertigo** in downtown Jelsa is beginning to shift the focus away from Carpe Diem and Hvar town harbour, and on to the north coast. Whatever next? Stringfellow's in Stari Grad?

Carpe Diem

Obala Oslobodenja, Hvar town (no phone, www.carpe-diem-hvar.com). **Open** June-Sept noon-3am daily.

Landmark cocktail-swigging hangout of celebs and the yachting fraternity. *See p234* **Cool clubs**.

Hula Hula Beach Bar

Majerovića, Hvar town (no phone). **Open** Summer noon-3am daily.

It might only look like a few sunshades and a bar, lapped by the sea, but the Hula Hula Beach Bar attracts in-the-know locals to this spot a short walk round the coast from the Hotel Amfora, on a reasonably isolated jut of coastland called Majerovića. It operates as a pre- and post-party joint but most of all attracts few tourists on the prowl for the scene. For now, anyway.

[stone house]

a place less ordinary... kamina kuca

holidays

courses

reunions

single-party stays

special interest groups

weddings

ozone pool and jacuzzi

inernational staff

private shoreline

secluded location

Hvar's best kept secret – the **Hula Hula Beach Bar**. *See p239.*

Veneranda

Hvar town (no phone). **Open** *Summer* 9pm-5am
daily.
Set in a hillside Venetian fortress behind the Hotel
Delfin east of Hvar town harbour, the Veneranda is
part culture centre, part open-air disco. The evening
kicks off with a film or a spoken-word performance,
and moves on to DJs, fire-eaters, dancers and so on.
Look out for flyers around town.

Vertigo

Off Pjaca, Jelsa (098 443 724 mobile). **Open** *June-
Sept* 8pm-5am Thur-Sat.
Opened in June 2005, Vertigo is cocktail and
lounge bar, plus cellar nightclub, all in one. Brit
owner Neil Lewis has brought London standards
to bear on his first serious enterprise on Hvar:
proper decor, proper cocktails, proper DJs – and
all at Croatian prices. Set in a small alley a short
walk from Jelsa harbour – walk across the main
square towards the church, turn right then right
again – Vertigo is free entry except for high season when a post-midnight nominal door price of
40kn is levied. Once inside, you can choose
between the garden cocktail bar – great mixing at
fair prices – and distinctive White Room of stark
hue, relaxed character and extensive global wine
list. Chill-out sundowner tracks and occasional
French jazz provide the musical backdrop. The
stone cellar club opens at midnight for dance
anthems, happy house and general party tomfoolery. Finish off with breakfast at harbour café Hit
or hit the 6.30am catamaran to Split.

Where to stay

The recent acquisition of the Sunčani Hvar
hotel conglomerate (www.suncanihvar.hr)
by the Orco property group will see all nine
venues upgraded in time. By the summer of
2006, the Slavija will be a four-star design hotel,
the Amfora a three- (and later four-) star leisure
one and the Adriatic a four-star spa venue. The
Dalmacija is still the best mid-range choice,
with easy access to the beach, and the **Palace**
has architectural character. Check the company
website for prices and availability. Arrivals at
Hvar harbour are bombarded with offers of
private rooms.

The hotel stock in Stari Grad, Jelsa and
Vrboska is to holiday standard. The four
package hotels in Stari Grad are in the Helios
group (021 765 555, www.stari-grad-faros.hr/
hoteli_en.htm) – the Arkada is the one three-
star. Austrian group Azalea (www.azalea-
hotels.com) operates four main ones there
– of them, the **Mina** is the most preferable.

Boutique hotels will soon be an option:
stonehouse (*see p238* **Hot hotels**) near Jelsa
in 2006 and one to be run by Blanch House
(www.blanchhouse.co.uk) in Stari Grad by 2007.

Hotel Palace

*Trg sv Stjepana, Hvar town (021 741 966/fax 021
742 420/www.suncanihvar.hr).* **Rates** €55-€80
single; €75-€140 double. **Credit** AmEx, DC, MC, V.

The most characterful of the Sunčani Hvar chain, the Palace occupies part of a Venetian loggia, hence the lovely façade facing the harbour. Inside you'll find an indoor pool with warm seawater, a gym, sauna and massage treatments. The standard rooms are adequate and a snip out of high season – although rates for the sea-view suites are heftier than you would expect in a three-star.

Hotel Podstine

Pod Stine, Hvar town (021 740 400/fax 021 740 499/www.podstine.com). Closed Nov-Feb. **Rates** *Mar-Oct* €60-€160 double. **Credit** AmEx, DC, MC, V.
Not tied to the Suncani Hvar chain, the family-run Podstine is tucked away by its own beach a 15-minute walk down the coast from Hvar town harbour. Prices for sea-view rooms increase €20 with each of the four seasons from 1 May to 31 October, but you're also getting a lovely terrace restaurant, tennis courts and any number of rental and excursion options, including the hotel's own yacht. The buffet breakfast is included.

Mina

Jelsa (021 761 024/www.azalea-hotels.com). **Closed** Nov-late Mar. **Rates** *late Mar-Oct* €47-€119 double. **Credit** AmEx, DC, MC, V.
The best of the Azalea hotel quartet in the same area, the Mina is a well-equipped three-star. It boasts indoor and outdoor pools, an exercise room and a children's club. All 206 rooms have balconies, most with a sea view. Beaches are a hop away. The Mina insists on a minimum four nights' stay for high summer, but quotes nightly rates at other times. Give them a call. Details on the other three venues are on the website.

Pansion Murvica

Jelsa (021 761 405). **Rates** 525kn-600kn double. **No credit cards**.
Set behind the bus station, and signposted on the right as you enter town, this comfortable family-run pension consists of three studios (all with a kitchenette) and a double room. There's not much of a view but if you prefer character to package hotels, choose the Murvica.

Pension Laguna Ložna

098 962 0489 mobile/091 151 1202 mobile/ www.lozna.ws. **Rates** *Rooms* €32-€40; *apartments* €60-€100. **No credit cards**.
If you want seclusion with Hvar town's nightlife on your doorstep, the Ložna on the north coast is ideal. Set with its own beach 6km (3.5 miles) from town, the Laguna has standard rooms, three- and four-bed terrace apartments, and a restaurant for the half-board deal at an extra €17 a day. Breakfast is €7.

stonehouse

Mudri Dolac, Vrbanj (098 443 724 mobile/www. stonehousehvar.com). **Closed** Dec-Mar. **Rates** *Apr-June, Sept-Nov half-board per room* €300. *July-Aug 7-night full hire* €30,000. **Credit** AmEx, DC, MC, V.
Ambitious boutique hotel due to be opened in July 2006. *See p238* **Hot hotels**.

Resources

Information

Hvar Tourist Office *Trg sv Stjepana (021 741 059/www.hvar.hr).* **Open** *July, Aug* 8am-2pm, 3.30-9pm Mon-Sat; 8am-1pm, 4-9pm Sun. *June, Sept* 8am-1pm, 4-7pm Mon-Fri; 8am-noon, 4-7pm Sat; 9am-noon Sun. *Oct-May* 8am-1pm Mon-Sat.
This modest bureau on the harbourside corner of the main square is overrun in summer but copes as best as it can with details of accommodation, tourist sights and excursions.

Jelsa Tourist Office *Mala Banda (021 761 017/www.tzjelsa.hr).* **Open** *Summer* 8am-9pm Mon-Sat; 10am-noon, 7.30-9pm Sun. *Winter* 8am-12.30pm Mon-Fri.
Set by the harbour, this should be your first point of call for local information.

Stari Grad Tourist Office *Nova Riva 2 (021 765 763/www.stari-grad-faros.hr).* **Open** *Summer* 8am-2pm, 4-10pm Mon-Sat; 9am-noon, 5-8pm Sun. *Winter* 8am-noon Mon-Sat.
Located near the harbour in the town centre, some 3km (2 miles) from the ferry terminal.

Internet

CIMA *Novo Ribo, Stari Grad (021 717 242/www. cimahvar.hr).* **Open** *Summer* 10am-2pm, 5.30pm-midnight daily.
The Centre for Youth Initiatives is in a grand building by the marina – inside you'll find six computers. Similar projects are set for Hvar town, Jelsa and Vrboska.

Leon *Trg sv Stjepana, Hvar town (021 741 824).* **Open** *Summer* 9am-midnight daily.
Just behind the landmark Kavana Pjaca facing the marina, this is a handy little place to check your mail.

Getting there & around

As traffic is barred from the centre of Hvar town, car ferries arrive at Stari Grad, 16km (ten miles) to the east. The quickest way to get to Hvar town from **Split** is by Jadrolinija hydrofoil (May-Sept, 50mins journey time, 30kn). It leaves in the late morning from the Split Riva and turns around soon afterwards. The main daily Jadrolinija car ferry from Split to Vela Luka at the far western tip of Korčula and Lastovo also calls at Hvar town but only foot passengers are allowed to disembark.

Between three and five ferries a day operate from the main harbour in Split to Stari Grad (1hr 45mins journey time, 25kn foot passengers, 220kn car). Ferries running on the main coastal line down from **Rijeka** or up from **Dubrovnik** also call at Stari Grad.

International services from **Ancona**, **Bari** and **Pescara** on the Italian coast also call at Stari Grad, operated by the three companies of Jadrolinija, SEM Marina and SNAV.

Jelsa is accessible from Bol on Brač by Jadrolinija catamaran (45mins, about 30kn) in summer. On Hvar's far eastern tip, Sućuraj is linked by regular ferry to the mainland at Drvenik on the Makarska Riviera (40min, 30kn).

Hvar island is poorly served by local **buses**. Incoming ferries are met by a bus at Stari Grad harbour – but it doesn't always work the other way round. About three buses a day head from Hvar town (*trajekt* on timetables) and Stari Grad town (30mins, 15kn-20kn), with a couple more on summer weekends. A taxi between Hvar town and Stari Grad costs between 150kn and 200kn. Agree a price with **Tihi Taxis** (021 741 888, 021 742 902, 098 338 824 mobile) beforehand.

From Stari Grad harbour to Stari Grad town, the bus (6kn) covers the 3km (2-mile) journey before calling at or linking with Vrboska and Jelsa. Sućuraj is practically isolated as far as local buses are concerned.

Makarska Riviera

Riding south on the main coastal road from Split to Dubrovnik, just past Omiš a big blue sign announces: 'Makarska Riviera'. Thus begins the 60km (37-mile) stretch of (mainly) purpose-built hotels with the nightlife hub of Makarska town in the middle. Few historic monuments survived the Turkish occupation of the 1500s or the earthquake of 1962, a decade after which a decision was taken to turn this section of the coast – some of it quite pretty, with palm-fringed pebble beaches – over to package tourism. This generally either takes the form of bland, white hotel blocks or campsites full of Czechs amazed to find the same prices here year after year. A number of hotels have been improved to four-star standard – the Makarska coast can make for a cut-price shoulder-season break within easy reach of Split airport.

Every few kilometres from Brela to Gradac down the dangerous coast road dotted with car wrecks, the welcome/farewell signposts pop up in quick succession: **Brela**, revered by locals; **Baška Voda**; **Makarska**, **Tučepi**; **Podgora**; **Drvenik**, **Zaostrog**, **Brist** and **Gradac**.

The islands of Brač, Hvar (both connected to the coast by ferry) and Pelješac come into jaw-dropping view to your right. To your left rises the constant, imposing, grey façade of the Biokovo mountain range. If you do find a tranquil spot, the natural backdrop is stunning in both directions.

Biokovo, its dozen high summits topped by the 1762-metre (5,781-foot) peak of Sveti Jure, contains a series of karst caves and the Botanical Gardens at Kotosina near Tučepi, and forms part of the testing hiking territory

of the **Biokovo Nature Park** (www.biokovo. com). It divides this narrow coastal strip of Croatia from the border with Bosnia-Hercegovina. The main towns over the border, including nearby Mostar (*see p244* **Mostar: A bridge too near**), are easily accessible from the ugly transport hub of Ploče just south of the riviera. As part of the Dayton Agreement to end the conflict in 1995, Bosnia was awarded a 22-km (14-mile) stretch of access to the Adriatic, centrepieced by the white honeycomb of tourist hotels in the anomalous resort of **Neum** (*see p247* **Neum: A bridge too far?**). Prepare your passports as you pass through coastal Bosnia to Dubrovnik. Any visa requirements are generally waived. To head to inland Bosnia, EU, American, Canadian, Australian and New Zealand citizens do not require visas anyway; South Africans currently do.

Beaches

The most attractive pebble beach is at **Brela**, approached through pine trees; the longest is at **Tučepi**. Other lovely stretches include the 3km (two miles) south of Makarska; the coves between Drvenik and Zaostrog; and the beach between Brist and Gradac. Activities are not as widespread as on the islands – there are **diving clubs** in Makarska (More Sub, Kralja Petra Krešimira IV 43, 021 611 727, 098 265 241 mobile, www.more-sub-makarska.hr) and at Pisak (021 480 683, 098 447 287 mobile, www.inet.hr/~govlahov).

Where to eat

Food with a view is on offer at every spot along the riviera – some places, set back from the coastal road, with a panoramic vista. Terrace restaurants invariably have a grill, so you can see your fish or meat being sizzled as you sip local wine and stare at the Adriatic. Nearly all hotels have a restaurant as well – half-board prices are extremely attractive. Notable venues include the upmarket **Jeny** in Gornje Tučepi and **Jež** in Makarska town.

Biston

Bast 76, Bast (021 621 517/091 2522 279 mobile). **Open** 2-11pm daily. **No credit cards.**
Set in the small village of Bast in the woods overlooking Baška Voda, this traditional *konoba* offers 'only local delicacies', according to the motto on the door. Suitably simply decorated, it features food that grandmother used to make: lamb's belly, a local lamb stew and lamb on the spit, with home-baked bread. The place has a pitch for *bocce*, a regional version of bowls, and numbers many aficionados among the dining regulars.

Mostar: A bridge too near

The most iconic attraction in what was Yugoslavia, the symbol of its collapse and a fragile sign of post-war hope, stands a couple of hours from Dalmatia into Bosnia-Hercegovina: the **Stari Most** of **Mostar**.

The Stari Most (Old Bridge) of Mostar ('bridge-keeper') has been the town's heart and identity for nearly half a millennium. It was constructed over nine years in the middle of the 16th century by Turkish architect Mimar Hayruddin, under the orders of the Sultan, as a symbol of the benevolence and power of the then ruling Ottoman empire. If the bridge had collapsed, Hayruddin would have been executed. He needn't have worried. The Stari Most stood for over 400 years, linking the then relatively harmonious tripartite local community of Bosnian Muslims, or Bosniaks, Croats and Serbs – until 1993. Croat and Bosniak forces, former allies in Mostar's defence against invading Serbian units of the Yugoslav Army, were fighting each other across opposite sides of the river. A direct hit from a Croatian tank caused the bridge to collapse into the turquoise Neretva river below. Symbolically, it blew the city apart. The old Muslim east of the city was besieged from the Croat west, much of it destroyed.

After a peace deal and subsequent international security forces and monitoring, relative stability, if not normality, returned to Mostar. The Muslims kept to the east, the Croats to the west. Separate school systems, separate hospitals, separate bus stations. Different mobile phone prefixes, different football teams, even different versions of Mostar's home page (www.mostar.ba), in similar versions of what was until recently a common language.

With $13m worth of international financial backing, the bridge was painstakingly reconstructed, using the same methods and materials as the Ottomans had. Hungarian military divers recovered the original blocks of white limestone, which had to be left to dry over several months. For years, a trickle of curious visitors would sit over a long, strong Turkish coffee at one of the many vantage point cafés and gawp at the scaffolding. Local lads would show off their prowess by diving into the river from the support planks, coming up to ask for a couple of convertible marks (KM), the currency for a newly independent, cantoned Bosnia-Hercegovina.

Finally, on 23 July 2004, with a lavish ceremony involving 2,000 dancers, singers and high divers from both sides of town, the Stari Most, looking as elegant and ingenious as four-odd centuries ago, was reopened.

Whether it can eventually help reconcile two sides after such bitter conflict is debatable. For the time being, it provides tourists in Dalmatia with an excellent reason to visit one of Europe's most fascinating crossroads, a world away from the coast. You can take a bus from Split or Dubrovnik, a daily 90-minute train from the transport hub of Ploče past the southern tip of the Makarska Riviera, or drive. Traffic can be heavy in high season.

Bosnia and Hercegovina (here in Hercegovina, do mention the full title) offers a taste of the Orient. Turkish coffeehouses

abound, local food such as *čevapi* (high-quality kebabs) and *burek* (filo pie with cheese) reflect the centuries of Ottoman rule, and the urban landscape is highlighted with bazaars, mosques and hammams. In Mostar, the **Koski Mehmed-Pasha mosque** just north of the Stari Most, was built in 1617. Open to men and women, it is beautifully detailed, with a minaret that can also be entered and (precariously) climbed for the ideal view across the Neretva. It stands beside the workshops of cobbled **Kujundžiluk**, where you can find copperware goods and carpets, and close to **Tepa market**, with its stalls of figs, pomegranates and local organic honey. Through the café-lined street of Fejića, you reach **Bišćevića**, a 17th-century Turkish house and open museum overlooking the river. This surviving example of residential Ottoman architecture is full of painted furniture and elaborately carved wooden ceilings.

Many of Mostar's other Muslim sights – the **Karadjozbegova** mosque, the **Tabhana** Turkish Baths – are still undergoing post-war reconstruction.

To dine on something other than the ubiquitous delicious Turkish snacks and sweets, try the traditional **Taurus** by Mostar's oldest stone bridge, the **Kriva Cuprija** or, with its stepped terraces overlooking Stari Most, **Babilon**.

If you're staying, the four-star **Bevanda** (Stara Ilička, 00 387 36 332 332, www.hotelbevanda.com) is the best in town, with double rooms about €140. For somewhere cheap, friendly, central and comfortable, the **Pansion Rose** (Bulevar, 00 387 36 578 300, www.pansion-rose.ba) has double rooms near the Stari Most for about €25.

The **tourist information office** is at Rade Bitange 5 (00 387 36 580 275). The website www.bhtourism.ba has basic, generic information. Mostar's official home page is in Croatian, Bosnian – but sadly not in English.

EU citizens, Americans, Canadians, Australians and New Zealanders can enter Bosnia with a valid passport – South Africans require a visa as well. The local currency is the convertible mark, exchange rate roughly 1KM to €2.

Feral
Obala Kneza Domagoja, Brela (021 618 909). **Open** *Summer* noon-midnight daily. **No credit cards**.
This rustic *konoba* serves something for everyone at all price ranges, from small and cheap (pilchard) to pricy white fish (sole), and lobster. Set in a small harbour, it is renowned for local specialities and the strict rule that all herbs used in cooking must be exclusively from Dalmatian gardens. Meat dishes include lamb cutlets, steaks and home-made stews.

Hrpina
Trg Hrpina 2, Makarska town (021 611 619).
Open *June-Sept* 8am-2pm, 6pm-1am daily. *Oct-May* 8am-2pm, 4-11pm daily. **No credit cards**.
Named after the neat square in the heart of town that it overlooks, this family-run restaurant is an ideal place to enjoy authentic Dalmatian food on a small shaded terrace. Opening early for coffee, it's suitable for a healthy brunch of octopus salad while watching holidaymakers bicker on the way to the beach.

Ivo
Ante Starčevića 41, Makarska town (021 611 257).
Open 9am-midnight daily. **No credit cards**.
As local as it gets, this simple restaurant offers traditional, home-made treats such as tripe, lamb or beef *na lečo* (boiled in soup), veal stew and grilled veal liver. Once regulars are finished with *marenda*, or Croatian elevenses, tourists drift in for authentic daily specials. There's a standard à la carte menu too, steaks, grilled fish and so on. Recommended.

Jeny
Gornje Tučepi 49 (021 623 704). **Open** *May-Sept* 6pm-midnight daily. *Mar, Apr, Oct-Dec* 5-11pm Tue-Sat. **Credit** AmEx, DC, MC, V.
One of the best restaurants in Central Dalmatia is set some 250m (820 ft) above the sea with a beautiful view of the Hvar Channel. The menu is divided into seasonal specialities and à la carte of Dalmatian and French cuisine. Dishes in the latter category are served with a wine by the glass recommended by the experienced waitstaff. The fish is fresh, the fish soup outstanding and meat options include curiosities such as veal in black olive sauce. Excellent wine list.

Jež
Petra Krešimira IV 90, Makarska town (021 611 741). **Open** 11am-midnight daily. **Credit** AmEx, MC.
Regularly honoured with a listing in the national top 100 establishments, this is primarily a fish restaurant, offering 20 fish hors d'oeuvres (including carpaccios) and soups (including cream shrimp). Meat dishes include steak 'à la Marco Polo' (with shrimps and basil) and medallions filled with ham and four types of cheese. Desserts are another speciality, prepared to old recipes. You won't find a better wine list on the whole riviera. Closed in January.

Naše Male Misto
Stari porat 1, Gradac (021 697 374). **Open** *Apr-Oct* noon-midnight daily. **Credit** MC, V.

The best place to eat in is this harbourfront *konoba*, offering traditional Dalmatian dishes at very reasonable prices. The speciality is soups and risottos, particularly fish and seafood varieties, and the service is impeccable. Upstairs are 40 rooms for rent (021 697 148), all with a sea-view balcony.

Palac

Obala sv Nikole 9, Baška Voda (021 620 544/ 098 371 783 mobile). **Open** 8am-11pm daily. **No credit cards.**
Under leafy shade on the waterfront, the Palac offers typical Dalmatian meat and fish specialities accompanied by an extensive wine list. The owner insists on fresh ingredients, usually sourced from that day's produce market – do make sure to ask your waiter for recommendations.

Point

Kačićev trg 7A, Makarska town (021 611 823). **Open** *May-Sept* 10am-3pm, 6pm-1am daily. **No credit cards.**
With the most scenic terrace on the main square, the seasonally run Point provides standard Med fare (risotto, seafood pasta) along with substantial grilled dishes. The house speciality is a huge plate of meat, more than enough for one person.

Porat

Obala Kralja Tomislava 2, Makarska town (021 615 088). **Open** 7am-midnight daily. **No credit cards.**
Home-made domestic food makes this centrally located restaurant. Neighbours arrive with empty pots to take away local delicacies such as *pašticada* (stuffed beef with home-made macaroni), mixed fish *brodet*, cod-fish stew or marinated fish – everything according to old, authentic recipes. Daily changing menu. Recommended.

PŠRD Arbun

Šetalište sv Petra 2, Makarska town (021 613 550). **Open** *Summer* 8pm-1am daily. **No credit cards.**
This informal open restaurant of the local club for fishing and water sports boasts regulars ranging from professors to fishermen. The tables among the pine trees are set by the grill, and waited on by club members. Informal service (eventually) brings any of six types of seafood (shark, sea bass, mackerel, squids, grouper and pilchards), always fresh. Prices for each range from 25kn to 50kn, a bargain, and make it worth overlooking the fact that there will be only one side dish or salad, and one wine type of each colour. It operates as a café during the day.

Rajski vrt

Obala Kneza Domagoja 44, Brela (091 582 8956 mobile). **Open** *Mar-Oct* 10am-midnight daily. **No credit cards.**
'Heaven's garden', referring to the nice surrounding greenery, is a slightly more upmarket dining option near the Hotel Soline, a short walk from Brela's fine beach. Grilled fish is the speciality, but there are risottos, pastas and pizzas, too. The

in-house baker's means that the range of cakes is far more extensive than you would otherwise expect of a seafood restaurant.

Ranč

Gornje Tučepi (021 623 563/098 286 118 mobile). **Open** *Summer* 6pm-midnight daily. **No credit cards.**
Located by Tučepi, near the main coastal road dividing the riviera below from the depopulated communities above, Ranč is looking to revive village life by creating a gastronomic centre of authentic local atmosphere and domestic specialities. Superb rural food is served in huge portions on a tranquil, tree-lined terrace. Grilled meats and steaks are the order here, along with fresh fish and soups (especially shrimp).

Roko

Branimirova obala 43, Podgora (no phone). **Open** *May-Oct* 8am-midnight Mon-Sat; 9am-midnight Sun. **No credit cards.**
This typical Dalmatian restaurant offers a few a typical dishes – anglerfish in champagne, for one. Grilled meats are the mainstay, though, vast portions served up by the owner sweating under billows of smoke. A portion for two will be enough for four. Pastas and pizzas of equal quality.

Stari mlin

Prvosvibanjska 43, Makarska town (021 611 509/ 098 781 360 mobile). **Open** *Summer* 10am-1am Mon-Sat. **No credit cards.**
This family-run fish and steak restaurant is based in a grade-I listed baroque house from the 18th century, once used to press olives. Here local and international cuisine combine. Well-travelled owner Goga has staffed the place with Croatian returnees, allowing for diversity such as surf & turf, vegetarian and Thai food. The grill is set on the summer terrace, so guests can enjoy seeing how Goga's dad prepares the food. Cosy, year-round interior.

Susvid

Kačićev trg 9, Makarska town (021 612 732). **Open** *Summer* 7am-1am daily. *Winter* 9am-11pm daily. **No credit cards.**
This popular terrace steakhouse by the church on the main square is known for its T-bone steaks, shark medallions and strict policy of using no frozen food. The owner insists on fresh ingredients from the surrounding area, ideally products from organic farms. The same management also runs the Peskera (Šetalište Donja luka, 021 613 028) down on the seafront.

Where to drink

Although each resort will have its modest scattering of cafés, recommended venues listed below are all in the riviera's nightlife hub of Makarska town. Most other resorts lock their doors from October to April.

Neum: A bridge too far?

Just past the Makarska Riviera, two-thirds of the way southbound from Split to Dubrovnik, bus passengers or car drivers will be surprised to come up against a border crossing – they thought they were travelling between two major hubs in the same country. The place looks nothing like the classic Venetian towns along the coast of southern Dalmatia. Bulk-buy supermarkets and ugly hotel blocks abound. Whichever way you look at it, **Neum** (www.neum.ba) is an anomaly.

Built as a retreat for the Yugoslav Communist elite, Neum is the only settlement along the 22km (13.5 miles) of coastline awarded to Bosnia-Hercegovina after the conflict of the 1990s. Equidistant from Dubrovnik and Mostar (see p244 **A bridge too near**), this otherwise anonymous resort has always been sandwiched by history. The border judgement is a hangover from one made 300 years previously. The Treaty of Karlowitz of 1699 had the Republic of Dubrovnik give Neum and area to the Turks as a buffer to the encroaching Venetians.

But the dispute has not ended here. The fact that people must cross Bosnia to reach the southern tip of Croatia – although passport checks are light and visa requirements waived – has caused the

Croatian government to look into building a bridge from the nearby village of Klek to the Pelješac peninsula, circumventing Neum. The plan would contravene international laws of the sea, as it would suspend navigation between Bosnia's territorial continental shelf and the open sea. After years of discussions, the bridge may yet go ahead.

So, if they build the bridge, what would you be missing out on? Not much. Neum has steep hills, beaches and several large tourist hotels, the main ones being the **Neum**, the **Sunce** and the **Zenit**. Charm doesn't really come into it. Its best buildings are the modern villas built for Yugoslav politicians.

Neum does rank among the sunniest coastal towns, protected from high winds and the open sea by an enclosed bay. You can rent boats, go scuba diving and indulge in other water sports, all arranged at the major hotels. The area behind it is untouched wilderness and little else.

Prices in Neum are lower than in Croatia. Bus drivers stop at the Orka or Kuzman *trgovinska centar* for cheap cigarettes, as passengers stretch their legs and gaze at the stark blocks in this bizarre buffer between two border posts. Shops accept kuna and Bosnian marks – for the time being at least.

Makarska Riviera

Bety

Lištun 1, Makarska town (021 612 185). **Open**
Summer 7am-1pm, 5pm-3am daily. *Winter* 7am-1am.
This small café with a long tradition has a strong
local following thanks to its regular Saturday DJ
nights – even out of season. In summer working
hours are flexible. If there are guests, they serve.
Only the summer afternoon siesta is sacrosanct.

Café OZ

*Šetalište Dr Franje Tudjmana 3, Makarska town
(021 611 202).* **Open** *Summer* 6am-2am daily.
Winter 8am-1am daily.
One of the oldest cocktail bars on the Dalmatian
coast, the former Marocco is opposite the city beach
and children's playground. The current cocktail
selection numbers 100 and complements a regular
agenda of decent local DJs. Food includes pizzas,
pastas and standard Mexican offerings.

Kačić café

Kačićev trg, Makarska town (021 616 186). **Open**
Summer 7am-3am daily. *Winter* 7am-midnight daily.
This busy café on the main square has a spacious
terrace with views of the nearby church and the
Biokovo Nature Park above. It's the ideal place to
see what's going on in town while drinking your
morning coffee or evening cocktails.

Kostela

*Tina Ujevića 6, Makarska town (098 347 554
mobile).* **Open** 6.30am-1am daily.
Right on the Riva, this easygoing café in the shade
of an ancient elm (*kostela*) tree provides a panoramic terrace for lazy drinking through the day. After
dark, the daily charm is dispensed with for a more
lively atmosphere.

Marineta

Marineta, Makarska town (021 616 886).
Open *June-Sept* 7am-4am daily. *Oct-May* hours vary.
Marineta covers all bases to cater for the summer
season. Café, pizzeria, cocktail bar and nightclub all
in one, it runs almost 24 hours day, serving pizzas
in the main room and cocktails under a roofed
terrace. In winter it catches its breath, locals taking
their time over a quiet coffee and brandy until the
last one goes home.

Pink Panter

Lištun 2, Makarska town (no phone). **Open** *Summer*
7am-noon, 5pm-3am daily. *Winter* 7am-11pm daily.
This small and pleasant lounge bar is centrally
located in a lively street between the main square
and the waterfront. It's the ideal choice for
morning coffee – the noisy surrounding cafés tend
to drown it out after nightfall.

Popeye

Mala obala 3b, Makarska town (no phone). **Open**
Summer 7pm-4am daily. *Winter* 4pm-midnight daily.
This showy place is the centre of Makarska nightlife,
right on the esplanade. Inside the space is divided
between a line of small tables and a large dancefloor,
with two platforms for professional dancers. Outside
by the main entrance a cocktail bar is manned by
juggling barmen.

Rockatansky

Fra Filipa Grabovca, Makarska town (no phone).
Open *Summer* 5pm-3am daily. *Winter* 3pm-
midnight.
This rock 'n' roll, jazz and blues pub is just behind
Lištun near the main square. 'Rocky' is where local
musicians meet, joined by toe-tapping tourists in
summer. If there's no live music, expect a DJ. Get a
place on the small terrace – the inside is tiny.

Nightlife

Again, Makarska town is the centre of activity,
mainly along Marineta waterfront and Lištun
immediately behind. The places listed below are
all close by, and provide an unchallenging spot
to go on to after an easy barhop.

Deep

*Osejava peninsula, Makarska town (098 320 055
mobile).* **Open** *Summer* 9am-4am daily.
This all-day bar and club is set in natural cave on
the Osejava peninsula at the end of the esplanade,
on the opposite side to the city beach. It's an interesting spot by day and popular place by night.

Grotta

Sv Petar, Makarska town (091 569 4657 mobile).
Open *Summer* 10am-4am daily.
Another nightclub in a natural cave, but this one is
on the St Peter peninsula, on the opposite side of the
bay to the town. On the agenda is live music (blues,
rock, jazz, funk or soul) and DJ nights. During the
day you can swim from the lower terrace.

Opera

Šetalište fra Jure Radića, Makarska town (no phone).
Open *Summer* 10pm-5am daily.
This huge mirrored disco has barely changed since
the 1980s. The vast terrace is packed with teenagers,
whatever the varying quality of DJs.

Where to stay

The Makarska Riviera is lined with purpose-
built hotels. The majority open for the summer
season in April and close by October – few of
them stay open all year round. In this section
we indicate which close and which stay open.
Nearly all establishments offer attractive half-
board deals with prices set per person – an
individual traveller can stay for bargain rates
in May or September, with swimming pool,

sauna and other leisure facilities thrown in.
Most also operate a tariff of 30 per cent for
stays of less than three nights.
  If you're turning up on spec in Makarska
town, there are any number of agencies that
will find you a private room – and there's
usually space at one of the larger hotels.
  Among the bland tourist blocks, noteworthy
hotels do exist. Try the lovely **Porin** in
Makarska town, the **Bacchus** and fabulous
Aparthotel Milenij in Baška Voda, historic
Kaštelet in Tučepi and secluded **Riva** in Brist.

Alga

*Dračevice 35, Tučepi (021 601 202/fax 021 601
204/www.hotelitucepi.com).* **Closed** Nov-mid Mar.
Rates €86-€164 double. **No credit cards.**
Just behind the Hotel Kaštelet (*see p250*), Alga is also
a four-star, but of completely different character. A
large complex of 323 rooms and seven suites, it was
built as a result of the switch to mass family tourism
in the 1970s. All suites are of the same acceptable
quality, while standard room rates vary according to
balcony and sea-view availability. The services
include an indoor and outdoor pool, sauna and gym
and organised events for children. It's an ideal choice
for families with children.

Aparthotel Milenij

*Šetalište Kralja Petra Krešimira IV 5, Baška Voda
(021 620 644/404/fax 021 620 399/www.hotel-
milenij.com).* **Closed** Nov-Feb. **Rates** vary.
Credit AmEx, DC, MC, V.
The luxurious Aparthotel Milenij, opened on the
beach in 2001, has 27 four-star apartments spread
over five floors, which range from 36sq m to 73sq m
(387-785sq ft) in size. To rent the smallest in May is
a reasonable €71, rising to €140 in August. There's
24-hour room service, internet access, a restaurant,
two cocktail bars (one on the beach), a TV lounge
with a billiard table, gym, sauna, outdoor swimming
pool and an underground garage. The UK tour oper-
ator Holiday Options voted it Best Hotel in Croatia
a couple of years ago.

Apartel Park Osejava

*Šetalište fra Jure Radića 21, Makarska town
(021 695 140/+ 49 173 524 3253 mobile/
www.makarska-park-osejava.de).* **Closed** mid Nov-
mid Mar. **Rates** *Studio* €35-€75. **No credit cards.**
This new, German-owned complex contains nine
studios, of up to four-person capacity, at the end of
the waterfront on the Osejava peninsula, between
Makarska harbour and a sports centre, with tennis
courts immediately below. There are great weekly
rates in April and early May, and October and
November. All the studios are set on the third and
fourth floors with views to the sea or the park.

Aparthotel Tamaris

*Slatina 2, Tučepi (021 678 222/fax 021 623 415/
www.hotel-tamaris.hr).* **Closed** mid Oct-mid May.
Rates vary. **No credit cards.**

This four-star aparthotel is nicely set between the Biokovo mountain range and extensive Tučepi beach. There are 40 sea-view apartments and five double rooms, with shared restaurant, sauna, fitness and massage rooms, plus an outdoor swimming pool with children's pool and jacuzzi, bar and internet café. Rates vary according to the size of apartment.

Bacchus

Obala sv Nikole 89, Baška Voda (021 695 190/ fax 021 679 150/www.hotel-bacchus.hr). **Closed** Nov-Mar. **Rates** *Per person half-board* €90-€210. **No credit cards.**

Hotel Villa Bacchus is a new stylish four-star hotel, built in 2003, located 20m (65ft) from the beach and 200m (655ft) from the centre of Baška Voda. It has 27 air-conditioned single, double and triple rooms, suites and apartments. Each contains king-size beds, and the usual facilities. Rates vary wildly; April and October are half the price of July. On site are an à la carte restaurant with a sea-facing terrace, an indoor swimming pool, water massage and sauna. Sun loungers on the beach outside are free for guests.

Berulia

Frankopanska, Brela (021 603 599/fax 021 619 005/www.brelahotels.com). **Closed** Nov-Mar. **Rates** *Per person half-board* €48-€134. **No credit cards.**

The best option of the quartet under the Brela Hotels umbrella. Set in pine trees opposite the other three, the Berulia has an indoor pool, sauna and gym. Other activities include minigolf, bowling and table tennis, and there are tennis courts five minutes away. Although only graded as three-star (€48 a night for half-board in mid May is ludicrous), it's a nice, comfortable place to stay. 200 rooms.

Biokovka

Put Cvitačke 9, Makarska town (021 602 446/ biokovka@st.htnet.hr). **Open** all year. **Rates** vary. **No credit cards.**

Biokovka is registered as a medical institution for rehabilitation and therapy, but also works as a year-round hotel. In high season, nearly all guests are tourists, while winter sees it used by sufferers of arthritis and any number of neurological ailments. It is set on Makarska beach, 15 minutes from the centre, with its own gym, two swimming pools (one therapeutic) and a restaurant with a daily vegetarian menu. Room rates vary wildly during the five set seasons, from 175kn per person in winter to 700kn in summer. Treatments are on offer to guests too.

Biokovo

Obala Kralja Tomislava, Makarska town (021 615 244/fax 021 615 081/www.hotelbiokovo.hr). **Open** all year. **Rates** €64-€144 double. **No credit cards.**

Open year-round, this is a reasonably priced, simple modern three-star set on the waterfront. In the cheapest season of May and September, you can get the best of the four categories of double – with a sea-facing terrace – for €90. There are five suites as well. Facilities include a pizzeria, restaurant, a terrace café facing the sea and internet access.

Conté

Žbanjica 4, Promajna (021 695 444/fax 021 695 445/www.promajna-hoteli.hr). **Closed** Nov-Mar. **Rates** 500kn-900kn double. **No credit cards.**

Conté is a well-appointed four-star some 100m (330ft) from the sea, in the village of Promajna. Baška Voda is some 2km (1.25 miles) away, walking across the beach or the embankment. Facilities for guests in the 30 rooms are impressive; those staying in the three suites have their own jacuzzi and internet access. Communal services include an outdoor pool with jacuzzi, indoor pool, sauna, gym, children's playground, internet access and roof terrace for naturists.

Dalmacija

Kralja Petra Krešimira IV, Makarska town (021 615 777/fax 021 612 211/www.hoteli-makarska.hr). **Closed** Nov-Easter. **Rates** €62-€100 double. **No credit cards.**

This three-star beach hotel, fully refurbished in 2004, contains 190 rooms and has access to a few extra amenities along with the standard tourist-hotel facilities of two swimming pools, a casino and two restaurants. As well as proximity to a small harbour for boats, the Dalmacija is attached to the main diving centre on the riviera, More Sub (021 611 727, 098 265 241 mobile, www.more-sub-makarska.hr).

Horizont

Stjepana Radića 2, Baška Voda (021 604 555/fax 021 604 923/www.hoteli-baskavoda.hr). **Closed** Nov-Mar. **Rates** €92-€164 double. **No credit cards.**

This four-star set 50m (165ft) from the main beach at Baška Voda, a large resort hotel of classic 1970s vintage, underwent a complete renovation in 1997/98 and is due for major investment in 2006. Spa and fitness facilities are expected to be in place for the summer season. Already here are an indoor and outdoor pool, sauna and children's play area.

Hrvatska

Dr Šimuna Sikavice 2, Baška Voda (021 611 340/fax 021 620 841/www.club-adriatic.hr). **Closed** Nov-Apr. **Rates** 300kn-530kn double. **No credit cards.**

This seasonal two-star 100m (330ft) from the sea has 128 standard doubles at reasonable rates, even in high season. The eight suites, all with a sea-view balcony, aren't even less than 100kn more expensive. Facilities include a pizzeria on the beach and a restaurant with a daily changing menu.

Kaštelet

Dračevice 35, Tučepi (021 601 090/fax 021 601 113/www.hotelitucepi.com). **Closed** Nov-Feb. **Rates** €92-€172 double. **No credit cards.**

Right in the middle of Tučepi beach, Kaštelet was built in 1766 by Don Klement Grubišić, a renowned philologist and writer, and was later eulogised by Alberto Fortis in his famed travelogue *A Journey Through Dalmatia*. It now operates as a four-star hotel, with 24 rooms and four apartments, all fully facilitated, with its own in-house restaurant, beer hall and bowling alley.

Labineca

Jadranka Cesta 2, Gradac (021 601 005/fax 021 601 663/www.azalea-hotels.com). **Closed** Nov-Apr. **Rates** €42-€83 single; €112-€222 double. **Credit** V.

The better of the two Gradac hotels incorporated into the Austrian Azalea chain and upgraded, the four-star Labineca comprises 144 rooms and eight suites. All have balconies. Amenities include three floodlit tennis courts, an indoor pool and a kidney-shaped outdoor one, as well as a sauna, restaurant and three bars. Cycle and canoe hire are included in the price, as steep as it gets on the riviera – although the Labineca is a boon for families, with a kids' club, playground and regular entertainment.

Laguna

Jadranska Cesta 18, Gradac (021 601 222/fax 021 601 268/www.azalea-hotels.com). **Closed** Nov-Apr. **Rates** €30-€59 single; €78-€144 double. **Credit** MC, V.

The cheaper of the two Azalea chain hotels in town, the three-star Laguna comprises two buildings of some 100 rooms each. All have a balcony, most a sea view. The Laguna shares some of the facilities of its nearby sister hotel, the Labineca (*see above*), in particular three tennis courts and water sports. Right on the beach and close to the handful of bars and restaurants in Gradac.

Laurentum

Kraj 43, Tučepi (021 605 900/fax 021 605 902/www.hotellaurentum.com). **Closed** Dec-Mar. **Rates** €71-€157 double. **No credit cards**.

A cut above the bland, tourist-standard block, this stylish new four-star is set in the middle of Tučepi, right by a pebble beach and a yacht marina. All 40 rooms have a sea-view balcony, king-size beds and – hooray! – a bath as well as a shower. The restaurant has a spacious patio, there's an outdoor pool and sunbathing terrace; inside are a gym and sauna.

Marco Polo

Obala 18, Gradac (021 695 060/fax 021 697 502/www.hotel-marcopolo.com). **Open** all year. **Rates** €45-€93 double. **Credit** MC, V.

The nicest hotel in Gradac is a friendly little place of 32 rooms, half of them with a sea view. Rarely for these parts, it's open all year round. There's a recently installed rooftop sauna and gym, but most guests are happy to spend time on the adjacent beach. The terrace restaurant is open to the public. Fishing trips are organised in the summer.

Maestral

Filipinska cesta, Brela (021 603 671/fax 021 603 688/www.brelahotels.com). **Closed** Nov-Mar. **Rates** €56-€110 double. **No credit cards.**

A rare moment of quiet on the **Makarska Riviera**.

Renovated in 2002, this standard three-star beach hotel contains 69 simple rooms, most with sea views, all with balconies. It has its own restaurant, car park, outdoor pool and mini-golf.

Makarska

Potok 17, Makarska town (021 616 622/fax 021 616 360/www.makarska-hotel.com). **Closed** Nov-Apr. **Rates** €56-€72 double. **No credit cards**.

This simple, cheap family-run three-star is in the old part of the city, five minutes from the beach. All 20 rooms have air-conditioning and a balcony – the half-board deals are a giveaway. Two apartments also available. Free parking places for 18 cars.

Marina

Filipinska cesta, Brela (021 608 891/fax 021 608 880/www.brelahotels.com). **Closed** Nov-Mar. **Rates** €50-€124 double. **No credit cards**.

Close to its partner hotel the Maestral (*see above*), this comparatively new and considerably larger three-star beach venue offers a different set of facilities – massage treatments to go with the sauna, for one. Nearly 300 rooms, so it can feel intimidating – but the prices are reasonable.

Meteor

Kralja Petra Krešimira IV, Makarska town (021 615 344/fax 021 611 419/www.hoteli-makarska.hr). **Rates** €60-€130 double. **Open** all year. **No credit cards**.

Reopened in February 2006 after redecoration, this Socialist-era ziggurat is now pretty luxurious – international football clubs use it in the winter. It's a four-star, with spa facilities, pools outdoor and in, two restaurants and the Tropicana disco. The rooms vary from boxy singles to quite spacious doubles with a terrace.

Minerva

Branimirova obala, Podgora (021 602 111/fax 021 625 311/www.hoteli-podgora.com). **Closed** Nov-Easter. **Rates** €58-€102 double. **No credit cards**.

Of the three establishments under the Hoteli Podgora umbrella, this three-star is the best. Set right on the beach, it has 165 standard rooms and five suites. Most come here for the glass-roofed indoor pool, gym, sauna and massage facilities. The two-star Podgorka nearby and Mediteran (see the same website) also operate Easter to October.

Neptun

Slatina 2, Tučepi (021 605 500/fax 021 605 700/www.hotelitucepi.com). **Closed** Nov-Apr. **Rates** €96-€198 double. **No credit cards**.

The best riviera venue for children, this beach-side three-star is closer in spirit to a holiday camp – kids' clubs, organised entertainment, a playground and child-friendly swimming pool – but with hotel facilities. For the price, it's a steal – and most under-14s accompanied by two adults are accommodated for free or for a nominal sum. There are basketball courts and five-a-side football pitches, volleyball and tennis, plus a terrace bar and restaurant.

Porin

Marineta 2, Makarska town (021 613 744/fax 021 613 688/www.hotel-porin.hr). **Open** all year. **Rates** 550kn-750kn double. **No credit cards**.

Lovely, central three-star in a late 19th-century Renaissance-style palace-cum-fortress, once used as the town library. Renovated into a hotel in 2002, this palace offers two dozen beds in seven rooms, with one two-floored apartment. It's right by the sea, its restaurant is spot-on, it has terraces either side and a panoramic one on the roof – and in high season, it's affected by noise from the bars immediately downstairs. Come before the crowds.

Primordia

Branimirova obala 111, Podgora (021 625 144/fax 021 678 983/www.hotel-primordia.com). **Closed** Nov-Mar. **Rates** €94-€164 double. **Credit** V.

This pretty house dates back to 1922 and, according to the plaque mounted 50 years later, has had an eventful past. Tranquillity itself these days, surrounded by pine trees and set by a sandy beach, during World War II the Primordia was the navy station for the local Partisan battalion. Today this three-star contains 25 accommodation units – 16 apartments and nine standard rooms. Eight apartments on the third floor are split-level, with a living room below and bedroom above, and all 16 have a balcony with a sea view.

Riva

Slakovac, Brist (021 695 598/www.hotel-riva.brist.hr). **Closed** Oct-Mar. **Rates** €46-€78 double. **Credit** MC, V.

A lovely little place this, its loggia-style restaurant terrace lapped by a relatively secluded stretch of the Adriatic, below the balconies of each of its neat, recently renovated rooms. The half-board rates here are absolute bargains, out of season, when the only sound you will hear is the occasional fishing boat. Ask about weekly rates, too – sometimes the management offers seven nights for six. It's a short stroll downhill from the Zvijezda Mora bar right by the southbound Brist bus stop, an easy beach walk from Gradac.

Rivijera

Put Cvitačke, Makarska town (021 616 000/fax 021 611 028/www.hoteli-makarska.hr). **Closed** Oct-May. **Rates** €62-€78 double. **No credit cards**.

This high-season two-star, popular with Czech tour companies, is an ideal for sporting types, with basketball and volleyball courts, a five-a-side football pitch, mini-golf and local bowls, or *bocce*. Rooms are standard, all ensuite, and the hotel is nicely shaded, with a beachside location.

Rosina

Vukovarska ulica 38, Makarska town (021 695 450/fax 021 695 455/www.hotel-rosina.com). **Open** all year. **Rates** vary. **No credit cards**.

Elevated above the promenade for nice sea views, two minutes from the beach and ten from Makarska town centre, the Rosina is a simple resort hotel of 12

Split & Islands

Konoba Bako, Komiža

Seemingly raised just inches above the sea, the beachside **Bako** (*see p257*) offers some of the best views of the bay of Komiža and some of the best meals on all Vis. Prices are not much higher than elsewhere. The service is attentive and professional and there is still a friendly, family-run feel about the place. Then there are the views of the sea, lapping at the rocks just below the terrace.

Restaurant founder Tonko Borčić Bako has been collecting finds from dives around Vis for the 30 years, and many are mounted inside the restaurant. The collection includes ancient Greek and Roman amphorae, two-handled water vessels, including one said to date back to the fifth century BC. Ships' bells and a rare altar are also on display.

The softly lit, stone-and-wood interior complements the sea view out front. There's a large rock-lined pool in the back where lobsters are humanely kept alive, and a wood-fired grill conveniently nearby where lobsters are inhumanely cooked alive. The squeamish can choose to ignore the busy chef at work but lobster diners may find it perversely fascinating to stand by and watch their dinner struggling to keep away from the flames.

A simple menu includes langouste lobsters, grilled, broiled or served in a *brodet*, Dalmatian stew. There's no bad choice, though grilled may be the simplest and most popular. You can also choose from grilled grouper, snapper, rockfish and breaded anglerfish, plus a choice of steaks and meat-free pasta sauces. Appetisers include octopus in wine sauce and *komižka pogača*, the local fish-filled bread. It's also an ideal place to sample the famed Vis vintages, featured in a long list of Croatian wines.

Bako is located next door to **Konoba Jastožera** (*see p257*), the better-known of the harbourfront restaurants, forming a miniature gourmet enclave near Pol Kalafotovo beach. Both are popular, so if you want to get a table for either during the high season, make sure you book ahead.

Split & Islands

spacious family rooms, three suites and six standard rooms. Package tour companies account for much of the year-round occupancy but individual travellers should be able to find something by phoning ahead. Restaurant and underground parking too.

Slavija

Obala sv Nikole 71, Baška Voda (021 604 888/ fax 021 620 740/www.hoteli-baskavoda.hr). **Open** all year. **Rates** €88-€140 double. **No credit cards**.
A mix of the new and the austere – the website still boasts of an award given to Slavija's predecessor at a London trades exhibition in 1936 – the 'Glory' was way past its sell-by date until the current management picked it up by the scruff of the neck and renovated it in time for the 2006 season. The main feature is now the spa and fitness facility, giving the hotel a four-star rating and allowing it to be open year round. Close to the beach too.

Soline

Trg Gospe od Karmela 1, Brela (021 603 207/ fax 021 602 208/www.brelahotels.com). **Closed** Dec-Feb. **Rates** €52-€126 double. **No credit cards**.
Of the four hotels in the Brela group, this is the most basic, but makes up for it with the activities it offers.

Komiža, Vis. *See p255.*

Its 200 rooms are standard – with either bath or shower – although all have a balcony, some of them sea-facing. The main attraction is a diving school, as well as an indoor pool, sauna and massage facilities. Tennis courts are nearby.

Urania

Petra Krešimira IV 9, Baška Voda (021 695 500/ fax 021 620 009/www.hoteli-baskavoda.hr). **Closed** Oct-mid May. **Rates** *Bungalows* €68-€96 double. **No credit cards**.
Although advertised as a 'tourist settlement', it's far less grim than that. The Urania comprises renovated two-storey bungalows and new self-catering apartments, located among pine woods close to the beach. Prices for the self-catering units, accommodating three to five people, begin at €54 and run up to €150. The main building contains a beer cellar and self-service restaurant, so you needn't live off bread, cheese and cheap wine for the whole holiday. Open from mid May to early October.

Vila Kristina

Petra Krešimira IV 1A, Baška Voda (021 620 120/ 091 512 0283 mobile/www.vilakristina.hr). **Open** all year. **Rates** €30-€140 double. **No credit cards**.
Twelve studio apartments comprise this three-star, three-storey complex at Baška Voda beach, opened in 2004. Off-season prices – the Vila Kristina stays open in the winter but do phone ahead – are very reasonable, and under-12s are accommodated free. Ask about half-board rates, as the house has a restaurant, the Tamarillo (021 620 350), also open to non-residents. Underground parking.

Villa Andrea

Kamena 46, Tučepi (021 623 008/098 356 71 mobile/fax 021 695 259/www.villa-andrea.info). **Closed** Nov-Easter. **Rates** €35-€130 single; €60-€86 double. **No credit cards**.
Opened in 2005, the Villa Andrea has 16 well-equipped rooms (ten doubles and six suites, one superior), although falls somewhat short of its claim to be 'the newest true boutique hotel'. Furnishings are comfortable, to be sure, but hardly inventive. The terrace restaurant is nice, 24-hour reception a rarity – although with a minibar already equipped, what could you possibly want at three in the morning? – and the Villa Andrea is trying to lift itself above the bog standard for the Makarska coast without pricing itself out of the market. And for that, it should be praised. It has parking facilities too. Open late April to mid October.

Villa Bacchus

Obala sv Nikole 89, Baška Voda (021 695 190/ fax 021 679 150/www.hotel-bacchus.hr). **Closed** Nov-Mar. **Rates** €90-€190 double. **Credit** AmEx, DC, MC, V.
Bacchus is a stylish new four-star hotel, built in 2003, 20m (65ft) from the beach and 200m (655ft) from the centre of Baška Voda. Each of the 27 air-conditioned single, double or triple rooms, family suites and apartments, have large beds. The terrace

restaurant faces the sea, there's an indoor swimming pool with a sauna nearby, and sunbeds on the beach. Prices double in high season, so get here in May to make the most of it.

Villa Marija
Donji Ratac 24, Tučepi (021 623 200/fax 021 623 004/www.hotelvillamarija.com). **Closed** Oct-mid May. **Rates** €90-€140 double. **No credit cards**.
Definitely a cut above, the Villa Marija is a four-star hotel with 30 nicely furnished rooms accessed by a panoramic lift. Communal facilities include a roof terrace, indoor and outdoor pools, gym, sauna and billiard room. It is run by the Simic family, whose renovated homestead is visible in the Biokovo highlands, and who encourage guests to take part in olive gathering and fruit picking. The restaurant is unsurprisingly traditional Dalmatian.

Resources

Information
Each resort on the riviera (www.makarska-riviera.com) has its own modest tourist office: **Brela** (021 618 337, www.brela.hr); **Baška Voda** (021 620 713, www.baskavoda.com); **Makarska** (Obala Kralja Tomislava 16, 021 612 002, www.makarska.hr); **Tučepi** (021 623 100, www.tucepi.com); **Zaostrog** (021 697 511); and **Gradac** (021 697 511, www.gradac.hr).

Atlas Travel Agency *Kačićev trg 9, Makarska town (021 617 038).* **Open** 8am-1pm, 5-9pm Mon-Sat; 8am-noon, 6-9pm Sun.
Accommodation booked and excursions arranged.

Internet
Internet Club Master *Jadranska 1, Makarska town (no phone).* **Open** *Summer* 9am-midnight daily.
Modest place near the Hotel Biokovo.

Getting there & around

The riviera is served almost hourly by buses between **Split** and **Dubrovnik**, all year round. Makarska town is 75mins from Split (about 35kn) and three hours from Dubrovnik (about 100kn). For short hops down the riviera, simply flag down a passing bus at the bus shelter on the coast road with the town's name on it – and pay the nominal fee once on board.

In summer at least three ferries a day (30mins, about 25kn) run from Makarska town to **Sumartin** in the eastern tip of **Brač**. In winter you can count on two. From **Drvenik** further down there is an almost hourly service (40mins, about 30kn) to **Sućuraj** on the eastern tip of Hvar, usually three or four a day in winter. There is little bus service across Hvar from there. Another service runs to **Korčula** (2hrs 15mins, about 35kn) once a day in spring and autumn, at least twice a day in summer.

Vis

The remote rocky island of Vis is being transformed from a forbidden army base to a holiday hotspot for the rich and famous. Trade is centred on two bay-blessed settlements at either end of this 13-kilometre-long (eight-mile) outcrop: to the north, **Vis town**, a port with quirky bars and quality restaurants; and to the west, the quiet fishing town of **Komiža**.

Obscure historic remains relate to the island's strategic importance since 500 BC. You can find Greek vessels, Roman baths, baroque Austrian architecture and, revived by an Australian returnee and lucky new expat homeowners, the Sir William Hoste Cricket Club. Like a number of fortified spots near the harbour (or 'Luka' – even once called 'Engleska Luka') side of Vis town, the club is named after one of the naval commanders during short-lived British rule after Napoleon.

Vis was spared the grim fate of becoming an Adriatic Gibraltar. After passing to the Italians, in 1944 Vis was used as a base by Tito and his Partisans. It remained a military facility, off-limits to foreigners, until 1989. You can visit **Tito's cave headquarters**, halfway up Mount Hum – ask at any travel agency listed (*see p260*). Vis' appeal is thus its seclusion and undeveloped tourism – making it ideal for independent travellers, many of them Croats. And despite the arriviste posh crowd, prices are not much higher than elsewhere on the coast. You can dine where John Malkovich does or dock where Tom Cruise and fiancée Katie Holmes parked their yacht in 2005.

The most popular spot for yachters is Vis town, with great beaches and noteworthy bars and restaurants, particularly in **Kut**, 500 metres (550 yards) east of the harbour. The only real sights are the **Archaeological Museum** in the Austrian fortress, on Baterija (021 711 729, open summer 9am-1pm, 5-7pm Tue-Sun, 10kn), featuring pottery, jewellery and sculpture from the Greek and Roman eras, including a 400 BC bronze head of a Greek goddess; and, in Kut, **St Cyprian's church**, a lovely mid 18th-century baroque affair with a campanile. Just beyond Kut lies a British naval cemetery, with graves of those who fell fighting Napoleon and during World War II.

The quieter Komiža is a stone-built, sunburnt old town that has supported fishing for a millennium. Local fishermen still supply Komiža's restaurants as the hospitality industry quickly becomes the main business. On the seafront, in the stubby Venetian fortress, or **Kaštel**, you'll find the **Fishing Museum** (no phone, open summer 9am-noon, 5-10pm daily, 10kn), with old boats, nets, sardine cans and other memorabilia from Komiža's glory days as a fishing centre. There are superb views from the tower, erected three centuries after the fortress in 1585.

Komiža isn't yet overrun with visitors, even in high season. The narrow, stone-paved streets downtown are free of cars, and even motor scooters rarely interrupt the peaceful sound of waves hitting the shore.

Beyond, a short hop from Komiža, lies the islet of **Biševo**, with its **Blue Cave** (Modra špilja). *See p258* **The big blue**.

Beaches

Small downtown beaches lie just north of Komiža harbour. Further along, near the **Hotel Biševo** (*see p260*), are a couple of busy beaches, **Uvala Pod Gospu** and **Bjažičevo**, both with small pebbles that are easy on the feet. In the other direction are the less busy pebble beaches of **Jucica** and **Jurkovica**. South from town is

popular **Kamenica** beach, a pleasant mix of sand and small pebbles, and further south still is a nudist beach and secluded swimming spots with rocky beaches – take your sandals.

On the west side of Vis harbour, you'll find a busy public beach near the **Hotel Issa** (*see p260*). This is a bit close to town but still comfortable and not too crowded. Past the hotel are more rocky beaches, a nudist swimming area and wild, more private beaches beyond. Again, you'll need sandals. On the other side of the bay, past the British Naval Cemetery, there's a good pebble beach at **Grandovac**.

Away from the main towns, beaches are only accessible by boat, car or motor scooter. There are inviting sand beaches in the narrow inlet of **Stončica** and near the village of **Milna**. There are stony ones south of Milna and along the whole southern coast of the island. These include **Srebrna**, a beach in an inlet near the village of **Rukavac**, with flat, pale stones and the most beautiful views.

Vis.

Excursions

To explore Vis, rent a boat or scooter from one of the travel agencies listed above. The island is surrounded by shipwrecks, caves and sites of natural or archaeological interest, so diving is extremely popular. Beyond, a short hop from Komiža, lies the islet of Biševo, with its **Blue Cave** (Modra špilja), a stunning if hugely popular attraction especially when bathed in late-morning light. *See p258* **The big blue**.

Further away, much further away, halfway across the Adriatic to Italy and the most remote spot in Croatia, is an island called **Palagruža**, dominated by a lighthouse where you can rent rooms for a week (www.adriatica.net). **Alter Natura tours** (*see p260*) arranges day trips from Komiža by boat.

Dodoro Diving Center
Kranjčevića 4, Vis town (091 251 2263 mobile/ www.dodoro-diving.com).
Equipment rental, classes, accommodation packages and guided trips.

Issa Diving Center
At Hotel Biševo, Ribarska 96, Komiža (021 713 144/www.scubadiving.hr).
Equipment rental, diving classes and 22 itineraries for guided diving trips around the island.

Where to eat

Good seafood and pizzas are plentiful around the harbours of both towns. Head to **Kut**, east of Vis harbour, for a clutch of good restaurants. Yacht owners enjoy the many high-end eateries scattered around Vis town.

The local speciality, *pogača*, also known as *viska pogača* or *komižka pogača*, is a square of dough with a filling of fish (ideally sardines), onion, tomatoes and other local ingredients – similar to a focaccia. It's prepared with pride all around Vis and is generally delicious.

The sandy hills of Vis produce great local wines, the dry white Vugava and the full-flavoured red Plavac, providing the ideal accompaniment to any meal.

Keynote venues include the **Konoba Jastožera** and adjoining **Konoba Bako** (*see p253* **Top tables**) in the gourmet enclave by Komiža's **Pol Kalafotovo** beach, as well as Vis town's upmarket **Villa Kaliopa**, set in a garden attached to a 16th-century mansion. In Kut, look out for **Pojoda**, scenic but secluded.

Konoba Bako
Gundulićeva 1, Komiža (021 713 008/021 713 742). **Open** *Summer* 11am-2am daily. *Winter* 5pm-midnight daily. **Credit** AmEx, DC, MC, V.
Some of the best food – and best views – to be had on Vis. *See p253* **Top tables**.

Kantun, Vis

Vis produces some of the most drinkable dry red and white wines served in Croatia – and you don't have to splash out for a full meal just to sample the local grape. At **Kantun** (*see p259*), the owners understand that wine can be the main attraction, but it doesn't stop them taking equal care over the food they serve.

Set by the meeting point of Luka and Kut in Vis town, in a beautiful old building on the harbour, Kantun entices customers off the street with its thick, shaded grape arbour. Grab a seat under the vines or in the softly lit, antique-filled interior with old stone walls, and let a member of the outgoing staff recommend a vintage.

The sandy soil, dry summers and warm climate of Vis nourish wonderful grapes. The most commonly grown on the island are Vugava, which makes a dry white that is the perfect accompaniment to fish, and Plavac Mali, genetically linked to Californian Zinfandel, and creates a dry red. The wine is sold by the glass, at 20kn each, so you can sample many vintages without breaking a hole in your holiday budget.

More a bar than a restaurant, Kantun operates in a relaxed atmosphere, encouraging guests to mingle. The food is basically light, tapas-style dishes that help soak up the tipple: locally produced capers, olives, cheese and fish. Like the wines, all the food served at the Kantun originates from Vis island.

Kantun's intoxicating ambience has such a strong pull that you can pop in to get out of the sun for a minute and find yourself happily sipping away an entire evening.

Konoba Jastožera
Gundulićeva 6, Komiža (021 713 859/www. jastozera.com). **Open** *Spring-summer* 6pm-1am daily. **Credit** AmEx, DC, MC, V.
No longer a local *konoba*, far from it. This is one of the most talked-up restaurants in Croatia, a former lobster pot-house where dining tables are placed on a floor of planks raised above the turquoise sea. Waiters happily discuss the ingredients, merits and history of every item on the menu, in particular the several tantalising versions of lobster: the langouste lobster with spaghetti au gratin and the grilled lobster with four sauces. As well as lobster, there are crabs, clams and fabulous octopus salad appetisers, plus grills and steaks, and an extensive selection of wines from Vis and elsewhere in Croatia. Celebrities

love it – note the pictures by the entrance of John Malkovich and other notable Croatophiles to have visited – so it is essential to book well ahead.

Nono
Obala Pape Aleksandra III, Komiža (098 203 122 mobile). **Open** *Spring-summer* 8am-1am daily. **No credit cards**.
Ideally priced and idyllically located, the simple Nono offers local domestic fare at its best. Low-frills, friendly and family-run, this seafront restaurant located between Lucica and Jurkovica beaches is known for its excellent seafood, which can compete with any on Vis. The delightful terrace, by a boathouse, is a great place to sip a carafe of local white wine and order lobster, red fish, snapper or grouper. Non-seafood offerings include hearty steaks stuffed with prosciutto and cheese. The early

opening hours mean that this is a perfect choice for breakfast or lunch by the sea. Make sure you book ahead for dinner in high season.

Pojoda
Don Cvjetka Marasovića 8, Kut (021 711 575). **Open** *Summer* noon-3pm, 5pm-1am daily. *Winter* 5pm-midnight daily. **No credit cards**.
Just off a street full of restaurants in Kut, hidden behind a tall stone wall, an attractive garden faces a cheerful, half-opened interior with modern decor. Within, a busy flame grill produces delicious Dalmatian-style seafood and barbecued meat. Tempting appetisers include octopus salad, seafood cocktail and prosciutto, enjoyed with good, local wines. Repeat business is generated by friendly, efficient service in a homely atmosphere. Book a table upstairs to admire the scenery.

The big blue

No visit to Vis would be complete without seeing the **Blue Cave** of **Biševo**. Set on the east coast of this tiny island, the Blue Cave (Modra špilja) is accessible by sea from Komiža. Boats leave Komiža harbour at 9am, as the time to arrive is from about 11am. With the sun gaining height, it shines through the waters of a submerged side entrance and the cave is bathed in a fabulous blue light.

At this point, many dive in, although the high volume can make this impossible in July or August. Every Komiža travel agency (*see* p260) arranges day tours, at about 90kn per head, including lunch and an afternoon at a beach near Biševo. Alternatively, take the taxi boat from Komiža to Biševo, walk to the cave entrance and take a little boat from there. Never risk it if the sea is choppy.

Restaurant Val

Don Cvjetka Marasovića 1, Kut (021 711 763).
Open *Summer* 6pm-1am daily. **No credit cards.**
Val, in an old stone house with a beautiful seaside terrace, offers a good selection of the kind of seafood served in many Vis restaurants. Skilled gastronomy and a beautiful location set this place above its neighbours, and the service is also superior. Friendly owners, who clearly take an interest in the business, are usually on hand to make sure everything goes smoothly. Festive music too.

Vila Kaliopa

Vladimira Nazora 32, Vis town (021 711 755/099 529 667 mobile). **Open** *Summer* 5pm-1am daily.
No credit cards.
This is where the yachting crowd goes to splash out. You'll pay a good 300kn per head all-in to enjoy the shade of the palm trees, bamboo and statues in this enclosed garden between Kut and Luka, attached to the 16th-century mansion of Milanese nobleman Francesco Garibaldi – but the location and the food are memorable. The cuisine is Dalmatian, with a lot of seafood, and Goran Pecarević ensures his kitchen strives to use local ingredients. The menu changes regularly according to what's fresh that day – and you're in the ideal place to sample the strong selection of Vis island vintages.

Where to drink

In Vis town, **Kut** is probably the best neighbourhood for drinking earlier on, before you drift down to the late-opening harbourfront hostelries of **Luka**. Here bars are still going when most of the island has gone to bed, particularly the landmark **Bejbi**. If you're keen on sampling the local wines, you won't do better than **Kantun** (*see p257* **Best bars**).

In Komiža, restaurants go until 1am and provide all the drinking you need to do for a night. If you're up for post-dinner socialising, the main square known locally as **Škor** is the place to be. The terraces of three small bars bump up against each other in this tight space, creating the sensation of a big outdoor party. Namesake **Škor** is the bar of choice.

Caffè Bar Bejbi

Šetalište Stare Isse 9, Komiža (no phone).
Open *Summer* 8am-4am daily.
A comfortable dive on the working section of the harbour by the docks, Bejbi ('bay-bee') bustles day and night with people who like to drink and gab. The thatched terrace has its own bar and harbour view, and a mural with an African motif. There's pinball and pool tables in the large indoor bar. This is usually the last place to close, so it's where all the other parties continue. Come the wee hours, relaxed patrons are ready to dance on the tables, sing Dalmatian folk tunes in four-part harmony and meet new people. A worthy stop on any serious bar crawl.

Caffè Bar Martin

Ribarska 5, Vis town (no phone). **Open** *Summer* 7am-2am daily.
This café with a little indoor bar and a comfortable terrace shares a small square with Lambik (*see below*), and revellers can shift back and forth between the two throughout the long evenings. Friendly staff play good dance tracks and fast jazz inspiring a young crowd to get down under the stars.

Kantun

Biskupa Mihe Psica 17, Vis town (021 711 306).
Open 8am-midnight daily. **No credit cards.**
Fabulous selection of local wines and tasty, light snacks. *See p257* **Best bars.**

Lambik

Pod Ložu 2, Vis town (no phone). **Open** *Summer* 7am-late daily.
This ancient-looking courtyard and grape arbour is one of the more entertaining and idiosyncratic bars on the island, ably run by a charming young brother-and-sister team who enjoy partying with their equally young guests late into the evening. Drunken singing and snogging take place on the terrace, the big tables under the vines induce conversation, and the indoor bar area encourages mingling and dancing. If the fun is still going on, the bar serves past closing time, and you may be offered home-made grappa. Decent dance music is often provided by local DJs.

Malibu Bar

Trg 30.Svibnja 1992 1, Vis town (no phone). **Open** *Summer* 8am-1am daily.
A lot of work and no little neon went into designing this large, dark bar with a studiously casual appearance and a big terrace near the harbour in Luka. A decent mix of electronic and rock music, and general seaside buzz, make this a fine place for morning coffees or late-night drinking. Friendly staff and a sociable core of regulars add to the fun. Palatable and cheap dinners – pastas, risottos and some seafood – are served from 7pm.

Škor

Škor 11, Komiža (no phone). **Open** *Summer* 7.30am-2am daily.
The bar that started it all has a quirky interior, a nice terrace and a fun, friendly management. The staff have good taste in music, and the fast-paced rock and dance tunes help set a happy, energetic atmosphere. Local slackers start the day here over coffee and gossip about the night before.

Nightlife

Aquarius

Kamenica beach, Komiža (no phone). **Open** *Summer* from 9pm Fri-Sat and for special occasions.
Foreign acts and DJs supplement the local talent and turn this disco by the beach into an all-night party. A predominantly younger crowd is peppered

with up-for-it boating types and occasional celebrities who populate Komiža in the summer. Open weekends and sporadically on weekdays. Check the bars around Škor for posters announcing special parties.

Where to stay

The family-run **Paula**, in Kut, Vis town, is a delightful option. The other two hotels here, the **Issa** and the **Tamaris**, run by the same company, are decent and reasonably priced. The smaller Tamaris is preferable.

Komiža only contains one main hotel, the **Biševo**, and not particularly fancy at that. The most common lodging is one of the private apartments and guest rooms for rent. Some of them can be surprisingly luxurious and expensive. As for Vis town, book from one of the travel agencies listed below – and well ahead in high season.

Hotel Biševo

Ribarska 96, Komiža (021 713 144/fax 021 713 098/modra.spilja@st.t-com.hr). **Rates** €25-€46 single; €44-€72 double. **Credit** AmEx, DC, V.
Komiža's one big hotel is a three-star resort-style complex with 280 beds. Located on a harbourfront of pretty old stone houses, next to one of the busier beaches, the modern Biševo has its own sports pitch plus all kinds of equipment available for rent nearby. Private parking is also on offer. The restaurant serves the breakfast included in the price and decent seafood dishes twice a day. Although there's no air-conditioning, the rooms are comfortable and the rates pretty reasonable.

Hotel Issa

Apolonija Zanelle 5, Vis town (021 711 124/fax 021 717 740). **Rates** €36-€62 single; €54-€110 double. **Credit** AmEx, DC, MC, V.
This boxy, modern structure with 256 beds offers low-frills resort-style accommodation. Tennis courts, volleyball, basketball, mini-golf are among the many sports facilities, plus cycle and diving rental nearby. There's private parking and a restaurant too. Breakfast is included in the price.

Hotel Paula

Petra Hektorovića 2, Vis town (021 711 362/www. paula-hotel.htnet.hr). **Rates** €66 single; €95 double. **Credit** AmEx, DC, MC, V.
This charming, family-run, 35-bed hotel in an old stone building in Kut, is easily the best option on the island. The 12 recently renovated rooms have carefully and individually designed interiors, the service is good and there's fine seafood at the lovely walled terrace restaurant – or kitchenettes in some rooms.

Hotel Tamaris

Obala sv Jurja 30, Vis town (021 711 350/fax 021 711 349). **Rates** €36-€62 single; €54-€110 double. **Credit** AmEx, DC, MC, V.

In the same family as the Issa (*see above*), the Tamaris, in an old harbourside building, is more attractive. With 54 beds, Tamaris is somewhat smaller and you don't feel as if you're jammed into a tourist factory. All rooms have air-conditioning. There's private parking for hotel guests and a decent restaurant with harbour-side terrace where the inclusive breakfast is served.

Villa Nonna

Ribarska 50, Komiža (021 713 500/098 380 046 mobile/www.villa-nonna.com). **Rates** €35-€55 single; €60-€100 double. **No credit cards**.
Affordable, comfortable and central accommodation is available in this pretty old townhouse one block from the harbour. There are seven apartments for rent, each one more distinctive than a hotel room. Kitchenettes allow you you cook up the fish and produce available in the local market. The management also looks after private rooms around town – enquire here.

Resources

Information

Alter Natura *Hrvatskih mučenika 2, Komiža (021 717 239/091 250 3809 mobile/www.alternatura.hr).* **Open** *Summer* 8am-9pm daily.
Accommodation, unusual excursions, rentals and currency exchange.

Darlić & Darlić Travel Agency *Riva sv Mikule 13, Komiža (021 713 760/098 784 664 mobile/ www.darlic-travel.hr).* **Open** *Summer* 8am-9pm daily.
Accommodation, excursions, rentals and currency exchange.

Navigator *Šetalište Stare Isse, Vis town (021 717 786/098 942 6315 mobile/www.navigator.hr).* **Open** *Summer* 8am-10pm daily.
On the harbour, close to the ferry. Accommodation in hotels or private rooms, plus tours and rental of scooters, cars and diving equipment.

Internet

Biliba *Trg Klapavića, Vis town (021 711 357).* **Open** *Summer* 6am-1am daily.
Lively harbour café also serving sandwiches.

Getting there & around

In summer Jadrolinija runs a couple of ferries a day from **Split** to Vis town. The two-hour trip costs about 35kn per person and about 250kn with a car. You can only do the round trip in a day in July and August – out of high season, ferries run every other day. Also in July and August, SEM catamarans (90mins, about 30kn) run the same route. Note that out of season the sea can be very choppy indeed. Ferries and hydrofoils also run from Ancona and Pescara in summer. It's a 20-minute bus ride from the ferry dock in Vis town to Komiža (20kn). For a taxi, call Ivanisević, 021 711 544, 098 784 662 mobile.

Dubrovnik & Islands

Features

Maps

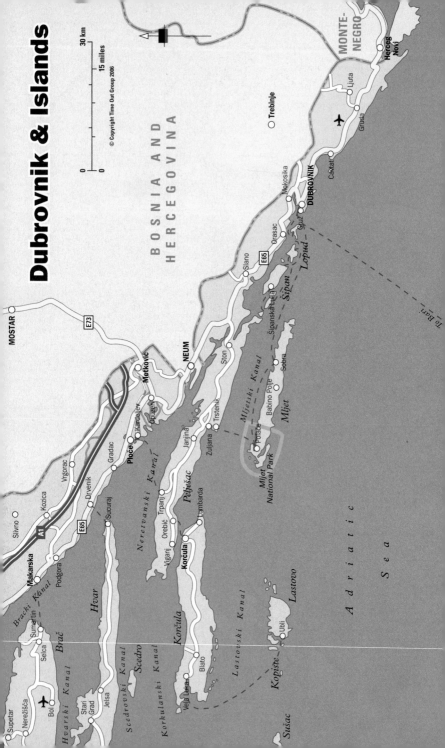

Dubrovnik & Islands

© Copyright Time Out Group 2006

0   15 miles   30 km

BOSNIA AND HERCEGOVINA

MONTE-NEGRO

MOSTAR

E3

Supetar
Nerežišća
Bol
Sumartin
Selca
Brač
Brački Kanal
Podgora
Makarska
A1
E65
Silvno
Kozica
Vrgorac
Drvenik
Gradac
Ploče
Metković
NEUM
Kardeljevo
Opuzen
Neretvanski Kanal

Stari Grad
Jelsa
Hvar
Hvarski Kanal
Ščedro
Ščedrovski Kanal
Sučuraj
Viganj
Orebić
Trpanj
Janjina
Pelješac
Ston
Trstenik
Žuljana

Korkulanski Kanal
Vela Luka
Blato
Korčula
Korčula
Lumbarda

Lastovski Kanal
Ubli
Lastovo
Sušac
Kopište

Adriatic Sea

Mljet
Mljet National Park
Pomena
Polače
Babino Polje
Sobra
Mljetski Kanal

Slano
E65
Špansla luka
Šipan
Lopud
Koločep
Orašac
Mokošika
DUBROVNIK
Cavtat

Trebinje

Gruda
Ljuta
Herceg Novi

To Bari

Dubrovnik & Islands

The pearl of the Adriatic surrounded by pristine islands in a sea of pure blue.

Strikingly beautiful southern Dalmatia, where Croatia tapers down to Montenegro, appeals to an older, more genteel tourist. Hedonists head to Hvar, Vis and the party islands an easy hop from Split. South of the Makarska Riviera, the islands are relatively undeveloped, the coast free of mass tourism. Industry – apart from wine, olives and shellfish – is minimal. Locals live from fishing and tourism.

Dubrovnik is a one-town tourist industry on its own. As stunning as the clear blue sea around it, the former centre of the independent Republic of Ragusa invites superlatives and attracts the lion's share of year-round visitors. When a foreigner thinks of Croatia, he thinks of Dubrovnik's proud, pristine fortifications set on an azure background. The travel brochure covers need little touching up. Anti-clockwise currents running up the coast from Albania mean that the Adriatic is crystal clear here. Islands such as Korčula and Mljet – one a living museum, the other a verdant wilderness – produce little to mess up Mother Nature.

Island hopping is done as day trips from Dubrovnik, either to Lokrum or the Elafiti Islands nearby, or to Mljet. Hotels are few and open seasonally. None have a must-see museum or photogenic ruin. The pleasure is seeing it all in the flesh, as the Romans or Venetians would have done before you.

Dubrovnik, of course, is a case apart. As Ragusa, it was a hub of cultural, architectural and scientific achievement, backed by lucrative maritime trading and a progressive urban infrastructure. Bending to the Napoleonic Code, moribund under the Habsburgs, Ragusa faded until reinventing itself under Tito as tourist-friendly Dubrovnik. In 1991 these same tourists watched the news in horror as Dubrovnik was shelled day after day during a six-month siege. Painstakingly rebuilt, it welcomes back visitors, preferably high-end ones, with a string of new and renovated luxury hotels.

Its top restaurants benefit from proximity to Croatia's finest oyster beds, at Ston where the Pelješac peninsula meets the mainland. A favourite with weekending locals, Ston, and the wine cellars and tourist-free shingle beaches of Pelješac, is a relatively undiscovered treasure of the region – as are some of its restaurants.

Nothing illustrates the cosmopolitan spirit of Dubrovnik more than its Summer Festival (www.dubrovnik-festival.hr). Moving towards its 60th year, the festival is as prestigious as Edinburgh's – past performers include the London, Vienna and Moscow Philharmonics, Isaac Stern, David Oistrakh, Dizzy Gillespie and Duke Ellington. And it's every bit as fun. The 45-day fest (10 July-25 Aug) takes up every space in town, outdoor and in – book your hotel room and performance tickets online as soon as you can. Even if you're just passing through, you're bound to catch any number of traditional *klapa* singers, street performers and folk dancers.

Dubrovnik

Where Boškovićeva meets the north flank of the iconic city walls that encircle Dubrovnik's Old Town, a map plots the exact points where the shells fell during the six-month Serb and

At the hop

Dubrovnik's main harbour at Gruž (*see p285*) serves Croatia's southernmost islands down the Adriatic coast: Korčula and Mljet. One Jadrolinija car ferry a day serves each island. There is also a quicker and more convenient Atlantagent catamaran to Korčula. There is also a ferry and catamaran service to the nearer Elafiti Islands. Vela Luka on Korčula and the remote Lastovo are accessible on a daily service from Split and Hvar (*see p294*).

From the old harbour in the Old Town, taxi boats hop over to Lokrum. One bus a day leaves Dubrovnik for Korčula (*see p294*), crossing the water at ferry point Orebić on Pelješac.

►The phone code for the Dubrovnik & Islands area is 020. In this chapter we provide the full phone number for each venue – drop the first '0' if dialling from abroad, followed by the six-digit number. If you're dialling within the area, you don't need the 020. Numbers beginning 091 or 098 are Croatian mobiles and expensive to call from most foreign phones.

Dubrovnik & Islands

Things to do

Take a walking tour high up around **Dubrovnik's city walls** (*see p266*). Jump on one of the taxi boats to the undeveloped island of **Lokrum** (*see p269*), 15 minutes from Dubrovnik's old harbour – or venture further afield to the mainly uninhabited **Elafiti Islands** (*see p270*). Watch traditional **Moreška** dancing (*see p289* **Do the Moreška**) with real swords in Korčula. Nudists feed deer on beautiful **Badija** island (*see p290*) off Korčula – join them, clad or otherwise. Head for the remote island of **Lastovo** (*see p290*), closed to foreigners until fairly recently. Spend a week at a working farm near **Lumbarda**, Korčula (*see p293*). Row across a saltwater lake to a 12th-century monastery (*see p297*) on **Mljet**. Buy Croatia's finest oysters fresh at 5kn a piece from the roadside in **Ston** (*see p298*). Visit Dalmatia's most prestigious wine cellars to sample the wares on **Pelješac** (*see p298*). See the beautiful botanical gardens at **Trsteno** (*see p271*). Hire **Pločica Lighthouse** off Korčula, surrounded by old fig trees (*see p291* **Getting away from it all**).

Places to stay

The **Pucić Palace** (*see p283* **Hot hotels**) and the **Hotel Dubrovnik Palace** (*see p280* **Hot hotels**) are as good as it gets in Croatia – which is very good indeed. The **Hotel Kompas** (*see p282*) welcomes families and is a snip off-season. The **Hotel Bellevue** (*see p280*) is Dubrovnik's first boutique lodging. The **Villa Kvarternik** in Cavtat (*see p271*) is a superb conversion. **Sveti Stefan** in Montenegro (*see p286* **Misty mountain hop**) is a hotel of honeymoon material – get hitched quick or get rich, it'll be platinum card only by 2007.

Places to eat

Atlas Club Nautika (*see p274* **Top tables**), **Defne** (*see p271*) and **Porat** (*see p274*) offer top-drawer dining in Dubrovnik. **Lokanda Peskarija** (*see p272*) provides local dishes at local prices on Dubrovnik's old harbour. **Leut** in Cavtat (*see p271*) has stupendous fish and a view to match. Dine sumptuously and swim to your heart's delight at the **Gverović-Orsan** in Zaton Mali (*see p299* **Top tables**). **Kapetanova Kuća** (*see p300* **Top tables**) in Mali Ston offers new Adriatic cuisine by one of Croatia's most renowned chefs. The **Melita** (*see p297*) in Mljet is set in an old monastery in the middle of a lake.

Nightlife

Although the heart of Dubrovnik nightlife is at Lazareti beach and the **East-West** club (*see p279*), you shouldn't miss out on paying a visit to the two cliff-face bars cut into the Old Town fortifications, **Buža I** and **Buža II** (*see p284* **The hole in the wall gang**). The **Troubador** (*see p276* **Best bars**) is a Dubrovnik Old Town landmark. On the edge of town, the **Sunset Lounge** (*see p279* **Best bars**) has its sights on the 21st century – and the Elafiti Islands from the panoramic window. The **Massimo Cocktail Bar** (*see p293*) in a 15th-century tower in Korčula is so high up they winch the drinks up to you.

Culture

The biggest cultural event of the year is the **Dubrovnik Summer Festival** (*see p263*). Take time to see Dubrovnik's finest display of 20th-century art at the **Modern Art Gallery** (*see p267*), with sculptures by Ivan Meštrović and paintings by local realist painter Vlaho Bukovac. Meštrović has his own masterwork, the **Račić Mausoleum**, at Cavtat (*see p271*). More **Bukovac** work can be seen in Dubrovnik's **Dominican monastery** (*see p268*) – and he has his own **gallery** in his native Cavtat (*p271*). In Dubrovnik Old Town, **War Photo Limited** (*see p267*) shows images of conflict captured by award-winning photographers. To learn more about the 1991 siege of Dubrovnik, visit the **Memorial Room of the Dubrovnik Defenders** (*see p267*) in the Sponza Palace. You'll find a couple of Tintorettos in **St Mark's Cathedral** (*see p289*) in Korčula. There's modern Croatian art aplenty at the **Memorial Collection of Maksimilijan Vanka** (*see p289*) in Korčula. Vela Luka's **Culture Centre** (*see p290*) on Korčula contains a couple of Henry Moores in its collection.

Sport & activities

Try **kayaking** out to sea right from Dubrovnik's **Pile Gate** (*see p271*). The **Epidaurum Diving Club** (*see p271*) in Cavtat is one of Croatia's best – clear waters and Roman finds. The **Ladesta Hotel** (*see p290*) near Ubli, Lastovo, runs a diving centre at waters so clear people used to dive for coral there. The **Hotel Odisej** (*see p298*) on Mljet organises diving and windsurfing activities. **Viganj** (*see p300*), not far from Orebić, is the centre of Dalmatia's windsurfing scene.

Montenegrin bombardment 15 years ago. It looks like a dartboard. Two out of every three buildings in the city were damaged. Today only the shinier red roof tiles indicate the brutality. Dubrovnik has been restored to its finest medieval glory and is fully open for business – as the summer hordes of tourists testify.

The year 2005 was Dubrovnik's most prosperous since 1989. The five-star **Hilton Imperial** was opened, many other key hotels were renovated and the compact Old Town overflowed from May until October. In 2006, high-end chain Adriatic Luxury Hotels will open the boutique **Bellevue**, a rather classy conversion of a well-located three-star. In a town bereft of destination restaurants, the former grand coffeehouse Gradska Kavana, now modernised and trendily tagged **graDskavana**, has opened a fashionable wine bar-eaterie behind it, the **Taverna Arsenal**. Other venues near the old harbour also attempt to veer away from a norm imposed by the introduction of mass tourism in the 1960s.

The tourists Dubrovnik is cultivating arrive by cruise ship or private boat. The rest fly in to an airport being upgraded in 2007. Its Old Town centrepieced by one high-end hotel and surrounded by half-a-dozen, Dubrovnik is still a city without any rail link. Backpackers make do with private rooms.

This independently minded former city state of 35,000 people has ambitious plans, knowing that high-end tourism is its bread and butter. The expansion of the harbour at **Gruž** to accommodate the biggest cruise ships and two million passengers a year by 2010, a golf course and the reopening of the cablecar to Mount Srdj, all are priorities. First, though, the bottleneck around the Pile Gate by the Old Town must be cleared. Even the city buses – quaint, orange, Doris Day-era Libertas ones somehow still in operation – will circumnavigate the centre. Access will be created for the transport hub of Gruž, site of the new bus station and main ferry terminal; **Lapad**, home of the family-oriented beach and tourist hotels; and the huge new suspension bridge link to the outside world already in place over the Rijeka Dubrovačka.

For now, not the summer swarm, nor the pretend pubs, nor the daft faux-historic maroon signs in medieval script on every side street corner can ruin the moment. As you stride down the smooth, polished marble of the spinal street **Stradun**, you thank your lucky stars for all the international effort that went into rebuilding this Adriatic gem. Venice sinking would be of similar tragedy and magnitude to the fate that befell Dubrovnik in 1991. And Venice is the key to its history.

STATE OF INDEPENDENCE

For 1,000 years Dubrovnik was the city state of Ragusa, the name given to it by the Italianate refugees who had fled Epidaurum, today's Cavtat, in the seventh century. A wily maritime power run by an enlightened council of local noblemen, Ragusa vied with Venice for Adriatic trade. Many think Dubrovnik to be a Venetian creation, but the 150-year sovereignty of La Serenissima was a distant one. Ragusa had its own currency and institutions. Rid of the Venetians in 1358, Ragusa quickly blossomed.

The noblemen spoke a local version of Italian, sent their children to study at the Sorbonne and governed one of Europe's most progressive centres of learning and commerce. The lower classes resided on the lower slopes of Mount Srdj and the streets north of Stradun, the dividing line. Although a strict class system was in force, slavery had been abolished. There was a public health service, an orphanage, a home for old people, Europe's first pharmacy and an advanced water supply. And all this in the 1400s. Onofrio della Cava's water fountains still stand on Stradun; in 1991 they helped supply besieged residents with water more than 500 years after their installation.

With no royal intrigue – the Old Town is still free of grandiose statues – Ragusa thrived. Whenever the Turks threatened, Ragusa paid them off. Citizenship was bestowed upon the skilled and the entrepreneurial, Jews included. Buildings of marble and stone replaced wooden ones. More than anything, Ragusa produced superb sailors, who worked a highly profitable fleet of 300 ships. Some worked aboard Columbus' ships that sailed to the New World in 1492 – ironically, the first step in robbing Ragusa of its riches when Atlantic trade links began to replace Mediterranean ones in importance.

As the economic tide was turning, a great earthquake struck in 1667. The rebuilding programme called for height restrictions in case of further disaster. A century later, Napoleon took Venice. The writing was on the wall. His forces entered Ragusa in 1806. Soon afterwards the republic was abolished.

As in Split, short French rule saw a swift improvement in the urban infrastructure. After Napoleon's defeat, the Habsburgs moved in to control Ragusa for 100 years until their demise in 1918. During this time, although the local nobility was dying out, the city was central to the Croatian revival against Vienna and Budapest. When it became part of the new south Slav state, it took its Slav name of Dubrovnik. Ruled from Belgrade, its lack of overland transport links with Yugoslavia and outdated trades saw economic decline and mass emigration to the Americas. The city claimed by Croatian Fascists, Mussolini, Hitler and Tito's Partisans was a living museum.

SIEGE AND REVIVAL

Post-war mass tourism put Dubrovnik back on the map, its Old Town a familiar sight in travel brochures. Few Westerners could believe their eyes when the news bulletins of November 1991 showed it billowing with smoke, under siege from Serbian and Montenegrin forces strategically positioned overlooking the town. Retaliating against the blockade of their bases in Croatia, and hoping to break the will of the Croatian people, the Belgrade-backed Yugoslav army, aided by Montenegrin soldiers after booty, seized key resorts in southern Dalmatia and began to shell Dubrovnik. Few Serbs lived in the town, a demilitarised resort.

Blockaded by sea and cut off by land, locals were forced to fend for themselves. Supplies of water and electricity were cut. Citizens going about their business along Stradun were hit by shells. At the same time, little-known towns in Slavonia – in particular Vukovar (*see p108* **Vukovar before and after**) – were being flattened. But Dubrovnik was the historic gem. International outrage was prompt, Belgrade lost the propaganda war and within weeks an independent Croatia was recognised by the EU.

With occasional ceasefires, the siege lasted until the summer of 1992 when Croatian forces pushed the Serbs and Montenegrins. More than two-thirds of the buildings in the Old Town had been hit and nearly half-a-million tiles had to be replaced. Rebuilding lasted seven years and cost an approximate $18.5 million, some of it from UNESCO – the Old Town is on the World Heritage list. From the late 1990s, tourists have trickled back, turning into a steady stream by the summer of 2005. Dubrovnik is familiar territory for the now fiftysomethings who came in droves before 1991, who are happy to follow each other round the Old Town sights and are not too fussy when it comes to inventive cuisine.

SIGHTS AND SOUNDS

Almost everything worth seeing is centred on the Old Town. To get the best view, and one of a stupendously clear, blue Adriatic lapping the rocks below and stretching way beyond, take the **walking tour** of the city walls (summer 9am-7pm daily, winter 9am-3pm daily, 30kn). Audio-guides (30kn) are available at the main entrance inside the Pile Gate to the left. An hour should suffice but take as long as you like.

You'll spend the bulk of your time within the 15th-century ring of fortifications, in the small square half-mile (1.3sq km) of gleaming medieval space bisected by 300-metre-long

(985-foot) Stradun. As you flit between the main gates of Pile and Ploče, guided by the list of places on the maroon flags, each venue with its own logoed white lamp, barkers on every side street corner call you up to the bland tourist restaurants on Prijeko. Cats scatter in from the old harbour, a cacophony of tour guides, many French, give their spiels. All is free of traffic until you reach the bus-choked hub outside the Pile Gate. Beyond, over the drawbridge, stand the Lovrijenac Fortress, used for productions of Shakespeare classics during the Summer Festival, and the main road to Gruž and Lapad.

Beyond the Ploče Gate stretches Lazareti beach, the nightlife centre, then a string of luxury hotels. Beside it is the attractive old harbour, where taxi boats set off for the nearby island of Lokrum. Just inside the walls is the main square and crossing point of Luža, where you'll find the landmark astronomical clock tower (sadly, a modern rebuild of the 1444 original), Orlando's Column where all state declarations were read and the smaller of Onofrio's fountains. Surrounding it are the main historic attractions of the **Rector's Palace**; the **Cathedral** and **Treasury**; the **Sponza Palace**; and the **Dominican monastery**.

The other sights are within easy reach. On the south side of the harbour, round the corner from the Rector's Palace, St John's Fortress (Damjana Jude 2) houses both the **Maritime Museum** (020 426 465, open 9am-2pm Tue-Sun, 15kn) and the **Aquarium** (020 427 937, open summer 9am-9pm daily, winter 9am-1pm Mon-Sat, 15kn). While downstairs is a gloomy collection of tanks containing mainly Adriatic sealife, upstairs is an attractive collection of ships' models, paintings and photographs detailing Dubrovnik's seafaring history through the Golden Age to the somewhat less glorious modern one.

In front of the clock tower, the baroque **Church of St Blaise** (open 8am-noon, 5-7pm daily), named after the protector of Dubrovnik through the centuries of trade, torment and tourism, was rebuilt after the 1667 earthquake. Inside, the altar, with a statue of the saint, is the biggest attraction. The stained-glass windows are a modern addition.

On the other side of St Blaise, the adjoining squares of Gundulićeva poljana and Bunićeva poljana are busy day and night. Market stalls cover the pavement in the morning, constant entertainment for diners and coffee drinkers at nearby terraces; bars kick into action after dark.

At the other end of Stradun, by the Pile Gate built in the 15th century, the main drawbridged entrance to the Old Town, stands **Onofrio's Great Fountain**, less ornate than how it looked before the 1667 earthquake. Behind the Franciscan church nearby, the **Franciscan**

Luxury lodgings – the **Villa Shererezade** of the **Hotel Grand Villa Argentina**. *See p282.*

monastery (020 321 410, 9am-3pm daily, 10kn), embellished with beautiful cloisters, houses what is claimed to be the world's oldest pharmacy and a museum of religious artefacts.

Dubrovnik's contemporary attractions include the **Modern Art Gallery** (Frana Supila 23, 020 426 590, open summer 10am-1pm, 5-9pm Tue-Sun, winter 10am-5pm Tue-Sun, 15kn), past Lazareti beach, with sculptures by Ivan Meštrović and paintings by Cavtat-born Vlaho Bukovac, whose 19th-century portraits are the highlight of this collection; and **War Photo Limited** (Antuninska 6, 020 322 166, www.warphotoltd.com, open May-Sept 9am-9pm daily, Mar, Apr, Oct 10am-4pm Tue-Sat, 10am-2pm Sun, closed Nov-Apr, 25kn), two floors of war photography, of Dubrovnik and other recent conflicts. Works by renowned photographers are displayed in temporary exhibitions throughout the summer.

Rector's Palace

Pred Dvorom 3 (020 321 497). **Open** *Summer* 9am-6pm daily. *Winter* 9am-2pm daily. **Admission** 20kn; under-12s 7kn.

The most historic monument in Dubrovnik, the Rector's Palace was rebuilt twice. The first, by Onofrio della Cava of fountain fame, was in Venetian-Gothic style, visible in the window design once you ascend the grand staircase to the Rector's living quarters. The second was by Florentine Michelozzo Michelozzi, responsible for the loggia façade. On the ground floor, either side of a light-filled courtyard, are the prison and courtrooms of the Ragusa Republic, and a separate exhibition of Neolithic Age findings from the Vela Špilja on Korčula. More Neolithic and Bronze Age finds from Gudnja Cave near Ston are on display upstairs. Here, where each Rector resided for his month's stint, is a strange assortment of items: sedan chairs, carriages, magistrates' robes and wigs, portraits of local notables and Ivo Rudenjak's beautifully carved bookcase, in the otherwise staid reception and administration rooms. One curiosity is the clocks, some set at quarter to six, the time in the evening when Napoleon's troops entered in 1806.

Sponza Palace

Luža (020 321 032). **Open** 9am-2pm daily.

The attractive, 16th-century former customs house and Ragusa mint is used to house the extensive state archives (by appointment only, phone ahead) and temporary exhibitions. Free to enter, a current long-term exhibition has been given space in a small room opposite the ticket office: the Memorial Room of the Dubrovnik Defenders. Covering the terrible 12 months from October 1991 (although keen to point out that isolated attacks continued until the summer of 1995), the exhibition contains portraits of the 300 defenders and civilians who died during the siege and the tattered remnant of the Croatian flag that flew atop strategic Mount Srdj. Napoleon's Imperial Fort there is still a ruin and closed to the public.

Cathedral

Poljana Marina Držića (no phone). **Open** 8am-8pm daily. **Admission** treasury 7kn.

The original church, allegedly funded by Richard the Lionheart in recognition of the local hospitality when shipwrecked on Lokrum in the 1190s, was lost to the 1667 earthquake. In its place was built a somewhat bland, baroque affair, free but unenticing to walk around. The main draw is the treasury at one end, a somewhat grotesque collection of holy relics. The arm, skull and lower leg of patron St Blaise are kept in jewel-encrusted casings, another box contains one of Christ's nappies, and wood from the Holy Cross is incorporated into a finely crafted crucifix from the 16th century. Perhaps the most bizarre artefact is the creepy dish and jug designed as a gift for the Hungarian King Mátyás Corvinus, who died before he could receive it.

Dominican Monastery

Sv Dominika 4 (020 321 423). **Open** *Summer* 9am-6pm daily. *Winter* 9am-3pm daily. **Admission** 10kn.

Between the Sponza Palace and the Ploče Gate, this monastery is best known for its late Gothic cloisters and late 15th-century paintings of the Dubrovnik School in the museum. On the walls of the monastery church are a beautiful wooden crucifix by Paolo Veneziano from 1358 and a painting by renowned fin-de-siècle artist Vlaho Bukovac from Cavtat, *The Miracle of St Dominic*.

Beaches

The main city beach is just past the Ploče Gate at **Lazareti**, named after the 16th-century quarantine buildings at street level. The pebbly

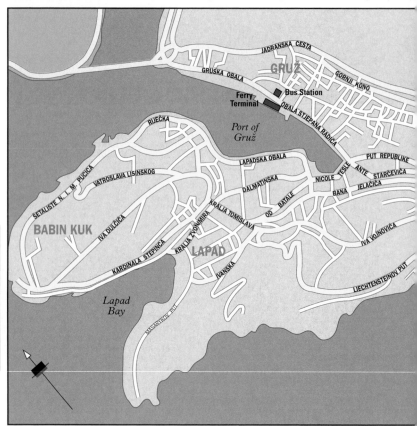

beach here, **Banje**, is packed in summer and a main feature of the **East-West** beach club (*see p279*) and restaurant.

Walking round from the old harbour, along the rocks fringing the sea-lapped city walls, are several spots used by bathers and divers. The most popular is by one of the Buža bars (*see p284* **The hole in the wall gang**), its jagged stones planed flat for sunbathers and metal steps cut into the rock to help you clamber back up.

The main hotel complexes within a short bus journey of town, Lapad and Babin Kuk, both have popular, well-maintained public beaches, the best equipped being the child-friendly **Copacabana** near the Hotel Minčeta. If you're serious about beaches, take the regular taxi boat from the old harbour to unspoiled **Lokrum** (*see below* **Excursions**). There are a handful of beaches within easy walk of the harbour, including a naturist one at the far eastern edge.

Venturing further afield to the Elafiti Islands (*see p270*), Lopud has a lovely, sandy beach at Sunj, 2km (1.2 miles) south of the main village.

Excursions

The easiest trip is to take a taxi boat (every 30mins, 15mins journey time, 9am-9pm daily, 35kn return) to unspoilt Lokrum from the old harbour. Covered in pine trees and dotted with rocky beaches, including a naturist one on the east coast, Lokrum's attractions have crowds packing the taxi boats through the summer. Centrepieced by a ruined Napoleonic fort and botanical gardens (still filled with exotic plants and peacocks) set up by fated Habsburg royal Maximilian, Lokrum is big enough to swallow the masses even in high season. A restaurant is set by the 11th-century Benedictine monastery closed by the French 200 years ago. The monks

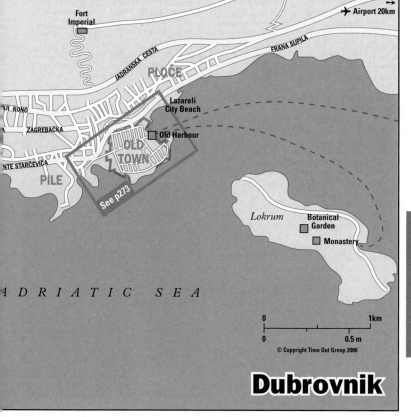

are said to have left a curse on the island – Maximilian (famously shot by firing squad in Mexico) is one of a dozen notables connected with it who came to a sticky end. No local will spend the night on Lokrum.

Until the cablecar link is restored, scaling nearby **Mount Srdj** is a strenuous, mainly unshaded two-hour climb from the Pile Gate, up Jadranksa cesta. Don't stray from the footpath as there may still be unexploded missiles on the hillside. At the top is a ruined Napoleonic fort, the hilltop cross you see illuminated at night from town and a breathtaking view. On hot afternoons, don't forget to pack water.

To escape the crowds, take a foot-passenger ferry from the main harbour at Gruž for the three (barely) inhabited of the 14-island Elafiti archipelago: **Koločep**, **Lopud** and **Šipan**. The nearest, Koločep, consists of a couple of modest settlements: Donje Čelo, site of the ferry port and only hotel; and Gornje Čelo, accessible by a pine-shaded footpath. Secluded pebble beaches, some naturist, mark the coastline. To stay over, the three-star Villa Koločep (020 757 025, fax 020

Dubrovnik in one day

Start the day as locals do – with a coffee and a cigarette on the terrace of the **graDskavana** (*see p276*). Dubrovnik's three main sights – the **Rector's Palace** (*see p267*), the **Sponza Palace** (*see p267*) and the **Cathedral** (*see p268*) – are all within two minutes' walk. Allow 30 minutes to one hour for each. If you start getting peckish, the excellent **Dubrovački kantun** (*see p272*) has takeaway sandwiches, which you can take to the old harbourfront nearby. As you're on Boškovićeva, though, perhaps you could quickly climb to the top and take a look at the diagram of where the bombs fell in 1991 to give you an idea of the pristine repair job around you.

By now the sun should be high – but not too high – in the sky, time for a tour around the **city walls** (*see p266*), allowing you to stride down the gleaming pavement of Stradun to the Pile Gate. Before you start, book a sea-view table at the snazzy **Atlas Club Nautika** (*see p274*) for its cut-price light lunch. Do a circuit of the walls in an hour or so, and heaven will be waiting on a plate.

You're off sightseeing duty for the afternoon so spend it at the beach. You can either go back to the old harbour for the hourly taxi boat to unspoiled **Lokrum** (*see p269*) or head for the main harbour at Gruž and a longer trek to the **Elafiti Islands** (*see p270*) – perhaps better appreciated with a two- or three-day visit. Sailing back from Lokrum, you can beat the crowds by tucking into an early-evening meal at the **Lokanda Peskarija** (*see p272*) right on the old harbour – or try any number of local wines with a snack at the **Taverna Arsenal** (*see p274*) behind.

If you want a panoramic sunset drink, head for Buža II, saving Buža I for post-midnight dives into the moonlit Adriatic and beers (for both, *see p284* **The hole in the wall gang**). Those serious about their sunsets and cocktails can make a detour, 20 minutes by bus from the Pile Gate to Lapad and the stupendous **Sunset Lounge** (*see p279*).

Back on Stradun, the **Troubador** (*see p276*) is best attempted early. If the tourists get too much, try the lesser known **Libertina** (*see p276*) nearby. **Talir** (*see p277*) is another good bet. If dining later on, the **Defne** (*see p271*) roof-terrace restaurant of the Pucić Palace is outstanding.

Unless you've made the two detours to Gruž and Lapad, the schedule has kept you within ten minutes' walk of your first morning coffee. Your nightclub is equally close: the **East-West** (*see p279*), on Lazareti beach. Taxis await at the Ploče Gate afterwards.

Dubrovnik & Islands

757 027, open May-Oct, half-board €60-€120) or a few private rooms can accommodate.

The most developed, but by no means built-up, is Lopud. Dotted with medieval churches, it was popular with local noblemen who built villas on the island, including the Rector, whose summer palace is in ruins. Nearby, the Grand Hotel is being restored; your only option, apart from private rooms, is the three-star Lafodia hotel complex (open May-Oct, 020 759 022, fax 020 759 026, half-board €65-€100), with a pool, a short walk from the ferry port. A path near the Grand Hotel leads over the hill to the other side of the island, and the lovely sandy beach of **Šunj** 15 minutes away. It faces Šipan, the largest of the islands, similarly dotted with a few old churches, noblemen's villas, Roman remains and two villages: Šipanska Luka and Sudjuradj. A five-kilometre (three-mile) road through a valley of olive groves links the two. Ferries stop at both. The Hotel Šipan (020 758 000, fax 020 758 003, open May-Oct, €50-€90 double) overlooks the harbour at Šipanska Luka. Private rooms are plentiful.

Adventure Croatia (091 526 3813 mobile, 091 546 4110 mobile, www.crochallenge. com) organise sea kayaking and snorkelling excursions from the Pile Gate. The **Dubrovnik Diving Club** (www.dubrovnikreception.com/main/diving_en.html) is based in Babin Kuk.

Down the coast, **Cavtat** is an easy day trip, either by hourly bus No.10 (40mins, 12kn) or boat from the old harbour (50mins, 30kn). The southernmost resort in Croatia, Cavtat is an old Greek and Roman settlement, sacked by tribes in the seventh century. Refugees flooded to Ragusa and built Dubrovnik. It's the birthplace of realist painter Vlaho Bukovac, who has a gallery on the Riva (020 478 646, open summer 9am-1pm, 5-9pm daily, winter 9am-1pm daily, 10kn). The key sight is the **Račić Mausoleum** (020 478 646, summer 10am-noon, 6-8pm Mon-Sat, 10am-noon Sun), under renovation in 2005. Set on the hilltop tip of the peninsula, it's a Meštrović masterpiece in white marble dominating the town cemetery.

Close to the main airport at Čilipi, Cavtat is a reasonably cheap and convenient place to base yourself. If you want to stay in style, it has two classy hotels: the beautiful six-room Villa Kvarternik (Kvarternikova 3, 020 479 800, fax 020 479 808, www.dub.iz.hr, €83-€160 double) and the five-star Hotel Croatia (Frankopanska 10, 020 475 555, fax 020 478 213, www.hoteli-croatia.hr, €130-€442 double), a massive, multi-tiered year-round resort hotel with pools, tennis courts and two beaches. The best table in town is the Leut (Trumbićev put 11, 020 478 477, closed Jan), a fish restaurant with a lovely seafront terrace.

The sea here is particularly clear. Just outside Cavtat is the Hotel Epidaurus, linked to one of Croatia's best diving centres, Epidaurum (020 471 386, 098 427 550 mobile, www.epidaurum-diving-cavtat.hr). Roman ruins and sunken ships line the seabed nearby.

Further south, and you're in **Montenegro** (*see p286* **Misty mountain hop**), definitely worth a day trip. Head north from Dubrovnik and you find the village of **Trsteno**, known for its **Arboretum** (020 751 019, open summer 8am-6pm daily, winter 8am-3pm daily, 15kn), 16th-century botanical gardens. You either visit as part of an excursion from Dubrovnik or ask the driver to drop you 45 minutes out of town on the regular service to Split. Near Trsteno, at Brsečine, is Veliki Žal beach, with a summer DJ scene. Between Trsteno and Dubrovnik is **Zaton Mali**, a small fishing village best known for the **Gverović-Orsan** restaurant, one of the best in south Dalmatia (*see p299* **Top tables**).

Where to eat

Dubrovnik is overflowing with tourist-friendly restaurants – which is half the problem. Barkers work Stradun, persuading passing tourists to head to a side-street restaurant that will differ little in character from any other in the Old Town. Prijeko, parallel to Stradun, and sundry downtown squares are lined with characterless terrace restaurants. You won't be poisoned, nor will you come away looking forward to a revisit. Watch out for wine prices. There are exceptions – **Atlas Club Nautika**, **Labirint**, **Proto** – but they provide a pricy formal dining experience hardly conducive to a relaxed evening with your holiday companions.

With this in mind, the three key venues around the old harbour – **Lokanda Peskarija**, **Poklisar** and the newly opened **Taverna Arsenal** – offer atmosphere, location and, for the price, good quality (mainly) seafood specialities. For quality Mediterranean cuisine, head to the signature restaurants of the **Pucić Palace** and the **Hilton Imperial** hotels: **Defne** and **Porat**.

Atlas Club Nautika

Brsalje 3 (020 442 526). **Open** Mid Jan-mid Dec noon-midnight daily. **Credit** AmEx, DC, MC, V. Just outside the Pile Gate, this is Dubrovnik's most prestigious place. *See p274* **Top tables**.

Defne

Pucic Palace, Od Puča 1 (020 326 200/www.thepucic palace.com). **Open** May-Oct 11am-midnight daily. **Credit** AmEx, DC, MC, V.
Defne occupies the roof terrace in the Old Town's five-star hotel, one of its three restaurants. Its accent on eastern Mediterranean cuisine comes with a whole

philosophy, starting with its name from the ancient Greek laurel-tree-nurturing nymph, passing by the presence of a waterpipe and mint teas at dinner, and ending, thankfully, with the rather splendid food itself. Under the ambitious stewardship of chef Ozgur Donertas, it has plenty of flavoursome meat options from Turkey and the Levant (grilled lamb chops with fresh mint, kebabs of meatballs and beef steak with mint yoghurt sauce and garlic tomatoes, chicken breast marinated with lavender and sage, upmarket meze) as well as maritime ones from closer to home. Mljet lobster is grilled with a white wine risotto or poached with black risotto and saffron sauce. Defne prides itself on its traditional seafood soup with real sea stone – the edible contents are certainly fresh, both seafood and garden vegetables. Other starters, also under 50kn, such as octopus carpaccio with handmade black tagliolini served with truffle honey vinaigrette, put similarly priced standard ones in the vicinity to shade. Most mains are under 100kn. A diner can toddle downstairs after a completely memorable meal only 300kn the lighter. The year-round Café Royale and Razonada wine bar also feature a selection of Ozgur Donertas' stellar creations.

Dubrovački kantun

Boškovićeva 5 (020 331 911/091 699 4966 mobile). **Open** 10.30am-4pm, 6.30pm-midnight daily. **Credit** MC, V.
Andrej Di Leo's delightful little eaterie in the heart of the Old Town is a real treat. Not ten minutes from the tourist traps of Prijeko, the kantun offers healthy local vegetables, meats and cheeses in a homely atmosphere. Ignore the silly chef sign outside and walk into a wooden interior tastefully decorated with strings of garlic and framed pictures. Appetisers are a speciality – dive into a Dubrovački kantun platter (99kn for two) of smoked ham, cheeses, anchovies and rocket. Fish, such as Dalmatian-style cod (55kn), can be a starter or a main (90kn), accompanied with seasonal vegetables. The house specialities are traditional beef dishes (69kn): *pastičada* alla Dubrovački kantun, marinated beef stew; or *brasol* with gnocchi, beef steak with bacon and parmesan. Dalmatian flans (15kn) follow. It has a takeaway sandwich bar, too. Recommended.

Labirint

Sv Dominika (020 322 222/www.labirint dubrovnik.com). **Open** noon-midnight daily. **Credit** AmEx, DC, MC, V.
After 13 years of renovation, this prime space opposite the Dominican monastery opened for business in 2005. Restaurant, bar and nightclub, the Labirint boasts a fabulous location, overlooking the old harbour from the Sv Luka battlement. Given its classy site, the nightclub is old-school tacky really, while the restaurant does a fair job at sometimes twice the price you'd be paying elsewhere. Pastas, standard fish dishes and grilled meats are served in the stone alcoves or on the starry terrace, but it's the setting you're paying for – and the setting (and the bill) you'll be talking about afterwards.

Lokanda Peskarija

Na Ponti (020 324 750). **Open** 8am-midnight daily. **No credit cards**.
Queues around the old harbour for this one, and so there should be. Nothing fancy at all here, just good domestic dishes at knockdown prices swiftly served by overworked staff. Outside, rows of tables line a courtyard overlooking the bobbing boats of the harbour; within, a large bar counter and top floor with rustic touches. The kitchen knocks out simple seafood risottos and grilled squid at 50kn-70kn a go, equally cheap but drinkable domestic wine gets sunk by the jug-load and everyone wanders off satisfied. The motto in local dialect over the door says: 'Here we eat, drink and party.' Exactly.

Mea Culpa

Za Rokom 3 (020 323 430). **Open** 9am-midnight daily. **Credit** MC, V.
Run by the same management as the Lokanda Peskarija (*see above*), this is generally considered the best pizzeria in town. It certainly serves the biggest pizzas. It's a simple wooden venue at the Pile Gate end of the Old Town, providing a straightforward 50kn dining fix. If you don't fancy pizza, there's not much else to choose from, but with a scattering of tables outside on a summer's eve, Mea Culpa makes for a pleasant, cheap and communal dining choice.

Penatur

Lučarica 2 (020 323 700). **Open** noon-11pm daily. **No credit cards**.
Although it's the promise of 35kn lunches that draws you in, this modest place isn't a bad or expensive choice for dinner either, and as close to the heart of Dubrovnik as you can get. With a few tables in the shadow of St Blaise's church and another door in Lučarica, the Penatur is both prominent and intimate, its simple interior of oil paintings and shelves of Pelješac wine comprising a dozen tables at most. Most opt for fish, fresh and 280kn by the kilo, although decent meaty mains (rib steak, 65kn, veal medallions, 70kn) are also available. Throw in a bottle of Dingač (170kn) or Pošip (140kn) and you've got a satisfying supper all round.

Poklisar

Ribarnica 1 (020 322 176). **Open** 8am-midnight daily. **Credit** AmEx, DC, MC, V.
With its twin terraces occupying both sides of a prominent square overlooking the old harbour, the Poklisar cannot fail to make a decent turnover in high season. The prices, given the location, are reasonable – pizzas at 45kn, sea fish of the day at 230kn for two people, even grilled lobster is 430kn a kilo, and that can be astronomical elsewhere. Among the standard choice of mains is the odd interesting dish, such as shrimps in saffron sauce or home-made gnocchi with gorgonzola and rocket, and desserts deserve a detour once you step off the boat back from Lokrum: walnut pancakes, hazelnut or wild fruit parfaits. Try and get here early on, before the cheesy live music drowns out the lovely lap of the sea.

Central Dubrovnik

1   2   3   4

F   E   D   C   B   A

Airport 22km
FRANA SUPILA

Lazareli
City Beach

Kaše

POROPORELA

St John's
Fortress

Old
Harbour

Revelin
Fortress

TRG
ORUŽJA

DOMINIKANSKA

IZA GRADA

Dominican
Monastery

Sponza
Palace

Rector's
Palace

KNEZA DAMJANA JUDE

OD PUSTIJERNE

ANDRIJIĆA

Orlando
Tower

St Blaise
Church

PRED
DVOROM

POLJANA
M. DRŽIĆA

Cathedral

ILIJE SARAKE

ZLATARSKA

KOVAČKA

ŽUDIOSKA

BOŠKOVIĆEVA

DROPČEVA

ZAMANJINA

VETRANOVIĆEVA

PETILOVRIJENCI

MLINIČEVA

LUČARICA

GUNDULIĆEVA
POLJANA

C. ZUZORIĆ

BUNIĆEVA
POLJANA

HRVASKA

ZAGREBAČKA

IZA GRADA

Minčeta
Fortress

PRIJEKO

PELINE

NALJEŠKOVIĆA

ANTUNINSKA

PALMOTIĆEVA

CELESTINA MEDOVIĆA

OD SIGURATE

STRADUN

ZLATARIĆEVA

GETALDIĆEVA

OD PUČA

DOBRIČEVA

ŠIROKA

MIHA PRACATA

M. KABOGE

OD DOMINA

STROSSMAYEROVA

SVETE MARIJE

ZVIJEZDIĆEVA

KASTELA

POLJANA
R. BOSKOVIĆA

DRŽIĆEVA

Jesuit Church
and Monastery

Franciscan
Monastery

Onofrio's
Fountain

St Claire's
Nunnery

ZLATARIĆEVA

OD PUČA

OD SIGURATE

ZAGROM

OD RUPA

OD SORTE

Buža 1

Buža 2

PUTNIŠĆA

FRANKOPANSKA

UZ POSAT

ZVJEZDANA BOSKOVIĆA

UZ POSAT

ANTE STARČEVIĆA

Bokar
Fortress

Lovrijenac
Fortress

Adriatic
Sea

100 m

100 yds

© Copyright Time Out Group 2006

To Ferry Terminal &
Bus Station 2.5km

Atlas Club Nautika

This is the snazziest place in town, fantastically positioned with two panoramic terraces, impeccably staffed with starched white-tablecloth formality, and, naturally, vastly expensive. Set between the Pile Gate and the Lovrijenac fortress, the **Nautika** (see p271) is worth the big blow-out (400kn-500kn per head à la carte, with wine) – provided you reserve a sea-view table, Nos.30-38 on the Penatur terrace or Nos.56, 57 or 64 on the Lovrijenac/Brsalje terrace. The interior dining rooms are quite plain. If you're going à la carte, chef Nikola Ivanišević insists on the freshest fish (ask the waiter for recommendations), some of which are used in the 500kn-700kn five-course menus. Shellfish are a speciality, particularly in dishes from the nearby Elafiti Islands, such as Lopud brodet with polenta. Truffles are used with abandon – the cream of scampi soup with black truffles is outstanding. Ivanišević makes a big fuss of desserts, too: strawberries in maraschino with mint or strudel with dry figs and sour cherries. For those who don't have 500kn to throw around, the Nautika has introduced a concept since followed by other high-end establishments here: the 'light lunch'. Available until 4pm, it offers the chance to sample Dubrovnik's best without breaking the bank – Adriatic salad or tagliatelle with mushrooms and truffles at 60kn-70kn a throw, for example.

Porat

Hilton Imperial, Marijana Blažica 2 (020 320 320/ www.hilton.com). **Open** 7am-11pm daily. **Credit** AmEx, DC, MC, V.

The signature restaurant of the recently opened Hilton offers something that few others seem to do in Dubrovnik: contemporary, inventive cuisine. Although you can find Dalmatian treats aplenty – the air-dried, smoked ham and cheese starter, for example – the accent is on the pan-seared and the rosemary-tinted. The grilled lamb ribs, one of a handful of carnivorous delicacies from the lava-stone grill, have a rosemary lard crust, the pan-seared tuna has been marinated in lime and rosemary. With appetisers, such as the octopus carpaccio with grilled peppers and spicy wild rocket, in the 90kn bracket, and mains, such as the pork belly with vegetable caponata, 140kn, you won't have much change from 400kn, but worth every lipa if you're looking for international quality. Also equipped with a summer terrace, it should give the Nautika (see above) a run for its money. Superb food offered in the lounge bar too.

Proto

Široka 1 (020 323 234). **Open** 11am-11pm daily. **Credit** AmEx, DC, MC, V.

From the same family as the upmarket Nautika, the fish-oriented Proto cannot fail to be classy. It's in the Old Town, so the view from the first-floor terrace is of Dubrovnik's familiar masonry, but the food more than makes up for it. As well as mussels, squid and lobster in simple but superbly balanced sauces, there are more unusual finds from nearby Pelješac, snails for example. The fish soup (48kn) might be the best you'll find in town. An easy option might be to dive in with the fish plate for two (288kn) and spend an enjoyable hour over it. Superb selection of wines, three meal choices for children, light lunches – and booking essential.

Taverna Arsenal

Pred Dvorom 1 (020 321 065). **Open** noon-midnight daily. **Credit** AmEx, DC, MC, V.

The Mea Culpa group, which runs the pizzeria of the same name (see p272), and which recently trendified the landmark coffeehouse graDskavana (see p276) operating from this same historic building, opened this fabulous place towards the end of 2005. A weaponry overlooking the old harbour has existed since the 13th century; the archways were added in the 15th century, but by the 19th this was a theatre. In recent times it was left to cats and fishermen repairing their nets until Mea Culpa transformed it to resemble a post-modern taverna. A huge vaulted wooden interior with a few maritime knick-knacks and an aquarium or two is neatly divided between diners and wine drinkers. The wine list is huge, some 20 (mainly local) varieties of each colour, eight each by the glass, from a simple white Vrbnička (14kn/105kn) to a Pinot Siri Batić (262kn). Reds run up to a Plavac Mali Ergić (457kn). Local spirits are equally well represented, with all kinds of *rakija* and Istrian bitters. Unsurprisingly, given the location, fish is the speciality, fresh, grilled varieties at 300kn a kilo, fillets of *brancin* (sea bass) and *sabljarka* (swordfish) at 60kn-90kn, plus top-notch versions of ubiquitous standards. You can equally call up a T-bone steak (110kn) or rumpsteak salad (50kn). Smart but unpretentious clientele, snappy staff and at last a buzz in the dreary local dining scene.

Where to drink

For the seasoned bar hopper, Dubrovnik Old Town and vicinity offer a surprisingly unusual array of venues to investigate. Stylish cafés at the clock-tower end of Stradun do a brisk trade from breakfast time past dusk – even the once traditional **graDskavana** has undergone a modern revamp to compete. Behind it, you can sample the best local wines at the **Taverna Arsenal** (*see p274*), both bar and restaurant. During the day, escape or enjoy the heat at Dubrovnik's two rocky terrace beach bars cut into its seafacing city walls, named simply **Buža I** and **Buža II** (*see p284* **The Hole in the wall gang**). Both stay open late in summer, although by then half the world has flocked to the landmark **Troubador** (*see p276* **Best bars**). The handful of nearby bars in the adjoining square of Bunićeva poljana cope with the overflow. Bizarre Old Town gems abound: the idiosyncratic **Libertina**, the total grunge of **Ludwig** and the luvvies' favourite **Talir**, all within five minutes of each other.

A short walk from the city walls, Lazareti beach offers seaside cocktails at the **East-West** (*see p279*), while in the other direction towards Gruž, a strip of bars on Bana Jelačića includes the hard-drinking **Roxy**, favoured by the leather-

jacketed fraternity. Kralja Zvonimira towards Lapad, and the beach itself, throng with late bars, although no award-winners. By contrast, the **Sunset Lounge** of the high-end Hotel Dubrovnik Palace (*see p279* **Best bars**), at the end of the No.4 bus route, is text-your-mates-immediately material. Once-in-a-lifetime view, great service, excellent cocktails at reasonable prices – and half-price happy hour too.

Gaffe Pub

Miha Pracata 4 (020 323 867). **Open** 10am-11pm daily.

The best example of what passes for a pub in these parts – preferable to the Irish one nearby – the unfortunately named Gaffe comprises a corridor terrace and shiny wood interior with little booths. Hajduk Split and Everton football souvenirs lend a suitably sporting touch, DJ decks provide conversation-level evening entertainment, Strongbow cider and Guinness are the cross-Channel draught options,

Dubrovnik by night – the **Cathedral** and the **Rector's Palace** (*left*). *See p267 and p268.*

Troubador

The most famous bar in Dalmatia now looks like a billboard for T-Mobile, and if you didn't know that this was the lovely old **Troubador**, you wouldn't touch it with a bargepole. But lovely old Troubador it is, and visit it you must. Run by Marco, a member of renowned 1960s group the Dubrovački Trubadori, it's a touchstone for the pre-conflict generation, and all Dubrovnik's musicians and entertainers of a certain age pass through and say hello. In summer, the corner of terrace is given over to free jazz concerts, waiters rushing between tables packed with tourists. Inside is now only a tiny, seen-it-all bar, room enough for three tables, a piano, a slap bass and a few pictures of the Trubadori of Eurovision yore. An atmospheric, back area of wooden alcoves has been blocked off by a large fridge of beer bottles (Heineken, Karlovačko, Corona), hopefully just a temporary measure. Cocktails (50kn-60kn) and sandwiches (15kn-20kn) also available. *See p277 for listings.*

and Kodak snaps nod towards the concept of a regular clientele. The growing number of expat residents propping up the bar here testify to that. Local prices on local brews, Karlovačko at 12kn a glass, for example. Happy hour 5-7pm.

Galerie

Kunićeva 7 (no phone). **Open** noon-midnight daily.
A rather stylish off-Stradun option this one, popular with a young, local party crowd, and ideal for a

pre-club couple of swifties. Chat-friendly rap and dance music fills a modest interior decorated with striking line drawings by Nikolina Šimunović, while friends relax in the wicker chairs at the back. Brown stools surround a busy bar counter that dispenses standard, reasonably priced cocktails and draught Laško. It's a better option than the dozens of tourist-filled spots on similar side streets.

graDskavana

Luža 2 (020 321 414). **Open** Summer 8am-2am daily. Winter 8am-11pm daily.
A handful of café terraces surround the focal square of Luža, offering the ideal morning pick-me-up. The Cele has the best cakes, the Dubrava the best sandwiches, but the newly renovated graDskavana has ambience. Not long ago, this was the landmark Gradska Kavana, a coffeehouse of Habsburg vintage, given what passed for classy decor in the Communist era. Each main town has one, a prominent meeting place where locals spend hours observing each other. This one is by the clock tower. In 2005 it had a modern revamp. Neat red-and-blue chairs now line the terrace, the interior of wrought-iron and pastel colours has lost the decorative fuss of yesteryear, and the name has gone all lower-case. Drinks, too, have caught up with contemporary mores – the handful of classic cocktails (70kn), Manhattans, Negronis and Daiquiris, are well prepared and well concocted. This doesn't mean that a trendy element now flocks here, but any Gradska Kavana has always been for every strata of society.

Hemingway Bar

Pred Dvorom (no phone). **Open** noon-1am daily.
Prominent cocktail bar opposite the Rector's Palace, round the corner from the Troubador (*see left*). Given its name and location, you would expect the Hemingway to be pricy and snobby, but not a bit of it. The most comprehensive range of cocktails in the Old Town features a long list of drinks, nearly all in the 50kn bracket, with the possibility of a 150kn-200kn pitcher for four. No real surprises among the selection, Daiquiris and Mojitos mixed with Havana 3, a tidy combination of Pernod and champagne in the Death in the Afternoon, and a pleasant buzz around the bar and terrace.

Kavana Kino Slavica

Ante Starčićeva 42 (no phone). **Open** Summer 6-11pm daily.
On the main road into the Old Town stands a huge stone terrace equipped with an almost equally expansive cinema screen. Here film-goer and barfly alike can gawp at the jaw-dropping panoramic view of the sea while enjoying a drink at local bar prices. Order a 7kn spritzer or 12kn beer from the basic bar inside, take it up to the terrace and you've the perfect start to the evening set apart from the tourist swarm ten minutes away in the Old Town.

Libertina

Zlatarska 3 (no phone). **Open** noon-midnight daily.

Dubrovnik & Islands

This characterful shoebox of a bar is affectionately known by locals as 'Luci' after Luci Capurso, the bar-owning former member of vintage local beat combo Dubrovački Trubaduri. Although just as much part of Dubrovnik's pop heritage as the landmark Troubador (*see p276*) the other side of Stradun, this is off the tourist track. They wouldn't fit in anyway – there's just enough room for an Ožujsko beertap, a Gaggia coffee machine, a TV, weird retro souvenirs and a wall of cuttings dedicated to Luci's glory years. Shying away from any mention of his Eurovision Song Contest past, Luci just serves the regulars, pleasingly oblivious to the piles of money being made at inferior bars on his doorstep.

Ludwig
Zamanjina 7 (no phone). **Open** noon-midnight daily.
Even this grunge bar in a Stradun side street has its own dinky little lantern, although you can't see any middle-aged couples lingering over a pint. Gogol, Mogwai, *Kill Bill* and Hendrix all get a decorative look-in, but it's the hard-living drinkers hunched around the counter that make the place. Unthreatening if occasionally entertainingly edgy, Ludwig offers welcome respite from the dainty tourist traps nearby.

Roxy
Bana Jelačića 9 (no phone). **Open** 6pm-2am daily.
If Croatia had roadhouses, this would be a road-house. The main rockers' hangout, the Roxy celebrates 20 years of hard-core drinking in 2006. Set on a small stretch of street lined with party bars just past the junction on the Lapad side of the Hilton Imperial, the Roxy is more for musos than bikers, with letters from the Beatles Fan Club, an old Animals album and an original *Penny Lane* 45, all

framed and mounted. There's a Seeburg jukebox, too, just for show – the aural background from the CD player is at conversation level.

Sunset Lounge
Hotel Dubrovnik Palace, Masarykov put 20 (020 430 000/www.dubrovnikpalace.hr). **Open** noon-1am daily.
Fab view, chic surroundings, mellow piano player – and happy-hour cocktails. See *p279* **Best bars**.

Talir
Antuninska 5 (020 323 293). **Open** noon-1am daily.
Classic actors' bar in the Old Town. Diagonally opposite the gallery of the same name, the Talir has been the scene of many a good time since opening in 1983 – just look at the snapshots on the walls. You're just as likely to rub shoulders with the unpretentious party crowd as any local theatre star, as the Talir has a constant buzz and bonhomie about it. The cosy, wooden interior is packed on summer nights, drinkers blocking the stepped passageway outside, so get in early and find a seat.

Troubador
Bunićeva poljana 2 (020 323 476). **Open** *Summer* 9am-3am daily. *Winter* 5-11pm daily.
Landmark bar with an impeccable local pedigree. See *p276* **Best bars**.

Nightlife

Nightclubs in Dubrovnik are typified by places such as the **Latino Club Fuego** (www.fuego-dubrovnik.com) by the Pile Gate, live music shows or mainstream discos, or slick places such as **Labirint** (*see p272*). There's a young discobar

Dubrovnik.

FORGET THE FORMALITIES.
JUST ASK FOR JACK.

Best bars — Sunset Lounge
Sunset Lounge

For those not staying at the seriously high-end five-star Dubrovnik Palace, the **Sunset Lounge** (*see p277*) may come as something of a shock, particularly after the bone-shaking ride on a rickety old city bus No.4 from the Pile Gate to its terminus here. Walking through the swish lobby in reasonably smart dress – T-shirts OK, shorts and flip-flops a probable no-no – your eyes are immediately drawn to a floor-to-ceiling panoramic glass façade of idyllic sea-blue view, interspersed by the occasional boat drifting towards any one of several lush Elafiti islands. It's not a painting and you're not dreaming. Find a chair, open up the drinks menu.

Cocktails are 45kn-52kn, Manhattans, Mojitos, Daiquiris, you name it, and the management even has the temerity to offer them half-price from 4 to 6pm. There's a questionable taste for Beck's beer varieties, justifiably named Enigma (mixed with Bacardi), Dubbio (with Havana Club) and Questione (Campari and Triple Sec), but you could just order a simple 15kn Bavaria beer or house white and gawp for the afternoon. All flavours of Absolut vodkas and vintage malts line the shelves, and you're bound to linger until the piano player comes on in the evening. Food is pricy, 75kn for a club sandwich, but this is once-in-a-holiday stuff.

scene in Lapad, along Šetalište Kralja Zvonimira towards the sea, but compared to what's going on in the islands further north, it's tame. The only exception is the **East-West Beach Club** at Lazareti, a short walk from Ploče Gate, but it likes to think itself quite snazzy and you may feel more comfortable with late drinks at **Buža I** (*see p284* **The Hole in the wall gang**).

East-West

Frana Supila (020 412 220/www.ew-dubrovnik.com). **Open** *Summer* 5pm-3am daily.
The only nightspot worthy of the name in Dubrovnik, East-West is a café and restaurant by day (spaghetti with lobster, calamari, pizzas, open from 9am) and a clubby beachside cocktail bar by night. The location, right on Banje beach within five minutes of the Old Town, is perfect. The clientele tends to be pretty glitzy – it's often hired for fashion parties – but the place is comfortable rather than intimidating and prices are the same as anywhere

else. Thirty-odd cocktails are 45kn each, the lethal house East-West of vodka, gin, tequila, rum, Triple Sec, Sprite and an energy drink is 100kn, and the music is unobtrusive.

Where to stay

Downtown Dubrovnik is firmly aimed at high-end tourism. It boasts some of the best hotels in Croatia – the **Pucić Palace**, the **Hilton Imperial**, the **Hotel Dubrovnik Palace** – at justifiably high prices, given the setting and services. All offer relatively reasonable rates for the shoulder- and off-peak seasons. Note that the best rooms are often taken during the Summer Festival, from 10 July to 25 August.

Accommodation is clustered around three main areas – the Old Town isn't one of them. Here you will only find the **Pucić Palace** and little **Hotel Stari Grad**, whose eight rooms are soon booked up. On the other side of the Ploče

Dubrovnik & Islands

Hotel Dubrovnik Palace

It doesn't get any better, not in Croatia anyway. Voted Croatia's best hotel at the World Travel Market in 2005, the **Dubrovnik Palace** (*see right*) was opened the year before following a 13-year, €45-million renovation programme. The result is a ten-floor, 308-room luxury hotel equally suited to business and pleasure. Business is done in the well-equipped conference and meeting rooms. The pleasure is in the setting. Saying that all rooms have a sea view doesn't do it justice. When Vincek came up with the original design in 1972, he placed the Dubrovnik Palace in a tangle of woodland paths at the south-west tip of Lapad, with a phenomenal vista of the Elafiti Islands.

This is what everyone sees from their balcony, from the 11 bars, three restaurants, four pools and the fitness centre. Even the 234 standard rooms are spacious, and all have flat-screen TVs, internet access and a laptop; all have been touched by the creative hand of renowned designer Renata Štrok. The main presidential suite, one of two, is the size of a small house. The off-season rates (3 Jan-24 Mar), compare favourably with the price of a boxy three-star in London. In high season, your budget may not stretch to prices at twice that rate, but any reasonably dressed visitor to Dubrovnik is welcome to a drink in the panoramic **Sunset Lounge** (*see p279*). In fact, it's obligatory.

Gate, along the main road of Frana Supila, are a string of four-stars: **Hotel Excelsior**, **Hotel Villa Orsula**, **Hotel Grand Villa Argentina** and, further along, the **Villa Dubrovnik**.

Tourist hotels and a luxury establishment or two can be found in the other hubs of Lapad and Babin Kuk, on the headland overlooking beaches. The renovated **Hotel Kompas** is a well-priced, family-friendly choice for a short-term stay. All are an easy 15-minute bus journey from the Old Town, although you'll probably need a taxi later in the evening.

A new hotel zone is developing the other side of the Pile Gate from the Old Town.

As well as the Hilton, opened in 2005, a boutique hotel will be unveiled in July 2006 by high-end chain Adriatic Luxury Hotels: the **Bellevue**, a classy conversion of a well-located three-star. Nearby, the **Lero** is a handy mid-range choice.

You'll find private rooms in Dubrovnik to be the most expensive in Croatia – you can find yourself paying well over €50 a night in the Old Town in high season. If you weren't bombarded by old ladies at the bus station, look out for the blue 'Sobe' bed signs dotted on front doors or go to **Atlas Travel** (*see p284*) near the Pile Gate.

The following hotels are open all year round, with the exception of the **Argosy**, the **Uvala** and the **Villa Dubrovnik**.

Hilton Imperial

Marijana Blažica 2 (020 320 320/fax 020 320 220/ www.hilton.co.uk/Dubrovnik). **Rates** €170-€360 double. **Credit** AmEx, DC, MC, V.

Swish and business-like, the Hilton's first operation in Croatia launched in 2005. Occupying a grand, caramel-coloured, fin-de-siècle building set in from the sea and a short walk from the Pile Gate, it has location without the beachside grace of other five-star establishments in town. With its gym and indoor pool open 24 hours, this is a place for execs to convene. They have their own fourth-floor lounge, and can make use of five meeting rooms, three ballrooms for presentations and exhibitions, a boardroom and business centre. And the bedrooms? Simple, modern with large beds, they are comfortable but unmemorable, many standard ones without sea views. You will remember the Porat restaurant, though (*see p274*), its stand-out Med cuisine a rarity in the staid, local dining scene. The lobby bar has a panoramic terrace, there's a gym and sauna, too, and the pool is flooded with natural light. Current weekend deals for €149 a room.

Hotel Argosy

Iva Dolčića 41 (020 446 100/fax 020 435 578/ www.babinkuk.com). **Rates** €80-€195 double. **Credit** AmEx, DC, MC, V.

The furthest of the Babin Kuk resort hotels, tucked in behind the Dubrovnik President, the Argosy looks plain but it has access to the beach and tennis courts, plus two pools, one for children. The standard three-star rooms are comfortable enough, all have balconies, some with sea views.

Hotel Bellevue

Pera Čingrije 7 (020 330 000/fax 020 330 100/ www.hotel-bellevue.hr). **Rates** from €250 double. **Credit** AmEx, DC, MC, V.

This boutique hotel is being unveiled in July 2006 after a €12 million refurbishment. Dubrovnik's eighth and newest five-star will be its most chic. The co-owner Renata Štrok has undertaken the interior design, which will feature Dalmatian stone, a combination of antique and modern furniture and Gharani Štrok linen (her daughter Vanja is one half of the London fashion duo) – all of which points to a tasteful take on Mediterranean decor. What's guaranteed is the cliff-top property's enchanting sea views.

Hotel Dubrovnik Palace

Masarykov put 20 (020 430 000/fax 020 430 100/ www.dubrovnikpalace.hr). **Rates** €159-€317 double. **Credit** AmEx, DC, MC, V.

Superbly equipped flagship of the Adriatic Luxury Hotels group. *See left* **Hot hotels**.

Hotel Dubrovnik President

Iva Dulčića 39 (020 441 100/fax 020 435 600/ www.babinkuk.com). **Rates** €155-€320 double. **Credit** AmEx, DC, MC, V.

The leading hotel of the Babin Kuk group, this one ruled the roost on the Babin Kuk headland until the Dubrovnik Palace (*see left*) came along. Set right on the western tip, it commands its own section of beach, and each of the 181 rooms has a balcony view of the sea and Elafiti Islands beyond. In essence, it's a high-end resort hotel, with an indoor pool, children's entertainment and playground, and access to nearby tennis courts. If turning up on spec, for these rates you're better off in the Dubrovnik Palace – unless you're with the kids.

Hotel Excelsior

Frana Supila 12 (020 353 353/fax 020 353 555/ www.hotel-excelsior.hr). **Rates** €243-€365 double. **Credit** AmEx, DC, MC, V.

More of an old-style five-star this one, on the main road up from the Ploče Gate with a perfect view of the fortifications, Lokrum island and the sea around. As not all rooms have a sea view, and without the high-tech facilities of recently opened rivals, the Excelsior plays up its heritage. Built by hotel owner Robert Odak in 1913, his villa became the Hotel Excelsior in 1930. The royals, Richard and Liz, assorted Habsburgs, they've all stayed here. In 1998 it became Croatia's first five-star hotel. The 154 bedrooms are tasteful and comfortable, without cause for flat-screen TVs or power showers; each of the 18 suites has a jacuzzi. The hotel boasts its own section of beach, outdoor pool for kids, indoor one for adults, gym and sauna. The Zagreb

Old school **Hotel Excelsior**. *See above.*

of the outdoor pool (there's an indoor one, too), nearby tennis courts and popular pebbly beach a few steps away. Nearly half the 115 rooms boast balconies with a sea view.

Hotel Lero

Iva Vojnovića 14 (020 341 333/fax 020 332 133/ www.hotel-lero.hr). **Rates** €64-€140 double. **Credit** AmEx, DC, MC, V.
The advantage of this Socialist-style, 152-room hotel is location – and price. Equidistant between the Old Town and the main bus station and ferry terminal at Gruž, the three-star Lero offers simple, comfortable rooms, half with a sea view, a surprisingly extensive buffet breakfast and bargain €12 full-board deals all year round at the traditional adjoining Taverna Nava. And it's only a short walk to the sheltered stretch of beach on the other side of the bay from the Pile Gate.

Hotel Minčeta

Iva Dulčića 18 (020 447 100/fax 020 447 603/ www.babinkuk.com). **Rates** €53-€147 double. **Credit** AmEx, DC, MC, V.
Perfect choice for families, the three-star Minčeta is part of the cluster of Babin Kuk hotels, set in its own patch of woodland. It is also the one nearest to the Copacabana beach, with its water chutes, banana rides and pedalos. The hotel itself has a large, outdoor pool, children's pool and a full summer programme for kids. Many of the 300-plus rooms have a sea view. The Minčeta shares sports facilities – a dozen tennis courts, a small football pitch, mini-golf and a diving centre – with the other group hotels nearby.

Hotel Petka

Obala Stjepana Radića 38 (020 410 500/fax 020 410 127/www.croatia-vacation.com). **Rates** €72-€112 double. **Credit** AmEx, DC, MC, V.
A convenient place to flop after that long bus or ferry journey, the three-star Petka now has a few extras after its recent upgrade. Most of the 100-plus rooms have a balcony overlooking Gruž bay and harbour, there is a modest gym and simple restaurant. The full-board supplement at €8-€11 is a snip.

Hotel Uvala

Masarykov put 6 (020 433 580/fax 020 433 590/ www.hotelimaestral.com). **Closed** Nov-Mar. **Rates** €120-€252 double. **Credit** AmEx, DC, MC, V.
The newest and only four-star of the Maestral group, the Uvala boasts a decent and spacious spa centre with aromatherapy and massage treatments, indoor and outdoor pools, a steam room, sauna and solarium. The other four – Adriatic, Komodor, Splendid and Vis – are resort hotels on the same main road towards the coast at Lapad. Their details are all on this website.

Hotel Zagreb

Šetalište Kralja Zvonimira 27 (020 438 930/fax 020 436 006/www.hotels-sumratin.com). **Closed** Nov-Mar. **Rates** €95-€143 double. **Credit** DC, MC, V.

Tourists in Dubrovnik **Old Town**.

restaurant does a classy job, but perhaps the best feature is the palm terrace, ideal for a sunset drink.

Hotel Grand Villa Argentina

Frana Supila 14 (020 440 555/fax 020 432 524/ www.gva.hr). **Rates** €190-€340 double. **Credit** AmEx, DC, MC, V.
This five-star villa-and-hotel complex has been ameliorated by the grand opening of the Villa Sheherezade. Behind its intricately renovated oriental façade, a banquet hall, two terraces and five luxury bedrooms with marble bathrooms accommodate up to a dozen people – all yours for a total of €6,000 a day. The main rates given above are for the two sister villas, the Argentina and the Glavic, with beautifully appointed rooms, a little pool, gym, sauna and terrace overlooking a wide stretch of private beach. The Villa Orsula and Hotel Argentina are slightly cheaper.

Hotel Kompas

Šetalište Kralja Zvonimira 56 (020 352 000/fax 020 435 877/www.hotel-kompas.hr). **Rates** €82-€178 double. **Credit** AmEx, DC, MC, V.
Formerly a standard package-tour hotel, since taken over by the Adriatic Luxury Hotels group (note the fragrant Gharani Štrok soap in the bathroom), the refurbished Kompas and expansive terrace restaurant dominate Lapad beach. Now boasting a sauna, gym and conference facilities, the Kompas is still a good, reasonably priced choice for families in the shoulder months, when you can take advantage

Set in its own pleasant grounds in from the main drag through Lapad down to the beach nearby, the Zagreb seems a bit pricy for its two-star status. But once installed in one of its 23 rooms, you'll enjoy the homely surroundings, access to floodlit tennis courts and proximity to buses for the Old Town. The back garden and terrace provide handy respite from the holiday swarms, and half-board rates are a reasonable 30kn-40kn extra. The nearby Sumratin is under the same management.

Pucić Palace

Od Puča 1 (020 326 200/fax 020 326 323/ www.thepucicpalace.com). **Rates** €273-€582 double. **Credit** AmEx, DC, MC, V.
The most tasteful choice, wonderfully located in the heart of the Old Town. *See right* **Hot hotels.**

Hotel Stari Grad

Od Sigurate 4 (020 321 373/fax 020 321 256/ www.hotelstarigrad.com). **Rates** €80-€133 single; €115-€190 double. **Credit** AmEx, DC, MC, V.
Apart from the Pucić Palace, the dinky Stari Grad is the only other choice in the Old Town. It is comprised of eight quiet bedrooms, large enough for an extra bed (€35-€57) if necessary, and a panoramic fifth-floor roof terrace where breakfast is served in the warmer months. The rooms are tastefully furnished but none have a view. In winter you may find yourself spending more time out of the hotel than you would if you were spending the same amount of money for a sea vista in Lapad or Babin Kuk. Still, with half its rooms for single travellers, and set only a few minutes from the Pile Gate, the Stari Grad is ideal for independent visitors here to nose around the treasures of the Old Town.

Villa Dubrovnik

Vlaha Bukovaca 6 (020 422 933/fax 020 423 465/ www.villa-dubrovnik.hr). **Closed** Oct-Mar. **Rates** €190-€280 double. **Credit** MC, V.
Distant enough away from the Old Town (1.5km/ 1 mile) to warrant a handy complimentary boat service there and back five times a day, the summer-only Villa Dubrovnik allows tranquillity and isolation. Beautifully set over an accessible, secluded rocky outcrop lapped by the sea, all 40 rooms of the Villa Dubrovnik, set on descending terraces, have sea and Old Town views, and all are beautifully appointed without much by way of man-made amenity – hence the five-star prices for three-star status. The most attractive facility is the Bistro Giardino, a verdant, panoramic terrace and the ideal spot for a sunset cocktail before the last boat to town at 8.30pm. Rates in high season are for half-board only.

Resources

Hospital

Roka Misetica, Lapad (020 431 777).
Dubrovnik's main hospital is some 4km (2.4 miles) out of town in Lapad.

Hot hotels Pucić Palace

A beautifully crafted five-star in the heart of the Old Town, the **Pucić Palace** combines old-world heritage with 21st-century convenience. The 19 individually and tastefully decorated rooms feature spacious bathrooms of Italian mosaic tiles, Egyptian cotton towels and thick bathrobes hanging on heated towel racks and baroque-style furnishings in the bedrooms. Wi-Fi internet and DVD players provide technology, comfort comes from ample beds and sumptuous linens (choose your colour). Large, soundproofed windows allow views of the market scenes below – this former nobleman's pile faces prominent Gundulićeva poljana, which lends its name to the first-floor suite (€772-€978). On the roof terrace, the **Defne** restaurant (*see p271*) is one of the best in town, the kitchen also serving the Razonada wine bar downstairs. *See left for listings.*

Dubrovnik & Islands

The hole in the wall gang

Striding down Stradun, rubbing shoulder after shoulder after shoulder with half of *France métropolitaine* in slacks and sandals, you do wonder where any downtown action might be in Dubrovnik. True, a random turn into any Stradun side street may turn up a curiosity – but try getting into the **Talir** (*see p277*) on a hot July night.

There is nothing for it but to flee the unfashionable flock, duck down a couple of hidden passages and find the bar table of your dreams. Escaping the nearby Stradun swarm is only half the fun, for what you find are two virtually nameless terraces with jaw-dropping vistas set on the seafacing rocky promontory propping up the city walls: **Buža I** and **Buža II**. Once you've found your niche, and you're settled in for an evening's gawp at the sunset sinking over paradise, there is no need to move – unless you fancy stripping off to dive naked into a moonlit Adriatic from Buža I. And it's three euros a beer once you clamber out again.

Buža, meaning 'hole in the wall', suits boozers, swimmers and sunbathers alike. Of the two, Buža I is the most basic but perhaps the most enjoyable – maybe because of the easy access to the Adriatic, metal steps fixed to the rocks. From the cathedral, walk down Ilije Šarake; at No.10 you'll find the dining terrace of the Konoba Ekvinocijo. Diagonally opposite is a doorway saying simply '8-20'. Poke your head in and the words 'Topless Nudist' are scrawled on the wall. Negotiate the stone staircase and lo! A scattering of tables set at various levels according to the rock formation – and a bar counter. And also, sadly, Sadé. Somehow they always seem to be playing Sadé. There may even be a modest impromptu performance of jazz standards in what passes for a corner. Laško is 22kn, Beck's 30kn and not even Sadé can ruin the moonlit moment. Open daily till 3am in high season.

Of the two, Buža II is the more well known – and its music considerably better. Invariably, it's Elvis, or possibly Gene Pitney, yet the place does seem more formal, more confined. Perhaps it's because they've made a fuss with the straw roof, or serve wine cups in dinky little wooden trays. The waiters even have their own white logoed T-shirts. From the south-west corner of the open square of Rudjera Boškovića, behind the Jesuit church, is a sign saying 'Cold Drinks With The Most Beautiful View'.

Internet

Ante Starčićeva 7 (020 427 591/www.tzdubrovnik.hr). **Open** *July, Aug* 8am-midnight daily. *June, Sept* 8am-10pm daily. *Oct-May* 9am-9pm Mon-Fri; 9am-7pm Sat.
In the same room as the main tourist office (*see below*) near the Pile Gate, with enough space for a dozen or so computers at reasonable hourly rates.

Pharmacy

Kod Zvonika, Stradun (020 321 133). **Open** 7am-8pm Mon-Fri; 7.30am-8pm Sat.
Located right in the Old Town, this is the main late-opening chemist.

Post office

Put republike 32 (020 413 960). **Open** 7am-8pm Mon-Fri; 8am-4pm Sat; 8am-noon Sun.
Near the old bus station halfway between the Old Town and Gruž harbour, this is the town's main post office. It has a branch closer to the Old Town at the Pile Gate at Ante Starčićeva 2 (open 8am-3pm Mon-Fri).

Tourist information

Atlas Travel *Brsalje 17 (020 442 574/www.atlas-croatia.com)*. **Open** *Summer* 8am-8pm Mon-Fri; 8am-3pm Sat. *Winter* 8am-7pm Mon-Fri; 8am-3pm Sat.

Near the Pile Gate, this travel agency books private rooms and arranges tours and excursions.
Dubrovnik Tourist Office *Ante Starčićeva 7 (020 427 591/www.tzdubrovnik.hr)*. **Open** *Summer* 8am-8pm. *Winter* 9am-4pm Mon-Fri; 9am-1pm Sat.
With internet facilities, too, this main tourist office a short walk towards Lapad from the Pile Gate has young, friendly staff providing all information including the free monthly *Dubrovnik Guide* and a similar one issued by *In Dubrovnik*. Staff in the branch office on Stradun (020 321 561, same hours) can be quite brusque.

Getting there and around

Dubrovnik **airport** is 22km (13 miles) south-east of town, down the coast at **Čilipi**. Buses (30mins, 30kn) meet all incoming Croatia Airlines and British Airways flights, stopping in town near the Pile Gate before going on to the main new bus station, three kilometres (two miles) west of the Old Town at **Gruž**. Gruž is also the site of the main ferry terminal.

Buses leave bay Nos.6-8 of Gruž bus station two hours before flights on BA and other foreign carriers, 90 minutes before Croatia

Buža II.

Buža I.

Walk through the passage, across a makeshift football pitch and ahead of you will be another sign pointing to 'Cold Drinks'. The sign has gone down in local lore – even the staff down the stone steps bear the 'Cold Drinks Buža' embroidered badge with pride. The cold drinks in question are Ožujsko and Heineken, both under 30kn, although many stick to wine, Malvazija or

Babić, at around the same price. Buža II tends to attract an older crowd – couples not talking, bickering newly weds, that kind of thing.

Rumour has it that the conservative city fathers are not best pleased with such untamed establishments and may move to close them. Join the Hole in the Wall gang before the whole shooting match goes up.

Airlines ones. They also stop at the old bus station halfway to the Old Town, then at a municipal bus stop on the main road just north of the city walls, opposite the shop Oleviri Logorio. This is the nearest jump-on point from the centre of town.

A taxi costs about 250kn, probably nearer to 350kn if you're at a hotel on the Lapad or Babin Kuk headland. Call one on 970.

All ferries and catamarans use Gruž except for the **taxi boat** to **Lokrum** and service to **Cavtat**, which leave from the old harbour near the Ploče Gate in the Old Town. A coastal ferry runs daily in the summer, four times a week in winter, all the way up to Rijeka, a journey of 20-24 hours. Jadrolinija foot passenger ferries make regular runs to the Elafiti Islands, namely Koločep (25mins, 12kn), Lopud (50mins, 20kn) and the two harbours on Šipan (1hr-1hr 45mins, 14kn-20kn). For the same price, **Atlantagent catamarans** run at 9am on Saturdays. A daily Jadrolinija car ferry leaves in the afternoon for **Sobra** on Mljet (2hrs 15mins, 35kn), turning around at 6am, requiring you to spend the night. An Atlantagent catamaran runs at

9am every morning, calling at Sobra (1hr, 22kn) and Polače (1hr 40mins, 60kn), returning at 6.20pm from Polače and 7pm from Sobra. The Saturday service takes 45 minutes longer as it calls at each of the main Elafiti Islands.

The main bus station is near the ferry terminal, a short walk in the opposite direction from town. Both are three kilometres (two miles) west of the Old Town. Buses run hourly services to Split (4.5hrs, about 110kn, depending on the bus company). Remember to keep your passport handy as you pass through Bosnia on the way.

Orange Libertas city buses link Gruž, Babin Kuk, Lapad and Ploče to the Old Town. Buy a ticket (14kn for two journeys) at any newsstand or in exact change (10kn) from the driver. Gruž is a deceptively long walk to and from town – allow 40 minutes and don't count on easily making it by taxi if you're running late. Although there are cabs aplenty at the Pile Gate, the road to Gruž is always busy and often gridlocked. Taxis start at 25kn and charge 8kn per km – expect a 50kn-70kn bill for Gruž. Bus Nos.1a, 3 and 8 do the same journey.

Misty mountain hop

After post-conflict political isolation, **Montenegro** is now an attractive coastal detour for visitors to Dubrovnik and southern Dalmatia. A handful of travel companies in Dubrovnik run one-day tours (*see p284*). For independent travel, check the new website www.tourism-montenegro.com for details of hotel information.

The continuation from Croatia seems natural: the two countries are more visually similar than they would like to admit. Walled old coastal towns like **Kotor** and **Budva** show an age-old trade and maritime partnership and a visual resemblance with Dubrovnik; the blue waters of the Adriatic lap sandy and pebbly beaches, while church spires stab the cloudless sky as if letting in air on hot summer days.

The country is currently one half of the fraught federation of Serbia and Montenegro, in existence since the two republics stopped calling themselves Yugoslavia in 2003. But May 2006 sees a referendum on independence. Local opposition and government parties have held talks with European Union envoys and the glue of brotherhood that has kept Serbia and Montenegro united seems to be losing its hold. Montenegro's official currency is the euro (Serbia still uses the dinar) and its ATMs offer a menu in 'Montenegrin', a linguistic proposition inconceivable a decade ago when everyone considered they were speaking Serbian. But whatever happens in the future, it's certain that Montenegro has its own, individual history.

Even in the Ottoman tide that engulfed the region for 400 years from the 14th century, Montenegro managed to keep a degree of autonomy. The Montenegrins earned themselves a reputation as good warriors, something they are still proud of (and often mocked for). They were valiant fighters in World War II, mainly in Tito's Partisan army, earning republic status within Yugoslavia in 1945. The Montenegrins often used the country's tall and remote mountains as their base and hiding place, and these mountains are synonymous with the country's name and image. Montenegro (Crna Gora), or 'Black Mountain', got its name from the dark pine-covered Mount Lovcen, on top of which the nation's most revered ruler, prince and poet, Petar Petrovic Njegoš, now lies buried.

Montenegrin culture is a cocktail of Montenegrin, Serb, Albanian and Croat, with a relaxed Mediterranean air. Orthodoxy, Catholicism and Islam live alongside each other in relative harmony. Since Yugoslavia's break-up, the country has struggled with its image as Serbia's wartime companion – Montenegrins were partly responsible for the siege of Dubrovnik. Realising the error of its ways, this tiny republic has seen what tourist riches can do to a post-war place – Dubrovnik is only 40km (24 miles) away.

Montenegro has all the ingredients for an exotic and relaxing break: long, sandy beaches or small pebbly coves; historical walks around Kotor, Budva and **Cetinje**; skiing and snowboarding on Durmitor mountain, and white-water rafting on the foamy waters in the Tara and Piva canyons. Fishing and ornithology are also popular – rare birds rest on the shores of Skadar lake after their long flight north.

Montenegro is very popular with crowds cascading on to the beaches from Serbia's main cities in high season. Explore it when it's quietest and cheapest, in May, June or September.

The most seductive part of the coast is the Kotor Bay (Boka Kotorska), Europe's largest fjord, where moody mountains surround an indigo sea. At its centre is the town of Kotor, a fortified labyrinth of marble streets and hidden piazzas, with a towering cliff crested by an ancient wall. The town was once a Mediterranean naval power – in the 18th century the Bay of Kotor sent out over 400 ships to sail the world's seas. The most important building is **St Tryphon's Cathedral**, sitting in the centre of town and dating back to the 11th century. A thumping nightlife claims the streets in the summer, when the dreaded sounds of turbofolk (a sorry mix of cheap folk music and techno) weave with live music and DJ electronica in the narrow streets. A popular and fashionable hangout is **Cesare** (Stari Grad 327, 00 381 82 325 913, www.adn-cesare.com), an elongated bar-club with a space-shuttle capsule for a toilet. Just about any of the town's squares has a DJ bar and an eager crowd, so take your pick.

The nearby small town of **Perast** is a perfect slice of the old Mediterranean, with marble houses surrounding the exquisite church of **St Nikola**. Opposite Perast are two tiny tuft-like islets floating on the sea's surface: **Gospa od Skrpjela** (Lady of Rock) and **St George**. Legend says that the Gospa od Skrpjela island was artificially created over 550 years, by seamen who kept an ancient oath and dropped a rock in the water every year. The neighbouring St George is balanced on a natural reef and houses the Benedictine monastery of St George shaded by cypress trees. Near Perast, the small village of Risan has third-century mosaics remaining from the floor of an ancient villa rustica.

From Kotor, a terrifying hairpin drive leads all the way up to Cetinje. The former capital is now a quiet little town but its mansions used to house embassies and consulates. You can still find the mausoleum of legendary poet prince Petar Petrovic Njegoš. His grave is atop Mount Lovcen, 1,500 steps up from Cetinje.

Back on the coast, Budva throbs with tourists in high season. A miniature Dubrovnik, the town's smooth marble and limestone streets were carefully reconstructed after a heavy earthquake almost flattened the town. Surrounding it are two fabulous little towns: the village hotel resort of **Sveti Stefan**, and the small town of **Petrovac**. Sveti Stefan (00 381 86 420 000, www.budvanska-rivijera.co.yu) is an idyllic resort of the old school, an outcrop of villas

and hotel rooms built from a picturesque 15th-century fishing village. It's honeymoon material, expensive but not extortionate. As an indication of how Montenegro is heading, for 2007 it will be transformed into a seriously high-end hotel. 2006 is the last summer of the Sophia Loren era. Petrovac is perfect in September, when the late summer sun glows over a red sand beach full of health-improving minerals. Oleander and citrus trees line the lush promenade.

Further south stretch olive groves, stopping at Ulcinj, a mixed Albanian-Montenegrin town with the longest sandy beach in the country. Velika Plaža measures 12.5km (7.5 miles) and welcomes clothed or nude bathers. After that, those with an adventurous spirit can cross the border and see the gorgeous coast of Albania.

EU citizens, Americans, Canadians, Australians and New Zealanders do not need a visa for a 30-day stay in Montenegro. In Dubrovnik, day trips are advertised in tourist hubs such as the old harbour or Lapad beach. **Atlas Travel** (*see p284*) also organises excursions. There are two types of tours, one by bus (Kotor, Budva and Cetinje); the other returning by boat (Herceg Novi, Perast, Risan, Gospa od Skrpjela and St George islands). Both cost 340kn.

Korčula

As you approach Korčula from the mainland nearby, the crowded little houses on the edge of the island seem to be pushing each other out of the way to see if you are friend or foe. Holding them in, a stern medieval fortress centrepieced by the slim belltower of St Mark's Cathedral stands guard over the narrow Pelješac Channel, protecting the riches contained on the sixth largest island in the Croatian Adriatic. So lush with dark pine forests, vineyards and olive groves the ancient Greek settlers called it *Kerkyra Melaina* ('Black Corfu'), Korčula has managed to avoid the tourist trap tendencies of its original Greek namesake 480 kilometres (300 miles) south.

No longer fought over by Turk or Venetian, Napoleon's troops or Prince-Bishop Petar Njegoš' Montenegrins, Habsburg Austrians or Mussolini's Italians, by Partisan or German, Korčula is one of Dalmatia's most relaxing getaways, best enjoyed by an older generation of tourist. The main town of the same name, set on the north-eastern tip of the island opposite the Pelješac peninsula, has one of the best-preserved medieval centres in Dalmatia. It is the most popular regional destination after Dubrovnik, with which it is often compared.

Unlike Dubrovnik, Korčula was governed by the Venetians, responsible for the layout of the Old Town, no more than few hundred metres across. Within the oval walls, streets are laid out in a herringbone pattern. Those running west are straight to let in the cool westerly breeze on burning summer days; those running east are curved to keep out the chilly winter Bura wind from the north-east. Those facing north allowed locals to rush up and quickly defend the Pelješac Channel.

Little is made of Korčula's Venetian heritage, compared to the overkill granted to what locals see as their claim to fame: the birthplace of Marco Polo. Whether the famed traveller was born on the island in 1254 cannot be proven (*see p295* **Marco Polo: The myth with the hole**) but the story has elements of truth. In any case, funding to convert his supposed family home into a museum is now in place.

Not that Korčula is without authentic historic attractions, thanks to a medieval building programme begun by one of Polo's contemporaries, ruling Venetian nobleman Count Marsilije Zorzi. Entering the Old Town from the south, you pass through the **Kopnena Vrata** (Land Gate), erected to mark the island's gallant defence against the Turkish navy at the Battle of Lepanto. It leads to the **Punat**, or stone bridge, and the **Veliki Revelin Tower** bearing the Venetian coat of arms. By the gate is a fruit and vegetable market; in summer it is the setting for performances of the Moreška sword dance (*see p289* **Do the Moreška**). Through it is the square of Sv Mihovil, lined with municipal buildings. A small chapel here dedicated to the Miraculous Virgin of the Island was built after Lepanto. Every 15 August a procession runs from the chapel to mark the Virgin's Ascension.

The main street, Ulica Korčulanskog Statuta, leads to **St Mark's Cathedral** (020 711 049, open summer 8am-9pm daily, winter 8am-noon, 4-6.30pm daily), one of the finest examples of Croatian church architecture and design. Taking three centuries to build, it features several styles, including Gothic, Romanesque and baroque. Most notable is the work by local stonemason Marko Andrijić, responsible for the canopy set on four columns above the altar, or ciborium. Beneath it is the sarcophagus of St Theodore, the protector of Korčula. You can

Korčula Punat. *See above.*

Do the Moreška

As you pass by Korčula's Land Gate of a balmy summer evening you may wonder what the strange locals in funny costume are doing – and why they're doing it with swords. The answer is the **Moreška**, and Korčula is the only place where this age-old dance is still performed in the traditional way, with real blades.

Moreška has its origins in Moorish Spain, when battles won by the Christians were celebrated and re-enacted in folk dance and drama. By the time it got to Dalmatia, the Turk was at the door, so the victorious Battle of Lepanto in 1571 has been played out in

sword and swing ever since. Perhaps Lepanto is apt, for the story is an age-old pantomime between two kings over a betrothed princess. While respective soldiers do a war dance and swords clash, a blasting brass band accompanies the drama – modern-day Moreška has undergone a few modifications. King Korčula gets the girl and the Turk is given the royal heave-ho.

Each Korčula community has an annual sword dance festival. In Korčula town, it's 29 July, but shows are also staged every Thursday evening in summer.

also see here *St Mark with St Bartholomew and St Jerome*, an early work by Tintoretto, whose *Annunciation* also stands in the south nave. Cannonballs and weapons from wars with the Turks are also placed here, and a 13th-century icon of the Virgin, prayed to for salvation when the Turks threatened in 1571. Next door is the **Abbey Treasury** (summer 9am-7pm daily, 10kn) with a collection of Dalmatian art from the 15th and 16th centuries.

Opposite the cathedral, the **Town Museum** (020 711 420, open 9am-1.30pm Mon-Sat, 10kn),

set in a 16th-century Venetian palace, contains a copy of the fourth-century Greek tablet from Lumbarda, the earliest evidence of civilisation on the island, various Roman ceramics and a reconstruction of a Korčula peasant kitchen. Behind the cathedral stands the house claimed to be Marco Polo's birthplace, currently under reconstruction while a museum is being built.

Korčula's best modern sight stands on the seafront, ten minutes from the cathedral. The **Memorial Collection of Maksimilijan Vanka** (Put Sv Nikole, open summer 9am-noon, 6-9pm daily, 10kn) shows the art nouveau and Expressionist works by this 20th-century painter and hosts temporary exhibitions by key Croatian artists in summer.

Korčula's other hub is **Vela Luka**, the ferry port for Split, Hvar town and Lastovo. If you've a while to wait for the next bus to Korčula town 80 minutes away, pop to the **Culture Centre** by the Church of St John (020 813 001, open summer 9am-noon, 6-10pm Mon-Sat, 6-10pm Sun, winter 9am-noon Mon-Sat, 10kn). Set in an old school, it has two Henry Moores in its art collection and archaeological finds from the nearby Vela Špilja (Big Cave), inhabited in Neolithic times. There are no beaches in town, but a couple within fair proximity (*see below*).

Beaches

In Korčula town **Banje** beach, by the Hotel Marko Polo (*see p293*), is crowded and not particularly attractive. The nicer, shingle one by the Bon Repos (*see p293*) is a trek; locals pack sandy **Luka Korčulanska**, 15 minutes away towards Dominče. If you take the regular 15-minute taxi boat to **Badija** (*see below*), round the corner from the quay are paths leading to little coves and pebble beaches, one naturist. Deer roam free and are fed by nudists.

Regular boats run from Korčula town to Orebić (*see p300*), 15 minutes away on Pelješac, with a long stretch of pebble beach.

Either side of the village of Lumbarda (*see below*), 6km (3.6 miles) from Korčula town, are three sandy beaches: modest **Tatinja** to the east, and **Bilin Žal** and **Vela Pržina** on either side of the headland. Either is 15 minutes from Lumbarda. Head south from the village until you reach a fork – take the left-hand one for the rockier Bilin Žal and continue south-east for the lovely, sandy Vela Pržina. Ask in Korčula town about the bus service to Bilin Žal.

A more infrequent bus runs the 15km (9.5 miles) to **Pupnat**, on the south shore, with its beautifully clear swimming spot in the bay of **Pupnatska Luka**. The north shore village of **Racisce** contains what is probably Korčula's best beach, Vaja. Walk north of Racisce harbour for 15 minutes to find gleaming white pebbles lapped by an indigo sea.

Near Vela Luka, the two small islands of **Proizd** and **Osjak** have clean beaches of white pebbles. Proizd, 30 minutes away by taxi boat (every 2hrs, 30kn) is used by naturists.

Excursions

An easy day trip, from the smaller east harbour, is the quick, regular taxi boat to **Badija**. This lovely pine-forested island, its 14th-century

monastery converted into a residential sports centre, is a haven for deer and naturists. Another is to take the taxi boat or hourly bus to the early Greek settlement of **Lumbarda**, 6km (3.6 miles) away. Surrounded by vineyards, Lumbarda is famous for producing the dry, white Grk variety. It's best enjoyed at the one good restaurant in the village: Zure (020 712 008, 091 512 8712 mobile, open 6-11pm Mon-Sat).

To explore Korčula, you can rent a boat, car or moped from Rent a Djir (Obala Hrvatskih mornara, 020 711 908, www.korcula-rent.com). The two main diving schools are British-run **Dupin** (020 716 247, 098 812 496 mobile), based at the Hotel Bon Repos (*see p301*) and **MM Sub** (Tatinja 65, 020 712 288, 098 285 011 mobile, www.mm-sub.hr) based in Lumbarda. Viganj (*see p300*) near Orebić, opposite Korčula by a short ferry hop, is a centre for windsurfing.

The daily ferry and catamaran from Split to Vela Luka go on to the island immediately south of Korčula, **Lastovo**. Like Vis (*see p255*), remote Lastovo was a military base. The ferry port is at tiny Ubli, although whatever life there is is concentrated on Lastovo town 10km (6 miles) north-east. There is a clutch of old stone houses, many of them empty, a couple of churches, a couple of *konobas* and that's it. In summer, a boatman will take you out to the uninhabited **Lastovci** islets just off the coast. One of them, Šaplun, has a lovely beach of fine shingle. The island is famous for February's **Poklad** carnival, named after the straw puppet knifed and burned by dancing islanders. The island has one hotel, the **Ladesta** (Uvala Pasadur, 020 802 100, 098 220 120 mobile, www.diving-paradise.net), near Ubli, open from May to October. It is also a diving centre.

Where to eat

Korčula Old Town is not short of standard pizzerias and tourist-friendly restaurants serving ubiquitous seafood dishes. You'll find a string of them on central Ulica Korčulanskog Statuta or the surrounding street of Šetalište Petra Kanavelića. If the **Adio Mare** is full (in high season it will be), try the **Morski Konjić**. Whatever you choose, do try the famous local dry white wines Grk, Pošip and Rukatac.

The island is also famous for its sweet cakes, *cukarini*, such as *prikle*, deep-fried dough with almonds and raisins, and *lumblija*, sweet bread with wine and spices.

Adio Mare

Ulica sv Roka (020 711 253). **Open** *Mid Apr-mid Oct* 6-11.30pm Mon-Sat; 6-11pm Sun. **Credit** AmEx, DC, MC, V.

Getting away from it all

The conversion of Croatia's remote 19th-century lighthouses into lodgings allows for the ideal away-from-it-all break. In the case of **Pločica**, off Korčula, you can bring along a group of friends, too. With a maximum capacity of 14, it is the biggest of the ten on the roster of local booking agency adriatica.net, which specialises in unique breaks around Croatia.

Pločica is certainly unique. One of the few of adriatica's venues not to have a lighthouse keeper, there's nothing but you, the lighthouse and the small island you're both standing on. Fortunately, at least one happens to be beautiful, its land plotted with old fig trees, its waters perfect for diving and fishing. There's a sandy lagoon with shallow waters on the northern side, ideal for children's swimming, and a rocky seabed to the south for divers.

The lighthouse has two three-star apartments, of three and four double rooms each. Choose the bedroom in the north-east corner of the first floor – at dusk, you can see lighthouse signals from as away as Hvar and Pelješac. Bring your own provisions and a fishing rod. Check prices and availability on the website below.

You reach it by making your way to Prigradića on Korčula's north coast near Vela Luka. From there, Ante Petković, a local on hand for any help and emergencies (mobiles, eh?), will pick you up and whisk you off in a speedy dinghy the 15 minutes to Pločica. Price of the transfer both ways is €120 per apartment. An extra 200kn is charged if you want to be fetched from Vela Luka.

Pločica Lighthouse

+385 1 241 5611/in UK 0207 183 0437/www.adriatica.net. **Rates** *per person/day from €12.48.*

Around the corner from Marco Polo's house, this most popular of restaurants has queues around the block in high season. As you watch from a high-ceilinged maritime-themed dining room, the cooks in the open-plan kitchen flame-grill your fish or stew your beef in *prošek* (sherry) and prunes, the famous house *pastičada*, served up with sticky gnocchi.

Gradski Podrum

Trg Antuna/Kaporova (020 711 222). **Open** *Apr-Oct* 11am-2pm, 6-10.30pm daily. **Credit** AmEx, DC, MC, V.
Extensive menu, a terrace on an open square by the Town Hall and St Michael's church just inside the Land Gate, excellent service, there's a reason why the Gradski is just that bit dearer than everywhere else. Equal emphasis given to fish and meat, with sauces prepared just right. Recommended.

Morski Konjić

Šetalište Petra Kanavelića (020 711 878). **Open** *Summer* 9am-1am daily. *Winter* 6pm-1am daily. **Credit** MC, V.

At the northern tip of the Old Town, its little terrace overlooking the sea, the Morski serves what is probably the best food in town. After complimentary fish pâté and warm bread you can choose from the high-grade versions of Dalmatia's seafood favourites. Mussels are a rich starter but a light main, the grilled squid is a treat, and if you're having the *brodet*, fish stew, mind the bones. Round it off with a glass of the house digestif, a *rakija* of figs and carobs. A smaller place of the same name sits in the Old Town.

Planjak

Plokata 19.Travnja (020 711 015). **Open** *Summer* 9am-11pm daily. *Winter* 9am-10pm daily. **No credit cards**.
On a shaded terrace in a square just behind the market, this is the place to tuck into cheap, authentic Balkan food. Choose any of the grilled meats – go for seafood elsewhere – and you can't go wrong. There's a 60kn daily menu or regular dishes such as stuffed peppers or *ćevapčići*, minced rissoles.

Dubrovnik & Islands

Korčula.

Where to drink

There is little problem finding somewhere to drink in Korčula. There are any number of bars and cafés around the Old Town, particularly on Plokata 19.Travnja by the market. The terrace café of the **Hotel Korčula** (*see below*) is a great place to start or end the day. Apart from that, the problem is finding somewhere special, particularly after dark – which is why Korčula is better suited to older couples and young families. Hotels house what seems to pass for discotheques in these parts.

Cukarin

Hrvatske bratske zajednice (020 711 055). **Open** 8.30am-noon, 6-9pm Mon-Fri; 8.30am-noon Sat.
In a side street just outside the Old Town, this pâtisserie serves strong coffee and local sweet cakes such as *klajun* (a pastry filled with walnuts) or *amareta* (an almond cake). Tables inside and out allow for a relaxed sugar-rush breakfast.

Fresh

Kod kina Liburne 1 (091 799 2086 mobile/ www.igotfresh.com). **Open** 9am-11pm daily. **No credit cards.**
Backpacker-friendly Canadian-Japanese-Croatian venture recently opened opposite the bus station, Fresh combines the need for real breakfast (tortilla wraps, smoothies) with after-dark DJ music and cocktails. It's only a kiosk with happy-hour drinks but at least it's somewhere geared to the party crowd.

Massimo Cocktail Bar

Kula Zakerjan, Šetalište Petra Kanavelića (020 715 073). **Open** *May-Oct* 6pm-2am daily.
The only destination bar to speak of, reaching Massimo is more interesting than sampling the bog-standard cocktails it serves (40kn-50kn). Set under the turrets of the 15th-century Zakerjan Tower in the northern fortifications, Massimo is accessible by stairs, then ladder. Drinks come to you by pulley as you take in the fine view as far as Pelješac. The problem might be getting down again afterwards.

Where to stay

The limited hotels, most in the HTP group (www.htp-korcula.hr), are unrenovated hangovers from the Communist era, pricy for what little they have to offer. All except the Korčula are a distance from the Old Town, and all slap on a supplement for short stays. Many go for the private room option. Marko Polo (see below) can help with booking. Expect to pay 250kn for a double in high season. The link www.korcula.net/firme/p_index.htm gives a list of family homes. Recommended are the Villa Sole (Soline, www.korcula-croatia.com/ villasole, Mar-Oct 207kn-414kn) and Pansion Marinka (020 712 007, 098 344 712

mobile) in Lumbarda. Here you can spend a relaxing time on Frano Bire's working farm, enjoying his smoked fish, smoked ham, wines, cheeses and home-made brandy. For isolation, hook up with www.adriatica.net and lodging at one of its few unmanned lighthouses, Pločica (*see p291* **Getting away from it all**).

Hotel Bon Repos

Lumbarda road (020 711 102/fax 020 711 122/ www.htp-korcula.hr). **Closed** mid Oct-mid Apr. **Rates** (per night for 3-7 night stays) €25-€72 single; €38-€96 double. **Credit** AmEx, DC, MC, V.
This labyrinthine 1970s hotel is 2km (1.2 miles) from town on the main road to Lumbarda – it's a good 20-minute walk, an occasional taxi boat or the bus driver will drop you off. Set in greenery, it's divided into four pavilions, two renovated to three-star status in 1998. All 278 rooms are pretty basic, but en-suite, there's a large, seawater pool, two tennis courts and diving school.

Hotel Korčula

Obala dr Franje Tudjmana 5 (020 711 078/fax 020 711 026/www.htp-korcula.hr). **Closed** Oct-Mar. **Rates** per night for 3-7 night stays single €42-€106; double €60-€142. **Credit** AmEx, DC, MC, V.
The best hotel in town, the Korčula was also the first hotel to be built on the island in 1912 and has been a local landmark ever since. Behind a pristine, palm-fringed exterior, the 20 rooms have seen better days, but mahogany beds and tall ceilings give a comfortable feel. Little old television sets replace the sea views in some of them and there are no lifts. The terrace is a real boon but your best bet might be to find a private room and use the beautifully located café and restaurant as a local would.

Hotel Liburna

Put od Luke 17 (020 726 006/fax 020 726 026/ www.htp-korcula.hr). **Closed** Nov-Mar. **Rates** *per night for 3-7 night stays* €42-€96 single; €60-€128 double. **Credit** AmEx, DC, MC, V.
Built out of gleaming white Dalmatian stone and surrounded by pine trees, the Liburna is great for sports. As well as sailing and windsurfing schools, the Communist-era hotel runs a tennis school on its two courts, and has facilities for mini-golf, bowling, table tennis and pool. A small sea-water pool complements the modest pebble beach just outside. Cycle, moped and motor boat hire can also be arranged. The rooms are rather uneventful, but guests spend most of their time outdoors. A ten-minute walk from Korčula town.

Hotel Marko Polo

Šetalište Frana Kršinića (020 726 100/fax 020 726 026/www.htp-korcula.hr). **Closed** Nov-Mar. **Rates** *per night for 3-7 night stays* €42-€96 single; €60-€128 double. **Credit** AmEx, DC, MC, V.
Linked to the nearby Hotel Park (*see p294*), the three-star, three-floor Marko Polo offers a sea view from most of its 100 rooms. Two-phase renovation either side of the summer season in 2006 will see new

bathrooms fitted, indoor and outdoor pools, a gym and sauna. The hotel shares a rocky beach with the Park. About 1km (half a mile) from Korčula bus station, it's the closest of the out-of-town hotels.

Hotel Park

Šetalište Frana Kršinića (020 726 004/fax 020 726 286/www.htp-korcula.hr). **Closed** Nov-Mar. **Rates** *per night for 3-7 night stays* €36-€85 single; €52-€114 double. **Credit** AmEx, DC, MC, V.

Huge great four-pavilion complex of 150 rooms, half of them three-star, half of them two-star, many with sea-view balconies. Although you can hire canoes and take a dip from the rocky beach nearby, there's not much by way of facilities. This is fine in the shoulder season, as prices are relatively low, but €85 for a single room here in August is frankly absurd.

Resources

Information

Korčula Tourist Office *Obala Franje Tudjmana (020 715 701/www.korcula.net).* **Open** *June-mid Oct* 8am-3pm, 4-10pm Mon-Sat; 8am-2pm Sun. *Mid Oct-May* 8am-2pm Mon-Sat.

Located in an old customs house by the Hotel Korčula on the west quay, this helpful office dispenses free maps and information.

Marko Polo *Biline 5 (020 715 400).* **Open** *Summer* 9am-6pm daily.

Between the market and the east harbour, this agency can find you private accommodation and organise day trips.

Internet

Tino Computers *Šetalište Fr. Kršinića (020 716 188/www.tinocomputers.hr).* **Open** 9am-8pm daily.

Handy little place by the marina. There's another branch at Tri Sulara near Plokata 19.Travnja.

Getting there & around

The main ferry down the Adriatic coast from Rijeka takes 18 hours to reach Korčula town. The service runs once a day in summer, twice a week in winter. Prices range from the best cabins at €102-€125 and the basic deck ticket of €23.50-€28. From Split, in summer a catamaran three to five times a week takes just over two hours to reach Korčula town (about 60kn).

The quickest hop from the mainland for foot passengers to Korčula town is the boat shuttle from **Orebić** on Pelješac (summer only, Mon-Fri, every 1-2hrs, 15mins, 15kn). The car ferry from Orebić lands at **Dominče** (daily every 1-2hrs, 20mins, 10kn) – a shuttle bus takes you the 2km (1.2 miles) to Korčula town.

From **Dubrovnik**, a daily **bus** runs to Korčula town (3hrs, 80kn), ferry price included. The other port is Vela Luka. A car ferry runs from Split via Hvar town (3hrs 45mins, 40kn). A catamaran does the same journey five times a

week in summer (2hrs 45mins, 55kn). Both then go on to Lastovo, an hour or so away. Between Vela Luka and Korčula town, a bus runs every one to two hours (80mins, 24kn).

Between Korčula town and **Lumbarda**, you can take an hourly bus (15mins, 10kn) or a regular water taxi (15mins, 30kn). There is also a taxi boat (every 30mins, 15mins, 30kn) to **Badija**. Boat taxis leave from the east harbour, on Obala korčulanskih Brodograditelja.

Mljet

If you're after urban fun, forget Mljet. But if you dream of silence, rest and relaxation, get the afternoon ferry from Dubrovnik and don't worry about the one back in the morning – Mljet is the next best thing to a desert island.

Mljet is Dalmatia's most southern, most verdant and, some would argue, most beautiful isle. More than 70 per cent of this thin, 37km-long (22-mile) one-road idyll is covered in pine forest. A third of it is national park. Before Tito chose Brijuni as his place for leisure, luxury and safari animals (*see p118* **Tito's Xanadu**), Mljet was a prime candidate for the prestigious role. And though it never got to see zebras, elephants and giraffes, Mljet remained a natural escape, underdeveloped and underpopulated.

According to legend, Odysseus was so enchanted by Mljet that he stayed here for seven years. Locals tend to stay for the day, arriving in someone's boat in the morning, spending the day cycling and swimming, before heading back for dinner in Dubrovnik. Tourists coming with the ferry are plonked at sombre **Sobra**, on the north-east coast. Those in the catamaran go on to the western tip and **Polače**, named after mildly interesting Roman ruins. This is your best arrival point, with private rooms and cycle hire (although there's a steep hill to start off with). It is 5km (3 miles) to the new port of **Pomena**, where you'll find the island's only hotel, the Odisej, plus more private rooms, cycle hire places and restaurants. The hotel (*see p298*) is the island's link with civilisation, boasting a cashpoint and internet access. Note that the hotel closes for the winter.

Halfway between the two is the main ticket office (020 744 041, www.np-mljet.hr) for the national park at **Govedjari**. Kiosks are also dotted elsewhere. Entry in summer is 65kn/45kn for children, 45kn/30kn in winter, with the boat trip to a Benedictine monastery (*see below*) included. If you're spending the night on the island, you do not pay for park entry. The park is open 24 hours in summer, 7am-3pm Monday to Friday in winter.

Near Govedjari are the island's main attractions, the twin saltwater lakes of **Veliko**

Marco Polo: The myth with the hole

Dubrovnik has its cultural cachet. Mljet has its nature. Hvar has its party scene. And Korčula? Korčula must have something. Well, Korčula is the home of the world's most famous traveller, Marco Polo.

That's the theory, anyway. Born here – or in Šibenik or in Venice – in c1254, the intrepid voyager was living with his family of merchants in Venice by the early 1270s, when he joined his father and his uncle on their second journey to the Orient, along the Silk Road to meet Kubla Kahn. The young Polo stayed in the Far East for nearly two decades, travelling in the region as a diplomat, before coming back to Europe laden with riches and exotic tales.

Shortly after his homecoming, he fought for the Venetians at the Battle of Korčula in 1298. Captured by the rival Genoese, he was thrown in jail for a year. Incarcerated, he told his adventures to his cellmate Rusticello. The Pisan scribe had an ear for a story, and had them published in French, popularising Polo's accounts. The travelogue was in common currency from the 13th century onwards. Nearly 200 years later, it inspired Columbus. Polo died in Venice in 1324.

Korčula's connection with Polo is tenuous but not impossible. DePolo is a family name on the island, as it is in Šibenik. The fact that he was fighting off Lumbarda may be a red herring – he had been given command of a galley by the Doge of Venice in recognition of his achievements and the Genoese fleet happened to be raiding Korčula. That is all we know.

Columbus was certainly Genoese, born in or near Genoa. Marco Polo was certainly Venetian, perhaps born in the trading outpost of Korčula.

Convinced of Polo's quirky birthplace, an English scholar and Polo obsessive by the name of James A Gilman has been trying to establish a Visitor Information Centre on the island. In 1995, on the 700th anniversary of Polo's epic trek back from China to Europe, Gilman failed to launch an expedition in Polo's footsteps from the shores of Korčula. Bizarrely, in raising awareness for this project, Gilman did manage to bring together a certain Mate DePolo from Korčula and Dashzeveg Delegsuren, a Mongol and allegedly a Khan descendant, by a lake in Wales in 1993.

Meanwhile, the Croats decided that a prominent 17th-century house fitted with a watchtower was Marco Polo's. Conveniently located one block behind the island's real main sight, the cathedral, on DePolo Street, it made a panoramic detour from the light sightseeing duties required of any tourist on Korčula. The trouble was, it didn't contain anything relating to the intrepid traveller.

It's one thing to have a hotel, a travel agency, a ferry boat and a festival every May named after your famous son – an empty house from a different century to his is not quite the same. After the firework celebrations to mark Polo's 750th anniversary in 2004, the locals closed it down.

Realising they needed to open a proper tourist attraction, Korčulans began lobbying the government for funding. In December 2005 backing for a museum was provisionally approved by the state. The first step is to unveil a replica of Polo's galleon (nothing about China, then?), the intricate building of which may take until Polo's 760th anniversary.

In the meantime, every summer the tourists politely ignore the poor chaps dressed up in medieval breeches and floppy hats and wonder what all the fuss is about.

Badija. *See p290.*

Mljet. *See p294.*

Jezero and **Malo Jezero**, attached by a channel of water. Veliko Jezero is connected to the Adriatic by the Soline Canal and, like the sea, it has tidal flows. Make sure you know which way the current is going and don't get swept out. Malo Jezero is safe for children. There isn't much of a shore. Take a deep breath and plunge in – the water is quite warm.

In the centre of Veliko Jezero is the tiny islet of **St Mary** with the church of the same name and a 12th-century **Benedictine monastery** on it. Beneath the church is the former monastery, abandoned in the 19th century, now occupied by the Melita restaurant (*see below*). The monastery building used to house the government offices for forest management until 1941. After World War II it was turned into a hotel, only to be looted and ruined during the Yugoslav war. Most visit the monastery islet by an hourly boat that goes from the little bridge on Malo Jezero. You can also hire a small canoe from the same place and row there.

Around the lakes, the little stone-house settlements of Babine Kuće and Soline are nice for a wander. From Veliko Jezera, a hiking path leads to the 253-metre-high (830-foot) high point of Montokuc, allowing fine views of Pelješac and Korčula. Hiking maps (30kn) of the islands are sold at kiosks in Polače and Pomena. Other sports activities – windsurfing, diving – can be organised from the Hotel Odisej (*see p298*).

The rest of the island contains a few small settlements, centrepieced by the administrative capital of **Babino Polje**, and nothing else but nature. As nearly all tourists hang around the lakes, this is pretty much yours. There's nothing by way of transport or refreshments but the reward is three sandy beaches near **Sapunara**, on Mljet's far eastern tip. The main one can get a little crowded, but the other two, **Podkućica** and the beautiful **Blace**, are quieter, the latter

attracting nudists. Locals can find you a private room or there is apartment rental (*see p300*).

On the south coast, a hard walk from Babino Polje or an easy boat excursion from the Hotel Odisej (*see p298*), is **Ulysses Cave**, where the nymph Calypos is said to have held Odysseus captive. Seven years stuck in paradise, maybe it was the itch that made him leave.

Where to eat

Mljet's dining scene is modest but you can find fresh, local dishes at serene lakeside taverns. Most venues are in Pomena where most tourists plot up. The best two are **Mali Raj** (020 744 115), a small *konoba* serving Dalmatian staples with gorgeous views of the lake, and **Nine** (020 744 037), opposite the Hotel Odisej. This is the place to come for fresh lobster, kept in wells outside and fished out at your request. It's a favoured haunt of the yachting fraternity.

Another favourite is the **Melita** (020 744 037), set in the old monastery in the middle of Veliko Jezero, with a terrace by the water. You can eat fish or grilled meat while dipping your toes in the water. Although it's quite out of the way, the **Konoba Barba** (020 746 200) is like dining in somebody's house. Fresh fish and friendly conversation from the old lady are provided in equal measure. It's in the village of **Prožura**, between Sobra and the island's only petrol pumps.

The few local *konobas* are where the drinking gets done. There is nothing by way of nightlife.

Where to stay

The only hotel on the island is the **Odisej**, located in Pomena. Private rooms are generally available in Polače and Pomena, although they can be scarce in Sobra. Expect to pay 200kn-250kn for a double. We recommend you phone

Naughty finger food

Pelješac is not only known for its marvellous mussels and outstanding oysters. You may also find a local delicacy, known in Croatian as *prstaci* ('fingers'), and in English as date shells – that is, if you look under the table.

Prstaci are an endangered species and collecting or selling them is illegal. The *prstac* grows on rocks or large stones in the Mediterranean, the Red Sea and the Adriatic. It can grow up to 12 centimetres (4.7 inches) but it takes 15-20 years for it to grow to a commercially interesting length of 5-6

centimetres (2-2.4 inches), and 50 years to reach 7-8 centimetres (2.8-3.2 inches). Because of this slow process and because a rock has to be smashed in order to take the *prstaci* out, collecting them has long been banned elsewhere in Europe. In Croatia, gathering *prstaci* was legal until the 1990s when restrictions came in.

Fines run from 6,000kn to 30,000kn. The trouble is that *prstaci* taste delicious and can still be found (shhh!) at a number of Croatian restaurants. Just don't ask too loudly.

ahead in high season – you can book at one of Dubrovnik's travel agencies (*see p284*).

There are several basic apartments for rent. **Srsen Apartments** (020 747 025/€45 per flat) in Soline stands out because the large limestone house contains sleek, modern flats of a better standard. The balconies have views of the lake and the sea. **Apartmani Pitarević** (020 764 015/€50 per flat) in Saplunara are more basic but have the advantage of being close to the only sandy beaches on the island.

Hotel Odisej

Pomena (020 744 022/362 111/fax 020 362 042/ www.hotelodisej.hr). **Closed** Nov-Easter. **Rates** €38-€102 single; €56-€147 double. **Credit** AmEx, DC, MC, V.

With 156 rooms and one four-person apartment (€169-€313), the island's only hotel is a decent enough place to stay. A modern, 1970s three-star, it has a concrete beach with a bar, loungers and a children's pool. The pricier rooms have sea-view balconies. Staff can organise excursions and numerous sports activities, including diving and windsurfing.

Resources

Tourist information

Mljet Tourist Office *Polače (020 744 086/ www.mljet.hr)*. **Open** *Mid June-mid Sept* 8am-noon, 5-8pm Mon-Sat; 9.30-11.30am Sun. *Mid Sept-mid June* 8am-1pm Mon-Fri.

Private room details and reservation, as well as national park information.

Getting there & around

The best option for foot passengers to Mljet is to take the **Atlantagent catamaran**. It leaves Dubrovnik (1hr 40mins) at 9am daily, the Saturday service stopping at each main Elafiti island and taking 45 minutes longer. It stops at Sobra (22kn) then goes on to Polače (60kn). You can just make the 45-minute Sobra–Polače leg (10am Mon-Fri, Sun, 10.45am Sat) for 50kn. It leaves Polače at 6.20pm and Sobra at 7pm daily.

The **Jadrolinija car ferry** from Dubrovnik (2hrs, 32kn, cars 215kn) runs once a day, generally in the afternoon six days a week, landing at Sobra. It turns around at 6am the next day. The Dubrovnik-Bari international line also calls at Sobra three times a week. In high season there is also a service from Korčula (2hrs, about 40kn) three times a week. A bus shuttles between Sobra, Polače and Pomena for arrivals and departures of Jadrolinija ferries – but it can be full in high season. There is no other public transport.

An additional Jadrolinija service is being introduced from Prapratno on Pelješac to Sobra in summer 2006 (5 times a day, 30 mins).

Between mid June and mid September, an **SEM Marina ferry** service runs twice a day from Trstenik on Pelješac to Polače (1hr 20mins, about 30kn).

You can rent a bike from several places, such as Polače harbour, the Hotel Odisej or the main ticket office for the national park. All places charge 15kn per hour or 90kn per day.

Pelješac

Pelješac is passed over by most visitors to Korčula and Dubrovnik but locals are drawn to its very lack of tourists, fine wines, long shingle beaches and, most of all, the best mussels and oysters in Croatia. They are farmed at **Ston**, one of the two key destinations on the Pelješac peninsula, which sticks out some 90km (56 miles) towards Korčula. The other is **Orebić**, a resort in its own right, a quick hop and a quieter alternative to Korčula. A windsurfing scene nearby gives it the younger edge that Korčula lacks. One road runs the length of the peninsula, and unless you have a car, your best bet is to head for Ston, where Pelješac meets the mainland, by bus from Dubrovnik, or take the regular water hop from Korčula to Orebić.

With your own transport, you can drive the 65km (40 miles) of vineyard-lined road, stopping at wine cellars serving the famed Postup and Dingač reds. Pošip and Plavac Mali are available at the Grgić Cellar just before you reach Trstenik (020 748 090), open 10am-5pm every day in summer.

Excellent beaches stretch either side of the main road too. On the north side, **Divna**, near the two-house village of Duba, some 6km (3.5 miles) from Trpanj, is secluded and sandy. **Prapratno**, 3km (2 miles) west of Ston, is also sandy. On the south side, **Žuljana**, before Trstenik, is a lovely village in a bay where you'll find several beaches. The most beautiful is **Vučine**, 15 minutes' walk south. Campsites and private rooms abound.

Ston is really two towns in one, linked by hilltop fortifications. Ston, called Veliki ('Great') to distinguish it from its smaller sister of Mali Ston, has its own historic walls, built to protect the lucrative salt pans there. Half the original 14th-century towers and walls remain, some 20 towers and 3km (2 miles) of wall surviving the earthquake of 1996 that destroyed houses in both towns. Many are still boarded up.

The natural lake-like bay has hosted mussel and oyster farms since Roman times. In summer, locals sell 5kn oysters by the side of the road. Renowned restaurants from here to Dubrovnik feature Ston oysters on their menus. Fifteen minutes from Veliki Ston, Mali Ston boasts the best tables – the **Kapetanova Kuća**

Gverović-Orsan, Zaton Mali

Zaton Mali is a small fishing village 7km (4.5 miles) north-west of Dubrovnik where Ragusa noblemen had their summer houses. It's a bohemian community with no hotels and a disproportionate number of artists in its midst. And here you will also find one of the best restaurants in the region, beautifully located, reasonably priced, family-run and a gastronomic winner.

Gverović-Orsan is an old noblemen's boathouse cut into the cliff, converted into a restaurant by Niko Gverović in 1966. Niko, having worked in some of Germany's top restaurants, chose this prime location by the clear water of the Zaton Bay, built a terrace and filled the grotto with restored maritime artefacts, galley sails and a piano.

Forty years on, his son Niko now runs the place with his mother, Mira, and the traditional dishes are just as sublime. The house speciality is black risotto Orsan, four kinds of shells and shrimps sautéed in wine and lemon and mixed with rice soaked in black squid ink. There are lesser known dishes, such as milk-fish carpaccio, made from a tiny fish eaten whole and dressed with local olive oil. Motar salad is made from a plant that only grows on rocks near the sea. Desserts include Dubrovnik *rožata*, a domestic and home-made crème caramel. The wine list is huge, 120 local, Italian and French varieties, including a blue-label brand produced exclusively on Hvar for the restaurant.

The venue even has its own beach (and shower), so you can take a dip while your dinner is cooking, and enjoy a contemplative digestif afterwards on the terrace jutting out into the water.

Stilkovića 43, Zaton Mali (020 891 267/www.gverovic-orsan.hr). **Closed** *Jan, Feb.* **Open** *Mar-Dec* noon-midnight Mon-Sat. **Credit** AmEx, MC, V.

Kapetanova Kuća, Mali Ston

Known throughout Croatia, the **Kapetanova Kuća** is named after the old villa that the Kralj family converted 20 years ago: the Captain's House. The waterfront location and fishermen's nets accentuate the theme.

The reason why it fills with Croatian day-trippers every weekend is award-winning chef Lidija Kralj's modern take on traditional regional recipes. Essential to it all, of course, are the oysters of local renown, but Ms Kralj presents them with chilli and lemon, or uses them in a wonderful cream of oyster soup with myrtle. Oysters are even used in a flambé. The kitchen is equally adept at turning out a *škampi na buzaru*, the langoustines ladelled with a wonderfully rich tomato sauce. Octopuses feature heavily, either in a salad with capers, rocket and tomatoes, or in the warm starter of octopus burger with tartare sauce. Ston walnut pancake is a speciality house dessert – nut trees grow with abandon around the town.

It's not cheap – one of the regulars is Princess Stéphanie of Monaco – and you're looking at least 400kn per head. But you'll have a meal to write home about, and if you choose to stay at the Kralj's luxurious Hotel Ostrea, too, you've only got a two-minute walk home along the seafront.

Mali Ston (020 754 555/www.ostrea.hr). **Open** 10am-11pm daily. **Credit** AmEx, DC, MC, V.

(*see above* **Top tables**) is pick of the bunch. It's attached to the best hotel here, the **Ostrea** (020 754 555, fax 020 754 575, www.ostrea.hr, 450kn-700kn). The **Vila Koruna** (020 754 359, fax 020 754 642, www.vilakoruna.cjb.net, 500kn-1,000kn) is also comfortable, with a lovely terrace restaurant.

Orebić has package hotels and standard restaurants, but has more to pack into a weekend. A major trading centre until the late 19th century, it contains a cluster of grand villas festooned with greenery, built by retired sea captains. Its main sight is a **Franciscan monastery** (summer 9am-noon, 4-7pm Mon-Sat, 4-7pm Sun, 10kn) on a hilltop 20 minutes' walk from the Hotel Bellevue. Built in the late 15th century, it houses Our Lady of the Angels, an icon said to protect sailors in the Pelješac Channel picturesquely spread down below. Before you reach it, another trail leads to the summit of **Sv Ilija**, with panoramic views from 961 metres (3,153 feet) high.

Locals come to Orebić and surroundings for its beaches. The nicest one near is **Trstenica**, pebbly and sandy, with a few bars and a section for naturists. It's a 20-minute stroll east of the ferry terminal. Boats make regular journeys to the village of **Viganj**, the most popular spot for windsurfing in Croatia apart from Bol on Brač. A north-western afternoon wind makes it ideal for intermediate surfers. Beginners are best going out on summer mornings, when a mild wind from the south-east blows. Beach bars abound, the most lively being **Karmela**. Locals tend to nip over to Korčula for the evening, foreigners tend to stay put – there's a significant number of Brit expats in the village.

There are campsites aplenty. **Liberan** (020 719 330, www.liberan-camping.com) rents boards and has a windsurfing school. **Perna** (098 395 807 mobile, www.perna-surf.com), a campsite between Viganj and Orebić, specialises in kite-surf. The main diving club, **OreBeach**, outside Orebić (Šetalište Kralja Krešimira 121, 020 713 985, 091 1543 5532 mobile, www.orebeach clubhotel.com), is a modern Dutch-run centre with a 30-room hotel and restaurant.

Resources

Tourist information

Orebić Tourist Office *Trg Mimbelli (020 713 718/www.tz-orebic.net).* **Open** *Summer* 8am-1pm, 4-8pm Mon-Sat. *Winter* 8am-1pm Mon-Fri.

Ston Tourist Office *Pelješki put 1 (020 754 452/www.tzo-ston.hr).* **Open** *Summer* 9am-1pm, 5-7pm Mon-Sat; 8am-noon Sun. *Winter* 8am-noon Mon-Sat.

Getting there & around

Pelješac is served by **bus** from **Dubrovnik**. Ston is an hour and a half away, Orebić another hour. Three services a day run the length of the peninsula, one going over to Korčula two hours from Ston. There are no other buses.

From Korčula, there are regular **foot passenger** and **ferry boats** hopping the 30 minutes to Orebić (*see p298*).

There is a regular **Jadrolinija** ferry from the transport hub of **Ploče**, just south of the Makarska Riviera on the mainland, to **Trpanj** on the north coast of Pelješac. The crossing lasts 50 minutes. From 2006 there will be two services between **Prapratno** on Pelješac and **Mljet** (*see p298*).

Directory

Directory

Getting There & Around

The easiest way is to reach Croatia is to fly. Direct flight times from the UK are under three hours. As well as the two national carriers, **British Airways** and **Croatia Airlines**, low-cost companies **easyJet**, **flyglobespan** and **Wizz Air** fly directly from UK. There are currently no direct flights from the United States to Croatia.

Alternative methods are by bus, rail or ferry from central Europe or Italy. However, unless you are touring Europe, these can be lengthy options.

Once in Croatia, transport consists of **Jadrolinija** ferries running down to coast or hopping to islands near the main ports of **Rijeka**, **Zadar**, **Split** and **Dubrovnik**; a cheap, extensive bus network; and a minimal rail network. **Croatia Airlines** keep back a number of cheap seats on their internal flights.

By air

The main international airports for arrivals from the UK are **Dubrovnik** (*see p284*); **Pula** (*see p127*); **Rijeka** (*see p161*); **Split** (*see p226*); **Zadar** (*see p192*) and **Zagreb** (*see p94*). **Brač** (*see p233*) is used for domestic internal and budget central European services. All but Pula have easy and cheap transfers into town; not all have easy links back from town to airport, Split being notoriously difficult.

British Airways
UK office *0870 850 9 850*
Croatia office *Dubrovnik airport (020 773 212/www.british airways.com.* **Open** *all year 10am-5pm daily.*

Flies from London Gatwick to Dubrovnik and Split.

Croatia Airlines
UK office *020 870 4100 310*
Croatia office *01 487 27 27*
www.croatiaairlines.hr
Flies from London (Gatwick, Heathrow, Stansted) to: Dubrovnik; Pula; Rijeka; Split; Zadar and Zagreb; from Manchester to Dubrovnik, Pula and Split; and from East Midlands to Dubrovnik and Split.

EasyJet
0905 821 0905/www.easyjet.com
Flies from London Gatwick to Split; from London Luton to Rijeka; from Bristol to Rijeka.

Excel Airways
0870 169 0169/www.excelairways.com
Flies from London Gatwick to Split.

Flyglobespan
08705 561 522/www.flyglobespan.com
Flies from Glasgow and Edinburgh to Pula.

GB Airways
www.gbairways.com
Flies from Manchester to Dubrovnik.

Wizz Air
Poland *+48 22 351 9499*
Hungary *+36 1 470 9499*
www.wizzair.com
Polish airline flies direct from London Luton to Split and Zagreb.

By boat

Croatia is accessible from Italy by sea. There are a number of routes, the main ones being from Ancona, Pescara and Bari to Split, Hvar and Dubrovnik

Croatia's main passenger line is **Jadrolinija** (051 666 111, www.jadrolinija.hr). Other companies operating routes to and from Croatia include **SEM Marina** (www.sem-marina.hr) and Italian companies such as **Adriatic** (www.adriatica.it), **Sanmar** (www.sanmar.it) and **Tirrenia** (www.tirrenia.it).

By rail

Croatia has direct train connections with Austria, Bosnia-Hercegovina, Germany, Hungary, Italy, Serbia and Montenegro, Slovenia and Switzerland. The domestic rail network is not very developed, so while Zagreb, Rijeka and Split are linked by train, you cannot get to Dubrovnik.

On the routes it does run, the train service is reasonably efficient and competitively priced. A first-class ticket on the new InterCity service from Zagreb to Split costs around 225kn, second-class 150kn, with three trains a day. Some routes don't run on Sundays and public holidays.

Information on rail links between Croatia and other countries, as well as on internal routes, can be found from **Croatian Railways** (060 333 444, www.hznet.hr).

If you intend visiting Croatia on an Inter-rail pass, you'll need to buy a pass that includes Zone D. For details see **www.raileurope.co.uk**. Getting to Croatia from London involves three or four changes. To make bookings you will need to call Rail Europe on 08708 371 371 as you can't book this route on the internet.

By road

Croatia's road system is improving dramatically, with many major motorway constructions underway or recently completed. The most notable is the new motorway between Zagreb and Split, opened in June 2005.

The rules of the road are stringent: seat belts must be used front and rear, and using a mobile while driving is forbidden. No under-12s are allowed in the front seat. You must always drive with your lights on. Croatia also has a zero tolerance approach to drink driving, which amounts to no drinking *at all* before getting in your car.

The speed limit is 50km/h (30mph) in built up areas, 90km/h (56mph) outside built up areas, 110km/h (70mph) on major motor routes designed for motor vehicles, and 130km/h (80mph) on motorways. In the event of an accident, you must contact the police on 92.

English-language traffic reports are given on **radio HR2** (*see p307*) throughout the day. Updates are also posted on the website of the **Croatian Automobile Club** (01 464 0800, www.hak.hr), or call for information.

Bringing your own car

To enter Croatia by car you need a valid driving licence with a photograph, vehicle registration documents and insurance documents (including a Green Card).

Car hire

Car hire in Croatia is expensive – about 500kn a day for an average family car. Try and get some quotes online before you travel to avoid any nasty surprises when you arrive. Rental requirements are that drivers must be over 21 and must have held their driving licence for at least one year.

The following car hire companies operate in Croatia:
Avis UK *0870 60 60 100/ www.avis.co.uk*; **Croatia** *062 222 226/www.avis.com*.
Dollar Rent a Car Croatia *021 399 000/www.subrosa.hr*.
Thrifty Car Rental Croatia *021 398 800/www.subrosa.hr*.

Travel advice

For up-to-date information on travelling to a specific country – including the latest news on safety and security, health issues, local laws and customs – make sure you contact your home country government's department of foreign affairs. Most have websites packed with useful advice for would-be travellers.

Australia
www.smartraveller.gov.au

Canada
www.voyage.gc.ca

New Zealand
www.mft.govt.nz/travel

Republic of Ireland
http://foreignaffairs.gov.ie

UK
www.fco.gov.uk/travel

USA
www.state.gov/travel

Petrol stations

Petrol stations are open 7am-7pm, or 10pm in the summer. Some stations in the cities and on international routes are open 24hrs. Stations sell Super 95, Eurosuper 95, Super 98, Super Plus 98, Diesel and Euro Diesel. Gas is available in major towns.

By bus

Croatia is part of the Eurolines network but journey times can be immense; London to Croatia for example takes more than 36 hours. Coaches depart London's Victoria station for destinations including Zagreb, Split and Dubrovnik. For more details contact Euroline's UK partner **National Express** (08705 143 219, www.national express.com). For travel from elsewhere in Europe visit **www.eurolines.com**.

Within Croatia, several private companies run frequently between the main towns. The leading one is AutoTrans, www.autotrans.hr.

Taxis

Taxis can be found in all towns and resorts. They are not cheap but can be lifeline if you've missed the last bus on an island. A tip is expected – round up the fare as you would do anywhere else.

In rural areas especially, your taxi driver may not wear his seat belt. You should buckle up all the same.

By bicycle

Cycling isn't big with the locals and the main roads are not particularly cycle friendly. Cycling for tourists is growing, as is mountain biking – especially on the islands. Information on bike tracks and mountain biking in central Dalmatia can be found at **www.dalmatia.hr**. Try also **www.findcroatia.com** for a list of links for agencies and websites with more useful cycling information.

Walking

Large parts of Croatia are best experienced on foot, whether it's the national parks or the old towns like Dubrovnik. For more on hiking see *p52*.

Cicerone (01539 562 069, www.cicerone.co.uk) publish *Walking In Croatia*, while another UK publisher, Sunflower books (01392 274 686, www.sunflowerbooks. co.uk), issues the hiking guide *Landscapes of Croatia*.

Directory

Resources A-Z

Age restrictions

The age of consent in Croatia is 18. You must be 18 to smoke or drink alcohol.

Attitude & etiquette

Croats are hospitable. If sometimes they seem a little abrupt, it's just their manner – a Croat is more likely to profer a curt 'Sit!' rather than 'Please take a seat'.

Unless you really know what you're talking about, avoid talking about Croatia's recent turbulent history. With frequent justification, Croats consider most Western Europeans and Americans ill-informed. It's not that they'll take offence but you're likely to be on the receiving end of a long and rambling lecture to set you straight.

Business

Since the end of Communism, Croatia has readily embraced market capitalism. Some of the inefficiencies of the old systsem remain, but Croats are in fact natural-born capitalists.

Personal relationships are important – getting to know each other well over meals or simply coffee goes a long way to ensuring smooth business relations.

There are a number of organisations offering advice and contacts. In Zagreb, there's the **British Croatian Business Network** (01 46 66 440, www.bcbn.org) and the **American Chamber of Commerce** (01 48 36 777, www.amcham.hr). In London a good point of first contact is the **British Croatian Chamber of Commerce** (0208 908 1151, www.british croatianchamber.co.uk).

Other sources of information are the subscription-only *Croatia Business Report* (www.croatiabusinessreport. com) and the book *Doing Business with Croatia* published by Global Market Briefings (www.globalmarket briefings.com).

Children

Croatians have a very Mediterranean attitude to children and treat them as little grown-ups. They are generally allowed into restaurants and cafés without any fuss.

Croatia may be a major holiday destination, with a clean sea, but its beaches (*see pp47-49*) are mainly stony and children should wear plastic sandals to avoid any sharp rocks or spiky urchins.

As well as providing pools and water slides, the larger package hotels usually lay on summer entertainment for kids. Outside, there are few theme parks or funfairs. **Dubrovnik** (*see p266*) and **Rovinj** (Obala G Paliage 5, 052 804 712, www.more.cim.irb.hr, open summer 9am-9pm daily) have aquariums. **Brijuni** (*see p118* **Tito's Xanadu**) has all kinds of safari animals. Zagreb's **Maksimir Park** (*see p78*) contains a zoo. Few of the museums are particularly child-friendly, with the praiseworthy exception of the **Bunari Museum** (*see p201*) in **Šibenik**. The town also hosts an **International Children's Festival**; *see p305*. Carnivals include the main one in Rijeka (*see p161* **Rio in Rijeka**).

Customs

Customs in Croatia has been harmonised with the European Union. Foreign currency can be taken freely in and out of the country, and local currency up to an amount of 15,000kn. You are permitted 200 cigarettes or cigarillos or 50 cigars or 250g of tobacco, and one litre of spirits, two litres of liqueur or dessert or sparkling wine and two litres of table wine. Valuable professional and technical equipment needs to be declared at the border (just to be sure that it leaves with you again and you don't sell it while you're in Croatia).

Anything that might be considered a cultural artefact, art or archaeological finds, can only be exported with the necessary approval. For more information visit the customs website at www.carina.hr.

Disabled travellers

Croatia is not as enlightened as other countries in providing facilities for the disabled. That is changing as a result of the large number of people left handicapped by the fighting in the 1990s.

It's vital that prior to travel you make enquiries with your hotel as to whether it has disabled access and facilities – a number of hotels do, but certainly not all.

Savez organizacija invalida Hrvatske

Savska 3, 10000 Zagreb (01 482 9394/www.soih.hr).
The association of organisations of disabled people of Croatia.

Drugs

Croatia, set between the Middle East and Europe, is a transit point for drug smuggling. Penalties for use, possession and trafficking of drugs are severe. Offenders can expect prison sentences and/or large fines. Since the war, Croatia has had to cope with a significant drugs problem among its youth.

Electricity

Croatia uses a 220V, 50Hz voltage and continental two-pin plugs. Visitors from the UK require an adaptor.

Embassies & consulates

Australian Embassy

Kaptol Centar, Nova Ves 11, Zagreb (01 48 91 200/ www.auembassy.hr). **Open** 8.30am-4.30pm Mon-Fri.

British Embassy

Ivana Lučića 4, Zagreb (01 60 09 100/british.embassyzagreb@fco. gov.uk). **Open** 8.30am-5pm Mon-Thur; 8.30am-2pm Fri. **Consulate** *Obala Hrvatskog Narodnog Preporoda 10/III, Split (021 346 007/british-consulat-st@st.htnet.hr).*

Canadian Embassy

Prilaz Gjure Deželića 4, Zagreb (01 48 81 200). **Open** 8am-noon, 1.30-3pm Mon-Fri.

Irish Honorary Consul

Miramarska 23, Zagreb (01 63 10 025/irish. consulate.zg@inet.hr). **Open** 8am-noon, 2-3pm Mon-Fri.

New Zealand Consulate

c/o Hrvatska matica iseljenika, Trg Stjepana Radića 3, Zagreb (01 61 51 382). **Open** 8am-noon, 1.30-3pm Mon-Fri.

US Embassy

Ulica Thomas Jeffersona 2, Zagreb (01 66 12 200/ www.usembassy.hr). **Open** 8am-noon, 1.30-3pm Mon-Fri.

Emergencies

Call **92** for the police, **93** for the fire brigade and **94** for an ambulance.

Festivals & events

World Festival of Animated Films

June or Oct
Croatia is internationally renowned for its contribution to animation, so it's fitting that Zagreb has hosted a world animation festival for more than 30 years. For further details visit **www.animafest.hr**.

International Children's Festival

Mid June-July
Held in Šibenik, the festival includes puppetry, music, film, theatre, literature, workshops and visual arts from Croatia and around the world. For more details visit **www.mdf-si.org**.

International Folklore Festival

July
Held in Zagreb and running for 40 years, the festival showcases both Croatian and foreign folk dance and music. For further details visit **www.msf.hr**.

Pula Film Festival

July
Croatian and international films, some screened at the Roman ampitheatre, with seating for up to 7,000. The festival's heyday was in the 1960s when stars such as Richard Burton, Elizabeth Taylor, Orson Welles and Sophia Loren were regular guests. For details visit **www.pulafilmfestival.hr**.

Dubrovnik Summer Festival

Early July-mid Aug
This world famous festival has been running since 1950. It encompasses music, theatre, folklore and dance, not only from Croatia but from all around the world. Although the events tend to be quite highbrow – you're guaranteed Shakespeare – there is plenty of street entertainment too. For more details visit **www.dubrovnik-festival.hr**.

Motovun Film Festival

A cross between Sundance and Glastonbury, this five-day celebration of independent film takes place in a little hilltop Istrian village in late July. *See p128* **Motovun Film Festival**. For more info see **www.motovun filmfestival.com**.

Split Summer Festival

July/August
This is Split's major cultural festival and consists of operas, theatre and music, much of it performed in the atmospheric open-air setting of Diocletian's Palace. For more details visit **www.splitsko-ljeto.hr**.

Gay & lesbian

Homosexuality was decriminalised in Croatia in 1977, and it is forbidden to discriminate against anyone on the grounds of their sexuality. However, it's only in the last few years that gay and lesbian groups have had any sort of profile and begun to make assertions of their rights – and not without opposition. June's Gay Pride march through Zagreb, established in 2001, was set upon by homophobic protesters a year later. The group **Queer Zagreb** (www.queerzagreb.org) organises a festival of gay art in Zagreb every April, and screenings of gay films every third weekend of the month at the Tuškanać cinema (Tuškanać 1, Zagreb, www.queerzagreb.org/film).

Outside of the capital conservatism reigns and gay travellers will need to use their discretion.

For an excellent web-based gay guide to Croatia go to **http://travel.gay.hr/en**.

Health

Croatia has a reciprocal agreement with the UK that means – in theory – British passport holders are entitled to free hospital and dental treatment in Croatia. Even so, we recommend investing in travel insurance because public facilities are not always available and, particularly in the case of an emergency, you may need to go private. The standard of medical care in Croatia is generally good.

Contraception

Condoms are available from pharmacies and groceries.

Dentists & doctors

Pharmacists (*see below*) are usually able to help with minor complaints, but for proper medical care your best bet is to go to the local hospital or emergency unit where a duty doctor can have a look at you.

The address and telephone numbers of general hospitals in **Dubrovnik** (*see p283*), **Pula** (*see p127*), **Rijeka** (*see p161*) and **Zadar** (*see p192*) are given in their relevant chapters in this *Guide*.

Opticians

You will need to pay for optical care. Evey main town centre has at least one optician (*optičar*) and you should be able to get replacement lenses and frames easily In **Zagreb**, Kraljević (Trg Stjepana Konzula 4, 01 48 19 912) is as good as any.

Pharmacies

Pharmacies are usually open from 8am to 7pm weekdays, and until 2pm on Saturdays. In larger towns some are open 24hrs. Prescriptions need to be paid for.

The address and telephone numbers of pharmacies in **Dubrovnik** (*see p284*), **Pula** (*see p127*), **Rijeka** (*see p161*), **Zadar** (*see p192*) and **Zagreb** (*see p94*) are given in their relevant chapters in this *Guide*.

STDs, HIV & AIDS

Croatia has one of the lowest rates of HIV/AIDS in Europe. The first AIDS cases were diagnosed in 1985. By the end of 2004, there were 486 HIV cases, 223 AIDS cases and 116 AIDS-related deaths.

Most cases have been attributed to male-to-male sex, 14 per cent due to intravenous drugs use. Of the heterosexual cases, 90 per cent of men were infected outside of Croatia.

Hotels

Croatia has been a popular holiday spot for decades and is used to accommodating foreigners. The problem is that Croatia is not yet fully geared to the independent traveller, catering more for families coming here for package holidays in high season.

Scores of hotels have recently undergone renovation following a period of neglect. While Dubrovnik and Zagreb may contain a good number of high-end establishments, in the mid-range and budget category there is vast room for improvement everywhere. In fact, if you're on a budget you might be better off ignoring hotels and looking for a private room (*see p15* **Zimmer frei**).

The Croatian tourist board website (**www.croatia.hr**) has a decent accommodation search facility that includes both hotels and private rooms. Website **www.adriatica.net** offers similar.

Note that most local tourist offices will not book a hotel (or private) room for you, but provide you with a list of places and phone numbers. Private travel agencies, set up in all main towns, should be able to accommodate.

ID

Although it's unlikely that you will ever be asked to show it, you are supposed to carry some form of picture ID on your person while in Croatia. Rather than carry around your passport and risk losing it, UK residents are recommended to get the credit-card style photo driving licence.

Insurance

Travellers should take out comprehensive travel insurance, especially if you are going to indulge in any risky sports – climbing, skiing,

mountain biking – although check the small print first to see if such activities are covered by your policy. If you are going to take expensive equipment make sure that it's also covered. In the event that you need to claim, make sure you get all the relevant paperwork from medical staff or the police.

Internet access

Most towns have a handful of internet cafés and rates are usually reasonable. Wi-Fi is available too, with over 40 hotspots around the country at various hotels, airports and marinas: a list can be found at www.t-mobile.hr. If your laptop is not Wireless Local Area Network-enabled, cards are available from T-Mobile.

Language

English is widely spoken, especially by Croats in the tourist industry. Most, if not all, tourist offices will have an English speaker and tourist information material is usually also available in English. A fair number of Croats in Istria and on the coast speak Italian.

Left luggage

Left luggage facilities are available at most train stations; they typically charge around 10kn per item. Have your passport ready for staff to take down your details.

Legal help

If you get in trouble with the authorities you should get in touch immediately with your local embassy or consulate (*see p305*) for advice and assistance.

Lost property

There no lost and found offices at stations or airports.

Media

Croatian newspapers and magazines are available from kiosks. The best selling national daily paper is *Večernji List* followed by *Jutarnji List*. Both are European-owned and follow the line of their publishers. The third best-seller is *Slobodna Dalmacija*, which is a conservative, Dalmatia-based paper with a Zagreb edition.

Sportske Novosti is the main sports daily, carrying the football results from across Europe including the top two divisions in England.

Croatia also has a number of weeklies. The most significant is *Nacional*, which has pulled off some major scoops in recent times. Most notable was an interview with Croat general Ante Gotovina, while he was a fugitive from UN prosecutors. Another weekly, *Globus*, competes with *Nacional* for stories. Other weeklies include the left wing *Feral Tribune* – known for its run ins with the government of Franjo Tudjman (*see p222* **Tribute to the *Tribune***). A recent arrival on the scene is the right-wing *Hrvatski List*, which has antagonised UN prosecutors so much that they issued indictments for contempt against certain members of their staff.

Croatian papers are less prudish than mid-range British ones – expect bare flesh now and then. Pornographic magazines are more openly on display in Croatia than would be expected in Britain.

A surprising number of British and European newspapers and magazines are also available from Tisak kiosks, usually one, sometimes two days late. In Zagreb, **Algoritam** (*see p91*) carries the city's most comprehensive selection of UK and US publications on fashion, sport and music.

Radio

There are approximately 191 licensed radio stations in Croatia. Of the three main state-run stations, HR1 and HR2 broadcast politics, documentaries, entertainment music and sport. HR3 has a cultural and spiritual agenda. HR1 also carries occasional English-language broadcasts. Some of these are also available on Glas Hrvatska, HRT's external service.

There are plenty of commercial alternatives, notably Radio 101 (www.radio101.hr), Otvoreni Radio (www.otvoreni.hr) and Narodni Radio (www.narodni.hr). Fiddle with your tuner and you'll usually find a station to your taste.

Television

In Croatia there are four main TV stations. HRT1 and HRT2 are state-run and screen news, drama, documentaries and sports programmes. There are also a number of local TV stations.

Croatian TV shows a lot of imported TV series and films from the US and Britain. These are subtitled rather than dubbed. So you can expect Hollywood blockbusters as well as familiar series such as *Frasier*, *The West Wing* and *Only Fools and Horses* with their original dialogues.

Money

The Croatian kuna (kn) is divided into 100 lipa. Coins are issued in in denominations of 1, 2, 5, 10, 20 and 50 lipa and 1, 2 and 5kn. Notes come in denominations of 5, 10, 20, 50, 100, 200, 500 and 1,000kn.

Euros are accepted in the posher hotels and some restaurants but the currency in everyday use is the kuna.

Prices in Croatia can roughly be compared with those in Western Europe. Local goods and those from central Europe and neighbouring states are a little cheaper; goods imported from other parts of Europe and the US are a little more expensive. Public transport, cinema, drinking and dining out in standard places generally cost less in Croatia than in the West.

Foreign currency can be exchanged in banks, post offices, most tourist agencies, bureaux de change and at some hotels.

ATMs

ATMs are easy enough to find in major cities and towns, but a lot scarcer in the provinces. Instructions appear in English, and they accept Eurocard, MasterCard, Diners Club, American Express and Visa, as well as Cirrus, Maestro and Plus. There is usually a charge for withdrawing money from a local ATM.

Banks

Banks are usually open 7am-7pm Monday to Friday.

Credit & debit cards

Most hotels, shops and restaurants accept Eurocard, MasterCard, Diners Club, American Express and Visa, as well as debit cards.

Tax

Foreign visitors can claim a tax refund on any goods costing more than 500kn. Be sure to get a 'tax cheque' at the time of purchase.

Natural hazards

There are mosquitoes in Croatia, so it's a good idea to pack repellent. Croatia also has two species of poisonous snake, the horned viper and the common adder. In the

Directory

unlikely event of being bitten, try not to panic, keep the bitten area as still as possible and get to a hospital immediately.

The only hazard you're likely to see regularly are sea urchins, small spiky black creatures who sit on the rocks just below the water surface of the shore. *See p48* **Urchins!**

Opening times

Public sector offices and most businesses usually work from 8am to 4pm Monday to Friday. Post offices are open from 7am to 7pm, and generally close at weekends. Shops open from 8am to 8pm weekdays and until 2 or 3pm on Saturdays, although in summer some stay open much longer.

Postal services

Stamps are available from post offices, and from newspaper and tobacco kiosks. Mail across Europe takes less than a week; to the US it's about seven to ten days. Postcards and letters should cost less than 5kn for Europe and around 10kn to the US.

Poste restante

Items (bar express mail) can be delivered for holding at a post office. The letter must clearly be marked 'Poste Restante' in the address. It will be kept in the destination post office for 30 days and is returned if the addressee does not claim it in that time. More details can be found on the Croatian Post Office website www.posta.hr.

Public holidays

See p310 **When to go**; *see p305* **Festivals & events**.

Religion

Croatia is 87.8% Roman Catholic (4.4% Orthodox, 0.4% other Christian and 1.3%

Muslim). Most towns and villages have a patron saint whose saint's day will be celebrated once year, usually with a procession followed by feasting and drinking.

Safety

Croatia has a low crime rate. Even so, don't be too showy with expensive possessions and don't wander around poorly lit city areas. Follow the same rules that you would at home and you'll be OK.

Foreign women may not appreciate the amount of attention they get from local men, especially those in coastal areas. If it's in danger of crossing the line between flirtatious and harrassment don't be shy of making your displeasure known.

Landmines

Landmines are a problem in the countryside. Look out for signs bearing a skull and crossbones and stay well clear. However, not all minefields are marked and it is definitely not advisable to wander around any abandoned villages or wander across any uncultivated fields. In war-affected areas such as eastern and western Slavonia, the area between Karlovac and Split, and around Zadar, do not stray from main roads or clearly marked footpaths.

Smoking

A large proportion of Croats smoke and it is a far more socially acceptable habit than in the UK or US. No smoking is permitted in public buildings and cinemas, and on public transport. Only a certain number of restaurants, cafés and bars have a no-smoking area. Cigarettes are bought from kiosks marked 'Duhan' (tobacco). Most major Western brands are available.

Study

If you are looking to study Croatian, many local universities offer summer schools and short courses, including the University of Zagreb (www.croaticum.com.hr). The Croatian Heritage Foundation (01 61 15 116, www.matis.hr) also runs summer schools in conjunction with the university.

In London, the Croatian Language School (020 8948 5771, www.easycroatian.com) runs immersion courses.

University of Osijek *Trg Sv Trojstva 3, HR-31000 Osijek (031 224 102/www.unios.hr).*
University of Rijeka *Trg braće Mažuranića 10, HR-51000 Rijeka (051 406 500/www.uniri.hr).*
University of Split *Livanjska 5, 21000 Split (021 558 222/www.unist.hr).*
University of Zadar *Ulica Mihovila Pavlinovica, 23000 Zadar (023 200 534/www.unizd.hr).*
University of Zagreb *Trg maršala Tita 14, HR-10000 Zagreb (01 45 64 111/www.unizg.hr).*

Telephones

The dialling code for Croatia is +385. Croatian town and city codes have a zero in front of them that must left off when calling from overseas.

When calling overseas from Croatia, the prefix 00 is the international access code.

Public phones

Public telephones use cards bought from post offices and kiosks. They come in units ('*impulsa*') from 25 to 500. Units run down fast calling internationally and you need a card of at least 50 *impulsa*, which should cost about 50kn.

It may be more convenient to place a call from a booth set up at most post offices.

Mobile phones

Croatia relies on the mobile. Roaming agreements exist with foreign companies and if you have a roaming facility on your mobile, the only problem should be the hideous expense.

An alternative is to purchase a local SIM card with a pre-paid subscription; you can usually buy a card with some starter airtime, although you should make sure your mobile is unlocked. A Simpa (T-Mobile) SIM card costs 120kn including 100kn worth of free airtime, although this is added at 20kn after your first call and then 10kn for the next 10 months. If you're only in Croatia for a short while, you may need to buy top-up vouchers at a cost of 50kn or 100kn. For further details visit www.t-mobile.hr.

Time

Croatia is an hour ahead of Greenwich Mean Time and six hours ahead of Eastern Standard Time. The clocks go forward an hour in spring and back an hour in autumn.

Tipping

Tipping is expected by taxi drivers and waiters in restaurants. Round up bills to the next 10kn-20kn, or by about 10 per cent.

You don't need to tip in pubs and cafés, unless you have received special service and have been there for a while.

Toilets

Most cafés and bars have toilets – although the staff would probably prefer it if you bought a drink before or after using them. Toilets in train stations, airports and other public areas will sometimes have a lady stationed at the door to collect a user fee of around 2kn – keep a few coins handy on long bus journeys. Universal signs will be placed on the toilet doors to indicate men's and ladies', or look out for *M* (men's) and *Ž* (ladies').

Tourist information

All cities, towns and even a number of villages have tourist information offices. There will usually be at least one person who speaks English. Levels and quality of service are variable. There's also an additional call service **Croatian Angels** (0385 62 999 999) that offers tourist information in English. The website www.croatia.hr is reasonably comprehensive.
Croatian National Tourist Office (UK) *Croatia House, 162-4 Fulham Palace Road, London W6 9ER (020 8563 7979).*
Croatian National Tourist Office (USA) *350 Fifth Avenue, Suite 4003, New York 10118 (212 279 8672).*

Tour operators

There are more than 100 tour operators selling all kinds of holidays in Croatia – 15 new ones were set up in 2005 alone. The list below can be no more than a sample. The Croatian National Tourist Office in London (*see above*) has a more extensive register.
adriatica.net *(+385 1 24 15 614/www.adriatica.net).* Zagreb-based company specialising in lighthouse holidays and trips for special events.
Adventure Company *(01420 541 007/www.adventurecompany.co.uk).* Active breaks around Dalmatia: rafting; diving; canoeing; mountain biking and horse riding.
Andante Travels *(01722 713 800/www.andantetravels.co.uk).* Archaeological tours of Dalmatia including Split, Salona and Brač.
Arblaster & Clarke Wine Tours *(01730 893 244/www.winetours.co.uk).* Wine cruises in Croatia.
Bond Tours *(01372 745 300/ www.bondtours.com).* Includes tailor-made trips, apartments, fly drive and adventure tours.
Bosere Travel *(0143 834 094/ www.bosmeretravel.co.uk).* Specialist trips to Croatia including naturist, scuba diving, painting and trekking.
Hidden Croatia *(0871 208 0075/ www.hiddencroatia.com).* City breaks and tailor-made holidays.
Holiday Options *(0870 0130 450/ www.holidayoptions.co.uk).* Large range of holidays in Croatia.

Nautilus Yachting *(01732 867 445/www.nautilus-yachting.com).* Sailing holidays.
Peng Travel *(0845 345 8345/ www.pengtravel.co.uk).* Naturist breaks in Istria.
Saga Holidays *(0800 300 500/ www.saga.co.uk).* Large list of destinations in Croatia.
Sail Croatia *(020 7751 9988/0871 733 8686/www.sailcroatia.net).* Specialists in sailing holidays from beginners upwards.
Scuba En Cuba *(01895 624 100/www.scuba-en-cuba).* Since moved into Croatia, offering diving holidays in Dubrovnik and on Korčula island.
Simply Croatia *(020 8541 2214/ www.simplytravel.com).* Flights from Bristol, London and Manchester to well chosen properties in rural Istria, Kvarner and Dalmatia.
Thomson Holidays *(0870 060 0847/www.thomson.co.uk).* Large range of holidays in Croatia.
Travelsphere *(01858 410 818/ www.travelsphere.co.uk).* Coach travel.
2 Wheel Treks Cycling *(0845 612 6106/www.2wheeltreks.co.uk).* Cycling and cruise trips to Istria and Dalmatia.

Visas

Visitors from the European Union, Canada, USA, Australia and New Zealand do not need a visa if staying in Croatia for less than 90 days. If you're travelling between Split and Dubrovnik, you have to pass a small stretch of coastline around **Neum** (*see p247*), in the territory of Bosnia-Hercegovina. Buses and cars are stopped and identity documents checked. Bosnia-Hercegovina has similar visa requirements to Croatia but it's wise to check beforehand on current regulations.

Weights & measures

Croatia uses the metric system.

What to take

Pack sun cream, sunglasses and sandals or flip-flops – most of Croatia's beaches are rocky. You may also want to

Directory

Weather

	Av daily max temp °C/°F	Av daily min temp °C/°F	Av daily hrs of sunshine	Av monthly rainfall mm/in
Jan	10/50	5/41	3	102/4
Feb	11/52	6/43	4	102/4
Mar	13/56	7/45	5	76/3
Apr	17/63	11/52	6	102/4
May	22/72	15/59	7	76/3
June	26/79	18/65	8	51/2
July	29/85	21/70	9	51/2
Aug	29/85	21/70	9	51/2
Sept	25/77	18/65	7	76/3
Oct	20/68	14/58	4	102/4
Nov	14/58	9/49	3	127/5
Dec	11/52	6/43	2	102/4

take mosquito repellent. If you're spending most of the time in budget or private-room accommodation, take a universal plug for washing in the sink. For electrical equipment, UK visitors will need an adaptor.

General stores in small towns – in any towns, in fact – tend to be poorly stocked, so don't count on being able to pick things up while you're away on holiday.

When to go

The Adriatic coast benefits from a Mediterranean climate, with hot summers. The average summer temperature is about 25C and in winter 12C. To avoid the crowds go in May or September, when the weather is slightly cooler and hotels are much cheaper.

Public holidays

The following are all national public holidays:
1 Jan New Year's Day; **6 Jan** Epiphany; **Easter Sunday**; **Easter Monday**; **1 May** Labour Day; **Corpus Christi** (movable feast); **22 June** Anti-Fascist Resistance Day; **25 June** Statehood Day; **5 Aug** Victory Day/National Thanksgiving Day;
15 Aug Assumption; **8 Oct** Independence Day; **1 Nov** All Saints' Day; **25, 26 Dec** Christmas holidays.

Working in Croatia

Croatia is a highly desirable place to live and an increasing number of people are settling here and setting up businesses. Aside from tourism, in which you will find a number of expats in sailing and diving clubs, there's also the property sector and the old stand-by of English-language teaching.

Also see the website **www.moj-posao.net** for further opportunities. Although it's aimed primarily at Croats, it's worth a look as you will find bilingual job opportunities posted from international employers, generally based in Zagreb.

Work permits

Working in Croatia requires a work or business permit. To work without one is illegal and can result in a fine or even deportation. To obtain a permit the first port of call is the Croatian Embassy, which in the UK is at 21 Conway Street, London W1T 6BN (020 7387 2022).

Residence permit

A temporary residence permit is required for anyone staying in Croatia for more than three months, whether for work or any other reasons. If you're a long-term tourist, the solution to this might be to nip over the border, have your passport stamped and come back.

If you have a work permit then the temporary residence is available to British citizens for whatever the length of duration of the work permit. Permanent residence can be applied for once you've been in Croatia for five years.

To apply for residence you need a copy of your birth certificate issued within the last three months. The certificate must bear an apostille stamp, which you can only get at the Foreign Office's Legalisation office in London: call 020 7008 1111 for more information. Applicants also need proof of health insurance and a letter confirming that you don't have a criminal record. For more information you can contact the **British Embassy** in Zagreb (*see p305*) or the local department for foreigners at the Croatian Ministry of the Interior.

Vocabulary

The official language of Croatia is Croatian. It has dialects in Dalmatia, Zagreb and Zagorje, and Slavonia, but there is a standardised version used in official documents. Road signs are given in Croatian. In Istria they are often in Italian and Croatian.

English is widely spoken in holiday areas but less so in the interior, where if you learn a few phrases, it is likely to be appreciated.

For food terms, *see p38-39* **What's on the menu?**

Pronunciation

Croatian is a phonetic language and has no silent letters. For English speakers, the difficulty comes with some of the sibilant consonants, which have different sound to the English ones:
c is 'ts' as in 'hats'.
ć is a light 'ch' as 'future'.
č is 'ch' as in 'church'.
š is a soft 'sh' as in 'shoe'.
ž is 'zh' as in 'pleasure'.
Other letters are lj, as in the 'lli' of million, nj as in the 'ny' of canyon and đ, as in the j of jury. This is often rendered in English as 'dj' (as in Tudjman), a practice we follow in this *Guide*. The Croatian letter j is pronounced as an English 'y'.

Basics

Yes *da*
No *ne*
Hello/good day *dobar dan*
Goodbye *do vidjenja*
Hello (when answering the phone) *molim*
Hello! (familiar) *bok!*
Good morning *dobro jutro*
Good evening *dobra večer*
Good night *laku noć*
Please *molim*
Great/OK *dobro*
Thank you (very much) *hvala (lijepo)*
I don't know *Ne znam*

Do you speak English?
Govorite li engleski?
I'm sorry, I don't speak Croatian *Izvinite, ne govorim hrvatski*
I don't understand *Ne razumijem*
What's your name? (polite) *Kako se zovete?*
What's your name? (familiar) *Kako se zoveš?*
My name is... *Zovem se...*
Excuse me/sorry *Oprostite*
Where are you from? (polite) *Odakle ste?*
Where are you from? (familiar) *Odakle si?*
When? *kada?*
How much is it? *Koliko košta?*
Large *veliko*
Small *malo*
More *više*
Less *manje*
Expensive *skupo*
Cheap *jeftino*
Hot (*food, drink*) *toplo*
Cold *hladno*
With/without *sa/bez*
Open *otvoreno*
Closed *zatvoreno*
Can I book a room? *Mogu li rezervati sobu?*

Getting around

Where is? *Gdje je...?*
Where to? *kamo?*
Here *ovdje*
There *tamo*
Left *levo*
Right *desno*
Straight on *pravo*
Backwards *natrag*
A ticket to... *Jednu kartu za...*
Single *u jednom pravcu*
Return *povratnu kartu*
When does the next bus/ferry/train leave for...? *Kada polazi sljedeći autobus/trajekt/vlak za...?*
I'm lost *Izgubio same se* (masc)/*Izgubila sam se* (fem)
How far is it? *Koliko je daleko?*
Arrival *polazak*
Departure *odlazak*

Station *kolodvor*
Airport *zračna luka*
Port *luka*; ferry terminal *trajektna luka*

Time

In Croatian, half-hours mean half to the next hour, so it may be easier to say *deset i trideset* ('10.30') instead of *pola jedanaest* ('half-to-eleven').
What time is it? *Koliko je sati?*
Ten o'clock *deset sati*
Day *dan*; week *tjedan*
Today *danas*
Tomorrow *sutra*
Yesterday *jučer*
In the morning *ujutro*
In the evening *uvečer*
Early *rano*
Late *kasno*

Numbers

1 *jedan*; 2 *dva*; 3 *tri*; 4 *četiri*; 5 *pet*; 6 *šest*; 7 *sedam*; 8 *osam*; 9 *devet*; 10 *deset*; 11 *jedanaest*; 12 *dvanaest*; 13 *trinaest*; 14 *četrnaest*; 15 *petnaest*; 16 *šesnaest*; 17 *sedamnaest*; 18 *osamnaest*; 19 *devetnaest*; 20 *dvadeset*; 21 *dvadeset i jedan*; 30 *trideset*; 40 *četrdeset*; 50 *pedeset*; 60 *šezdeset*; 70 *sedamdeset*; 80 *osamdeset*; 90 *devedeset*; 100 *sto*; 200 *dvjesta*; 1,000 *tisuća*

Days, months

Monday *ponedjelak*
Tuesday *utorak*
Wednesday *srijeda*
Thursday *četvrtak*
Friday *petak*
Saturday *subota*
Sunday *nedjelja*

January *sljęčanj*; February *veljača*; March *ožujak*; April *travanj*; May *svibanj*; June *lipanj*; July *srpanj*; August *kolovoz*; September *rujan*; October *listopad*; November *studeni*; December *prosinac*

Further Reference

Books

Fiction

Andrić, Ivo
The Days of the Consuls Tales of 19th-century Ottoman-ruled Travnik, by the man Serbs and Croats claim as their own. Andrić is best known for his masterpiece *Bridge over the Drina.*

Drakulić, Slavenka
As If I am not there Harrowing story of a Bosnian rape victim from the Yugoslav war, by one of Croatia's leading contemporary writers

Franolić, Branko
An Historical Survey of Literary Croatian Offers precisely what it says on the cover.

Krleža, Miroslav
The Return of Philip Latinovicz A classic work, a set novel in schools, by the acknowledged master of 20th-century Croatian literature.

Krleža, Miroslav
The Banquet in Blitva Satire of Europe in the Age of the Dictators, written in the 1930s.

Ugrešić, Dubravka
Fording the Stream of Consciousness The most striking work of this exiled Croatian writer, also known for *In the Jaws of Life.* Ugrešić is criticised in Croatia for her neutral stance in the 1990s.

History

Banać, Ivo
The National Question in Yugoslavia In-depth exploration of national identities.

Bracewell, Catherine
The Uskoks of Senj History of the pirate sea-kings of the Adriatic in the 16th century.

Despalatović, Elinor
Ljudevit Gaj and the Illyrian Movement Croatia's national awakening in the turbulent 1830s and 1840s.

Glenny, Misha
The Fall of Yugoslavia Colourful account of how it all ended in carnage, and why.

Goldstein, Ivo
Croatia, A History By a Zagreb historian, an overview from the earliest times.

Hall, Brian
The Impossible Country Touching travelogue of Hall's travels around Yugoslavia in the build-up to war, 1991.

Harris, Robin
Dubrovnik, a History Recently published coffee-table volume on the Pearl of the Adriatic.

Jelavich, Barbara
History of the Balkans Sets everything in a broad context.

Little, Allan and **Silber, Laura**
The Death of Yugoslavia Fly-on-the-wall account to accompany the BBC TV series of the break-up of Yugoslavia.

Ridley, Jasper
Tito – A biography Sympathetic portrayal of the long-time Communist dictator

Tanner, Marcus
Croatia A Nation Forged in War From Roman times to today, by the former Balkans correspondent of *The Independent.* The best general history currently in print.

Thompson, Mark
Forging War – The Media in Serbia, Croatia and Bosnia-Hercegovina The role played by the local press in manipulating the population. Look out also for Thompson's *A Paper House,* one of the better travelogue histories as Yugoslavia was collapsing.

Religion

Alexander, Stella
The Triple Myth – A Life of Archbishop Alojzije Stepinac Fair account of the rise and fall of Croatia's war-time primate.

Alexander, Stella
Church and State in Yugoslavia since 1945 Well researched account of confessional relations, written before the killing began again.

Travelogue

Donley, Michael
Marco Polo's Isle Impressions from a year spent on Korčula.

West, Rebecca
Black Lamb and Grey Falcon The benchmark for all Balkan travelogues, researched in the late 1930s.

Websites

www.croatia.hr Official tourist website – excellent hotel database.

www.croatiabusiness report.com English-language site devoted to Croatia's economic and business affairs.

www.croatiafocus.com Pro-Croatia political articles in English.

www.croatianworld.net English-language news articles concerning Croatia.

www.csypn.org.uk UK-based Croatian expat group that organises cultural and social events.

www.dalmatia-cen.com Dalmatia Regional Tourist Board.

www.hic.hr Croatian news in English.

www.hina.hr Croatian state news agency, English items.

www.istra.hr Istrian Regional Tourist Board.

www.kvarner.hr Kvarner Regional Tourist Board.

www.titoville.com Cult site dedicated to the old leader.

www.visit-croatia.co.uk Large website devoted to Croatian tourism.

www.zadar.hr Zadar Regional Tourist Board.

www.zagreb.hr The Zagreb municipal site.

Index

Advertisers' Index